FREEDOM VS. NATIONAL SECURITY

Morton H. Halperin is currently Director of the American Civil Liberties Project on National Security and Civil Liberties. He was formerly a Deputy Assistant Secretary of Defense in the Johnson Administration and a Senior Staff member of the National Security Council under Henry A. Kissinger whom he later sued for wiretapping his private home telephone for 21 months. His academic credentials include a Ph.D from Yale University and an assistant Professorship of Government at Harvard. He is the author of numerous books and articles on foreign policy and defense strategy.

Daniel Hoffman, co-author with Mr. Halperin of Top Secret, *is a graduate of the Harvard Law School and received his Ph.D from MIT. He was formerly editor of the Selective Service Law Reporter and is now teaching political science at the University of Vermont.*

FREEDOM VS. NATIONAL SECURITY

SECRECY AND SURVEILLANCE

MORTON H. HALPERIN
DANIEL HOFFMAN

Chelsea House Publishers
New York London
1977

Acknowledgments
Among the many who assisted in various ways, we wish to express our thanks in particular to Leon Friedman, Florence Oliver, Christine Marwick, Maria Mossaides and David Schaefer.

Consulting Editor: Leon Friedman
Project Editor: Karyn Gullen Browne
Managing Editor: Laurie Likoff
Art Director: Susan Lusk

Library of Congress Cataloging in Publication Data

Halperin, Morton H.
Freedom vs. national security.

1. Privacy, Right of—United States. 2. United States—National security. I. Hoffman, Daniel, 1942-joint author. II. Title.

JC599.U5H254 323.44'0973 77-13281
ISBN 0-87754-037-3

CHELSEA HOUSE PUBLISHERS

Harold Steinberg, Chairman and Publisher Andrew Norman, President
A Division of Chelsea House Educational Communications, Inc.
70 West 40th Street, New York, N.Y. 10018

Contents

NATIONAL SECURITY AND CIVIL LIBERTIES: AN OVERVIEW

by Morton H. Halperin
Daniel N. Hoffman

The plan of this book is to explain how the courts have attempted to balance the requirements of national security, as determined by the President and the Congress, against the constitutional rights of Americans. The framers of the Constitution were deeply concerned about protecting the rights of citizens even in times of danger and crisis. Thus, in a letter to Thomas Jefferson written in 1798 James Madison noted that "perhaps it is a universal truth that the loss of liberty at home is to be charged to provisions against danger, real or pretended, from abroad."

At several critical periods in our history, dominant parties in government have discerned threats from abroad or from internal subversion, and have sought to deal with them by constricting the freedoms guaranteed by the Bill of Rights. In the early days of the Republic, the Federalist party saw in war with France an opportunity to suppress domestic opposition. The resulting fight over the Alien and Sedition Acts marked the first major struggle between national security and civil liberties. Later, in order to preserve the Union, Lincoln placed most areas under military government, and greatly expanded the powers of the commander-in-chief. In both cases, the courts validated much of what had been done. Their rulings carefully preserved the fundamental powers of Congress and the courts themselves. Yet, as to the rights of native Americans, Blacks, alien immigrants, soldiers, women and children, the Supreme Court was slow to find in the Bill of Rights a mandate to intervene, and sometimes they found in the Constitution a bar to the benevolent interventions of Congress. In addition, the Court began to develop doctrines limiting its power to overturn the policy judgments of the "political branches," especially in the national security field. Yet the Court never compromised its power to protect the personal constitutional rights of Americans.

During and after World War I, the rise of judicial activity in the First Amendment area surfaced as the Government moved against organized labor and Socialist party activities and instituted novel programs such as a military draft. The courts began to carve out limits to government control of political speech and action alleged to threaten domestic security. The "clear and present danger" test for judicial protection of political speech was the most durable constitutional legacy of this period. The upgraded priority of personal, vis-a-vis property interests led the Court also, after some hesitation, to uphold New Deal legislation expanding the joint powers of Congress and the Presidency. The security crisis during World War II saw a further acceleration of this trend, as the Supreme Court upheld the mass internment of American citizens of Japanese ancestry—a decision, like the upholding by the Judges of the 1798 Sedition Act, that few would defend today. The cold war period led to new creativity in internal security legislation and Congressional investigations and also to vast loyalty, security, secrecy and surveillance programs based solely on executive order—all prompted by the apparent threat of international communism and trenching severely on the civil liberties of Americans. Because those claiming constitutional protection often bore the stigma of communism, the courts' response was at best equivocal.

More recently, the Vietnam war resistance movement, Watergate, and the disclosures of the crimes of the intelligence agencies have heightened public and judicial consciousness of issues involving a clash between national security and civil liberties. The intelligence agency scandals highlighted a new aspect of the problem. The internment of Japanese Americans, the Smith Act prosecutions, the loyalty and security oaths, were, at least, publicly stated policies of the President and Congress, which could be challenged in the courts and at the polls. However, the deprivations of constitutional rights by the intelligence agencies went on in secret, without any possibility, until the recent revelations, that they could be challenged.

So far, few new, definitive judicial rulings have emerged. In the 1970's, the Supreme Court has issued landmark rulings limiting executive claims of secrecy privilege and of inherent power to wiretap. The claim of Nixon administration officials, that the burglary of the office of Daniel Ellsberg's psychiatrist was justified on national security grounds, led to an especially well-argued ruling by Judge Gesell of the United States District Court, District of Columbia, which we reprint following this introduction. *United States v. Ehrlichman,* 376 F. Supp 29 (1974), *aff'd,* 546 F. 2d. 910 (1976), cert. denied, 429 U.S. 1120 (1977).

The main presentation begins with our analysis of the issue of inherent presidential power, of the sweeping claim that when the President draws upon his power as commander-in-chief and representative of the nation in foreign affairs, he can take whatever action he deems necessary and is not subject to congressional limitation or judicial review. Such an approach has, in our view, no place in a constitutional democracy, and the courts with heartening unanimity have agreed.

We also deal at considerable length with the government's power to control access to information relating to national security matters in Chapter 3. This issue has only recently become a subject of broad discussion. The unauthorized release of the Pentagon Papers triggered a wide debate in and out of government on the government's right to prevent publication of such material and to punish those who make it available. Subsequently, through amendments to the Freedom of Information Act, Congress for the first time established a statutory right to such information, but only if its release could not be said to threaten the national security.

In Chapter 4 we discuss more familiar, national-security related limitations on the rights of Americans. Chapter 4 begins with a consideration of political surveillance—a subject which has received surprisingly little attention from the courts, from Congress, or from legal commentators. We then discuss the rights to speak, to travel abroad, to remain a citizen, to work, and to decline to serve in the Armed Forces. On the whole the controversy over these questions has subsided for the time being, and we present only a few cases which highlight the current state of the law.

Chapter 5 considers the rights of certain special groups: aliens and members of the military. For national security reasons the courts have generally given them less protection than that afforded to other persons; but they have not been left entirely to the tender mercies of the political branches of government.

Finally, in Chapter 6 we consider the question of whether persons whose rights have been violated in the name of national security can vindicate those rights in court. We deal with such legal obstacles to relief as standing, sovereign immunity, and the "good-faith" defense. This is a subject, as some readers have been aware, on which one of us cannot write in a completely disinterested way. Morton Halperin was the subject of a wiretap purportedly justified on national security grounds. The suit which was brought on his behalf and that of his family by the American Civil Liberties Union led to a finding by a federal district court that the surveillance was unconstitutional, and that the Halperins were entitled to damages from former President Nixon, former Attorney General John Mitchell, and White House aide H. R. Haldeman.

The approach of this study is not historical. Rather our effort has been to assemble the cases and other materials that most usefully illuminate the main issues of the day, as regards the clash between personal liberties and the perceived requirements of national security. We have not attempted to provide a bibliography or extensive notes, since that task is ably performed in Emerson, Haber, and Dorsen's *Political and Civil Rights in the United States.*

We prepared this book in the hope that it would help alert a new generation to the danger which too many of us ignored for too long. The legacy of our constitutional system is stronger than we dared hope when we began this inquiry; but "it can happen here," and it will, unless we understand how precious our rights are, and how easy it is to surrender them on the altar of security. We cannot preserve our security by surrendering our freedom; but we can preserve that security while observing fully the limitations which the Constitution places on those to whom we entrust the power to govern.

United States v. Ehrlichman

376 F. Supp. 29 (D.D.C. 1974)

Gesell, District Judge.

Five defendants stand indicted for conspiring to injure a Los Angeles psychiatrist in the enjoyment of his Fourth Amendment righs by entering his offices without a warrant for the purpose of obtaining the doctor's medical records relating to one of his patients, a Daniel Ellsberg, then under Federal indictment for revealing top secret documents. They now claim that broad pretrial discovery into the alleged national security aspects of this case is essential to the presentation of their defense, in that it will establish (1) that the break-in was legal under the Fourth Amendment because the President authorized it for reasons of national security, and (2) that even in the absence of such authorization the national security information available to the defendants at that time led them to the good-faith, reasonable belief that the break-in was legal and justified in the national interest. The Court has carefully considered these assertions, which have been fully briefed and argued over a two-day period, and finds them to be unpersuasive as a matter of law.[1]

In approaching these issues, it is well to recall the origins of the Fourth Amendment and the crucial role that it has played in the development of our constitutional democracy. That Amendment provides:

> The right of the people to be secure in their persons, houses, papers, and effects, against unreasonable searches and seizures, shall not be violated, and no Warrants shall issue, but upon probable cause, supported by Oath or affirmation, and particularly describing the place to be searched, and the persons or things to be seized.

The Fourth Amendment protects the privacy of citizens against unreasonable and unrestrained intrusion by Government officials and their agents. It is not theoretical. It lies at the heart of our free society. As the Supreme Court recently remarked, "no right is held more sacred." Terry v. Ohio, 392 U.S. 1, 9, 88 S.Ct. 1868, 1873, 20 L.Ed. 2d 889 (1968), quoting from Union Pacific R. Co. v. Botsford, 141 U.S. 250, 251, 11 S.Ct. 1000, 35 L.Ed. 734 (1891). Indeed, the American Revolution was sparked in part by the complaints of the colonists against the issuance of writs of assistance, pursuant to which the King's revenue officers conducted unrestricted, indiscriminate searches of persons and homes to uncover contraband. James Otis' famous argument in *Lechmere's Case,* challenging the writ as a "monster of oppression" and a "remnant of Star Chamber tyranny,"[2] sowed one of the seeds of the coming rebellion. The Fourth Amendment was framed against this background; and every state in the Union, by its own constitution, has since reinforced the protections and the security which that Amendment was designed to achieve.

Thus the security of one's privacy against arbitrary intrusion by governmental authorities has proven essential to our concept of ordered liberty. When officials have attempted to justify law enforcement methods that ignore the strictures of this Amendment on grounds of necessity, such excuses have proven fruitless, for the Constitution brands such conduct as lawless, irrespective of the end to be served. Throughout the years the Supreme Court of the United States, regardless of changes in its composition or contemporary issues, has steadfastly applied the Amendment to protect a citizen against the warrantless invasion of his home or office, except under carefully delineated emergency circumstances. Coolidge v. New Hampshire, 403 U.S. 443, 91 S.Ct. 2022, 29 L.Ed.2d 564 (1971); Warden v. Hayden, 387 U.S. 294, 87 S.Ct. 1642, 18 L.Ed.2d 782 (1967); Agnello v. United States, 269 U.S. 20, 46 S.Ct. 4, 70 L.Ed. 145 (1925). No right so fundamental should now, after the long struggle against governmental trespass, be diluted to accommodate conduct of the very type the Amendment was designed to outlaw.

The break-in charged in this indictment involved an unauthorized entry and search by agents of the Executive branch of the Federal Government. It is undisputed that no warrant was obtained and no Magistrate gave his approval. Moreover, none of the traditional exceptions to the warrant requirement are claimed and none existed; however desirable the break-in may have appeared to its instigators, there is no indication that it had to be carried out quickly, before a warrant could have been obtained. On the contrary, it had been meticulously planned over a period of more than a month. The search of Dr. Fielding's office was therefore clearly illegal under the unambiguous mandate of the Fourth Amendment. *See* Wolf v. People, 117 Colo. 279, 187 P.2d 926 (1947), aff'd sub nom., Wolf v. Colorado, 338 U.S. 25, 69 S.Ct. 1359, 93 L.Ed. 1782 (1949).

Defendants contend that even though the Fourth Amendment would ordinarily prohibit break-ins of this nature, the President has the authority, by reason of his special responsibilities over foreign relations and national defense, to suspend its requirements, and that he did so in this case. Neither assertion is accurate. Many of the landmark Fourth Amendment cases in this country and in England concerned citizens accused of disloyal or treasonous conduct, for history teaches that such suspicions foster attitudes within a government that generate conduct inimical to individual rights. *See* United States v. United States District Court, 407 U.S. 297, 314, 92 S.Ct. 2125, 32 L.Ed.2d 752 (1972). The judicial response to such Executive overreaching has been consistent and emphatic: the Government must comply with the strict constitutional and statutory limitations on trespassory searches and arrests even when known foreign agents are involved. *See, e.g.,* Abel v. United States, 362 U.S. 217, 226, 80 S.Ct. 683, 4 L.Ed.2d 668 (1960); United States v. Coplon, 185 F.2d 629 (2d Cir. 1950), cert. denied, 342 U.S. 920, 72 S.Ct. 362, 96 L.Ed. 688 (1952). To hold otherwise, except under the most exigent circumstances, would be to abandon the Fourth Amendment to the whim of the Executive in total disregard of the Amendment's history and purpose.

Defendants contend that, over the last few years, the courts have begun to carve out an exception to this traditional rule for purely intelligence-gathering searches deemed necessary for the conduct of foreign affairs. However, the cases cited are carefully limited to the issue of wiretapping, a relatively nonintrusive search, United States v. Butenko, 494 F.2d 593 (3d Cir. 1974); United States v. Brown, 484 F.2d 418 (5th Cir. 1973); Zweibon v. Mitchell, 363 F.Supp. 936 (D.D.C. 1973), and the Supreme Court has reserved judgment in this unsettled area. United States v. United States District Court, 407 U.S. 297, 322 n. 20, 92 S.Ct. 2125, 32 L.Ed.2d 752 (1972).[3] The Court cannot find that this recent, controversial judicial response to the special problem of national security wiretaps indicates an intention to obviate the entire Fourth Amendment whenever the President determines that an American citizen, personally innocent of wrongdoing, has in his possession information that may touch upon foreign policy concerns.[4] Such a doctrine, even in the context of purely information-gathering searches, would give the Executive a blank check to disregard the very heart and core of the Fourth Amendment and the vital privacy interests that it protects. Warrantless criminal investigatory searches—which this break-in may also have been[5]—would, in addition, undermine vital Fifth and Sixth Amendment rights.

The facts presented pretrial lead the Court to conclude as a matter of law that the President not only lacked the authority to authorize the Fielding break-in but also that he did not in fact give any specific directive permitting national security break-ins, let alone this particular intrusion. The President has repeatedly and publicly denied prior knowledge or authorization of the Fielding break-in, and the available transcripts of the confidential tape recordings support that claim.[6] No defendant has presented any evidence to the contrary, and either Ehrlichman nor Colson, the two defendants who had the greatest access to the President, contend that such specific authorization was given to anyone. The Special Prosecutor has uncovered nothing to the contrary. Although there is no recording of the crucial San Clemente meeting between the President, Ehrlichman and Krogh, their similar accounts of that conversation reflect intense Presidential concern with the need to plug the national security leaks and a belief that Dr. Ellsberg might be involved, but no specific reference either to Dr. Fielding or to trespassory searches. The President described that meeting in the following terms:

> I considered the problem of such disclosures most critical to the national security of the United States and it was my intent, which I believe I conveyed, that the fullest authority of the President under the Constitution and the law should be used if necessary to bring a halt to these disclosures. I considered the successful prosecution of anyone responsible for such unauthorized disclosures a necessary part of bringing to an end this dangerous practice of making such unauthorized disclosures.
>
> I did not have prior knowledge of the break-in of Dr. Fielding's office, nor was I informed of it until March 17, 1973.[7]

Such comments simply cannot be interpreted to direct a break-in in violation of the Fourth Amendment.

Defendants adopt the fall-back position that even if the President did not specifically authorize the Fielding break-in, he properly delegated to one or more of the defendants or unindicted co-conspirators the authority to approve national security break-ins. Of course, since the President had no such authority in the first place, he could not have delegated it to others. Beyond this, however, the Court rejects the contention that the President could delegate his alleged power to suspend constitutional rights to non-law enforcement officers in the vague, informal, inexact terms noted above. Even in the wiretap cases the courts have stressed the fact that the President had specifically delegated the authority over "national security" wiretaps to his chief legal officer, the Attorney General, who approved each such tap. *See, e.g.,* Katz v. United States, 389 U.S. 347, 364, 88 S.Ct. 507, 19 L.Ed.2d 576 (1967) (White, J., concurring). *Cf.* United States v. Chavez, 416 U.S. 562, 94 S.Ct. 1849, 40 L.Ed.2d 380, 42 U.S.L.W. 4660 (1974). Whatever accommodation is required between the guarantees of the Fourth Amendment and the conduct of foreign affairs, it cannot justify a casual, ill-defined assignment to White House aides and part-time employees granting them an uncontrolled discretion to select, enter and search the homes and offices of innocent American citizens without a warrant. *Cf.* Ex parte Milligan, 71 U.S. (4 Wall.) 2, 18 L.Ed. 281 (1866); Ex parte Merryman, 17 Fed. Cas. p. 144, 161 (No. 9,487) (C.C.Md. 1861).

Defendants contend that, even if the break-in was illegal, they lacked the specific intent necessary to violate section 241 because they reasonably *believed* that they had been authorized to enter and search Dr. Fielding's office. As explained above, however, such authorization was not only factually absent but also legally insufficient, and it is well established that a mistake of law is no defense in a conspiracy case to the knowing performance of acts which, like the unauthorized entry and search at issue here, are *malum in se. See, e.g.,* Hamburg-American Steam Packet Co. v. United States, 250 F. 747, 758-759 (2d Cir.), cert. denied, 246 U.S. 662, 38 S.Ct. 333, 62 L.Ed. 927 (1918); Chadwick v. United States, 141 F. 225, 243 (6th Cir. 1905); United States v. DePietro 36 F.Supp. 389 (W.D.N.Y. 1941); Commonwealth v. O'Rourke, 311 Mass. 213, 40 N.E.2d 883, 887 (1942); People v. McLaughlin, 111 Cal.App.2d 781, 245 P.2d 1076 (1952); G. Williams, Criminal Law 288 n. 4 (2d ed. 1961). As the Supreme Court said in Screws v. United States, 325 U.S. 91, 106, 65 S.Ct. 1031, 1037, 80 L.Ed. 1495 (1945). "[t]he fact that the defendants may not have been thinking in constitutional terms is not material [to a charge under § 242, a related specific intent statute.] where their aim was not to enforce local law but to deprive a citizen of a right and that right was protected by the Constitution." Here, defendants are alleged to have intended to search Dr. Fielding's office without a warrant, and their mistaken belief that such conduct did not offend the Constitution would not protect them from prosecution under section 241. *See also* Williams v. United States, 341 U.S. 97, 101-102, 71 S.Ct. 576, 95 L.Ed. 774 (1951).

The cases cited by the defendants are not to the contrary. United States v. Guest, 383 U.S. 745, 86 S.Ct. 1170, 16 L.Ed.2d 239 (1966), requires only that the acts which violate federal rights must have been the primary purpose of the conspiracy rather than an incidental side effect. And United States v. Murdock, 290 U.S. 389, 54 S.Ct. 223, 78 L.Ed. 381 (1933), merely reflects the rule that mistake of law often *is* a defense to *malum prohibitum* crimes requiring specific intent, such as those created by the federal tax laws. *See also* Commonwealth v. Rudnick, 318 Mass. 45, 60 N.E.2d 353 (1945). *But see* Chadwick v. United States, *supra,* at 243.

Mistake of law may also excuse an act if it resulted from good faith reliance upon a court order or decision, United States v. Mancuso, 139 F.2d 90 (3d Cir.

1943); State v. O'Neil, 147 Iowa 513, 126 N.W. 454 (1910), or upon the legal advice of an executive officer charged with interpreting or enforcing the law in question. *See* Cox v. Louisiana, 379 U.S. 559, 85 S.Ct. 476, 13 L.Ed.2d 487 (1965); Raley v. Ohio, 360 U.S. 423, 79 S.Ct. 1257, 3 L.Ed.2d 1344 (1959). This principle however, cannot be stretched to encompass a mistake based upon the assurances of an alleged co-conspirator with regard to the criminality of acts that are *malum in se. See* United States v. Konovsky, 202 F.2d 721, 730-731 (7th Cir. 1953) (obedience to the orders of a superior does not necessarily negate the specific intent requirement set forth in *Screws*).

Defendants nonetheless are entitled to present factual material that negatives the claim that they conspired to break in. This will, of course, permit them to explain contacts and activities which may imply collaboration as to the break-in but which they contend was collaboration in pursuit of different, more legitimate efforts to tighten security and prevent leaks within the Government establishment. This material, of course, will necessarily also reflect upon the underlying questions of intent and apparently will require the presentation of some evidence bearing on the defendant's knowledge and authority in national security areas. Discovery to this end—within strict limits—should be permitted by specific, particularized documentary discovery adequate to corroborate their factual contentions as to the legitimate reasons for their association.

To the extent that the Special Prosecutor has not already produced all material relevant to these limited issues within the possession of his office, the Department of Justice and the F.B.I., defendants may demand such production under Brady v. Maryland, 373 U.S. 83, 83 S.Ct. 1194, 10 L.Ed.2d 215 (1963), and Rule 16 of the Federal Rules of Criminal Procedure. Defendants may pursue such material in the possession of other government agencies or private parties by means of tightly framed subpoenas *duces tecum,* in accordance with Rule 17 of the Federal Fules of Criminal Procedure. These subpoenas must be confined to documents the defendants wrote, received, or read, and a strict rule of relevance and materiality will be applied. Cumulative material will be rejected. These subpoenas should give adequate notice and be returnable in open court on June 6, 1974, at 9:30 a. m. At that time the Court will hear any objections and make rulings, document-by-document, following such *in camera* inspection as may be necessary. All documents subpoenaed shall be produced in court.

Defendants, while expressing some willingness to go along with this procedure, claim that the Special Prosecutor is required by *Brady* to obtain all of this material himself and disclose it to the defendants. Although the issue is unsettled, there is some support for the contention that the prosecutor's duty of production under *Brady* applies not only to documents in the possession of any federal investigative agency, United States v. Bryant, 142 U.S.App.D.C. 132, 439 F.2d 642, 650 (1971), but also to those held by any agency closely connected to the allegations in the indictment. United States v. Deutsch, 475 F.2d 55, 57 (5th Cir. 1973). While this rule would undoubtedly be reasonable in most federal prosecutions, it cannot be applied to the instant case. Here the Government is prosecuting itself, and those in the Government who have evidence needed by the defense are in an adversary position toward the Special Prosecutor and perhaps in some instance toward the defendants as well. Under such circumstances, in which the customary informal requests within the Government would be to no avail, the subpoena approach set forth above best serves the purposes of *Brady* by providing a prompt, orderly and enforceable procedure for obtaining the necessary disclosures prior to trail.

While the Court is thus limiting the Prosecutor's duty to demand exculpatory evidence from other government agencies, it is not limiting the Government's ultimate duty to produce such material: if evidence relevant and material to the defense is suppressed despite a sufficiently specific demand from one of the defendants, the Court will use the full range of its sanctions, including dismissal, if necessary, to insure that defendants received a fair trial. *See* United States v. Coplon, 185 F.2d 629 (2d Cir. 1950), cert. denied, 342 U.S. 920, 72 S.Ct. 362, 96 L.Ed. 688 (1952); United States v. Andolschek, 142 F.2d 503 (2d Cir. 1944).

Defendants' motions for discovery are granted to the extent set forth above and are denied in all other respects. The motion for dismissal because of the danger of exposing national security information is denied.

So ordered.

---

[1]The Court also rejects the claim that this indictment must be dismissed because the judiciary has no right to risk the public disclosure of the sensitive national security information required for the prosecution and defense of the case. Totten v. United States, 92 U.S. 105, 23 L.Ed. 605 (1875), cited by defendants, is inapplicable to criminal actions and has been modified by a century of legal experience, which teaches that the courts have broad authority to inquire into national security matters so long as proper safeguards are applied to avoid unwarranted disclosures. Nixon v. Sirica, 487 F.2d 700, 713 (D.C. Cir. 1973). *See also* United States v. Reynolds, 345 U.S. 1, 73 S.Ct. 528, 97 L.Ed. 727 (1953).

[2]Otis' argument was abstracted by John Adams. *See* Legal Papers of John Adams 134-44.

[3]While the Fourth Amendment undoubtedly encompasses nontrespassory surveillance, "physical entry of the home is the chief evil against which the wording of the Fourth Amendment is directed. . . ." United States v. United States District Court, *supra,* at 313.

[4]The doctrine of the President's inherent authority as "the sole organ of the nation in its external relations." 10 Annals of Cong. 613 (1800) (remarks of John Marshall), has been developed by a series of Supreme Court decisions dealing with the President's power to enter into international agreements and to prohibit commercial contracts which impede American foreign policy. Chicago & So. Air Lines, Inc. v. Waterman Steamship Corp., 333 U.S. 103, 68 S.Ct. 431, 92 L.Ed. 568 (1948); United States v. Pink, 315 U.S. 203, 62 S.Ct. 552, 86 L.Ed. 796 (1942); United States v. Belmont, 301 U.S. 324, 57 S.Ct. 758, 81 L.Ed. 1134 (1937); United States v. Curtiss-Wright Export Corp., 299 U.S. 304, 57 S.Ct. 216, 81 L.Ed. 255 (1936). None of these cases purport to deal with the constitutional rights of American citizens or with Presidential action in defiance of congressional legislation. When such issues have arisen, Executive assertions of inherent authority have been soundly rejected. *See* Kent v. Dulles, 357 U.S. 116, 78 S.Ct. 1113, 2 L.Ed.2d 1204 (1958); Youngstown Sheet & Tube Co. v. Sawyer, 343 U.S. 579, 72 S.Ct. 863, 96 L.Ed. 1153 (1952).

[5]This possibility is strongly suggested by that portion of the President's letter to the Court set forth at p. 34, *infra.*

[6]The President has called the break-in "illegal, unauthorized, as far as I am concerned, and completely deplorable" (Presidential news conference, August 22, 1973), and has repeatedly insisted that he gave no approval and had no prior knowledge of that incident (*see, e.g.,* President's letter to the Court, *infra,* p. 34: President's Statements of May 22, 1973, and August 15, 1973). On March 21, 1973, while discussing the break-in long after the fact, the President stated, "I don't know what the hell we did that for," and the possibility of claiming a national security justification was thereafter considered (Tape Transcript of March 21, 1973, meeting between the President, John Dean and H. R. Haldeman).

[7]Letter to the Court from President Richard M. Nixon, dated April 29, 1974.

CONSTITUTIONAL RESTRICTIONS ON THE NATIONAL SECURITY POWERS OF THE GOVERNMENT

CONSTITUTIONAL RESTRICTIONS ON THE NATIONAL SECURITY POWERS OF THE GOVERNMENT

Recent events—Watergate, the Huston Plan, intelligence agency abuses—have raised questions about the impact of the national security powers of the government upon the liberties guaranteed by the Bill of Rights. Courts have in the past few years dealt with a growing number of cases involving these questions, including the Pentagon Papers civil and criminal litigations.

The most important and controversial constitutional issues concern what are called the "inherent" powers of the President stemming from his role as commander-in-chief and representative of the nation in foreign affairs. Two extreme positions have emerged at various times in American history. One of these—the "presidential" perspective—argues essentially that:

> The President has broad powers stemming from his constitutional responsibilities in defense and foreign policy;
>
> These powers increase substantially in times of war or other emergency;
>
> When the President is exercising these powers he does not need congressional authorization;
>
> Congress cannot limit the exercise of these powers by legislation;
>
> Courts cannot question or limit such presidential actions and must support them (e.g., by injunctions) when requested to do so.

The other perspective argues the contrary, in short, that:

> The President's foreign policy and national defense powers are no greater than his powers in other areas;
>
> Presidential actions must be authorized by Congress;
>
> Presidential action (even when supported by legislation) is subject to the constraints imposed by the Bill of Rights;
>
> Courts can examine actions in this area as in any other.

The Supreme Court has never consistently adopted either position. In dicta—that is, opinion not essential for its decision—and in wartime, it has occasionally come close to the "presidential" view. In times of peace or when presidential action seemed to break the bounds of the constitutional strictures, it has moved toward the other extreme. Nevertheless, despite the inevitable inconsistencies and lack of cohesion there are a number of principles which emerge clearly from what the Supreme Court has said about the role of the President and the Congress as they relate to national security.

In evaluating various claims of power based on national security concerns, the courts have resorted mainly to four factors. However, these have been applied in an ad hoc rather than a systematic manner. It is unusual for more than two dimensions to be explored in any given case, even where the others seem also relevant. When we consider the underlying complications introduced by the political sensitivity of these cases, the lack of textual guidance for judicial discretion, and the historical shifts in judicial temper regarding "strict construction" and the appropriate functions of the several branches, we can better understand the unusual fragmentation and analytical weakness of the cases to be discussed.

The four factors mentioned above are as follows:

1. *The nature and scope of the power that is asserted, and the ease with which that power can fairly be inferred from the constitutional or statutory text.*

It is often said that ours is a government of enumerated powers, that implied powers generally are repugnant to our Constitution. Thus Madison wrote regarding the infamous seditious libel law:

> [I]t is urged that every Government possess an inherent power of self-preservation, entitling it to do whatever it shall judge necessary for that purpose.
>
> This is a repetition of the doctrine of implication and expediency in different language, and admits of a similar and decisive answer, namely, that as the powers of Congress are defined, powers inherent, implied, or expedient, are obviously the creatures of ambition; because the care expended in defining powers would otherwise have been superfluous.[1]

While this principle may safely be advanced as a true one, it must be admitted that it does not state the whole truth. First, the specific grants of power in the Constitution are inevitably ambiguous to some extent, and the courts are often required to interpret their scope. As we shall see, it is *not* a canon of constitutional law that *all* grants of power are to be given the narrowest possible reading. In the national security realm, the contrary rule has often been applied.

Second, there is an important difference between the legislature and the other branches with respect to implied powers, for Congress is specifically empowered to do everything "necessary and proper" to the accomplishment of its enumerated powers. The Supreme Court established as early as *McCullough v. Maryland* (1819) that the "necessary and proper" clause would be given an expansive reading. The other branches have no such textual mandate, apart from the vesting in them of "executive power" and the "judicial power," respectively. However, it is possible for Congress, within uncertain limits, to delegate its powers to the executive branch, just as the President may delegate his power to subordinate officials.

The analytical question posed by this first factor can be roughly summarized as follows: whether the power asserted by the government, a branch, or an official can be fairly said to be comprehended in (implied by) an express grant of power; or, in the case of Congress, whether it is necessary and proper to the exercise of a granted power.

2. *The exigency—the degree and urgency of need for the power that is asserted; the social costs of a decision adverse to the government.*

In a sense a claim of power without explicit constitutional or legislative authority is always an attempt simply to do something faster. In principle, any power sought could be securely established by constitutional amendment. Even this would not be required if it is simply a case of the executive trying to do without congressional authority what it clearly could do if such authority existed. In practice, the political support for an amendment or an act of Congress may be lacking; or it may be simply a matter of avoiding delay.

At any rate, it is not surprising that the courts have been more willing to adopt an expansive reading of a grant of power when it appeared that disaster might result from a contrary decision. This legitimate tendency has, of course, sometimes encouraged the government to exaggerate the perils that impend, in order to circumvent the checks and balances deliberately designed into the constitutional plan.

3. *The separation of powers factor—whether the power claimed is at the expense of another branch of government, or of the states; whether it is to be exclusive or concurrent; or whether it relates solely to the internal affairs of the affected branch.*

The doctrine of separated powers, a fundamental of the constitutional order, has two ramifications of importance here. First, a claim of power is suspect to the extent that it can be regarded as a usurpation of the powers, or invasion of the autonomy, of another governmental body. Second, a claim is strengthened to the extent that the asserted power is in aid of the integrity of the claimant, and does not interfere with the legitimate powers of other branches.

Cases where the separation of powers doctrine has worked in favor of implied powers include the power of courts and of Congress to hold recalcitrant witnesses in contempt, and the power of Congress to conduct investigations in aid of legislation. These powers have been held to exist in the absence of legislation, and to be partly immune to interference by the other branches, though such powers are nowhere mentioned in the Constitution.

4. *The impact on individual rights of a proposed extension of governmental power.*

The gist of the matter is that national security powers are subject to essentially the same substantive and procedural limitations as are other implied or explicit powers of the federal government. Thus a claim of national security powers requires the traditional balancing of the public interest involved against any private interests that will be adversely affected. Just as some public interests are more compelling than others, so is this true of the interests on the other side. Here we deal with cases where the interests on both sides have tended to be exceptionally grave. The status of the complaining party, whether private citizen, business concern, or government official, national or alien, has profoundly affected the result in many cases, although these distinctions do not always enjoy support in the constitutional text. Easier to rationalize is the special regard that has usually been shown for favored rights such as freedom of speech and trial by jury.

In discussing how the Court has dealt with national security issues in applying these principles, we organize our discussion around four questions of central concern to our inquiry, viz.:

1. What can the President do absent congressional authorization?

2. To what degree can the Congress limit the powers of the President?

3. What powers can the Congress delegate and with what precision must they be delegated?

4. What is the role of the courts in assessing the constitutionality of presidential action and congressional legislation.

We begin with the more modest form of inherent presidential powers—what the President can do in areas in which Congress has not legislated. Next we turn to the question of the more extreme claim that in the national security area Congress cannot limit the President's inherent powers. Then we consider cases where the President and Congress act together; and finally, we consider limitations on the courts' powers in the national security field.

The President Acting Alone

The Constitution says surprisingly little about the powers of the President. It vests in him the "executive power" and charges him to "take care that the laws be faithfully executed." It permits him to secure in writing the opinions of the principal officer of each executive department and to appoint officers with the advice and consent of the Senate.[2]

Many of the enumerated presidential powers relate to what is now called national security—a concept that lumps together what the Founders thought of as the quite distinct military and foreign affairs powers. These are, in their entirety:

> The President shall be Commander in Chief of the Army and Navy of the United States, and of the militia of the several States, when called into the actual service of the United States.
>
> * * *
>
> He shall have power, by and with the Advice and Consent of the Senate, to make treaties, provided two-thirds of the Senators present concur; and he shall nominate, and by and with the advice and consent of the Senate, shall appoint ambassadors. . . .
>
> * * *
>
> . . . he shall receive ambassadors and other public ministers.[3]

From these humble beginnings the Supreme Court has defined the President as an active military leader and as the sole representative of the nation in foreign affairs with substantial powers to act on his own, particularly in wartime. At the same time the Court has interpreted the "executive power" clause as a grant of additional power.

The two most important cases establishing the right of the President to act in the absence of legislation in support of his general executive power and his duty to see that the laws be faithfully executed are *In re Neagle,* 135 U.S. 1 (1890) and *In re Debs,* 158 U.S. 564 (1895).

In *Re Neagle* the Court held that the President had power without legislation to assign a U.S. Marshall to protect a Supreme Court Justice whose life had been threatened. The Marshall was acting under "a law of the United States" in that he was performing a duty fairly inferrable from the Constitution; for the President's duties include "all the protection implied by the nature of the government under the

Constitution," such as protecting the mails and the national forests against robbery, or suing those who defraud the United States.

Justice Lamar, in dissent, insisted that Congress was the depository of implied and constructive powers. He stressed the failure of Congress to respond to requests for legislation in this area.

The case of *In re Debs* (1895) pushed the Court's reasoning in *Neagle* to its ultimate extent. Here the President intervened in a labor dispute in Illinois, for the avowed purpose of protecting interstate commerce. Yet he acted in the face of vehement protests by the state governor, and ignored the applicable criminal laws passed by Congress to deal with such situations, in order to seek an injunction, for which there was no statutory authority. The Court found that Congress's scheme had preempted the state from authority, and that the President's action was in aid of congressional policy.[4]

In the area of foreign affairs the President is conceded to be the sole organ for negotiating with foreign governments. In this capacity he can, without authorizing legislation, grant recognition to foreign governments, appoint personal agents, including secret agents, to gather information, negotiate treaties, terminate treaties and negotiate executive agreements. All of this is relatively non-controversial. Difficulty arises only when the execution of these powers clashes with claimed rights of private parties. Such conflict stemming from the executive agreements signed by President Franklin D. Roosevelt in connection with the establishment of diplomatic relations with the Soviet Union drew from the Court two sweeping opinions often cited by proponents of inherent presidential power.[5]

In *United States v. Belmont,* 301 U.S. 324 (1937) and *United States v. Pink,* 315 U.S. 203 (1934) the issue was whether the compact, not ratified by the Congress, took precedence over state laws in determining the rights of Soviet companies. The Supreme Court held that the President had the right to sign such a compact without the consent of Congress and that it took precedence over state laws just as a treaty would.

While often cited in support of sweeping presidential powers, these decisions rest firmly on the treaty power. The Court argued that the President could sign executive agreements and that such agreements should be treated as the supreme law of the land, subject only, as all such laws are, to the constitutional rights of individuals. Moreover, the Court in both cases emphasized that in its view no constitutional rights of Americans were at stake. Thus, in the *Belmont* case Justice Sutherland wrote:

> So far as the record shows, only the rights of the Russian corporation have been affected by what has been done; and it will be time enough to consider the rights of our nationals when, if ever, by proper judicial proceedings, it should be made to appear that they are so affected as to entitle them to judicial relief.[6]

Since the President's foreign policy and commander-in-chief powers are often viewed together, we postpone our attempt to summarize what the President can do acting alone until we have considered the cases involving military matters.

The original notion of the commander-in-chief clause, supported by even as strong a proponent of executive power as Alexander Hamilton, was that it simply designated him as commander of the troops. As Hamilton wrote, this clause "would amount to nothing more than the supreme command and direction of the military and naval forces, as first general and admiral of the confederacy."[7] The Supreme Court adopted this position as late as 1850.[8]

Under the pressure of the assertions of war powers by Presidents Abraham Lincoln and Theodore and Franklin Roosevelt, the court has come to accept a broader conception of the commander-in-chief power, although it has not quite accepted Theodore Roosevelt's "stewardship theory" that the President's power in wartime is to do "whatever the needs of the people demand, unless the Constitution or the laws explicitly forbid him to do it."[9]

Thus, the President now is conceded the power, without specific congressional authority, to employ military force, at least when U.S. territory or forces are under attack, to create executive offices necessary to prosecute a war, to issue regulations affecting industry and labor in wartime, to requisition property in a theatre of war, to establish procedures for military government in occupied territory, and to end hostilities by armistice.[10]

The President has the power to set up a system to exclude loyalty and security risks from government employment, but only with procedures conforming to due process, or so the Court seemed to be saying in a case rejecting summary dismissal of a Defense Department employee.[11]

The Court has also put other limits on the President's power as commander-in-chief. He cannot suspend habeas corpus, deny passports to communists, seize property beyond the war zone, annex territory, or engage in warrantless surveillance of citizens not agents of a foreign power.[12]

The Court has never attempted to codify these cases in a single opinion. Nevertheless, they seem to suggest broad powers for the President to act in the absence of legislation to represent the nation in its foreign affairs and to take the steps necessary to secure victory in wartime. The Court will restrain the President where his actions impinge on constitutional rights, where the exigency does not appear severe, or where the action impinges directly on legislative power. All of this is on the assumption that Congress has not acted. When it has, the situation is substantially different, as we shall now observe.

The President Acting Contrary to Legislation

One extreme version, of relatively recent origin, of inherent presidential powers in the national security field is the doctrine that Congress may not legislate to constrain the President. We are told that if the President has authority to act deriving from his role as commander-in-chief or organ of foreign policy, Congress can do nothing to affect what the President can do.

President Gerald Ford presented just such an interpretation of his powers in vetoing a revision of the Freedom of Information Act. He argued *inter alia* that the Act was unconstitutional because it gave the courts a role in determining what national security information could be kept secret.[13] Similarly, executive branch spokesmen have suggested that Congress cannot constrain the President's power to engage in electronic surveillance of foreign embassies.[14]

The Constitution itself makes it abundantly clear that Congress can legislate to limit the President's powers as commander-in-chief and organ of foreign policy. While designating the President commander-in-chief, the Constitution grants all legislative power to the Congress and specifically grants it the powers:

> To declare war, grant letters of marque and reprisal, and make rules concerning captures on land and water;

> To raise and support armies, but no appropriation of money to that use shall be for a longer term than two years;
>
> To provide and maintain a navy;
>
> To make rules for the government and regulation of the land and naval forces;
>
> To provide for calling forth the militia to execute the laws of the Union, suppress insurrections and repel invasions;
>
> To provide for organizing, arming, and disciplining the militia, and for governing such part of them as may be employed in the service of the United States, reserving to the States respectively, the appointment of the officers, and the authority of training the militia according to the discipline prescribed by Congress.[15]

In addition, the Third Amendment provides that soldiers can be quartered in private homes only "in a manner to be prescribed by law."

The foreign policy power is, of course, limited by the Senate's role in approving treaties and appointments of executive branch officials as well as ambassadors.

If the Constitution provides no basis for the belief that Congress cannot interfere with the President's national security powers, neither has the Supreme Court ever accepted this doctrine.

Only twice in its history has the Court held an act of Congress unconstitutional on the grounds that it interfered with the powers of the President. The first instance involved the President's pardon power. In a line of cases decided shortly after the Civil War, the Supreme Court invalidated congressional attempts to control the President's discretion, first in pardoning individuals who participated in the rebellion and later in issuing a blanket, unconditional amnesty.[15a]

In the second instance, the statute at issue provided that postmasters appointed with the advice and consent of the Senate could only be removed with the Senate's consent. In *Myers v. United States,* 272 U.S. 52 (1926) Chief Justice Taft, speaking for a divided Court, stated that as far as executive officers appointed by the President, the power of removal was not susceptible constitutionally of any restraint or limitation by Congress. Taft based what Corwin terms this "sweeping doctrine" in large part on Madison's argument in the First Congress that the removal power belonged to the President alone since he could be impeached for the acts of his subordinates.

Much of the force of this opinion has been by the Court, most notably in *Humphrey's Executor v. United States,* where it held that the President could not fire a member of the Federal Communications Commission appointed for a fixed term set by Congress. What remains is "that the President's constitutionally illimitable power of removal reaches only two classes of officials: (1) those whose statutory powers are ministerial merely; (2) those who exercise the President's own powers, whether of statutory or constitutional origin."[16]

The Court, as noted, has not found any other illimitable power. Hence, it follows that the Court has never held any congressional act to be unconstitutional on the grounds that it infringed on the President's powers as commander-in-chief or agent of foreign policy. Indeed, such claims have rarely been raised before the Court,[17] at least not in a pure form. Sometimes a presidential action challenged in court is defended both as pursuant to an act of Congress and as based on the President's own constitutional powers. Confronted by such claims the Court has tended to ignore the assertion of inherent powers and to decide the issue on the basis of what Congress intended and the constitutionality of the act. For example, in a series of cases involving the President's right to fire those he decided to be security risks, the majority consistently ignored the claim that the President's power to fire employees on security grounds could not be limited by the Congress.[18] However, in finding dismissals unconstitutional or unauthorized by statute the Court implicitly rejected the claim of illimitable presidential power to fire employees. This occurred most clearly in *Cole v. Young* where the Court ordered an employee reinstated on the grounds that the Congress had not authorized his firing without a hearing. Here, as Justice Clark pointed out in dissent, the Court confronted and, at least by implication, rejected an executive branch claim that Congress could not constitutionally prohibit the President from acting as he had.

If the Court has seldom ruled explicitly on claims of illimitable power, it has dealt with situations where Congress has prescribed executive branch behavior. Often in such cases the Court's opinions have stated explicitly that the President had the contested power before Congress acted but did not have it once legislation was enacted. The Court has reasoned that until Congress acted to meet a particular threat to the nation's safety, the President could proceed on his own; but once the Congress acted either to prescribe a method of dealing with a danger or proscribe a particular remedy, the President was bound by the legislation.

The first such decision in the national security field came in 1804 in the case of *Little v. Barreme,* 6 U.S. 170. Congress had authorized the seizure of ships bound *to* French ports. The issue before the Court was the legality of a seizure by the U.S. Navy of a ship bound *from* a French port. Chief Justice Marshall speaking for the Court noted that the President as commander-in-chief might well have had the power to order the seizure in the absence of legislation. However, Congress having laid out the rules for the seizure of ships trading with France, the President was bound to follow them. This was the case even though the legislation did not specifically prohibit seizure of ships leaving French ports.

The Supreme Court addressed the issue even more explicitly some years later in a case not involving national security. In *United States v. Tingey,* 30 U.S. 115 (1831), the Court held that revenue officers could be required to put surety bonds in the absence of legislation—but that where Congress had acted, the executive could not go beyond the law by imposing additional requirements.

The ability of Congress to limit the power of the President or even to reverse his actions extends even to activities stemming from his role as sole organ for foreign policy including the power to negotiate treaties and executive agreements. One case, *La Abra Silver Mining Co. v. United States,* 175 U.S. 423 (1899), involved an American company's claim against a foreign government, which claim the President had sponsored and brought to a successful conclusion before an international arbitration board. However, persistent rumors of fraud on the company's part led Congress to investigate the case, and ultimately to direct the government to take the company into court, with a view to causing the return of the award to Mexico. The company protested that Congress lacked power to undo the work of the President and the arbitration tribunal, but a unanimous Court held that the matter was not committed by the Constitution to the President's exclusive control; rather, Congress "undoubtedly" had power to intervene, just as it could by statute abrogate treaties at any time. In another case, involving the deportation of aliens, the Court held unanimously that where Congress had established procedures the President was obliged to follow them.[19]

One way in which Congress can limit the President's power is to provide for judicial review of his actions. Thus in refusing judicial review in two cases, one involving deportation of aliens and the other the awarding of airline routes, the Court's decisions turned on congressional intent. In both the Court made it clear that Congress could provide for judicial review if it wanted to do so.[20]

The most important case involving Congress' ability to limit presidential war powers and to do so by establishing procedures for dealing with a threat to the nation's safety is the *Steel Seizure* case. In 1952, during the middle of the Korean War, the steelworkers went on strike. President Harry S. Truman found that a prolonged strike would jeopardize the war effort and he ordered the Secretary of Commerce to seize and operate the mills. The Solicitor General in argument before the Court relied on the President's inherent powers as chief executive and commander-in-chief and conceded that no statute authorized the seizure. Justice Black, speaking for the Court, rejected this claim of inherent power, asserting that only Congress could authorize a seizure of property. In a concurring opinion which has come to be regarded as a definitive statement on "inherent" powers, Justice Jackson laid great stress on the fact that Congress had legislated in this area. He began by distinguishing three different situations, an analysis on which this chapter relies, and which is well worth quoting in full:

> 1. When the President acts pursuant to an express or implied authorization of Congress, his authority is at its maximum, for it includes all that he possesses in his own right plus all that Congress can delegate. In these circumstances, and in these only, may he be said (for what it may be worth) to personify the federal sovereignty. If his act is held unconstitutional under these circumstances, it usually means that the Federal Government as an undivided whole lacks power. A seizure executed by the President pursuant to an Act of Congress would be supported by the strongest of presumptions and the widest latitude of judicial interpretation, and the burden of persuasion would rest heavily upon any who might attack it.
>
> 2. When the President acts in absence of either a congressional grant or denial of authority, he can only rely upon his own independent powers, but there is a zone of twilight in which he and Congress may have concurrent authority, or in which its distribution is uncertain. Therefore, congressional inertia, indifference or quiescence may sometimes, at least as a practical matter, enable, if not invite, measures on independent presidential responsibility. In this area, any actual test of power is likely to depend on the imperatives of events and contemporary imponderables rather than on abstract theories of law.
>
> 3. When the President takes measures incompatible with the expressed or implied will of Congress, his power is at its lowest ebb, for then he can rely only upon his own constitutional powers minus any constitutional powers of Congress over the matter. Courts can sustain exclusive presidential control in such a case only by disabling the Congress from acting upon the subject. Presidential claim to a power at once so conclusive and preclusive must be scrutinized with caution, for what is at stake is the equilibrium established by our constitutional system.[21]

In Justice Jackson's view the steel seizure clearly fit into the third category and could be sustained only if the seizure was in the President's domain and "beyond control of Congress." After reviewing the constitutional provisions cited above, Jackson concluded that the Congress had clear authority to limit the war power, especially when it was turned inward and affected constitutional rights.

Thus we find no basis in the Constitution or in the opinions of the Supreme

Court to sustain the argument that when the President exercises his national security powers Congress is powerless to act to constrain or even reverse his actions. On the contrary, if there is any limit to Congress' power in this area, it has yet to be found and certainly would not affect actions which impinge on constitutional rights.

Congressional Delegation of Powers

Two questions arise in connection with the delegation by Congress to the President of authority to take action in connection with foreign or military affairs:

1. What are the limits, if any, of Congress' power to delegate responsibility to the President?
2. With what specificity must Congress delegate?

On the first question the Supreme Court has been quite clear. Whatever limits might apply to delegation in the domestic sphere, the power to delegate in the national security field is very broad. *Curtiss-Wright,* a case often cited to justify very broad inherent presidential powers in the national security field stands for this principle but only this principle.[22] Justice Jackson in a footnote to a portion of his concurring opinion in the *Steel Seizure* case describes the holding of *Curtiss-Wright* as follows:

> *United States v. Curtiss-Wright Corp.,* 299 U.S. 304, involved, not the question of the President's power to act without congressional authority, but the question of his right to act under and in accord with an Act of Congress. The constitutionality of the Act under which the President had proceeded was assailed on the ground that it delegated legislative powers to the President. Much of the Court's opinion is *dictum,* but the *ratio decidendi* is contained in the following language:
>
> "When the President is to be authorized by legislation to act in respect of a matter intended to affect a situation in foreign territory, the legislator properly bears in mind the important consideration that the form of the President's action—or, indeed, whether he shall act at all—may well depend, among other things, upon the nature of the confidential information which he has or may thereafter receive, or upon the effect which his action may have upon our foreign relations. This consideration in connection with what we have already said on the subject, discloses the unwisdom of requiring Congress in this field of governmental power to lay down narrowly definite standards by which the President is to be governed. As this court said in *Mackenzie v. Hare,* 239 U.S. 299, 311. 'As a government, the United States is invested with all the attributes of sovereignty. As it has the character of nationality it has the powers of nationality, especially those which concern its relations and intercourse with other countries. *We should hesitate long before limiting or embarrassing such powers.*' (Italics supplied)" *Id.,* at 321-22.
>
> That case does not solve the present controversy. It recognized internal and external affairs as being in separate categories, and held that the strict limitation upon congressional delegations of power to the President over internal affairs does not apply with respect to delegations of power in external affairs. It was intimated that the President might act in external affairs without congressional authority, but not that he might act contrary to an Act of Congress.[23]

On the question of the explicitness of delegation, the Court has in general shown a willingness to find congressional sanction where it can plausibly be said to exist.

Thus delegation can be retroactive, it can be read into the appropriation of funds to carry out the activity, into the appropriation of funds for a general program, or the general authorization of a program when Congress is aware of executive branch actions.[24]

However, where constitutional rights are involved the Court has required more precision. In a Civil War case involving the powers of the military governor of South Carolina, the Court stated that "the clearest language would be necessary to satisfy us that Congress intended that the power given by these acts should be so exercised."[25]

The Court has applied this principle in a variety of situations. After sanctioning various aspects of the Japanese internment program during World War II on the grounds that they had been authorized by Congress, the Court ordered the release of an American citizen of Japanese descent who had been found to be loyal. The Court argued that Congress had not authorized such detentions and that it could not read such a delegation into the legislation.[26] The Court similarly struck down a State Department regulation denying passports to communists on the grounds that no such power had been delegated to the President.[27] The Court in another case denied that the President had been given the power to dismiss all government employees on security grounds, finding that Congress had intended to authorize dismissal only from truly sensitive positions.[28]

Our discussion thus far has focussed on the relationship between the powers of the President vis-à-vis the Congress and on the ability of the Congress to delegate its powers to the President. Implicit in this discussion is the notion that the Congress and the President acting together had the constitutional power to act. In general the Court has been less concerned about the distribution of power between the political branches where their power together is not in doubt. Where the actions of the government clash with constitutional rights, the Court is less willing to sanction action by the President alone or with a vague mandate from Congress. And even when Congress' intent is clear, the Court is not always willing to find the action constitutional, as we shall see in turning to the question of judicial restraint.

Judicial Restraint

The Court's restraint in the national security area stems in part from what the Justices have referred to as the "political question" doctrine, i.e., that in certain areas the nation must speak with one voice; or that some issues are not susceptible to legal reasoning or solutions and should be left to the political branches.[29]

The earliest statement of what later came to be called the political question doctrine is in the famous case of *Marbury v. Madison.* In a passage quoted first in most expositions of inherent presidential powers beyond the reach of the Court, Chief Justice Marshall declared:

> By the Constitution of the United States, the President is invested with certain important political powers in the exercise of which he is to use his own discretion, and is accountable only to his country in his political character and to his own conscience.[30]

But Marshall immediately went on to make a distinction whose importance we have already stressed and to which we shall return: "The subjects are political. They respect the nation, and not individual rights."[31]

The first application of the political question doctrine to national security matters came in 1829 when the Court held that it was bound to accept the President's interpretation of the meaning of a treaty.[32]

In *Oetjen v. Central Leather Co.*, 246 U.S. 297 (1918), another case in the litany of inherent powers decisions, the Court refused to consider whether an act of the Mexican government, accepted by the executive branch, was legal. In an oft-quoted sentence the Court declared:

> The conduct of the foreign relations of our Government is committed by the Constitution to the Executive and Legislative—'the political'—Departments of the Government, and the propriety of what may be done in the exercise of this political power is not subject to judicial inquiry or decision.[33]

The range of holdings based on the application of the political question doctrine to foreign policy and military affairs is summarized by Corwin as follows:

> On this principle the Court has subsequently held at one time or another that it must accept as final and binding on itself the determinations of one or other or both of "the political departments," with respect to all such questions as whether a certain newly constituted community was a qualified belligerent at international law; what was the correct boundary of a certain country; what country was the sovereign of a particular region; whether a certain community was entitled to be considered as a "belligerent" or as an independent state; who was the *de jure*, who the *de facto* ruler of a certain country; whether a particular person was a duly accredited diplomatic agent to the United States; how long a military occupation of a certain region should continue in order to fulfill the terms of a treaty; whether a certain treaty was in effect; and so on.[34]

A second class of cases in which the Court exercises great restraint are those which involve individuals or groups who the Court decides are not entitled to the full protection of the Bill of Rights. Most notable in this regard is the question of the rights of aliens to enter or remain in the United States. The Court has consistently held that the President and the Congress had inherent power to exclude aliens and that in deportation or exclusion matters aliens were not entitled to the protections of the Bill of Rights. In a recent case involving the asserted First Amendment right of American citizens to bring an alien to the United States to hear his views, a divided court held that, with regard to the exclusion of aliens, "the courts will neither look behind the exercise of that discretion nor test it by balancing its justification against the First Amendment interests of those who seek personal communications with the applicant.[35] Other groups who can expect only limited protection from the Courts include enemy aliens in regard to their property, and prisoners of war.[36]

A third area of judicial restraint relates to findings of fact which the government has already announced and the Court could not contradict without causing serious embarrassment in our foreign affairs; or findings which depend on information which, in the Court's view, can properly be kept secret in the interests of national security. Thus the Court has declined to review factual findings in a number of situations where the legislation ruled out such review or simply did not explicitly provide for it. Among the situations in which the Court has so ruled are findings justifying deportation of aliens, a finding by the President that there was imminent danger of invasion and, more generally, a finding that the international situation required the seizure of telegraph lines. Nor would the Court review findings justifying invocation of the Trading With the Enemy Act.[37]

In the most widely quoted of such cases—another of the select list used to justify inherent powers—the Court declined to review a finding regarding the awarding of an overseas airline route. The basis of the decision in *Chicago and Southern Airlines v. Waterman Steamship Corp.*, 333 U.S. 103 (1948), was that Congress had not provided for judicial review. Justice Jackson explained why the Court would accept this limit on its power:

> The President, both as Commander in Chief and as the Nation's organ for foreign affairs, has available intelligence services which reports are not, and ought not to be, published to the world. It would be intolerable that courts, without relevant information, should review and perhaps nullify actions of the executive taken on information properly held secret. Nor can the court sit in camera in order to be taken into executive confidences. But even if the courts could require full disclosure, the very nature of executive decisions as to foreign policy is political, not judicial. Such decisions are wholly confined by our Constitution to the political departments of the government, executive and legislature. They are delicate, complex, and involve large elements of policy. They are and should be undertaken only by those directly responsible to the people whose welfare and lives are in peril. They are decisions of a kind for which the judiciary has neither aptitude, facilities nor responsibilities, and which has long been held to belong to the domain of political power not subject to judicial intrusion or inquiry.[38]

The limit to the Court's willingness to exercise restraint when Congress and the President are acting together comes when it sees an infringement of constitutional rights. The Court has consistently stressed that the clash between national security powers and constitutional rights is no different than the clash between any other state interest and the Bill of Rights. It is for the Court to balance the interests and decide if the law is constitutional.

As early as 1919 the Court declared that the war power is subject to the "applicable constitutional limitations."[39]

In 1934 Chief Justice Hughes in an opinion for the Court wrote:

> Emergency does not create power. Emergency does not increase granted power or remove or diminish the restrictions imposed upon power granted or reserved. The Constitution was adopted in a period of grave emergency. Its grants of power to the Federal Government and its limitations of the power of the States were determined in the light of emergency and they are not altered by emergency. . . . [E]ven the war power does not remove constitutional limitations safeguarding essential liberties.[40]

More recently, in *Kennedy v. Mendoza-Martinez,* 372 U.S. 144 (1963), Justice Goldberg reaffirmed this principle in overturning a law designed to strip of their citizenship draft avoiders who fled the country:

> It is fundamental that the great powers of Congress to conduct war and to regulate the nation's foreign relations are subject to the constitutional requirements of due process.[40a]

In *United States v. Robel,* 389 U.S. 258 (1967), the Court held unconstitutional a statute making it unlawful for a member of a communist organization to work in a defense facility. It said:

> [T]he phrase "war power" cannot be invoked as a talismanic incantation to support any exercise of congressional power which can be brought within its ambit. . . . Even the war power does not remove constitutional limitations safeguarding essential liberties.[41]

To be sure, in applying a constitutional balancing the Court has usually given great weight to findings of fact made pursuant to legislation. Thus the Court refused to overturn the action by a base commander summarily denying access to a military base to an employee of a private firm operating a cafeteria on the base.[42]

The Court has also been reluctant to intervene in moments of great national danger. Thus, the Supreme Court refused to overturn any of Lincoln's actions during the Civil War except for his efforts to try civilians in military courts and then only after the war.[43] The Court, in two decisions which in retrospect have come into increasing disrepute, sanctioned aspects of the Japanese internment program during World War II.[44]

When balancing security interests against a constitutional right, the Court will give great weight to a congressional finding of evil and of necessity for action, but it will not be bound by it. Thus in the first Supreme Court decision striking down an act of Congress on First Amendment grounds, *Lamont v. Postmaster General,* 381 U.S. 301 (1965) the Court found unconstitutional a provision in congressional legislation authorizing the Postmaster General not to deliver overseas mail which contained communist propaganda to an American citizen unless he certified in writing that he wanted to receive that material. The Court held that the government had not shown a sufficient danger that would result from private citizens reading communist propaganda to authorize an interference with the First Amendment right to receive the material.[45]

Even if it accepts the existence of an overriding state interest, the Court will insist that the legislation be drawn to cover only that behavior which must be prohibited to deal with the evil, and not cover other actions as well. In the words of the Court, the problem of overbreadth must be avoided if the legislation is to be found constitutional. Thus in *Aptheker v. United States,* 378 U.S. 500 (1964), the Court held that legislation banning a person who was a member of a subversive organization from applying for a passport was void for overbreadth. It stated Congress could ban the travel of those individuals about whom there was a reasonable basis to believe that they would use the opportunity to travel in ways which would threaten the security of the United States. This was a far smaller class than all of those who belonged to organizations listed by the government as subversive. That list included many people who did not even know that their organizations were on such a list and were not active members who would pursue the interests of the organization when traveling abroad.

Similarly, in *United States v. Robel,* 389 U.S. 258 (1967), the Court held unconstitutional a statute saying that it would be unlawful for members of a communist organization "to engage in any employment in any defense facility." The Court held again that the action was overbroad in that it covered too large a class.[46]

In perhaps a needed effort to remind the executive branch and Congress of the Court's role in this area, the Court declared:

> When Congress's exercise of one of its enumerated powers clashes with the individual liberties protected by the Bill of Rights, it is "our delicate and difficult task" to determine whether the resulting restrictions on freedom can be tolerated.[47]

It should be clear from the preceding discussion that these limitations applicable to exercises of Congressional power will be applied by the Court with at least equal rigor where the President, for some valid reason, acts on his own.

Summary and Conclusion

The general conclusions which emerge from our discussion of the war and foreign policy powers may be summarized as follows:

1. Where Congress has not acted, the President has broad powers to represent the nation in foreign affairs and to take steps necessary to secure victory in wartime.

2. Even where Congress has not legislated, the Court will restrain the President when his actions impinge on constitutional rights, where the exigency is not great or where the action impinges directly on legislative power.

3. The Congress has very broad powers to constrain presidential behavior in the national security field.

4. The Congress can delegate very broadly to the President in the national security field.

5. The Court will insist on precision in delegation when the power of the two branches together is in doubt and particularly when it sees a need to balance state action against constitutional rights.

6. The Court will exercise great restraint in dealing with political questions, in cases of unprotected individuals such as aliens being deported, and where the issue is judicial review of sensitive factual findings or of policy decisions to which the government is publicly committed in the international arena.

7. When it sees the case as one involving a balancing of state power against constitutional rights the Court insists on doing its own balancing and has not hesitated to find acts of Congress unconstitutional because of a lack of showing of sufficient danger or because the statute is overbroad.

---

[1]"Address of the General Assembly to the People of the Commonwealth of Virginia, *Letters and Other Writings of James Madison,* Vol. 4, 1829-1836, (New York: 1865), 510-11.

[2]Unless the Congress vests the power of appointment in the President alone or in the heads of departments.

[3]Constitution, Article II, Sections 2 and 3.

[4]The vitality of *Debs* after the *Steel Seizure Case,* discussed herein, may be regarded as doubtful.

[5]There is a series of cases generally cited by the Justice Department in support of claims of presidential powers. These cases are: *Marbury v. Madison,* 5 U.S. (1 Cranch) 137 (1803); *In re Debs,* 158 U.S. 554 (1895); *Oetjen v. Central Leather Co.,* 264 U.S. 297 (1918); *United States v. Curtiss-Wright,* 299 U.S. 304 (1937); *United States v. Belmont,* 301 U.S. 324 (1937); *United States v. Pink,* 315 U.S. 203 (1942); *Hirabayashi v. United States,* 320 U.S. 81 (1942); *Chicago and Southern Airlines v. Waterman Steamship Co.,* 333 U.S. 103 (1948); and *Cafeteria Workers v. McElroy,* 367 U.S. 886 (1961).

We analyze each of these cases as they arise in treating the questions discussed in this chapter. Here we wish to note that nothing in the decisions in the cases even suggests that there is an area of presidential power beyond judicial review or congressional limitation. Moreover, in none of these cases did the court define the issue as requiring the balancing of a presidential action against a constitutional right and then conclude that the presidential action was constitutional. Indeed, we know of no such case. On the limited significance of these cases on issues affecting constitutional rights see *United States v. United States District Court,* 444 F.2d 651 (denying the relevance of many of these cases on the question of warrantless wiretaps in domestic security cases); *United States v. Ehrlichman,* 376 F. Supp. 29 (1974) (memorandum opinion of Judge Gesell discussing relevance of these cases to civil liberties issues); and *Minority Memorandum on Facts and Law,* Hearings before the House Committee on the Judiciary on the Impeachment of Richard Nixon, July 22, 1974, 93rd Congress, 2nd Session, citing *Waterman, Pink, Belmont,* and *Curtiss-Wright* and concluding that "none of these cases, however, involved liberties guaranteed by the Bill of Rights," 57, n. 15.

[6]301 U.S. at 232.

[7]The Federalist, No. 69. See also Story *Commentaries* §§1492.

[8]*Fleming v. Page*, 50 U.S. 603 (9 How) 603, 615, 618 (1850).

[9]T. Roosevelt, *An Autobiography*, New York, 1914, 479.

[10]See generally, Edwin S. Corwin, *The President: Office and Powers, 1787-1957*, 4th Rev. Ed., New York, 227-62.

[11]*Greene v. McElroy*, 360 U.S. 474 (1959).

[12]*Ex parte Milligan*, 71 U.S. 2 (1866), *Duncan v. Kahanamoku*, 327 U.S. 304 (1946), *Kent v. Dulles*, 375 U.S. 116 (1958), *Raymond v. Thomas*, 91 U.S. 712 (1876), *Fleming v. Page*, 50 U.S. 603 (1850), *United States v. United States District Court*, 407 U.S. 297 (1972). The Court reserved on the President's right to engage in warrantless electronic surveillance of agents of a foreign power.

[13]We consider this specific issue elsewhere.

[14]Nor is the executive branch alone in making such assertions. Members of Congress on occasion fall into using such rhetoric. See for example the debate over the national security exemption to the 1968 wiretap law in which Senators seem agreed that if the President has the power to wiretap without a warrant Congress could not take it away. See the quotations from the debate in *United States v. United States District Court*.

[15]Article I, Section 7, paragraphs 11 through 16.

[15A]*Ex parte Garland*, 71 U.S. (4 Wall.) 333 (1867); *United States v. Klein*, 80 U.S. (13 Wall.) 128 (1871); *Knote v. United States*, 95 U.S. 149 (1877).

[16]295 U.S. 602 (1935); see Corwin, p. 92. In a footnote Corwin expresses doubts as to whether the presumption holds for the first class. See footnote 86, p. 377.

[17]Even on the wiretap issue, Robert Mardian arguing for the government conceded that the Congress could limit or even take away entirely whatever power to wiretap without a warrant the President has. See the concurring opinion of Justice White. *United States v. United States District Court*, 407 U.S. 297, 339 n. 3 (1972).

[18]*Peters v. Hobby*, 349 U.S. 331 (1955), *Cole v. Young*, 351 U.S. 536 (1956), *Service v. Dulles*, 354 U.S. 363 (1957), *Greene v. McElroy*, 360 U.S. 474 (1959).

[19]*Mahler v. Eby*, 264 U.S. 32 (1924).

[20]*Chicago & Southern Airlines v. Waterman*, 333 U.S. 103 (1948); *Knauff v. Shaughnessy*, 338 U.S. 537 (1950).

[21]*Youngstown Sheet and Tube Co. v. Sawyer*, 343 U.S. 579 (1952), 635-38.

[22]*United States v. Curtiss-Wright*, 299 U.S. 304 (1936); on the war powers see *Yakus v. United States*, 321 U.S. 414 (1944); *Lichter v. United States*, 334 U.S. 742 (1948).

[23]*Youngstown Sheet & Tube Co. v. Sawyer*, 343 U.S. 579, at n.2 (1952).

[24]See for example, *Swayne & Hoyt v. United States*, 300 U.S. 297 (1937), *Prize Cases*, 67 U.S. 635 (1863), *United States v. Midwest Oil*, 236 U.S. 459 (1915), *Zemel v. Rusk*, 381 U.S. 1 (1965). For cases in which various lower federal courts applied this principle to the Vietnam War, see Leon Friedman and Burt Neuborne, *Unquestioning Obedience to Authority*, 1972.

[25]*Raymond v. Thomas*, 91 U.S. 712 (1876). The governor had sought to annul a decree issued by a state court in a civil action.

[26]*Ex parte Endo*, 323 U.S. 283 (1944). The earlier cases are discussed herein.

[27]*Kent v. Dulles*, 357 U.S. 116 (1958). In a later case, *Zemel v. Rusk*, 381 U.S. 1 (1965), the Court upheld a regulation under which the State Department refused to validate passports to Cuba. Here the Court found a pattern of executive branch behavior extending over a period of years of precluding travel to particular regions. At least where citizens were not being discriminated against on the basis of political beliefs, the Court was prepared to interpret Congress' renewals of the Passport Act as sanction for the practice.

[28]*Cole v. Young*, 351 U.S. 536 (1956). See also *Duncan v. Kahanamoku*, 327 U.S. 304 (1945) holding that civilians could not be tried in military courts even though Congress had authorized martial law.

[29]For a modern effort to codify a series of disparate decisions and to present a coherent view of the political question doctrine see the opinion of the Court in *Baker v. Carr*, 369 U.S. 186 (1962), in which the Court reversed its position that reapportionment was a political question.

[30]5 U.S. (1 Cranch) 137, 165-66 (1803).

[31]*Ibid.*, at 166.

[32] *Foster & Elam v. Nielson,* 2 Pet. (27 U.S.) 253 (1829).

[33] p. 302.

[34] Corwin, *op. cit.*, p. 177. See also *Baker v. Carr,* at 211, and *Holmes v. Laird,* 459 F.2d 1211, at 1215 n. 26 (1972), *cert. denied,* 409 U.S. 869 (1972).

[35] *Kleindienst v. Mandel,* 408 U.S. 753 (1972). See also *Fong Yue Ting v. United States,* 149 U.S. 698 (1893), *Knauff v. Shaughnessy,* 338 U.S. 537 (1950), *Harisiades v. Shaughnessy,* 342 U.S. 580 (1952).

[36] *Miller v. United States,* 78 U.S. 268 (1871), *Ex parte Quirin,* 317 U.S. 1 (1942), *Hirota v. MacArthur,* 338 U.S. 197 (1948).

[37] *Knauff v. Shaughnessy,* 338 U.S. 537 (1950), *Martin v. Mott,* 25 U.S. 19 (1827), *Dakota Central Telephone Co. v. South Dakota ex rel. Payne,* 250 U.S. 163 (1919), *United States v. Chemical Foundation,* 272 U.S. 1 (1926).

[38] p. 111. "Though Waterman has not been over-ruled by the Supreme Court, its apparently sweeping contours have been eroded by recent circuit court opinions." *Pan American World Airlines v. CAB,* 392 F.2d 483, 492 (D.C. Cir. 1968).

[39] *Hamilton v. Kentucky Distilleries & Warehouse Co.,* 251 U.S. 146 (1919).

[40] *Home Building and Loan Association v. Blaisdell,* 290 U.S. 398 (1934).

[40a] 372 U.S. 144, 164-5 (1963).

[41] 389 U.S. 258, 263 (1967).

[42] The decision rested on the fact that both the Congress and the President had authorized the action and on the belief that the deprivation to the worker was slight, since she was eligible for employment at another restaurant operated by the same firm. *Cafeteria Workers v. McElroy,* 367 U.S. 886 (1961).

[43] *Ex parte Milligan,* 71 U.S. 402 (1866).

[44] *Hirabayashi v. United States,* 320 U.S. 81 (1943) and *Korematsu v. United States,* 323 U.S. 214 (1944).

[45] See *Kennedy v. Mendoza-Martinez,* 372 U.S. 144, holding a bill which deprived citizens of their right to be citizens without due process as unconstitutional.

[46] The Court, in a rare limit on the delegation of power in the national security field, held that it was an unlawful delegation of the right to define the phrase "defense facility."

[47] p. 264.

INHERENT PRESIDENTIAL POWERS

INHERENT PRESIDENTIAL POWERS

CASES

Oetjen v. Central Leather Company

246 U.S. 297 (1918)

Mr. Justice Clarke delivered the opinion of the court:

These two cases, involving the same question, were argued and will be decided together. They are suits in replevin and involve the title to two large consignments of hides, which the plaintiff in error claims to own as assignee of Martinez & Company, a partnership engaged in business in the city of Torreon, Mexico, but which the defendant in error claims to own by purchase from the Finnegan-Brown Company, a Texas corporation, which it is alleged purchased the hides in Mexico from General Francisco Villa, on January 3, 1914.

The cases were commenced in a circuit court of New Jersey, in which judgments were rendered for the defendants, which were affirmed by the court of errors and appeals, and they are brought to this court on the theory that the claim of title to the hides by the defendant in error is invalid because based upon a purchase from General Villa, who, it is urged, confiscated them contrary to the provisions of the Hague Convention of 1907 respecting the laws and customs of war on land; that the judgment of the state court denied to the plaintiff in error this right which he "set up and claimed" under the Hague Convention or Treaty; and that this denial gives him the right of review in this court.

A somewhat detailed description will be necessary of the political conditions in Mexico prior to and at the time of the seizure of the property in controversy by the military authorities. It appears in the record, and is a matter of general history, that on February 23, 1913, Madero, President of the Republic of Mexico, was assassinated; that immediately thereafter General Huerta declared himself Provisional President of the Republic and took the oath of office as such; that on the 26th day of March following General Carranza, who was then governor of the state of Coahuila, inaugurated a revolution against the claimed authority of Huerta and in a "Manifesto addressed to the Mexican Nation" proclaimed the organization of a constitutional government under "The Plan of Guadalupe," and that civil war was at once entered upon between the followers and forces of the two leaders. When General Carranza assumed the leadership of what were called the Constitutionalist forces he commissioned General Villa his representative, as "Commander of the North," and assigned him to an independent command in that part of the country. Such progress was made by the Carranza forces that in the autumn of 1913 they were in military possession, as the record shows, of approximately two thirds of the area of the entire country, with the exception of a few scattered towns and cities, and after a battle lasting several days the city of Torreon in the state of Coahuila was captured by General Villa on October 1 of that year. Immediately after the capture of Torreon, Villa proposed levying a military contribution on the inhabitants, for the support of his army, and thereupon influential citizens, preferring to provide the required money by an assessment upon the community, to having their property forcibly seized, called together a largely attended meeting and after negotiations with General Villa as to the amount to be paid, an assessment was made on the men of property of the city, which was in large part promptly paid. Martinez, the owner from whom the plaintiff in error claims title to the property involved in this case, was a wealthy resident of Torreon and was a dealer in hides in a large way. Being an adherent of Huerta, when Torreon was captured Martinez fled the city and failed to pay the assessment imposed upon him, and it was to satisfy this assessment that, by order of General Villa, the hides in controversy were seized and on January 3, 1914, were sold in Mexico to the Finnegan-Brown Company. They were paid for in Mexico, and were thereafter shipped into the United States and were replevied, as stated.

This court will take judicial notice of the fact that since the transactions thus detailed and since the trial of this case in the lower courts, the government of the United States recognized the government of Carranza as the de facto government of the Republic of Mexico, on October 19, 1915, and as the de jure government on August 31, 1917. Jones v. United States, 137 U.S. 202, 34 L. ed. 691, 11 Sup. Ct. Rep. 80; Underhill v. Hernandez, 168 U.S. 250, 42 L. ed. 456, 18 Sup. Ct. Rep. 83.

On this state of fact the plaintiff in error argues that the "regulations" annexed to the Hague Convention of 1907 "Respecting Laws and Customs of War on Land" constitute a treaty between the United States and Mexico; that these "regulations" forbid such seizure and sale of property as we are considering in this case; and that, therefore, somewhat vaguely, no title passed by the sale made by General Villa, and the property may be recovered by the Mexican owner or his assignees when found in this country.

It would, perhaps, be sufficient answer to this contention to say that the Hague Conventions are international in character, designed and adapted to regulate international warfare, and that they do not, in terms or in purpose, apply to a civil war. Were it otherwise, however, it might be effectively argued that the declaration relied upon that "private property cannot be confiscated," contained in article 46 of the regulations, does not have the scope claimed for it, since article 49 provides that "money contributions . . . for the needs of the army" may be levied upon occupied territory, and article 52 provides that "requisitions in kind and services may be demanded for the needs of the army of occupation," and that contributions in kind shall, as far as possible, be paid for in cash, and when not so paid for a receipt shall be given and payment of the amount due shall be made as soon as possible. And also for the reason that the "Convention" to which the "regulations" are annexed, recognizing the incomplete character of the results arrived at, expressly provides that until a more complete code is agreed upon, cases not provided for in the "regulations" shall be governed by the principles of the law of nations.

But, since claims similar to the one before us are being made in many cases in this and in other courts, we prefer to place our decision upon the application of three clearly settled principles of law to the facts of this case as we have stated them.

The conduct of the foreign relations of our government is committed by the Constitution to the executive and legislative—"the political"—departments of the government, and the propriety of what may be done in the exercise of this policial power is not subject to judicial inquiry or decision. United States v. Palmer, 3 Wheat. 610, 4 L. ed. 471; Foster v. Neilson, 2 Pet. 253, 307, 309, 7 L. ed. 415, 433, 434; Garcia v. Lee, 12 Pet. 511, 517, 520, 9 L. ed. 1176, 1178, 1179; Williams v. Suffolk Ins. Co. 13 Pet. 415, 420, 10 L. ed. 226, 228; Re Cooper, 143 U.S. 472, 499, 36 L. ed. 232, 240, 12 Sup. Ct. Rep. 453. It has been specifically decided that "who is the sovereign de jure or de facto of a territory is not a judicial but a political question, the determination of which by the legislative and executive departments of any government conclusively binds the judges, as well as all other officers, citizens, and subjects of that government. This principle has always been upheld by this court, and has been affirmed under a great variety of circumstances." Jones v. United States, 137 U.S. 202, 212, 34 L. ed. 691, 695, 11 Sup. Ct. Rep. 80.

It is also the result of the interpretation by this court of the principles of international law that when a government which originates in revolution or revolt is recognized by the political department of our government as the de jure government of the country in which it is established, such recognition is retroactive in effect and validates all the actions and conduct of the government so recognized from the commencement of its existence. Williams v. Bruffy, 96 U.S. 176, 186, 24 L. ed. 716, 718; Underhill v. Hernandez, 168 U.S. 250, 253, 42 L. ed. 456, 457, 18 Sup. Ct. Rep. 83. See s. c. 38 L.R.A. 405, 13 C. C. A. 51, 26 U.S. App. 573, 65 Fed. 577.

To these principles we must add that "every sovereign state is bound to respect the independence of every other sovereign state, and the courts of one country will not sit in judgment on the acts of the government of another, done within its own territory. Redress of grievances by reason of such acts must be obtained through the means open to be availed of by sovereign powers as between themselves." Underhill v. Hernandez, 168 U.S. 250, 252, 42 L. ed. 456, 457, 18 Sup. Ct. Rep. 83; American Banana Co. v. United Fruit Co. 213 U.S. 347, 53 L. ed. 826, 29 Sup. Ct. Rep. 511, 16 Ann. Cas. 1047.

Applying these principles of law to the case at bar; we have a duly commissioned military commander of what must be accepted as the legitimate government of Mexico, in the progress of a revolution, and when conducting active independent operations, seizing and selling in Mexico, as a military contribution, the property in controversy, at the time owned and in the possession of a citizen of Mexico, the assignor of the plaintiff in error. Plainly this was the action, in Mexico, of the legitimate Mexican government when dealing with a Mexican citizen, and, as we have seen, for the soundest reasons, and upon repeated decisions of this court, such action is not subject to reexamination and modification by the courts of this country.

The principle that the conduct of one independent government cannot be successfully questioned in the courts of another is as applicable to a case involving the title to property brought within the custody of a court, such as we have here, as it was held to be to the cases cited, in which claims for damages were based upon acts done in a foreign country; for it rests at last upon the highest considerations of international comity and expediency. To permit the validity of the acts of one sovereign state to be re-examined and perhaps condemned by the courts of another would very certainly "imperil the amicable relations between governments and vex the peace of nations."

It is not necessary to consider, as the New Jersey court did, the validity of the levy of the contribution made by the Mexican commanding general, under rules of international law applicable to the situation, since the subject is not open to re-examination by this or any other American court.

The remedy of the former owner, or of the purchaser from him, of the property in controversy, if either has any remedy, must be found in the courts of Mexico or through the diplomatic agencies of the political department of our government. The judgments of the Court of Errors and Appeals of New Jersey must be affirmed.

Home Building and Loan Assn. v. Blaisdell

398 U.S. 290 (1934)

Mr. Chief Justice Hughes delivered the opinion of the Court.

Appellant contests the validity of Chapter 339 of the Laws of Minnesota of 1933, p. 514, approved April 18, 1933, called the Minnesota Mortgage Moratorium Law, as being repugnant to the contract clause (Art. I, § 10) and the due process and equal protection clauses of the Fourteenth Amendment, of the Federal Constitution. The statute was sustained by the Supreme Court of Minnesota, 189 Minn. 422, 448; 249 N.W. 334, 893, and the case comes here on appeal.

The Act provides that, during the emergency declared to exist, relief may be had through authorized judicial proceedings with respect to foreclosures of mortgages, and execution sales, or real estate; that sales may be postponed and periods of redemption may be extended. The Act does not apply to mortgages subsequently made nor to those made previously which shall be extended for a period ending more than a year after the passage of the Act (Part One, § 8). There are separate provisions in Part Two relating to homesteads, but these are to apply "only to cases not entitled to relief under some valid provision of Part One." The Act is to remain in effect "only during the continuance of the emergency and in no event beyond May 1, 1935." No extension of the period for redemption and no postponement of sale is to be allowed which would have the effect of extending the period of redemption beyond that date. Part Two, § 8.

The Act declares that the various provisions for relief are severable; that each is to stand on its own footing with respect to validity. Part One, § 9. We are here concerned with the provisions of Part One, § 4, authorizing the District Court of the county to extend the period of redemption from foreclosure sales "for such additional time as the court may deem just and equitable," subject to the above described limitation. The extension is to be made upon application to the court, on notice, for an order determining the reasonable value of the income on the property involved in the sale, or if it has no income, then the reasonable rental value of the property, and directing the mortgagor "to pay all or a reasonable part of such income or rental value, in or toward the payment of taxes, insurance, interest, mortgage . . . indebtedness at such times and in such manner" as shall be determined by the court. The section also provides that the time for redemption from foreclosure sales theretofore made, which otherwise would expire less than thirty days after the approval of the Act shall be extended to a date thirty days after its approval, and application may be made to the court within that time for a further extension as provided in the section. By another provision of the Act, no action, prior to May 1, 1935, may be maintained for a deficiency judgment until the period of redemption as allowed by existing law or as extended under the provisions of the Act has expired. Prior to the expiration of the extended period of redemption the court may revise or alter the terms of the extension as changed circumstances may require. Part One, § 5.

The state court upheld the statute as an emergency measure. Although conceding that the obligations of the mortgage contract were impaired, the court decided that what it thus described as an impairment was, notwithstanding the contract clause of the Federal Constitution, within the police power of the State as that power was called into exercise by the public economic emergency which the legislature had found to exist. Attention is thus directed to the preamble and first section of the statute, which described the existing emergency in terms that were deemed to justify the temporary relief which the statute affords. The state court, declaring that it could not say that this legislative finding was without basis, supplemented that finding by its own statement of conditions of which it took judicial notice. The court said:

"In addition to the weight to be given the determination of the legislature that an economic emergency exists which demands relief, the court must take notice of other considerations. The members of the legislature come from every community of the state and from all the walks of life. They are familiar with conditions generally in every calling, occupation, profession, and business in the state. Not only they, but the courts must be guided by what is common knowledge. It is common knowledge that in the last few years land values have shrunk enormously. Loans made a few years ago upon the basis of the then going values cannot possibly be replaced on the basis of present values. We all know that when this law was enacted the large financial companies, which had made it their business to invest in mortgages, had ceased to do so. No bank would directly or indirectly loan on real estate mortgages. Life insurance companies, large investors in such mortgages, had even declared a moratorium as to the loan provisions of their policy contracts. The President had closed banks temporarily. The Congress, in addition to many extraordinary measures looking to the relief of the economic emergency, had passed an act to supply funds whereby mortgagors may be able within a reasonable time to refinance their mortgages or redeem from sales where the redemption has not expired. With this knowledge the court cannot well hold that the legislature had no basis in fact for the conclusion that an economic emergency existed which called for the exercise of the police power to grant relief." [189 Minn. 429; 249 N.W. 336.]

We approach the questions thus presented upon the assumption made below, as required by the law of the State, that the mortgage contained a valid power of sale to be exercised in case of default; that this power was validly exercised; that under the law then applicable the period of redemption from the sale was one year and that it has been extended by the judgment of the court over the opposition of the mortgagee-purchaser; and that during the period thus extended, and unless the order for extension is modified, the mortgagee-purchaser will be unable to obtain possession, or to obtain or convey title in fee, as he would have been able to do had the statute not been enacted. The statute does not impair the integrity of the mortgage indebtedness. The obligation for interest remains. The statute does not affect the validity of the sale or the right of a mortgagee-purchaser to title in fee, or his right to obtain a deficiency judgment, if the mortgagor fails to redeem within the prescribed period. Aside from the extension of time, the other conditions of redemption are unaltered. While the mortgagor remains in possession he must pay the rental value as that value has been determined, upon notice and hearing, by the court. The rental value so paid is devoted to the carrying of the property by the application of the required payments to taxes, insurance, and interest on the mortgage indebtedness. While the mortgagee-purchaser is debarred from actual possession, he has, so far as rental value is concerned, the equivalent of possession during the extended period.

In determining whether the provision for this temporary and conditional relief exceeds the power of the State by reason of the clause in the Federal Constitution prohibiting impairment of the obligations of contracts, we must consider the relation of emergency to constitutional power, the historical setting of the contract clause, the development of the jurisprudence of this Court in the construction of that clause, and the principles of construction which we may consider to be established.

Emergency does not create power. Emergency does not increase granted power or remove or diminish the restrictions imposed upon power granted or reserved. The Constitution was adopted in a period of grave emergency. Its grants of power to the Federal Government and its limitations of the power of the States were determined in the light of emergency and they are not altered by emergency. What power was thus granted and what limitations were thus imposed are questions which have always been, and always will be, the subject of close examination under our constitutional system.

While emergency does not create power, emergency may furnish the occasion for the exercise of power. "Although an emergency may not call into life a power which has never lived, nevertheless emergency may afford a reason for the exertion of a living power already enjoyed." *Wilson v. New,* 243 U.S. 332, 348. The constitutional question presented in the light of an emergency is whether the power possessed embraces the particular exercise of it in response to particular conditions. Thus, the war power of the Federal Government is not created by the emergency of war, but it is a power given to meet that emergency. It is a power to wage war successfully, and thus it permits the harnessing of the entire energies of the people in a supreme cooperative effort to preserve the nation. But even the war power does not remove constitutional limitations safeguarding essential liberties. When the provisions of the Constitution, in grant or restriction, are specific, so particularized as not to admit of construction, no question is presented. Thus, emergency would not permit a State to have more than two Senators in the Congress, or permit the election of President by a general popular vote without regard to the number of electors to which the States are respectively entitled, or permit the States to "coin money" or to "make anything but gold and silver coin a tender in payment of debts." But where constitutional grants and limitations of power are set forth in general clauses, which afford a broad outline, the process of construction is essential to fill in the details. That is true of the contract clause. The necessity of construction is not obviated by the fact that the contract clause is associated in the same section with other and more specific prohibitions. Even the grouping of subjects in the same clause may not require the same application to each of the subjects, regardless of differences in their nature. See *Groves v. Slaughter,* 15 Pet. 449, 505; *Atlantic Cleaners & Dyers v. United States,* 286 U.S. 427, 434.

* * *

United States v. Curtiss-Wright Corp.

299 U.S. 304 (1936)

Mr. Justice Sutherland delivered the opinion of the Court.

On January 27, 1936, an indictment was returned in the court below, the first count of which charges that appellees, beginning with the 29th day of May, 1934, conspired to sell in the United States certain arms of war, namely fifteen machine guns, to Bolivia, a country then engaged in armed conflict in the Chaco, in violation of the Joint Resolution of Congress approved May 28, 1934, and the provisions of a proclamation issued on the same day by the President of the United States pursuant to authority conferred by § 1 of the resolution. In pursuance of the conspiracy, the commission of certain overt acts was alleged, details of which need not be stated. The Joint Resolution (c. 365, 48 Stat. 811) follows:

"*Resolved by the Senate and House of Representatives of the United States of America in Congress assembled,* That if the President finds that the prohibition of the sale of arms and munitions of war in the United States to those countries now engaged in armed conflict in the Chaco may contribute to the reestablishment of peace between those countries, and if after consultation with the governments of other American Republics and with their cooperation, as well as that of such other governments as he may deem necessary, he makes proclamation to that effect, it shall be unlawful to sell, except under such limitations and exceptions as the President prescribes, any arms or munitions of war in any place in the United States to the countries now engaged in that armed conflict, or to any person, company, or association acting in the interest of either country, until otherwise ordered by the President or by Congress.

"Sec. 2. Whoever sells any arms or munitions of war in violation of section 1 shall, on conviction, be punished by a fine not exceeding $10,000 or by imprisonment not exceeding two years, or both."

The President's proclamation (48 Stat. 1744), after reciting the terms of the Joint Resolution, declares:

* * *

Appellees severally demurred to the first count of the indictment on the grounds (1) that it did not charge facts sufficient to show the commission by appellees of any offense against any law of the United States; (2) that this count of the indictment charges a conspiracy to violate the joint resolution and the Presidential proclamation, both of which had expired according to the terms of the joint resolution by reason of the revocation contained in the Presidential proclamation of November 14, 1935, and were not in force at the time when the indictment was found. The points urged in support of the demurrers were, first, that the joint resolution effects an invalid delegation of legislative power to the executive; second, that the joint resolution never became effective because of the failure of the

President to find essential jurisdictional facts; and third, that the second proclamation operated to put an end to the alleged liability under the joint resolution.

The court below sustained the demurrers upon the first point, but overruled them on the second and third points. 14 F. Supp. 230. The government appealed to this court under the provisions of the Criminal Appeals Act of March 2, 1907, 34 Stat. 1246, as amended, U. S. C. Title 18, § 682. That act authorizes the United States to appeal from a district court direct to this court in criminal cases where, among other things, the decision sustaining a demurrer to the indictment or any count thereof is based upon the invalidity or construction of the statute upon which the indictment is founded.

First. It is contended that by the Joint Resolution, the going into effect and continued operation of the resolution was conditioned (a) upon the President's judgment as to its beneficial effect upon the reestablishment of peace between the countries engaged in armed conflict in the Chaco; (b) upon the making of a proclamation, which was left to his unfettered discretion, thus constituting an attempted substitution of the President's will for that of Congress; (c) upon the making of a proclamation putting an end to the operation of the resolution, which again was left to the President's unfettered discretion; and (d) further, that the extent of its operation in particular cases was subject to limitation and exception by the President, controlled by no standard. In each of these particulars, appellees urge that Congress abdicated its essential functions and delegated them to the Executive.

Whether, if the Joint Resolution had related solely to internal affairs it would be open to the challenge that it constituted an unlawful delegation of legislative power to the Executive, we find it unnecessary to determine. The whole aim of the resolution is to affect a situation entirely external to the United States, and falling within the category of foreign affairs. The determination which we are called to make, therefore, is whether the Joint Resolution, as applied to that situation, is vulnerable to attack under the rule that forbids a delegation of the law-making power. In other words, assuming (but not deciding) that the challenged delegation, if it were confined to internal affairs, would be invalid, may it nevertheless be sustained on the ground that its exclusive aim is to afford a remedy for a hurtful condition within foreign territory?

It will contribute to the elucidation of the question if we first consider the differences between the powers of the federal government in respect of foreign or external affairs and those in respect of domestic or internal affairs. That there are differences between them, and that these differences are fundamental, may not be doubted.

The two classes of powers are different, both in respect of their origin and their nature. The broad statement that the federal government can exercise no powers except those specifically enumerated in the Constitution, and such implied powers as are necessary and proper to carry into effect the enumerated powers, is categorically true only in respect of our internal affairs. In that field, the primary purpose of the Constitution was to carve from the general mass of legislative powers *then possessed by the states* such portions as it was thought desirable to vest in the federal government, leaving those not included in the enumeration still in the states. *Carter v. Carter Coal Co.*, 298 U.S. 238, 294. That this doctrine applies only to powers which the states had, is self evident. And since the states severally never possessed international powers, such powers could not have been carved from the mass of state powers but obviously were transmitted to the United States from some other source. During the colonial period, those powers were possessed exclusively by and were entirely under the control of the Crown. By the Declaration of Independence, "the Representatives of the United States of America" declared the United [not the several] Colonies to be free and independent states, and as such to have "full Power to levy War, conclude Peace, contract Alliances, establish Commerce and to do all other Acts and Things which Independent States may of right do."

As a result of the separation from Great Britain by the colonies acting as a unit, the powers of external sovereignty passed from the Crown not to the colonies severally, but to the colonies in their collective and corporate capacity as the United States of America. Even before the Declaration, the colonies were a unit in foreign affairs, acting through a common agency—namely the Continental Congress, composed of delegates from the thirteen colonies. That agency exercised the powers of war and peace, raised an army, created a navy, and finally adopted the Declaration of Independence. Rulers come and go; governments end and forms of government change; but sovereignty survives. A political society cannot endure without a supreme will somewhere. Sovereignty is never held in suspense. When, therefore, the external sovereignty of Great Britain in respect of the colonies ceased, it immediately passed to the Union. See *Penhallow v. Doane,* 3 Dall. 54, 80-81. That fact was given practical application almost at once. The treaty of peace, made on September 23, 1783, was concluded between his Britanic Majesty and the "United States of America." 8 Stat.—European Treaties—80.

The Union existed before the Constitution, which was ordained and established among other things to form "a more perfect Union." Prior to that event, it is clear that the Union, declared by the Articles of Confederation to be "perpetual," was the sole possessor of external sovereignty and in the Union it remained without change save in so far as the Constitution in express terms qualified its exercise. The Framers' Convention was called and exerted its powers upon the irrefutable postulate that though the states were several their people in respect of foreign affairs were one. Compare *The Chinese Exclusion Case,* 130 U.S. 581, 604, 606. In that convention, the entire absence of state power to deal with those affairs was thus forcefully stated by Rufus King:

"The states were not 'sovereigns' in the sense contended for by some. They did not possess the peculiar features of sovereignty,—they could not make war, nor peace, nor alliances, nor treaties. Considering them as political beings, they were dumb, for they could not speak to any foreign sovereign whatever. They were deaf, for they could not hear any propositions from such sovereign. They had not even the organs or faculties of defence or offence, for they could not of themselves raise troops, or equip vessels, for war." 5 Elliott's Debates 212.[1]

It results that the investment of the federal government with the powers of external sovereignty did not depend upon the affirmative grants of the Constitution. The powers to declare and wage war, to conclude peace, to make treaties, to maintain diplomatic relations with other sovereignties, if they had never been mentioned in the Constitution, would have vested in the federal government as necessary concomitants of nationality. Neither the Constitution nor the laws passed in pursuance of it have any force in foreign territory unless in respect of our own citizens (see *American Banana Co. v. United Fruit Co.,* 213 U.S. 347, 356); and operations of the nation in such territory must be governed by treaties, international understandings and compacts, and the principles of international law. As a member of the family of nations, the right and power of the United States in that field are equal to the right and power of the other members of the international family. Otherwise, the United States is not completely sovereign. The power to acquire territory by discovery and occupation (*Jones v. United States,* 137 U.S. 202, 212), the power to expel undesirable aliens (*Fong Yue Ting v. United States,* 149 U.S. 698, 705 *et seq.*), the power to make such international agreements as do not constitute treaties in the constitutional sense (*Altman & Co. v. United States,* 224 U.S. 583, 600-601; Crandall, Treaties, Their Making and Enforcement, 2d ed., p. 102 and note 1), none of which is expressly affirmed by the Constitution, nevertheless exist as inherently inseparable from the conception of nationality. This the court recognized, and in each of the cases cited found the warrant for its conclusions not in the provisions of the Constitution, but in the law of nations.

In *Burnet v. Brooks,* 288 U.S. 378, 396, we said, "As a nation with all the attributes of sovereignty, the United States is vested with all the powers of government necessary to maintain an effective control of international relations." Cf. *Carter v. Carter Coal Co., supra,* p. 295.

Not only, as we have shown, is the federal power over external affairs in origin and essential character different from that over internal affairs, but participation in the exercise of the power is significantly limited. In this vast external realm, with its important, complicated, delicate and manifold problems, the President alone has the power to speak or listen as a representative of the nation. He *makes* treaties with the advice and consent of the Senate; but he alone negotiates. Into the field of negotiation the Senate cannot intrude; and Congress itself is powerless to invade it. As Marshall said in his great argument of March 7, 1800, in the House of Representatives, "The President is the sole organ of the nation in its external relations, and its sole representative with foreign nations." Annals, 6th Cong., col. 613. The Senate Committee on Foreign Relations at a very early day in our history (February 15, 1816), reported to the Senate, among other things, as follows:

"The President is the constitutional representative of the United States with regard to foreign nations. He manages our concerns with foreign nations and must necessarily be most competent to determine when, how, and upon what subjects negotiation may be urged with the greatest prospect of success. For his conduct he is responsible to the Constitution. The committee consider this responsibility the surest pledge for the faithful discharge of his duty. They think the interference of the Senate in the direction of foreign negotiations calculated to diminish that responsibility and thereby to impair the best security for the national safety. The nature of transactions with foreign nations, moreover, requires caution and unity of design, and their success frequently depends on secrecy and dispatch." U.S. Senate, Reports, Committee on Foreign Relations, vol. 8, p. 24.

It is important to bear in mind that we are here dealing not along with an authority vested in the President by an exertion of legislative power, but with such an authority plus the very delicate, plenary and exclusive power of the President as the sole organ of the federal government in the field of international relations—a power which does not require as a basis for its exercise an act of Congress, but which, of course, like every other governmental power, must be exercised in subordination to the applicable provisions of the Constitution. It is quite apparent that if, in the maintenance of our international relations, embarrassment—perhaps serious embarrassment—is to be avoided and success for our aims achieved, congressional legislation which is to be made effective through negotiation and inquiry within the international field must often accord to the President a degree of discretion and freedom from statutory restriction which would not be admissible were domestic affairs alone involved. Moreover, he, not Congress, has the better opportunity of knowing the conditions which prevail in foreign countries, and especially is this true in time of war. He has his confidential sources of information. He has his agents in the form of diplomatic, consular and other officials. Secrecy in respect of information gathered by them may be highly necessary, and the premature disclosure of it productive of harmful results. Indeed, so clearly is this true that the first President refused to accede to a request to lay before the House of Representatives the instructions, correspondence and documents relating to the negotiation of the Jay Treaty—a refusal the wisdom of which was recognized by the House itself and has never since been doubted. In his reply to the request, President Washington said:

"The nature of foreign negotiations requires caution, and their success must often depend on secrecy; and even when brought to a conclusion a full disclosure of all the measures, demands, or eventual concessions which may have been proposed or contemplated would be extremely impolitic; for this might have a pernicious influence on future negotiations, or produce immediate inconveniences, perhaps danger and mischief, in relation to other powers. The necessity of such caution and secrecy was one cogent reason for vesting the power of making treaties in the President, with the advice and consent of the Senate, the principle on which that body was formed confining it to a small number of members. To admit, then, a right in the House of Representatives to demand and to have as a matter of course all the papers respecting a negotiation with a foreign power would be to establish a dangerous precedent." 1 Messages and Papers of the Presidents, p. 194.

The marked difference between foreign affairs and domestic affairs in this respect is recognized by both houses of Congress in the very form of their requisitions for information from the executive departments. In the case of every department except the Department of State, the resolution *directs* the official to furnish the information. In the case of the State Department, dealing with foreign affairs, the President is *requested* to furnish the information "if not incompatible with the public interest." A statement that to furnish the information is not compatible with the public interest rarely, if ever, is questioned.

When the President is to be authorized by legislation to act in respect of a matter intended to affect a situation in foreign territory, the legislator properly bears in mind the important consideration that the form of the President's action—or, indeed, whether he shall act at all—may well depend, among other things, upon the nature of the confidential information which he has or may thereafter receive, or upon the effect which his action may have upon our foreign relations. This consideration, in connection with what we have already said on the subject, discloses the unwisdom of requiring Congress in this field of governmental power to lay down narrowly definite standards by which the President is to be governed. As this court said in *Mackenzie v. Hare,* 239 U.S. 299, 311, "As a government, the United States is invested with all the attributes of sovereignty. As it has the character of nationality it has the powers of nationality, especially those which concern its relations and intercourse with other countries. *We should hesitate long before limiting or embarrassing such powers.*" (Italics supplied.)

In the light of the foregoing observations, it is evident that this court should not be in haste to apply a general rule which will have the effect of condemning legislation like that under review as constituting an unlawful delegation of legislative power. The principles which justify such legislation find overwhelming support in the unbroken legislative practice which has prevailed almost from the inception of the national government to the present day.

Practically every volume of the United States Statutes contains one or more acts or joint resolutions of Congress authorizing action by the President in respect of subjects affecting foreign relations, which either leave the exercise of the power to his unrestricted judgment, or provide a standard far more general than that which has always been considered requisite with regard to domestic affairs. Many, though not all, of these acts are designated in the footnote.

The result of holding that the joint resolution here under attack is void and unenforceable as constituting an unlawful delegation of legislative power would be to stamp this multitude of comparable acts and resolutions as likewise invalid. And while this court may not, and should not, hesitate to declare acts of Congress, however many times repeated, to be unconstitutional if beyond all rational doubt it finds them to be so, an impressive array of legislation such as we have just set forth, enacted by nearly every Congress from the beginning of our national existence to the present day, must be given unusual weight in the process of reaching a correct determination of the problem. A legislative practice such as we have here, evidenced not by only occasional instances, *Ames v. Kansas,* 111 U.S. 449, 469; *McCulloch v. Maryland,* 4 Wheat. 316, 401; *Downes v. Bidwell,* 182 U.S. 244, 286.

The uniform, long-continued and undisputed legislative practice just disclosed rests upon an admissible view of the Constitution which, even if the practice found far less support in principle than we think it does, we should not feel at liberty at this late day to disturb.

We deem it unnecessary to consider, *seriatim,* the several clauses which are said to evidence the unconstitutionality of the Joint Resolution as involving an unlawful delegation of legislative power. It is enough to summarize by saying that, both upon principle and in accordance with precedent, we conclude there is sufficient warrant for the broad discretion vested in the President to determine whether the enforcement of the statute will have a beneficial effect upon the reestablishment of peace in the affected countries; whether he shall make proclamation to bring the resolution into operation; whether and when the resolution shall cease to operate and to make proclamation accordingly; and to prescribe limitations and exceptions to which the enforcement of the resolution shall be subject.

United States v. Belmont

301 U.S. 324 (1937)

Mr. Justice Sutherland delivered the opinion of the Court.

This is an action at law brought by petitioner against respondents in a federal district court to recover a sum of money deposited by a Russian corporation (Petrograd Metal Works) with August Belmont, a private banker doing business in New York City under the name of August Belmont & Co. August Belmont died in 1924; and respondents are the duly-appointed executors of his will. A motion to dismiss the complaint for failure to state facts sufficient to constitute a cause of action was sustained by the district court, and its judgment was affirmed by the court below. 85 F. (2d) 542. The facts alleged, so far as necessary to be stated, follow.

The corporation had deposited with Belmont, prior to 1918, the sum of money which petitioner seeks to recover. In 1918, the Soviet Government duly enacted a decree by which it dissolved, terminated and liquidated the corporation (together with others), and nationalized and appropriated all of its property and assets of every kind and wherever situated, including the deposit account with Belmont. As a result, the deposit became the property of the Soviet Government, and so remained until November 16, 1933, at which time the Soviet Government released and assigned to petitioner all amounts due to that government from American nationals, including the deposit account of the corporation with Belmont. Respondents failed and refused to pay the amount upon demand duly made by petitioner.

The assignment was effected by an exchange of diplomatic correspondence between the Soviet Government and the United States. The purpose was to bring about a final settlement of the claims and counterclaims between the Soviet Government and the United States; and it was agreed that the Soviet Government would take no steps to enforce claims against American nationals; but all such claims were released and assigned to the United States, with the understanding that the Soviet Government was to be duly notified of all amounts realized by the United States from such release and assignment. The assignment and requirement for notice are parts of the larger plan to bring about a settlement of the rival claims of the high contracting parties. The continuing and definite interest of the Soviet Government in the collection of assigned claims is evident; and the case, therefore, presents a question of public concern, the determination of which well might involve the good faith of the United States in the eyes of a foreign government. The court below held that the assignment thus effected embraced the claim here in question; and with that we agree.

That court, however, took the view that the situs of the bank deposit was within the State of New York; that in no sense could it be regarded as an intangible property right within Soviet territory; and that the nationalization decree, if enforced, would put into effect an act of confiscation. And it held that a judgment for the United States could not be had, because, in view of that result, it would be contrary to the controlling public policy of the State of New York. The further contention is made by respondents that the public policy of the United States would likewise be infringed by such a judgment. The two questions thus presented are the only ones necessary to be considered.

First. We do not pause to inquire whether in fact there was any policy of the State of New York to be infringed, since we are of opinion that no state policy can prevail against the international compact here involved.

This court has held, Underhill v. Hernandez, 168 U.S. 250, 42 L. ed. 456, 18 S. Ct. 83, that every sovereign state must recognize the independence of every other sovereign state; and that the courts of one will not sit in judgment upon the acts of the government of another, done within its own territory.

That general principle was applied in Oetjen v. Central Leather Co. 246 U.S. 297, 62 L. ed. 726, 38 S. Ct. 309, to a case where an action in replevin had been brought in a New Jersey state court to recover a consignment of hides purchased in Mexico from General Villa. The title of the purchaser was assailed on the ground that Villa had confiscated the hides. Villa, it appeared, had seized the hides while conducting independent operations under the Carranza government, which at the time of the seizure had made much progress in its revolution in Mexico. The government of the United States, after the trial of the case in the state court, had recognized the government of Carranza, first as the de facto government of the Republic of Mexico, and later as the government de jure. This court held that the conduct of foreign relations was committed by the Constitution to the political departments of the government, and the propriety of what may be done in the exercise of this political power was not subject to judicial inquiry or decision; that who is the sovereign of a territory is not a judicial question, but one the determination of which by the political departments conclusively binds the courts; and that recognition by these departments is retroactive and validates all actions and conduct of the government so recognized from the commencement of its existence. "The principle," we said, p. 303, "that the conduct of one independent government cannot be successfully questioned in the courts of another is as applicable to a case involving the title to property brought within the custody of a court, such as we have here, as it was held to be to the cases cited, in which claims for damages were based upon acts done in a foreign country, for it rests at last upon the highest considerations of international comity and expediency. To permit the validity of the acts of one sovereign State to be reexamined and perhaps condemned by the courts of another would very certainly 'imperil the amicable relations between governments and vex the peace of nations.' " Ricaud v. American Metal Co. 246 U.S. 304, 308-310, 62 L. ed. 733, 736, 737, 38 S. Ct. 312, is to the same effect.

In Aksionairnoye Obschestvo v. James Sagor & Co. [1921] 3 K. B. 532, 11 B. R. C. 666, the English Court of Appeal expressly approved and followed our decision in the Oetjen Case. The English case involved that part of the same decree of the Soviet Government here under consideration which declared certain private woodworking establishments to be the property of the Republic. Under that decree the Government seized plaintiff's factory in Russia together with a stock of wood therein. Agents of the Republic sold a quantity of the stock so seized to the defendants, who imported it into England. Thereafter, the British Government recognized the Soviet Government as the de facto government of Russia. Upon these facts, the court held that, the British Government having thus recognized the Soviet Government, existing at a date before the decree in question, the validity of that decree and the sale of the wood to the defendants could not be impugned, and gave judgment for defendants accordingly. The court regarded the decree as one of confiscation, but was unable to see (Bankes, L. J., p. 546) how the courts could treat the decree "otherwise than as the expression by the de facto government of a civilized country of a policy which it considered to be in the best interest of that country. It must be quite immaterial for present purposes that the same views are not entertained by the Government of this country, are repudiated by the vast majority of its citizens, and are not recognized by our laws." Lord Justice Scrutton, in his opinion, discusses (pp. 557-559) the contention that the courts should refuse to recognize the decree and the titles derived under it as confiscatory and unjust, and concludes that the question is one not for the judges but for the action of the sovereign through his ministers. "I do not feel able," he said, "to come to the conclusion that the legislation of a state recognized by my Sovereign as an independent sovereign state is so contrary to moral principle that the judges ought not to recognize it. The responsibility for recognition or non-recognition with the consequences of each rests on the political advisers of the Sovereign and not on the judges." Further citation of authority seems unnecessary.

We take judicial notice of the fact that coincident with the assignment set forth in the complaint, the President recognized the Soviet Government, and normal diplomatic relations were established between that government and the Government of the United States, followed by an exchange of ambassadors. The effect of this was to validate, so far as this country is concerned, all acts of the Soviet Government here involved from the commencement of its existence. The recognition, establishment of diplomatic relations, the assignment, and agreements with respect thereto, were all parts of one transaction, resulting in an international compact between the two governments. That the negotiations, acceptance of the assignment and agreements and understandings in respect thereof were within the competence of the President may not be doubted. Governmental power over internal affairs is distributed between the national government and the several states. Governmental power over external affairs is not distributed, but is vested exclusively in the national government. And in respect of what was done here, the Executive had authority to speak as the sole organ of that government. The assignment and the agreements in connection therewith did not, as in the case of treaties, as that term is used in the treaty making clause of the Constitution (Art. 2, § 2), require the advice and consent of the Senate.

A treaty signifies "a compact made between two or more independent nations with a view to the public welfare." B. Altman & Co. v. United States, 224 U.S. 583, 600, 56 L. ed. 894, 910, 32 S. Ct. 593. But an international compact, as this was, is not always a treaty which requires the participation of the Senate. There are many such compacts, of which a protocol, a modus vivendi, a postal convention, and agreements like that now under consideration are illustrations. See 5 Moore, International Law Dig. 210-221. The distinction was pointed out by this court in the B. Altman & Co. Case, supra, which arose under § 3 of the Tariff Act of [July 24], 1897 [30 Stat. at L. 151, 203, chap. 11], authorizing the President to conclude commercial agreements with foreign countries in certain specified matters. We held that although this might not be a treaty requiring ratification by the Senate, it was a compact negotiated and proclaimed under the authority of the President, and as such was a "treaty" within the meaning of the Circuit Court of Appeals Act, the construction of which might be reviewed upon direct appeal to this court.

Plainly, the external powers of the United States are to be exercised without regard to state laws or policies. The supremacy of a treaty in this respect has been recognized from the beginning. Mr. Madison, in the Virginia Convention, said that if a treaty does not supersede existing state laws, as far as they contravene its operation, the treaty would be ineffective. "To counteract it by the supremacy of the state laws, would bring on the Union the just charge of national perfidy, and involve us in war." 3 Elliot, Debates, 515. And see Ware v. Hylton, 3 Dall. 199, 236, 237, 1 L. ed. 568, 584, 585. And while this rule in respect of treaties is established by the express language of cl. 2, Art. 6, of the Constitution, the same rule would result in the case of all international compacts and agreements from the very fact that complete power over international affairs is in the national government and is not and cannot be subject to any curtailment or interference on the part of the several states. Compare United States v. Curtiss-Wright Export Corp. 299 U.S. 304, 316, et seq., ante, 255, 57 S. Ct. 216. In respect of all international negotiations and compacts, and in respect of our foreign relations generally, state lines disappear. As to such purposes the State of New York does not exist. Within the field of its powers, whatever the United States rightfully undertakes, it necessarily has warrant to consummate. And when judicial authority is invoked in aid of such consummation, state constitutions, state laws, and state policies are irrelevant to the inquiry and decision. It is inconceivable that any of them can be interposed as an obstacle to the effective operation of a federal constitution power. Cf. Missouri v. Holland, 252

U.S. 416, 64 L. ed. 641, 60 S. Ct. 382, 11 A.L.R. 984; Asakura v. Seattle, 265 U.S. 332, 341, 68 L. ed. 1041, 1044, 44 S. Ct. 515.

Second. The public policy of the United States relied upon as a bar to the action is that declared by the Constitution, namely, that private property shall not be taken without just compensation. But the answer is that our Constitution, laws and policies have no extraterritorial operation, unless in respect of our own citizens. Compare United States v. Curtiss-Wright Export Corp. supra, at p. 318. What another country has done in the way of taking over property of its nationals, and especially of its corporations, is not a matter for judicial consideration here. Such nationals must look to their own government for any redress to which they may be entitled. So far as the record shows, only the rights of the Russian corporation have been affected by what has been done; and it will be time enough to consider the rights of our nationals when, if ever, by proper judicial proceeding, it shall be made to appear that they are so affected as to entitle them to judicial relief. The substantive right to the moneys, as now disclosed, became vested in the Soviet Government as the successor to the corporation; and this right that government has passed to the United States. It does not appear that respondents have any interest in the matter beyond that of a custodian. Thus far no question under the Fifth Amendment is involved.

It results that the complaint states a cause of action and that the judgment of the court below to the contrary is erroneous. In so holding, we deal only with the case as now presented and with the parties now before us. We do not consider the status of adverse claims, if there be any, of others not parties to this action. And nothing we have said is to be construed as foreclosing the assertion of any such claim to the fund involved, by intervention or other appropriate proceeding. We decide only that the complaint alleges facts sufficient to constitute a cause of action against the respondents.

Judgment reversed.

United States v. Pink

315 U.S. 203 (1942)

Mr. Justice Douglas delivered the opinion of the Court:

This action was brought by the United States to recover the assets of the New York branch of the First Russian Insurance Co. which remained in the hands of respondent after the payment of all domestic creditors. The material allegations of the complaint were in brief as follows:

The First Russian Insurance Co., organized under the laws of the former Empire of Russia, established a New York branch in 1907. It deposited with the Superintendent of Insurance, pursuant to the laws of New York, certain assets to secure payment of claims resulting from transactions of its New York branch. By certain laws, decrees, enactments and orders in 1918 and 1919 the Russian Government nationalized the business of insurance and all of the property, wherever situated, of all Russian insurance companies (including the First Russian Insurance Co.), and discharged and cancelled all the debts of such companies and the rights of all shareholders in all such property. The New York branch of the First

Russian Insurance Co. continued to do business in New York until 1925. At that time respondent, pursuant to an order of the Supreme Court of New York, took possession of its assets for a determination and report upon the claims of the policyholders and creditors in the United States. Thereafter all claims of domestic creditors, i.e., all claims arising out of the business of the New York branch, were paid by respondent, leaving a balance in his hands of more than $1,000,000. In 1931 the New York Court of Appeals (255 NY 415, 175 NE 114) directed respondent to dispose of that balance as follows: first, to pay claims of foreign creditors who had filed attachment prior to the commencement of the liquidation proceeding and also such claims as were filed prior to the entry of the order on remittitur of that court; and second, to pay any surplus to a quorum of the board of directors of the company. Pursuant to that mandate, respondent proceeded with the liquidation of the claims of the foreign creditors. Some payments were made thereon. The major portion of the allowed claims, however, were not paid, a stay having been granted pending disposition of the claim of the United States. On November 16, 1933, the United States recognized the Union of Soviet Socialist Republics as the de jure Government of Russia and as an incident to that recognition accepted as assignment (known as the Litvinov Assignment) of certain claims. The Litvinov Assignment was in the form of a letter, dated November 16, 1933, to the President of the United States from Maxim Litvinov, People's Commissar for Foreign Affairs, reading as follows:

* * *

On November 14, 1934, the United States brought an action in the federal District Court for the Southern District of New York, seeking to recover the assets in the hands of respondent. This Court held in United States v. Bank of New York & T. Co. 296 U.S. 463, 80 L ed 331, 56 S Ct 343, that the well settled "principles governing the convenient and orderly administration of justice require that the jurisdiction of the state court should be respected" (p. 480); and that whatever might be "the effect of recognition" of the Russian Government, it did not terminate the state proceedings. p. 479. The United States was remitted to the state court for determination of its claim, no opinion being intimated on the merits. p. 481. The United States then moved for leave to intervene in the liquidation proceedings. Its motion was denied "without prejudice to the institution of the time-honored form of action." That order was affirmed on appeal.

Thereafter the present suit was instituted in the Supreme Court of New York. The defendants, other than respondent, were certain designated policyholders and other creditors who had presented in the liquidation proceedings claims against the corporation. The complaint prayed, inter alia, that the United States be adjudged to be the sole and exclusive owner entitled to immediate possession of the entire surplus fund in the hands of the respondent.

Respondent's answer denied the allegations of the complaint that title to the funds in question passed to the United States and that the Russian decrees had the effect claimed. It also set forth various affirmative defenses—that the order of distribution pursuant to the decree in 255 NY 415, 175 NE 114, could not be affected by the Litvinov Assignment; that the Litvinov Assignment was unenforceable because it was conditioned upon a final settlement of claims and counterclaims which had not been accomplished; that under Russian law the nationalization decrees in question had no effect on property not factually taken into possession by the Russian Government prior to May 22, 1922; that the Russian decrees had no extraterritorial effect, according to Russian law; that if the decrees were given extraterritorial effect, they were confiscatory and their recognition would be unconstitutional and contrary to the public policy of the United States and of the State of New York; and that the United States under the Litvinov Assignment acted merely as a collection agency for the Russian Government and hence was foreclosed from asserting any title to the property in question.

The answer was filed in March 1938. In April, 1939, the New York Court of Appeals decided Moscow F. Ins. Co. v. Bank of New York & T. Co. 280 NY 286, 20 NE(2d) 758. In May, 1939, respondent (but not the other defendants) moved pursuant to Rule 113 of the Rules of the New York Civil Practice Act and § 476 of that Act for an order dismissing the complaint and awarding summary judgment in favor of respondent "on the ground that there is no merit to the action and that it is insufficient in law." The affidavit in support of the motion stated that there was "no dispute as to the facts;" that the separate defenses to the complaint "need not now be considered for the complaint standing alone is insufficient in law;" that the facts in the Moscow F. Ins. Co. Case and the instant one, so far as material, were "parallel" and the Russian decrees the same; and that the Moscow F. Ins. Co. Case authoritatively settled the principles of law governing the instant one. The affidavit read in opposition to the motion stated that a petition for certiorari in the Moscow F. Ins. Co. Case was about to be filed in this Court; that the motion was premature and should be denied or decision thereon withheld pending the final decision of this Court. On June 29, 1939, the Supreme Court of New York granted the motion and dismissed the complaint "on the merits," citing only the Moscow F. Ins. Co. Case in support of its action. On September 2, 1939, a petition for certiorari in the Moscow F. Ins. Co. Case was filed in this Court. The judgment in that case was affirmed here by an equally divided Court. 309 U.S. 624, 84 L ed 986, 60 S Ct 725. Subsequently the Appellate Division of the Supreme Court of New York affirmed, without opinion, the order of dismissal in the instant case. The Court of Appeals affirmed with a per curiam opinion (284 NY 555, 32 NE (2d) 552) which after noting that the decision below was "in accord with the decision" in the Moscow F. Ins. Co. Case stated:

"Three of the judges of this court concurred in a forceful opinion dissenting from the court's decision in that case, but the decision left open no question which has been argued upon this appeal. We are agreed that without again considering such questions this court should, in determining title to assets of First Russian Insurance Company, deposited in this State, apply in this case the same rules of law which the court applied in the earlier case in determining title to the assets of Moscow Fire Insurance Company deposited here."

We granted the petition for certiorari because of the nature and public importance of the questions raised.

First. Respondent insists that the complaint in this action was identical in substance and sought the same relief as the petition of the United States in the Moscow F. Ins. Co. Case, and that his answer set up the same defenses as were successfully sustained against the United States by the defendants in that case. He also maintains that both parties agreed on the motion for summary judgment that the decision in the Moscow F. Ins. Co. Case governed this cause, leaving no issues to be tried. We agree with those contentions. It is in accord not only with the motion papers but also with the ruling of the New York Court of Appeals that the Moscow F. Ins. Co. Case "left open no question which has been argued upon this appeal." In view of that ruling we are not free to inquire, as petitioner suggests, into the propriety under New York practice of grounding the motion for summary judgment on the record in the Moscow F. Ins. Co. Case. That is distinctly a question of state law on which New York has the last word.

But it does not follow, as respondent urges, that the writ should be dismissed as improvidently granted. The Moscow F. Ins. Co. Case is not res judicata since respondent was not a party to that suit. Stone v. Farmers' Bank, 174 U.S. 409, 43 L ed 1027, 19 S Ct 880; Rudd v. Cornell, 171 NY 114, 127, 128, 63 NE 823; St. John v. Fowler, 229 NY 270, 274, 128 NE 199. Nor was our affirmance of the judgment in that case by an equally divided court an authoritative precedent. While it was conclusive and binding upon the parties as respects that controversy (Durant v. Essex Co. 7 Wall. (U.S.) 107, 19 L ed 154), the lack of an agreement by a majority of the Court on the principles of law involved prevents it from being an authoritative determination for other cases. Hertz v. Woodman, 218 U.S. 205, 213, 214, 54 L ed 1001, 1005, 1006, 30 S Ct 621.

The upshot of the matter is that we now reach the issues in the Moscow F. Ins. Co. Case in so far as they are embraced in the pleadings in this case. And there is no reason why we cannot take judicial notice of the record in this Court of the Moscow F. Ins. Co. Case. Bienville Water Supply Co. v. Mobile, 186 U.S. 212, 217, 46 L ed 1132, 1134, 22 S Ct 820; Dimmick v. Tompkins, 194 U.S. 540, 548, 48 L ed 1110, 1113, 24 S Ct 780; Freshman v. Atkins, 269 U.S. 121, 124, 70 L ed 193, 195, 46 S Ct 41, 6 Am Bankr Rep(NS) 744.

Second. The New York Court of Appeals held in the Moscow F. Ins. Co. Case that the Russian decrees in question had no extraterritorial effect. If that is true, it is decisive of the present controversy. For the United States acquired under the Litvinov Assignment only such rights as Russia had. Guaranty Trust Co. v. United States, 304 U.S. 126, 143, 82 L ed 1224, 1234, 58 S Ct 785. If the Russian decrees left the New York assets of the Russian insurance companies unaffected, then Russia had nothing here to assign. But that question of foreign law is not to be determined exclusively by the state court. The claim of the United States based on the Litvinov Assignment raises a federal question. United States v. Belmont, 301 U.S. 324, 81 L ed 1134, 57 S Ct 758. This Court will review or independently determine all questions on which a federal right is necessarily dependent. United States v. Ansonia Brass & Copper Co. 218 U.S. 452, 462, 463, 471, 54 L ed 1107, 1111, 1112, 1114, 31 S Ct 49; Ancient Egyptian Arabic Order v. Michaux, 279 U.S. 737, 744, 745, 73 L ed 931, 935, 936, 49 S Ct 485; Broad River Power Co. v. South Carolina, 281 U.S. 537, 540, 74 L ed 1023, 1029, 50 S Ct 401; Pierre v. Louisiana, 306 U.S. 354, 358, 83 L ed 757, 760, 59 S Ct 536. Here title obtained under the Litvinov Assignment depends on a correct interpretation of Russian law. As in cases arising under the full faith and credit clause (Huntington v. Attrill, 146 U.S. 657, 684, 36 L ed 1123, 1133, 13 S Ct 224; Adam v. Saenger, 303 U.S. 59, 64, 82 L ed 649, 652, 58 S Ct 454), these questions of foreign law on which the asserted federal right is based are not peculiarly within the cognizance of the local courts. While deference will be given to the determination of the state court, its conclusion is not accepted as final.

We do not stop to review all the evidence in the voluminous record of the Moscow F. Ins. Co. Case bearing on the question of the extraterritorial effect of the Russian decrees of nationalization, except to note that the expert testimony tendered by the United States gave great credence to its position. Subsequently to the hearings in that case, however, the United States, through diplomatic channels, requested the Commissariat for Foreign Affairs of the Russian Government to obtain an official declaration by the Commissariat for Justice of the R.S.F.S.R. which would make clear, as a matter of Russian law, the intended effect of the

Russian decree nationalizing insurance companies upon the funds of such companies outside of Russia. The official declaration, dated November 28, 1937, reads as follows:

"The People's Commissariat for Justice of the R.S.F.S.R. certifies that by virtue of the laws of the organs of the Soviet Government all nationalized funds and property of former private enterprises and companies, in particular, by virtue of the decree of November 28, 1918 (Collection of Laws of the R.S.F.S.R., 1918, No. 86, Article 904), the funds and property of former insurance companies, constitute the property of the State, irrespective of the nature of the property, irrespective of whether it was situated within the territorial limits of the R.S.F.S.R. or abroad."

The referee in the Moscow F. Ins. Co. Case found, and the evidence supported his finding, that the Commissariat for Justice has power to interpret existing Russian law. That being true this official declaration is conclusive so far as the intended extraterritorial effect of the Russian decree is concerned. This official declaration was before the court below though it was not a part of the record. It was tendered pursuant to § 391 of the New York Civil Practice Act as amended by Laws 1933, chap. 690. In New York it would seem that foreign law must be found by the court (or in case of a jury trial, binding instructions must be given), though procedural considerations require it to be presented as a question of fact. Fitzpatrick v. International R. Co. 252 NY 127, 169 NE 112, 68 ALR 801; Petrogradsky Mejdunarodny Kommerchesky Bank v. National City Bank, 253 NY 23, 1970 NE 479. And under § 391 as amended it is clear that the New York appellate court has authority to consider appropriate decisions interpreting foreign law even though they are rendered subsequent to the trial. Los Angeles Invest. Securities Corp. v. Joslyn, 282 NY 438, 26 NE(2d) 968. We can take such notice of the foreign law as the New York court could have taken. Adam v. Saenger, 303 U.S. 59, 82 L ed 649, 58 S Ct 454, supra. We conclude that this official declaration of Russian law was not only properly before the court on appeal but also that it was embraced within those "written authorities" which § 391 authorizes the court to consider, even though not introduced in evidence on the trial. For while it was not "printed," it would seem to be "other written law" of unquestioned authenticity and authority within the meaning of § 391.

We hold that so far as its intended effect is concerned the Russian decree embraced the New York assets of the First Russian Insurance Co.

Third: The question of whether the decree should be given extraterritorial effect is of course a distinct matter. One primary issue raised in that connection is whether under our constitutional system New York law can be allowed to stand in the way.

The decision of the New York Court of Appeals in the Moscow F. Ins. Co. Case is unequivocal. It held that "under the law of this State such confiscatory decrees do not affect the property claimed here" (280 NY 314, 20 NE(2d) 758); that the property of the New York branch acquired a "character of its own" which was "dependent" on the law of New York (p. 310); that no "rule of comity and no act of the United States government constrains this State to abandon any part of its control or to share it with a foreign State" (p. 310); that although the Russian decree effected the death of the parent company, the situs of the property of the New York branch was in New York; and that no principle of law forces New York to forsake the method of distribution authorized in the earlier appeal (255 NY 415, 175 NE 114) and to hold that "the method which in 1931 conformed to the exactions of justice and equity must be rejected because retroactively it has become unlawful" (p. 312).

It is one thing to hold as was done in Guaranty Trust Co. v. United States, supra

(304 U.S. p. 142, 82 L ed 1233, 58 S Ct 785), that under the Litvinov Assignment the United States did not acquire "a right free of a preexisting infirmity" such as the running of the statute of limitations against the Russian Government, its assignor. Unlike the problem presented here and in the Moscow F. Ins. Co. Case, that holding in no way sanctions the asserted power of New York to deny enforcement of a claim under the Litvinov Assignment because of an overriding policy of the State which denies validity in New York of the Russian decrees on which the assigned claims rest. That power was denied New York in United States v. Belmont, 301 U.S. 324, 81 L ed 1134, 57 S Ct 758, supra. With one qualification to be noted, the Belmont Case is determinative of the present controversy.

That case involved the right of the United States under the Litvinov Assignment to recover from a custodian or stakeholder in New York funds which had been nationalized and appropriated by the Russian decrees.

This Court, speaking through Mr. Justice Sutherland, held that the conduct of foreign relations is committed by the Constitution to the political departments of the Federal Government; that the propriety of the exercise of that power is not open to judicial inquiry; and that recognition of a foreign sovereign conclusively binds the courts and "is retroactive and validates all actions and conduct of the government so recognized from the commencement of its existence." p. 328. It further held (p. 330) that recognition of the Soviet Government, the establishment of diplomatic relations with it, and the Litvinov Assignment were "all parts of one transaction, resulting in an international compact between the two governments." After stating that "in respect of what was done here, the Executive had authority to speak as the sole organ" of the national government, it added (p. 330): "The assignment and the agreements in connection therewith did not, as in the case of treaties, as that term is used in the treaty making clause of the Constitution (Art. 2, § 2), require the advice and consent of the Senate." It held (p. 331) that the "external powers of the United States are to be exercised without regard to state laws or policies. The supremacy of a treaty in this respect has been recognized from the beginning." And it added that "all international compacts and agreements" are to be treated with similar dignity for the reason that "complete power over international affairs is in the national government and is not and cannot be subject to any curtailment or interference on the part of the several states." p. 331. This Court did not stop to inquire whether in fact there was any policy of New York which enforcement of the Litvinov Assignment would infringe since "no state policy can prevail against the international compact here involved." p. 327.

The New York Court of Appeals in the Moscow F. Ins. Co. Case (280 NY 309, 20 NE(2d) 758) distinguished the Belmont Case on the ground that it was decided on the sufficiency of the pleadings, the demurrer to the complaint admitting that under the Russian decree the property was confiscated by the Russian Government and then transferred to the United States under the Litvinov Assignment. But, as we have seen, the Russian decree in question was intended to have an extraterritorial effect and to embrace funds of the kind which are here involved. Nor can there be any serious doubt that claims of the kind here in question were included in the Litvinov Assignment. It is broad and inclusive. It should be interpreted consonantly with the purpose of the compact to eliminate all possible sources of friction between these two great nations. See Tucker v. Alexandroff, 183 U.S. 424, 437, 46 L ed 264, 270, 22 S Ct 195; Jordan v. Tashiro, 278 U.S. 123, 127, 73 L ed 214, 218, 49 S Ct 47. Strict construction would run counter to that national policy. For, as we shall see, the existence of unpaid claims against Russia and its nationals which were held in this country and which the Litvinov assignment was intended to secure, had long been one impediment to resumption of friendly relations between these two great powers.

The holding in the Belmont Case is therefore determinative of the present controversy unless the stake of the foreign creditors in this liquidation proceeding and the provision which New York has provided for their protection call for a different result.

Fourth: The Belmont Case forecloses any relief to the Russian corporation. For this Court held in that case (301 U.S. at p. 332, 81 L ed 1140, 57 S Ct 758): ". . . our Constitution, laws and policies have no extraterritorial operation, unless in respect of our own citizens. . . . What another country has done in the way of taking over property of its nationals, and especially of its corporations, is not a matter for judicial consideration here. Such nationals must look to their own government for any redress to which they may be entitled."

But it is urged that different considerations apply in case of the foreign creditors to whom the New York Court of Appeals (255 NY 415, 175 NE 114) ordered distribution of these funds. The argument is that their rights in these funds have vested by virtue of the New York decree; that to deprive them of the property would violate the Fifth Amendment which extends its protection to aliens as well as to citizens; and that the Litvinov Assignment cannot deprive New York of its power to administer the balance of the fund in accordance with its laws for the benefit of these creditors.

At the outset it should be noted that, so far as appears, all creditors whose claims arose out of dealings with the New York branch have been paid. Thus we are not faced with the question whether New York's policy of protecting the so-called local creditors by giving them priority in the assets deposited with the State (People v. Norske Llody Ins. Co. (Re Stoddard) 242 NY 148, 158, 159, 151 NE 159, 45 ALR 622) should be recognized within the rule of Clark v. Williard, 294 U.S. 211, 79 L ed 865, 55 S Ct 356, 98 ALR 347, or should yield to the Federal policy expressed in the international compact or agreement. Santovincenzo v. Eagan, 284 U.S. 30, 40, 76 L ed 151, 155, 52 S Ct 81; United States v. Belmont, 301 U.S. 324, 81 L ed 1134, 57 S Ct 758, supra. We intimate no opinion on that question. The contest here is between the United States and creditors of the Russian corporation who, we assume, are not citizens of this country and whose claims did not arise out of transactions with the New York branch. The United States is seeking to protect not only claims which it holds but also claims of its nationals. H. Rep. No. 865, 76th Cong. 1st Sess. Such claims did not arise out of transactions with this Russian corporation; they are, however, claims against Russia or its nationals. The existence of such claims and their non-payment had for years been one of the barriers to recognition of the Soviet regime by the Executive Department. Graham, Russian-American Relations, 1917-1933: An interpretation, 28 Am. Pol. Sc. Rev. 387; 1 Hackworth, Digest of International Law (1940) pp. 302-304. The purpose of the discussions leading to the policy of recognition was to resolve "all questions outstanding" between the two nations. Establishment of Diplomatic Relations with the Union of Soviet Socialist Republics, Dept. of State, Eastern European Series, No. 1 (1933), p. 1. Settlement of all American claims against Russia was one method of removing some of the prior objections to recognition based on the Soviet policy of nationalization. The Litvinov Assignment was not only part and parcel of the new policy of recognition (id. p. 13); it was also the method adopted by the Executive Department for alleviating in this country the rigors of nationalization. Congress tacitly recognized that policy. Acting in anticipation of the realization of funds under the Litvinov Assignment (H. Rep. No. 865, 76th Cong., 1st Sess.) it authorized the appointment of a Commissioner to determine the claims of American nationals against the Soviet Government. Joint Resolution of August 4, 1939, 53 Stat. at L. 1199, chap. 421.

If the President had the power to determine the policy which was to govern the question of recognition, then the Fifth Amendment does not stand in the way of giving full force and effect to the Litvinov Assignment. To be sure, aliens as well as citizens are entitled to the protection of the Fifth Amendment. Russian Volunteer Fleet v. United States, 282 U.S. 481, 75 L ed 473, 51 S Ct 229. A State is not precluded, however, by the Fourteenth Amendment from according priority to local creditors as against creditors who are nationals of foreign countries and whose claims arose abroad. Disconto Gesellschaft v. Umbreit, 208 U.S. 570, 52 L ed 625, 28 S Ct 337. By the same token, the Federal Government is not barred by the Fifth Amendment from securing for itself and our nationals priority against such creditors. And it matters not that the procedure adopted by the Federal Government is globular and involves a regrouping of assets. There is no Constitutional reason why this Government need act as the collection agent for nationals of other countries when it takes steps to protect itself or its own nationals on external debts. There is no reason why it may not through such devices as the Litvinov Assignment make itself and its nationals whole from assets here before it permits such assets to go abroad in satisfaction of claims of aliens made elsewhere and not incurred in connection with business conducted in this country. The fact that New York has marshaled the claims of the foreign creditors here involved and authorized their payment does not give them immunity from that general rule.

If the priority had been accorded American claims by treaty with Russia, there would be no doubt as to its validity. Cf. Santovincenzo v. Egan, 284 U.S. 30, 76 L ed 151, 52 S Ct 81, supra. The same result obtains here. The powers of the President in the conduct of foreign relations included the power, without consent of the Senate, to determine the public policy of the United States with respect to the Russian nationalization decrees. "What government is to be regarded here as representative of a foreign sovereign state is a political rather than a judicial question, and is to be determined by the political department of the government." Guaranty Trust Co. v. United States, supra (304 U.S. p. 137, 82 L ed 1231, 58 S Ct 785). That authority is not limited to a determination of the government to be recognized. It includes the power to determine the policy which is to govern the question of recognition. Objections to the underlying policy as well as objections to recognition are to be addressed to the political department and not to the courts. See Guaranty Trust Co. v. United States, supra (304 U.S. 138, 82 L ed 1231, 58 S Ct 785); Kennett v. Chambers, 14 How (U.S.) 38, 50, 51, 14 L ed 316, 321, 322. As we have noted, this Court in the Belmont Case recognized that the Litvinov Assignment was an international compact which did not require the participation of the Senate. It stated (301 U.S. pp. 330, 331, 81 L ed 1139, 1140, 57 S Ct 758): "There are many such compacts, of which a protocol, a modus vivendi, a postal convention, and agreements like that now under consideration are illustrations." And see Monaco v. Mississippi, 292 U.S. 313, 331, 78 L ed 1282, 1290, 54 S Ct 745; United States v. Curtiss-Wright Export Corp. 299 U.S. 304, 318, 81 L ed 255, 261, 57 S Ct 216. Recognition is not always absolute; it is sometimes conditional. 1 Moore, International Law Dig. (1906), pp. 73, 74; 1 Hackworth, Digest of International Law (1940), pp. 192-195. Power to remove such obstacles to full recognition as settlement of claims of our nationals (Levitan, Executive Agreements, 35 Ill. L. Rev. 365,

382-385) certainly is a modest implied power of the President who is the "sole organ of the federal government in the field of international relations." United States v. Curtiss-Wright Export Corp. supra (299 U.S. p. 320, 81 L ed 262, 57 S Ct 216). Effectiveness in handling the delicate problems of foreign relations requires no less. Unless such a power exists, the power of recognition might be thwarted or seriously diluted. No such obstacle can be placed in the way of rehabilitation of relations between this country and another nation, unless the historic conception of the powers and responsibilities of the President in the conduct of foreign affairs (see Moore, Treaties and Executive Agreements, 20 Pol. Sc. Q. 385, 403-417) is to be drastically revised. It was the judgment of the political department that full recognition of the Soviet Government required the settlement of all outstanding problems including the claims of our nationals. Recognition and the Litvinov Assignment were interdependent. We would usurp the executive function if we held that that decision was not final and conclusive in the courts.

"All constitutional acts of power whether in the executive or in the judicial department, have as much legal validity and obligation as if they proceeded from the legislature, . . ." The Federalist, No. 64. A treaty is a "Law of the Land" under the supremacy clause (Art. 6, Cl. 2) of the Constitution. Such international compacts and agreements as the Litvinov Assignment have a similar dignity. United States v. Belmont, supra (301 U.S. pp. 331, 81 L ed 1139, 57 S Ct 758). See Corwin, The President, Office & Powers (1940) pp. 228-240.

It is of course true that even treaties with foreign nations will be carefully construed so as not to derogate from the authority and jurisdiction of the States of this nation unless clearly necessary to effectuate the national policy. Guaranty Trust Co. v. United States, supra (304 U.S. p. 143, 82 L ed 1234, 58 S Ct 785) and cases cited. For example in Todok v. Union State Bank, 281 U.S. 449, 74 L ed 956, 50 S Ct 363, this Court took pains in its construction of a treaty, relating to the power of an alien to dispose of property in this country, not to invalidate the provisions of state law governing such dispositions. Frequently the obligation of a treaty will be dependent on state law. Prevost v. Greneaux, 19 How U.S. 1, 15 L ed 572. But state law must yield when it is inconsistent with or impairs the policy or provisions of a treaty or of an international compact or agreement. See Nielsen v. Johnson, 279 U.S. 47, 73 L ed 607, 49 S Ct 223. Then the power of a State to refuse enforcement of rights based on foreign law which runs counter to the public policy of the forum (Griffin v. McCoach, 313 U.S. 498, 506, 85 L ed 1481, 1486, 61 S Ct 1023, 134 ALR 1462) must give way before the superior Federal policy evidenced by a treaty or international compact or agreement. Santovincenzo v. Egan, 284 U.S. 30, 76 L ed 151, 52 S Ct 81, and United States v. Belmont, 301 U.S. 324, 81 L ed 1134, 57 S Ct 758, supra.

Enforcement of New York's policy as formulated by the Moscow case would collide with and subtract from Federal policy, whether it was premised on the absence of extraterritorial effect of the Russian decrees, the conception of the New York branch as a distinct juristic personality, or disapproval by New York of the Russian program of nationalization. For the Moscow F. Ins. Co. Case refuses to give effect or recognition in New York to acts of the Soviet Government which the United States by its policy of recognition agreed no longer to question. Enforcement of such state policies would indeed tend to restore some of the precise impediments to friendly relations which the President intended to remove on inauguration of the policy of recognition of the Soviet Government. In the first place, such action by New York, no matter what gloss be given it, amounts to official disapproval or non-recognition of the nationalization program of the Soviet Government. That disapproval or non-recognition is in the face of a disavowal by the United States of any official concern with that program. It is in the face of the underlying policy adopted by the United States when it recognized the Soviet Government. In the second place, to the extent that the action of the State in refusing enforcement of the Litvinov Assignment results in reduction or non-payment of claims of our nationals, it helps keep alive one source of friction which the policy of recognition intended to remove. Thus the action of New York tends to restore some of the precise irritants which had long affected the relations between these two great nations and which the policy of recognition was designed to eliminate.

We recently stated in Hines v. Davidowitz, 312 U.S. 52, 68, 85 L ed 581, 587, 61 S Ct 399, that the field which affects international relations is "the one aspect of our government that from the first has been most generally conceded imperatively to demand broad national authority;" and that any state power which may exist "is restricted to the narrowest of limits." There we were dealing with the question as to whether a state statute regulating aliens survived a similar federal statute. We held that it did not. Here we are dealing with an exclusive federal function. If state laws and policies did not yield before the exercise of the external powers of the United States, then our foreign policy might be thwarted. These are delicate matters. If state action could defeat or alter our foreign policy, serious consequences might ensue. The nation as a whole would be held to answer if a State created difficulties with a foreign power. Cf. Chy Lung v. Freeman, 92 U.S. 275, 279, 280, 23 L ed 550, 551, 552. Certainly the conditions for "enduring friendship" between the nations, which the policy of recognition in this instance was designed to effectuate, are not likely to flourish where contrary to national policy a lingering atmosphere of hostility is created by state action.

Such considerations underlie the principle of Oetjen v. Central Leather Co. 246 U.S. 297, 302, 303, 62 L ed 726, 731, 732, 38 S Ct 309, that when a revolutionary government is recognized as a de jure government, "such recognition is retroactive in effect and validates all the actions and conduct of the government so recognized from the commencement of its existence." They also explain the rule expressed in Underhill v. Hernandez, 168 U.S. 250, 252, 42 L ed 456, 457, 18 S Ct 83, that "the courts of one country will not sit in judgment on the acts of the government of another done within its own territory."

The action of New York in this case amounts in substance to a rejection of a part of the policy underlying recognition by this nation of Soviet Russia. Such power is not accorded a State in our constitutional system. To permit it would be to sanction a dangerous invasion of Federal authority. For it would "imperil the amicable relations between governments and vex the peace of nations." Oetjen v. Central Leather Co. supra (246 U.S. p. 304, 62 L ed 733, 38 S Ct 309). It would tend to disturb that equilibrium in our foreign relations which the political departments of our national government had diligently endeavored to establish.

We repeat that there are limitations on the sovereignty of the States. No state can rewrite our foreign policy to conform to its own domestic policies. Power over external affairs is not shared by the States; it is vested in the national government exclusively. It need not be so exercised as to conform to state laws or state policies whether they be expressed in constitutions, statutes, or judicial decrees. And the policies of the States become wholly irrelevant to judicial inquiry, when the United States, acting within its constitutional sphere, seeks enforcement of its foreign policy in the courts. For such reasons, Mr. Justice Sutherland stated in United

States v. Belmont, supra (301 U.S. p. 331, 81 L ed 1139, 57 S Ct 758), "In respect of all international negotiations and compacts, and in respect of our foreign relations generally, state lines disappear. As to such purposes the State of New York does not exist."

We hold that the right to the funds or property in question became vested in the Soviet Government as the successor to the First Russian Insurance Co.; that this right has passed to the United States under the Litvinov Assignment; and that the United States is entitled to the property as against the corporation and the foreign creditors.

The judgment is reversed and the cause is remanded to the Supreme Court of New York for proceedings not inconsistent with this opinion.

Reversed.

Hirabayashi v. United States

320 U.S. 81 (1943)

Mr. Chief Justice Stone delivered the opinion of the Court.

Appellant, an American citizen of Japanese ancestry, was convicted in the district court of violating the Act of Congress of March 21, 1942, 56 Stat. 173, which makes it a misdemeanor knowingly to disregard restrictions made applicable by a military commander to persons in a military area prescribed by him as such, all as authorized by an Executive Order of the President.

The questions for our decision are whether the particular restriction violated, namely that all persons of Japanese ancestry residing in such an area be within their place of residence daily between the hours of 8:00 p. m. and 6:00 a. m., was adopted by the military commander in the exercise of an unconstitutional delegation by Congress of its legislative power, and whether the restriction unconstitutionally discriminated between citizens of Japanese ancestry and those of other ancestries in violation of the Fifth Amendment.

The indictment is in two counts. The second charges that appellant, being a person of Japanese ancestry, had on a specified date, contrary to a restriction promulgated by the military commander of the Western Defense Command, Fourth Army, failed to remain in his place of residence in the designated military area between the hours of 8:00 o'clock p. m. and 6:00 a. m. The first count charges that appellant, on May 11 and 12, 1942, had, contrary to a Civilian Exclusion Order issued by the military commander, failed to report to the Civil Control Station within the designated area, it appearing that appellant's required presence there was a preliminary step to the exclusion from that area of persons of Japanese ancestry.

By demurrer and plea in abatement, which the court overruled (46 F. Supp. 657), appellant asserted that the indictment should be dismissed because he was an American citizen who had never been a subject of and had never borne allegiance to the Empire of Japan, and also because the Act of March 21, 1942, was an unconstitutional delegation of Congressional power. On the trial to a jury it appeared that appellant was born in Seattle in 1918, of Japanese parents who had come from Japan to the United States, and who had never afterward returned to Japan; that he was educated in the Washington public schools and at the time of his arrest was a senior in the University of Washington; that he had never been in Japan or had any association with Japanese residing there.

The evidence showed that appellant had failed to report to the Civil Control Station on May 11 or May 12, 1942, as directed, to register for evacuation from the military area. He admitted failure to do so, and stated it had at all times been his belief that he would be waiving his rights as an American citizen by so doing. The evidence also showed that for like reason he was away from his place of residence after 8:00 p. m. on May 9, 1942. The jury returned a verdict of guilty on both counts and appellant was sentenced to imprisonment for a term of three months on each, the sentences to run concurrently.

On appeal the Court of Appeals for the Ninth Circuit certified to us questions of law upon which it desired instructions for the decision of the case. See § 239 of the Judicial Code as amended, 28 U. S. C. § 346. Acting under the authority conferred upon us by that section we ordered that the entire record be certified to this Court so that we might proceed to a decision of the matter in controversy in the same manner as if it had been brought here by appeal. Since the sentences of three months each imposed by the district court on the two counts were ordered to run concurrently, it will be unnecessary to consider questions raised with respect to the first count if we find that the conviction on the second count, for violation of the curfew order, must be sustained. *Brooks v. United States*, 267 U.S. 432, 441; *Gorin v. United States,* 312 U.S. 19, 33.

The curfew order which appellant violated, and to which the sanction prescribed by the Act of Congress has been deemed to attach, purported to be issued pursuant to an Executive Order of the President. In passing upon the authority of the military commander to make and execute the order, it becomes necessary to consider in some detail the official action which preceded or accompanied the order and from which it derives its purported authority.

On December 8, 1941, one day after the bombing of Pearl Harbor by a Japanese air force, Congress declared war against Japan. 55 Stat. 795. On February 19, 1942, the President promulgated Executive Order No. 9066. 7 Federal Register 1407. The Order recited that "the successful prosecution of the war requires every possible protection against espionage and against sabotage to national-defense material, national-defense premises, and national-defense utilities as defined in Section 4, Act of April 20, 1918, 40 Stat. 533, as amended by the Act of November 30, 1940, 54 Stat. 1220, and the Act of August 21, 1941, 55 Stat. 655." By virtue of the authority vested in him as President and as Commander in Chief of the Army and Navy, the President purported to "authorize and direct the Secretary of War, and the Military Commanders whom he may from time to time designate, whenever he or any designated Commander deems such action necessary or desirable, to prescribe military areas in such places and of such extent as he or the appropriate Military Commander may determine, from which any or all persons may be excluded, and with respect to which, the right of any person to enter, remain in, or leave shall be subject to whatever restrictions the Secretary of War or the appropriate Military Commander may impose in his discretion."

On February 20, 1942, the Secretary of War designated Lt. General J. L. DeWitt as Military Commander of the Western Defense Command, comprising the Pacific Coast states and some others, to carry out there the duties prescribed by Executive Order No. 9066. On March 2, 1942, General DeWitt promulgated Public Proclamation No. 1. 7 Federal Register 2320. The proclamation recited that the entire Pacific Coast "by its geographical location is particularly subject to attack, to attempted invasion by the armed forces of nations with which the United States is now at war, and, in connection therewith, is subject to espionage and acts of sabotage, thereby requiring the adoption of military measures necessary to establish safeguards against such enemy operations." It stated that "the present situation requires as a matter of military necessity the establishment in the territory embraced by the Western Defense Command of Military Areas and Zones thereof"; it specified and designated as military areas certain areas within the Western Defense Command; and it declared that "such persons or classes of persons as the situation may require" would, by subsequent proclamation, be excluded from certain of these areas, but might be permitted to enter or remain in certain others, under regulations and restrictions to be later prescribed. Among military areas so designated by Public Proclamation No. 1 was Military Area No. 1, which embraced, besides the southern part of Arizona, all the coastal region of three Pacific Coast states, including the City of Seattle, Washington, where appellant resided. Military Area No. 2 designated by the same proclamation, included those areas of the coastal states and of Arizona not placed with Military Area No. 1.

Public Proclamation No. 2 of March 16, 1942, issued by General DeWitt, made like recitals and designated further military areas and zones. It contained like provisions concerning the exclusion, by subsequent proclamation, of certain persons or classes of persons from these areas, and the future promulgation of regulations and restrictions applicable to persons remaining within them. 7 Federal Register 2605.

An Executive Order of the President, No. 9102, of March 18, 1942, established the War Relocation Authority, in the Office for Emergency Management of the Executive Office of the President; it authorized the Director of War Relocation Authority to formulate and effectuate a program for the removal relocation, maintenance and supervision of persons designated under Executive Order No. 9066, already referred to; and it conferred on the Director authority to prescribe regulations necessary or desirable to promote the effective execution of the program. 7 Federal Register 2165.

Congress, by the Act of March 21, 1942, provided: "That whoever shall enter, remain in, leave, or commit any act in any military area or military zone prescribed, under the authority of an Executive order of the President, by the Secretary of War, or by any military commander designated by the Secretary of War, contrary to the restrictions applicable to any such area or zone or contrary to the order of the Secretary of War or any such military commander, shall, if it appears that he knew or should have known of the existence and extent of the restrictions or order and that his act was in violation thereof, be guilty of a misdemeanor and upon conviction shall be liable" to fine or imprisonment, or both.

Three days later, on March 24, 1942, General DeWitt issued Public Proclamation No. 3. 7 Federal Register 2543. After referring to the previous designation of military areas by Public Proclamations Nos. 1 and 2, it recited that ". . . the present situation within these Military Areas and Zones requires as a matter of military necessity the establishment of certain regulations pertaining to all enemy aliens and all persons of Japanese ancestry within said Military Areas and Zones. . . ." It accordingly declared and established that from and after March 27, 1942, "all alien Japanese, all alien Germans, all alien Italians, and all persons of Japanese ancestry residing or being within the geographical limits of Military Area No. 1 . . . shall be within their place of residence between the hours of 8:00 P. M. and 6:00 A. M., which period is hereinafter referred to as the hours of curfew." It also imposed certain other restrictions on persons of Japanese ancestry, and provided that any person violating the regulations would be subject to the criminal penalties provided by the Act of Congress of March 21, 1942.

Beginning on March 24, 1942, the military commander issued a series of Civilian Exclusion Orders pursuant to the provisions of Public Proclamation No. 1. Each such order related to a specified area within the territory of his command. The order applicable to appellant was Civilian Exclusion Order No. 57 of May 10, 1942. 7 Federal Register 3725. It directed that from and after 12:00 noon, May 16, 1942, all persons of Japanese ancestry, both alien and non-alien, be excluded from a specified portion of Military Area No. 1 in Seattle, including appellant's place of residence, and it required a member of each family, and each individual living alone, affected by the order to report on May 11 or May 12 to a designated Civil Control Station in Seattle. Meanwhile the military commander had issued Public Proclamation No. 4 of March 27, 1942, which recited the necessity of providing for the orderly evacuation and resettlement of Japanese within the area, and prohibited all alien Japanese and all persons of Japanese ancestry from leaving the military area until future orders should permit. 7 Federal Register 2601.

Appellant does not deny that he knowingly failed to obey the curfew order as charged in the second count of the indictment, or that the order was authorized by the terms of Executive Order No. 9066, or that the challenged Act of Congress purports to punish with criminal penalties disobedience of such an order. His contentions are only that Congress unconstitutionally delegated its legislative power to the military commander by authorizing him to impose the challenge regulation, and that, even if the regulation were in other respects lawfully authorized, the Fifth Amendment prohibits the discrimination made between citizens of Japanese descent and those of other ancestry.

It will be evident from the legislative history that the Act of March 21, 1942, contemplated and authorized the curfew order which we have before us. The bill which became the Act of March 21, 1942, was introduced in the Senate on March 9th and in the House on March 10th at the request of the Secretary of War who, in letters to the Chairman of the Senate Committee on Military Affairs and to the Speaker of the House, stated explicitly that its purpose was to provide means for the enforcement of orders issued under Executive Order No. 9066. This appears in the committee reports on the bill, which set out in full the Executive Order and the Secretary's letter. 88 Cong. Rec. 2722, 2725; H. R. Rep. No. 1906, 77th Cong., 2d Sess.; S. Rep. No. 1171, 77th Cong., 2d Sess. And each of the committee reports expressly mentions curfew orders as one of the types of restrictions which it was deemed desirable to enforce by criminal sanctions.

When the bill was under consideration, General DeWitt had published his Proclamation No. 1 of March 2, 1942, establishing Military Areas Nos. 1 and 2, and that Proclamation was before Congress. S. Rep. No. 1171, 77th Cong., 2d Sess., p. 2; see also 88 Cong. Rec. 2724. A letter of the Secretary to the Chairman of the House Military Affairs Committee, of March 14, 1942, informed Congress that "General DeWitt is strongly of the opinion that the bill, when enacted, should be broad enough to enable the Secretary of War or the appropriate military commander to enforce curfews and other restrictions within military areas and zones"; and that General DeWitt had "indicated that he was prepared to enforce certain restrictions at once for the purpose of protecting certain vital national defense interests but did not desire to proceed until enforcement machinery had been set up." H. R. Rep. No. 1906, 77th Cong., 2d Sess., p. 3. See also letter of the Acting Secretary of War to the Chairman of the Senate Military Affairs Committee, March 13, 1942, 88 Cong. Rec. 2725.

The Chairman of the Senate Military Affairs Committee explained on the floor of the Senate that the purpose of the proposed legislation was to provide means of enforcement of curfew orders and other military orders made pursuant to Executive Order No. 9066. He read General DeWitt's Public Proclamation No. 1, and statements from newspaper reports that "evacuation of the first Japanese aliens and American-born Japanese" was about to begin. He also stated to the Senate that "reasons for suspected widespread fifth-column activity among Japanese" were to be found in the system of dual citizenship which Japan deemed applicable to American-born Japanese, and in the propaganda disseminated by Japanese consuls, Buddhist priests and other leaders, among American-born children of Japanese. Such was stated to be the explanation of the contemplated evacuation from the Pacific Coast area of persons of Japanese ancestry, citizens as well as aliens. 88 Cong. Rec. 2722-26; see also pp. 2729-30. Congress also had before it the Preliminary Report of a House Committee investigating national defense migration, of March 19, 1942, which approved the provisions of Executive Order No. 9066, and which recommended the evacuation, from military areas established under the Order, of all persons of Japanese ancestry, including citizens. H. R. Rep. No. 1911, 77th Cong., 2d Sess. The proposed legislation provided criminal sanctions for violation of orders, in terms broad enough to include the curfew order now before us, and the legislative history demonstrates that Congress was advised that curfew orders were among those intended, and was advised also that regulation of citizen and alien Japanese alike was contemplated.

The conclusion is inescapable that Congress, by the Act of March 21, 1942, ratified and confirmed Executive Order No. 9066. *Prize Cases*, 2 Black 635, 671; *Hamilton v. Dillin,* 21 Wall. 73, 96-97; *United States v. Heinszen & Co.,* 206 U.S. 370, 382-84; *Tiaco v. Forbes,* 228 U.S. 549, 556; *Isbrandtsen-Moller Co. v. United States*, 300 U.S. 139, 146-48; *Swayne & Hoyt, Ltd. v. United States,* 300 U.S. 297, 300-03; *Mason Co. v. Tax Comm'n,* 302 U.S. 186, 208. And so far as it lawfully could, Congress authorized and implemented such curfew orders as the commanding officer should promulgate pursuant to the Executive Order of the President. The question then is not one of Congressional power to delegate to the President the promulgation of the Executive Order, but whether, acting in coöperation, Congress and the Executive have constitutional authority to impose the curfew restriction here complained of. We must consider also whether, acting together, Congress and the Executive could leave it to the designated military commander to appraise the relevant conditions and on the basis of that appraisal to say whether, under the circumstances, the time and place were appropriate for the promulgation of the curfew order and whether the order itself was an appropriate means of carrying out the Executive Order for the "protection against espionage and against sabotage" to national defense materials, premises and utilities. For reasons presently to be stated, we conclude that it was within the constitutional power of Congress and the executive arm of the Government to prescribe this curfew order for the period under consideration and that its promulgation by the military commander involved no unlawful delegation of legislative power.

Executive Order No. 9066, promulgated in time of war for the declared purpose of prosecuting the war by protecting national defense resources from sabotage and espionage, and the Act of March 21, 1942, ratifying and confirming the Executive

Order, were each an exercise of the power to wage war conferred on the Congress and on the President, as Commander in Chief of the armed forces, by Articles I and II of the Constitution. See *Ex parte Quirin*, 317 U.S. 1, 25-26. We have no occasion to consider whether the President, acting alone, could lawfully have made the curfew order in question, or have authorized others to make it. For the President's action has the support of the Act of Congress, and we are immediately concerned with the question whether it is within the constitutional power of the national government, through the joint action of Congress and the Executive, to impose this restriction as an emergency war measure. The exercise of that power here involves no question of martial law or trial by military tribunal. Cf. *Ex parte Milligan*, 4 Wall. 2; *Ex parte Quirin, supra.* Appellant has been tried and convicted in the civil courts and has been subjected to penalties prescribed by Congress for the acts committed.

The war power of the national government is "the power to wage war successfully." See Charles Evans Hughes, War Powers Under the Constitution, 42 A. B. A. Rep. 232, 238. It extends to every matter and activity so related to war as substantially to affect its conduct and progress. The power is not restricted to the winning of victories in the field and the repulse of enemy forces. It embraces every phase of the national defense, including the protection of war materials and the members of the armed forces from injury and from the dangers which attend the rise, prosecution and progress of war. *Prize Cases, supra; Miller v. United States,* 11 Wall. 268, 303-14; *Stewart v. Kahn,* 11 Wall. 493, 506-07; *Selective Draft Law Cases*, 245 U.S. 366; *McKinley v. United States,* 249 U.S. 397; *United States v. Macintosh*, 283 U.S. 605, 622-23. Since the Constitution commits to the Executive and to Congress the exercise of the war power in all the vicissitudes and conditions of warfare, it has necessarily given them wide scope for the exercise of judgment and discretion in determining the nature and extent of the threatened injury or danger and in the selection of the means for resisting it. *Ex parte Quirin, supra,* 28-29; cf. *Prize Cases, supra,* 670; *Martin v. Mott*, 12 Wheat. 19, 29. Where, as they did here, the conditions call for the exercise of judgment and discretion and for the choice of means by those branches of the Government on which the Constitution has placed the responsibility of war-making, it is not for any court to sit in review of the wisdom of their action or substitute its judgment for theirs.

The actions taken must be appraised in the light of the conditions with which the President and Congress were confronted in the early months of 1942, many of which, since disclosed, were then peculiarly within the knowledge of the military authorities. On December 7, 1941, the Japanese air forces had attacked the United States Naval Base at Pearl Harbor without warning, at the very hour when Japanese diplomatic representatives were conducting negotiations with our State Department ostensibly for the peaceful settlement of differences between the two countries. Simultaneously or nearly so, the Japanese attacked Malaysia, Hong Kong, the Philippines, and Wake and Midway Islands. On the following day their army invaded Thailand. Shortly afterwards they sank two British battleships. On December 13th, Guam was taken. On December 24th and 25th they captured Wake Island and occupied Hong Kong. On January 2, 1942, Manila fell, and on February 10th Singapore, Britain's great naval base in the East, was taken. On February 27th the battle of the Java Sea resulted in a disastrous naval defeat to the United Nations. By the 9th of March Japanese forces had established control over the Netherlands East Indies; Rangoon and Burma were occupied; Bataan and Corregidor were under attack.

Although the results of the attack on Pearl Harbor were not fully disclosed until much later, it was known that the damage was extensive, and that the Japanese by their successes had gained a naval superiority over our forces in the Pacific which might enable them to seize Pearl Harbor, our largest naval base and the last stronghold of defense lying between Japan and the west coast. That reasonably prudent men charged with the responsibility of our national defense had ample ground for concluding that they must face the danger of invasion, take measures against it, and in making the choice of measures consider our internal situation, cannot be doubted.

The challenged orders were defense measures for the avowed purpose of safeguarding the military area in question, at a time of threatened air raids and invasion by the Japanese forces, from the danger of sabotage and espionage. As the curfew was made applicable to citizens residing in the area only if they were of Japanese ancestry, our inquiry must be whether in the light of all the facts and circumstances there was any substantial basis for the conclusion, in which Congress and the military commander united, that the curfew as applied was a protective measure necessary to meet the threat of sabotage and espionage which would substantially affect the war effort and which might reasonably be expected to aid a threatened enemy invasion. The alternative which appellant insists must be accepted is for the military authorities to impose the curfew on all citizens within the military area, or on none. In a case of threatened danger requiring prompt action, it is a choice between inflicting obviously needless hardship on the many, or sitting passive and unresisting in the presence of the threat. We think that constitutional government, in time of war, is not so powerless and does not compel so hard a choice if those charged with the responsibility of our national defense have reasonable ground for believing that the threat is real.

When the orders were promulgated there was a vast concentration, within Military Areas Nos. 1 and 2, of installations and facilities for the production of military equipment, especially ships and airplanes. Important Army and Navy bases were located in California and Washington. Approximately one-fourth of the total value of the major aircraft contracts then let by Government procurement officers were to be performed in the State of California. California ranked second, and Washington fifth, of all the states of the Union with respect to the value of shipbuilding contracts to be performed.

In the critical days of March 1942, the danger to our war production by sabotage and espionage in this area seems obvious. The German invasion of the Western European countries had given ample warning to the world of the menace of the "fifth column." Espionage by persons in sympathy with the Japanese Government had been found to have been particularly effective in the surprise attack on Pearl Harbor. At a time of threatened Japanese attack upon this country, the nature of our inhabitants' attachments to the Japanese enemy was consequently a matter of grave concern. Of the 126,000 persons of Japanese descent in the United States, citizens and non-citizens, approximately 112,000 resided in California, Oregon and Washington at the time of the adoption of the military regulations. Of these approximately two-thirds are citizens because born in the United States. Not only did the great majority of such persons reside within the Pacific Coast states but they were concentrated in or near three of the large cities, Seattle, Portland and Los Angeles, all in Military Area No. 1.

There is support for the view that social, economic and political conditions which have prevailed since the close of the last century, when the Japanese began to come to this country in substantial numbers, have intensified their solidarity and have in large measure prevented their assimilation as an integral part of the white population. In addition, large numbers of children of Japanese parentage are sent to Japanese language schools outside the regular hours of public schools in the locality. Some of these schools are generally believed to be sources of Japanese nationalistic propaganda, cultivating allegiance to Japan. Considerable numbers, estimated to be approximately 10,000, of American-born children of Japanese parentage have been sent to Japan for all or a part of their education.

Congress and the Executive, including the military commander, could have attributed special significance, in its bearing on the loyalties of persons of Japanese descent, to the maintenance by Japan of its system of dual citizenship. Children born in the United States of Japanese alien parents, and especially those children born before December 1, 1924, are under many circumstances deemed, by Japanese law, to be citizens of Japan. No official census of those whom Japan regards as having thus retained Japanese citizenship is available, but there is ground for the belief that the number is large.

The large number of resident alien Japanese, approximately one-third of all Japanese inhabitants of the country, are of mature years and occupy positions of influence in Japanese communities. The association of influential Japanese residents with Japanese Consulates has been deemed a ready means for the dissemination of propaganda and for the maintenance of the influence of the Japanese Government with the Japanese population in this country.

As a result of all these conditions affecting the life of the Japanese, both aliens and citizens, in the Pacific Coast area, there has been relatively little social intercourse between them and the white population. The restrictions, both practical and legal, affecting the privileges and opportunities afforded to persons of Japanese extraction residing in the United States, have been sources of irritation and may well have tended to increase their isolation, and in many instances their attachments to Japan and its institutions.

Viewing these data in all their aspects, Congress and the Executive could reasonably have concluded that these conditions have encouraged the continued attachment of members of this group to Japan and Japanese institutions. These are only some of the many considerations which those charged with the responsibility for the national defense could take into account in determining the nature and extent of the danger of espionage and sabotage, in the event of invasion or air raid attack. The extent of that danger could be definitely known only after the event and after it was too late to meet it. Whatever views we may entertain regarding the loyalty to this country of the citizens of Japanese ancestry, we cannot reject as unfounded the judgment of the military authorities and of Congress that there were disloyal members of that population, whose number and strength could not be precisely and quickly ascertained. We cannot say that the war-making branches of the Government did not have ground for believing that in a critical hour such persons could not readily be isolated and separately dealt with, and constituted a menace to the national defense and safety, which demanded that prompt and adequate measures be taken to guard against it.

Appellant does not deny that, given the danger, a curfew was an appropriate measure against sabotage. It is an obvious protection against the perpetration of sabotage most readily committed during the hours of darkness. If it was an appropriate exercise of the war power its validity is not impaired because it has restricted the citizen's liberty. Like every military control of the population of a dangerous zone in war time, it necessarily involves some infringement of individual liberty, just as does the police establishment of fire lines during a fire, or the confinement of people to their houses during an air raid alarm—neither of which could be thought to be an infringement of constitutional right. Like them, the validity of the restraints of the curfew order depends on all the conditions which obtain at the time the curfew is imposed and which support the order imposing it.

But appellant insists that the exercise of the power is inappropriate and unconstitutional because it discriminates against citizens of Japanese ancestry, in violation of the Fifth Amendment. The Fifth Amendment contains no equal protection clause and it restrains only such discriminatory legislation by Congress as amounts to a denial of due process. *Detroit Bank v. United States,* 317 U.S. 329, 337-38, and cases cited. Congress may hit at a particular danger where it is seen, without providing for others which are not so evident or so urgent. *Keokee Coke Co. v. Taylor,* 234 U.S. 224, 227.

Distinctions between citizens solely because of their ancestry are by their very nature odious to a free people whose institutions are founded upon the doctrine of equality. For that reason, legislative classification or discrimination based on race alone has often been held to be a denial of equal protection. *Yick Wo v. Hopkins,* 118 U. S. 356; *Yu Cong Eng v. Trinidad*, 271 U.S. 500; *Hill v. Texas*, 316 U.S. 400. We may assume that these considerations would be controlling here were it not for the fact that the danger of espionage and sabotage, in time of war and of threatened invasion, calls upon the military authorities to scrutinize every relevant fact bearing on the loyalty of populations in the danger areas. Because racial discriminations are in most circumstances irrelevant and therefore prohibited, it by no means follows that, in dealing with the perils of war, Congress and the Executive are wholly precluded from taking into account those facts and circumstances which are relevant to measures for our national defense and for the successful prosecution of the war, and which may in fact place citizens of one ancestry in a different category from others. "We must never forget, that it is *a constitution* we are expounding," "a constitution intended to endure for ages to come, and, consequently, to be adapted to the various *crises* of human affairs." *McCulloch v. Maryland*, 4 Wheat. 316, 407, 415. The adoption by Government, in the crisis of war and of threatened invasion, of measures for the public safety, based upon the recognition of facts and circumstances which indicate that a group of one national extraction may menace that safety more than others, is not wholly beyond the limits of the Constitution and is not to be condemned merely because in other and in most circumstances racial distinctions are irrelevant. Cf. *Clarke v. Deckebach*, 274 U.S. 392, and cases cited.

Here the aim of Congress and the Executive was the protection against sabotage of war materials and utilities in areas thought to be in danger of Japanese invasion and air attack. We have stated in detail facts and circumstances with respect to the American citizens of Japanese ancestry residing on the Pacific Coast which support the judgment of the war-waging branches of the Government that some restrictive measure was urgent. We cannot say that these facts and circumstances, considered in the particular war setting, could afford no ground for differentiating citizens of Japanese ancestry from other groups in the United States. The fact alone that attack on our shores was threatened by Japan rather than another enemy power set these citizens apart from others who have no particular associations with Japan.

Our investigation here does not go beyond the inquiry whether, in the light of all the relevant circumstances preceding and attending their promulgation, the challenged orders and statute afforded a reasonable basis for the action taken in imposing the curfew. We cannot close our eyes to the fact, demonstrated by experience, that in time of war residents having ethnic affiliations with an invading enemy may be a greater source of danger than those of a different ancestry. Nor can we deny that Congress, and the military authorities acting with its authorization, have constitutional power to appraise the danger in the light of facts of public notoriety. We need not now attempt to define the ultimate boundaries of the war power. We decide only the issue as we have defined it—we decide only that the curfew order as applied, and at the time it was applied, was within the boundaries of the war power. In this case it is enough that circumstances within the knowledge of those charged with the responsibility for maintaining the national defense afforded a rational basis for the decision which they made. Whether we would have made it is irrelevant.

What we have said also disposes of the contention that the curfew order involved an unlawful delegation by Congress of its legislative power. The mandate of the Constitution that all legislative power granted "shall be vested in Congress" has never been thought, even in the administration of civil affairs, to preclude Congress from resorting to the aid of executive or administrative officers in determining by findings whether the facts are such as to call for the application of previously adopted legislative standards or definitions of Congressional policy.

The purpose of Executive Order No. 9066, and the standard which the President approved for the orders authorized to be promulgated by the military commander—as disclosed by the preamble of the Executive Order—was the protection of our war resources against espionage and sabotage. Public Proclamations Nos. 1 and 2 by General DeWitt, contain findings that the military areas created and the measures to be prescribed for them were required to establish safeguards against espionage and sabotage. Both the Executive Order and the Proclamations were before Congress when the Act of March 21, 1942, was under consideration. To the extent that the Executive Order authorized orders to be promulgated by the military commander to accomplish the declared purpose of the Order, and to the extent that the findings in the Proclamations establish that such was their purpose, both have been approved by Congress.

It is true that the Act does not in terms establish a particular standard to which orders of the military commander are to conform, or require findings to be made as a prerequisite to any order. But the Executive Order, the Proclamations and the statute are not to be read in isolation from each other. They were parts of a single program and must be judged as such. The Act of March 21, 1942, was an adoption by Congress of the Executive Order and of the Proclamations. The Proclamations themselves followed a standard authorized by the Executive Order—the necessity of protecting military resources in the designated areas against espionage and sabotage. And by the Act, Congress gave its approval to that standard. We have no need to consider now the validity of action if taken by the military commander without conforming to this standard approved by Congress, or the validity of orders made without the support of findings showing that they do so conform. Here the findings of danger from espionage and sabotage, and of the necessity of the curfew order to protect against them, have been duly made. General DeWitt's Public Proclamation No. 3, which established the curfew, merely prescribed regulations of the type and in the manner which Public Proclamations Nos. 1 and 2 had announced would be prescribed at a future date, and was thus founded on the findings of Proclamations Nos. 1 and 2.

The military commander's appraisal of facts in the light of the authorized standard, and the inferences which he drew from those facts, involved the exercise of his informed judgment. But as we have seen, those facts, and the inferences which could be rationally drawn from them, support the judgment of the military commander, that the danger of espionage and sabotage to our military resources was imminent, and that the curfew order was an appropriate measure to meet it.

Where, as in the present case, the standard set up for the guidance of the military commander, and the action taken and the reasons for it, are in fact recorded in the military orders, so that Congress, the courts and the public are assured that the orders, in the judgment of the commander, conform to the standards approved by the President and Congress, there is no failure in the performance of the legislative function. *Opp Cotton Mills v. Administrator,* 312 U.S. 126, 142-46, and cases cited. The essentials of that function are the determination by Congress of the legislative policy and its approval of a rule of conduct to carry that policy into execution. The very necessities which attend the conduct of military operations in time of war in this instance as in many others preclude Congress from holding committee meetings to determine whether there is danger, before it enacts legislation to combat the danger.

The Constitution as a continuously operating charter of government does not demand the impossible or the impractical. The essentials of the legislative function are preserved when Congress authorizes a statutory command to become operative, upon ascertainment of a basic conclusion of fact by a designated representative of the Government. Cf. *The Aurora,* 7 Cranch 382; *United States v. Chemical Foundation*, 272 U.S. 1, 12. The present statute, which authorized curfew orders to be made pursuant to Executive Order No. 9066 for the protection of war resources from espionage and sabotage, satisfies those requirements. Under the Executive Order the basic facts, determined by the military commander in the light of knowledge then available, were whether that danger existed and whether a curfew order was an appropriate means of minimizing the danger. Since his findings to that effect were, as we have said, not without adequate support, the legislative function was performed and the sanction of the statute attached to violations of the curfew order. It is unnecessary to consider whether or to what extent such findings would support orders differing from the curfew order.

The conviction under the second count is without constitutional infirmity. Hence we have no occasion to review the conviction on the first count since, as already stated, the sentences on the two counts are to run concurrently and conviction on the second is sufficient to sustain the sentence. For this reason also it is unnecessary to consider the Government's argument that compliance with the order to report at the Civilian Control Station did not necessarily entail confinement in a relocation center.

Affirmed.

Korematsu v. United States

323 U.S. 214 (1944)

Mr. Justice Black delivered the opinion of the Court.

The petitioner, an American citizen of Japanese descent, was convicted in a federal district court for remaining in San Leandro, California, a "Military Area," contrary to Civilian Exclusion Order No. 34 of the Commanding General of the Western Command, U.S. Army, which directed that after May 9, 1942, all persons of Japanese ancestry should be excluded from that area. No question was raised as to petitioner's loyalty to the United States. The Circuit Court of Appeals affirmed, and the importance of the constitutional question involved caused us to grant certiorari.

It should be noted, to begin with, that all legal restrictions which curtail the civil rights of a single racial group are immediately suspect. That is not to say that all such restrictions are unconstitutional. It is to say that courts must subject them to the most rigid scrutiny. Pressing public necessity may sometimes justify the existence of such restrictions; racial antagonism never can.

In the instant case prosecution of the petitioner was begun by information charging violation of an Act of Congress, of March 21, 1942, 56 Stat. 173, which provides that

". . . whoever shall enter, remain in, leave, or commit any act in any military area or military zone prescribed, under the authority of an Executive order of the President, by the Secretary of War, or by any military commander designated by the Secretary of War, contrary to the restrictions applicable to any such area or zone or contrary to the order of the Secretary of War or any such military commander, shall, if it appears that he knew or should have known of the existence and extent of the restrictions or order and that his act was in violation thereof, be guilty of a misdemeanor and upon conviction shall be liable to a fine of not to exceed $5,000 or to imprisonment for not more than one year, or both, for each offense."

Exclusion Order No. 34, which the petitioner knowingly and admittedly violated, was one of a number of military orders and proclamations, all of which were substantially based upon Executive Order No. 9066, 7 Fed. Reg. 1407. That order, issued after we were at war with Japan, declared that "the successful prosecution of the war requires every possible protection against espionage and against sabotage to national-defense material, national-defense premises, and national-defense utilities. . . ."

One of the series of orders and proclamations, a curfew order, which like the exclusion order here was promulgated pursuant to Executive Order 9066, subjected all persons of Japanese ancestry in prescribed West Cost military areas to remain in their residences from 8 p. m. to 6 a. m. As is the case with the exclusion order here, that prior curfew order was designed as a "protection against espionage and against sabotage." In *Hirabayashi v. United States,* 320 U.S. 81, we sustained a conviction obtained for violation of the curfew order. The Hirabayashi conviction and this one thus rest on the same 1942 Congressional Act and the same basic executive and military orders, all of which orders were aimed at the twin dangers of espionage and sabotage.

The 1942 Act was attacked in the *Hirabayashi* case as an unconstitutional delegation of power; it was contended that the curfew order and other orders on which it rested were beyond the war powers of the Congress, the military authorities and of the President, as Commander in Chief of the Army; and finally that to apply the curfew order against none but citizens of Japanese ancestry amounted to a constitutionally prohibited discrimination solely on account of race. To these questions, we gave the serious consideration which their importance justified. We upheld the curfew order as an exercise of the power of the government to take steps necessary to prevent espionage and sabotage in an area threatened by Japanese attack.

In the light of the principles we announced in the *Hirabayashi* case, we are unable to conclude that it was beyond the war power of Congress and the Executive to exclude those of Japanese ancestry from the West Coast war area at the time they did. True, exclusion from the area in which one's home is located is a far greater deprivation than constant confinement to the home from 8 p. m. to 6 a. m. Nothing short of apprehension by the proper military authorities of the gravest imminent danger to the public safety can constitutionally justify either. But exclusion from a threatened area, no less than curfew, has a definite and close relationship to the prevention of espionage and sabotage. The military authorities, charged with the primary responsibility of defending our shores, concluded that curfew provided inadequate protection and ordered exclusion. They did so, as pointed out in our *Hirabayashi* opinion, in accordance with Congressional authority to the military to say who should, and who should not, remain in the threatened areas.

In this case the petitioner challenges the assumptions upon which we rested our conclusions in the *Hirabayashi* case. He also urges that by May 1942, when Order No. 34 was promulgated, all danger of Japanese invasion of the West Coast had disappeared. After careful consideration of these contentions we are compelled to reject them.

Here, as in the *Hirabayashi* case, *supra,* at p. 99, ". . . we cannot reject as unfounded the judgment of the military authorities and of Congress that there were disloyal members of that population, whose number and strength could not be precisely and quickly ascertained. We cannot say that the war-making branches of the Government did not have ground for believing that in a critical hour such persons could not readily be isolated and separately dealt with, and constituted a menace to the national defense and safety, which demanded that prompt and adequate measures be taken to guard against it."

Like curfew, exclusion of those of Japanese origin was deemed necessary because of the presence of an unascertained number of disloyal members of the group, most of whom we have no doubt were loyal to this country. It was because we could not reject the finding of the military authorities that it was impossible to bring about an immediate segregation of the disloyal from the loyal that we sustained the validity of the curfew order as applying to the whole group. In the instant case, temporary exclusion of the entire group was rested by the military on the same ground. The judgment that exclusion of the whole group was for the same reason a military imperative answers the contention that the exclusion was in the nature of group punishment based on antagonism to those of Japanese origin. That there were members of the group who retained loyalties to Japan has been confirmed by investigations made subsequent to the exclusion. Approximately five thousand American citizens of Japanese ancestry refused to swear unqualified allegiance to the United States and to renounce allegiance to the Japanese Emperor, and several thousand evacuees requested repatriation to Japan.

We uphold the exclusion order as of the time it was made and when the petitioner violated it. Cf. *Chastleton Corporation v. Sinclair,* 264 U.S. 543, 547; *Block v. Hirsh,* 256 U.S. 135, 154-5. In doing so, we are not unmindful of the hardships imposed by it upon a large group of American citizens. Cf. *Ex parte Kawato,* 317 U.S. 69, 73. But hardships are part of war, and war is an aggregation of hardships. All citizens alike, both in and out of uniform, feel the impact of war in greater or lesser measure. Citizenship has its responsibilities as well as its privileges, and in time of war the burden is always heavier. Compulsory exclusion of large groups of citizens from their homes, except under circumstances of direst emergency and peril, is inconsistent with our basic government institutions. But when under conditions of modern warfare our shores are threatened by hostile forces, the power to protect must be commensurate with the threatened danger.

It is argued that on May 30, 1942, the date the petitioner was charged with remaining in the prohibited area, there were conflicting orders outstanding, forbidding him both to leave the area and to remain there. Of course, a person cannot be convicted for doing the very thing which it is a crime to fail to do. But the outstanding orders here contained no such contradictory commands.

There was an order issued March 27, 1942, which prohibited petitioner and others of Japanese ancestry from leaving the area, but its effect was specifically limited in time "until and to the extent that a future proclamation or order should so permit or direct." 7 Fed. Reg. 2601. That "future order," the one for violation of which petitioner was convicted, was issued May 3, 1942, and it did "direct" exclusion from the area of all persons of Japanese ancestry, before 12 o'clock noon, May 9; furthermore it contained a warning that all such persons found in the prohibited area would be liable to punishment under the March 21, 1942 Act of Congress. Consequently, the only order in effect touching the petitioner's being in the area on May 30, 1942, the date specified in the information against him, was the May 3 order which prohibited his remaining there, and it was that same order, which he stipulated in his trial that he had violated, knowing of its existence. There is therefore no basis for the argument that on May 30, 1942, he was subject to punishment, under the March 27 and May 3 orders, whether he remained in or left the area.

It does appear, however, that on May 9, the effective date of the exclusion order, the military authorities had already determined that the evacuation should be effected by assembling together and placing under guard all those of Japanese ancestry, at central points, designated as "assembly centers," in order "to insure the orderly evacuation and resettlement of Japanese voluntarily migrating from Military Area No. 1, to restrict and regulate such migration." Public Proclamation No. 4, 7 Fed. Reg. 2601. And on May 19, 1942, eleven days before the time petitioner was charged with unlawfully remaining in the area, Civilian Restrictive Order No. 1, 8 Fed. Reg. 982, provided for detention of those of Japanese ancestry in assembly or relocation centers. It is now argued that the validity of the exclusion order cannot be considered apart from the orders requiring him, after departure from the area, to report and to remain in an assembly or relocation center. The contention is that we must treat these separate orders as one and inseparable; that, for this reason, if detention in the assembly or relocation center would have illegally deprived the petitioner of his liberty, the exclusion order and his conviction under it cannot stand.

We are thus being asked to pass at this time upon the whole subsequent detention program in both assembly and relocation centers, although the only issues framed at the trial related to petitioner's remaining in the prohibited area in violation of the exclusion order. Had petitioner here left the prohibited area and gone to an assembly center we cannot say either as a matter of fact or law that his presence in that center would have resulted in his detention in a relocation center. Some who did report to the assembly center were not sent to relocation centers, but were released upon condition that they remain outside the prohibited zone until the military orders were modified or lifted. This illustrates that they pose different problems and may be governed by different principles. The lawfulness of one does not necessarily determine the lawfulness of the others. This is made clear when we analyze the requirements of the separate provisions of the separate orders. These separate requirements were that those of Japanese ancestry (1) depart from the area; (2) report to and temporarily remain in an assembly center; (3) go under military control to a relocation center there to remain for an indeterminate period until released conditionally or unconditionally by the military authorities. Each of these requirements, it will be noted, imposed distinct duties in connection with the separate steps in a complete evacuation program. Had Congress directly incorporated into one Act the language of these separate orders, and provided sanctions for their violations, disobedience of any one would have constituted a separate offense. Cf. *Blockburger v. United States,* 284 U.S. 299, 304. There is no reason why violations of these orders, insofar as they were promulgated pursuant to Congressional enactment, should not be treated as separate offenses.

The *Endo* case, *post,* p. 283, graphically illustrates the difference between the validity of an order to exclude and the validity of a detention order after exclusion has been effected.

Since the petitioner has not been convicted of failing to report or to remain in an assembly or relocation center, we cannot in this case determine the validity of those separate provisions of the order. It is sufficient here for us to pass upon the order which petitioner violated. To do more would be to go beyond the issues raised, and to decide momentous questions not contained within the framework of the pleadings or the evidence in this case. It will be time enough to decide the serious constitutional issues which petitioner seeks to raise when an assembly or relocation order is applied or is certain to be applied to him, and we have its terms before us.

Some of the members of the Court are of the view that evacuation and detention in an Assembly Center were inseparable. After May 3, 1942, the date of Exclusion Order No. 34, Korematsu was under compulsion to leave the area not as he would choose but via an Assembly Center. The Assembly Center was conceived as a part of the machinery for group evacuation. The power to exclude includes the power to do it by force if necessary. And any forcible measure must necessarily entail some degree of detention or restraint whatever method of removal is selected. But whichever view is taken, it results in holding that the other under which petitioner was convicted was valid.

It is said that we are dealing here with the case of imprisonment of a citizen in a concentration camp solely because of his ancestry, without evidence or inquiry concerning his loyalty and good disposition towards the United States. Our task would be simple, our duty clear, were this a case involving the imprisonment of a loyal citizen in a concentration camp because of racial prejudice. Regardless of the true nature of the assembly and relocation centers—and we deem it unjustifiable to call them concentration camps with all the ugly connotations that term implies—we are dealing specifically with nothing but an exclusion order. To cast this case into outlines of racial prejudice, without reference to the real military dangers which were presented, merely confuses the issue. Korematsu was not excluded from the Military Area because of hostility to him or his race. He *was* excluded because we are at war with the Japanese Empire, because the properly constituted military authorities feared an invasion of our West Coast and felt constrained to take proper security measures, because they decided that the military urgency of the situation demanded that all citizens of Japanese ancestry be segregated from the West Coast temporarily, and finally, because Congress, reposing its confidence in this time of war in our military leaders—as inevitably it must—determined that they should have the power to do just this. There was evidence of disloyalty on the part of some, the military authorities considered that the need for action was great, and time was short. We cannot—by availing ourselves of the calm perspective of hindsight—now say that at that time these actions were unjustified.

Ex Parte Endo

323 U.S. 283 (1944)

Mr. Justice Douglas delivered the opinion of the Court:

This case comes here on a certificate of the Court of Appeals for the Ninth Circuit, certifying to us questions of law upon which it desires instructions for the decision of the case. Judicial Code, § 239, 28 USCA § 346, 8 FCA title 28, § 346. Acting under that section we ordered the entire record to be certified to this Court so that we might proceed to a decision, as if the case had been brought here by appeal.

Mitsuye Endo, hereinafter designated as the appellant, is an American citizen of Japanese ancestry. She was evacuated from Sacramento, California, in 1942, pursuant to certain military orders which we will presently discuss, and was removed to the Tule Lake War Relocation Center located at Newell, Modoc County, California. In July, 1942, she filed a petition for a writ of habeas corpus in the District Court of the United States for the Northern District of California, asking that she be discharged and restored to liberty. That petition was denied by the District Court in July, 1943, and an appeal was perfected to the Circuit Court of Appeals in August, 1943. Shortly thereafter appellant was transferred from the Tule Lake Relocation Center to the Central Utah Relocation Center located at Topaz, Utah, where she is presently detained. The certificate of questions of law was filed here on April 22, 1944, and on May 8, 1944, we ordered the entire record to be certified to this Court. It does not appear that any respondent was ever served with process or appeared in the proceedings. But the United States Attorney for the Northern District of California argued before the District Court that the petition should not be granted. And the Solicitor General argued the case here.

The history of the evacuation of Japanese aliens and citizens of Japanese ancestry from the Pacific coastal regions, following the Japanese attack on our Naval Base at Pearl Harbor on December 7, 1941, and the declaration of war against Japan on December 8, 1941 (55 Stat 795, c 561, 50 USCA Appx note, prec. § 1), has been reviewed in Hirabayashi v. United States, 320 U.S. 81, 87 L ed 1774, 63 S Ct 1375. It need be only briefly recapitulated here. On February 19, 1942, the President promulgated Executive Order No. 9066, 7 Fed Reg 1407. It recited that "the successful prosecution of the war requires every possible protection against espionage and against sabotage to national-defense material, national-defense premises, and national-defense utilities as defined in § 4, Act of April 20, 1918, 40 Stat 533, c 59, as amended by the Act of November 30, 1940, 54 Stat 1220, c 926, and the Act of August 21, 1941, 55 Stat 655, c 388 (50 USCA § 104, 11 FCA title 50, § 104)."

And it authorized and directed "the Secretary of War, and the Military Commanders whom he may from time to time designate, whenever he or any designated Commander deems such action necessary or desirable, to prescribe military areas in such places and of such extent as he or the appropriate Military Commander may determine, from which any or all persons may be excluded, and with respect to which, the right of any person to enter, remain in, or leave shall be subject to whatever restrictions the Secretary of War or the appropriate Military Commander may impose in his discretion. The Secretary of War is hereby authorized to provide for residents of any such area who are excluded therefrom, such transportation, food, shelter, and other accommodations as may be necessary, in the judgment of the Secretary of War or the said Military Commander, and until other arrangements are made, to accomplish the purpose of this order."

Lt. General J. L. De Witt, Military Commander of the Western Defense Command, was designated to carry out the duties prescribed by that Executive Order. On March 2, 1942, he promulgated Public Proclamation No. 1 (7 Fed Reg 2320) which recited that the entire Pacific Coast of the United States "by its geographical location is particularly subject to attack, to attempted invasion by the armed forces of nations with which the United States is now at war, and, in connection therewith, is subject to espionage and acts of sabotage, thereby requiring the adoption of military measures necessary to establish safeguards against such enemy operations."

It designated certain Military Areas and Zones in the Western Defense Command and announced that certain persons might subsequently be excluded from these areas. On March 16, 1942, General De Witt promulgated Public Proclamation No. 2 which contained similar recitals and designated further Military Areas and Zones. 7 Fed Reg 2405.

On March 18, 1942, the President promulgated Executive Order No. 9102 which established in the Office for Emergency Management of the Executive Office of the President the War Relocation Authority. 7 Fed Reg 2165. It recited that it was made "in order to provide for the removal from designated areas of persons whose removal is necessary in the interests of national security." It provided for a Director and authorized and directed him to "formulate and effectuate a program for the removal, from the areas designated from time to time by the Secretary of War or appropriate military commander under the authority of Executive Order No. 9066 of February 19, 1942, of the persons or classes of persons designated under such Executive Order, and for their relocation, maintenance, and supervision."

The Director was given the authority, among other things, to prescribe regulations necessary or desirable to promote effective execution of the program.

Congress shortly enacted legislation which, as we pointed out in Hirabayashi v. United States, supra, ratified and confirmed Executive Order No. 9066. See 320 U.S. pp 87-91, 87 L ed 1779-1781, 63 S Ct 1375. It did so by the Act of March 21, 1942 (56 Stat 173, c 191, 18 USCA § 97a, FCA title 18, § 97a) which provided:

"That whoever shall enter, remain in, leave, or commit any act in any military area or military zone prescribed, under the authority of an Executive Order of the President, by the Secretary of War, or by any military commander designated by the Secretary of War, contrary to the restrictions applicable to any such military commander, shall, if it appears that he knew or should have known of the existence and extent of the restrictions or order and that his act was in violation thereof, be guilty of a misdemeanor and upon conviction shall be liable to a fine of not to exceed $5,000 or to imprisonment for not more than one year, or both, for each offense."

Beginning on March 24, 1942, a series of 108 Civilian Exclusion Orders were issued by General De Witt pursuant to Public Proclamation Nos. 1 and 2. Appellant's exclusion was effected by Civilian Exclusion Order No. 52, dated May

7, 1942. It ordered that "all persons of Japanese ancestry, both alien and non-alien" be excluded from Sacramento, California, beginning at noon on May 16, 1942. Appellant was evacuated to the Sacramento Assembly Center on May 15, 1942, and was transferred from there to the Tule Lake Relocation Center on June 19, 1942.

On May 19, 1942, General De Witt promulgated Civilian Restrictive Order No. 1 (8 Fed Reg 982) and on June 27, 1942, Public Proclamation No. 8. 7 Fed Reg 8346. These prohibited evacuees from leaving Assembly Centers or Relocation Centers except pursuant to an authorization from General De Witt's, headquarters. Public Proclamation No. 8 recited that "the present situation within these military areas requires as a matter of military necessity" that the evacuees be removed to "Relocation Centers for their relocation, maintenance and supervision," that those Relocation Centers be designated as War Relocation Project Areas, and that restrictions on the rights of the evacuees to enter, remain in, or leave such areas be promulgated. These restrictions were applicable to the Relocation Centers within the Western Defense Command and included both of those in which appellant has been confined—Tule Lake Relocation Center at Newell, California and Central Utah Relocation Center at Topaz, Utah. And Public Proclamation No. 8 purported to make any person who was subject to its provisions and who failed to conform to it liable to the penalties prescribed by the Act of March 21, 1942.

By letter of August 11, 1942, General De Witt authorized the War Relocation Authority to issue permits for persons to leave these areas. By virtue of that delegation and the authority conferred by Executive Order No. 9102, the War Relocation Authority was given over the ingress and egress of evacuees from the Relocation Centers where Mitsuye Endo was confined.

The program of the War Relocation Authority is said to have three main features: (1) the maintenance of Relocation Centers as interim places of residence for evacuees; (2) the segregation of loyal from disloyal evacuees; (3) the continued detention of the disloyal and so far as possible the relocation of the loyal in selected communities. In connection with the latter phase of its work the War Relocation Authority established a procedure for obtaining leave from Relocation Centers. That procedure so far as indefinite leave is concerned, presently provides as follows:

Application for leave clearance is required. An investigation of the applicant is made for the purpose of ascertaining "the probable effect upon the war program and upon the public peace and security of issuing indefinite leave" to the applicant. The grant of leave clearance does not authorize departure from the Relocation Center. Application for indefinite leave must also be made. Indefinite leave may be granted under 14 specified conditions. For example, it may be granted (1) where the applicant proposes to accept an employment offer or an offer of support that has been investigated and approved by the Authority; or (2) where the applicant does not intend to work but has "adequate financial resources to take care of himself" and a Relocation Officer has investigated and approved "public sentiment at his proposed destination," or (3) where the applicant has made arrangements to live at a hotel or in a private home approved by a Relocation Officer while arranging for employment; or (4) where the applicant proposes to accept employment by a federal or local governmental agency; or (5) where the applicant is going to live with designated classes of relatives.

But even if an applicant meets those requirements, no leave will issue when the proposed place of residence or employment is within a locality where it has been ascertained that "community sentiment is unfavorable" or when the applicant plans to go to an area which has been closed by the Authority to the issuance of indefinite leave. Nor will such leave issue if the area where the the applicant plans to reside or work is one which has not been cleared for relocation. Moreover, the applicant agrees to give the Authority prompt notice of any change of employment or residence. And the indefinite leave which is granted does not permit entry into a prohibited military area, including those from which these people were evacuated.

Mitsuye Endo made application for leave clearance on February 19, 1943, after the petition was filed in the District Court. Leave clearance was granted her on August 16, 1943. But she made no application for indefinite leave.

Her petition for a writ of habeas corpus alleges that she is a loyal and law-abiding citizen of the United States, that no charge has been made against her, that she is being unlawfully detailed, and that she is confined in the Relocation Center under armed guard and held there against her will.

It is conceded by the Department of Justice and by the War Relocation Authority that appellant is a loyal and law-abiding citizen. They make no claim that she is detained on any charge or that she is even suspected of disloyalty. Moreover, they do not contend that she may be held any longer in the Relocation Center. They concede that it is beyond the power of the War Relocation Authority to detain citizens against whom no charges of disloyalty or subversiveness have been made for a period longer than that necessary to separate the loyal from the disloyal and to provide the necessary guidance for relocation. But they maintain that detention for an additional period after leave clearance has been granted is an essential step in the evacuation program. Reliance for that conclusion is placed on the following circumstances.

When compulsory evacuation from the West Coast was decided upon, plans for taking care of the evacuees after their detention in the Assembly Centers, to which they were initially removed, remained to be determined. On April 7, 1942, the Director of the Authority held a conference in Salt Lake City with various state and federal officials including the Governors of the intermountain states. "Strong opposition was expressed to any type of unsupervised relocation and some of the Governors refused to be responsible for maintenance of law and order unless evacuees brought into their States were kept under constant military surveillance." Sen Doc No. 96, supra, note 7, p 4. As stated by General De Witt in his report to the Chief of Staff:

"Essentially, military necessity required only that the Japanese population be removed from the coastal area and dispersed in the interior, where the danger of action in concert during any attempted enemy raids along the coast, or in advance thereof as preparation for a full scale attack, would be eliminated. That the evacuation program necessarily and ultimately developed into one of complete Federal supervision, was due primarily to the fact that the interior states would not accept an uncontrolled Japanese migration."

Final Report, supra, note 2, pp 43, 44. The Authority thereupon abandoned plans for assisting groups of evacuees in private colonization and temporarily put to one side plans for aiding the evacuees in obtaining private employment. As an alternative the Authority "concentrated on establishment of Government-operated centers with sufficient capacity and facilities to accommodate the entire evacuee population." Sen Doc No. 96, supra, note 7, p 4. Accordingly, it undertook to care for the basic needs of these people in the Relocation Centers, to promote as rapidly as possible the permanent resettlement of as many as possible in normal communities, and to provide indefinitely for those left at the Relocation Centers. An effort was made to segregate the loyal evacuees from the others. The leave program which we have discussed was put into operation and the resettlement program commenced.

It is argued that such a planned and orderly relocation was essential to the success of the evacaution program; that but for such supervision there might have been a dangerously disorderly migration of unwanted people to unprepared communities; that unsupervised evacuation might have resulted in hardship and disorder; that the success of the evacuation program was thought to require the knowledge that the Federal government was maintaining control over the evacuated population except as the release of individuals could be effected consistently with their own peace and well-being and that of the nation; that although community hostility towards the evacuees has diminished, it has not disappeared and the continuing control of the Authority over the relocation process is essential to the success of the evacuation program. It is argued that supervised relocation, as the chosen method of terminating the evacuation, is the final step in the entire process and is a consequence of the first step taken. It is conceded that appellant's detention pending compliance with the leave regulations is not directly connected with the prevention of espionage and sabotage at the present time. But it is argued that Executive Order No. 9102 confers power to make regulations necessary and proper for controlling situations created by the exercise of the powers expressly conferred for protection against espionage and sabotage. The leave regulations are said to fall within that category.

First. We are of the view that Mitsuye Endo should be given her liberty. In reaching that conclusion we do not come to the underlying constitutional issues which have been argued. For we conclude that, whatever power the War Relocation Authority may have to detain other classes of citizens, it has no authority to subject citizens who are concededly loyal to its leave procedure.

It should be noted at the outset that we do not have here a question such as was presented in Ex parte Milligan, 4 Wall. (U.S.) 2, 18 L ed 281, or in Ex parte Quirin, 317 U.S. 1, 87 L ed 3, 63 S Ct 2, where the jurisdiction of military tribunals to try persons according to the law of war was challenged in habeas corpus proceedings. Mitsuye Endo is detained by a civilian agency, the War Relocation Authority, not by the military. Moreover, the evacuation program was not left exclusively to the military; the Authority was given a large measure of responsibility for its execution and Congress made its enforcement subject to civil penalties by the Act of March 21, 1942. Accordingly, no questions of military law are involved.

Such power of detention as the Authority has stems from Executive Order No. 9066. That order is the source of the authority delegated by General De Witt in his letter of August 11, 1942. And Executive Order No. 9102 which created the War Relocation Authority purported to do no more than to implement the program authorized by Executive Order No. 9066.

We approach the construction of Executive Order No. 9066 as we would approach the construction of legislation in this field. That Executive Order must indeed be considered along with the Act of March 21, 1942, which ratified and confirmed it (Hirabayashi v. United States, supra (320 U.S. pp 87-91, 87 L ed 1779, 1781, 63 S Ct 1375)) as the Order and the statute together laid such basis as there is for participation by civil agencies of the federal government in the evacuation program. Broad powers frequently granted to the President or other executive officers by Congress so that they may deal with the exigencies of war time problems have been sustained. And the Constitution when it committed to the Executive and to Congress the exercise of the war power necessarily gave them wide scope for the exercise of judgment and discretion so that war might be waged effectively and successfully. Hirabayashi v. United States, supra (320 U.S. p 93, 87 L ed 1782, 63 L ed 1375). At the same time, however, the Constitution is as specific in its enumeration of many of the civil rights of the individual as it is in its enumeration of the powers of his government. Thus it has prescribed procedural safeguards surrounding the arrest, detention and conviction of individuals. Some of these are contained in the Sixth Amendment, compliance with which is essential if convictions are to be sustained. Tot v. United States, 319 U.S. 463, 87 L ed 1519, 63 S Ct 1241. And the Fifth Amendment provides that no person shall be deprived of liberty (as well as life or property) without due process of law. Moreover, as a further safeguard against invasion of the basic civil rights of the individual it is provided in Art. 1, § 9 of the Constitution that "The Privilege of the Writ of Habeas Corpus shall not be suspended, unless when in Cases of Rebellion or Invasion the public Safety may require it." See Ex parte Milligan, 4 Wall. (U.S.) 2, 18 L ed 281, supra.

We mention these constitutional provisions not to stir the constitutional issues which have been argued at the bar but to indicate the approach which we think should be made to an Act of Congress or an order of the Chief Executive that touches the sensitive area of rights specifically guaranteed by the Constitution. This Court has quite consistently given a narrower scope for the operation of the presumption of constitutionality when legislation appeared on its face to violate a specific prohibition of the Constitution. We have likewise favored that interpretation of legislation which gives it the greater chance of surviving the test of constitutionality. Those analogies are suggestive here. We must assume that the Chief Executive and members of Congress, as well as the courts, are sensitive to and respectful of the liberties of the citizen. In interpreting a war-time measure we must assume that their purpose was to allow for the greatest possible accommodation between those liberties and the exigencies of war. We must assume, when asked to find implied powers in a grant of legislative or executive authority, that the law makers intended to place no greater restraint on the citizen than was clearly and unmistakably indicated by the language they used.

The Act of March 21, 1942, was a war measure. The House Report (H. Rep. No. 1906, 77th Cong. 2d Sess p. 2) stated, "The necessity for this legislation arose from the fact that the safe conduct of the war requires the fullest possible protection against either espionage or sabotage to national defense material, national defense premises, and national defense utilities." That was the precise purpose of Executive Order No. 9066, for, as we have seen, it gave as the reason for the exclusion of persons from prescribed military areas the protection of such property "against espionage and against sabotage." And Executive Order No. 9102 which established the War Relocation Authority did so, as we have noted, "in order to provide for the removal from designated areas of persons whose removal is necessary in the interests of national security." The purpose and objective of the Act and of these orders are plain. Their single aim was the protection of the war effort against espionage and sabotage. It is in light of that one objective that the powers conferred by the orders must be construed.

Neither the Act nor the orders use the language of detention. The Act says that no one shall "enter, remain in, leave, or commit any act" in the prescribed military areas contrary to the applicable restrictions. Executive Order No. 9066 subjects the right of any person "to enter, remain in, or leave" those prescribed areas to such restrictions as the military may impose. And apart from those restrictions the

Secretary of War is only given authority to afford the evacuees "transportation, food, shelter, and other accommodations." Executive Order No. 9102 authorizes and directs the War Relocation Authority "to formulate and effectuate a program for the removal" of the persons covered by Executive Order No. 9066 from the prescribed military areas and "for their relocation, maintenance, and supervision." And power is given the Authority to make regulations "necessary or desirable to promote effective execution of such program." Moreover, unlike the case of curfew regulations (Hirabayashi v. United States, 320 U.S. 81, 87 L ed 1774, 63 S Ct 1375, supra), the legislative history of the Act of March 21, 1942, is silent on detention. And that silence may have special significance in view of the fact that detention in Relocation Centers was no part of the original program of evacuation but developed later to meet what seemed to the officials in charge to be mounting hostility to the evacuees on the part of the communities where they sought to go.

We do not mean to imply that detention in connection with no phase of the evacuation program would be lawful. The fact that the Act and the orders are silent on detention does not of course mean that any power to detain is lacking. Some such power might indeed be necessary to the successful operation of the evacuation program. At least we may so assume. Moreover, we may assume for the purposes of this case that initial detention in Relocation Centers was authorized. But we stress the silence of the legislative history and of the Act and the Executive Orders on the power to detain to emphasize that any such authority which exists must be implied. If there is to be the greatest possible accommodation of the liberties of the citizen with this war measure, any such implied power must be narrowly confined to the precise purpose of the evacuation program.

A citizen who is concededly loyal presents no problem of espionage or sabotage. Loyalty is a matter of the heart and mind, not of race, creed, or color. He who is loyal is by definition not a spy or a saboteur. When the power to detain is derived from the power to protect the war effort against espionage and sabotage, detention which has no relationship to that objective is unauthorized.

Nor may the power to detain an admittedly loyal citizen or to grant him a conditional release be implied as a useful or convenient step in the evacuation program, whatever authority might be implied in case of those whose loyalty was not conceded or established. If we assume (as we do) that the original evacuation was justified, its lawful character was derived from the fact that it was an espionage and sabotage measure, not that there was community hostility to this group of American citizens. The evacuation program rested explicitly on the former ground not on the latter as the underlying legislation shows. The authority to detain a citizen or to grant him a conditional release as protection against espionage or sabotage is exhausted at least when his loyalty is conceded. If we held that the authority to detain continued thereafter, we would transform an espionage or sabotage measure into something else. That was not done by Executive Order No. 9066 or by the Act of March 21, 1942, which ratified it. What they did not do we cannot do. Detention which furthered the campaign against espionage and sabotage would be one thing. But detention which has no relationship to that campaign is of a distinct character. Community hostility even to loyal evacuees may have been (and perhaps still is) a serious problem. But if authority for their custody and supervision is to be sought on that ground, the Act of March 21, 1942, Executive Order No. 9066, and Executive Order No. 9102, offer no support. And none other is advanced.[24] To read them that broadly would be to assume that the Congress and the President intended that this discriminatory action should be taken against these people wholly on account of their ancestry even though the government conceded their loyalty to this country. We cannot make such an assumption. As the President has said of these loyal citizens:

"Americans of Japanese ancestry, like those of many other ancestries, have shown that they can, and want to, accept our institutions and work loyally with the rest of us, making their own valuable contribution to the national wealth and well-being. In vindication of the very ideals for which we are fighting this war it is important to us to maintain a high standard of fair, considerate, and equal treatment for the people of this minority as of all other minorities. . . .

The judgment is reversed and the cause is remanded to the District Court for proceedings in conformity with this opinion.

Reversed.

---

[24]It is argued, to be sure, that there has been Congressional ratification of the detention of loyal evacuees under the leave regulations of the Authority through the appropriation of sums for the expenses of the Authority. 57 Stat 533, c 228, PL 139, 78th Cong 1st Sess approved July 12, 1943 and PL 372, 78th Cong 2d Sess approved June 28, 1944. It is pointed out that the regulations and procedures of the Authority were disclosed in reports to the Congress and in Congressional hearings. See, for example, Sen. Doc. No. 96, supra, note 7; Report and Minority Views of the Special Committee on Un-American Activities on Japanese War Relocation Centers, H. Rep. No. 717, 78th Cong. 1st Sess, pp 23-26; Hearings, Subcommittee of the Senate Military Affairs Committee on S. 444, 78th Cong. 1st Sess. pp 45, 46; Japanese War Relocation Centers, Subcommittee Report on S. 444 and S. 101 and 111, 78th Cong. 1st Sess. pp 4, 5 et seq. And it is shown that the leave program of the authority was mentioned both in the House and Senate Committee hearings on the 1944 Appropriation Act (Hearings, Subcommittee of the House Committee on Appropriations, National War Agencies Appropriation Bill for 1944, 78th Cong. 1st Sess. pp 698, 699, 710; Hearings of the Senate Subcommittee on Appropriations, National War Agencies Appropriation Bill for 1944, 78th Cong. 1st Sess. p 382) and on the floor of the House prior to passage of the 1944 Act. 89 Cong. Rec. pp 5983-5985. Congress may of course do by ratification what it might have authorized. Swayne & Hoyt v. United States, 300 U.S. 297, 301, 302, 81 L ed 659, 662, 663, 57 S Ct 478. And ratification may be effected through appropriation acts. Isbrandtsen-Moller Co. v. United States, 300 U.S. 139, 147, 81 L ed 562, 568, 57 S Ct 407; Brooks v. Dewar, 313 U.S. 354, 361, 85 L ed 1399, 1403, 61 S Ct 979. But the appropriation must plainly show a purpose to bestow the precise authority which is claimed. We can hardly deduce such a purpose here where a lump appropriation was made for the overall program of the Authority and no sums were earmarked for the single phase of the total program which is here involved. Congress may support the effort to take care of these evacuees without ratifying every phase of the program.

Duncan v. Kahanamo Ku

327 U.S. 304 (1946)

Mr. Justice Black delivered the opinion of the Court.

The petitioners in these cases were sentenced to prison by military tribunals in Hawaii. Both are civilians. The question before us is whether the military tribunals had power to do this. The United States district court for Hawaii in habeas corpus proceedings held that the military tribunals had no such power and ordered that they be set free. The circuit court of appeals reversed, and ordered that the petitioners be returned to prison. 146 F. 2d 576. Both cases thus involve the rights of individuals charged with crime and not connected with the armed forces to have their guilt or innocence determined in courts of law which provide established procedural safeguards, rather than by military tribunals which fail to afford many of these safeguards. Since these judicial safeguards are prized privileges of our system of government we granted certiorai.

The following events led to the military tribunals' exercise of jurisdiction over the petitioners. On December 7, 1941, immediately following the surprise air attack by the Japanese on Pearl Harbor, the Governor of Hawaii by proclamation undertook to suspend the privilege of the writ of habeas corpus and to place the Territory under "martial law." Section 67 of the Hawaiian Organic Act, 31 Stat. 141, 153,[1] authorizes the Territorial Governor to take this action "in case of rebellion or invasion, or imminent danger thereof, when the public safety requires it . . ." His action was to remain in effect only "until communication can be had with the President and his decision thereon made known." The President approved the Governor's action on December 9th.[2] The Governor's proclamation also authorized and requested the Commanding General, "during the . . . emergency and until danger of invasion is removed, to exercise all the powers normally exercised" by the Governor and by the "judicial officers and employees of this territory."

Pursuant to this authorization the commanding general immediately proclaimed himself Military Governor and undertook the defense of the Territory and the maintenance of order. On December 8th, both civil and criminal courts were forbidden to summon jurors and witnesses and to try cases. The Commanding General established military tribunals to take the place of the courts. These were to try civilians charged with violating the laws of the United States and of the Territory, and rules, regulations, orders or policies of the Military Government. Rules of evidence and procedure of courts of law were not to control the military trials. In imposing penalties the military tribunals were to be "guided by, but not limited to the penalties authorized by the courts martial manual, the laws of the United States, the Territory of Hawaii, the District of Columbia, and the customs of war in like cases." The rule announced was simply that punishment was to be "commensurate with the offense committed" and that the death penalty might be imposed "in appropriate cases." Thus the military authorities took over the government of Hawaii. They could and did, by simply promulgating orders, govern the day to day activities of civilians who lived, worked, or were merely passing through there. The military tribunals interpreted the very orders promulgated by the military authorities and proceeded to punish violators. The sentences imposed were not subject to direct appellate court review, since it had long been established that military tribunals are not part of our judicial system. *Ex parte Vallandigham,* 1 Wall. 243. The military undoubtedly assumed that its rule was not subject to any judicial control whatever, for by orders issued on August 25, 1943, it prohibited even accepting of a petition for writ of habeas corpus by a judge or judicial employee or the filing of such a petition by a prisoner or his attorney. Military tribunals could punish violators of these orders by fine, imprisonment or death.

Both White and Duncan challenged the power of the military tribunals to try them by petitions for writs of habeas corpus filed in the district court for Hawaii on March 14 and April 14, 1944, respectively. Their petitions urged both statutory and constitutional grounds. The court issued orders to show cause. Returns to these orders contended that Hawaii had become part of an active theatre of war constantly threatened by invasion from without; that the writ of habeas corpus had therefore properly been suspended and martial law had validly been established in accordance with the provisions of the Organic Act; that consequently the district court did not have jurisdiction to issue the writ; and that the trials of petitioners by military tribunals pursuant to orders by the Military Governor issued because of military necessity were valid. Each petitioner filed a traverse to the returns, which traverse challenged among other things the suspension of habeas corpus, the establishment of martial law and the validity of the Military Governor's orders, asserting that such action could not be taken except when required by military necessity due to actual or threatened invasion, which even if it did exist on December 7, 1941, did not exist when the petitioners were tried; and that, whatever the necessity for martial law, there was no justification for trying them in military tribunals rather than the regular courts of law. The district court, after separate trials, found in each case, among other things, that the courts had always been able to function but for the military orders closing them, and that consequently there was no military necessity for the trial of petitioners by military tribunals rather than regular courts.[4] It accordingly held the trials void and ordered the release of the petitioners.

The circuit court of appeals, assuming without deciding that the district court had jurisdiction to entertain the petitions, held the military trials valid and reversed the ruling of the district court. 146 F. 2d 576. It held that the military orders providing for military trials were fully authorized by § 67 of the Organic Act and the Governor's actions taken under it. The court relied on that part of the section which, as we have indicated, authorizes the Governor with the approval of the President to proclaim "martial law" whenever the public safety requires it. The circuit court thought that the term "martial law" as used in the Act denotes among other things the establishment of a "total military government" completely displacing or subordinating the regular courts, that the decision of the executive as to what the public safety requires must be sustained so long as that decision is based on reasonable grounds and that such reasonable grounds did exist.

In presenting its argument before this Court the Government for reasons set out in the margin[5] abandons its contention as to the suspension of the writ of habeas corpus and advances the argument employed by the circuit court for sustaining the trials and convictions of the petitioners by military tribunals. The petitioners contend that "martial law" as provided for by § 67 did not authorize the military to try and punish civilians such as petitioners and urge further that if such authority should be inferred from the Organic Act, it would be unconstitutional. We need decide the constitutional question only if we agree with the Government that Congress did authorize what was done here.

Did the Organic Act during the period of martial law give the armed forces power to supplant all civilian laws and to substitute military for judicial trials under the conditions that existed in Hawaii at the time these petitioners were tried? The relevant conditions, for our purposes, were the same when both petitioners were tried. The answer to the question depends on a correct interpretation of the Act. But we need not construe the Act, insofar as the power of the military might be used to meet other and different conditions and situations. The boundaries of the situation with reference to which we do interpret the scope of the Act can be more sharply defined by stating at this point some different conditions which either would or might conceivably have affected to a greater or lesser extent the scope of the authorized military power. We note first that at the time the alleged offenses were committed the dangers apprehended by the military were not sufficiently imminent to cause them to require civilians to evacuate the area or even to evacuate any of the buildings necessary to carry on the business of the courts. In fact, the buildings had long been open and actually in use for certain kinds of trials. Our question does not involve the well-established power of the military to exercise jurisidiction over members of the armed forces,[6] those directly connected with such forces,[7] or enemy belligerents, prisoners of war, or others charged with violating the laws of war.[8] We are not concerned with the recognizes power of the military to try civilians in tribunals established as a part of a temporary military government over occupied enemy territory or territory regained from an enemy where civilian government cannot and does not function.[9] For Hawaii since annexation has been held by and loyal to the United States. Nor need we here consider the power of the military simply to arrest and detain civilians interfering with a necessary military function at a time of turbulence and danger from insurrection or war.[10] And finally, there was no specialized effort of the military, here, to enforce orders which related only to military functions, such as, for illustration, curfew rules or blackouts. For these petitioners were tried before tribunals set up under a military program which took over all government and superseded all civil laws and courts. If the Organic Act, properly interpreted, did not give the armed forces this awesome power, both petitioners are entitled to their freedom.

I.

In interpreting the Act we must first look to its language. Section 67 makes it plain that Congress did intend the Governor of Hawaii, with the approval of the President, to invoke military aid under certain circumstances. But Congress did not specifically state to what extent the army could be used or what power it could exercise. It certainly did not explicitly declare that the Governor in conjunction with the military could for days, months or years close all the courts and supplant them with military tribunals. Cf. *Coleman v. Tennessee,* 97 U.S. 509, 514. If a power thus to obliterate the judicial system of Hawaii can be found at all in the Organic Act, it must be inferred from § 67's provision for placing the Territory under "martial law." But the term "martial law" carries no precise meaning. The Constitution does not refer to "martial law" at all and no Act of Congress has defined the term. It has been employed in various ways by different people and at different times. By some it has been identified as "military law" limited to members of, and those connected with, the armed forces. Others have said that the term does not imply a system of established rules but denotes simply some kind of day to day expression of a general's will dictated by what he considers the imperious necessity of the moment. See *United States v. Diekelman,* 92 U.S. 520, 526. In 1857 the confusion as to the meaning of the phrase was so great that the Attorney General in an official opinion had this to say about it: "The common law authorities and commentators afford no clue to what martial law, as understood in England, really is . . . In this country it is still worse." 8 Op. Atty. Gen. 365, 367, 368. What was true in 1857 remains true today.[11] The language of § 67 thus fails to define adequately the scope of the power given to the military and to show whether the Organic Act provides that courts of law be supplanted by military tribunals.

II.

Since the Act's language does not provide a satisfactory answer, we look to the legislative history for possible further aid in interpreting the term "martial law" as used in the statute. The Government contends that the legislative history shows that Congress intended to give the armed forces extraordinarily broad powers to try civilians before military tribunals. Its argument is as follows: That portion of the language of § 67 which prescribes the prerequisites to declaring martial law is identical with a part of the language of the original Constitution of Hawaii. Before Congress enacted the Organic Act the supreme court of Hawaii had construed that language as giving the Hawaiian President power to authorize military tribunals to try civilians charged with crime whenever the public safety required it. *In re Kalanianaole,* 10 Hawaii 29. When Congress passed the Organic Act it simply enacted the applicable language of the Hawaiian Constitution and with it the interpretation of that language by the Hawaiian supreme court.

In disposing of this argument we wish to point out at the outset that even had Congress intended the decision in the *Kalanianaole* case to become part of the Organic Act, that case did not go so far as to authorize military trials of the petitioners for these reasons. There the defendants were insurrectionists taking part in the very uprising which the military were to suppress, while here the petitioners had no connection with any organized resistance to the armed forces or the established government. If, on the other hand, we should take the *Kalanianaole* case to authorize the complete supplanting of courts by military tribunals, we are certain that Congress did not wish to make that case part of the Organic Act. For that case did not merely uphold military trials of civilians but also held that courts were to interfere only when there was an obvious abuse of discretion which resulted in cruel and inhuman practices or the establishment of military rule for the personal gain of the President and the armed forces. But courts were not to review whether the President's action, no matter how unjustifiable, was necessary for the public safety. As we shall indicate later, military trials of civilians charged with crime, especially when not made subject to judicial review, are so obviously contrary to our political traditions and our institution of jury trials in courts of law, that the tenuous circumstance offered by the Government can hardly suffice to persuade us that Congress was willing to enact a Hawaiian supreme court decision permitting such a radical departure from our steadfast beliefs.[12]

Partly in order to meet this objection the Government further contends that Congress, in enacting the *Kalanianaole* case, not only authorized military trials of civilians in Hawaii, but also could and intended to provide that "martial law" in Hawaii should not be limited by the United States Constitution or by established constitutional practice. But when the Organic Act is read as a whole and in the light of its legislative history it becomes clear that Congress did not intend the Constitution to have a limited application to Hawaii. Along with § 67 Congress enacted § 5 of the Organic Act which provides "that the Constitution . . . shall have the same force and effect within the said Territory as elsewhere in the United States . . ." 31 Stat. 141. Even when Hawaii was first annexed Congress had provided that the Territory's existing laws should remain in effect unless contrary to the Constitution. 30 Stat. 750. And the House Committee Report in explaining § 5 of the Organic Act stated: "Probably the same result would obtain without this provision under section 1891, chapter 1, Title XXIII, of the Revised Statutes, *but to prevent possible question,* the section is inserted in the bill."[13] (Italics supplied.) Congress thus expressed a strong desire to apply the Constitution without qualification.

It follows that civilians in Hawaii are entitled to the constitutional guarantee of a fair trial to the same extent as those who live in any other part of our country. We are aware that conditions peculiar to Hawaii might imperatively demand extraordinarily speedy and effective measures in the event of actual or threatened invasion. But this also holds true for other parts of the United States. Extraordinary measures in Hawaii, however necessary, are not supportable on the mistaken premise that Hawaiian inhabitants are less entitled to constitutional protection than others. For here Congress did not in the Organic Act exercise whatever power it might have had to limit the application of the Constitution. Cf. *Hawaii v. Mankichi,* 190 U.S. 197. The people of Hawaii are therefore entitled to constitutional protection to the same extent as the inhabitants of the 48 States. And Congress did not enact the Hawaiian supreme court's decision in the *Kalanianaole* case and thus authorize the military trials of petitioners. Whatever power the Organic Act gave the Hawaiian military authorities, such power must therefore be construed in the same way as a grant of power to troops stationed in any one of the States.

III.

Since both the language of the Organic Act and its legislative history fail to indicate that the scope of "martial law" in Hawaii includes the supplanting of courts by military tribunals, we must look to other sources in order to interpret that term. We think the answer may be found in the birth, development and growth of our governmental institutions up to the time Congress passed the Organic Act. Have the principles and practices developed during the birth and growth of our political institutions been such as to persuade us that Congress intended that loyal civilians in loyal territory should have their daily conduct governed by military orders substituted for criminal laws, and that such civilians should be tried and punished by military tribunals? Let us examine what those principles and practices have been, with respect to the position of civilian government and the courts and compare that with the standing of military tribunals throughout our history.

People of many ages and countries have feared and unflinchingly opposed the kind of subordination of executive, legislative and judicial authorities to complete military rule which, according to the Government, Congress has authorized here. In this country that fear has become part of our cultural and political institutions. The story of that development is well known and we see no need to retell it all. But we might mention a few pertinent incidents. As early as the 17th Century our British ancestors took political action against aggressive military rule. When James I and Charles I authorized martial law for purposes of speedily punishing all types of crimes committed by civilians the protest led to the historic Petition of Right[14] which in uncompromising terms objected to this arbitrary procedure and prayed that it be stopped and never repeated.[15] When later the American colonies declared their independence one of the grievances listed by Jefferson was that the King had endeavored to render the military superior to the civil power. The executive and military officials who later found it necessary to utilize the armed forces to keep order in a young and turbulent nation, did not lose sight of the philosophy embodied in the Petition of Right and the Declaration of Independence, that existing civilian government and especially the courts were not to be interfered with by the exercise of military power. In 1787, the year in which the Constitution was formulated, the Governor of Massachusetts Colony used the militia to cope with Shay's Rebellion. In his instructions to the Commander of the troops the Governor listed the "great objects" of the mission. The troops were to "protect the judicial courts, . . ." "to assist the civil magistrates in executing the laws, . . ." and to "aid them in apprehending the disturbers of the public peace . . ." The Commander was to consider himself "constantly as under the direction of the civil officer, saving where any armed force shall appear and oppose . . . [his] marching to execute these orders."[16] President Washington's instructions to the Commander of the troops sent into Pennsylvania to suppress the Whiskey Rebellion of 1794 were to the same effect. The troops were to see to it that the laws were enforced and were to deliver the leaders of armed insurgents to the regular courts for trial. The President admonished the Commanding General "that the judge can not be controlled in his functions . . ."[17] In the many instances of the use of troops to control the activities of civilians that followed, the troops were generally again employed merely to aid and not to supplant the civilian authorities.[18] The last noteworthy incident before the enactment of the Organic Act was the rioting that occurred in the spring of 1899 at the Coeur d'Arlene mines of Shoshone County, Idaho. The President ordered the regular troops to report to the Governor for instructions and to support the civil authorities in preserving the peace. Later the State Auditor as agent of the Governor, and not the Commanding General, ordered the troops to detain citizens without trial and to aid the Auditor in doing all he thought necessary to stop the riot.[19] Once more, the military authorities did not undertake to supplant the courts and to establish military tribunals to try and punish ordinary civilian offenders.[20]

Courts and their procedural safeguards are indispensable to our system of government. They were set up by our founders to protect the liberties they valued. *Ex parte Quirin,* 317 U.S. 1, 19. Our system of government clearly is the antithesis of total military rule and the founders of this country are not likely to have contemplated complete military dominance within the limits of a territory made part of this country and not recently taken from an enemy. They were opposed to governments that placed in the hands of one man the power to make, interpret and enforce the laws. Their philosophy has been the people's throughout our history. For that reason we have maintained legislatures chosen by citizens or their representatives and courts and juries to try those who violate legislative enactments. We have always been especially concerned about the potential evils of summary criminal trials and have guarded against them by provisions embodied in the Constitution itself. See *Ex parte Milligan,* 4 Wall. 2; *Chambers v. Florida,* 309 U.S. 227. Legislatures and courts are not merely cherished American institutions; they are indispensable to our Government.

Military tribunals have no such standing. For as this Court has said before: ". . . the military should always be kept in subjection to the laws of the country to which it belongs, and that he is no friend to the Republic who advocates the contrary. The established principle of every free people is, that the law shall alone govern; and to it the military must always yield." *Dow v. Johnson,* 100 U.S. 158, 169. Congress prior to the time of the enactment of the Organic Act had only once authorized the supplanting of the courts by military tribunals. Legislation to that effect was enacted immediately after the South's unsuccessful attempt to secede from the Union. Insofar as that legislation applied to the Southern States after the war was at an end it was challenged by a series of Presidential vetoes as vigorous as any in the country's history.[21] And in order to prevent this Court from passing on the constitutionality of this legislation Congress found it necessary to curtail our appellate jurisdiction.[22] Indeed, prior to the Organic Act, the only time this Court had ever discussed the supplanting of courts by military tribunals in a situation other than that involving the establishment of a military government over recently occupied enemy territory, it had emphatically declared that "civil liberty and this kind of martial law cannot endure together; the antagonism is irreconcilable; and, in the conflict, one or the other must perish." *Ex parte Milligan,* 4 Wall. 2, 124-125.

We believe that when Congress passed the Hawaiian Organic Act and authorized the establishment of "martial law" it had in mind and did not wish to exceed the boundaries between military and civilian power, in which our people have always believed, which responsible military and executive officers had heeded, and which had become part of our political philosophy and institutions prior to the time Congress passed the Organic Act. The phrase "martial law" as employed in that Act, therefore, while intended to authorize the military to act vigorously for the maintenance of an orderly civil government and for the defense of the Islands against actual or threatened rebellion or invasion, was not intended to authorize the supplanting of courts by military tribunals. Yet the Government seeks to justify the punishment of both White and Duncan on the ground of such supposed congressional authorization. We hold that both petitioners are now entitled to be released from custody.

Reversed.

Mr. Justice Jackson took no part in the consideration or decision of these cases.

Mr. Justice Murphy, concurring.

---

[1]"That the governor shall be responsible for the faithful execution of the laws of the United States and of the Territory of Hawaii within the said Territory, and whenever it becomes necessary he may call upon the commanders of the military and naval forces of the United States in the Territory of Hawaii, or summon the posse comitatus, or call out the militia of the Territory to prevent or suppress lawless violence, invasion, insurrection, or rebellion in said Territory, and he may, in case of rebellion or invasion, or imminent danger thereof, when the public safety requires it, suspend the privilege of the writ of habeas corpus, or place the Territory, or any part thereof, under martial law until communication can be had with the President and his decision thereon made known."

[2]The district court heard much evidence and from it found as follows on this subject: "By radio the Governor of Hawaii on December 7, 1941, notified the President of the United States simply that he had placed the Territory under martial law and suspended the writ. The President's approval was requested and it was granted by radio on December 8, 1941. Not until 1943 was the text of the Governor's December 7 proclamation furnished Washington officials, and it is still doubtful if it has yet been seen by the President."

[4]We do not set out the other grounds of challenge since under the view we take we do not reach them.

[5]The Government points out that since the privilege of the writ was restored and martial law terminated by Presidential Proclamation on October 24, 1944, petitioners are entitled to their liberty if the military tribunals were without jurisdiction to try them. We therefore do not pass upon the validity of the order suspending the privilege of habeas corpus or the power of the military to detain persons under other circumstances and conditions.

[6]*Wiles v. Dinsman*, 7 How. 89; *Ex parte Reed*, 100 U.S. 13; *Martin v. Mott*, 12 Wheat. 19; *In re Grimley*, 137 U.S. 147; *Johnson v. Sayre*, 158 U.S. 109; *Carter v. McClaughry*, 182 U.S. 365.

[7]*Ex parte Gerlach*, 247 F. 616; *Ex parte Falls*, 251 F. 415; *Ex parte Jochen*, 257 F. 200; *Hines v. Mikell*, 259 F. 28. See cases and statutes collected and discussed in Underhill, *infra*, note 11, 12 Cal. L. Rev. 81-98.

[8]*Ex parte Quirin*, 317 U.S. 1; *In re Yamashita*, 327 U.S. 1. See 10 U.S.C. §§ 1553, 1554. See also cases and statutes collected and discussed in Underhill, *infra*, note 11, 12 Cal. L. Rev. 81-98.

[9]*Cross v. Harrison*, 16 How. 164; *Leitensdorfer v. Webb*, 20 How. 176; *The Prize Cases*, 2 Black 635; *Mrs. Alexander's Cotton*, 2 Wall. 404; *Ford v. Surget*, 97 U.S. 594, 604; *New Orleans v. Steamship Co.*, 20 Wall. 387, 393; *Dow v. Johnson*, 100 U.S. 158, 166; *The Grapeshot*, 9 Wall. 129; *Mechanics' & Traders' Bank v. Union Bank*, 22 Wall. 276. Nor is this a case where violators of military orders are to be tried by regular courts. Cf. *Hirabayashi v. United States*, 320 U.S. 81.

[10]*Moyer v. Peabody*, 212 U.S. 78; *Ex parte Milligan*, 4 Wall. 2, 125, 126; *Luther v. Borden*, 7 How. 1, 45, 46; see *Sterling v. Constantin*, 287 U.S. 378, 400; Fairman, The Law of Martial Rule, Chicago 1943, 209-218.

[11]For discussions of the great contrast of views see the following writings: Fairman, *supra*, Ch. II; Wiener, A Practical Manual of Martial Law, Harrisburg 1940, Ch. 1; Military Aid to the Civil Power, Fort Leavenworth 1925, pp. 230-232; Underhill, *Jurisdiction of Military Tribunals in the United States over Civilians* (1924) 12 Cal. L. Rev. 75, 163-178; Ballentine, *Qualified Martial Law*

(1915) 14 Mich. L. Rev. 102, 203, 204; Max Radin, *Martial Law and the State of Siege* (1942) 30 Cal. L. Rev. 634.

[12]We point out in this connection that by § 83 of the Organic Act Congress provided how juries should be constituted and provided for the drawing of grand juries and for unanimous jury verdicts in criminal cases. 31 Stat. 141, 157.

[13]*Government for the Territory of Hawaii,* H. Rep. No. 305, 56th Cong., 1st Sess., p. 10. In the House, Representative Knox, the Republican leader for the bill, stated: "This bill, in so many words, extends the Constitution to Hawaii; so that there has not been practically a moment of time since the Hawaiian Islands were annexed to the United States that the Constitution has not been the standard by which all the laws of that country must be measured . . . *The decisions of the Supreme Court of the United States will be equally operative in Hawaii as in any portion of the United States as to any constitutional right which he possesses.*" 33 Cong. Rec. 3704, 3709 (1900). See the following decisions of this Court relating to the applicability of the Constitution to United States Territories. *Hawaii v. Mankichi,* 190 U.S. 197; *Rassmussen v. United States,* 197 U.S. 516; *Farrington v. Tokushige,* 273 U.S. 284. See also Frank, *Ex parte Milligan v. The Five Companies: Martial Law in Hawaii* (1944) 44 Col. L. Rev. 639, 658-660.

[14]3 Chas. I, c. 1.

[15]Hallam, Constitutional History, (2d ed.) Vol. I, c. vii, pp. 531, 532, 533. See also discussions in dissent in *Luther v. Borden,* 7 How. 1, 48, 63; *In re McDonald,* 49 Mont. 454, 468, 143 P. 947.

[16]Federal Aid in Domestic Disturbances, Senate Document No. 263, 67th Cong., 2d Sess., 10.

[17]*Id.* pp. 31, 32. See also on the same subject the dissent in *Luther v. Borden, supra,* 7 How. at 77-81.

[18]This appears from the facts related throughout Senate Document No. 263, 67th Cong., 2d Sess., *supra.*

After the passing of the Organic Act disturbances in the coal fields of West Virginia, a longshoremen's strike in Galveston and a packers' strike in Nebraska City, all led to criminal trials of civilians by military tribunals which were upheld by decisions of state and lower federal courts. *State ex rel. Mays v. Brown,* 71 W. Va. 519, 77 S. E. 243; *Ex parte Jones,* 71 W. Va. 567, 77 S. E. 1029; *United States ex rel. McMaster v. Wolters,* 268 F. 69; *United States ex rel. Seymour v. Fischer,* 280 F. 208. But cf. *In re McDonald,* 49 Mont. 454. All these cases rested on the ground that the Governor's determination of the existence of insurrection conclusively established that all the Governor had done was legal. The basis of these decisions was definitely held erroneous in *Sterling v. Constantin,* 287 U.S. 378, where this Court said: "What are the allowable limits of military discretion, and whether or not they have been overstepped in a particular case, are judicial questions." 287 U.S. at 401. As one commentator puts it, this Court "has knocked out the prop" on which these aforementioned cases rested. Wiener, A Practical Manual of Martial Law, 1940, p. 116.

[19]Senate Document No. 263, 67th Cong., 2d Sess., 190 ff., 210 ff.

[20]Even as late as 1937 when the War Department promulgated regulations concerning the employment of troops in aid of civil authorities, it was aware of this tradition. A. R. 500-50, ¶ 7e stated: ". . . Persons not normally subject to military law, taken into custody by the military forces incident to the use of troops contemplated by these regulations, should be turned over to the civil authorities. Punishment in such cases belongs to the courts of justice and not to the armed forces." But cf. A. R. 500-50, ¶ 8 (1945).

[21]In one of these vetoes President Johnson said: "The trials having their origin under this bill are to take place without the intervention of a jury and without any fixed rules of law or evidence. The rules on which offenses are to be 'heard and determined' by the numerous agents are such rules and regulations as the President, through the War Department, shall prescribe. No previous presentment is required nor any indictment charging the commission of a crime against the laws; but the trial must proceed on charges and specifications. The punishment will be, not what the law declares, but such as a court-martial may think proper; and from these arbitrary tribunals there lies no appeal, no writ of error to any of the courts in which the Constitution of the United States vests exclusively the judicial power of the country." Messages and Papers of the Presidents, Richardson, Vol. VI, 399. In another he said: "It is plain that the authority here given to the military officer amounts to absolute despotism. But to make it still more unendurable, the bill provides that it may be delegated to as many subordinates as he chooses to appoint, for it declares that he shall 'punish or cause to be punished.' Such a power has not been wielded by any monarch in England for more than five hundred years. . . . This broad principle limits all our functions and applies to all subjects. It protects not only the citizens of States which are within the Union, but it shields every human being who comes or is brought under our jurisdiction. We have no right to do in one place more than in another that which the Constitution says we shall not do at all." *Id.,* pp. 502-503.

[22]*Ex parte McCardle,* 6 Wall. 318. See also Warren, The Supreme Court in United States History, Vol. 2, 464, 484.

Youngstown Sheet and Tube Co. v. Sawyer

343 U.S. 579 (1952)

Mr. Justice Black delivered the opinion of the Court.

We are asked to decide whether the President was acting within his constitutional power when he issued an order directing the Secretary of Commerce to take possession of and operate most of the Nation's steel mills. The mill owners argue that the President's order amounts to lawmaking, a legislative function which the Constitution has expressly confided to the Congress and not to the President. The Government's position is that the order was made on findings of the President that his action was necessary to avert a national catastrophe which would inevitably result from a stoppage of steel production, and that in meeting this grave emergency the President was acting within the aggregate of his constitutional powers as the Nation's Chief Executive and the Commander in Chief of the Armed Forces of the United States. The issue emerges here from the following series of events.:

In the latter part of 1951, a dispute arose between the steel companies and their employees over terms and conditions that should be included in new collective bargaining agreements. Long-continued conferences failed to resolve the dispute. On December 18, 1951, the employees' representative, United Steelworkers of America, C. I. O., gave notice of an intention to strike when the existing bargaining agreements expired on December 31. The Federal Mediation and Conciliation Service then intervened in an effort to get labor and management to agree. This failing, the President on December 22, 1951, referred the dispute to the Federal Wage Stabilization Board[1] to investigate and make recommendations for fair and equitable terms of settlement. This Board's report resulted in no settlement. On April 4, 1952, the Union gave notice of a nation-wide strike called to begin at 12:01 a. m. April 9. The indispensability of steel as a component of substantially all weapons and other war materials led the President to believe that the proposed work stoppage would immediately jeopardize our national defense and that governmental seizure of the steel mills was necessary in order to assure the continued availability of steel. Reciting these considerations for his action, the President, a few hours before the strike was to begin, issued Executive Order 10340, a copy of which is attached as an appendix, *post,* p. 589. The order directed the Secretary of Commerce to take possession of most of the steel mills and keep them running. The Secretary immediately issued his own possessory orders, calling upon the presidents of the various seized companies to serve as operating managers for the United States. They were directed to carry on their activities in accordance with regulations and directions of the Secretary. The next morning the President sent a message to Congress reporting his action. Cong. Rec., April 9, 1952, p. 3962. Twelve days later he sent a second message. Cong. Rec., April 12, 1952, p. 4192. Congress has taken no action.

Obeying the Secretary's orders under protest, the companies brought proceedings against him in the District Court. Their complaints charged that the seizure was not authorized by an act of Congress or by any constitutional provisions. The District Court was asked to declare the orders of the President and the Secretary invalid and to issue preliminary and permanent injunctions restraining their enforcement. Opposing the motion for preliminary injunction, the United States asserted that a strike disrupting steel production for even a brief period would so endanger the well-being and safety of the Nation that the President had "inherent power" to do what he had done—power "supported by the Constitution, by historical precedent, and by court decisions." The Government also contended that in any event no preliminary injunction should be issued because the companies had made no showing that their available legal remedies were inadequate or that their injuries from seizure would be irreparable. Holding against the Government on all points, the District Court on April 30 issued a preliminary injunction restraining the Secretary from "continuing the seizure and possession of the plants . . . and from acting under the purported authority of Executive Order No. 10340." 103 F. Supp. 569. On the same day the Court of Appeals stayed the District Court's injunction. 90 U.S. App. D.C. , F. 2d Deeming it best that the issues raised be promptly decided by this Court, we granted certiorari on May 3 and set the cause for argument on May 12. 343 U.S. 937.

Two crucial issues have developed: *First.* Should final determination of the constitutional validity of the President's order be made in this case which has proceeded no further than the preliminary injunction stage? *Second.* If so, is the seizure order within the constitutional power of the President?

I.

It is urged that there were non-constitutional grounds upon which the District Court could have denied the preliminary injunction and thus have followed the customary judicial practice of declining to reach and decide constitutional questions until compelled to do so. On this basis it is argued that equity's extraordinary injunctive relief should have been denied because (a) seizure of the companies' properties did not inflict irreparable damages, and (b) there were available legal remedies adequate to afford compensation for any possible damages which they might suffer. While separately argued by the Government, these two contentions are here closely related, if not identical. Arguments as to both rest in large part on the Government's claim that should the seizure ultimately be held unlawful, the companies could recover full compensation in the Court of Claims for the unlawful taking. Prior cases in this Court have cast doubt on the right to recover in the Court of Claims on account of properties unlawfully taken by government officials for public use as these properties were alleged to have been. See *e.g., Hooe v. United States,* 218 U.S. 322, 335-336; *United States v. North American Co.,* 253 U.S. 330, 333. But see *Larson v. Domestic & Foreign Corp.,* 337 U.S. 682, 701-702. Moreover, seizure and governmental operation of these going businesses were bound to result in many present and future damages of such nature as to be difficult, if not incapable, of measurement. Viewing the case this way, and in the light of the facts presented, the District Court saw no reason for delaying decision of the constitutional validity of the orders. We agree with the District Court and can see no reason why that question was not ripe for determination on the record presented. We shall therefore consider and determine that question now.

II.

The President's power, if any, to issue the order must stem either from an act of Congress or from the Constitution itself. There is no statute that expressly authorizes the President to take possession of property as he did here. Nor is there any act of Congress to which our attention has been directed from which such a power can fairly be implied. Indeed, we do not understand the Government to rely on statutory authorization for this seizure. There are two statutes which do authorize the President to take both personal and real property under certain conditions.[2] However, the Government admits that these conditions were not met and that the President's order was not rooted in either of the statutes. The Government refers to the seizure provisions of one of these statutes (§ 201 (b) of the Defense Production Act) as "much too cumbersome, involved, and time-consuming for the crisis which was at hand."

Moreover, the use of the seizure technique to solve labor disputes in order to prevent work stoppages was not only unauthorized by any congressional enactment; prior to this controversy, Congress had refused to adopt that method of settling labor disputes. When the Taft-Hartley Act was under consideration in 1947, Congress rejected an amendment which would have authorized such governmental seizures in cases of emergency.[3] Apparently it was thought that the technique of seizure, like that of compulsory arbitration, would interfere with the process of collective bargaining.[4] Consequently, the plan Congress adopted in that Act did not provide for seizure under any circumstances. Instead, the plan sought to bring about settlements by use of the customary devices of mediation, conciliation, investigation by boards of inquiry, and public reports. In some instances temporary injunctions were authorized to provide cooling-off periods. All this failing, unions were left free to strike after a secret vote by employees as to whether they wished to accept their employers' final settlement offer.[5]

It is clear that if the President had authority to issue the order he did, it must be found in some provision of the Constitution. And it is not claimed that express constitutional language grants this power to the President. The contention is that presidential power should be implied from the aggregate of his powers under the Constitution. Particular reliance is placed on provisions in Article II which says that "The executive Power shall be vested in a President . . ."; that "he shall take Care that the Laws be faithfully executed"; and that he "shall be Commander in Chief of the Army and Navy of the United States."

The order cannot properly be sustained as an exercise of the President's military power as Commander in Chief of the Armed Forces. The Government attempts to do so by citing a number of cases upholding broad powers in military commanders engaged in day-to-day fighting in a theater of war. Such cases need not concern us here. Even though "theater of war" be an expanding concept, we cannot with faithfulness to our constitutional system hold that the Commander in Chief of the Armed Forces has the ultimate power as such to take possession of private property in order to keep labor disputes from stopping production. This is a job for the Nation's lawmakers, not for its military authorities.

Nor can the seizure order be sustained because of the several constitutional provisions that grant executive power to the President. In the framework of our Constitution, the President's power to see that the laws are faithfully executed refutes the idea that he is to be a lawmaker. The Constitution limits his functions in the lawmaking process to the recommending of laws he thinks wise and the vetoing of laws he thinks bad. And the Constitution is neither silent nor equivocal about who shall make laws which the President is to execute. The first section of the first article says that "All legislative Powers herein granted shall be vested in a Congress of the United States. . . ." After granting many powers to the Congress, Article I goes on to provide that Congress may "make all Laws which shall be necessary and proper for carrying into Execution the foregoing Powers, and all other Powers vested by this Constitution in the Government of the United States, or in any Department or Officer thereof."

The President's order does not direct that a congressional policy be executed in a manner prescribed by Congress—it directs that a presidential policy be executed in a manner prescribed by the President. The preamble of the order itself, like that of many statutes, sets out reasons why the President believes certain policies should be adopted, proclaims these policies as rules of conduct to be followed, and again, like a statute, authorizes a government official to promulgate additional rules and regulations consistent with the policy proclaimed and needed to carry that policy into execution. The power of Congress to adopt such public policies as those proclaimed by the order is beyond question. It can authorize the taking of private property for public use. It can make laws regulating the relationships between employers and employees, prescribing rules designed to settle labor disputes, and fixing wages and working conditions in certain fields of our economy. The Constitution does not subject this lawmaking power of Congress to presidential or military supervision or control.

It is said that other Presidents without congressional authority have taken possession of private business enterprises in order to settle labor disputes. But even if this be true, Congress has not thereby lost its exclusive constitutional authority to make laws necessary and proper to carry out the powers vested by the Constitution "in the Government of the United States, or any Department or Officer thereof."

The Founders of this Nation entrusted the lawmaking power to the Congress alone in both good and bad times. It would do no good to recall the historical events, the fears of power and the hopes for freedom that lay behind their choice. Such a review would but confirm our holding that this seizure order cannot stand.

The judgment of the District Court is

Affirmed.

[1]This Board was established under Executive Order 10233, 16 Fed. Reg. 3503.

[2]The Selective Service Act of 1948, 62 Stat. 604, 625-627, 50 U. S. C. App. (Supp. IV) § 468; the Defense Production Act of 1950, Tit. II, 64 Stat. 798, as amended, 65 Stat. 132.

[3]93 Cong. Rec. 3637-3645.

[4]93 Cong. Rec. 3835-3836.

[5]Labor Management Relations Act, 1947, 61 Stat. 136, 152-156, 29 U. S. C. (Supp. IV) §§ 141, 171-180.

Mr. Justice Frankfurter.

Although the considerations relevant to the legal enforcement of the principle of separation of powers seem to me more complicate and flexible than may appear from what Mr. Justice Black has written, I join his opinion because I thoroughly agree with the application of the principle to the circumstances of this case. Even though such differences in attitude toward this principle may be merely differences in emphasis and nuance, they can hardly be reflected by a single opinion for the Court. Individual expression of views in reaching a common result is therefore important.

Mr. Justice Jackson, concurring in the judgment and opinion of the Court.

That comprehensive and undefined presidential powers hold both practical advantages and grave dangers for the country will impress anyone who has served as legal adviser to a President in time of transition and public anxiety. While an interval of detached reflection may temper teachings of that experience, they probably are a more realistic influence on my views than the conventional materials of judicial decision which seem unduly to accentuate doctrine and legal fiction. But as we approach the question of presidential power, we half overcome mental hazards by recognizing them. The opinions of judges, no less than executives and publicists, often suffer the infirmity of confusing the issue of a power's validity with the cause it is invoked to promote, of confounding the permanent executive office with its temporary occupant. The tendency is strong to emphasize transient results upon policies—such as wages or stabilization—and lose sight of enduring consequences upon the balanced power structure of our Republic.

A judge, like an executive adviser, may be surprised at the poverty of really useful and unambiguous authority applicable to concrete problems of executive power as they actually present themselves. Just what our forefathers did envision, or would have envisioned had they foreseen modern conditions, must be divined from materials almost as enigmatic as the dreams Joseph was called upon to interpret for Pharaoh. A century and a half of partisan debate and scholarly speculation yields no net result but only supplies more or less apt quotations from respected sources on each side of any question. They largely cancel each other.[1] And court decisions are indecisive because of the judicial practice of dealing with the largest questions in the most narrow way.

The actual art of governing under our Constitution does not and cannot conform to judicial definitions of the power of any of its branches based on isolated clauses or even single Articles torn from context. While the Constitution diffuses power the better to secure liberty, it also contemplates that practice will integrate the dispersed powers into a workable government. It enjoins upon its branches separateness but interdependence, autonomy but reciprocity. Presidential powers are not fixed but fluctuate, depending upon their disjunction or conjunction with those of Congress. We may well begin by a somewhat over-simplified grouping of practical situations in which a President may doubt, or others may challenge, his powers, and by distinguishing roughly the legal consequences of this factor of relativity.

1. When the President acts pursuant to an express or implied authorization of Congress, his authority is at its maximum, for it includes all that he possesses in his own right plus all that Congress can delegate.[2] In these circumstances, and in these only, may he be said (for what it may be worthy) to personify the federal sovereignty. If his act is held unconstitutional under these circumstances, it usually means that the Federal Government as an undivided whole lacks power. A seizure executed by the President pursuant to an Act of Congress would be supported by the strongest of presumptions and the widest latitude of judicial interpretation, and the burden of persuasion would rest heavily upon any who might attack it.

2. When the President acts in absence of either a congressional grant or denial of authority, he can only rely upon his own independent powers, but there is a zone of twilight in which he and Congress may have concurrent authority, or in which its distribution is uncertain. Therefore, congressional inertia, indifference or quiescence may sometimes, at least as a practical matter, enable, if not invite, measures on independent presidential responsibility. In this area, any actual test of power is likely to depend on the imperatives of events and contemporary imponderables rather than on abstract theories of law.[3]

3. When the President takes measures incompatible with the expressed or implied will of Congress, his power is at its lowest ebb, for then he can rely only upon his own constitutional powers minus any constitutional powers of Congress over the matter. Courts can sustain exclusive presidential control in such a case only by disabling the Congress from acting upon the subject. Presidential claim to a power at once so conclusive and preclusive must be scrutinized with caution, for what is at stake is the equilibrium established by our constitutional system.[4]

Into which of these classifications does this executive seizure of the steel industry fit? It is eliminated from the first by admission, for it is conceded that no congressional authorization exists for this seizure. That takes away also the support of the many precedents and declarations which were made in relation, and must be confined, to this category.[5]

Can it then be defended under flexible tests available to the second category? It seems clearly eliminated from that class because Congress has not left seizure of private property an open field but has covered it by three statutory policies inconsistent with this seizure. In cases where the purpose is to supply needs of the Government itself, two courses are provided: one, seizure of a plant which fails to comply with obligatory orders placed by the Government;[6] another, condemnation of facilities, including temporary use under the power of eminent domain.[7] The third is applicable where it is the general economy of the country that is to be protected rather than exclusive governmental interests.[8] None of these were invoked. In choosing a different and inconsistent way of his own, the President cannot claim that it is necessitated or invited by failure of Congress to legislate upon the occasions, grounds and methods for seizure of industrial properties.

This leaves the current seizure to be justified only by the severe tests under the third grouping, where it is to be supported only by any remainder of executive power after subtraction of such powers as Congress may have over the subject. In short, we can sustain the President only by holding that seizure of such strike-bound industries is within his domain and beyond control by Congress. Thus, this Court's first review of such seizures occurs under circumstances which leave presidential power now vulnerable to attack and in the least favorable of possible constitutional postures.

I did not suppose, and I am not persuaded, that history leaves it open to question, at least in the courts, they, the executive branch, like the Federal Government as a whole, possesses only delegated powers. The purpose of the Constitution was not only to grant power, but to keep it from getting out of hand. However, because the President does not enjoy unmentioned powers does not mean that the mentioned ones should be narrowed by a niggardly construction. Some clauses could be made almost unworkable, as well as immutable, by refusal to indulge some latitude of interpretation for changing times. I have heretofore, and do now, give to the enumerated powers the scope and elasticity afforded by what seem to be reasonably practical implications instead of the rigidity dictated by a doctrinaire textualism.

The Solicitor General seeks the power of seizure in three clauses of the Executive Article, the first reading, "The executive Power shall be vested in a President of the United States of America." Lest I be thought to exaggerate, I quote the interpretation which his brief puts upon it: "In our view, this clause constitutes a grant of all the executive powers of which the Government is capable." If that be true, it is difficult to see why the forefathers bothered to add several specific items, including some trifling ones.[9]

The example of such unlimited executive power that must have most impressed the forefathers was the prerogative exercised by George III, and the description of its evils in the Declaration of Independence leads me to doubt that they were creating their new Executive in his image. Continental European examples were no more appealing. And if we seek instruction from our own times, we can match it only from the executive powers in those governments we disparagingly describe as totalitarian. I cannot accept the view that this clause is a grant in bulk of all conceivable executive power but regard it as an allocation to the presidential office of the generic powers thereafter stated.

The clause on which the Government next relies is that "The President shall be Commander in Chief of the Army and Navy of the United States. . . ." These cryptic words have given rise to some of the most persistent controversies in our constitutional history. Of course, they imply something more than an empty title. But just what authority goes with the name has plagued presidential advisers who would not waive or narrow it by nonassertion yet cannot say where it begins or ends. It undoubtedly puts the Nation's armed forces under presidential command. Hence, this loose appellation is sometimes advanced as support for any presidential action, internal or external, involving use of force, the idea being that it vests power to do anything, anywhere that can be done with an army or navy.

That seems to be the logic of an argument tendered; our bar—that the President having, on his own responsibility, sent American troops abroad derives from the act "affirmative power" to seize the means of producing a supply of steel for them. To quote, "Perhaps the most forceful illustration of the scope of Presidential power in this connection is the fact that American trools in Korea, whose safety and effectiveness are so directly involved here, were sent to the field by an exercise of the President's constitutional powers." Thus, it is said, he has invested himself with "war powers."

I cannot foresee all that it might entail if the Court should indorse this argument. Nothing in our Constitution is plainer than that declaration of a war is entrusted only to Congress. Of course, a state of war may in fact exist without a formal declaration. But no doctrine that the Court could promulgate would seem to me more sinister and alarming than that a President whose conduct of foreign affairs is so largely uncontrolled, and often even is unknown, can vastly enlarge his mastery over the internal affairs of the country by his own commitment of the Nation's armed forces to some foreign venture.[10] I do not, however, find it necessary or appropriate to consider the legal status of the Korean enterprise to discountenance argument based on it.

Assuming that we are in a war *de facto*, whether it is or is not a war *de jure*, does that empower the Commander in Chief to seize industries he thinks necessary to supply our army? The Constitution expressly places in Congress power "to raise and *support* Armies" and "to *provide* and *maintain* a Navy." (Emphasis supplied.) This certainly lays upon Congress primary responsibility for supplying the armed forces. Congress alone controls the raising of revenues and their appropriation and may determine in what manner and by what means they shall be spent for military and naval procurement. I suppose no one would doubt that Congress can take over war supply as a Government enterprise. On the other hand, if Congress sees fit to rely on free private enterprise collectively bargaining with free labor for support and maintenance of our armed forces, can the Executive, because of lawful disagreements incidental to that process, seize the facility for operation upon Government-imposed terms?

There are indications that the Constitution did not contemplate that the title Commander in Chief *of the Army and Navy* will constitute him also Commander in Chief of the country, its industries and its inhabitants. He has no monopoly of "war powers," whatever they are. While Congress cannot deprive the President of the command of the army and navy, only Congress can provide him an army or navy to command. It is also empowered to make rules for the "Government and Regulation of land and naval Forces," by which it may to some unknown extent impinge upon even command functions.

That military powers of the Commander in Chief were not to supersede representative government of internal affairs seems obvious from the Constitution and from elementary American history. Time out of mind, and even now in many parts of the world, a military commander can seize private housing to shelter his troops. Not so, however, in the United States, for the Third Amendment says, "No Soldier shall, in time of peace be quartered in any house, without the consent of the Owner, nor in time of war, but in a manner to be prescribed by law." Thus, even in war time, his seizure of needed military housing must be authorized by Congress. It also was expressly left to Congress to "provide for calling forth the Militia to execute the Laws of the Union, suppress Insurrections and repel Invasions. . . ."[11] Such a limitation on the command power, written at a time when the militia rather than a standing army was contemplated as the military weapon of the Republic, underscores the Constitution's policy that Congress, not the Executive, should control utilization of the war power as an instrument of domestic policy. Congress, fulfilling that function, has authorized the President to use the army to enforce certain civil rights.[12] On the other hand, Congress has forbidden him to use the army for the purpose of executing general laws except when *expressly* authorized by the Constitution or by Act of Congress.[13]

While broad claims under this rubric often have been made, advice to the President in specific matters usually has carried overtones that powers, even under this head, are measured by the command functions usual to the topmost officer of the army and navy. Even then, heed has been taken of any efforts of Congress to negative his authority.[14]

We should not use this occasion to circumscribe, much less to contract, the lawful role of the President as Commander in Chief. I should indulge the widest latitude of interpretation to sustain his exclusive function to command the instruments of national force, at least when turned against the outside world for the security of our society. But, when it is turned inward, not because of rebellion but because of a lawful economic struggle between industry and labor, it should have no such indulgence. His command power is not such an absolute as might be implied from that office in a militaristic system but is subject to limitations consistent with a constitutional Republic whose law and policy-making branch is a representative Congress. The purpose of lodging dual titles in one man was to insure that the civilian would control the military, not to enable the military to subordinate the presidential office. No penance would ever expiate the sin against free government of holding that a President can escape control of executive powers by law through assuming his military role. What the power of command may include I do not try to envision, but I think it is not a military prerogative, without support of law, to seize persons or property because they are important or even essential for the military and naval establishment.

The third clause in which the Solicitor General finds seizure powers is that "he shall take Care that the Laws be faithfully executed. . . ."[15] That authority must be matched against words of the Fifth Amendment that "No person shall be . . . deprived of life, liberty or property, without due process of law. . . ." One gives a governmental authority that reaches so far as there is law, the other gives a private right that authority shall go no farther. These signify about all there is of the principle that ours is a government of laws, not of men, and that we submit ourselves to rulers only if under rules.

The Solicitor General lastly grounds support of the seizure upon nebulous, inherent powers never expressly granted but said to have accrued to the office from the customs and claims of preceding administrations. The plea is for a resulting power to deal with a crisis or an emergency according to the necessities of the case, the unarticulated assumption being that necessity knows no law.

Loose and irresponsible use of adjectives colors all nonlegal and much legal discussion of presidential powers. "Inherent" powers, "implied" powers, "incidental" powers, "plenary" powers, "war" powers and "emergency" powers are used, often interchangeably and without fixed or ascertainable meanings.

The vagueness and generality of the clauses that set forth presidential powers afford a plausible basis for pressures within and without an administration for presidential action beyond that supported by those whose responsibility it is to defend his actions in court. The claim of inherent and unrestricted presidential powers has long been a persuasive dialectical weapon in political controversy. While it is not surprising that counsel should grasp support from such unadjudicated claims of power, a judge cannot accept self-serving press statements of the attorney for one of the interested parties as authority in answering a constitutional question, even if the advocate was himself. But prudence has counseled that actual reliance on such nebulous claims stop short of provoking a judicial test.[16]

The Solicitor General, acknowledging that Congress has never authorized the seizure here, says practice of prior Presidents has authorized it. He seeks color in legality from claimed executive precedents, chief of which is President Roosevelt's seizure on June 9, 1941, of the California plant of the North American Aviation Company. Its superficial similarities with the present case upon analysis, yield to distinctions so decisive that it cannot be regarded as even a precedent, much less an authority for the present seizure.[17]

The appeal, however, that we declare the existence of inherent powers *ex necessitate* to meet an emergency asks us to do what many think would be wise, although it is something the forefathers omitted. They knew what emergencies were, knew the pressures they engender for authoritative action, knew, too, how they afford a ready pretext for usurpation. We may also suspect that they suspected that emergency powers would tend to kindle emergencies. Aside from suspension of the privilege of the writ of hapeas corpus in time of rebellion or invasion, when the public safety may require it,[18] they made no express provision for exercise of extraordinary authority because of a crisis.[19] I do not think we rightfully may so amend their work, and, if we could, I am not convinced it would be wise to do so, although many modern nations have forthrightly recognized that war and economic crises may upset the normal balance between liberty and authority. Their experience with emergency powers may not be irrelevant to the argument here that we should say that the Executive, of his own volition, can invest himself with undefined emergency powers.

Germany, after the First World War, framed the Weimar Constitution, designed to secure her liberties in the Western tradition. However, the President of the Republic, without concurrence of the Reichstag, was empowered temporarily to suspend any or all individual rights if public safety and order were seriously disturbed or endangered. This proved a temptation to every government, whatever its shade of opinion, and in 13 years of suspension of rights was invoked on more than 250 occasions. Finally, Hitler persuaded President Von Hindenberg to suspend all such rights, and they were never restored.[20]

The French Republic provided for a very different kind of emergency government known as the "state of siege." It differed from the German emergency dictatorship, particularly in that emergency powers could not be assumed at will by the Executive but could only be granted as a parliamentary measure. And it did not, as in Germany, result in a suspension or abrogation of law but was a legal institution governed by special legal rules and terminable by parliamentary authority.[21]

Great Britain also has found both World Wars under a sort of temporary dictatorship created by legislation.[22] As Parliament is not bound by written constitutional limitations, it established a crisis government simply by delegation to its Ministers of a larger measure than usual of its own unlimited power, which is exercised under in supervision by Ministers whom it may dismiss. This had been called the "high-water mark in the voluntary surrender of liberty," but, as Churchill put it, "Parliament stands custodian of these surrendered liberties, and its most sacred duty will be to restore them in their fullness when victory has crowned our exertions and our perseverance."[23] Thus, parliamentary control made emergency powers compatible with freedom.

This contemporary foreign experience may be inconclusive as to the wisdom of lodging emergency powers somewhere in a modern government. But it suggests that emergency powers are consistent with free government only when their control is lodged elsewhere than in the Executive who exercises them. That is the safeguard that would be nullified by our adoption of the "inherent powers" formula. Nothing in my experience convinces me that such risks are warranted by any real necessity, although such powers would, of course, be an executive convenience.

In the practical working of our Government we already have evolved a technique within the framework of the Constitution by which normal executive powers may be considerably expanded to meet an emergency. Congress may and has granted extraordinary authorities which lie dormant in normal times but may be called into play by the Executive in war or upon proclamation of a national emergency. In 1939, upon congressional request, the Attorney General listed ninety-nine such separate statutory grants by Congress of emergency or wartime executive powers.[24] They were invoked from time to time as need appeared. Under this procedure we retain Government by law—special, temporary law, perhaps, but law nonetheless. The public may know the extent and limitations of the powers that can be asserted, and persons affected may be informed from the statute of their rights and duties.

In view of the ease, expedition and safety with which Congress can grant and has granted large emergency powers, certainly ample to embrace this crisis, I am quite unimpressed with the argument that we should affirm possession of them without statute. Such power either has no beginning or it has no end. If it exists, it need submit to no legal restraint. I am not alarmed that it would plunge us straightway into dictatorship, but it is at least a step in that wrong direction.

As to whether there is imperative necessity for such powers, it is relevant to note the gap that exists between the President's paper powers and his real powers. The Constitution does not disclose the measure of the actual controls wielded by the modern presidential office. That instrument must be understood as an Eighteenth-Century sketch of a government hoped for, not as a blueprint of the Government that is. Vast accretions of federal power, eroded from that reserved by the States, have magnified the scope of presidential activity. Subtle shifts take place in the centers of real power that do not show on the face of the Constitution.

Executive power has the advantage of concentration in a single head in whose choice the whole Nation has a part, making him the focus of public hopes and expectations. In drama, magnitude and finality his decisions so far overshadow any others that almost alone he fills the public eye and ear. No other personality in public life can begin to compete with him in access to the public mind through modern methods of communications. By his prestige as head of state and his influence upon public opinion he exerts a leverage upon those who are supposed to check and balance his power which often cancels their effectiveness.

Moreover, rise of the party system has made a significant extraconstitutional supplement to real executive power. No appraisal of his necessities is realistic which overlooks that he heads a political system as well as a legal system. Party loyalties and interests, sometimes more binding than law, extend his effective control into branches of government other than his own and he often may win, as a political leader, what he cannot command under the Constitution. Indeed, Woodrow Wilson, commenting on the President as leader both of his party and of the Nation, observed, "If he rightly interpret the national thought and boldly insist upon it, he is irresistible. . . . His office is anything he has the sagacity and force to make it."[25] I cannot be brought to believe that this country will suffer if the Court refuses further to aggrandize the presidential office, already so potent and so relatively immune from judicial review,[26] at the expense of Congress.

But I have no illusion that any decision by this Court can keep power in the hands of Congress if it is not wise and timely in meeting its problems. A crisis that challenges the President equally, or perhaps primarily, challenges Congress. If not good law, there was worldly wisdom in the maxim attributed to Napoleon that "The tools belong to the man who can use them." We may say that power to legislate for emergencies belongs in the hands of Congress, but only Congress itself can prevent power from slipping through its fingers.

The essence of our free Government is "leave to live by no man's leave, underneath the law"—to be governed by those impersonal forces which we call law. Our Government is fashioned to fulfill this concept so far as humanly possible. The Executive, except for recommendation and veto, has no legislative power. The executive action we have here originates in the individual will of the President and represents an exercise of authority without law. No one, perhaps not even the President, knows the limits of the power he may seek to exert in this instance and the parties affected cannot learn the limit of their rights. We do not know today what powers over labor or property would be claimed to flow from Government possession if we should legalize it, what rights to compensation would be claimed or recognized, or on what contingency it would end. With all its defects, delays and inconveniences, men have discovered no technique for long preserving free government except that the Executive be under the law, and that the law be made by parliamentary deliberations.

Such institutions may be destined to pass away. But it is the duty of the Court to be last, not first, to give them up.[27]

Mr. Justice Burton, concurring in both the opinion and judgment of the Court.

[1]A Hamilton may be matched against a Madison. 7 The Works of Alexander Hamilton, 76-117; 1 Madison, Letters and Other Writings, 611-654. Professor Taft is counterbalanced by Theodore Roosevelt. Taft, Our Chief Magistrate and His Powers, 139-140; Theodore Roosevelt, Autobiography, 388-389. It even seems that President Taft cancels out Professor Taft. Compare his "Temporary Petroleum Withdrawal No. 5" of September 27, 1909, *United States v. Midwest Oil Co.*, 236 U.S. 459, 467, 468, with his appraisal of executive power in "Our Chief Magistrate and His Powers" 139-140.

[2]It is in this class of cases that we find the broadest recent statements of presidential power, including those relied on here. *United States v. Curtiss-Wright Corp.*, 299 U.S. 304, involved, not the question of the President's power to act without congressional authority, but the question of his right to act under and in accord with an Act of Congress. The constitutionality of the Act under which the President had proceeded was assailed on the ground that it delegated legislative powers to the President. Much of the Court's opinion is *dictum*, but the *ratio decidendi* is contained in the following language:

"When the President is to be authorized by legislation to act in respect of a matter intended to affect a situation in foreign territory, the legislator properly bears in mind the important consideration that the form of the President's action—or, indeed, whether he shall act at all—may well depend, among other things, upon the nature of the confidential information which he has or may thereafter receive, or upon the effect which his action may have upon our foreign relations. This consideration, in connection with what we have already said on the subject, discloses the unwisdom of requiring Congress in this field of governmental power to lay down narrowly definite standards by which the President is to be governed. As this court said in *Mackenzie v. Hare*, 239 U.S. 299, 311, 'As a government, the United States is invested with all the attributes of sovereignty. As it has the character of nationality it has the powers of nationality, especially those which concern its relations and intercourse with other countries. *We should hesitate long before limiting or embarrassing such powers.*' (Italics supplied.)" *Id.*, at 321-322.

That case does not solve the present controversy. It recognized internal and external affairs as being in separate categories, and held that the strict limitation upon congressional delegations of power to the President over internal affairs does not apply with respect to delegations of power in external affairs. It was intimated that the President might act in external affairs without congressional authority, but not that he might act contrary to an Act of Congress.

Other examples of wide definition of presidential powers under statutory authorization are *Chicago & Southern Air Lines, Inc. v. Waterman Steamship Corp.*, 333 U.S. 103, and *Hirabayashi v. United States*, 320 U.S. 81. But see, *Jecker v. Montgomery*, 13 How. 498, 515; *United States v. Western Union Telegraph Co.*, 272 F. 311; aff'd, 272 F. 893; rev'd on consent of the parties, 260 U.S. 754; *United States Harness Co. v. Graham*, 288 F. 929.

[3]Since the Constitution implies that the writ of habeas corpus may be suspended in certain circumstances but does not say by whom, President Lincoln asserted and maintained it as an executive function in the face of judicial challenge and doubt. *Ex parte Merryman*, 17 Fed. Cas. 144; *Ex parte Milligan*, 4 Wall. 2, 125; see *Ex parte Bollman*, 4 Cranch 75, 101. Congress eventually ratified his action. Habeas Corpus Act of March 3, 1863, 12 Stat. 755. See Hall, Free Speech in War Time, 21 Col. L. Rev. 526. Compare *Myers v. United States*, 272 U.S. 52, with *Humphrey's Executor v. United States*, 295 U.S. 602; and *Hirabayashi v. United States*, 320 U.S. 81, with the case at bar. Also compare *Ex parte Vallandigham*, 1 Wall. 243, with *Ex parte Milligan, supra*.

[4]President Roosevelt's effort to remove a Federal Trade Commissioner was found to be contrary to the policy of Congress and impinging upon an area of congressional control, and so his removal power was cut down accordingly. *Humphrey's Executor v. United States*, 295 U.S. 602. However, his exclusive power of removal in executive agencies, affirmed in *Myers v. United States*, 272 U.S. 52, continued to be asserted and maintained. *Morgan v. Tennessee Valley Authority*, 115 F. 2d 990, cert. denied, 312 U.S. 701; *In re Power to Remove Members of the Tennessee Valley Authority*, 39 Op. Atty. Gen. 145; President Roosevelt's Message to Congress of March 23, 1938, The Public Papers and Addresses of Franklin D. Roosevelt, 1938 (Rosenman), 151.

[5]The oft-cited Louisiana Purchase had nothing to do with the separation of powers as between the President and Congress, but only with state and federal power. The Louisiana Purchase was subject to rather academic criticism, not upon the ground that Mr. Jefferson acted without authority from Congress, but that neither had express authority to expand the boundaries of the United States by purchase or annexation. Mr. Jefferson himself had strongly opposed the doctrine that the States' delegation of powers to the Federal Government could be enlarged by resort to implied powers. Afterwards in a letter to John Breckenridge, dated August 12, 1803, he declared:

"The Constitution has made no provision for our holding foreign territory, still less for incorporating foreign nations into our Union. The executive in seizing the fugitive occurrence which so much advances the good of their country, have done an act beyond the Constitution. The Legislature in casting behind them metaphysical subtleties, and risking themselves like faithful servants, must ratify and pay for it, and throw themselves on their country for doing for them unauthorized, what we know they would have done for themselves had they been in a situation to do it." 10 The Writings of Thomas Jefferson 407, 411.

[6]Selective Service Act of 1948, § 18, 62 Stat. 625, 50 U. S. C. App. (Supp. IV) § 468 (c).

[7]Defense Production Act of 1950, § 201, 64 Stat. 799, amended, 65 Stat. 132, 50 U. S. C. App. (Supp. IV) § 2081. For the latitude of the condemnation power which underlies this Act, see *United States v. Westinghouse Co.*, 339 U.S. 261, and cases therein cited.

[8]Labor Management Relations Act, 1947, §§ 206-210, 61 Stat. 136, 155, 156, 29 U. S. C. (Supp. IV) §§ 141, 176-180. The analysis, history and application of this Act are fully covered by the opinion of the Court, supplemented by that of Mr. Justice Frankfurter and of Mr. Justice Burton, in which I concur.

[9]". . . he may require the Opinion, in writing, of the principal Officer in each of the executive Departments, upon any Subject relating to the Duties of their respective Offices. . . ." U.S. Const., Art. II, § 2. He ". . . shall Commission all the Officers of the United States." U.S. Const., Art II, § 3. Matters such as those would seem to be inherent in the Executive if anything is.

[10]How widely this doctrine espoused by the President's counsel departs from the early view of presidential power is shown by a comparison. President Jefferson, without authority from Congress, sent the American fleet into the Mediterranean, where it engaged in a naval battle with the Tripolitan fleet. He sent a message to Congress on December 8, 1801, in which he said:
"Tripoli, the least considerable of the Barbary States, had come forward with demands unfounded either in right or in compact, and had permitted itself to denounce war on our failure to comply before a given day. The style of the demand admitted but one answer. I sent a small squadron of frigates into the Mediterranean . . . with orders to protect our commerce against the threatened attack. . . . Our commerce in the Mediterranean was blockaded and that of the Atlantic in peril. . . . One of the Tripolitan cruisers having fallen in with and engaged the small schooner *Enterprise*, . . . was captured, after a heavy slaughter of her men. . . . Unauthorized by the Constitution, without the sanction of Congress, to go beyond the line of defense, the vessel, being disabled from committing further hostilities, was liberated with its crew. The Legislature will doubtless consider whether, by authorizing measures of offense also, they will place our force on an equal footing with that of its adversaries. I communicate all material information on this subject, that in the exercise of this important function confided by the Constitution to the Legislature exclusively their judgment may form itself on a knowledge and consideration of every circumstance of weight." I Richardson, Messages and Papers of the Presidents, 314.

[11]U.S. Const., Art. I, § 8, cl. 15.

[12]14 Stat. 29, 16 Stat. 143, 8 U. S. C. § 55.

[13]20 Stat. 152, 10 U. S. C. § 15.

[14]In 1940, President Roosevelt proposed to transfer to Great Britain certain overage destroyers and small patrol boats then under construction. He did not presume to rely upon any claim of constitutional power as Commander in Chief. On the contrary, he was advised that such destroyers—if certified not to be essential to the defense of the United States—could be "transferred, exchanged, sold, or otherwise disposed of," because Congress had so authorized him. Accordingly, the destroyers were exchanged for air bases. In the same opinion, he was advised that Congress had prohibited the release or transfer of the so-called "mosquito boats" then under construction, so those boats were not transferred. *Acquisition of Naval and Air Bases in Exchange for Over-age Destroyers*, 39 Op. Atty. Gen. 484. See also *Training of British Flying Students in the United States*, 40 Op. Atty. Gen. 58.

[15]U.S. Const., Art. II, § 3.

[16]President Wilson, just before our entrance into World War I, went before the Congress and asked its approval of his decision to authorize merchant ships to carry defensive weapons. He said:

"No doubt I already possess that authority without special warrant of law, by the plain implication of my constitutional duties and powers; but I prefer, in the present circumstances, not to act upon general implication. I wish to feel that the authority and the power of the Congress are behind me in whatever it may become necessary for me to do. We are jointly the servants of the people and must act together and in their spirit, so far as we can divine and interpret it." XVII Richardson, *op. cit.*, 8211.

When our Government was itself in need of shipping whilst ships flying the flags of nations overrun by Hitler, as well as belligerent merchantmen, were immobilized in American harbors where they had taken refuge, President Roosevelt did not assume that it was in his power to seize such foreign vessels to make up our own deficit. He informed Congress: "I am satisfied, after consultation with the heads of the interested departments and agencies of the Government, that we should have statutory authority to take over any such vessels as our needs may require. . . ." 87 Cong. Rec. 3072 (77th Cong., 1st Sess.); The Public Papers and Addresses of Franklin D. Roosevelt, 1941 (Rosenman), 94. The necessary statutory authority was shortly forthcoming. 55 Stat. 242.

In his first inaugural address President Roosevelt pointed out two courses to obtain legislative remedies, one being to enact measures he was prepared to recommend, the other to enact measures "the Congress may build out of its experience and wisdom." He continued, "But in the event that the Congress shall fail to take one of these two courses, and in the event that the national emergency is still critical, I shall not evade the clear course of duty that will then confront me. *I shall ask the Congress for the one remaining instrument to meet the crisis*—broad Executive power to wage a war against the emergency, as great as the power that would be given to me if we were in fact invaded by a foreign foe." (Emphasis supplied.) The Public Papers and Address of Franklin D. Roosevelt, 1933 (Rosenman), 15.

On March 6, 1933, President Roosevelt proclaimed the Bank Holiday. The Proclamation did not invoke constitutional powers of the Executive but expressly and solely relied upon the Act of Congress of October 6, 1917, 40 Stat. 411, § 5 (b), as amended. He relied steadily on legislation to empower him to deal with economic emergency. The Public Papers and Addresses of Franklin D. Roosevelt, 1933 (Rosenman), 24.

It is interesting to note Holdsworth's comment on the powers of legislation by proclamation when in the hands of the Tudors. "The extent to which they could be legally used was never finally settled in this century, because the Tudors made so tactful a use of their powers that no demand for the settlement of this question was raised." 4 Holdsworth, History of English Law, 104.

[17]The North American Aviation Company was under direct and binding contracts to supply defense items to the Government. No such contracts are claimed to exist here. Seizure of plants which refused to comply with Government orders had been expressly authorized by Congress in § 9 of the Selective Service Act of 1940, 54 Stat. 885, 892, so that the seizure of the North American plant was entirely consistent with congressional policy. The company might have objected on technical grounds to the seizure, but it was taken over with acquiescence, amounting to all but consent, of the owners who had admitted that the situation was beyond their control. The strike involved in the North American case was in violation of the union's collective agreement and the national labor leaders approved the seizure to end the strike. It was described as in the nature of an insurrection, a Communist-led political strike against the Government's lend-lease policy. Here we have only a loyal, lawful, but regrettable economic disagreement between management and labor. The North American plant contained government-owned machinery, material and goods in the process of production to which workmen were forcibly denied access by picketing strikers. Here no Government property is protected by the seizure. See New York Times of June 10, 1941, pp. 1, 14 and 16, for substantially accurate account of the proceedings and the conditions of violence at the North American plant.

The North American seizure was regarded as an execution of congressional policy. I do not regard it as a precedent for this, but, even if I did, I should not bind present judicial judgment by earlier partisan advocacy.

Statements from a letter by the Attorney General to the Chairman of the Senate Committee on Labor and Public Welfare, dated February 2, 1949, with reference to pending labor legislation, while not cited by any of the parties here, are sometimes quoted as being in support of the "inherent" powers of the President. The proposed bill contained a mandatory provision that during certain investigations the disputants in a labor dispute should continue operations under the terms and conditions of employment existing prior to the beginning of the dispute. It made no provision as to how continuance should be enforced and specified no penalty for disobedience. The Attorney General advised that in appropriate circumstances the United States would have access to the courts to protect the national health, safety and welfare. This was the rule laid down by this Court in *Texas & N. O. R. Co. v. Brotherhood of Railway Clerks,* 281 U.S. 548. The Attorney General observed:

"However, with regard to the question of the power of the Government under Title III, I might point out that the inherent power of the President to deal with emergencies that affect the health, safety and welfare of the entire Nation is exceedingly great. See Opinion of Attorney General Murphy of October 4, 1939 (39 Op. A. G. 344, 347); *United States v. United Mine Workers of America,* 330 U.S. 258 (1947)." See Hearings before the Senate Committee on Labor and Public Welfare on S. 249, 81st Cong., 1st Sess. 263.

Regardless of the general reference to "inherent powers," the citations were instances of congressional authorization. I do not suppose it is open to doubt that power to see that the laws are faithfully executed was ample basis for the specific advice given by the Attorney General in this letter.

[18]U.S. Const., Art. I, § 9, cl. 2.

[19]I exclude, as in a very limited category by itself, the establishment of martial law. Cf. *Ex parte Milligan,* 4 Wall. 2; *Duncan v. Kahanamoku,* 327 U.S. 304.

[20]1 Nazi Conspiracy and Aggression 126-127; Rossiter, Constitutional Dictatorship, 33-61; Brecht, Prelude to Silence, 138.

[21]Rossiter, Constitutional Dictatorship, 117-129.

[22]Defence of the Realm Act, 1914, 4 & 5 Geo. V, c. 29, as amended, c 63; Emergency Powers (Defence) Act, 1939, 2 & 3 Geo. VI, c. 62; Rossiter, Constitutional Dictatorship, 135-184.

[23]Churchill, The Unrelenting Struggle, 13. See also *id.,* at 279-281.

[24]39 Op. Atty. Gen. 348.

[25]Wilson, Constitutional Government in the United States, 68-69.

[26]Rossiter, The Supreme Court and the Commander in Chief, 126.

[27]We follow the judicial tradition instituted on a memorable Sunday in 1612, when King James took offense at the independence of his judges and, in rage, declared: "Them I am to be *under* the law—which it is treason to affirm." Chief Justice Coke replied to his King: "Thus wrote Bracton, 'The King ought not to be under any man, but he is under God and the Law.' " 12 Coke 65 (as to its verity, 18 Eng. Hist. Rev. 664-675); 1 Campbell, Lives of the Chief Justices (1849), 272.

Baker v. Carr

369 U.S. 186 (1962)

Mr. Justice Brennan delivered the Opinion of the Court.

* * *

Our discussion, even at the price of extending this opinion, requires review of a number of political question cases, in order to expose the attributes of the doctrine—attributes which, in various settings, diverge, combine, appear, and disappear in seeming disorderliness. Since that review is undertaken solely to demonstrate that neither singly nor collectively do these cases support a conclusion that this apportionment case is nonjusticiable, we of course do not explore their implications in other contexts. That review reveals that in the Guaranty Clause cases and in the other "political question" cases, it is the relationship between the judiciary and the coordinate branches of the Federal Government, and not the federal judiciary's relationship to the States, which gives rise to the "political question."

We have said that "In determining whether a question falls within [the political question] category, the appropriateness under our system of government of attributing finality to the action of the political departments and also the lack of satisfactory criteria for a judicial determination are dominant considerations." Coleman v Miller, 307 U.S. 433, 454, 455, 83 L ed 1385, 1396, 1397, 59 S Ct 972, 122 ALR 695. The nonjusticiability of a political question is primarily a function of the separation of powers. Much confusion results from the capacity of the "political question" label to obscure the need for case-by-case inquiry. Deciding whether a matter has in any measure been committed by the Constitution to another branch of government, or whether the action of that branch exceeds whatever authority has been committed, is itself a delicate exercise in constitutional interpretation, and is a responsibility of this Court as ultimate interpreter of the Constitution. To demonstrate this requires no less than to analyze representative cases and to infer from them the analytical threads that make up the political question doctrine. We shall then show that none of those threads catches this case.

Foreign relations: There are sweeping statements to the effect that all questions touching foreign relations are political questions. Not only does resolution of such issues frequently turn on standards that defy judicial application, or involve the exercise of a discretion demonstrably committed to the executive or legislature; but many such questions uniquely demand single-voiced statement of the Government's views. Yet it is error to suppose that every case or controversy which touches foreign relations lies beyond judicial cognizance. Our case in this field seem invariably to show a discriminating analysis of the particular question posed, in terms of the history of its management by the political branches, of its susceptibility to judicial handling in the light of its nature and posture in the specific case, and of the possible consequences of judicial action. For example, though a court will not ordinarily inquire whether a treaty has been terminated, since on that question "governmental action . . . must be regarded as of controlling importance," if there has been no conclusive "governmental action" then a court can construe a treaty and may find it provides the answer. Compare Terlinden v Ames, 184 U.S. 270, 285, 46 L ed 534, 543, 22 S Ct 484, with Society for Propagation of Gospel v New Haven (U.S.) 8 Wheat 464, 492-495, 5 L ed 662, 669, 670. Though a court will not undertake to construe a treaty in a manner inconsistent with a subsequent federal statute, no similar hesitancy obtains if the asserted clash is with state law. Compare Whitney v Robertson, 124 U.S. 190, 31 L ed 386, 8 S Ct 456, with Kolovrat v Oregon, 366 U.S. 187, 6 L ed 2d 218, 81 S Ct 922.

While recognition of foreign governments so strongly defies judicial treatment that without executive recognition a foreign state has been called "a republic of whose existence we know nothing," and the judiciary ordinarily follows the executive as to which nation has sovereignty over disputed territory, once sovereignty over an area is politically determined and declared, courts may examine the resulting status and decide independently whether a statute applies to that area. Similarly, recognition of belligerency abroad is an executive responsibility, but if the executive proclamations fall short of an explicit answer, a court may construe them seeking, for example, to determine whether the situation is such that statutes designed to assure American neutrality have become operative. The Three Friends (United States v The Three Friends) 166 U.S. 1, 63, 66, 41 L ed 897, 918, 919, 17 S Ct 495. Still again, though it is the executive that determines a person's status as representative of a foreign government, Ex parte Hitz, 111 U.S. 766, 28 L ed 592, 4 S Ct 698, the executive's statements will be construed where necessary to determine the court's jurisdiction, Re Baiz, 135 U.S. 403, 34 L ed 222, 10 S Ct 854. Similar judicial action in the absence of a recognizedly authoritative executive declaration occurs in cases involving the immunity from seizure of vessels owned by friendly foreign governments. Compare Ex parte Peru, 318 U.S. 578, 87 L ed 1014, 63 S Ct 793, with Mexico v Hoffman, 324 U.S. 30, 34, 35, 89 L ed 729, 734, 735, 65 S Ct 530.

Dates of duration of hostilities: Though it has been stated broadly that "the power which declared the necessity is the power to declare its cessation, and what the cessation requires," Commercial Trust Co. v Miller, 262 U.S. 51, 57, 67 L ed 858, 862, 43 S Ct 486, here too analysis reveals isolable reasons for the presence of political questions, underlying this Court's refusal to review the political departments' determination of when or whether a war has ended. Dominant is the need for finality in the political determination, for emergency's nature demands "A prompt and unhesitating obedience," Martin v Mott (U.S.) 12 Wheat 19, 30, 6 L ed 537, 540 (calling up of militia). Moreover, "the cessation of hostilities does not necessarily end the war power. It was stated in Hamilton v Kentucky Distilleries & W. Co., 251 U.S. 146, 161, that the war power includes the power 'to remedy the evils which have arisen from its rise and progress' and continues during that emergency. Stewart v Kahn, 11 Wall. 493, 507." Fleming v Mohawk Wrecking Co. 331 U.S. 111, 116, 91 L ed 1375, 1382, 67 S Ct 1129. But deference rests on reason, not habit. The question in a particular case may not seriously implicate considerations of finality—e.g., a public program of importance (rent control) yet not central to the emergency effort. Further, clearly definable criteria for decision may be available. In such case the political question barrier falls away: "[A] Court is not at liberty to shut its eyes to an obvious mistake, when the validity of the law depends upon the truth of what is declared. . . . [It can] inquire whether the exigency still existed upon which the continued operation of the law depended." Chastleton Corp. v Sinclair, 264 U.S. 543, 547, 548, 68 L ed 841, 843, 44 S Ct 405. Compare Woods v Cloyd W. Miller Co. 333 U.S. 138, 92 L ed 596, 68 S Ct 421. On the other hand, even in private litigation which directly implicates no feature of separation of powers, lack of judicially discoverable standards and the drive for even-handed application may impel reference to the political departments' determination of dates of hostilities' beginning and ending. The Protector (Freeborn v The Protector) (U.S.) 12 Wall 700, 20 L ed 463.

CONTROL OF GOVERNMENT INFORMATION

CONTROL OF GOVERNMENT INFORMATION

Preventing Release of Information

Commentary

Marbury v. Madison[1] decided in 1803, elicited the first judicial pronouncements on secrecy, but secrecy was not an issue directly presented in the case and purposefully submitted for judicial arbitration. The cause arose from the refusal of the newly elected President Thomas Jefferson to carry out certain "midnight" appointments made by the outgoing Federalist administration and ratified by the Senate. Marbury's judicial commission was signed but undelivered when Jefferson took office, and the President instructed the Secretary of State to withhold the commission; Marbury sought an order of mandamus for delivery of the same. To make his case, Marbury needed first to prove that he had in fact been appointed by President John Adams. This should have been a bare formality; but now a remarkable problem arose: neither the executive nor the Senate (now also Republican-controlled) was willing to supply Marbury with documentary proof of his appointment. He therefore required judicial assistance in extracting from the government the evidence he needed. Former Secretary of State (now Attorney General) Levi Lincoln appeared in Court, but refused to answer questions about the relevant transactions, on the ground that the separation of powers required that the proceedings of the executive branch be kept secret. Lincoln at first claimed "that he was not bound, and ought not to answer, as to any facts which came officially to his knowledge while acting as Secretary of State." To this the Court replied firmly that confidentiality was not an attribute of high office itself, but pertained only to particular communications for which the claim might be appropriate. The fact that a commission had been in the Secretary's possession did not impress the Court as a confidential matter. The Court ruled that "they had no doubt he ought to answer. There was nothing confidential required to be disclosed. If there had been he was not obliged to answer it; and if he thought that anything was communicated to him in confidence he was not bound to disclose it . . . but that the fact whether such commissions had been in the office or not, could not be a confidential fact; it is a fact which all the world have a right to know." In the end, Lincoln agreed to answer all the questions that had been put to him, save for that concerning the actual whereabouts of Marbury's commission—a matter the Court held immaterial to the litigation.

In its opinion, the Court stated simply in characterizing the litigation, that "so far from being an intrusion into the secrets of the cabinet, it respects a paper which, according to law, is upon record. . . ."[2]

Marbury established two general propositions about secrecy: that there exists, in principle, a category of privileged, "confidential" executive communications; but that the Court, in a proper case, has power to review the propriety of a claim of privilege.[3]

The next occasion on which judicial proceedings ran afoul of a claim of executive privilege (as it is currently termed) was the criminal trial of Aaron Burr, dutifully but reluctantly presided over by Chief Justice Marshall.[4]

Burr sought to introduce in evidence two letters written to President Jefferson by General Wilkinson, the main prosecution witness. Burr alleged that the letters reflected on Wilkinson's credibility; they also contained matter embarrassing to the administration, domestically and internationally. These requests engendered protracted negotiations between President Jefferson, U.S. Attorney George Hay, Justice Marshall, and the defense. Burr's counsel disclaimed any intent to force release of "state secrets". Despite the President's apparent wish to claim absolute privilege, Hay conceded that the issue was for the Court to decide. Marshall desperately wished to avoid a confrontation with the President and expressed himself guardedly in his rulings from the bench. He did not attempt to establish a detailed judicial doctrine of privileged information, nor did he hold that claims of privilege are for the executive finally to determine. His staunch insistence on the prerogatives of the judiciary within its own sphere dictated a commitment to independent judicial evaluation of the respective claims to withhold and to disclose, conceding "all proper respect" to the initial determination made by the President. Thus Marshall stipulated that any claim of privilege must be made by the President himself, not by his representatives, and that the accused is entitled to see the material in order to participate in the determination as to relevance. The next step was for the Court to inspect the documents and rule on the privilege claim:

> I can readily conceive that the president might receive a letter which would be improper to exhibit in public, because of the manifest inconveniences of its exposure. The occasion for demanding it ought, in such a case, be very strong, and to be fully shown to the court before its production could be insisted on. . . . Perhaps the court ought to consider the reasons, which would induce the president to refuse to exhibit such letter as conclusive on it, unless such letter could be shown to be absolutely necessary in the defense.

The President proceeded to forward the requested letter to the Court, but with portions already deleted; and there, at least as far as the printed record is concerned, the matter abruptly ended. Burr did not promptly move for the introduction of the letters, but was anyway acquitted by Justice Marshall. No ruling on the propriety of the President's conduct was forthcoming. If the letters were not essential to a just disposition of the case, Marshall's declining to force a drastic confrontation with the President was only sensible. To persist would have required measures so extreme, e.g., citing the President for contempt, as to seem unjustified by the particular instance of secrecy at stake. The contents of the letters were known to Burr and to the court. Their materiality to the case was in fact limited; and Burr's attempt to bring them before the public was in large part politically inspired. Neither the express rulings of Justice Marshall nor his prudent avoidance of confrontation lends any support to Presidential claims of absolute privilege.

Congress too showed restraint in pursuing its own inquiry into the Burr conspiracy, requesting from the President all pertinent information "except such as he may deem the public welfare to require not to be disclosed." The President, in responding, did take advantage of this permissive exception, for he noted that "neither safety nor justice will permit the exposing of names," other than that of Burr himself. Evidently his censored submission to the House was acceptable to that body, for no further demand is recorded.[5]

The next Supreme Court decision involving national security secrets was prompted by a contract suit instituted by an individual citizen. *Totten v. United States,*[6] decided by the Supreme Court in 1876, was a suit brought in the Court of Claims to collect the compensation allegedly agreed upon by President Abraham Lincoln and his secret agent, William A. Lloyd, for services performed by Lloyd behind enemy lines during the Civil War. Totten was the administrator of the deceased Lloyd's estate. The Court of Claims had denied relief, on the ground that the contract lacked statutory authority and so was invalid and unenforceable. The Supreme Court unanimously rejected this reasoning, while affirming the result on quite different grounds:

> We have no difficulty as to the authority of the President in the matter. He was undoubtedly authorized during the war, as Commander-in-Chief of the Armies of the United States, to employ secret agents to enter the rebel lines and obtain information respecting the strength, resources and movements of the enemy; and contracts to compensate such agents are so far binding upon the Government as to render it lawful for the President to direct payment of the amount stipulated out of the contingent fund under his control. Our objection is not to the contract, but to the action upon it in the Court of Claims. The service stipulated by the contract was a secret service; the information sought was to be obtained clandestinely, and was to be communicated privately; the employment and the service were to be equally concealed. Both employer and agent must have understood that the lips of the other were to be forever sealed respecting the relation of either to the matter. This condition of the engagement was implied from the nature of the employment, and is implied in all secret employments of the Government in time of war, or upon matters affecting our foreign relations, where a disclosure of the service might compromise or embarrass our Government in its public duties, or endanger the person or injure the character of the agent. If upon contracts of such a nature an action against the Government could be maintained in the Court of Claims, whenever an agent should deem himself entitled to greater or different compensation than that awarded to him, the whole service in any case, and the manner of its discharge, with the details of dealings with *individuals and officers, might be ex- [*107 posed, to the serious detriment of the public. A secret service, with liability to publicity in this way, would be impossible: and, as such services are sometimes indispensable to the Government, its agents in those services must look for their compensation to the contingent fund of the

> department employing them, and to such allowance from it as those who dispense that fund may award. The secrecy which such contracts impose precludes any action for their enforcement. The publicity produced by an action would itself be a breach of a contract of that kind, and thus defeat a recovery.
>
> It may be stated, as a general principle, that public policy forbids the maintenance of any suit in a court of justice, the trial of which would inevitably lead to the disclosure of matters which the law itself regards as confidential, and respecting which it will not allow the confidence to be violated.

On a careful reading, *Totten* simply held that in wartime and in the absence of contrary legislation, the President can, on his own authority, contract for the services of secret agents, to be paid out of his contingent fund; that the existence and nature of such arrangements is supposed to be kept strictly secret by all parties concerned; and that the courts will not condone a violation of the secrecy pact by entertaining contract suits on behalf of the agent's estate.

Some of the language in *Totten* suggests a far broader proposition, that no direct or indirect disclosure about intelligence activities could ever be appropriate in any judicial proceeding. However, the Court could scarcely have considered the ramifications of such an extreme doctrine.

The *Totten* opinion did not deal with any aspect of the interests of Congress and the public in access to information. Only a private monetary interest—and not even that of the deceased agent personally—needed to be balanced against the interest in confidentiality in order to support the conclusion reached by the Court. It is not difficult to imagine a range of cases where the interest in disclosure would be more compelling. In *Burr*, for example, the government's case relied largely on information obtained by the President through confidential channels. We have shown that Chief Justice Marshall, far from forbidding the introduction of any such material by the government, was even prepared to compel its production at the defendant's behest. Surely the Court in *Totten* never dreamed it was overruling *Burr*. Since the *Totten* opinion emphasizes the bilateral nature of the secrecy agreement implicit in intelligence work, it is not obvious that *Totten* allows the government to waive secrecy at its convenience. The tone of reciprocity carefully maintained in the Court's opinion would justify interpreting *Totten* to bar, by the same reasoning, an income tax suit against an agent who failed to report his earnings. But what of an action by the government to enforce an agreement that bars an agent from publishing his memoirs? Putting aside the First Amendment questions raised by this hypothetical, a literal reading of *Totten* would certainly preclude the suit. Yet the secrecy interest is scarcely served by such a result. In light of the omissions and inconsistencies of the *Totten* opinion, together with the singularity of the facts involved, the case is best viewed as *sui generis*. It expressed an understandable respect for the value of secrecy in the intelligence sphere, but contributed nothing further to the development of a sophisticated body of law on secrecy.

No further relevant Supreme Court discussion was forthcoming until 1948. In that year the Court decided the *Waterman Steamship* case,[7] concerning the administrative process whereby air carriers compete for foreign routes. In the case of awards to foreign carriers, judicial review was expressly denied by law. In *Waterman*, a majority of the Court construed the ambiguous statute as also barring judicial review of foreign awards to domestic carriers. In both cases, the President had final approval, and the Court stressed that a presidential decision might be based upon confidential foreign policy considerations not appropriate for judicial review. Absent an explicit congressional mandate, the President should not be required to disclose these considerations in litigation—even on a confidential, *in camera* basis.

Justice Jackson in a widely quoted paragraph explained why the Court would accept this limit on its power:

> The President, both as Commander in Chief and as the Nation's organ for foreign affairs, has available intelligence services which reports are not, and ought not to be, published to the world. It would be intolerable that courts, without the relevant information, should review and perhaps nullify actions of the executive taken on information properly held secret. Nor can the court sit in camera in order to be taken into executive confidences. But even if the courts could require full disclosure, the very nature of executive decisions as to foreign policy is political, not judicial. Such decisions are wholly confined by our Constitution to the political departments of the government, executive and legislature. They are delicate, complex, and involve large elements of policy. They are and should be undertaken only by those directly responsible to the people whose welfare and lives are in peril. They are decisions of a kind for which the judiciary has neither aptitude, facilities nor responsibilities, and which has long been held to belong to the domain of political power not subject to judicial intrusion or inquiry.[8]

Waterman is consistent with the earlier cases in its deference for executive policy-making autonomy, and its reluctance to compel production of confidential information where this can be avoided without impairing the integrity of a judicial proceeding. In the same traditional spirit, the Court was careful not to proclaim an absolute, irrebuttable privilege for state secrets. It held, in effect, that Congress had balanced the value of judicial review against that of confidentiality for this particular administrative process. Given that no systematic unfairness in the administrative process was alleged, and that the private interest involved was not of the first magnitude, the Court could only accept the congressional determination that confidentiality was in this case the more important value. Yet the case certainly did not involve the dangerous political undercurrents that so embarrassed the judiciary in *Marbury, Burr,* and *Totten*. Thus four Justices dissented in *Waterman,* finding the majority's approach excessively timid.[9]

The modern doctrine of state secrets privilege was most fully expounded in *United States v. Reynolds,*[10] a 1953 civil action arising out of the crash of an airplane that carried secret electronic equipment. Stating that the plaintiffs had made only a "dubious showing of necessity," a 6-3 majority of the Court upheld the government's refusal to produce the official Air Force report on the accident. Given a more impressive showing of necessity, they added, the claim of privilege would not be automatically accepted, for "the court itself must determine whether the circumstances are appropriate for the claim of privilege." But that determination need not always require judicial inspection of the documents; on this point the Court repeated their *Waterman* strictures that *in camera* review may be dispensed with, if the court is otherwise "satisfied" that to compel production would pose a "reasonable danger" of harm to the national security. Finally, if the court determines that a state secret is truly at stake, even "the most compelling necessity" of civil litigants would not overcome the privilege. The Court did not define "state secret," beyond indicating that it refers to information the release of which could endanger national security.

Reynolds thus adopted a standard of utmost judicial deference to national security values, but stopped short of relinquishing the essence of judicial power. The courts must determine for themselves whether "circumstances are appropriate" for recognition of the privilege. Moreover, the case was expressly based on the law of evidence and not on constitutional grounds, so that Congress could, if it wished, provide for a more aggressive judicial role. In the political cold-war climate then prevailing, this was as far as the majority of the Court felt prepared to go.

The subsequent Court of Appeals decision in *Halpern v. United States*[11] illustrates the provisional status of the privilege recognized in the preceding cases. Halpern was the inventor of an electronic device, and he sued to obtain the compensation specially authorized by Congress in lieu of a patent, where a patent is withheld in order to preserve the secrecy of the invention. The government interposed a state secrets claim, but the Second Circuit had no difficulty in holding that when Congress expressly afforded a right to compensation, it waived any barrier to the presentation of the evidence necessary to establish the claim. Thus, an *in camera* trial could properly be held on Halpern's claim. The contrast between this case and *Totten, Waterman,* and *Reynolds* is evident; it was the clear congressional sanction for judicial intervention that made the difference.

While no important "state secrets" case has been handed down since *Reynolds,* President Richard Nixon's claims of absolute "executive privilege" in connection with Watergate prosecutions and the House impeachment inquiry did elicit significant judicial dicta on the subject of state secrets. In *Nixon v. Sirica,*[12] the District of Columbia Court of Appeals rejected the President's claim of a constitutional, absolute "advice" privilege for his tapes, and held that the interest in disclosure in criminal cases was paramount. While no "state secrets" were claimed to be involved, the court noted in summarizing the law that "Courts have appreciated that the public interest in maintaining the secrecy of military and diplomatic plans *may* override private interests in litigation" (emphasis added), citing for this proposition *Totten, Reynolds,* and *Burr*.

Later the Supreme Court in *United States v. Nixon*[13] also held against the President. While affirming that "executive privilege" is a constitutional principle, they unanimously denied that it affords absolute protection for a President's conversations with his advisors. Striving for the narrowest possible ground, the Court cautiously noted that the question before them related to criminal litigation, not to a private civil suit and not to a congressional demand for information. They emphasized also that no claim of "state secrets" privilege was involved, and here the Court gratuitously repeated its *Waterman-Reynolds* dicta on the special status of national security information. Still, the Court in its final footnote expressly recognized that in many cases, *in camera* judicial evaluation of a state secrets claim is entirely appropriate. While noting that the interest in protecting state secrets is very great, the Court said nothing in derogation of its constitutional power, or of the power of Congress to regulate access to national security information.[14]

The cases presented here will clearly support only the most general conclusions. The courts have repeatedly and firmly rejected Presidents' claims to be sole judge of the need for confidentiality with respect to state secrets. The weighing of the interests involved is, in principle, always subject to judicial review. In practice, however, the courts have sought to escape this unpleasant duty when it could be at all gracefully done. Sometimes they have invoked doctrines of judicial restraint in order to avoid making any substantive decision; sometimes they have contrived to decide a case without having to inspect the documents. Judgments have typically been announced in the most vague and conclusory terms, emphasizing the courts' deference to official expertise and their preference for a pragmatic, case-by-case approach.

No doubt this record reflects a sincere judicial concern for national security and the separation of powers; and no doubt it also reflects, in at least equal degree, a concern for the political position of the courts, uniquely vulnerable as they are to charges of irresponsibility or ignorance of national security affairs. In the absence of a clear Congressional mandate and workable legislated guidelines, the courts have been unwilling to assume a vigorous role in supervising the release of national security information.

Freedom of Information Act

In 1967, Congress for the first time passed a statute which established a right of access for all citizens to information held by the executive branch of the federal government. The Freedom of Information Act (FOIA)[15] provides that information must be released upon request unless it fits within one or more exemptions.

The first exemption relates to national security information, and as originally passed in 1967, the exemption covered information

> specifically required by Executive Order to be kept secret in the interest of the national defense or foreign policy.[16]

In passing the FOIA, little attention was given to this exemption. There was general agreement that the executive branch had the right to keep national security information secret and to determine the criteria under which it would be kept secret. The FOIA in the early years after passage was rarely used to seek the release of national security documents and then usually for historical documents and generally without success.[17]

In 1973, a group of congresspersons made a determined effort, relying on the FOIA, to secure release of documents relating to a planned nuclear test explosion in Alaska. Release of the documents was refused and a suit was filed leading to the only Supreme Court decision on the national security exemption to the FOIA.

The Court in *EPA v. Mink*, 410 U.S. 73 (1973), held that Congress had provided for only very limited judicial review of (b) (1) exemptions. The Court, it said, could only determine if the requested material was in fact classified. Congress had not intended, the Supreme Court held, that judges go behind the stamp to determine if the classification was correct or even if the classification was, in the words of Justice Stewart's concurring opinion, "cynical, myopic or even corrupt."

The Court went on to note that "Congress could certainly have provided that the Executive Branch adopt new procedures or it could have established its own procedures—subject only to whatever limitations the Executive privilege may be held to impose upon such congressional ordering. Cf. *United States v. Reynolds*, 345 U.S. 1 (1953)."[18]

The release of the Pentagon Papers had already stirred Congressional interest in the classification system and a series of hearings were held to determine if the (b) (1) exemption should be amended.[19]

In 1974, Congress responded to the Court's invitation in *Mink* and amended the national security exemption to read as follows:

> a) specifically authorized under criteria established by executive order to be

kept secret in the interests of national defense and foreign policy, and b) are in fact properly classified pursuant to such executive order.[20]

The Conference Report accompanying the amendments stated that the court would be required to make its own de novo determination of whether "both procedural and substantive criteria" of Executive Order 11652 were properly applied. The report went on to explain:

In *Environmental Protection Agency v. Mink*, et al., 410 U.S. 73 (1973), the Supreme Court ruled that *in camera* inspection of documents withheld under section 552(b) (1) of the law, authorizing the withholding of classified information, would ordinarily be precluded in Freedom of Information cases, unless Congress directed otherwise. H.R. 12471 amends the present law to permit such *in camera* examination at the discretion of the court. While *in camera* examination need not be automatic, in many situations it will plainly be necessary and appropriate. Before the court orders *in camera* inspection, the Government should be given the opportunity to establish by means of testimony or detailed affidavits that the documents are clearly exempt from disclosure. The burden remains on the Government under this law.

* * *

However, the conferees recognize that the Executive departments responsible for national defense and foreign policy matters have unique insights into what adverse effects might occur as a result of public disclosure of a particular classified record. Accordingly, the conferees expect that Federal courts, in making *de novo* determinations in section 552 (b) (1) cases under the Freedom of Information law, will accord substantial weight to an agency's affidavit concerning the details of the classified status of the disputed record.[21]

President Ford vetoed the bill claiming that the revised (b) (1) exemption was unconstitutional. Congress over-rode the veto and the amended act went into effect on February 19, 1976.

Documents can now be withheld only if the procedures of Executive Order 11652 are followed and only if the release of the material could reasonably be expected to cause damage to the national defense or foreign relations of the United States—the order's definition of "Confidential," the lowest classification level.

The change in the (b) (1) exemption and other amendments relating to time limits for responding, fees, and release of segregable portions have led to a substantial number of requests for current national security documents and to release of some important materials.[22] A number of cases have been filed. The courts predictably have been reluctant to over-rule assertions in Executive branch affidavits that documents are properly classified. Moreover, information relating to national security matters can be withheld under other exemptions, particularly those relating to advice, law enforcement and material authorized to be kept secret by other legislation. The last category in particular is used to justify withholding much information related to intelligence and atomic energy.[23]

Prior Restraint

Thus far we have dealt with the executive branch's right to withhold information in its possession. We turn now to its right to seek the assistance of the courts in preventing private citizens in possession of national security information from further disseminating or publishing that information.

The Supreme Court has considered this issue only once in the Pentagon Papers case. It has been considered also by the Fourth Circuit and the District Court in the Eastern District of Virginia in connection with the successful effort of the CIA to prevent one of its former employees from publishing an uncensored book.

The Pentagon Papers Case

The case arose when the *New York Times* and then the *Washington Post* began publishing sections of a top secret Pentagon history of the Vietnam War. The government sought and obtained temporary restraining orders in both New York and Washington but some seventeen days later, the Supreme Court vacated the orders and permitted publication to continue.

The government began in the lower courts by arguing that the President's power derived from the espionage laws, but by the time the matter reached the Supreme Court, the government was basing its position entirely on the inherent powers of the President.[24] The Court voted 6-3 that the government was not entitled to an injunction against either newspaper. The temporary restraint was flatly disapproved by Justices Black and Douglas, in view of their position that the constitutional ban against prior restraint is absolute. However, a clear majority of the Supreme Court were of the view that prior restraint is permissible under some circumstances, and that a restraining order was therefore appropriate pending evaluation of the substantive issues.

The Supreme Court's unsigned *per curiam* opinion, representing the domain of agreement among the six majority justices, was breathtakingly short. Its substantive discussion read as follows:

> "Any system of prior restraints of expression comes to this Court bearing a heavy presumption against its constitutional validity." *Bantam Books, Inc. v. Sullivan,* 372 U.S. 58, 70 (1963); see also *Near v. Minnesota,* 283 U.S. 697 (1931). The government "thus carries a heavy burden of showing justification for the enforcement of such a restraint." *Organization for a Better Austin v. Keefe,* 402 U.S. 415 (1971). The District Court for the Southern District of New York in the *New York Times* case and the District Court for the District of Columbia and the Court of Appeals for the District of Columbia Circuit in the *Washington Post* case held that the government had not met that burden. We agree.[25]

Each of the six majority Justices—Black, Douglas, Brennan, Stewart, White, and Marshall—expounded his individual views in a separate concurring opinion.

Mr. Justice Black approached the case on the basis of his "absolutist" view of the First Amendment, under which no limitations can be put on protected speech. Declaring that "every moment's continuation of the injunction against these newspapers amounts to a flagrant, indefensible, and continuing violation of the First Amendment," he argued that the restraining order against the *Times* should have been vacated without argument. "No one," he went on, "can read the history of the adoption of the First Amendment without being convinced beyond any doubt that it was injunctions like these sought here that Madison and his collaborators intended to outlaw in this nation for all time."

Only Justice Douglas was willing to agree with this absolutist position.[26] While joining in Justice Black's opinion, Justice Douglas also wrote a separate opinion, in which Justice Black concurred, presenting a supplemental or fallback position. Striking at the heart of the inherent powers argument, Justice Douglas emphasized that in the espionage laws, Congress had deliberately refrained from making criminal the "publication" of information related to the national defense.[27] Because prior restraints are even more offensive to First Amendment values than are criminal penalties, this Congressional judgment severely undercut the position of the executive branch. In the face of this indication of a contrary legislative policy, Justice Douglas concluded that the Court could not issue an injunction against publication.

Other Justices were equally unimpressed with the logic of inherent powers, and were therefore concerned to discover the intent of Congress. Justices White and Stewart, each of whom concurred in the other's separate opinion, were inclined to believe that section 793(e) of the espionage laws does apply to "publication," as well as to "communication," of information related to the national defense. While disagreeing with Justice Douglas on this point, however, they did not find the espionage law supportive of the government's injunction suit. Quite the contrary, they held it devastating to the government's case that Congress had specifically addressed the problem but had chosen only to establish criminal sanctions and had failed to provide for injunctive authority.[28]

As in the *Steel Seizure Case,*[29] where legislation defined the exclusive means to deal with labor disputes in defense plants, Congress had in the espionage laws provided an exclusive remedy for unauthorized disclosures of information. At least absent a very special showing of exigency, these Justices held it was not proper for the other branches to add injunctive power to the criminal penalties established by Congress.

Combining the thrust of these several analyses, Justice Marshall found it unnecessary to determine the scope of the espionage laws. Pointing out that the government had not committed itself as to whether the act of publication was a crime, he concluded that the injunction should be denied in either case. If Congress had not made publication a crime, then there was no legislative determination of grave danger, such as would be required to support an injunction. On the other hand if Congress had made the action a crime, this placed the Executive Branch in possession of a sufficient, constitutionally preferable, alternative means of dealing with unauthorized disclosures.

Justice Brennan, like Justice Black, did not discuss the intent of Congress. He urged that even a temporary restraining order should not be issued unless the court was convinced beyond a doubt that there would be "inevitably, directly, and immediately . . . irreparable damage to our nation or its people." The government, he added, must not submit a mere conclusion that such harm would result, but must make available sufficient supporting evidence for judicial scrutiny.

Each of the three dissenters also wrote a separate opinion. Justice Harlan's dissent, which Justices Burger and Blackmun joined, did not focus on the absence of congressional authorization for prior restraints. Instead, like Justice Brennan, he addressed himself directly to the question of the proper standard for judicial review. Justice Harlan argued that the Judiciary's role where foreign policy or national defense questions were concerned is a very limited one: it must accept a determination by the relevant agency head that disclosure "would irreparably impair the nation's security."

The dissenting opinions of Justices Burger and Blackmun stressed their discomfort at the unseemly pace of the litigation, the fragmentary nature of the factual record, and the poverty of applicable legal standards. They concluded that the cases should be remanded for further hearings. Chief Justice Burger addressed himself in passing to the issue of inherent powers, suggesting that in his view the absence of Congressional support was not especially damaging to the government's case.

This review of the separate opinions filed by the Justices suggests that the Court's position can be characterized as proceeding from four basic propositions:

1) rejection of the view that prior restraints are never permissible;
2) rejection of the view that it lies solely with the executive branch to determine the need for prior restraints in any given case;
3) recognition of the powerful, but not conclusive, weight of congressional judgment in determining when prior restraint is permissible;
4) insistence on the power of the judiciary to make its own judgment, founded on adequate evidence and argument, as to what the law is.[30]

It appears that the Court is most reluctant to validate prior restraints that lack an explicit congressional mandate, save possibly in the most uniquely pressing and grave emergency. Justice Brennan characterized the limiting case as one where the government could prove, with cogent evidence, that publication must "inevitably, directly and immediately" cause a harm equivalent in magnitude to a wartime disclosure imperiling the safety of American troops. Justice Stewart stated that in the absence of express congressional authorization, speech might be enjoined if it would "surely result in direct, immediate, and irreparable damage to our Nation or its people."

The Marchetti Case

While the government did not prevail in the Pentagon Papers case, the lacunae in the various concurring opinions encouraged further attempts at prior restraint. The case of Victor Marchetti shortly produced the first—and so far the only—successful suit to enjoin political speech in the United States.[31]

The facts of the case may be stated briefly. Victor Marchetti spent some 14 years with the CIA, rising to the level of staff assistant in the offices of the Director and the Deputy Director. After retiring in 1969, Mr. Marchetti wrote a novel, *The Rope Dancer,* about life in a fictional agency very much like the CIA. Later he decided to write a non-fictional account of CIA operations, particularly its covert intelligence gathering and covert political activities. An article and an outline for a larger study that he submitted to several publishers were forwarded to the CIA by a publisher's employee. Without contacting Marchetti, the agency went into court in the Eastern District of Virginia with a secret affidavit from its Deputy Director for Operations, Thomas H. Karamessines. That very day, on April 18, 1972, Judge Bryan granted a temporary restraining order prohibiting Marchetti from disclosing without CIA approval any information that he had learned by reason of his employment which related to intelligence activities, sources, or methods, except information subsequently disclosed by the United States. This order the Judge declined to dissolve after further argument, and the Fourth Circuit declined to intervene. Trial was held on May 15; and on May 19, 1972, Judge Bryan issued a permanent injunction, holding that Marchetti had waived his First Amendment rights when he went to work for the government, and again at the termination of his employment, by signing statements promising not to reveal classified information or information relating to intelligence matters.

On appeal, the Fourth Circuit Court of Appeals affirmed Judge Bryan's decision. They found the secrecy agreement a reasonable exercise of the President's power as commander-in-chief, and they pointed to the Director's statutory mandate to preserve the secrets of intelligence sources and methods.[32] This power could be exercised, they suggested, not merely to prevent "grave and irreparable harm" but whenever "disclosure may reasonably be thought to be inconsistent with the national interest."[33] However, they modified the injunction in one respect: it would apply only to *classified* intelligence information and not to all intelligence information. The court assumed that the CIA would simply determine which information was classified, and that ordinarily no serious controversy about this could arise. This assumption proved grossly unfounded.

When Marchetti, now working with John Marks, completed his manuscript, it was duly submitted to the CIA, which originally ordered some 339 deletions. Of these demands, all save 168 were dropped after negotiations. Mr. Marchetti and Mr. Marks, joined by their publisher, Knopf, were entitled under the Fourth Circuit's decision to dispute in court the government's assertion that the 168 still contested items were classified, and that they had not entered the public domain. Thus the second round of litigation began.

Prior to trial, Judge Bryan accepted the plaintiff's contention that there should be written proof of classification. He directed the government to turn over to the plaintiffs documentary proof that the information contained in the requested deletions was in fact classified. The CIA had at first objected to providing to Marks and Marchetti additional information of an extremely sensitive nature. To deal with this problem, the court issued a protective order preventing further disclosure of the information beyond the plaintiffs, their attorneys, and one consultant for the plaintiffs.[34]

The government thereupon turned over to the plaintiffs at least one document pertaining to each proposed deletion. Each document was stamped secret or top secret and, in some cases, bore additional code word designations as well.

As plaintiffs were quick to point out, the fact that information is contained in a stamped document does not prove that the particular piece of information was classified, or even classifiable. Under the rules of the classification system, every page in a document is to be stamped when any one sentence on any one page of it gets classified. Thus, many unclassified sentences appear on pages stamped at top and bottom.

Plaintiffs conceded that a few of the documents submitted by the government were marked in such a specific way that they did show that an authorized official had classified a contested item during the period of Marks's or Marchetti's access to the information. A few other documents showed that a senior official had issued a regulation prescribing that an entire relevant category of information, such as information relating to a certain kind of overseas base, was to be classified.[35] At trial, the government further presented testimony from the four deputy directors of the CIA as to the classifiability of the information. However, they were obliged to concede that not all classifiable information within the agency is in fact classified; and they lacked direct knowledge of the time and place where specific items might have been classified.

The court rejected this testimony as proof of the actual classification of the items. Based on the written evidence, the court accepted as classified only a few items besides those conceded by the plaintiffs. In all, only 28 of the deletions demanded by the CIA were proven to the court's satisfaction to be classified.

The Fourth Circuit had overlooked the fact that the classification procedures are designed, as they must be, to control the storage and dissemination of documents. The documents do not, and could not, reveal the classification status of bits of information. But, as Judge Bryan said:

> The result of this may be to release some sensitive information; however, the rationale underlying the fixing of *classification* as the dividing line between what could be revealed and what could not was the assumption that, at the time

the determination was made to classify, there had been a weighing of the competing interests of national defense and foreign relations on the one hand and the public's right to know on the other hand. It is not too much for the public and these plaintiffs to expect that such a determination *be in fact made* as to identifiable information, at an ascertainable time prior to the time of reviewing the manuscript, if that determination is to be the basis of denying the otherwise clear freedom to publish."[36]

The Judge ruled further, resolving an ambiguity in the Fourth Circuit's ruling, that the public domain defense applied only to matter *officially* released; but he held that the injunction did not cover seven items that, he ruled, were learned by plaintiffs independently of their official positions.[37]

Judge Bryan stayed his order, permitting publication of 140 of the 168 disputed items, pending appeal by both sides to the Fourth Circuit. The book was published at this juncture, with all 168 items deleted.[38]

When the Fourth Circuit's new opinion finally came down on February 7, 1975, nearly three years after Judge Bryan had issued his original restraining order against Marchetti and Marks, intervening developments had substantially changed the law applicable to the case.

The litigation had proceeded so far on the assumption that, under *EPA v. Mink*,[39] the courts were not to inquire whether information was properly classified; instead the mere fact of classification would be treated as conclusive against disclosure. Thus the controversy in the district court related primarily to whether the disputed items were in fact classified. As the Fourth Circuit now recognized, the new Freedom of Information Act had overturned the doctrine of *Mink*: under the new Act any citizen could now contest the propriety of the classification in question. It followed that the present plaintiffs must also be entitled to contest that issue, since "these plaintiffs should not be denied the right to publish information which any citizen could compel the CIA to produce and, after production, could publish."[40]

On the other hand, the Court of Appeals saw little merit in the district court's treatment of the classification question. While it had proved unexpectedly difficult for the government to prove that a specific item had in fact been deliberately classified, the relevance of such proof for the ultimate issues was obscure. If the deleted items were truly sensitive, a procedural irregularity on the agency's part would not soften the implications for national security of a court-ordered disclosure. The Fourth Circuit determined, therefore, that all the classifiable information in a stamped document should ordinarily be presumed classified.[41]

The Court of Appeals went on to approve the ruling of the court below, that information enters the public domain—the realm of protected speech, in effect—through official release only. They reasoned that even if rumors had already reached the public concerning a certain matter, confirmation of rumors by one in Marchetti's position could cause further harm to the national interest. Finally, the court ruled that the district judge had incorrectly allowed publication of seven items that first came to plaintiff's attention in the line of duty, but which they would have learned through unofficial channels in any event.

The court concluded by remanding the case to the trial court, where the issue of classifiability could be litigated under the appropriate standard—apparently the FOIA standard, whereby the court makes a *de novo* determination as to how each item should be classified under the Presidential guidelines. Subsequently, the Supreme Court declined to review the Fourth Circuit's judgment. When Plaintiffs declined to request a trial on the issue of classifiability, the district court issued an order denying release of the disputed materials. Thus the litigation came to an end, leaving in effect the permanent injunction issued in May, 1972.

Summary

Not only is there no textual authority for prior restraints on speech, but there is of course a constitutional provision that seems flatly to proscribe them. Yet in upholding the first judicially sanctioned prior restraint in our nation's history, the court pronounced the First Amendment irrelevant to the case. This curious conclusion was held to result from the operation of Marchetti's secrecy agreement; but the court failed to recognize that the force and effect of such an agreement must itself be determined in the light of First Amendment standards. The court thus assumed away the First Amendment rights not only of Marchetti himself, but of his publisher and the general public as well.

Three further considerations make the emphasis the court placed on the secrecy agreement seem even more inappropriate. First, the court stated that even without an explicit contract, a binding commitment not to reveal government secrets was implicit in Marchetti's acceptance of his employment. Second, even if there had been justification for characterizing the litigation as simply a contracts case, the court itself abandoned that position when it recognized the relevance of the Freedom of Information Act. If Marchetti's employment contract did not impair his rights, or those of the public, to obtain information under the FOIA, it would seem to follow *a fortiori* that the contract could not impair his or third parties' rights under the First Amendment either.[42] Third, and most important, is the court's failure to recognize that Congress has expressed its policy judgment by steadfastly refusing to authorize prior restraints.

In 1917, President Woodrow Wilson proposed an amendment to the espionage laws which appeared to sanction injunctions against publication. Congress rejected this proposal.[43] In 1950, when Congress undertook revision of the Internal Security Act, including various amendments to the espionage laws, it added a sentence specifically providing that nothing in the Act should be taken to imply authority for prior restraints on publication.[44] Congress has, however, legislated one very narrow authorization for prior restraint. In the Atomic Energy Act, Congress provided in 1954 that the Executive Branch could seek an injunction against violations of the criminal provisions of that Act.[45]

Congress has carefully chosen specific regulatory techniques and sanctions to meet specific problems. It authorized prior restraint only in this one instance; and the utterances sought to be restrained in *Marchetti* were not alleged to be within that area of specifically authorized prior restraint. In fact, both the absence of Congressional authority for prior restraints and the need for such authority have been implicitly recognized by the Director of the CIA, in that he developed a proposal for legislation, which would explicitly authorize injunctions on publication of intelligence information.[46] In February, 1976, President Gerald Ford proposed legislation which would permit the courts to enjoin the publication of information revealing intelligence sources and methods.

---

[1]5 U.S. (1 Cranch) 137 (1803).

[2]On the merits, the Court held that although the withholding of Marbury's commission was unlawful,

the Judiciary Act of 1789 had gone beyond the Constitution in attempting to give the Supreme Court original jurisdiction of mandamus cases. The Court thus deftly combined a finding that an act of Congress was unconstitutional with a declaration that the President had acted unlawfully, while at the same time limiting its own jurisdiction and declining to issue an order adverse to the administration.

[3]Later, in the course of the Burr trials, Marshall was to say of his *Marbury* ruling that "the principle there decided was that communications from the President to the Secretary of State could not be extorted from him." This dictum goes well beyond the bounds of any question actually presented or decided in *Marbury*. Marbury's counsel, it may be noted, had conceded that State Department clerks should not be compelled to testify to "the facts concerning foreign correspondences, and confidential communications between the head of the department and the President."

[4]*U.S. v. Burr*, 25 Fed. Cas. 30, 55, 187 (Cir. Ct. Va. 1807).

[5]The conduct of separate, parallel investigations by Congress and by those in charge of law enforcement is a straightforward, if sometimes awkward, consequence of the separation of powers. The historic reluctance of Congress, prior to the Nixon tapes controversy, to involve the courts directly in Congress's own investigative processes, at least where public officials are the object of investigation, is certainly due in part to Congressional respect for the integrity of the criminal law system. Moreover, the very gingerly manner in which Justice Marshall handled the secrecy problem in *Marbury* and *Burr* did not promise that the courts would necessarily emerge as a strong ally of Congress in time of need.

[6]92 U.S. 105 (1876).

[7]333 U.S. 103 (1948).

[8]333 U.S. at 11.

[9]"Though Waterman has not been over-ruled by the Supreme Court, its apparently sweeping contours have been eroded by recent circuit court opinions." *Pan American World Airlines v. CAB*, 392 F.2d 483, 492 (D.C. Cir. 1968).

[10]345 U.S. 1 (1953).

[11]258 F.2d 36 (2d Cir. 1958).

[12]487 F.2d 700 (D.C. Cir. 1973).

[13]418 U.S. 683 (1974).

[14]The Special Prosecutor's criminal investigations of course were not the only proceedings that led to demands for disclosure of President Nixon's tapes. Separate investigations were conducted both in the House of Representatives, with a view to possible impeachment of the President, and in the Senate, with a view to possible legislation respecting campaign reform and other subjects. It was the Senate Select Committee that reluctantly broke with precedent, by turning to the courts for assistance in obtaining information from the executive branch. Never before had Congress taken this step. This litigation, known as *Senate Select Committee on Presidential Campaign Activities v. Nixon*, is recorded at 366 F. Supp 51 (D.D.C. 1973), *aff'd.*, 498 F.2d 725 (D.C. Cir., 1973).

The justiciability of this direct, executive/congressional dispute about the boundaries of their respective powers, with no private interest represented in the case, did present a novel question. Strictly speaking, the court was free to decline jurisdiction on "political question" grounds. Yet the recent cases pointed strongly in the opposite direction. In modern times such politically explosive and internal matters as legislative reapportionment, congressional expulsion of a member, and congressional attempts to procure the removal of a high executive official by withholding his salary have fallen under judicial scrutiny. [*Baker v. Carr*, 369 U.S. 186 (1962); *Powell v. McCormack*, 395 U.S. 486 (1969); *United States v. Lovett*, 328 U.S. 303 (1946).] As it turned out, the courts had even less difficulty with the "political question" issue than might have been expected, holding it disposed of by the cases just mentioned. Nevertheless, the courts were not eager to undertake a head-on confrontation with the presidency. Their approach to the merits was guided by the realization that both the impeachment investigators in the House and the Special Prosecutor's office had a more urgent claim to the tapes than did the Select Committee. Either of the former might yet obtain the tapes by negotiation; failing this, either would be free to bring the case again before the courts. These circumstances obliged the Select Committee to support its own claim by showing an independent and urgent need for the tapes. Yet the Committee could only argue that, if they did not prevail in the present case, the development of legislative proposals on campaign reform would be frustrated. The Court of Appeals held that the Committee had not shown a compelling need for the tapes; and, instead of appealing to the Supreme Court, the Senate prudently let the House and the Special Prosecutor make the next move in the struggle.

[15]5 U.S.C. §552.

[16]5 U.S.C. §552 (b) (1).

[17]See eg. *Epstein v. Resor,* 421 F.2d 930 (9th Cir., 1970), cert. denied, 398 U.S. 965 (1970), *Wolfe v. Froehlke,* 510 F.2d 654 (D.C. Cir., 1974).

[18]410 U.S. 73, at 83. This ruling was interpreted as not preventing a court from inquiring into whether the procedures of the Executive Order were followed. See *Schaffer v. Kissinger,* 505 F.2d 389 (D.C. Cir., 1974).

[19]U.S. Government Information Policies and Practices, The Pentagon Papers, Hearings, Subcommittee of the House Committee on Government Operations, 92nd Cong., 1st Sess., Parts 1-3, 8, 9, 1971. Executive Privilege, Secrecy in Government, Freedom of Information, Hearings, Subcommittees of the Senate Committee on Government Operations and the Senate Committee on Judiciary, 93rd Cong., 1st Sess., Vol. 1-3, 1973. Security Classification Reform, Hearings, Subcommittee of the House Committee on Government Operations, 93rd Cong., 2nd Sess., 1974.

[20]5 U.S.C. §552 (b) (1).

[21]Senate Report No. 93-1200, 93d Cong. 2d sess. reprinted in Source Book: Legislative History, Texts and other Documents, House Committee on Government Operations and Senate Committee on the Judiciary, 94th Cong., 1st Sess., March 1975, 217.

[22]See e.g. "Abstracts of Documents Released Under the Freedom of Information Act Relating to Foreign Policy and National Defense" Washington, D.C. Project on National Security and Civil Liberties, September, 1976.

[23]See generally Christine M. Marwick (ed.) *Litigation Under the Amended Federal Freedom of Information Act,* (Washington, D.C., Project on National Security and Civil Liberties, 1976).

[24]The government's brief to the Supreme Court, and other briefs, orders, and opinions cited below, are reprinted in *The New York Times Company vs. United States, A Documentary History* (2 vols., Arno Press, 1971). The Supreme Court decision is reported officially at 403 U.S. 713 (1971).

[25]The three precedents cited had to do with publications allegedly obscene, libelous, and invasive of individual privacy, respectively. The *per curiam* opinion did not note that the motivation for speech was different in each case, ranging from the mainly commercial to political advocacy and information. However, it seems clear that if the government could once show a regulatory interest sufficiently compelling to pass the threshhold presumption against prior restraint, the strength of the specific, competing speech interest would become a critical issue.

[26]For one statement of the argument that the First Amendment was intended to ban absolutely all interferences with publication, see Meiklejohn, *The First Amendment Is an Absolute,* 1961 Supreme Court Review 245.

[27]See further discussion below at n. 43 and text.

[28]Except in the special case of Atomic Energy secrets.

[29]See further discussion in chapter 1.

[30]That the *New York Times* decision turned fundamentally on the question of separation of powers is also the conclusion of Junker, *Down Memory Lane: The Case of the Pentagon Papers,* 23 Case W. Res. L. Rev. 3 (1971).

[31]The litigation originated as United States v. Marchetti, No. 179-72-A (E.D.Va. 1972), *injunction affirmed,* 466 F.2d 1309 (4th Cir. 1972), *cert. denied,* 409 U.S. 1063 (1972) (three Justices dissenting). The subsequent proceedings are styled *Knopf, Inc. v. Colby,* No. 540-73-A (E.D.Va. 1974), *affirmed in part and vacated in part,* 509 F.2d 1362 (4th Cir., 1975), *cert. denied,* 421 U.S. 992 (1975), *order issued,* Oct. 22, 1975 (E.D.Va.).

[32]50 U.S.C. section 403(d)(3).

[33]466 F.2d at 1315.

[34]One plaintiff, the Knopf Publishing Company, was actually excluded by the protective order from seeing the documents; Knopf's attorneys, however, were eligible.

[35]Plaintiffs conceded only that such items were once classified. They did not by this concede that the classification was valid; that the item was not presently in the public domain; nor that the First Amendment allows censorship in any case.

[36]Memorandum, *Knopf v. Colby,* No. 540-73-A (E.D.Va. March 29, 1974) at 7.

[37]Memorandum, at 7, 12.

[38]See Victor Marchetti and John D. Marks, *The CIA and the Cult of Intelligence,* (New York, Alfred A.

Knopf, 1974), in particular the authors' prefaces and the introduction. See also John Marks, "On Being Censored," *Foreign Policy*, Summer 1974, 93.

[39]See above in Freedom of Information Act section.

[40]509 F.2d at 1367.

[41]The court did not dispute the district judge's finding that procedural requirements had not in fact been observed; nor did they discuss the significance of the Conference Report to the Freedom of Information Act, where it is specified that both substantive and procedural errors in classification will remove a document from the protection of the b(1) exemption.

[42]It can also be argued that the court failed to apply correctly the principles of contract law itself. The burden on Marchetti of a permanent censorship over both fiction and nonfiction writing on intelligence seems quite harsh. Private employers are not usually entitled to injunctive enforcement of such contractual terms as will prevent ex-employees from pursuing their professions. Yet the district court justified its injunction simply by noting the inadequacy of monetary damages to compensate the government for its loss. The appropriateness of this one-sided test was not discussed by the Fourth Circuit.

[43]See Edgar and Schmidt, *The Espionage Statutes and the Publication of Defense Information*, 73 Columbia Law Review 930, 952 (May 1973).

[44]*Ibid.*, at 1027.

[45]Atomic Energy Act, 42 U.S.C. section 2280.

[46]The proposal is part of the record in the *Marchetti* case.

STATUTES

Departmental Regulations on Documents

5 U.S.C. §301

The head of an Executive department or military department may prescribe regulations for the government of his department, the conduct of its employees, the distribution and performance of its business, and the custody, use, and preservation of its records, papers, and property. This section does not authorize withholding information from the public or limiting the availability of records to the public. Pub.L. 89-554, Sept. 6, 1966, 80 Stat. 379.

The Freedom of Information Act, As Amended in 1974

5 U.S.C. §552

Public information; agency rules, opinions, orders, records, and proceedings

(a) Each agency shall make available to the public information as follows:

(1) Each agency shall separately state and currently publish in the Federal Register for the guidance of the public—

(A) descriptions of its central and field organization and the established places at which, the employees (and in the case of a uniformed service, the members) from whom, and the methods whereby, the public may obtain information, make submittals or requests, or obtain decisions;

(B) statements of the general course and method by which its functions are channeled and determined, including the nature and requirements of all formal and informal procedures available;

(C) rules of procedure, descriptions of forms available or the places at which forms may be obtained, and instructions as to the scope and contents of all papers, reports, or examinations;

(D) substantive rules of general applicability adopted as authorized by law, and statements of general policy or interpretations of general applicability formulated and adopted by the agency; and

(E) each amendment, revision, or repeal of the foregoing.

Except to the extent that a person has actual and timely notice of the terms thereof, a person may not in any manner be required to resort to, or be adversely affected by, a matter required to be published in the Federal Register and not so published. For the purpose of this paragraph, matter reasonably available to the class of persons affected thereby is deemed published in the Federal Register when incorporated by reference therein with the approval of the Director of the Federal Register.

(2) Each agency, in accordance with published rules, shall make available for public inspection and copying—

(A) final opinions, including concurring and dissenting opinions, as well as orders, made in the adjudication of cases;

(B) those statements of policy and interpretations which have been adopted by the agency and are not published in the Federal Register; and

(C) administrative staff manuals and instructions to staff that affect a member of the public;

unless the materials are promptly published and copies offered for sale. To the extent required to prevent a clearly unwarranted invasion of personal privacy, an agency may delete identifying details when it makes available or publishes an opinion, statement of policy, interpretation, or staff manual or instruction. However, in each case the justification for the deletion shall be explained fully in writing. Each agency shall also maintain and make available for public inspection and copying current indexes providing identifying information for the public as to any matter issued, adopted, or promulgated after July 4, 1967, and required by this paragraph to be made available or published. Each agency shall promptly publish, quarterly or more frequently, and distribute (by sale or otherwise) copies of each index or supplements thereto unless it determines by order published in the Federal Register that the publication would be unnecessary and impracticable, in which case the agency shall nonetheless provide copies of such index on request at a cost not to exceed the direct cost of duplication. A final order, opinion, statement of policy, interpretation, or staff manual or instruction that affects a member of the public may be relied on, used, or cited as precedent by an agency against a party other than an agency only if—

(i) it has been indexed and either made available or published as provided by this paragraph; or

(ii) the party has actual and timely notice of the terms thereof.

(3) Except with respect to the records made available under paragraphs (1) and

(2) of this subsection, each agency, upon any request for records which (A) reasonably describes such records and (B) is made in accordance with published rules stating the time, place, fees (if any), and procedures to be followed, shall make the records promptly available to any person.

(4) (A) In order to carry out the provisions of this section, each agency shall promulgate regulations, pursuant to notice and receipt of public comment, specifying a uniform schedule of fees applicable to all constituent units of such agency. Such fees shall be limited to reasonable standard charges for document search and duplication and provide for recovery of only the direct costs of such search and duplication. Documents shall be furnished without charge or at a reduced charge where the agency determines that waiver or reduction of the fee is in the public interest because furnishing the information can be considered as primarily benefiting the general public.

(B) On complaint, the district court of the United States in the district in which the complainant resides, or has his principal place of business, or in which the agency records are situated, or in the District of Columbia, has jurisdiction to enjoin the agency from withholding agency records and to order the production of any agency records improperly withheld from the complainant. In such a case the court shall determine the matter de novo, and may examine the contents of such agency records in camera to determine whether such records or any part thereof shall be withheld under any of the exemptions set forth in subsection (b) of this section, and the burden is on the agency to sustain its action.

(C) Notwithstanding any other provision of law, the defendant shall serve an answer or otherwise plead to any complaint made under this subsection within thirty days after service upon the defendant of the pleading in which such complaint is made, unless the court otherwise directs for good cause shown.

(D) Except as to cases the court considers of greater importance, proceedings before the district court, as authorized by this subsection, and appeals therefrom, take precedence on the docket over all cases and shall be assigned for hearing and trial or for argument at the earliest practicable date and expedited in every way.

(E) The court may assess against the United States reasonable attorney fees and other litigation costs reasonably incurred in any case under this section in which the complainant has substantially prevailed.

(F) Whenever the court orders the production of any agency records improperly withheld from the complainant and assesses against the United States reasonable attorney fees and other litigation costs, and the court additionally issues a written finding that the circumstances surrounding the withholding raise questions whether agency personnel acted arbitrarily or capriciously with respect to the withholding, the Civil Service Commission shall promptly initiate a proceeding to determine whether disciplinary action is warranted against the officer or employee who was primarily responsible for the withholding. The Commission, after investigation and consideration of the evidence submitted, shall submit its findings and recommendations to the administrative authority of the agency concerned and shall send copies of the findings and recommendations to the officer or employee or his representative. The administrative authority shall take the corrective action that the Commission recommends.

(G) In the event of noncompliance with the order of the court, the district court may punish for contempt the responsible employee, and in the case of a uniformed service, the responsible member.

(5) Each agency having more than one member shall maintain and make available for public inspection a record of the final votes of each member in every agency proceeding.

(6) (A) Each agency, upon any request for records made under paragraph (1), (2), or (3) of this subsection, shall—

(i) determine within ten days (excepting Saturdays, Sundays, and legal public holidays) after the receipt of any such request whether to comply with such request and shall immediately notify the person making such request of such determination and the reasons therefor, and of the right of such person to appeal to the head of the agency any adverse determination; and

(ii) make a determination with respect to any appeal within twenty days (excepting Saturdays, Sundays, and legal public holidays) after the receipt of such appeal. If on appeal the denial of the request for records is in whole or in part upheld, the agency shall notify the person making such request of the provisions for judicial review of that determination under paragraph (4) of this subsection.

(B) In unusual circumstances as specified in this subparagraph, the time limits prescribed in either clause (i) or clause (ii) of subparagraph (A) may be extended by written notice to the person making such request setting forth the reasons for such extension and the date on which a determination is expected to be dispatched. No such notice shall specify a date that would result in an extension for more than ten working days. As used in this subparagraph, "unusual circumstances" means, but only to the extent reasonably necessary to the proper processing of the particular request—

(i) the need to search for and collect the requested records from field facilities or other establishments that are separate from the office processing the request;

(ii) the need to search for, collect, and appropriately examine a voluminous amount of separate and distinct records which are demanded in a single request; or

(iii) the need for consultation, which shall be conducted with all practicable speed, with another agency having a substantial interest in the determination of the request or among two or more components of the agency having substantial subject-matter interest therein.

(C) Any person making a request to any agency for records under paragraph (1), (2), or (3) of this subsection shall be deemed to have exhausted his administrative remedies with respect to such request if the agency fails to comply with the applicable time limit provisions of this paragraph. If the Government can show exceptional circumstances exist and that the agency is exercising due diligence in responding to the request, the court may retain jurisdiction and allow the agency additional time to complete its review of the records. Upon any determination by an agency to comply with a request for records, the records shall be made promptly available to such person making such request. Any notification of denial of any request for records under this subsection shall set forth the names and titles or positions of each person responsible for the denial of such request.

(b) This section does not apply to matters that are—

(1) (A) specifically authorized under criteria established by an Executive order

to be kept secret in the interest of national defense or foreign policy and (B) are in fact properly classified pursuant to such Executive order;

(2) related solely to the internal personnel rules and practices of an agency;

(3) specifically exempted from disclosure by statute;

(4) trade secrets and commercial or financial information obtained from a person and privileged or confidential;

(5) inter-agency or intra-agency memorandums or letters which would not be available by law to a party other than an agency in litigation with the agency;

(6) personnel and medical files and similar files the disclosure of which would constitute a clearly unwarranted invasion of personal privacy;

(7) investigatory records compiled for law enforcement purposes, but only to the extent that the production of such records would (A) interfere with enforcement proceedings, (B) deprive a person of a right to a fair trial or an impartial adjudication, (C) constitute an unwarranted invasion of personal privacy, (D) disclose the indentity of a confidential source and, in the case of a record compiled by a criminal law enforcement authority in the course of a criminal investigation, or by an agency conducting a lawful national security intelligence investigation, confidential information furnished only by the confidential source, (E) disclose investigative techniques and procedures, or (F) endanger the life or physical safety of law enforcement personnel;

(8) contained in or related to examination, operating, or condition reports prepared by, on behalf of, or for the use of an agency responsible for the regulation or supervision of financial institutions; or

(9) geological and geophysical information and data, including maps, concerning wells.

Any reasonably segregable portion of a record shall be provided to any person requesting such record after deletion of the portions which are exempt under this subsection.

(c) This section does not authorize withholding information or limit the availability of records to the public, except as specifically stated in this section. This section is not authority to withhold information from Congress.

(d) On or before March 1 of each calendar year, each agency shall submit a report covering the preceding calendar year to the Speaker of the House of Representatives and President of the Senate for referral to the appropriate committees of the Congress. The report shall include—

(1) the number of determinations made by such agency not to comply with requests for records made to such agency under subsection (a) and the reasons for each such determination;

(2) the number of appeals made by persons under subsection (a)(6), the result of such appeals, and the reason for the action upon each appeal that results in a denial of information;

(3) the names and titles or positions of each person responsible for the denial of records requested under this section, and the number of instances of participation for each;

(4) the results of each proceeding conducted pursuant to subsection (a)(4)(F), including a report of the disciplinary action taken against the officer or employee who was primarily responsible for improperly withholding records or an explanation of why disciplinary action was not taken;

(5) a copy of every rule made by such agency regarding this section;

(6) a copy of the fee schedule and the total amount of fees collected by the agency for making records available under this section; and

(7) such other information as indicates efforts to administer fully this section.

The Attorney General shall submit an annual report on or before March 1 of each calendar year which shall include for the prior calendar year a listing of the number of cases arising under this section, the exemption involved in each case, the disposition of such case, and the cost, fees, and penalties assessed under subsections (a)(4)(E), (F), and (G). Such report shall also include a description of the efforts undertaken by the Department of Justice to encourage agency compliance with this section.

(e) For purposes of this section, the term "agency" as defined in section 551(1) of this title includes any executive department, military department, Government corporation, Government controlled corporation, or other establishment in the executive branch of the Government (including the Executive Office of the President), or any independent regulatory agency.

Secrecy of Certain Inventions and Withholding of Patent

35 U.S.C. §181

Whenever publication or disclosure by the grant of a patent on an invention in which the Government has a property interest might, in the opinion of the head of the interested Government agency, be detrimental to the national security, the Commissioner upon being so notified shall order that the invention be kept secret and shall withhold the grant of a patent therefor under the conditions set forth hereinafter.

Whenever the publication or disclosure of an invention by the granting of a patent, in which the Government does not have a property interest, might, in the opinion of the Commissioner, be detrimental to the national security, he shall make the application for patent in which such invention is disclosed available for inspection to the Atomic Energy Commission, the Secretary of Defense, and the chief officer of any other department or agency of the Government designated by the President as a defense agency of the United States.

Each individual to whom the application is disclosed shall sign a dated acknowledgment thereof, which acknowledgment shall be entered in the file of the application. If, in the opinion of the Atomic Energy Commission, the Secretary of a Defense Department, or the chief officer of another department or agency so designated, the publication or disclosure of the invention by the granting of a patent therefor would be detrimental to the national security, the Atomic Energy Commission, the Secretary of a Defense Department, or such other chief officer shall notify the Commissioner and the Commissioner shall order that the invention be kept secret and shall withhold the grant of a patent for such period as the national interest requires, and notify the applicant thereof. Upon proper showing by the head of the department or agency who caused the secrecy order to be issued that the examination of the application might jeopardize the national interest, the Commissioner shall thereupon maintain the application in a sealed condition and notify the applicant thereof. The owner of an application which has been placed under a secrecy order shall have a right to appeal from the order to the Secretary of Commerce under rules prescribed by him.

An invention shall not be ordered kept secret and the grant of a patent withheld for a period of more than one year. The Commissioner shall renew the order at the end thereof, or at the end of any renewal period, for additional periods of one year upon notification by the head of the department or the chief officer of the agency who caused the order to be issued that an affirmative determination has been made that the national interest continues so to require. An order in effect, or issued, during a time when the United States is at war, shall remain in effect for the duration of hostilities and one year following cessation of hostilities. An order in effect, or issued, during a national emergency declared by the President shall remain in effect for the duration of the national emergency and six months thereafter. The Commissioner may rescind any order upon notification by the heads of the departments and the chief officers of the agencies who caused the order to be issued that the publication or disclosure of the invention is no longer deemed detrimental to the national security. July 19, 1952, c. 950, § 1, 66 Stat. 805.

Atomic Energy Act and Classification

42 U.S.C. §2256

Classification of Information

The Joint Committee may classify information originating within the committee in accordance with the standards used generally by the executive branch for classifying Restricted Data or defense information.

Aug. 1, 1946, c. 724, § 206, as added Aug. 30, 1954, c. 1073, § 1, 68 Stat. 957.

42 U.S.C. §2161

Policy of Commission

It shall be the policy of the Commission to control the dissemination and declassification of Restricted Data in such a manner as to assure the common defense and security. Consistent with such policy, the Commission shall be guided by the following principles:

(a) Until effective and enforceable international safeguards against the use of atomic energy for destructive purposes have been established by an international arrangement, there shall be no exchange of Restricted Data with other nations except as authorized by section 2164 of this title; and

(b) The dissemination of scientific and technical information relating to atomic energy should be permitted and encouraged so as to provide that free interchange of ideas and criticism which is essential to scientific and industrial progress and public understanding and to enlarge the fund of technical information.

Aug. 1,1946, c. 724, § 141, as added Aug. 30, 1954, c. 1073, § 1, 68 Stat. 940.

42 U.S.C. §2162

Classification and Declassification of Restricted Data—Periodic Determination

(a) The Commission shall from time to time determine the data, within the definition of Restricted Data, which can be published without undue risk to the common defense and security and shall thereupon cause such data to be declassified and removed from the category of Restricted Data.

Continuous Review

(b) The Commission shall maintain a continuous review of Restricted Data and of any Classification Guides issued for the guidance of those in the atomic energy program with respect to the areas of Restricted Data which have been declassified in order to determine which information may be declassified and removed from the category of Restricted Data without undue risk to the common defense and security.

Joint Determination on Atomic Weapons; Presidential Determination on Disagreement

(c) In the case of Restricted Data which the Commission and the Department of Defense jointly determine to relate primarily to the military utilization of atomic weapons, the determination that such data may be published without constituting an unreasonable risk to the common defense and security shall be made by the Commission and the Department of Defense jointly, and if the Commission and the Department of Defense do not agree, the determination shall be made by the President.

Same; Removal from Restricted Data Category

(d) The Commission shall remove from the Restricted Data category such data as the Commission and the Department of Defense jointly determine relates primarily to the military utilization of atomic weapons and which the Commission and Department of Defense jointly determine can be adequately safeguarded as defense information: *Provided, however,* That no such data so removed from the Restricted Data category shall be transmitted or otherwise made available to any nation or regional defense organization, while such data remains defense information, except pursuant to an agreement for cooperation entered into in accordance with section 2164(b) of this title.

Joint Determination on Atomic Energy Programs

(e) The Commission shall remove from the Restricted Data category such information concerning the atomic energy programs of other nations as the Commission and the Director of Central Intelligence jointly determine to be necessary to carry out the provisions of section 403(d) of Title 50 and can be adequately safeguarded as defense information.

Aug. 1, 1946, c. 724, § 142, as added Aug. 30, 1954, c. 1073, § 1, 68 Stat. 941.

42 U.S.C. §2163

Access to Restricted Data

The Commission may authorize any of its employees, or employees of any contractor, prospective contractor, licensee or prospective licensee of the Commission or any other person authorized access to Restricted Data by the Commission under section 2165(b) and (c) of this title to permit any employee of an agency of the Department of Defense or of its contractors, or any member of the Armed Forces to have access to Restricted Data required in the performance of his duties and so certified by the head of the appropriate agency of the Department of Defense or his designee: *Provided, however,* That the head of the appropriate agency of the Department of Defense or his designee has determined, in accordance with the established personnel security procedures and standards of such agency, that permitting the member or employee to have access to such Restricted Data will not endanger the common defense and security: *And provided further,* That the Secretary of Defense finds that the established personnel and other security procedures and standards of such agency are adequate and in reasonable conformity to the standards established by the Commission under section 2165 of this title.

Aug. 1, 1946, c. 724, § 143, as added Aug. 30, 1954, c. 1073, § 1, 68 Stat. 941, and amended Aug. 6, 1956, c. 1015, § 14, 70 Stat. 1071; Sept. 6, 1961, Pub.L. 87-206, § 5, 75 Stat. 476.

42 U.S.C. §2164

International Cooperation—By Commission

(a) The President may authorize the Commission to cooperate with another nation and to communicate to that nation Restricted Data on—

(1) refining, purification, and subsequent treatment of source material;

(2) civilian reactor development;

(3) production of special nuclear material;

(4) health and safety;

(5) industrial and other applications of atomic energy for peaceful purposes; and

(6) research and development relating to the foregoing:

Provided, however, That no such cooperation shall involve the communication of Restricted Data relating to the design or fabrication of atomic weapons: *And provided further,* That the cooperation is undertaken pursuant to an agreement for cooperation entered into in accordance with section 2153 of this title, or is undertaken pursuant to an agreement existing on August 30, 1954.

By Department of Defense

(b) The President may authorize the Department of Defense, with the assistance of the Commission, to cooperate with another nation or with a regional defense organization to which the United States is a party, and to communicate to that nation or organization such Restricted Data (including design information) as is necessary to—

(1) the development of defense plans;

42 U.S.C. §2275

Receipt of Restricted Data

Whoever, with intent to injure the United States or with intent to secure an advantage to any foreign nation, acquires, or attempts or conspires to acquire any document, writing, sketch, photograph, plan, model, instrument, appliance, note, or information involving or incorporating Restricted Data shall, upon conviction thereof be punished by imprisonment for life, or by imprisonment for any term of years or a fine of not more than $20,000 or both.

Aug. 1, 1946, c. 724, § 225, as added Aug. 30, 1954, c. 1073, § 1, 68 Stat. 959, and amended Dec. 24, 1969, Pub.L. 91-161, § 3(c), 83 Stat. 444.

42 U.S.C. §2276

Tampering with Restricted Data

Whoever, with intent to injure the United States or with intent to secure an advantage to any foreign nation, removes, conceals, tampers with, alters, mutilates, or destroys any document, writing, sketch, photograph, plan, model, instrument, appliance, or note involving or incorporating Restricted Data and used by any individual or person in connection with the production of special nuclear material, or research or development relating to atomic energy, conducted by the United States, or financed in whole or in part by Federal funds, or conducted with the aid of special nuclear material, shall be punished by imprisonment for life, or by imprisonment for any term of years or a fine of not more than $20,000 or both.

Aug. 1, 1946, c. 724, § 226, as added Aug. 30, 1954, c. 1073, § 1, 68 Stat. 959, and amended Dec. 24, 1969, Pub.L. 91-161, § 3(b), 83 Stat. 444.

42 U.S.C. §2277

Disclosure of Restricted Data

Whoever, being or having been an employee or member of the Commission, a member of the Armed Forces, an employee of any agency of the United States, or being or having been a contractor of the Commission or of an agency of the United States, or being or having been an employee of a contractor of the Commission or of an agency of the United States, or being or having been a licensee of the Commission, or being or having been an employee of a licensee of the Commission, knowingly communicates, or whoever conspires to communicate or to receive, any Restricted Data, knowing or having reason to believe that such data is Restricted Data, to any person not authorized to receive Restricted Data pursuant to the provisions of this chapter or under rule or regulation of the Commission issued pursuant thereto, knowing or having reason to believe such person is not so authorized to receive Restricted Data shall, upon conviction thereof, be punishable by a fine of not more than $2,500.

Aug. 1, 1946, c. 724, § 227, as added Aug. 30, 1954, c. 1073, § 1, 68 Stat. 959.

42 U.S.C. §2278

Statute of Limitations

Except for a capital offense, no individual or person shall be prosecuted, tried, or punished for any offense prescribed or defined in sections 2274 to 2276 of this title unless the indictment is found or the information is instituted within ten years next after such offense shall have been committed.

Aug. 1, 1946, c. 724, § 228, as added Aug. 30, 1954, c. 1073, § 1, 68 Stat. 959.

42 U.S.C. §2280

Injunction Proceedings

Whenever in the judgment of the Commission any person has engaged or is about to engage in any acts or practices which constitute or will constitute a violation of any provision of this chapter, or any regulation or order issued thereunder, the Attorney General on behalf of the United States may make application to the appropriate court for an order enjoining such acts or practices, or for an order enforcing compliance with such provision, and upon a showing by the Commission that such person has engaged or is about to engage in any such acts or practices, a permanent or temporary injunction, restraining order, or other order may be granted.

Aug. 1, 1946, c. 724 § 232, formerly 230, as added Aug. 30, 1954, c. 1073, § 1, 68 Stat. 959, and renumbered Aug. 6, 1956, c. 1015, § 6, 70 Stat. 1070.

National Security Council and the Central Intelligence Agency

50 U.S.C. §401

Congressional Declaration of Purpose

In enacting sections 401-403, 404, and 405 of this title and sections 1, 171-171d, 171e-171j, 171k-171n, 172-172j, 181-1, 181-2, 411a, 411b, 626-626c, and 626d of Title 5, it is the intent of Congress to provide a comprehensive program for the future security of the United States; to provide for the establishment of integrated policies and procedures for the departments, agencies, and functions of the Government relating to the national security; to provide three military departments, separately administered, for the operation and administration of the Army, the Navy (including naval aviation and the United States Marine Corps), and the Air Force, with their assigned combat and service components; to provide for their authoritative coordination and unified direction under civilian control of the Secretary of Defense but not to merge them; to provide for the effective strategic direction of the armed forces and for their operation under unified control and for their integration into an efficient team of land, naval, and air forces but not to establish a single Chief of Staff over the armed forces nor an armed forces general staff (but this is not to be interpreted as applying to the Joint Chiefs of Staff or Joint Staff). July 26, 1947, c. 343, § 2, 61 Stat. 496; Aug. 10, 1949, c. 412, § 2, 63 Stat. 579.

50 U.S.C. §402

National Security Council—(a) Establishment; Presiding Officer; Functions; Composition

There is established a council to be known as the National Security Council (hereinafter in this section referred to as the "Council").

The President of the United States shall preside over meetings of the Council: *Provided,* That in his absence he may designate a member of the Council to preside in his place.

The function of the Council shall be to advise the President with respect to the integration of domestic, foreign, and military policies relating to the national security so as to enable the military services and the other departments and agencies of the Government to cooperate more effectively in matters involving the national security.

The Council shall be composed of—

(1) the President;

(2) the Vice President;

(3) the Secretary of State;

(4) the Secretary of Defense;

(5) the Director for Mutual Security;

(6) the Chairman of the National Security Resources Board; and

(7) The Secretaries and Under Secretaries of other executive departments and of the military departments, the Chairman of the Munitions Board, and the Chairman

of the Research and Development Board, when appointed by the President by and with the advice and consent of the Senate, to serve at his pleasure.

Additional Functions

(b) In addition to performing such other functions as the President may direct, for the purpose of more effectively coordinating the policies and functions of the departments and agencies of the Government relating to the national security, it shall, subject to the direction of the President, be the duty of the Council—

(1) to assess and appraise the objectives, commitments, and risks of the United States in relation to our actual and potential military power, in the interest of national security, for the purpose of making recommendations to the President in connection therewith; and

(2) to consider policies on matters of common interest to the departments and agencies of the Government concerned with the national security, and to make recommendations to the President in connection therewith.

Executive Secretary; Appointment and Compensation; Staff Employees

(c) The Council shall have a staff to be headed by a civilian executive secretary who shall be appointed by the President, and who shall receive compensation at the rate of $10,000 a year. The executive secretary, subject to the direction of the Council, is authorized, subject to the civil-service laws and the Classification Act of 1949, to appoint and fix the compensation of such personnel as may be necessary to perform such duties as may be prescribed by the Council in connection with the performance of its functions.

Recommendations and Reports

(d) The Council shall, from time to time, make such recommendations, and such other reports to the President as it deems appropriate or as the President may require. July 26, 1947, c. 343, Title I, § 101, 61 Stat. 497; Aug. 10, 1949, c. 412, § 3, 63 Stat. 579; Oct. 28, 1949, c. 782, Title XI, § 1106(a), 63 Stat. 972; Oct. 10, 1951, c. 479, Title V, § 501(e) (1), 65 Stat. 378.

50 U.S.C. §403

Central Intelligence Agency—(a) Establishment; Director; Appointment and Compensation

There is established under the National Security Council a Central Intelligence Agency with a Director of Central Intelligence, who shall be the head thereof. The Director shall be appointed by the President, by and with the advice and consent of the Senate, from among the commissioned officers of the armed services or from among individuals in civilian life. The Director shall receive basic compensation at the rate of $16,000 per annum.

Commissioned Officer as Director; Powers and Limitations; Effect on Commissioned Status

(b) (1) If a commissioned officer of the armed services is appointed as Director then—

(A) in the performance of his duties as Director, he shall be subject to no supervision, control, restriction, or prohibition (military or otherwise) other than would be operative with respect to him if he were a civilian in no way connected with the Department of the Army, the Department of the Navy, the Department of the Air Force, or the armed services or any component thereof; and

(B) he shall not possess or exercise any supervision, control, powers, or functions (other than such as he possesses, or is authorized or directed to exercise, as Director) with respect to the armed services or any component thereof, the Department of the Army, the Department of the Navy, or the Department of the Air Force, or any branch, bureau, unit or division thereof, or with respect to any of the personnel (military or civilian) of any of the foregoing.

(2) Except as provided in paragraph (1) of this subsection, the appointment to the office of Director of a commissioned officer of the armed services, and his acceptance of and service in such office, shall in no way affect any status, office, rank, or grade he may occupy or hold in the armed services, or any emolument, prerequisite, right, privilege, or benefit incident to or arising out of any such status, office, rank, or grade. Any such commissioned officer shall, while serving in the office of Director, receive the military pay and allowances (active or retired, as the case may be) payable to a commissioned officer of his grade and length of service and shall be paid, from any funds available to defray the expenses of the Agency, annual compensation at a rate equal to the amount by which $16,000 exceeds the amount of his annual military pay and allowances.

Termination of Employment of Officers and Employees; Effect on Right of Subsequent Employment

(c) Notwithstanding the provisions of section 652 of Title 5, or the provisions of any other law, the Director of Central Intelligence may, in his discretion, terminate the employment of any officer or employee of the Agency whenever he shall deem such termination necessary or advisable in the interests of the United States, but such termination shall not affect the right of such officer or employee to seek or accept employment in any other department or agency of the Government if declared eligible for such employment by the United States Civil Service Commission.

Powers and Duties

(d) For the purpose of coordinating the intelligence activities of the several Government departments and agencies in the interest of national security, it shall be the duty of the Agency, under the direction of the National Security Council—

(1) to advise the National Security Council in matters concerning such intelligence activities of the Government departments and agencies as relate to national security;

(2) to make recommendations to the National Security Council for the coordination of such intelligence activities of the departments and agencies of the Government as relate to the national security;

(3) to correlate and evaluate intelligence relating to the national security, and provide for the appropriate dissemination of such intelligence within the Government using where appropriate existing agencies and facilities: *Provided,* That the Agency shall have no police, subpena, law-enforcement powers, or internal-security functions: *Provided further,* That the departments and other agencies of the Government shall continue to collect, evaluate, correlate, and disseminate depart-

mental intelligence: *And provided further,* That the Director of Central Intelligence shall be responsible for protecting intelligence sources and methods from unauthorized disclosure;

(4) to perform, for the benefit of the existing intelligence agencies, such additional services of common concern as the National Security Council determines can be more efficiently accomplished centrally;

(5) to perform such other functions and duties related to intelligence affecting the national security as the National Security Council may from time to time direct.

Inspection of Intelligence of Other Departments

(e) To the extent recommended by the National Security Council and approved by the President, such intelligence of the departments and agencies of the Government, except as hereinafter provided, relating to the national security shall be open to the inspection of the Director of Central Intelligence, and such intelligence as relates to the national security and is possessed by such departments and other agencies of the Government, except as hereinafter provided, shall be made available to the Director of Central Intelligence for correlation, evaluation, and dissemination: *Provided, however,* That upon the written request of the Director of Central Intelligence, the Director of the Federal Bureau of Investigation shall make available to the Director of Central Intelligence such information for correlation, evaluation, and dissemination as may be essential to the national security.

Termination of National Intelligence Authority; Transfer of Personnel, Property, Records, and Unexpended Funds

(f) Effective when the Director first appointed under subsection (a) of this section has taken office—

(1) the National Intelligence Authority (11 Fed. Reg. 1337, 1339, February 5, 1946) shall cease to exist; and

(2) the personnel, property, and records of the Central Intelligence Group are transferred to the Central Intelligence Agency, and such Group shall cease to exist. Any unexpended balances of appropriations, allocations, or other funds available or authorized to be made available for such Group shall be available and shall be authorized to be made available in like manner for expenditure by the Agency. July 26, 1947, c. 343, Title I, § 102, 61 Stat. 497; Oct. 15, 1949, c. 695, § 4, 63 Stat. 880.

50 U.S.C. §403a

Same; Definitions

When used in sections 403b-403j of this title, the term—

(a) "Agency" means the Central Intelligence Agency;

(b) "Director" means the Director of Central Intelligence;

(c) "Government agency" means any executive department, commission, council, independent establishment, corporation wholly or partly owned by the United States which is an instrumentality of the United States, board, bureau, division, service, office, officer, authority, administration, or other establishment, in the executive branch of the Government; and

(d) "Continental United States" means the States and the District of Columbia. June 20, 1949, c. 227, § 1, 63 Stat. 208.

50 U.S.C. §403b

Same; Seal of Office

The Director of Central Intelligence shall cause a seal of office to be made for the Central Intelligence Agency, of such design as the President shall approve, and judicial notice shall be taken thereof. June 20, 1949, c. 227, § 2, 63 Stat. 208.

50 U.S.C. §403c

Same; Procurement Authority

(a) In the performance of its functions the Central Intelligence Agency is authorized to exercise the authorities contained in sections 151(c) (1-6), (10), (12), (15), (17)-155 and 159 of Title 41.

(b) In the exercise of the authorities granted in subsection (a) of this section, the term "Agency head" shall mean the Director, the Deputy Director, or the Executive of the Agency.

(c) The determinations and decisions provided in subsection (a) of this section to be made by the Agency head may be made with respect to individual purchases and contracts or with respect to classes of purchases or contracts, and shall be final. Except as provided in subsection (d) of this section, the Agency head is authorized to delegate his powers provided in this section, including the making of such determinations and decisions, in his discretion and subject to his direction, to any other officer or officers or officials of the Agency.

(d) The power of the Agency head to make the determinations or decisions specified in sections 151(c) (12), (15) and 154(a) of Title 41 shall not be delegable. Each determination or decision required by sections 151(c) (12), (15), 153, or 154(a) of Title 41, shall be based upon written findings made by the official making such determinations, which findings shall be final and shall be available within the Agency for a period of at least six years following the date of the determination. June 20, 1949, c. 227, § 3, 63 Stat. 208.

50 U.S.C. §403d

Same; Education and Training of Officers and Employees

(a) Any officer or employee of the Agency may be assigned or detailed for special instruction, research, or training, at or with domestic or foreign public or private institutions; trade, labor, agricultural, or scientific associations; courses or training programs under the Department of Defense; or commercial firms.

(b) The Agency shall, under such regulations as the Director may prescribe, pay the tuition and other expenses of officers and employees of the Agency assigned or detailed in accordance with provisions of subsection (a) of this section, in addition to pay and allowances to which such officers and employees may be otherwise entitled. June 20, 1949, c. 227, § 4, 63 Stat. 208; Aug. 10, 1949, c. 412, § 12(a), 63 Stat. 591.

50 U.S.C. §403e

Same; Travel, Allowances, and Related Expenses

(a) Under such regulations as the Director may prescribe, the Agency, with respect to its officers and employees assigned to permanent-duty stations outside the continental United States, its territories, and possessions, shall—

(1) (A) pay the travel expenses of officers and employees of the Agency including expenses incurred while traveling pursuant to orders issued by the Director in accordance with the provisions of subsection (a) (3) of this section with regard to the granting of home leave;

(B) pay the travel expenses of members of the family of an officer or employee of the Agency when proceeding to or returning from his post of duty; accompanying him on authorized home leave; or otherwise traveling in accordance with authority granted pursuant to the terms of sections 403a-403j of this title or any other Act;

(C) pay the cost of transporting the furniture and household and personal effects of an officer or employee of the Agency to his successive posts of duty and, on the termination of his services, to his residence at time of appointment or to a point not more distant, or, upon retirement, to the place where he will reside;

(D) pay the cost of storing the furniture and household and personal effects of an officer or employee of the Agency who is absent under orders from his usual post of duty, or who is assigned to a post to which, because of emergency conditions, he cannot take or at which he is unable to use, his furniture and household and personal effects;

(E) pay the cost of storing the furniture and household and personal effects of an officer or employee of the Agency on first arrival at a post for a period not in excess of three months after such first arrival at such post or until the establishment of residence quarters, whichever shall be shorter;

(F) pay the travel expenses and transportation costs incident to the removal of the members of the family of an officer or employee of the Agency and his furniture and household and personal effects, including automobiles, from a post at which, because of the prevalence of disturbed conditions, there is imminent danger to life and property, and the return of such persons, furniture, and effects to such post upon the cessation of such conditions; or to such other post as may in the meantime have become the post to which such officer or employee has been assigned.

(2) Charge expenses in connection with travel of personnel, their dependents, and transportation of their household goods and personal effects, involving a change of permanent station, to the appropriation for the fiscal year current when any part of either the travel or transportation pertaining to the transfer begins pursuant to previously issued travel and transfer orders, notwithstanding the fact that such travel or transportation may not all be effected during such fiscal year, or the travel and transfer orders may have been issued during the prior fiscal year.

(3) (A) Order to the United States or its Territories and possessions on leave provided for in sections 30-30b of Title 5, or as such sections may hereafter be amended, every officer and employee of the Agency who was a resident of the United States or its Territories and possessions at time of employment, upon completion of two years' continuous service abroad, or as soon as possible thereafter: *Provided,* That such officer or employee has accrued to his credit at the time of such order, annual leave sufficient to carry him in a pay status while in the United States for at least a thirty-day period.

(B) While in the continental United States on leave, the service of any officer or employee shall not be available for work or duties except in the Agency or for training or for reorientation for work; and the time of such work or duty shall not be counted as leave.

(C) Where an officer or employee on leave returns to the United States or its Territories and possessions, leave of absence granted shall be exclusive of the time actually and necessarily occupied in going to and from the United States or its Territories and possessions, and such time as may be necessarily occupied in awaiting transportation.

(4) Notwithstanding the provisions of any other law, transport for or on behalf of an officer or employee of the Agency, a privately owned automobile in any case where it shall be determined that water, rail, or air transportation of the automobile is necessary or expedient for any part or of all the distance between points of origin and destination, and pay the costs of such transportation.

(5) (A) In the event of illness or injury requiring the hospitalization of an officer or full time employee of the Agency, not the result of vicious habits, intemperance, or misconduct on his part, incurred while on assignment abroad, in a locality where there does not exist a suitable hospital or clinic, pay the travel expenses of such officer or employee by whatever means he shall deem appropriate and without regard to the Standardized Government Travel Regulations and section 73b of Title 5, to the nearest locality where a suitable hospital or clinic exists and on his recovery pay for the travel expenses of his return to his post of duty. If the officer or employee is too ill to travel unattended, the Director may also pay the travel expenses of an attendant;

(B) Establish a first-aid station and provide for the services of a nurse at a post at which, in his opinion, sufficient personnel is employed to warrant such a station: *Provided,* That, in his opinion, it is not feasible to utilize an existing facility;

(C) In the event of illness or injury requiring hospitalization of an officer or full time employee of the Agency, not the result of vicious habits, intemperance, or misconduct on his part, incurred in the line of duty while such person is assigned abroad, pay for the cost of the treatment of such illness or injury at a suitable hospital or clinic;

(D) Provide for the periodic physical examination of officers and employees of the Agency and for the cost of administering inoculations or vaccinations to such officers or employees.

(6) Pay the costs of preparing and transporting the remains of an officer or employee of the Agency or a member of his family who may die while in travel status or abroad, to his home or official station, or to such other place as the Director may determine to be the appropriate place of interment, provided that in no case shall the expense payable be greater than the amount which would have been payable had the destination been the home or official station.

(7) Pay the costs of travel of new appointees and their dependents, and the transportation of their household goods and personal effects, from places of actual residence in foreign countries at time of appointment to places of employment and return to their actual residences at the time of appointment or a point not more distant: *Provided,* That such appointees agree in writing to remain with the United States Government for a period of not less than twelve months from the time of appointment.

Violation of such agreement for personal convenience of an employee or because of separation for misconduct will bar such return payments and, if determined by the Director or his designee to be in the best interests of the United States, any money expended by the United States on account of such travel and transportation shall be considered as a debt due by the individual concerned to the United States.

(b) In accordance with such regulations as the President may prescribe and notwithstanding the provisions of section 70 of Title 5, the Director is authorized to grant to any officer or employee of the Agency allowances in accordance with the provisions of section 1131(1), (2) of Title 22. June 20, 1949, c. 227, § 5, 63 Stat. 209.

50 U.S.C. §403f

Same; General Authorities of Agency

In the performance of its functions, the Central Intelligence Agency is authorized to—

(a) Transfer to and receive from other Government agencies such sums as may be approved by the Bureau of the Budget, for the performance of any of the functions or activities authorized under sections 403 and 405 of this title, and any other Government agency is authorized to transfer to or receive from the Agency such sums without regard to any provisions of law limiting or prohibiting transfers between appropriations. Sums transferred to the Agency in accordance with this paragraph may be expended for the purposes and under the authority of sections 403a-403j of this title without regard to limitations of appropriations from which transferred;

(b) Exchange funds without regard to section 543 of Title 31;

(c) Reimburse other Government agencies for services of personnel assigned to the Agency, and such other Government agencies are authorized, without regard to provisions of law to the contrary, so to assign or detail any officer or employee for duty with the Agency;

(d) Authorize couriers and guards designated by the Director to carry firearms when engaged in transportation of confidential documents and materials affecting the national defense and security;

(e) Make alterations, improvements, and repairs on premises rented by the Agency, and pay rent therefor without regard to limitations on expenditures contained in the Act of June 30, 1932, as amended: *Provided,* That in each case the Director shall certify that exception from such limitations is necessary to the successful performance of the Agency's functions or to the security of its activities.

(f) (1) Notwithstanding section 62 of Title 5, or any other law prohibiting the employment of any retired commissioned or warrant officer of the armed services, the Agency is authorized to employ and to pay the compensation of not more than fifteen retired officers or warrant officers of the armed services while performing service for the Agency, but while so serving such retired officer or warrant officer will be entitled to receive only the compensation of his position with the Agency, or his retired pay, whichever he may elect.

(2) Nothing in this section shall limit or affect the appointment of and payment of compensation to retired officers or warrant officers not presently or hereafter prohibited by law. June 20, 1949, c. 227, § 6, 63 Stat. 211; June 26, 1951, c. 151, 65 Stat. 89.

50 U.S.C. §403g

Same; Protection of Nature of Agency's Functions

In the interests of the security of the foreign intelligence activities of the United States and in order further to implement the proviso of section 403(d) (3) of this title that the Director of Central Intelligence shall be responsible for protecting intelligence sources and methods from unauthorized disclosure, the Agency shall be exempted from the provisions of section 654 of Title 5, and the provisions of any other law which require the publication or disclosure of the organization, functions, names, official titles, salaries, or numbers of personnel employed by the Agency: *Provided,* That in furtherance of this section, the Director of the Bureau of the Budget shall make no reports to the Congress in connection with the Agency under section 947(b) of Title 5. June 20, 1949, c. 227, § 7, 63 Stat. 211.

50 U.S.C. §403h

Same; Admission of Essential Aliens; Limitation on Number

Whenever the Director, the Attorney General, and the Commissioner of Immigration shall determine that the entry of a particular alien into the United States for permanent residence is in the interest of national security or essential to the furtherance of the national intelligence mission, such alien and his immediate family shall be given entry into the United States for permanent residence without regard to their inadmissibility under the immigration or any other laws and regulations, or to the failure to comply with such laws and regulations pertaining to admissibility: *Provided,* That the number of aliens and members of their immediate families entering the United States under the authority of this section shall in no case exceed one hundred persons in any one fiscal year. June 20, 1949, c. 227, § 8, 63 Stat. 212.

50 U.S.C. §403i

Same; Positions in Professional and Scientific Field; Number; Compensation

The Director is authorized to establish and fix the compensation for not more than three positions in the professional and scientific field, within the Agency, each such position being established to effectuate those scientific intelligence functions relating to national security, which require the services of specially qualified scientific or professional personnel: *Provided,* That the rates of compensation for positions established pursuant to the provisions of this section shall not be less than $13,100 per annum nor more than $15,000 per annum, and shall be subject to the approval of the Civil Service Commission. June 20, 1949, c. 227, § 9, 63 Stat. 212; Aug. 16, 1950, c. 719, 64 Stat. 450.

50 U.S.C. §403j

Same; Appropriations; Expenditures

(a) Notwithstanding any other provisions of law, sums made available to the Agency by appropriation or otherwise may be expended for purposes necessary to carry out its functions, including—

(1) personal services, including personal services without regard to limitations on types of persons to be employed, and rent at the seat of government and elsewhere; health-service program as authorized by section 150 of Title 5; rental of news-reporting services; purchase or rental and operation of photographic, reproduction, cryptographic, duplication and printing machines, equipment and devices, and radio-receiving and radio-sending equipment and devices, including telegraph and teletype equipment; purchase, maintenance, operation, repair, and hire of passenger motor vehicles, and aircraft, and vessels of all kinds; subject to policies established by the Director, transportation of officers and employees of the Agency in Government-owned automotive equipment between their domiciles and places of employment, where such personnel are engaged in work which makes such transportation necessary, and transportation in such equipment, to and from school, of children of Agency personnel who have quarters for themselves and their families at isolated stations outside the continental United States where adequate public or private transportation is not available; printing and binding; purchase, maintenance, and cleaning of firearms, including purchase, storage, and maintenance of ammunition; subject to policies established by the Director, expenses of travel in connection with, and expenses incident to attendance at meetings of professional, technical, scientific, and other similar organizations when such attendance would be a benefit in the conduct of the work of the Agency; association and library dues; payment of premiums or costs of surety bonds for officers or employees without regard to the provisions of section 14 of Title 6; payment of claims pursuant to Title 28; acquisition of necessary land and the clearing of such land; construction of buildings and facilities without regard to sections 259 and 267 of Title 40; repair, rental, operation, and maintenance of buildings, utilities, facilities, and appurtenances; and

(2) supplies, equipment, and personnel and contractual services otherwise authorized by law and regulations, when approved by the Director.

(b) The sums made available to the Agency may be expended without regard to the provisions of law and regulations relating to the expenditure of Government funds; and for objects of a confidential, extraordinary, or emergency nature, such expenditures to be accounted for solely on the certificate of the Director and every such certificate shall be deemed a sufficient voucher for the amount therein certified. June 20, 1949, c. 227, § 10, 63 Stat. 212.

50 U.S.C. §404

National Security Resources Board—(a) Establishment; Composition; Appointment and Compensation of Chairman

There is established a National Security Resources Board (hereinafter in this section referred to as the "Board") to be composed of the Chairman of the Board and such heads or representatives of the various executive departments and independent agencies as may from time to time be designated by the President to be members of the Board. The Chairman of the Board shall be appointed from civilian life by the President, by and with the advice and consent of the Senate, and shall receive basic compensation at the rate of $17,500 a year.

Employment and Compensation of Employees

(b) The Chairman of the Board, subject to the direction of the President, is authorized, subject to the civil-service laws and the Classification Act of 1949, to appoint and fix the compensation of such personnel as may be necessary to assist the Chairman of the Board in carrying out his functions.

Functions

(c) It shall be the function of the Chairman of the Board to advise the President concerning the coordination of military, industrial, and civilian mobilization, including—

(1) policies concerning industrial and civilian mobilization in order to assure the most effective mobilization and maximum utilization of the Nation's manpower in the event of war;

(2) programs for the effective use in time of war of the Nation's natural and industrial resources for military and civilian needs, for the maintenance and stabilization of the civilian economy in time of war, and for the adjustment of such economy to war needs and conditions;

(3) policies for unifying, in time of war, the activities of Federal agencies and departments engaged in or concerned with production, procurement, distribution, or transportation of military or civilian supplies, materials, and products;

(4) the relationship between potential supplies of, and potential requirements for, manpower, resources, and productive facilities in time of war;

(5) policies for establishing adequate reserves of strategic and critical material, and for the conservation of these reserves;

(6) the strategic relocation of industries, services, government, and economic activities, the continuous operation of which is essential to the Nation's security.

Utilization of Government Resources and Facilities

(d) In performing his functions, the Chairman of the Board shall utilize to the maximum extent the facilities and resources of the departments and agencies of the Government. July 26, 1947, c. 343, Title I, § 103, 61 Stat. 499; Oct. 15, 1949, c. 695, § 3, 63 Stat. 880; Oct. 28, 1949, c. 782, Title XI, § 1106(a), 63 Stat. 972; 1950 Reorg. Plan No. 25, eff. July 9, 1950, 15 F.R. 4366, 64 Stat. 1280.

50 U.S.C. §405

Advisory Committees; Appointment; Compensation of Part Time Personnel; Applicability of Other Laws

(a) The Chairman of the National Security Resources Board, the Director of Central Intelligence, and the National Security Council, acting through its Executive Secretary, are authorized to appoint such advisory committees and to employ, consistent with other provisions of sections 171-171d, 171e-171j, 171k-171n, 172-172j, 181-1, 181-2, 411a, 411b, 626-626c, and 626d of Title 5 and sections

401-403, 404, and 405 of this title, such part-time advisory personnel as they may deem necessary in carrying out their respective functions and the functions of agencies under their control. Persons holding other offices or positions under the United States for which they receive compensation, while serving as members of such committees, shall receive no additional compensation for such service. Other members of such committees and other part-time advisory personnel so employed may serve without compensation or may receive compensation at a rate not to exceed $50 for each day of service, as determined by the appointing authority.

(b) Service of an individual as a member of any such advisory committee, or in any other part-time capacity for a department or agency hereunder, shall not be considered as service bringing such individual within the provisions of section 198 or 203 of Title 18, or section 119, sixth paragraph, of Title 41, unless the act of such individual, which by such section is made unlawful when performed by an individual referred to in such section, is with respect to any particular matter which directly involves a department or agency which such person is advising or in which such department or agency is directly interested. July 26, 1947, c. 343, Title III, § 303, 61 Stat. 508; Aug. 10, 1949, c. 412, § 10(c), 63 Stat. 585.

Internal Security Act of 1950

64 Stat. 987*

Title I—Subversive Activities Control

Section 1. (a) This title may be cited as the "Subversive Activities Control Act of 1950".

(b) Nothing in this Act shall be construed to authorize, require, or establish military or civilian censorship or in any way to limit or infringe upon freedom of the press or of speech as guaranteed by the Constitution of the United States and no regulation shall be promulgated hereunder having that effect.

National Security Agency

73 Stat. 63
May 29, 1959

An Act

To provide certain administrative authorities for the National Security Agency, and for other purposes.

Be it enacted by the Senate and House of Representatives of the United States of America in Congress assembled, That section 202 of the Classification Act of 1949, as amended (5 U.S.C. 1082), is amended by changing the period at the end thereof to a semicolon and adding the following new paragraph:

"(32) the National Security Agency."

Sec. 2. The Secretary of Defense (or his designee for the purpose) is authorized to establish such positions, and to appoint thereto such officers and employees, in the National Security Agency, as may be necessary to carry out the functions of such agency. The rates of basic compensation for such positions shall be fixed by the Secretary of Defense (or his designee for the purpose) in relation to the rates of basic compensation contained in the General Schedule of the Classification Act of 1949, as amended, for positions subject to such Act which have corresponding levels of duties and responsibilities. Except as provided in section 4 of this Act, no officer or employee of the National Security Agency shall be paid basic compensation at a rate in excess of the highest rate of basic compensation contained in such General Schedule. Not more than fifty such officers and employees shall be paid basic compensation at rates equal to rates of basic compensation contained in grades 16, 17, and 18 of such General Schedule.

Sec. 3. Section 1581(a) of title 10, United States Code, as modified by section 12(a) of the Federal Employees Salary Increase Act of 1958 (72 Stat. 213), is amended by striking out ", and not more than fifty civilian positions in the National Security Agency," and the words "and the National Security Agency, respectively,".

Sec. 4. The Secretary of Defense (or his designee for the purpose) is authorized to establish in the National Security Agency not more than fifty civilian positions involving research and development functions, which require the services of specially qualified scientific or professional personnel, and fix the rates of basic compensation for such positions at rates not in excess of the maximum rate of compensation authorized by section 1581(b) of title 10, United States Code, as amended by paragraph (34)(B) of the first section of the Act of September 2, 1958 (72 Stat. 1456; Public Law 85-861).

Sec. 5. Officers and employees of the National Security Agency who are citizens or nationals of the United States may be granted additional compensation, in accordance with regulations which shall be prescribed by the Secretary of Defense, not in excess of additional compensation authorized by section 207 of the Independent Offices Appropriation Act, 1949, as amended (5 U.S.C. 118h), for employees whose rates of basic compensation are fixed by statute.

Sec. 6. (a) Except as provided in subsection (b) of this section, nothing in this Act or any other law (including, but not limited to, the first section and section 2 of the Act of August 28, 1935 (5 U.S.C. 654)) shall be construed to require the disclosure of the organization or any function of the National Security Agency, of any information with respect to the activities thereof, or of the names, titles, salaries, or number of the persons employed by such agency.

(b) The reporting requirements of section 1582 of title 10, United States Code, shall apply to positions established in the National Security Agency in the manner provided by section 4 of this Act.

Sec. 7. The total number of positions authorized by section 505(b) of the Classification Act of 1949, as amended (5 U.S.C. 1105(b)), to be placed in grades 16, 17, and 18 of the General Schedule of such Act at any time shall be deemed to have been reduced by the number of positions in such grades allocated to the National Security Agency immediately prior to the effective date of this section.

Sec. 8. The foregoing provisions of this Act shall take effect on the first day of the first pay period which begins later than the thirtieth day following the date of enactment of this Act.

Approved May 29, 1959.

Secrecy in Government

Executive Order 11652
37 Federal Register 5209 (1972)

Part 3—Classification of Information

Title 3—The President

Classification and Declassification of National Security Information and Material

The interests of the United States and its citizens are best served by making information regarding the affairs of Government readily available to the public. This concept of an informed citizenry is reflected in the Freedom of Information Act and in the current public information policies of the executive branch.

Within the Federal Government there is some official information and material which, because it bears directly on the effectiveness of our national defense and the conduct of our foreign relations, must be subject to some constraints for the security of our Nation and the safety of our people and our allies. To protect against actions hostile to the United States, of both an overt and covert nature, it is essential that such official information and material be given only limited dissemination.

This official information or material, referred to as classified information or material in this order, is expressly exempted from public disclosure by Section 552(b) (1) of Title 5, United States Code. Wrongful disclosure of such information or material is recognized in the Federal Criminal Code as providing a basis for prosecution.

To ensure that such information and material is protected, but only to the extent and for such period as is necessary, this order identifies the information to be protected, prescribes classification, downgrading, declassification and safeguarding procedures to be followed, and establishes a monitoring system to ensure its effectiveness.

Now, therefore, by virtue of the authority vested in me by the Constitution and statutes of the United States, it is hereby ordered:

Section 1. *Security Classification Categories.* Official information or material which requires protection against unauthorized disclosure in the interest of the national defense or foreign relations of the United States (hereinafter collectively termed "national security") shall be classified in one of three categories, namely "Top Secret," "Secret," or "Confidential," depending upon the degree of its significance to national security. No other categories shall be used to identify official information or material as requiring protection in the interest of national security, except as otherwise expressly provided by statute. These classification categories are defined as follows:

(A) *"Top Secret."* "Top Secret" refers to that national security information or material which requires the highest degree of protection. The test for assigning "Top Secret" classification shall be whether its unauthorized disclosure could reasonably be expected to cause exceptionally grave damage to the national security. Examples of "exceptionally grave damage" include armed hostilities against the United States or its allies: disruption of foreign relations vitally affecting the national security; the compromise of vital national defense plans or complex cryptologic and communications intelligence systems; the revelation of sensitive intelligence operations; and the disclosure of scientific or technological developments vital to national security. This classification shall be used with the utmost restraint.

(B) *"Secret."* "Secret" refers to that national security information or material which requires a substantial degree of protection. The test for assigning "Secret" classification shall be whether its unauthorized disclosure could reasonably be expected to cause serious damage to the national security. Examples of "serious damage" include disruption of foreign relations significantly affecting the national security; significant impairment of a program or policy directly related to the national security; revelation of significant military plans or intelligence operations; and compromise of significant scientific or technological developments relating to national security. The classification "Secret" shall be sparingly used.

(C) *"Confidential."* "Confidential" refers to that national security information or material which requires protection. The test for assigning "Confidential" classification shall be whether its unauthorized disclosure could reasonably be expected to cause damage to the national security.

Sec. 2. *Authority to Classify.* The authority to originally classify information or material under this order shall be restricted solely to those offices within the executive branch which are concerned with matters of national security, and shall be limited to the minimum number absolutely required for efficient administration. Except as the context may otherwise indicate, the term "Department" as used in this order shall include agency or other governmental unit.

(A) The authority to originally classify information or material under this order as "Top Secret" shall be exercised only by such officials as the President may designate in writing and by:

(1) The heads of the Departments listed below:

(2) Such of their senior principal deputies and assistants as the heads of such Departments may designate in writing; and

(3) Such heads and senior principal deputies and assistants of major elements of such Departments, as the heads of such Departments may designate in writing.

Such offices in the Executive Office of the President as the President may designate in writing
Central Intelligence Agency
Atomic Energy Commission
Department of State
Department of the Treasury
Department of Defense
Department of the Army
Department of the Navy
Department of the Air Force
United States Arms Control and Disarmament Agency
Department of Justice
National Aeronautics and Space Administration
Agency for International Development

(B) The authority to originally classify information or material under this order as "Secret" shall be exercised only by:

(1) Officials who have "Top Secret" classification authority;

(2) Such subordinates as officials with "Top Secret" classification authority under (A) (1) and (2) above may designate in writing; and

(3) The heads of the following named Departments and such senior principal deputies or assistants as they may designate in writing.

Department of Transportation
Federal Communications Commission
Export-Import Bank of the United States
Department of Commerce
United States Civil Service Commission
United States Information Agency
General Services Administration
Department of Health, Education, and Welfare
Civil Aeronautics Board
Federal Maritime Commission
Federal Power Commission
National Science Foundation
Overseas Private Investment Corporation

(C) The authority to originally classify information or material under this order as "Confidential" may be exercised by officials who have "Top Secret" or "Secret" classification authority and such officials as they may designate in writing.

(D) Any Department not referred to herein and any Department or unit established hereafter shall not have authority to originally classify information or material under this order, unless specifically authorized hereafter by an Executive order.

Sec. 3. *Authority to Downgrade and Declassify:* The authority to downgrade and declassify national security information or material shall be exercised as follows:

(A) Information or material may be downgraded or declassified by the official authorizing the original declassification, by a successor in capacity or by a supervisory official of either.

(B) Downgrading and declassification authority may also be exercised by an official specifically authorized under regulations issued by the head of the Department listed in Section 2 (A) or (B) hereof.

(C) In the case of classified information or material officially transferred by or pursuant to statute or Executive order in conjunction with a transfer of function and not merely for storage purposes, the receiving Department shall be deemed to be the originating Department for all purposes under this order including downgrading and declassification.

(D) In the case of classified information or material not officially transferred within (C) above, but originated in a Department which has since ceased to exist, each Department in possession shall be deemed to be the originating Department for all purposes under this order. Such information or material may be downgraded and declassified by the Department in possession after consulting with any other Departments having an interest in the subject matter.

(E) Classified information or material transferred to the General Services Administration for accession into the Archives of the United States shall be downgraded and declassified by the Archivist of the United States in accordance with this order, directives of the President issued through the National Security Council and pertinent regulations of the Departments.

(F) Classified information or material with special markings, as described in Section 8, shall be downgraded and declassified as required by law and governing regulations.

Sec. 4. *Classification.* Each person possessing classifying authority shall be held accountable for the propriety of the classifications attributed to him. Both unnecessary classification and over-classification shall be avoided. Classification shall be solely on the basis of national security considerations. In no case shall information be classified in order to conceal inefficiency or administrative error, to prevent embarrassment to a person or Department, to restrain competition or independent initiative or to prevent for any other reason the release of information which does not require protection in the interest of national security. The following rules shall apply to classification of information under this order:

(A) *Documents in General.* Each classified document shall show on its face its classification and whether it is subject to or exempt from the General Declassification Schedule. It shall also show the office of origin, the date of preparation and classification and, to the extent practicable, be so marked as to indicate which portions are classified, at what level, and which portions are not classified in order to facilitate excerpting and other use. Material containing references to classified materials, which references do not reveal classified information, shall not be classified.

(B) *Identification of Classifying Authority.* Unless the Department involved shall have provided some other method of identifying the individual at the highest level that authorized classification in each case, material classified under this order shall indicate on its face the identity of the highest authority authorizing the classification. Where the individual who signs or otherwise authenticates a document or item has also authorized the classification, no further annotation as to his identity is required.

(C) *Information or Material Furnished by a Foreign Government or International Organization.* Classified information or material furnished to the United States by a foreign government or international organization shall either retain its original classification or be assigned a United States classification. In either case, the classification shall assure a degree of protection equivalent to that required by the government or international organization which furnished the information or material.

(D) *Classification Responsibilities.*—A holder of classified information or material shall observe and respect the classification assigned by the originator. If a holder believes that there is unnecessary classification, that the assigned classification is improper, or that the document is subject to declassification under this order, he shall so inform the originator who shall thereupon re-examine the classification.

Sec. 5. *Declassification and Downgrading.* Classified information and material, unless declassified earlier by the original classifying authority, shall be declassified and downgraded in accordance with the following rules:

(A) *General Declassification Schedule.* (1) "Top Secret." Information or material originally classified "Top Secret" shall become automatically downgraded to "Secret" at the end of the second full calendar year following the year in which it was originated, downgraded to "Confidential" at the end of the fourth full calendar year following the year in which it was originated, and declassified at the end of the tenth full calendar year following the year in which it was originated.

(2) *"Secret."* Information and material originally classified "Secret" shall become automatically downgraded to "Confidential" at the end of the second full calendar year following the year in which it was originated, and declassified at the end of the eighth full calendar year following the year in which it was originated.

(3) *"Confidential."* Information and material originally classified "Confidential" shall become automatically declassified at the end of the sixth full calendar year following the year in which it was originated.

(B) *Exemptions from General Declassification Schedule.* Certain classified information or material may warrant some degree of protection for a period exceeding that provided in the General Declassification Schedule. An official authorized to originally classify information or material "Top Secret" may exempt from the General Declassification Schedule any level of classified information or material originated by him or under his supervision if it falls within one of the categories described below. In each case such official shall specify in writing on the material the exemption category being claimed and, unless impossible, a date or event for automatic declassification. The use of the exemption authority shall be kept to the absolute minimum consistent with national security requirements and shall be restricted to the following categories:

(1) Classified information or material furnished by foreign governments or international organizations and held by the United States on the understanding that it be kept in confidence.

(2) Classified information or material specifically covered by statute, or pertaining to cryptography, or disclosing intelligence sources or methods.

(3) Classified information or material disclosing a system, plan, installation, project or specific foreign relations matter the continuing protection of which is essential to the national security.

(4) Classified information or material the disclosure of which would place a person in immediate jeopardy.

(C) *Mandatory Review of Exempted Material.* All classified information and material originated after the effective date of this order which is exempted under (B) above from the General Declassification Schedule shall be subject to a classification review by the originating Department at any time after the expiration of ten years from the date of origin provided:

(1) A Department or member of the public requests a review;

(2) The request describes the record with sufficient particularity to enable the Department to identify it; and

(3) The record can be obtained with only a reasonable amount of effort.

Information or material which no longer qualifies for exemption under (B) above shall be declassified. Information or material continuing to qualify under (B) shall be so marked and, unless impossible, a date for automatic declassification shall be set.

(D) *Applicability of the General Declassification Schedule to Previously Classified Material.* Information or material classified before the effective date of this order and which is assigned to Group 4 under Executive Order No. 10501, as amended by Executive Order No. 10964, shall be subject to the General Declassification Schedule. All other information or material classified before the effective date of this order, whether or not assigned to Groups 1, 2, or 3 of Executive Order No. 10501, as amended, shall be excluded from the General Declassification Schedule. However, at any time after the expiration of ten years from the date of origin it shall be subject to a mandatory classification review and disposition under the same conditions and criteria that apply to classified information and material created after the effective date of this order as set forth in (B) and (C) above.

(E) *Declassification of Classified Information or Material After Thirty Years.* All classified information or material which is thirty years old or more, whether originating before or after the effective date of this order, shall be declassified under the following conditions:

(1) All information and material classified after the effective date of this order

shall, whether or not declassification has been requested, become automatically declassified at the end of thirty full calendar years after the date of its original classification except for such specifically identified information or material which the head of the originating Department personally determines in writing at that time to require continued protection because such continued protection is essential to the national security or disclosure would place a person in immediate jeopardy. In such case, the head of the Department shall also specify the period of continued classification.

(2) All information and material classified before the effective date of this order and more than thirty years old shall be systematically reviewed for declassification by the Archivist of the United States by the end of the thirtieth full calendar year following the year in which it was originated. In his review, the Archivist will separate and keep protected only such information or material as is specifically identified by the head of the Department in accordance with (E) (1) above. In such case, the head of the Department shall also specify the period of continued classification.

(F) *Departments Which Do Not Have Authority For Original Classification.* The provisions of this section relating to the declassification of national security information or material shall apply to Departments which, under the terms of this order, do not have current authority to originally classify information or material, but which formerly had such authority under previous Executive orders.

Sec. 6. *Policy Directives on Access, Marking, Safekeeping, Accountability, Transmission, Disposition and Destruction of Classified Information and Material.* The President acting through the National Security Council shall issue directives which shall be binding on all Departments to protect classified information from loss or compromise. Such directives shall conform to the following policies:

(A) No person shall be given access to classified information or material unless such person has been determined to be trustworthy and unless access to such information is necessary for the performance of his duties.

(B) All classified information and material shall be appropriately and conspicuously marked to put all persons on clear notice of its classified contents.

(C) Classified information and material shall be used, possessed, and stored only under conditions which will prevent access by unauthorized persons or dissemination to unauthorized persons.

(D) All classified information and material disseminated outside the executive branch under Executive Order No. 10865 or otherwise shall be properly protected.

(E) Appropriate accountability records for classified information shall be established and maintained and such information and material shall be protected adequately during all transmissions.

(F) Classified information and material no longer needed in current working files or for reference or record purposes shall be destroyed or disposed of in accordance with the records disposal provisions contained in Chapter 33 of Title 44 of the United States Code and other applicable statutes.

(G) Classified information or material shall be reviewed on a systematic basis for the purpose of accomplishing downgrading, declassification, transfer, retirement and destruction at the earliest practicable date.

Sec. 7. *Implementation and Review Responsibilities.* (A) The National Security Council shall monitor the implementation of this order. To assist the National Security Council, an Interagency Classification Review Committee shall be established, composed of representatives of the Departments of State, Defense and

Justice, the Atomic Energy Commission, the Central Intelligence Agency and the National Security Council Staff and a Chairman designated by the President. Representatives of other Departments in the executive branch may be invited to meet with the Committee on matters of particular interest to those Departments. This Committee shall meet regularly and on a continuing basis shall review and take action to ensure compliance with this order, and in particular:

(1) The Committee shall oversee Department actions to ensure compliance with the provisions of this order and implementing directives issued by the President through the National Security Council.

(2) The Committee shall, subject to procedures to be established by it, receive, consider and take action on suggestions and complaints from persons within or without the government with respect to the administration of this order, and in consultation with the affected Department or Departments assure that appropriate action is taken on such suggestions and complaints.

(3) Upon request of the Committee Chairman, any Department shall furnish to the Committee any particular information or material needed by the Committee in carrying out its functions.

(B) To promote the basic purposes of this order, the head of each Department originating or handling classified information or material shall:

(1) Prior to the effective date of this order submit to the Interagency Classification Review Committee for approval a copy of the regulations it proposes to adopt pursuant to this order.

(2) Designate a senior member of his staff who shall ensure effective compliance with and implementation of this order and shall also chair a Departmental committee which shall have authority to act on all suggestions and complaints with respect to the Department's administration of this order.

(3) Undertake an initial program to familiarize the employees of his Department with the provisions of this order. He shall also establish and maintain active training and orientation programs for employees concerned with classified information or material. Such programs shall include, as a minimum, the briefing of new employees and periodic reorientation during employment to impress upon each individual his responsibility for exercising vigilance and care in complying with the provisions of this order: Additionally, upon termination of employment or contemplated temporary separation for a sixty-day period or more, employees shall be debriefed and each reminded of the provisions of the Criminal Code and other applicable provisions of law relating to penalties for unauthorized disclosure.

(C) The Attorney General, upon request of the head of a Department, his duly designated representative, or the Chairman of the above described Committee, shall personally or through authorized representatives of the Department of Justice render an interpretation of this order with respect to any question arising in the course of its administration.

Sec. 8. *Material Covered by the Atomic Energy Act.* Nothing in this order shall supersede any requirements made by or under the Atomic Energy Act of August 30, 1954, as amended. "Restricted Data," and material designated as "Formerly Restricted Data," shall be handled, protected, classified, downgraded and declassified in conformity with the provisions of the Atomic Energy Act of 1954, as amended, and the regulations of the Atomic Energy Commission.

Sec. 9. *Special Departmental Arrangements.* The originating Department or other appropriate authority may impose, in conformity with the provisions of this order, special requirements with respect to access, distribution and protection of classified information and material, including those which presently relate to communications intelligence, intelligence sources and methods and cryptography.

Sec. 10. *Exceptional Cases.* In an exceptional case when a person or Department not authorized to classify information originates information which is believed to require classification, such person or Department shall protect that information in the manner prescribed by this order. Such persons or Department shall transmit the information forthwith, under appropriate safeguards, to the Department having primary interest in the subject matter with a request that a determination be made as to classification.

Sec. 11. *Declassification of Presidential Papers.* The Archivist of the United States shall have authority to review and declassify information and material which has been classified by a President, his White House Staff or special committee or commission appointed by him and which the Archivist has in his custody at any archival depository, including a Presidential Library. Such declassification shall only be undertaken in accord with: (i) the terms of the donor's deed of gift, (ii) consultations with the Departments having a primary subject-matter interest, and (iii) the provisions of Section 5.

Sec. 12. *Historical Research and Access by Former Government Officials.* The requirement in Section 6(A) that access to classified information or material be granted only as is necessary for the performance of one's duties shall not apply to persons outside the executive branch who are engaged in historical research projects or who have previously occupied policy-making positions to which they were appointed by the President: *Provided,* however, that in each case the head of the originating Department shall:

(i) determine that access is clearly consistent with the interests of national security; and

(ii) take appropriate steps to assure that classified information or material is not published or otherwise compromised.

Access granted a person by reason of his having previously occupied a policy-making position shall be limited to those papers which the former official originated, reviewed, signed or received while in public office.

Sec. 13. *Administrative and Judicial Action.* (A) Any officer or employee of the United States who unnecessarily classifies or overclassifies information or material shall be notified that his actions are in violation of the terms of this order or of a directive of the President issued through the National Security Council. Repeated abuse of the classification process shall be grounds for an administrative reprimand. In any case where the Departmental committee or the Interagency Classification Review Committee finds that unnecessary classification or overclassification has occurred, it shall make a report to the head of the Department concerned in order that corrective steps may be taken.

(B) The head of each Department is directed to take prompt and stringent administrative action against any officer or employee of the United States, at any level of employment, determined to have been responsible for any release or disclosure of national security information or material in a manner not authorized by or under this order or a directive of the President issued through the National Security Council. Where a violation of criminal statutes may be involved, Departments will refer any such case promptly to the Department of Justice.

Sec. 14. *Revocation of Executive Order No. 10501.* Executive Order No. 10501 of November 5, 1953, as amended by Executive Orders No. 10816 of May 8, 1959, No. 10901 of January 11, 1961, No. 10964 of September 20, 1961, No. 10985 of

January 15, 1962, No. 11097 of March 6, 1963 and by Section 1(a) of No. 11382 of November 28, 1967, is superseded as of the effective date of this order.

Sec. 15. *Effective date.* This order shall become effective on June 1, 1972.

Richard Nixon.

The White House, *March 8, 1972.*

National Security Council Directive on Classification

37 Federal Register 98 (1972)

The President has directed that Executive Order 11652, "Classification and Declassification of National Security Information and Material," approved March 8, 1972 (37 F.R. 5209, March 10, 1972) be implemented in accordance with the following:

I. Authority to Classify

A. *Personal and Non-delegable.* Classification authority may be exercised only by those officials who are designated by, or in writing pursuant to, Section 2 of Executive Order 11652 (hereinafter the "Order"). Such officials may classify information or material only at the level authorized or below. This authority vests only to the official designated under the Order, and may not be delegated.

B. *Observance of Classification.* Whenever information or material classified by an official designated under A above is incorporated in another document or other material by any person other than the classifier, the previously assigned security classification category shall be reflected thereon together with the identity of the classifier.

C. *Identification of Classifier.* The person at the highest level authorizing the classification must be identified on the face of the information or material classified, unless the identity of such person might disclose sensitive intelligence information. In the latter instance the Department shall establish some other record by which the classifier can readily be identified.

D. *Record Requirement.* Each Department listed in Section 2(A) of the Order shall maintain a listing by name of the officials who have been designated in writing to have Top Secret classification authority. Each Department listed in Section 2 (A) and (B) of the Order shall also maintain separate listings by name of the persons designated in writing to have Secret authority and persons designated in writing to have Confidential authority. In cases where listing of the names of officials having classification authority might disclose sensitive intelligence information, the Department shall establish some other record by which such officials can readily be identified. The foregoing listings and records shall be compiled beginning July 1, 1972, and updated at least on a quarterly basis.

E. *Resolution of Doubts.* If the classifier has any substantial doubt as to which security classification category is appropriate, or as to whether the material should be classified at all, he should designate the less restrictive treatment.

II. Downgrading and Declassification

A. *General Declassification Schedule and Exemptions.* Classified information and material shall be declassified as soon as there are no longer any grounds for continued classification within the classification category definitions set forth in Section 1 of the Order. At the time of origination the classifier shall, whenever possible, clearly mark on the information or material specific date or event upon which downgrading or declassification shall occur. Such dates or events shall be as early as is permissible without causing damage to the national security as defined in Section 1 of the Order. Whenever earlier dates or events cannot be determined, the General Declassification Schedule set forth in Section 5(A) of the Order shall apply. If the information or material is exempted under Section 5(B) of the Order from the General Declassification Schedule, the classifier shall clearly mark the material to show that it is exempt and indicate the applicable exemption category. Unless impossible, the exempted information or material shall be assigned and clearly marked by the classifier with a specific date or event upon which declassification shall occur. Downgrading and declassification dates or events established in accordance with the foregoing, whether scheduled or non-scheduled, shall to the extent possible be carried forward and applied whenever the classified information or material is incorporated in other documents or material.

B. *Extracts and Compilations.* When classified information or material from more than one source is incorporated into a new document or other material, the document or other material shall be classified, downgraded or declassified in accordance with the provisions of the Order and Directives thereunder applicable to the information requiring the greatest protection.

C. *Materially Not Officially Transferred.* When a Department holding classified information or material under the circumstances described in Section 3(D) of the Order notifies another Department of its intention to downgrade or declassify, it shall allow the notified Department 30 days in which to express its objections before taking action.

D. *Declassification of Material 30 Years Old.* The head of each Department shall assign experienced personnel to assist the Archivist of the United States in the exercise of his responsibility under Section 5(E) of the Order to systematically review for declassification all materials classified before June 1, 1972, and more than 30 years old. Such personnel will: (1) provide guidance and assistance to archival employees in identifying and separating those materials originated in their Departments which are deemed to require continued classification; and (2) develop a list for submission to the head of the Department which identifies the materials so separated, with recommendations concerning continued classification. The head of the originating Department will then make the determination required under Section 5(E) of the Order and cause a list to be created which identifies the documentation included in the determination, indicates the reason for continued classification and specifies the date on which such material shall be declassified.

E. *Notification of Expedited Downgrading or Declassification.* When classified information or material is downgraded or declassified in a manner other than originally specified, whether scheduled or exempted, the classifier shall, to the extent practicable, promptly notify all addressees to whom the information or material was originally officially transmitted. In turn, the addressees shall notify any other known recipient of the classified information or material.

III. Review of Classified Material for Declassification Purposes

A. *Systematic Reviews.* All information and material classified after the effective date of the Order and determined in accordance with Chapter 21, 44 U.S.C. (82 Stat. 1287) to be of sufficient historical or other value to warrant preservation shall be systematically reviewed on a timely basis by each Department for the purpose of making such information and material publicly available in accordance with the determination regarding declassification made by the classifier under Section 5 of the Order. During each calendar year each Department shall segregate to the maximum extent possible all such information and material warranting preservation and becoming declassified at or prior to the end of such year. Promptly after the end of such year the Department responsible, or the Archives of the United States if transferred thereto, shall make the declassified information and material available to the public to the extent permitted by law.

B. *Review for Declassification of Classified Material Over 10 Years Old.* Each Department shall designate in its implementing regulations an office to which members of the public or Departments may direct requests for mandatory review for declassification under Section 5 (C) and (D) of the Order. This office shall in turn assign the request to the appropriate office for action. In addition, this office or the office which has been assigned action shall immediately acknowledge receipt of the request in writing. If the request requires the rendering of services for which fair and equitable fees should be charged pursuant to Title 5 of the Independent Offices Appropriations Act, 1952, 65 Stat. 290, 31 U.S.C. 483a the requester shall be so notified. The office which has been assigned action shall thereafter make a determination within 30 days of receipt or shall explain the reasons why further time is necessary. If at the end of 60 days from receipt of the request for review no determination has been made, the requester may apply to the Departmental Committee established by Section 7(B) of the Order for a determination. Should the office assigned action on a request for review determine that under the criteria set forth in Section 5(B) of the Order continued classification is required, the requester shall promptly be notified, and whenever possible, provided with a brief statement as to why the requested information or material cannot be declassified. The requester may appeal any such determination to the Departmental Committee and the notice of determination shall advise him of this right.

C. *Departmental Committee Review for Declassification.* The Departmental Committee shall establish procedures to review and act within 30 days upon all applications and appeals regarding requests for declassification. The Department head, acting through the Departmental Committee shall be authorized to over-rule previous determinations in whole or in part when, in its judgment, continued protection is no longer required. If the Departmental Committee determines that continued classification is required under the criteria of Section 5(B) of the Order it shall promptly so notify the requester and advise him that he may appeal the denial to the Interagency Classification Review Committee.

D. *Review of Classified Material Over 30 Years Old.* A request by a member of the public or by a Department under Section 5 (C) or (D) of the Order to review for declassification documents more than 30 years old shall be referred directly to the Archivist of the United States, and he shall have the requested documents reviewed for declassification in accordance with Part II.D. hereof. If the information or material requested has not been transferred to the General Services Administration for accession into the Archives, the Archivist shall, together with the head of the Department having custody, have the requested documents reviewed for declassification. Classification shall be continued in either case only where the head of the Department concerned makes at that time the personal determination required by Section 5(E) (1) of the Order. The Archivist shall promptly notify the requester of such determination and of his right to appeal the denial to the Interagency Classification Review Committee.

E. *Burden of Proof for Administrative Determinations.* For purposes of administrative determinations under B., C., or D. above, the burden of proof is on the originating Department to show that continued classification is warranted within the terms of the Order.

F. *Availability of Declassified Material.* Upon a determination under B., C., or D. above that the requested material no longer warrants classification it shall be declassified and made promptly available to the requester, if not otherwise exempt from disclosure under Section 552(b) of Title 5 U.S.C. (Freedom of Information Act) or other provision of law.

G. *Classification Review Requests.* As required by Section 5(C) of the Order, a request for classification review must describe the document with sufficient particularity to enable the Department to identify it and obtain it with a reasonable amount of effort. Whenever a request is deficient in its description of the record sought the requester should be asked to provide additional identifying information whenever possible. Before denying a request on the ground that it is unduly burdensome, the requester should be asked to limit his request to records that are reasonably obtainable. If none-the-less the requester does not describe the records sought with sufficient particularity, or the record requested cannot be obtained with a reasonable amount of effort, the requester shall be notified of the reasons why no action will be taken and of his right to appeal such decision.

IV. Marking Requirements

A. *When Document or Other Material is Prepared.* At the time of origination, each document or other material containing classified information shall be marked with its assigned security classification and whether it is subject to or exempt from the General Declassification Schedule.

(1) For marking documents which are subject to the General Declassification Schedule, the following stamp shall be used:

(TOP SECRET, SECRET OR CONFIDENTIAL) CLASSIFIED

BY --

SUBJECT TO GENERAL DECLASSIFICATION SCHEDULE OF EXECUTIVE ORDER 11652 AUTOMATICALLY DOWNGRADED AT TWO YEAR INTERVALS AND DECLASSIFIED ON DEC. 31

(insert year)

----

(2) For marking documents which are to be automatically declassified on a given event or date earlier than the General Declassification Schedule the following stamp shall be used:

(TOP SECRET, SECRET OR CONFIDENTIAL) CLASSIFIED

BY____
AUTOMATICALLY DECLASSIFIED ON (effective date or event) _______________

(3) For marking documents which are exempt from the General Declassification Schedule the following stamp shall be used:

(TOP SECRET, SECRET OR CONFIDENTIAL) CLASSIFIED
____
BY____
EXEMPT FROM GENERAL DECLASSIFICATION SCHEDULE OF EXECUTIVE ORDER 11652 EXEMPTION CATEGORY (§ 5B (1), (2), (3), or (4)) AUTOMATICALLY DECLASSIFIED ON (effective date or event, if any)

Should the classifier inadvertently fail to mark a document with one of the foregoing stamps the document shall be deemed to be subject to the General Declassification Schedule. The person who signs or finally approves a document or other material containing classified information shall be deemed to be the classifier. If the classifier is other than such person he shall be identified on the stamp as indicated.

The "Restricted Data" and "Formerly Restricted Data" stamps (H. below) are, in themselves, evidence of exemption from the General Declassification Schedule.

(B) *Overall and Page Marking of Documents.* The overall classification of a document, whether or not permanently bound, or any copy or reproduction thereof, shall be conspicuously marked or stamped at the top and bottom of the outside of the front cover (if any), on the title page (if any), on the first page, on the back page and on the outside of the back cover (if any). To the extent practicable each interior page of a document which is not permanently bound shall be conspicuously marked or stamped at the top and bottom according to its own content, including the designation "Unclassified" when appropriate.

C. *Paragraph Marking.* Whenever a classified document contains either more than one security classification category or unclassified information, each section, part or paragraph should be marked to the extent practicable to show its classification category or that it is unclassified.

D. *Material Other Than Documents.* If classified material cannot be marked, written notification of the information otherwise required in markings shall accompany such material.

E. *Transmittal Documents.* A transmittal document shall carry on it a prominent notation as to the highest classification of the information which is carried with it, and a legend showing the classification, if any, of the transmittal document standing alone.

F. *Wholly Unclassified Material Not Usually Marked.* Normally, unclassified material shall not be marked or stamped "Unclassified" unless the purpose of the marking is to indicate that a decision has been made not to classify it.

G. *Downgrading, Declassification and Upgrading Markings.* Whenever a change is made in the original classification or in the dates of downgrading or declassification of any classified information or material it shall be promptly and conspicuously marked to indicate the change, the authority for the action, the date of the action, and the identity of the person taking the action. In addition, all earlier classification markings shall be cancelled, if practicable, but in any event on the first page.

(1) *Limited Use of Posted Notice for Large Quantities of Material.* When the volume of information or material is such that prompt remarking of each classified item could not be accomplished without unduly interfering with operations, the custodian may attach downgrading, declassification or upgrading notices to the storage unit in lieu of the remarking otherwise required. Each notice shall indicate the change, the authority for the action, the date of the action, the identity of the person taking the action and the storage units to which it applies. When individual documents or other materials are withdrawn from such storage units they shall be promptly remarked in accordance with the change, or if the documents have been declassified, the old markings shall be cancelled.

(2) *Transfer of Stored Quantities Covered by Posted Notice.* When information or material subject to a posted downgrading, upgrading or declassification notice are withdrawn from one storage unit solely for transfer to another, or a storage unit containing such documents or other materials is transferred from one place to another, the transfer may be made without remarking if the notice is attached to or remains with each shipment.

H. *Additional Warning Notices.* In addition to the foregoing marking requirements, warning notices shall be prominently displayed on classified documents or materials as prescribed below. When display of these warning notices on the documents or other materials is not feasible, the warnings shall be included in the written notification of the assigned classification.

(1) *Restricted Data.* For classified information or material containing Restricted Data as defined in the Atomic Energy Act of 1954, as amended:

> "Restricted Data"
>
> This document contains Restricted Data as defined in the Atomic Energy Act of 1954. Its dissemination or disclosure to any unauthorized person is prohibited.

(2) *Formerly Restricted Data.* For classified information or material containing solely Formerly Restricted Data, as defined in Section 142.d., Atomic EnergyAct of 1954, as amended:

> "Formerly Restricted Data"
>
> Unauthorized disclosure subject to Administrative and Criminal Sanctions. Handle as Restricted Data in Foreign Dissemination. Section 144.b., Atomic Energy Act, 1954.

(3) *Information Other Than Restricted Data or Formerly Restricted Data.* For classified information or material furnished to persons outside the Executive Branch of Government other than as described in (1) and (2) above:

> "National Security Information"
>
> Unauthorized Disclosure Subject to Criminal Sanctions.

(4) *Sensitive Intelligence Information.* For classified information or material relating to sensitive intelligence sources and methods, the following warning notice shall be used, in addition to and in conjunction with those prescribed in (1), (2), or (3), above, as appropriate: "WARNING NOTICE—SENSITIVE INTELLIGENCE SOURCES AND METHODS INVOLVED"

V. Protection and Transmission of Classified Information

A. *General.* Classified information or material may be used, held, or stored only where there are facilities or under conditions adequate to prevent unauthorized persons from gaining access to it. Whenever such information or material is not under the personal supervision of an authorized person, the methods set forth in *Appendix A* hereto shall be used to protect it. Whenever such information or material is transmitted outside the originating Department the requirements of *Appendix B* hereto shall be observed.

B. *Loss or Possible Compromise.* Any person who has knowledge of the loss or possible compromise of classified information shall immediately report the circumstances to a designated official of his Department or organization. In turn, the originating Department and any other interested Department shall be notified about the loss or possible compromise in order that a damage assessment may be conducted. An immediate inquiry shall be initiated by the Department in which the loss or compromise occurred for the purpose of taking corrective measures and appropriate administrative, disciplinary, or legal action.

VI. Access and Accountability

A. *General Access Requirements.* Except as provided in B. and C. below, access to classified information shall be granted in accordance with the following:

(1) *Determination of Trustworthiness.* No person shall be given access to classified information or material unless a favorable determination has been made as to his trustworthiness. The determination of eligibility, referred to as a security clearance, shall be based on such investigations as the Department may require in accordance with the standards and criteria of E.O. 10450 and E.O. 10865 as appropriate.

(2) *Determination of Need-to-Know.* In addition to a security clearance, a person must have a need for access to the particular classified information or material sought in connection with the performance of his official duties or contractual obligations. The determination of that need shall be made by officials having responsibility for the classified information or material.

(3) *Administrative Withdrawal of Security Clearance.* Each Department shall make provision for administratively withdrawing the security clearance of any person who no longer requires access to classified information or material in connection with the performance of his official duties or contractual obligations. Likewise, when a person no longer needs access to a particular security classification category, the security clearance shall be adjusted to the classification category still required for the performance of his duties and obligations. In both instances, such action shall be without prejudice to the person's eligibility for a security clearance should the need again arise.

B. *Access by Historical Researchers.* Persons outside the Executive Branch engaged in historical research projects may be authorized access to classified information or material provided that the head of the originating Department determines that:

(1) The project and access sought conform to the requirements of Section 12 of the Order.

(2) The information or material requested is reasonably accessible and can be located and compiled with a reasonable amount of effort.

(3) The historical researcher agrees to safeguard the information or material in a manner consistent with the Order and Directives thereunder.

(4) The historical researcher agrees to authorize a review of his notes and manuscript for the sole purpose of determining that no classified information or materials is contained therein.

An authorization for access shall be valid for the period required but no longer than two years from the date of issuance unless renewed under regulations of the originating Department.

C. *Access by Former Presidential Appointees.* Persons who previously occupied policy making positions to which they were appointed by the President, other than those referred to in Section 11 of the Order, may be authorized access to classified information or material which they originated, reviewed, signed or received while in public office. Upon the request of any such former official, such information and material as he may identify shall be reviewed for declassification in accordance with the provisions of Section 5 of the Order.

D. *Consent of Originating Department to Dissemination by Recipient.* Except as otherwise provided by Section 102 of the National Security Act of 1947, 61 Stat. 495, 50 U.S.C. 403, classified information or material originating in one Department shall not be disseminated outside any other Department to which it has been made available without the consent of the originating Department.

E. *Dissemination of Sensitive Intelligence Information.* Information or material bearing the notation "WARNING NOTICE—SENSITIVE INTELLIGENCE SOURCES AND METHODS INVOLVED" shall not be disseminated in any manner outside authorized channels without the permission of the originating Department and an assessment by the senior intelligence official in the disseminating Department as to the potential risk to the national security and to the intelligence sources and methods involved.

F. *Restraint on Special Access Requirements.* The establishment of special rules limiting access to, distribution and protection of classified information and material under Section 9 of the Order requires the specific prior approval of the head of a Department or his designee.

G. *Accountability Procedures.* Each Department shall prescribe such accountability procedures as are necessary to control effectively the dissemination of classified information or material. Particularly stringent controls shall be placed on information and material classified Top Secret.

(1) *Top Secret Control Officers.* Top Secret Control Officers shall be designated, as required, to receive, maintain current accountability records of, and dispatch Top Secret material.

(2) *Physical Inventory.* A physical inventory of all Top Secret material shall be made at least annually. As an exception, repositories storing large volumes of classified material, shall develop inventory lists or other findings aids.

(3) *Current Accountability.* Top Secret and Secret information and material shall be subject to such controls including current accountability records as the head of the Department may prescribe.

(4) *Restraint on Reproduction.* Documents or portions of documents containing Top Secret information shall not be reproduced without the consent of the originating office. All other classified material shall be reproduced sparingly and any stated prohibition against reproduction shall be strictly adhered to.

(5) *Restraint on Number of Copies.* The number of copies of documents containing classified information shall be kept to a minimum to decrease the risk of compromise and reduce storage costs.

VII. Data Index System

Each Department originating classified information or material shall undertake to establish a data index system for Top Secret, Secret and Confidential information in selected categories approved by the Inter-agency Classification Review Committee as having sufficient historical or other value appropriate for preservation. The index system shall contain the following data for each document indexed: (a) Identity of classifier, (b) Department of origin, (c) Addressees, (d) Date of classification. (e) Subject/Area, (f) Classification category and whether subject to or exempt from the General Declassification Schedule, (g) If exempt, which exemption category is applicable, (h) Date or event set for declassification, and (i) File designation. Information and material shall be indexed into the system at the earliest practicable date during the course of the calendar year in which it is produced and classified, or in any event no later than March 31st of the succeeding year. Each Department shall undertake to establish such a data index system no later than July 1, 1973, which shall index the selected categories of information and material produced and classified after December 31, 1972.

VIII. Combat Operations

The provisions of the Order and this Directive with regard to dissemination, transmission, or safekeeping of classified information or material may be so modified in connection with combat or combat-related operations as the Secretary of Defense may by regulations prescribe.

IX. Interagency Classification Review Committee

A. *Composition of Interagency Committee.* In accordance with Section 7 of the Order, an Interagency Classification Review Committee is established to assist the National Security Council in monitoring implementation of the Order. Its membership is comprised of senior representatives of the Department of State, Defense, and Justice, the Atomic Energy Commission, the Central Intelligence Agency, the National Security Council staff, and a Chairman designated by the President.

B. *Meetings and Staff.* The Interagency Committee shall meet regularly, but no less frequently than on a monthly basis, and take such actions as are deemed necessary to insure uniform compliance with the Order and this Directive. The Chairman is authorized to appoint an Executive Director, and to maintain a permanent administrative staff.

C. *Interagency Committee's Functions.* The Interagency Committee shall carry out the duties assigned it by Section 7(A) of the Order. It shall place particular emphasis on overseeing compliance with and implementation of the Order and programs established thereunder by each Department. It shall seek to develop means to (a) prevent overclassification, (b) ensure prompt declassification in accord with the provision of the Order, (c) facilitate access to declassified material and (d) eliminate unauthorized disclosure of classified information.

D. *Classification Complaints.* Under such procedures as the Interagency Committee may prescribe, it shall consider and take action on complaints from persons within or without the government with respect to the general administration of the Order including appeals from denials by Departmental Committees or the Archivist of declassification requests.

X. Departmental Implementation and Enforcement

A. *Action Programs.* Those Departments listed in Section 2 (A) and (B) of the Order shall insure that adequate personnel and funding are provided for the purpose of carrying out the Order and Directives thereunder.

B. *Departmental Committee.* All suggestions and complaints, including those regarding overclassification, failure to declassify, or delay in declassifying not otherwise resolved, shall be referred to the Departmental Committee for resolution In addition, the Departmental Committee shall review all appeals of requests for records under Section 522 of Title 5 U.S.C. (Freedom of Information Act) when the proposed denial is based on their continued classification under the Order.

C. *Regulations and Reports.* Each Department shall submit its proposed implementing regulations of the Order and Directives thereunder to the Chairman of the Interagency Classification Review Committee for approval by the Committee. Upon approval such regulations shall be published in the Federal Register to the extent they affect the general public. Each Department shall also submit to the said Chairman (1) copies of the record lists required under Part I.D. hereof by July 1, 1972 and thereafter quarterly, (2) quarterly reports of Departmental Committee actions on classification review requests, classification abuses and unauthorized disclosures, and (3) provide progress reports on information accumulated in the data index system established under Part VII hereof and such other reports as said Chairman may find necessary for the Interagency Classification Review Committee to carry out its responsibilities.

D. *Administrative Enforcement.* The Departmental Committees shall have responsibility for recommending to the head of the respective Departments appropriate administrative action to correct abuse or violation of any provision of the Order or Directives thereunder, including notifications by warning letter, formal reprimand, and to the extent permitted by law, suspension without pay and removal. Upon receipt of such a recommendation the head of the Department concerned shall act promptly and advise the Departmental Committee of his action.

Publication and Effective Date: This Directive shall be published in the Federal Register and become effective June 1, 1972.

Henry A. Kissinger,
Assistant to the President for
National Security Affairs.

May 17, 1972.

CASES

United States v. Totten

92 U.S. 105 (1876)

Mr. Justice Field delivered the opinion of the court.

This case comes before us on appeal from the Court of Claims. The action was brought to recover compensation for services alleged to have been rendered by the claimant's intestate, William A. Lloyd, under a contract with President Lincoln, made in July, 1861, by which he was to proceed South and ascertain the number of troops stationed at different points in the insurrectionary States, procure plans of forts and fortifications, and gain such other information as might be beneficial to the government of the United States, and report the facts to the President; for which services he was to be paid $200 a month.

The Court of Claims finds that Lloyd proceeded, under the contract, within the rebel lines, and remained there during the entire period of the war, collecting, and from time to time transmitting, information to the President; and that, upon the close of the war, he was only reimbursed his expenses. But the court, being equally divided in opinion as to the authority of the President to bind the United States by the contract in question, decided, for the purposes of an appeal, against the claim, and dismissed the petition.

We have no difficulty as to the authority of the President in the matter. He was undoubtedly authorized during the war, as commander-in-chief of the armies of the United States, to employ secret agents to enter the rebel lines and obtain information respecting the strength, resources, and movements of the enemy; and contracts to compensate such agents are so far binding upon the government as to render it lawful for the President to direct payment of the amount stipulated out of the contingent fund under his control. Our objection is not to the contract, but to the action upon it in the Court of Claims. The service stipulated by the contract was a secret service; the information sought was to be obtained clandestinely, and was to be communicated privately; the employment and the service were to be equally concealed. Both employer and agent must have understood that the lips of the other were to be for ever sealed respecting the relation of either to the matter. This condition of the engagement was implied from the nature of the employment, and is implied in all secret employments of the government in time of war, or upon matters affecting our foreign relations, where a disclosure of the service might compromise or embarrass our government in its public duties, or endanger the person or injure the character of the agent. If upon contracts of such a nature an action against the government could be maintained in the Court of Claims, whenever an agent should deem himself entitled to greater or different compensation than that awarded to him, the whole service in any case, and the manner of its discharge, with the details of dealings with individuals and officers, might be exposed, to the serious detriment of the public. A secret service, with liability to publicity in this way, would be impossible; and, as such services are sometimes indispensable to the government, its agents in those services must look for their compensation to the contingent fund of the department employing them, and to such allowance from it as those who dispense that fund may award. The secrecy which such contracts impose precludes any action for their emforcement. The publicity produced by an action would itself be a breach of a contract of that kind, and thus defeat a recovery.

It may be stated as a general principle, that public policy forbids the maintenance of any suit in a court of justice, the trial of which would inevitably lead to the disclosure of matters which the law itself regards as confidential, and respecting which it will not allow the confidence to be violated. On this principle, suits cannot be maintained which would require a disclosure of the confidences of the confessional, or those between husband and wife, or of communications by a client to his counsel for professional advice, or of a patient to his physician for a similar purpose. Much greater reason exists for the application of the principle to cases of contract for secret services with the government, as the existence of a contract of that kind is itself a fact not to be disclosed.

Judgment affirmed.

Chicago and Southern Air Lines, Inc. v. Waterman Steamship Corporation

333 U.S. 103 (1948)

Mr. Justice Jackson delivered the opinion of the Court.

The question of law which brings this controversy here is whether § 1006 of the Civil Aeronautics Act, 49 USCA § 646, 10A FCA title 49, § 646, authorizing judicial review of described orders of the Civil Aeronautics Board, includes those which grant or deny applications by citizen carriers to engage in overseas and foreign air transportation which are subject to approval by the President under § 801 of the Act. 49 USCA § 601, 10A FCA title 49, § 601.

By proceedings not challenged as to regularity, the Board, with express approval of the President, issued an order which denied Waterman Steamship Corporation a certificate of convenience and necessity for an air route and granted one to Chicago and Southern Air Lines, a rival applicant. Routes sought by both carrier interests involved overseas air transportation, § 1 (21) (b), 49 USCA § 401 (21) (b), 10A FCA title 49, § 401 (21) (b), between Continental United States and Caribbean possessions and also foreign air transportation, § 1 (21) (c), between the United States and foreign countries. Waterman filed a petition for review under § 1006 of the Act with the Circuit Court of Appeals for the Fifth Circuit. Chicago and Southern intervened. Both the latter and the Board moved to dismiss, the grounds pertinent here being that because the order required and had approval of the President, under § 801 of the Act, it was not reviewable. The Court of Appeals disclaimed any power to question or review either the President's approval or his disapproval, but it regarded any Board order as incomplete under court review, after which "the completed action must be approved by the President as to citizen air carriers in cases under § 801." 159 F2d 828. Accordingly, it refused to dismiss the petition and asserted jurisdiction. Its decision conflicts with one by the Court of Appeals for the Second Circuit. Pan American Airways Co. v. Civil Aeronautics Bd. 121 F2d 810. We granted certiorari both to the Chicago and Southern Air Lines, Inc. (No. 78) and to the Board (No. 88) to resolve the conflict.

Congress has set up a comprehensive scheme for regulation of common carriers by air. Many statutory provisions apply indifferently whether the carrier is a foreign air carrier or a citizen air carrier, and whether the carriage involved is "interstate air commerce," "overseas air commerce" or "foreign air commerce," each being appropriately defined. 49 USCA § 401 (20), 10A FCA title 49, § 401 (20). All air carriers by similar procedures must obtain from the Board certificates of convenience and necessity by showing a public interest in establishment of the route and the applicant's ability to serve it. But when a foreign carrier asks for any permit, or a citizen carrier applies for a certificate to engage in any overseas or foreign air transportation, a copy of the application must be transmitted to the President before hearing; and any decision, either to grant or to deny, must be submitted to the President before publication and is unconditionally subject to the President's approval. Also the statute subjects to judicial review "any order, affirmative or negative, issued by the Board under this Act, except any order in respect of any foreign air carrier subject to the approval of the President as provided in § 801 of this Act." It grants no express exemption to an order such as the one before us, which concerns a citizen carrier but which must have Presidential approval because it involves overseas and foreign air transportation. The question is whether an exemption is to be implied.

The Court long has held that statutes which employ broad terms to confer power of judicial review are not always to be read literally. Where Congress has authorized review of "any order" or used other equally inclusive terms, courts have declined the opportunity to magnify their jurisdiction, by self-denying constructions which do not subject to judicial control orders which; from their nature, from the context of the Act, or from the relation of judicial power to the subject-matter, are inappropriate for review. Examples are set forth by Chief Justice Hughes in Federal Power Commission v. Metropolitan Edison Co. 304 U.S. 375, 384, 82 L ed 1408, 1414, 58 S Ct 963. Cf. Rochester Teleph. Corp. v. United States, 307 U.S. 125, 130, 83 L ed 1147, 1152, 59 S Ct 754.

The Waterman Steamship Corporation urges that review of the problems involved in establishing foreign air routes are of no more international delicacy or strategic importance than those involved in routes for water carriage. It says, "It is submitted that there is no basic difference between the conduct of the foreign commerce of the United States by air or by sea." From this premise it reasons that we should interpret this statute to follow the pattern of judicial review adopted in relation to orders affecting foreign commerce by rail, Lewis-Simas-Jones Co. v. Southern P. Co. 283 U.S. 654, 75 L ed 1333, 51 S Ct 592; News Syndicate Co. v. New York C. R. Co. 275 U.S. 179, 72 L ed 225, 48 S Ct 39, or communications by wire, United States v. Western U. Teleg. Co (CCA2d NY) 272 F 893, or by radio, Mackay Radio & Teleg. Co. v. Federal Communications Commission, 68 App DC 336, 97 F2d 641; and it likens the subject-matter of aeronautics legislation of that of Title VI of the Merchant Marine Act of [June 29] 1936, 46 USCA § 1171, 10 FCA title 46, § 1171, and the function of the Aeronautics Board in respect to overseas and foreign air transportation to that of the Maritime Commission to such commerce when water-borne.

We find no indication that the Congress either entertained or fostered the narrow concept that airborne commerce is a mere outgrowth or overgrowth of surface-bound transport. Of course, air transportation, water transportation, rail transportation, and motor transportation all have a kinship in that all are forms of transportation and their common features of public carriage for hire may be amenable to kindred regulations. But these resemblances must not blind us to the fact that legally, as well as literally, air commerce, whether at home or abroad, soared into a different realm than any that had gone before. Ancient doctrines of private ownership of the air as appurtenant to land titles had to be revised to make aviation practically serviceable to our socicty. A way of travel which quickly escapes the bounds of local regulative competence called for a more penetrating, uniform and exclusive regulation by the nation than had been thought appropriate for the more easily controlled commerce of the past. While transport by land and by sea began before any existing government was established and their respective customs and practices matured into bodies of carrier law independently of legislation, air transport burst suddenly upon modern governments, offering new advantages, demanding new rights and carrying new threats which society could meet with timely adjustments only by prompt invocation of legislative authority. However useful parallels with older forms of transit may be in adjudicating private rights, we see no reason why the efforts of the Congress to foster and regulate development of a revolutionary commerce that operates in three dimensions should be judicially circumscribed with analogies taken over from two-dimensional transit.

The "public interest" that enters into awards of routes for aerial carriers, who in effect obtain also a sponsorship by our government in foreign ventures, is not confined to adequacy of transportation service, as we have held when that term is applied to railroads. Texas v. United States, 292 U.S. 522, 531, 78 L ed 1402, 1409, 54 S Ct 819. That aerial navigation routes and bases should be prudently correlated with facilities and plans for our own national defenses and raise new problems in conduct of foreign relations, is a fact of common knowledge. Congressional hearings and debates extending over several sessions and departmental studies of many years show that the legislative and administrative processes have proceeded in full recognition of these facts.

In the regulation of commercial aeronautics, the statute confers on the Board many powers conventional in other carrier regulation under the Congressional commerce power. They are exercised through usual procedures and apply settled standards with only customary administrative finality. Congress evidently thought of the administrative function in terms used by this Court of another of its agencies in exercising interstate commerce power: "Such a body cannot in any proper sense be characterized as an arm or an eye of the executive. Its duties are performed without executive leave and, in the contemplation of the statute, must be free from executive control." Humphrey v. United States, 295 U.S. 602, 628, 79 L ed 1611, 1619, 55 S Ct 869. Those orders which do not require Presidential approval are subject to judicial review to assure application of the standards Congress has laid down.

But when a foreign carrier seeks to engage in public carriage over the territory or waters of this country, or any carrier seeks the sponsorship of this Government to engage in overseas or foreign air transportation, Congress has completely inverted the usual administrative process. Instead of acting independently of executive control, the agency is then subordinated to it. Instead of its order serving as a final disposition of the application, its force is exhausted when it serves as a recommendation to the President. Instead of being handed down to the parties as the conclusion of the administrative process, it must be submitted to the President, before publication even can take place. Nor is the President's control of the ultimate decision a mere right of veto. It is not alone issuance of such authorizations that are subject to his approval, but denial, transfer, amendment, cancellation or suspension, as well. And likewise subject to his approval are the terms, conditions and limitations of the order. 49 USCA § 601, 10A FCA title 49, § 601. Thus, Presidential control is not limited to a negative but is a positive and detailed control over the Board's decisions, unparalleled in the history of American administrative bodies.

Congress may of course delegate very large grants of its power over foreign commerce to the President. Norwegian Nitrogen Products Co. v. United States, 288 U.S. 294, 77 L ed 796, 53 S Ct 350; United States v. George S. Bush & Co. 310 U.S. 371, 84 L ed 1259, 60 S Ct 944. The President also possesses in his own right certain powers conferred by the Constitution on him as Commander-in-Chief and as the Nation's organ in foreign affairs. For present purposes, the order draws vitality from either or both sources. Legislative and Executive powers are pooled obviously to the end that commercial strategic and diplomatic interests of the country may be coordinated and advanced without collision or deadlock between agencies.

These considerations seem controlling on the question whether the Board's action on overseas and foreign air transportation applications by citizens are subject to revision or overthrow by the courts.

It may be conceded that a literal reading of § 1006 subjects this order to re-examination by the courts. It also appears that the language was deliberately employed by Congress, although nothing indicates that Congress foresaw or intended the consequences ascribed to it by the decision of the Court below. The letter of the text might with equal consistency be construed to require any one of three things: first, judicial review of a decision by the President; second, judicial review of a Board order before it acquires finality through Presidential action, the court's decision on review being a binding limitation on the President's action; third, a judicial review before action by the President, the latter being at liberty wholly to disregard the court's judgment. We think none of these results is required by usual canons of construction.

In this case, submission of the Board's decision was made to the President, who disapproved certain portions of it and advised the Board of the changes which he required. The Board complied and submitted a revised order and opinion which the President approved. Only then were they made public, and that which was made public and which is before us is only the final order and opinion containing the President's amendments and bearing his approval. Only at that stage was review sought, and only then could it be pursued, for then only was the decision consummated, announced and available to the parties.

While the changes made at direction of the President may be identified, the reasons therefor are not disclosed beyond the statement that "because of certain factors relating to our broad national welfare and other matters for which the Chief Executive has special responsibility, he has reached conclusions which require" changes in the Board's opinion.

The court below considered, and we think quite rightly, that it could not review such provisions of the order as resulted from Presidential direction. The President, both as Commander-in-Chief and as the Nation's organ for foreign affairs, has available intelligence services whose reports are not and ought not to be published to the world. It would be intolerable that courts, without the relevant information, should review and perhaps nullify actions of the Executive taken on information properly held secret. Nor can courts sit in camera in order to be taken into executive confidences. But even if courts could require full disclosure, the very nature of executive decisions as to foreign policy is political, not judicial. Such decisions are wholly confided by our Constitution to the political departments of the government, Executive and Legislative. They are delicate, complex, and involve large elements of prophecy. They are and should be undertaken only by those directly responsible to the people whose welfare they advance or imperil. They are decisions of a kind for which the Judiciary has neither aptitude, facilities nor responsibility and which has long been held to belong in the domain of political power not subject to judicial intrusion or inquiry. Coleman v. Miller, 307 U.S. 433, 454, 83 L ed 1385, 1396, 59 S Ct 972, 122 ALR 695; United States v. Curtiss-Wright Export Corp. 299 U.S. 304, 319-321, 81 L ed 255, 262, 263, 57 S Ct 216; Oetjen v. Central Leather Co. 246 U.S. 297, 302, 62 L ed 726, 731, 38 S Ct 309. We therefore agree that whatever of this order emanates from the President is not susceptible of review by the Judicial Department.

The court below thought that this disability could be overcome by regarding the Board as a regulatory agent of Congress to pass on such matters as the fitness, willingness and ability of the applicant, and that the Board's own determination of these matters is subject to review. The court, speaking of the Board's action, said: "It is not final till the Board and the court have completed their functions. Thereafter the completed action must be approved by the President as to citizen air carriers in cases under § 801." The legal incongruity of interposing judicial review between the action by the Board and that by the President are as great as the practical disadvantages. The latter arise chiefly from the inevitable delay and obstruction in the midst of the administrative proceedings. The former arises from the fact that until the President acts there is no final administrative determination to review. The statute would hardly have forbidden publication before submission if it had contemplated interposition of the courts at this intermediate stage. Nor could it have expected the courts to stay the President's hand after submission while they deliberate on the inchoate determination. The difficulty is manifest in this case. Review could not be sought until the order was made available, and at that time it had ceased to be merely the Board's tentative decision and had become one finalized by Presidential discretion.

Until the decision of the Board has Presidential approval, it grants no privilege and denies no right. It can give nothing and can take nothing away from the applicant or a competitor. It may be a step, which if erroneous will mature into a prejudicial result, as an order fixing valuations in a rate proceeding may foreshow and compel a prejudicial rate order. But administrative orders are not reviewable unless and until they impose an obligation, deny a right or fix some legal relationship as a consummation of the administrative process. United States v. Los Angeles & S. L. R. Co. 273 U.S. 299, 71 L ed 651, 47 S Ct 413; United States v. Illinois C. R. Co. 244 U.S. 82, 61 L ed 1007, 37 S Ct 584; Rochester Teleph. Corp. v. United States, 307 U.S. 125, 131, 83 L ed 1147, 1151, 59 S Ct 754. The dilemma faced by those who demand judicial review of the Board's order is that, before Presidential approval, it is not a final determination even of the Board's ultimate action, and after Presidential approval, the whole order, both in what is approved without change, as well as in amendments which he directs, derives its vitality from the exercise of unreviewable Presidential discretion.

The court below considered that after it reviewed the Board's order, its judgment would be submitted to the President, that his power to disapprove would apply after as well as before the court acts, and hence that there would be no chance of a deadlock and no conflict of function. But if the President may completely disregard the judgment of the court, it would be only because it is one the courts were not authorized to render. Judgments, within the powers vested in courts by the Judiciary Article of the Constitution, may not lawfully be revised, overturned or refused faith and credit by another Department of Government.

To revise or review an administrative decision, which has only the force of a recommendation to the President, would be to render an advisory opinion in its most obnoxious form—advice that the President has not asked, tendered at the demand of a private litigant, on a subject concededly within the President's exclusive, ultimate control. This Court early and wisely determined that it would not give advisory opinions even when asked by the Chief Executive. It has also been the firm and unvarying practice of Constitutional Courts to render no judgments not binding and conclusive on the parties and none that are subject to later review or alteration by administrative action. Hayburn's Case, 2 Dall (U.S.) 409, 1 L ed 436; United States v. Ferreira, 13 How (U.S.) 40, 14 L ed 42; Gordon v. United States, 117 U.S. 697, and 76 L ed 1347; Re Sanborn, 148 U.S. 222, 37 L ed 429, 13 S Ct 577; Interstate Commerce Commission v. Brimson, 154 U.S. 447, 38 L ed 1047, 14 S Ct 1125, 4 Inters Com 545; La Abra Silver Min. Co. v. United States, 175 U.S. 423, 44 L ed 223, 20 S Ct 168; Muskrat v. United States, 219 U.S. 346, 55 L ed 246, 31 S Ct 250; United States v. Jefferson Electric Mfg. Co. 291 U.S. 386, 78 L ed 859, 54 S Ct 443.

We conclude that orders of the Board as to certificate for overseas or foreign air transportation are not mature and are therefore not susceptible of judicial review at any time before they are finalized by Presidential approval. After such approval has been given, the final orders embody Presidential discretion as to political matters beyond the competence of the courts to adjudicate. This makes it unnecessary to examine the other questions raised. The petition of the Waterman Steamship Corp. should be dismissed.

Judgment reversed.

Mr. Justice Douglas, with whom Mr. Justice Black, Mr. Justice Reed and Mr. Justice Rutledge concur, dissenting. . . .

Reynolds v. United States

192 F. 2d 987 (3d Cir. 1951)

Maris, Circuit Judge.

On October 6, 1948, a United States Air Force B-29 bomber, enroute from Robbins Air Force Base on a flight to Orlando, Florida, and return, crashed at Waycross, Georgia. The plane, carrying nine crew members and four civilian observers, had taken off for the purpose of an experimental testing of secret electronics equipment. Of the thirteen persons on board, nine were killed, including six members of the crew and three civilian observers who were engineer employees of private organizations involved in the research and development of the electronics equipment being tested. These consolidated suits under the Federal Tort Claims Act, 28 U.S.C. §§ 1346, 2671 et seq., were thereafter instituted in the United States District Court for the Eastern District of Pennsylvania by the widows of the three deceased civilian employees, each seeking damages for the alleged wrongful deaths of the deceased.

Subsequent to the filing of answers making general denials, detailed interrogatories pursuant to Civil Procedure Rule 33, 28 U.S.C., were served on the United States Attorney by the plaintiffs. One of the interrogatories requested that a copy of any investigation report of the accident be attached to the answer. Another similarly sought copies of statements of witnesses which might have been obtained in connection with the accident. In answering the interrogatories the United States declined to comply with those questions which required the production of documents on the ground that such production was not within the scope of Rule 33.

Following the filing of these answers, plaintiffs made a motion under Civil Procedure Rule 34 for production of the official investigation report prepared by officers of the Air Force and the statements of the surviving crew members taken in connection with that investigation. To show good cause the motion and supporting affidavits stated that those documents constituted or contained information and evidence necessary in preparation for trial, that the documents were in the possession and control of the United States and that plaintiffs knew no way to obtain knowledge of their contents or the cause of the accident other than by their production.

On June 30, 1950 the district court sustained plaintiffs' motions to produce, holding that good cause had been shown therefor. 10 F.R.D. 468. After deciding the matter of good cause, the district judge disposed of the questions as to the privileged status of the departmental records involved by reference to the views which he had expressed in O'Neill v. United States, D.C., 1948, 79 F.Supp. 827. An order requiring production was entered on July 20, 1950.

The Attorney General, upon being notified of the result reached by the district judge, notified the Department of the Air Force. On July 24, 1950 a letter from the Secretary of the Air Force to the district court stated:

> "Acting under the authority of Section 161 of the Revised Statutes (5 U.S.C. 22), it has been determined that it would not be in the public interest to furnish this report of investigation as requested by counsel in this case. This report was prepared under regulations which are designed to insure the collection of all pertinent information regarding aircraft accidents in order that all possible measures will be developed for the prevention of accidents and the optimum promotion of flying safety. Because this matter is one of such primary importance to the Air Force, it has been found necessary to restrict the use of aircraft accident reports to the official purpose for which they are intended. Under our regulations, this type of report is not available in courts-martial proceedings or other forms of disciplinary action or in the determination of pecuniary liability.
>
> "It is hoped that the extreme importance which the Department of the Air Force places upon the confidential nature of its official aircraft accident reports will be fully appreciated and understood by your Honorable Court."

Thereafter the district judge suggested that a hearing might be held so that this aspect of the case might be further considered. Accordingly a hearing was held by agreement in Washington, D.C., on August 9, 1950. At this hearing the district judge received a formal "claim of privilege" by the Secretary of the Air Force, setting forth the basis for the claim and the authority for the privilege, supported by his affidavit showing his right to promulgate regulations under Sec. 161, R.S., and the Act of March 1, 1875, 10 U.S.C.A. § 16, as head of the Department of the Air Force and describing the applicable regulations. In addition, an affidavit by the Judge Advocate General of the Air Force was filed which set forth the names and addresses of the survivors, undertook to make these witnesses available for interrogation at plaintiffs' will and at Government expense, and guaranteed to authorize the witnesses to testify to all matters pertaining to the cause of the accident except as to "classified" material. Further, the affidavit of the Judge Advocate General, after averring that all records, other than those classified or privileged, had already been made available to plaintiffs, specifically stated that the investigation board report and survivors' statements could not be furnished without seriously hampering national security, flying safety, and the development of highly technical and secret military equipment.

An amended order was issued by the district judge on September 21, 1950, to the effect that the United States should produce for examination by the court the documents in question, so that the court could determine whether the disclosure "would violate the Government's privilege against disclosure of matters involving the national or public interest." Compliance with this order was not forthcoming and, on October 12, 1950, the district judge issued an order, under Civil Procedure Rule 37, that the facts in plaintiffs' favor on the issue of negligence be taken as established and prohibiting the defendant from introducing evidence to controvert those facts. Subsequently, a hearing was held on the question of damages and judgment was entered for the plaintiffs on February 27, 1951. These appeals by the United States followed.

The appeals now before us raise a number of important and difficult questions for our determination. The first is whether the district judge erred in his ruling that the plaintiffs had shown good cause under Rule 34 for the production of the statements of witnesses and investigation report which they sought to have produced for their inspection and copying. In concluding that good cause had been shown, the district judge said, 10 F.R.D. 468, 470-471:

> "The plaintiffs have no knowledge of why the accident happened. So far as such knowledge is obtainable, the defendant has it. When the airplane crashed, it was wrecked and much of the evidence of what occurred was destroyed. Only persons with long experience in investigating airplane disasters could hope to get at the real cause of the accident under such circumstances. The Air Force appointed a board of investigators immediately after the accident and examined the surviving witnesses while their recollections were fresh. With their statements as a starting point the board was able to make an extensive investigation of the accident. These statements and the report of the board's investigation undoubtedly contain facts, information and clues which it might be extremely difficult, if not impossible, for the plaintiffs with their lack of technical resources to obtain merely by taking the depositions of the survivors.
>
> "I am not suggesting that the witnesses on deposition would not answer the questions asked them truthfully but, in a case like this, in which seemingly trivial things may, to the expert, furnish important clues as to the cause of the accident, the plaintiffs must have accurate and precise firsthand information as to every relevant fact, if they are to conduct their examination of witnesses properly and to get at the truth in preparing for trial. This only the statements can give them. I would not go so far as to say that the witnesses would necessarily be hostile. However, they are employees of the defendant, in military service and subject to military authority and it is not an unfair assumption that they will not be encouraged to disclose, voluntarily, any information which might fix responsibility upon the Air Force.
>
> "The answers to the interrogatories are far short of the full and complete disclosure of facts which the spirit of the rules requires. True, the defendant has produced a mass of documents but these refer to the past performance of the plane and service records of the pilots and are essentially negative. When it comes to the interrogatory 'Describe in detail the trouble experienced', the answer is, 'At between 18,500 or 19,000 feet manifold pressure dropped to 23 inches on No. one engine.' Obviously, the defendant, with the report and findings of its official investigation in its possession, knows more about the accident than this.
>
> "Beside all this, the accident happened more than 18 months ago and what the crew would remember now might well differ in important matters from what they told their officers when the event was fresh in their minds. Even in simple accident cases requiring no technical knowledge to prepare for trial, the fact that a long period of time has elapsed between the accident and the taking of the deposition of a witness gives a certain unique value to a statement given by him immediately after the accident when the whole thing was fresh—particularly when given to an employer before any damage suit involving negligence has begun."

We cannot say that in reaching his conclusion that good cause had been shown the district judge erred. The question, as we suggested in Alltmont v. United States, 3 Cir., 1950, 177 F.2d 971, 978, in every such case is whether special circumstances make it essential to the preparation of the party's case to see and copy the documents sought. In appraising for this purpose the circumstances of a particular case, the district court is necessarily vested with a wide discretion. Where, as here, the instrumentality involved in an accident was within the exclusive possession and control of the defendant so that it was as a practical matter virtually impossible for the plaintiffs to have made any independent investigation of the cause of the accident, considerations of justice may well demand that the plaintiffs should have had access to the facts, thus within the exclusive control of their opponent, upon which they were required to rely to establish their right of recovery. We agree with the district judge that it is not, under the circumstances of these cases, a sufficient answer to say that since the names of the witnesses whose statements were sought had been supplied in answer to the interrogatories, their depositions might have been taken by the plaintiffs. Obviously, this is no answer at all to their demand for the production of the investigation report. And under the circumstances here disclosed, as the district judge has cogently pointed out, it may well have been of vital importance to the plaintiffs to have knowledge of the contents of the statements made by the survivors immediately after the crash even though their depositions could also have been taken.

The Government's next contention is that even if it is held that good cause was shown by the plaintiffs for the production of the statements and report in question it was error to require their production because they were privileged. The Government points out that Rule 34 only authorizes the court to order the production of documents which are, in the language of the rule, "not privileged."

The Government's claim of privilege is based primarily on Section 161 of the Revised Statutes.[1] The primary contention is that this section in giving to the Secretary of the Air Force authority to prescribe regulations for the custody and use of the records and papers of his Department necessarily confers upon him full discretionary power in the public interest to refuse to produce any such records for examination and use in a judicial proceeding and that such records thereby become "privileged". The doctrine of separation of powers of the executive and judicial departments of the Government which is embodied in the Constitution is said to place the exercise of this discretionary power by the Secretary wholly beyond judicial review. In passing upon the validity, as applied to these cases, of this contention by the Government that it cannot be compelled to produce any records of the Department of the Air Force which the Secretary of that Department deems it not to be in the public interest to produce, it is necessary to consider the precise setting in which the contention is made.

In the first place it is clear that the validity of the regulations promulgated by the Secretary of the Air Force and his predecessor, the Secretary of War, with respect to the custody and production of papers and records of the Department is not an issue. For these regulations specifically provide that responsibility for the release of reports of boards of officers, special accident reports, or extracts therefrom regarding aircraft accidents to persons outside the authorized chain of command or administration, rests solely with the Secretary of the Air Force.[2] And since here the order to produce was directed to the United States as defendant, its execution, if lawfully demandable, obviously became the duty of the Secretary of the Air Force, the head of that department of the Government of the United States having custody of the records in question, who has full authority under the statute and the regulations to make such production. It is for this reason that the cases of Boske v. Comingore, 1900, 177 U.S. 459, 20 S.Ct. 701, 44 L.Ed. 846, and Touhy v. Ragen, 1951, 340 U.S. 462, 71 S.Ct. 416, 95 L.Ed. 417, both of which involved the refusal of a subordinate employee of a governmental department to produce records without the approval of his department head, are not in point.

Also it will be observed that we are not called upon to decide whether the Government's contention is available as a defense against the enforcement of the desired discovery through a subpoena duces tecum directed to the Secretary or a contempt proceeding against him for failure to obey it. Such a case would indeed, as the Government argues, raise difficult constitutional questions arising out of the separation of powers under our Constitution.[3] Here no such action against any officer of the executive branch of the Government has been asked for or taken. We are concerned in these cases merely with ascertaining the legal duty of the Secretary under the Federal Tort Claims Act to make the requested discovery in order that we may determine whether his refusal to do so justified the order made by the district court under Civil Procedure Rule 37(b)(2) that the negligence of the United States be taken as established. And, finally, we do not have to determine the validity of the Government's contention as applied to a demand for the production of documents in a suit between private parties.[4] For here the United States is the party defendant against which these suits have been brought pursuant to the express authority of the Federal Tort Claims Act.

The Federal Tort Claims Act provides that "The United States shall be liable . . . in the same manner and to the same extent as a private individual under like circumstances."[5] Thus by the express terms of the Act Congress has divested the United States of its normal sovereign immunity to the extent of making it liable in actions such as those now before us in the same manner as if it were a private individual. Moreover it has made the Federal Rules of Civil Procedure, including their discovery provisions, applicable to such actions against the United States.[6] We think that by so doing Congress has withdrawn the right of the executive departments of the Government in tort claims cases, even if under other circumstances such right exists,[7] to determine without judicial review the extent of the privilege against disclosure of Government documents sought to be produced for use in the litigation.

We come then to consider the propriety of the Government's claim of privilege in these cases. The principal basis of the Government's claim of immunity was set forth in the letter of the Secretary of the Air Force to the district judge dated July 24, 1950, from which we have already quoted. In that letter the Secretary stated that he had determined that it would not be in the public interest to furnish the documents requested. The basis which he stated for this determination was that it is necessary to restrict the use of aircraft accident reports so as to insure the collection of all pertinent information regarding aircraft accidents in order that all possible measures will be developed for the prevention of accidents and the optimum promotion of flying safety in the Air Force. The position of the Secretary in this regard is restated in the formal claim of privilege filed on August 9, 1950, as follows: "With regard to the demand for the production of the Report of Investigation (Report of Major Aircraft Accident, AF Form 14) and any other ancillary report or statement pertaining to this investigation, the respondent-defendant, the United States, has objected and still objects to the production of this report on the ground that it is privileged. The report of investigation (Report of Major Aircraft Accident, AF Form 14), together with all the statements of the witnesses, was prepared under regulations which are designed to insure the disclosure of all pertinent factors which may have caused, or which may have had a bearing on, the accident in order that every possible safeguard may be developed so that precautions may be taken for the prevention of future accidents and for the purpose of promoting the highest degree of flying safety. These statements are obtained in confidence, and these reports are prepared for intra-departmental use only, with the view of correcting deficiencies found to have existed and with the view of taking necessary corrective measures or additional precautions based on the opinions and conclusions of the Board of Officers convened to investigate such accidents. The disclosure of statements made by witnesses and air-crewmen before Accident Investigation Boards would have a deterrent effect upon the much desired objective of encouraging uninhibited statements in future inquiry proceedings instituted primarily in the interest of flying safety."

It will be seen that the privilege thus claimed is a broad one against any disclosure of the results of what the Government has aptly called its "housekeeping" investigations.[8] In support of its claim of privilege the Government points to paragraph 2 of Air Force Regulation No. 62-7 which contains the following provision: "Aircraft accident information is procured from reports of personnel who have waived their rights under the 24th Article of War in the interest of accident prevention upon the assurance that the reports will not be used in any manner in connection with any investigation or proceeding toward disciplinary action, determination of pecuniary liability, or line-of-duty status or reclassification." It seems clear to us, however, that this regulation has no bearing on the problem before us since it merely imposes restrictions upon the subsequent use within the department for disciplinary and other purposes of statements of Air Force personnel with respect to aircraft accidents.

It may be conceded that in addition to the privilege against divulging state secrets, to which we shall later advert, there is also a less clearly defined privilege against disclosing official information if such disclosure will actually be harmful to the interests of the nation.[9] But we do not think that in the present cases brought under the Federal Tort Claims Act the Department of the Air Force is entitled to the absolute "housekeeping" privilege which it asserts against disclosing any statements or reports relating to this airplane accident regardless of their contents.[10] It may well be more convenient and efficient in the conduct of accident investigations for the Department not to be required to disclose statements and reports of this character. But the same would be true in the case of any private person and the latter do not ordinarily enjoy that privilege. Where, as here, the United States has consented to be sued as a private person, whatever public interest there may be in avoiding any disclosure of accident reports in order to promote accident prevention must yield to what Congress evidently regarded as the greater public interest involved in seeing that justice is done to persons injured by governmental operations whom it has authorized to enforce their claims by suit against the United States.[11] When Congress has desired to bar the admission of airplane accident reports in evidence it has known how to do so[12] and it has also known how to give to department heads discretionary power to refuse to produce records in suits brought against the United States.[13] It has done neither in connection with suits under the Federal Tort Claims Act.

Moreover we regard the recognition of such a sweeping privilege against any disclosure of the internal operations of the executive departments of the Government as contrary to a sound public policy. The present cases themselves indicate the breadth of the claim of immunity from disclosure which one government department head has already made. It is but a small step to assert a privilege against any disclosure of records merely because they might prove embarrassing to government officers. Indeed it requires no great flight of imagination to realize that if the Government's contentions in these cases were affirmed the privilege against disclosure might gradually be enlarged by executive determinations until, as is the case in some nations today, it embraced the whole range of governmental activities.

We need to recall in this connection the words of Edward Livingston: "No nation ever yet found any inconvenience from too close an inspection into the conduct of its officers, but many have been brought to ruin, and reduced to slavery, by suffering gradual imposition and abuses, which were imperceptible, only because the means of publicity had not been secured."[14] And it was Patrick Henry who said that "to cover with the veil of secrecy the common routine of business, is an abomination in the eyes of every intelligent man and every friend to his country.[15]

It has been held that in criminal cases the Government has the choice either to reveal all evidence within its control which bears upon the charges or let the offense go unpunished, at least where the evidence is held by officials who are themselves charged with the administration of those laws for the violation of which the accused has been indicted.[16] We think that the Federal Tort Claims Act offers the Government an analogous choice in tort claims cases. The Government may decide to recognize the public interest involved in according justice to the private claimant who has brought suit against it by producing relevant documents in its possession upon an order of the court under Rule 34. On the other hand the Government may decide to give priority to the public interest which it believes to be involved in preserving the documents from disclosure by declining to produce them upon the order of the court at the cost, if its claim of privilege is overruled, of having the facts to which the documents are directed taken by the court to be established against the United States under Civil Procedure Rule 37(b)(2)(i). This last is the alternative which the Government chose in the cases now before us. The Federal Rules of Civil Procedure offer such a choice to private litigants under similar circumstances and we are satisfied that under the Federal Tort Claims Act the same choice is presented to the Government which, as we have seen, has been placed by Congress in this respect in the position of a private individual defending against a tort action.

At this point we must pause to notice a procedural contention of the Attorney General. It is that since the question which we have been discussing involves the duty of the Secretary of the Air Force to produce the documents in question it may only be decided in a proceeding in which that official is brought into court by direct process to answer the plaintiffs' demands for production of the documents. We find no merit in this contention, however, since the order to produce the documents which was made by the district court in these cases was not directed to the Attorney General or any other officer of the Government. On the contrary, it was directed to "defendant, the United States of America, its agents and attorneys." Since obviously the United States can respond only by its agents and since the Secretary of the Air Force is the agent of the United States concerned with the documents here ordered to be produced it seems quite clear that the order is directed to and binding upon him just as much as upon the Attorney General who in these cases is merely attorney for the United States. Moreover we think that the Secretary of the Air Force recognized this fact when he presented his claim of privilege to the district court for its consideration and approval stating that the defendant, the United States, objected to production on the ground that the documents were privileged. Under these circumstances it was clearly within the judicial power of the court to pass upon the question of privilege thus raised.

The formal claim of privilege filed with the district court by the Secretary of the Air Force on August 9, 1950, laid a second basis for the claim in the following language: "The defendant further objects to the production of this report, together with the statements of witnesses, for the reason that the aircraft in question, together with the personnel on board, were engaged in a confidential mission of the Air Force. The airplane likewise carried confidential equipment on board and any disclosure of its mission or information concerning its operation or performance would be prejudicial to this Department and would not be in the public interest."

The claim of privilege thus made is of a wholly different character from the one previously discussed. It asserts in effect that the documents sought to be produced contain state secrets of a military character. State secrets of a diplomatic or military nature have always been privileged from disclosure in any proceeding[17] and unquestionably come within the class of privileged matters referred to in Rule 34. Moreover this privilege, as well as the privilege previously mentioned against disclosure of official information which would be harmful to the interests of the United States, was fully recognized by the district judge in these cases in his final order. For as we have seen, he directed that the documents in question be produced for his personal examination so that he might determine whether all or any part of the documents contain, to use the words of his order, "matters of a confidential nature, discovery of which would violate the Government's privilege against disclosure of matters involving the national or public interest." The Government was thus adequately protected by the district court from the disclosure of any privileged matter contained in the documents in question.

The Government contends, as we have stated, that it is within the sole province of the Secretary of the Air Force to determine whether any privileged material is contained in the documents and that his determination of this question must be accepted by the district court without any independent consideration of the matter by it. We cannot accede to this proposition. On the contrary we are satisfied that a claim of privilege against disclosing evidence relevant to the issues in a pending law suit involves a justiciable question, traditionally within the competence of the courts,[18] which is to be determined in accordance with the appropriate rules of evidence,[19] upon the submission of the documents in question to the judge for his examination *in camera*.[20] Such examination must obviously be *ex parte* and *in camera* if the privilege is not to be lost in its assertion. But to hold that the head of an executive department of the Government in a suit to which the United States is a party may conclusively determine the Government's claim of privilege is to abdicate the judicial function and permit the executive branch of the Government to infringe the independent province of the judiciary as laid down by the Constitution.[21]

The Government presses upon us the contrary conclusion of the British House of Lords in Duncan v. Cammell, Laird & Co., (1942) A.C. 624. The case is distinguishable in that the plans of the submarine Thetis there involved were obviously military secrets and the suit was between private parties. But we do not regard the case as controlling in any event. For whatever may be true in Great Britain[22] the Government of the United States is one of checks and balances. One of the principal checks is furnished by the independent judiciary which the Constitution established. Neither the executive nor the legislative branch of the Government may constitutionally encroach upon the field which the Constitution has reserved for the judiciary by transferring to itself the power to decide justiciable questions which arise in cases or controversies submitted to the judicial branch for decision.[23] Nor is there any danger to the public interest in submitting the question of privilege to the decision of the courts. The judges of the United States are public officers whose responsibility under the Constitution is just as great as that of the heads of the executive departments. When Government documents are submitted to them *in camera* under a claim of privilege the judges may be depended upon to protect with the greatest of care the public interest in preventing the disclosure of matters which may fairly be characterized as privileged.[24] And if, as the Government asserts is sometimes the case, a knowledge of background facts is necessary to enable one properly to pass on the claim of privilege those facts also may be presented to the judge *in camera*.

One final point remains to be considered. The Government points to Civil Procedure Rule 55(e) which provides that "No judgment by default shall be entered against the United States . . . unless the claimant establishes his claim or right to relief by evidence satisfactory to the court." Its contention is that the order of the district court entered in these cases that the facts in plantiffs' favor on the issue of negligence be taken as established because of the Government's refusal to produce the documents in question amounted to the entry of judgment against the United States by default in violation of the rule. We do not agree. Paragraph (a) of Rule 55 in effect defines judgment by default as the judgment which the clerk enters when a party against whom a judgment for affirmative relief is sought has failed to plead or otherwise defend as provided by the rules. In the case before us the United States has filed answers and has vigorously defended the actions. The distinction is outlined in Rule 37 (b)(2). That rule sets forth the relief which the court may grant upon the refusal of a party to produce evidence after having been directed to do so, as follows:

> "(i) An order that the matters regarding which the questions were asked, or the character or description of the thing or land, or the contents of the paper, or the physical or mental condition of the party, or any other designated facts shall be taken to be established for the purposes of the action in accordance with the claim of the party obtaining the order;
>
> "(ii) An order refusing to allow the disobedient party to support or oppose designated claims or defenses, or prohibiting him from introducing in evidence designated documents or things or items of testimony, or from introducing evidence of physical or mental condition;
>
> "(iii) An order striking out pleadings or parts thereof, or staying further proceedings until the order is obeyed, or dismissing the action or proceeding or any part thereof, or rendering a judgment by default against the disobedient party."

It will be observed that the order made by the court in these cases is of the type authorized by subparagraphs (i) and (ii), whereas a judgment by default against a disobedient party is specifically authorized by subparagraph (iii). We think it is clear from the language of the rules that the order made by the district court in these cases did not amount to a judgment by default within the meaning of Rule 55(e).

We conclude (1) that the district court did not err in holding that good cause had been shown by the plaintiffs for production of the statements and the report in question which they asked the United States to produce, (2) that the district court rightly rejected the broad claim of privilege made by the United States not to produce any statements or reports regarding airplane accidents, (3) that the order of the district court entered on rehearing on plaintiffs' motions for the production of the documents rightly provided for the determination by the court of the Government's claim of privilege as to any particular parts of the documents and (4) that upon the election of the United States nonetheless not to produce the documents, the order of the court directing that certain facts be taken as established against the United States in these cases was authorized by Rule 37(b) (2) (i) and (ii) and was accordingly not erroneous.

Since we find no error the judgments entered in favor of the plaintiffs after trial of the issue of damages will be affirmed.

---

[1]"Sec. 161. The head of each department is authorized to prescribe regulations, not inconsistent with law, for the government of his department, the conduct of its officers and clerks, the distribution and performance of its business, and the custody, use, and preservation of the records, papers, and property appertaining to it." 5 U.S.C.A. § 22.

[2]AF Regulation, No. 62-7, December 17, 1947, paragraph 6.

[3]Compare Thompson v. German Valley R. Co., 1871, 22 N.J.Eq. 111; Appeal of Hartranft, 1877, 85 Pa. 433.

[4]Compare Marbury v. Madison, 1803, 1 Cranch. 137, 5 U.S. 137, 144, 2 L.Ed. 60; Gray v. Pentland, 1815, 2 Serg & R., Pa., 23.

[5]28 U.S.C. § 2674.

[6]United States v. Yellow Cab Co., 1951, 340 U.S. 543, 553, 71 S.Ct. 399, 95 L.Ed. 523; United States v. General Motors Corporation, D.C.N.D.Ill.1942, 2F.R.D. 528, 530.

[7]But see 8 Wigmore on Evidence, 3d Ed. § 2379; Berger and Krash, Government Immunity from Discovery, 1950, 59 Yale L.J. 1451.

[8]Bank Line v. United States, D.C.S.D.N.Y.1948, 76 F.Supp. 801, 803.

[9]As we shall point out later in this opinion this privilege was fully protected by the district judge in his amended order in these cases.

[10]See 8 Wigmore on Evidence, 3d Ed., § 2378a; Berger and Krash, Government Immunity from Discovery, 1950, 59 Yale L.J. 1451.

[11]Bank Line v. United States, D.C.S.D.N.Y.1948, 76 F.Supp. 801; Cresmer v. United States, D.C.E.D.N.Y.1949, 9 F.R.D. 203.

[12]Title VII of the Civil Aeronautics Act of 1938 contained the following provisions:

"Air Safety Board

* * *

"Sec. 701. . . .

"Preservation of Records and Reports

"(e) The records and reports of the Board shall be preserved in the custody of the secretary of the Authority in the same manner and subject to the same provisions respecting publication as the records and reports of the Authority, except that any publication thereof shall be styled 'Air Safety Board of the Civil Aeronautics Authority', and that no part of any report or reports of the Board or the Authority relating to any accident, or the investigation thereof, shall be admitted as evidence or used in any suit or action for damages growing out of any matter mentioned in such report or reports." 52 Stat. 1013, 49 U.S.C.A. § 581.

[13]For example, § 2507 of Title 28, United States Code, provides:

"§ 2507. Calls on departments for information.

"The Court of Claims may call upon any department or agency of the United States for any information or papers it deems necessary, and may use all recorded and printed reports made by the committees of the Senate or House of Representatives.

"The head of any department or agency may refuse to comply when, in his opinion, compliance will be injurious to the public interest."

[14]Edward Livingston, Works, I, p. 15.

[15]Elliot's Debates, vol. 3, p. 170.

[16]United States v. Andolschek, 2 Cir., 1944, 142 F.2d 503; United States v. Krulewitch, 2 Cir., 1944, 145 F.2d 76, 156 A.L.R. 337; United States v. Beckman, 2 Cir., 1946, 155 F.2d 580, 584; United States v. Grayson, 2 Cir., 1948, 166 F.2d 863.

[17]Totten v. United States, 1875, 92 U.S. 105, 107, 23 L.Ed. 605; Firth Sterling Steel Co. v. Bethlehem Steel Co., D.C.E.D.Pa.1912, 199 F. 353; Pollen v. Ford Instrument Co., D.C.E.D.N.Y.1939, 26 F.Supp. 583; 8 Wigmore on Evidence, 3d Ed., §§ 2212a, 2378; 1 Greenleaf on Evidence, Lewis' Ed., § 250.

[18]Cresmer v. United States, D.C.E.D.N.Y.1949, 9 F.R.D. 203; Evans v. United States, D.C.W.D.La.1950, 10 F.R.D. 255.

[19]Aaron Burr's Trial, Robertson's Rep. (1808), vol. 1, pp. 180-181; United States v. Ebeling, 2 Cir., 1944,

146 F.2d 254, 256-257; Wild v. Payson, D.C.S.D.N.Y.1946, 7 F.R.D. 495, 499; 2 Moore's Federal Practice (1938) 2641.

[20]"It would rather seem that the simple and natural process of determination was precisely such a private perusal by the judge. Is it to be said that even this much of disclosure cannot be trusted? Shall every subordinate in the department have access to the secret, and not the presiding officer of justice? Cannot the constitutionally coordinate body of government share the confidence?" 8 Wigmore on Evidence, 3d Ed., p. 799.

See also 4 Moore's Federal Practice, 2d Ed., p. 1178.

[21]United States v. Cotton Valley Operators Committee, D.C.W.D.La.1949, 9 F.R.D. 719, 720, affirmed by equally divided court, 339 U.S. 940, 70 S.Ct. 793, 94 L.Ed. 1356; 8 Wigmore on Evidence, 3d Ed., §2379.

[22]Compare Duncan v. Cammell, Laird & Co., (1942) A.C. 624, with Robinson v. State of South Australia (No. 2), (1931) A.C. 704.

See Note, Administrative Discretion and Civil Liberties in England, 1943, 56 Harv.L.R. 806.

[23]Kilbourn v. Thompson, 1880, 103 U.S. 168, 182, 190, 26 L.Ed. 377; Chicago & Southern Air Lines v. Waterman Corp., 1948, 333 U.S. 103, 113, 68 S.Ct. 431, 92 L.Ed. 568.

[24]See Berger and Krash, Government Immunity from Discovery, 1950, 59 Yale L.J. 1451, 1462-1464.

United States v. Reynolds

345 U.S. 1 (1952)

Mr. Chief Justice Vinson delivered the opinion of the Court.

These suits under the Tort Claims Act[1] arise from the death of three civilians in the crash of a B-29 aircraft at Waycross, Georgia, on October 6, 1948. Because an important question of the Government's privilege to resist discovery[2] is involved, we granted certiorari. 343 U.S. 918.

The aircraft had taken flight for the purpose of testing secret electronic equipment, with four civilian observers aboard. While aloft, fire broke out in one of the bomber's engines. Six of the nine crew members and three of the four civilian observers were killed in the crash.

The widows of the three deceased civilian observers brought consolidated suits against the United States. In the pretrial stages the plaintiffs moved, under Rule 34 of the Federal Rules of Civil Procedure,[3] for production of the Air Force's official accident investigation report and the statements of the three surviving crew members, taken in connection with the official investigation. The Government moved to quash the motion, claiming that these matters were privileged against disclosure pursuant to Air Force regulations promulgated under R. S. § 161.[4] The District Judge sustained plaintiff's motion, holding that good cause for production had been shown.[5] The claim of privilege under R. S. § 161 was rejected on the premise that the Tort Claims Act, in making the Government liable "in the same manner" as a private individual,[6] had waived any privilege based upon executive control over governmental documents.

Shortly after this decision, the District Court received a letter from the Secretary of the Air Force, stating that "it has been determined that it would not be in the public interest to furnish this report. . . ." The court allowed a rehearing on its earlier order, and at the rehearing the Secretary of the Air Force filed a formal "Claim of Privilege." This document repeated the prior claim based generally on R. S. § 161, and then stated that the Government further objected to production of the documents "for the reason that the aircraft in question, together with the personnel on board, were engaged in a highly secret mission of the Air Force." An affidavit of the Judge Advocate General, United States Air Force, was also filed with the court, which asserted that the demanded material could not be furnished "without seriously hampering national security, flying safety and the development of highly technical and secret military equipment." The same affidavit offered to produce the three surviving crew members, without cost, for examination by the plaintiffs. The witnesses would be allowed to refresh their memories from any statement made by them to the Air Force, and authorized to testify as to all matters except those of a "classified nature."

The District Court ordered the Government to produce the documents in order that the court might determine whether they contained privileged matter. The Government declined, so the court entered an order, under Rule 37 (b)(2)(i),[7] that the facts on the issue of negligence would be taken as established in plaintiffs' favor. After a hearing to determine damages, final judgment was entered for the plaintiffs. The Court of Appeals affirmed,[8] both as to the showing of good cause for production of the documents, and as to the ultimate disposition of the case as a consequence of the Government's refusal to produce the documents.

We have had broad propositions pressed upon us for decision. On behalf of the Government it has been urged that the executive department heads have power to withhold any documents in their custody from judicial view if they deem it to be in the public interest.[9] Respondents have asserted that the executive's power to withhold documents was waived by the Tort Claims Act. Both positions have constitutional overtones which we find it unnecessary to pass upon, there being a narrower ground for decision. *Touhy v. Ragen,* 340 U.S. 462 (1951); *Rescue Army v. Municipal Court of Los Angeles*, 331 U.S. 549, 574-585 (1947).

The Tort Claims Act expressly makes the Federal Rules of Civil Procedure applicable to suits against the United States.[10] The judgment in this case imposed liability upon the Government by operation of Rule 37, for refusal to produce documents under Rule 34. Since Rule 34 compels production only of matters "not privileged," the essential question is whether there was a valid claim of privilege under the Rule. We hold that there was, and that, therefore, the judgment below subjected the United States to liability on terms to which Congress did not consent by the Tort Claims Act.

We think it should be clear that the term "not privileged," as used in Rule 34, refers to "privileges" as that term is understood in the law of evidence. When the Secretary of the Air Force lodged his formal "Claim of Privilege," he attempted therein to invoke the privilege against revealing military secrets, a privilege which is well established in the law of evidence.[11] The existence of the privilege is conceded by the court below,[12] and, indeed, by the most outspoken critics of governmental claims to privilege.[13]

Judicial experience with the privilege which protects military and state secrets has been limited in this country.[14] English experience has been more extensive, but still relatively slight compared with other evidentiary privileges.[15] Nevertheless, the principles which control the application of the privilege emerge quite clearly from the available precedents. The privilege belongs to the Government and must be asserted by it; it can neither be claimed[16] nor waived[17] by a private party. It is not to be lightly invoked.[18] There must be a formal claim of privilege, lodged by the head of the department which has control over the matter,[19] after actual personal consideration by that officer.[20] The court itself must determine whether the circumstances are appropriate for the claim of privilege,[21] and yet do so without forcing a disclosure of the very thing the privilege is designed to protect.[22] The latter requirement is the only one which presents real difficulty. As to it, we find it helpful to draw upon judicial experience in dealing with an analogous privilege, the privilege against self-incrimination.

The privilege against self-incrimination presented the courts with a similar sort of problem. Too much judicial inquiry into the claim of privilege would force disclosure of the thing the privilege was means to protect while a complete abandonment of judicial control would lead to intolerable abuses. Indeed, in the earlier stages of judicial experience with the problem, both extremes were advocated, some saying that the bare assertion by the witness must be taken as conclusive, and others saying that the witness should be required to reveal the matter behind his claim of privilege to the judge for verification.[23] Neither extreme prevailed, and a sound formula of compromise was developed. This formula received authoritative expression in this country as early as the *Burr* trial.[24] There are differences in phraseology, but in substance it is agreed that the court must be satisfied from all the evidence and circumstances, and "from the implications of the question, in the setting in which it is asked, that a responsive answer to the question or an explanation of why it cannot be answered might be dangerous because injurious disclosure could result." *Hoffman v. United States*, 341 U.S. 479, 486-487 (1951).[25] If the court is so satisfied, the claim of the privilege will be accepted without requiring further disclosure.

Regardless of how it is articulated, some like formula of compromise must be applied here. Judicial control over the evidence in a case cannot be abdicated to the caprice of executive officers. Yet we will not go so far as to say that the court may automatically require a complete disclosure to the judge before the claim of privilege will be accepted in any case. It may be possible to satisfy the court, from all the circumstances of the case, that there is a reasonable danger that compulsion of the evidence will expose military matters which, in the interest of national security, should not be divulged. When this is the case, the occasion for the privilege is appropriate, and the court should not jeopardize the security which the privilege is meant to protect by insisting upon an examination of the evidence, even by the judge alone, in chambers.

In the instant case we cannot escape judicial notice that this is a time of vigorous preparation for national defense. Experience in the past war has made it common knowledge that air power is one of the most potent weapons in our scheme of defense, and that newly developing electronic devices have greatly enhanced the effective use of air power. It is equally apparent that these electronic devices must be kept secret if their full military advantage is to be exploited in the national interests. On the record before the trial court it appeared that this accident occurred to a military plane which had gone aloft to test secret electronic equipment. Certainly there was a reasonable danger that the accident investigation report would contain references to the secret electronic equipment which was the primary concern of the mission.

Of course, even with this information before him, the trial judge was in no position to decide that the report was privileged until there had been a formal claim of privilege. Thus it was entirely proper to rule initially that petitioner had shown probable cause for discovery of the documents. Thereafter, when the formal claim of privilege was filed by the Secretary of the Air Force, under circumstances indicating a reasonable possibility that military secrets were involved, there was certainly a sufficient showing of privilege to cut off further demand for the documents on the showing of necessity for its compulsion that had then been made.

In each case, the showing of necessity which is made will determine how far the court should probe in satisfying itself that the occasion for invoking the privilege is appropriate. Where there is a strong showing of necessity, the claim of privilege should not be lightly accepted, but even the most compelling necessity cannot overcome the claim of privilege if the court is ultimately satisfied that military secrets are at stake.[26] *A Fortiori,* where necessity is dubious, a formal claim of privilege, made under the circumstances of this case, will have to prevail. Here, necessity was greatly minimized by an available alternative, which might have given respondents the evidence to make out their case without forcing a showdown on the claim of privilege. By their failure to pursue that alternative, respondents have posed the privilege question for decision with the formal claim of privilege set against a dubious showing of necessity.

There is nothing to suggest that the electronic equipment, in this case, had any causal connection with the accident. Therefore, it should be possible for respondents to adduce the essential facts as to causation without resort to material touching upon military secrets. Respondents were given a reasonable opportunity to do just that, when petitioner formally offered to make the surviving crew members available for examination. We think that offer should have been accepted.

Respondents have cited us to those cases in the criminal field, where it has been held that the Government can invoke its evidentiary privileges only at the price of letting the defendant go free.[27] The rationale of the criminal cases is that, since the Government which prosecutes an accused also has the duty to see that justice is done, it is unconscionable to allow it to undertake prosecution and then invoke its governmental privileges to deprive the accused of anything which might be material to his defense. Such rationale has no application in a civil forum where the Government is not the moving party, but is a defendant only on terms to which it has consented.

The decision of the Court of Appeals is reversed and the case will be remanded to the District Court for further proceedings consistent with the views expressed in this opinion.

Reversed and remanded.

Mr. Justice Black, Mr. Justice Frankfurter, and Mr. Justice Jackson dissent, substantially for the reasons set forth in the opinion of Judge Maris below. 192 F. 2d 987.

* * *

[1]28 U.S.C. §§ 1346, 2674.

[2]Federal Rules of Civil Procedure, Rule 34.

[3]"Rule 34. *Discovery and Production of Documents and Things for Inspection, Copying, or Photographing.* Upon motion of any party showing good cause therefor and upon notice to all other parties, and subject to the provisions of Rule 30 (b), the court in which an action is pending may (1) order any party to produce and permit the inspection and copying or photographing, by or on behalf of the moving party, of any designated documents, papers, books, accounts, letters, photographs, objects, or tangible things, not privileged, which constitute or contain evidence relating to any of the matters within the scope of the examination permitted by Rule 26 (b) and which are in his possession, custody, or control; or (2) order any party to permit entry upon designated land or other property in his possession or control for the purpose of inspecting, measuring, surveying, or photo-

graphing the property or any designated object or operation thereon within the scope of the examination permitted by Rule 26 (b). The order shall specify the time, place, and manner of making the inspection and taking the copies and photographs and may prescribe such terms and conditions as are just."

4 5 U.S.C. § 22:

"The head of each department is authorized to prescribe regulations, not inconsistent with law, for the government of his department, the conduct of its officers and clerks, the distribution and performance of its business, and the custody, use, and preservation of the records, papers, and property appertaining to it."

Air Force Regulation No. 62-7 (5) (b) provides:

"Reports of boards of officers, special accident reports, or extracts therefrom will not be furnished or made available to persons outside the authorized chain of command without the specific approval of the Secretary of the Air Force."

5 10 F.R.D. 468.

6 28 U.S.C. § 2674:

"The United States shall be liable, respecting the provisions of this title relating to tort claims, in the same manner and to the same extent as a private individual under like circumstances, but shall not be liable for interest prior to judgment or for punitive damages."

7 "Rule 37. *Refusal to Make Discovery: Consequences.*

* * *

"(b) Failure to Comply With Order.

* * *

"(2) *Other Consequences. If any party or an officer or managing agent of a party refuses to obey . . . an order made under Rule 34 to produce any document . . . , the court may make such orders in regard to the refusal as are just, and among others the following:*

"(i) An order that the matters regarding which the questions were asked, or the character or description of the thing or land, or the contents of the paper, or the physical or mental condition of the party, or any other designated facts shall be taken to be established for the purposes of the action in accordance with the claim of the party obtaining the order; . . ."

8 192 F. 2d 987.

9 While claim of executive power to suppress documents is based more immediately upon R. S. § 161 (see *supra,* note 4), the roots go much deeper. It is said that R. S. § 161 is only a legislative recognition of an inherent executive power which is protected in the constitutional system of separation of power.

10 28 U. S. C. (1946 ed.) § 932; *United States v. Yellow Cab Co.,* 340 U.S. 543, 553 (1951).

11 *Totten v. United States,* 92 U.S. 105, 107 (1875); *Firth Sterling Steel Co. v. Bethlehem Steel Co.,* 199 F. 353 (D. C. E. D. Pa. 1912); *Pollen v. Ford Instrument Co.,* 26 F. Supp. 583 (D. C. E. D. N.Y. 1939); *Cresmer v. United States,* 9 F. R. D. 203 (D. C. E. D. N.Y. 1949); see *Bank Line v. United States,* 68 F. Supp. 587 (D. C. S. D. N.Y. 1946), 163 F. 2d 133 (C. A. 2d Cir. 1947). 8 Wigmore on Evidence (3d ed.) § 2212*a,* p. 161, and § 2378 (g) (5), at pp. 785 *et seq.*; 1 Greenleaf on Evidence (16th ed.) §§ 250-251; Sanford, Evidentiary Privileges Against the Production of Data Within the Control of Executive Departments, 3 Vanderbilt L. Rev. 73, 74-75 (1949).

12 192 F. 2d 987, 996.

13 See Wigmore, *op. cit. supra,* note 11.

14 See cases cited *supra,* note 11.

15 Most of the English precedents are reviewed in the recent case of *Duncan v. Cammell, Laird & Co.,* [1942] A. C. 624.

16 *Firth Sterling Steel Co. v. Bethlehem Steel Co.,* 199 F. 353 (D. C. E. D. Pa. 1912).

17 *In re Grove,* 180 F. 62 (C. A. 3d Cir. 1910).

18 Marshall, C. J., in the *Aaron Burr* trial, I Robertson's Reports 186: "That there may be matter, the production of which the court would not require, is certain. . . . What ought to be done, under such circumstances, presents a delicate question, the discussion of which, it is hoped, will never be rendered necessary in this country."

19 *Firth* case, *supra,* note 16.

20 "The essential matter is that the decision to object should be taken by the minister who is the political head of the department, and that he should have seen and considered the contents of the documents and himself have formed the view that on grounds of public interest they ought not to be produced. . . ." *Duncan v. Cammell, Laird & Co.,* [1942] A. C. 624, 638.

[21]*Id.*, at p. 642:

"Although an objection validly taken to production, on the ground that this would be injurious to the public interest, is conclusive, it is important to remember that *the decision ruling out such documents is the decisions of the judge*. . . . It is the judge who is in control of the trial, not the executive. . . ." (Emphasis supplied.)

[22]*Id.*, at pp. 638-642; cf. the language of this Court in *Hoffman v. United States*, 341 U.S. 479, 486 (1951), speaking of the analogous hazard of probing too far in derogation of the claim of privilege against self-incrimination:

"However, if the witness, upon interposing his claim, were required to prove the hazard in the sense in which a claim is usually required to be established in court, *he would be compelled to surrender the very protection which the privilege is designed to guarantee*." (Emphasis supplied.)

[23]Compare the expressions of Rolfe, B. and Wilde, C. J. in *Regina v. Garbett*, 2 Car. & K. 474, 492 (1847); see 8 Wigmore on Evidence (3d ed.) § 2271.

[24]I Robertson's Reports 244:

"When a question is propounded, it belongs to the court to consider and to decide, whether any direct answer to it can implicate the witness. If this be decided in the negative, then he may answer it without violating the privilege which is secured to him by law. If a direct answer to it *may* criminate himself, then he must be the sole judge what his answer would be. The court cannot participate with him in this judgment, because they cannot decide on the effect of his answer without knowing what it would be; and a disclosure of that fact to the judges would strip him of the privilege which the law allows, and which he claims."

[25]*Brown v. United States*, 276 U.S. 134 (1928); *Mason v. United States*, 244 U.S. 362 (1917).

[26]See *Totten v. United States*, 92 U.S. 105 (1875), where the very subject matter of the action, a contract to perform espionage, was a matter of state secret. The action was dismissed on the pleadings without ever reaching the question of evidence, since it was so obvious that the action should never prevail over the privilege.

[27]*United States v. Andolschek*, 142 F. 2d 503 (C. A. 2d Cir. 1944); *United States v. Beekman*, 155 F. 2d 580 (C. A. 2d Cir. 1946).

Jencks v. United States

353 U.S. 657 (1957)

* * *

The practice of producing government documents to the trial judge for his determination of relevancy and materiality, without hearing the accused, is disapproved.[15] Relevancy and materiality for the purposes of production and inspection, with a view to use on cross-examination, are established when the reports are shown to relate to the testimony of the witness. Only after inspection of the reports by the accused, must the trial judge determine admissibility—*e.g.*, evidentiary questions of inconsistency, materiality and relevancy—of the contents and the method to be employed for the elimination of parts immaterial or irrelevant. See *Gordon v. United States*, 344 U.S., at 418.

In the courts below the Government did not assert that the reports were privileged against disclosure on grounds of national security, confidential character of the reports, public interest or otherwise. In its brief in this Court, however, the Government argues that, absent a showing of contradiction, "[t]he rule urged by petitioner . . . disregards the legitimate interest that each party—including the Government—has in safeguarding the privacy of its files, particularly where the documents in question were obtained in confidence. Production of such documents, even to a court, should not be compelled in the absence of a preliminary showing by the party making the request." The petitioner's counsel, believing that Court of

Appeals' decisions imposed such a qualification, restricted his motions to a request for production of the reports to the trial judge for the judge's inspection and determination whether and to what extent the reports should be made available to the petitioner.

It is unquestionably true that the protection of vital national interests may militate against public disclosure of documents in the Government's possession. This has been recognized in decisions of this Court in civil causes where the Court has considered the statutory authority conferred upon the departments of Government to adopt regulations "not inconsistent with law, for . . . use . . . of the records, papers . . . appertaining" to his department.[16] The Attorney General has adopted regulations pursuant to this authority declaring all Justice Department records confidential and that no disclosure, including disclosure in response to subpoena, may be made without his permission.[17]

But this Court has noticed, in *United States v. Reynolds,* 345 U.S. 1, the holdings of the Court of Appeals for the Second Circuit[18] that, in criminal causes ". . . the Government can invoke its evidentiary privileges only at the price of letting the defendant go free. The rationale of the criminal cases is that, since the Government which prosecutes an accused also has the duty to see that justice is done, it is unconscionable to allow it to undertake prosecution and then invoke its governmental privileges to deprive the accused of anything which might be material to his defense. . . ." 345 U.S., at 12.

In *United States v. Andolschek,* 142 F. 2d 503, 506, Judge Learned Hand said:

> ". . . While we must accept it as lawful for a department of the government to suppress documents, even when they will help determine controversies between third persons, we cannot agree that this should include their suppression in a criminal prosecution, founded upon those very dealings to which the documents relate, and whose criminality they will, or may, tend to exculpate. So far as they directly touch the criminal dealings, the prosecution necessarily ends any confidential character the documents may possess; it must be conducted in the open, and will lay bare their subject matter. The government must choose; either it must leave the transactions in the obscurity from which a trial will draw them, or it must expose them fully. Nor does it seem to us possible to draw any line between documents whose contents bears directly upon the criminal transactions, and those which may be only indirectly relevant. Not only would such a distinction be extremely difficult to apply in practice, but the same reasons which forbid suppression in one case forbid it in the other, though not, perhaps, quite so imperatively. . . ."

We hold that the criminal action must be dismissed when the Government, on the ground of privilege, elects not to comply with an order to produce, for the accused's inspection and for admission in evidence, relevant statements or reports in its possession of government witnesses touching the subject matter of their testimony at the trial. Accord, *Roviaro v. United States,* 353 U.S. 53, 60-61. The burden is the Government's, not to be shifted to the trial judge, to decide whether the public prejudice of allowing the crime to go unpunished is greater than that attendant upon the possible disclosure of state secrets and other confidential information in the Government's possession.

Reversed.

Mr. Justice Frankfurter joins the opinion of the Court, but deeming that the questions relating to the instructions to the jury should be dealt with, since a new trial has been directed, he agrees with the respects in which, and the reasons for which, Mr. Justice Burton finds them erroneous.

Mr. Justice Whittaker took no part in the consideration or decision of this case.

Mr. Justice Burton, whom Mr. Justice Harlan joins, concurring in the result

* * *

Mr. Justice Clark, dissenting.

* * *

[15] See, *e.g.*, *United States v. Grayson*, 166 F. 2d 863, 869; *United States v. Beekman*, 155 F. 2d 580, 584; *United States v. Ebeling*, 146 F. 2d 254, 256; *United States v. Cohen*, 145 F. 2d 82, 92; *United States v. Krulewitch*, 145 F. 2d 76, 78.

[16] R. S. § 161, 5 U.S.C. § 22; *United States v. Reynolds*, 345 U.S. 1; cf. *Totten v. United States*, 92 U.S. 105.

[17] Atty. Gen Order No. 3229 (1939), 28 CFR, 1946 Supp., § 51.71; Atty. Gen. Order No. 3229, Supp. 2, Pike & Fischer Admin. Law 2d, Dept. of Justice 1 (1947); Atty. Gen. Order No. 3229, Rev., 18 Fed. Reg. 1368 (1953).

[18] *United States v. Beekman*, 155 F. 2d 580; *United States v. Andolschek*, 142 F. 2d 503.

New York Times Co. v. United States

403 U.S. 713 (1971)

Per Curiam.

We granted certiorari in these cases in which the United States seeks to enjoin the New York Times and the Washington Post from publishing the contents of a classified study entitled "History of U.S. Decision-Making Process on Viet Nam Policy." *Post*, pp. 942, 943.

"Any system of prior restraints of expression comes to this Court bearing a heavy presumption against its constitutional validity." *Bantam Books, Inc. v. Sullivan*, 372 U.S. 58, 70 (1963); see also *Near v. Minnesota*, 283 U.S. 697 (1931). The Government "thus carries a heavy burden of showing justification for the imposition of such a restraint." *Organization for a Better Austin v. Keefe*, 402 U.S. 415, 419 (1971). The District Court for the Southern District of New York in the *New York Times* case and the District Court for the District of Columbia and the Court of Appeals for the District of Columbia Circuit in the *Washington Post* case held that the Government had not met that burden. We agree.

The judgment of the Court of Appeals for the District of Columbia Circuit is therefore affirmed. The order of the Court of Appeals for the Second Circuit is reversed and the case is remanded with directions to enter a judgment affirming the judgment of the District Court for the Southern District of New York. The stays entered June 25, 1971, by the Court are vacated. The judgments shall issue forthwith.

So ordered.

Mr. Justice Black, with whom Mr. Justice Douglas joins, concurring.

I adhere to the view that the Government's case against the Washington Post should have been dismissed and that the injunction against the New York Times should have been vacated without oral argument when the cases were first presented to this Court. I believe that every moment's continuance of the injunctions against these newspapers amounts to a flagrant, indefensible, and continuing violation of the First Amendment. Furthermore, after oral argument, I agree completely that we must affirm the judgment of the Court of Appeals for the District of Columbia Circuit and reverse the judgment of the Court of Appeals for the Second Circuit for the reasons stated by my Brothers Douglas and Brennan. In my view it is unfortunate that some of my Brethren are apparently willing to hold that the publication of news may sometimes be enjoined. Such a holding would make a shambles of the First Amendment.

Our Government was launched in 1789 with the adoption of the Constitution. The Bill of Rights, including the First Amendment, followed in 1791. Now, for the first time in the 182 years since the founding of the Republic, the federal courts are asked to hold that the First Amendment does not mean what it says, but rather means that the Government can halt the publication of current news of vital importance to the people of this country.

In seeking injunctions against these newspapers and in its presentation to the Court, the Executive Branch seems to have forgotten the essential purpose and history of the First Amendment. When the Constitution was adopted, many people strongly opposed it because the document contained no Bill or Rights to safeguard certain basic freedoms.[1] They especially feared that the new powers granted to a central government might be interpreted to permit the government to curtail freedom of religion, press, assembly, and speech. In response to an overwhelming public clamor, James Madison offered a series of amendments to satisfy citizens that these great liberties would remain safe and beyond the power of government to abridge. Madison proposed what later became the First Amendment in three parts, two of which are set out below, and one of which proclaimed: "The people shall not be deprived or abridged of their right to speak, to write, or to publish their sentiments; *and the freedom of the press, as one of the great bulwarks of liberty, shall be inviolable.*"[2] (Emphasis added.) The amendments were offered to *curtail* and *restrict* the general powers granted to the Executive, Legislative, and Judicial Branches two years before in the original Constitution. The Bill of Rights changed the original Constitution into a new charter under which no branch of government could abridge the people's freedoms of press, speech, religion, and assembly. Yet the Solicitor General argues and some members of the Court appear to agree that the general powers of the Government adopted in the original Constitution should be interpreted to limit and restrict the specific and emphatic guarantees of the Bill of Rights adopted later. I can imagine no greater perversion of history. Madison and the other Framers of the First Amendment, able men that they were, wrote in language they earnestly believed could never be misunderstood: "Congress shall make no law . . . abridging the freedom . . . of the press . . . ." Both the history and language of the First Amendment support the view that the press must be left free to publish news, whatever the source, without censorship, injunctions, or prior restraints.

In the First Amendment the Founding Fathers gave the free press the protection it must have to fulfill its essential role in our democracy. The press was to serve the governed, not the governors. The Government's power to censor the press was abolished so that the press would remain forever free to censure the Government.

The press was protected so that it could bare the secrets of government and inform the people. Only a free and unrestrained press can effectively expose deception in government. And paramount among the responsibilities of a free press is the duty to prevent any part of the government from deceiving the people and sending them off to distant lands to die of foreign fevers and foreign shot and shell. In my view, far from deserving condemnation for their courageous reporting, the New York Times, the Washington Post, and other newspapers should be commended for serving the purpose that the Founding Fathers saw so clearly. In revealing the workings of government that led to the Vietnam war, the newspapers nobly did precisely that which the Founders hoped and trusted they would do.

The Government's case here is based on premises entirely different from those that guided the Framers of the First Amendment. The Solicitor General has carefully and emphatically stated:

> "Now, Mr. Justice [Black], your construction of ... [the First Amendment] is well known, and I certainly respect it. You say that no law means no law, and that should be obvious. I can only say, Mr. Justice, that to me it is equally obvious that 'no law' does not mean 'no law', and I would seek to persuade the Court that that is true. ... [T]here are other parts of the Constitution that grant powers and responsibilities to the Executive, and ... the First Amendment was not intended to make it impossible for the Executive to function or to protect the security of the United States."[3]

And the Government argues in its brief that in spite of the First Amendment, "[t]he authority of the Executive Departmet to protect the nation against publication of information whose disclosure would endanger the national security stems from two interrelated sources: the constitutional power of the President over the conduct of foreign affairs and his authority as Commander-in-Chief."[4]

In other words, we are asked to hold that despite the First Amendment's emphatic command, the Executive Branch, the Congress, and the Judiciary can make laws enjoining publication of current news and abridging freedom of the press in the name of "national security." The Government does not even attempt to rely on any act of Congress. Instead it makes the bold and dangerously far-reaching contention that the courts should take it upon themselves to "make" a law abridging freedom of the press in the name of equity, presidential power and national security, even when the representatives of the people in Congress have adhered to the command of the First Amendment and refused to make such a law.[5] See concurring opinion of Mr. Justice Douglas, *post*, at 721-722. To find that the President has "inherent power" to halt the publication of news by resort to the courts would wipe out the First Amendment and destroy the fundamental liberty and security of the very people the Government hopes to make "secure." No one can read the history of the adoption of the First Amendment without being convinced beyond any doubt that it was injunctions like those sought here that Madison and his collaborators intended to outlaw in this Nation for all time.

The word "security" is a broad, vague generality whose contours should not be invoked to abrogate the fundamental law embodied in the First Amendment. The guarding of military and diplomatic secrets at the expense of informed representative government provides no real security for our Republic. The Framers of the First Amendment, fully aware of both the need to defend a new nation and the abuses of the English and Colonial governments, sought to give this new society strength and security by providing that freedom of speech, press, religion, and assembly should not be abridged. This though was eloquently expressed in 1937 by

Mr. Chief Justice Hughes—great man and great Chief Justice that he was—when the Court held a man could not be punished for attending a meeting run by Communists.

> "The greater the importance of safeguarding the community from incitements to the overthrow of our institutions by force and violence, the more imperative is the need to preserve inviolate the constitutional rights of free speech, free press and free assembly in order to maintain the opportunity for free political discussion, to the end that government may be responsive to the will of the people and that changes, if desired, may be obtained by peaceful means. Therein lies the security of the Republic, the very foundation of constitutional government."[6]

---

[1]In introducing the Bill of Rights in the House of Representatives, Madison said: "[B]ut I believe that the great mass of the people who opposed [the Constitution], disliked it because it did not contain effectual provisions against the encroachments on particular rights. . . ." 1 Annals of Cong. 433. Congressman Goodhue added: "[I]t is the wish of many of our constituents, that something should be added to the Constitution, to secure in a stronger manner their liberties from the inroads of power." *Id.*, at 426.

[2]The other parts were:

"The civil rights of none shall be abridged on account of religious belief or worship, nor shall any national religion be established, nor shall the full and equal rights of conscience be in any manner, or on any pretext, infringed."

"The people shall not be restrained from peaceably assembling and consulting for their common good; nor from applying to the Legislature by petitions, or remonstrances, for redress of their grievances." 1 Annals of Cong. 434.

[3]Tr. of Oral Arg. 76.

[4]Brief for the United States 13-14.

[5]Compare the views of the Solicitor General with those of James Madison, the author of the First Amendment. When speaking of the Bill of Rights in the House of Representatives, Madison said: "If they [the first ten amendments] are incorporated into the Constitution, independent tribunals of justice will consider themselves in a peculiar manner the guardians of those rights; they will be an impenetrable bulwark against every assumption of power in the Legislative or Executive; they will be naturally led to resist every encroachment upon rights expressly stipulated for in the Constitution by the declaration of rights." 1 Annals of Cong. 439.

[6]*De Jonge v. Oregon*, 299 U.S. 353, 365.

Mr. Justice Douglas, with whom Mr. Justice Black joins, concurring.

While I join the opinion of the Court I believe it necessary to express my views more fully.

It should be noted at the outset that the First Amendment provides that "Congress shall make no law . . . abridging the freedom of speech, or of the press." That leaves, in my view, no room for governmental restraint on the press.[1]

There is, moreover, no statute barring the publication by the press of the material which the Times and the Post seek to use. Title 18 U.S.C. § 793 (e) provides that "[w]hoever having unauthorized possession of, access to, or control over any document, writing . . . or information relating to the national defense which information the possessor has reason to believe could be used to the injury of the United States or to the advantage of any foreign nation, willfully communicates . . . the same to any person not entitled to receive it . . . [s]hall be fined not more than $10,000 or imprisoned not more than ten years, or both."

The Government suggests that the word "communicates" is broad enough to encompass publication.

There are eight sections in the chapter on espionage and censorship, §§ 792-799. In three of those eight "publish" is specifically mentioned; § 794 (b) applies to "Whoever, in time of war, with intent that the same shall be communicated to the enemy, collects, records, *publishes*, or communicates . . . [the disposition of armed forces]."

Section 797 applies to whoever "reproduces, *publishes*, sells, or gives away" photographs of defense installations.

Section 798 relating to cryptography applies to whoever: "communicates, furnishes, transmits, or otherwise makes available . . . *or publishes*" the described material.[2] (Emphasis added.)

Thus it is apparent that Congress was capable of and did distinguish between publishing and communication in the various sections of the Espionage Act.

The other evidence that § 793 does not apply to the press is a rejected version of § 793. That version read: "During any national emergency resulting from a war to which the United States is a party, or from threat of such a war, the President may, by proclamation, declare the existence of such emergency and, by proclamation, prohibit the publishing or communicating of, or the attempting to publish or communicate any information relating to the national defense which, in his judgment, is of such character that it is or might be useful to the enemy." 55 Cong. Rec. 1763. During the debates in the Senate the First Amendment was specifically cited and that provision was defeated. 55 Cong. Rec. 2167.

Judge Gurfein's holding in the *Times* case that this Act does not apply to this case was therefore preeminently sound. Moreover, the Act of September 23, 1950, in amending 18 U. S. C. § 793 states in § 1 (b) that:

> "Nothing in this Act shall be construed to authorize, require, or establish military or civilian censorship or in any way to limit or infringe upon freedom of the press or of speech as guaranteed by the Constitution of the United States and no regulation shall be promulgated hereunder having that effect." 64 Stat. 987.

Thus Congress has been faithful to the command of the First Amendment in this area.

So any power that the Government possesses must come from its "inherent power."

The power to wage war is "the power to wage war successfully." See *Hirabayashi v. United States*, 320 U.S. 81, 93. But the war power stems from a declaration of war. The Constitution by Art. I, § 8, gives Congress, not the President, power "[t]o declare War." Nowhere are presidential wars authorized. We need not decide therefore what leveling effect the war power of Congress might have.

These disclosures[3] may have a serious impact. But that is no basis for sanctioning a previous restraint on the press. As stated by Chief Justice Hughes in *Near v. Minnesota*, 283 U.S. 697, 719-720:

> While reckless assaults upon public men, and efforts to bring obloquy upon those who are endeavoring faithfully to discharge official duties, exert a baleful influence and deserve the severest condemnation in public opinion, it cannot be said that this abuse is greater, and it is believed to be less, than that which characterized the period in which our institutions took shape. Meanwhile, the administration of government has become more complex, the opportunities for malfeasance and corruption have multiplied, crime has grown to most serious proportions, and the daner of its protection by unfaithful officials and of the impairment of the fundamental security of life

and property by criminal alliances and official neglect, emphasizes the primary need of a vigilant and courageous press, especially in great cities. The fact that the liberty of the press may be abused by miscreant purveyors of scandal does not make any the less necessary the immunity of the press from previous restraint in dealing with official misconduct."

As we stated only the other day in *Organization for a Better Austin v. Keefe,* 402 U.S. 415, 419, "[a]ny prior restraint on expression comes to this Court with a 'heavy presumption' against its constitutional validity."

The Government says that it has inherent powers to go into court and obtain an injunction to protect the national interest, which in this case is alleged to be national security.

Near v. Minnesota, 283 U.S. 697, repudiated that expansive doctrine in no uncertain terms.

The dominant purpose of the First Amendment was to prohibit the widespread practice of governmental suppression of embarrassing information. It is common knowledge that the First Amendment was adopted against the widespread use of the common law of seditious libel to punish the dissemination of material that is embarrassing to the powers-that-be. See T. Emerson, The System of Freedom of Expression, c. V (1970); Z. Chafee, Free Speech in the United States, c. XIII (1941). The present cases will, I think, go down in history as the most dramatic illustration of that principle. A debate of large proportions goes on in the Nation over our posture in Vietnam. That debate antedated the disclosure of the contents of the present documents. The latter are highly relevant to the debate in progress.

Secrecy in government is fundamentally anti-democratic, perpetuating bureaucratic errors. Open debate and discussion of public issues are vital to our national health. On public questions there should be "uninhibited, robust, and wide-open" debate. *New York Times Co. v. Sullivan,* 376 U.S. 254, 269-270.

I would affirm the judgment of the Court of Appeals in the *Post* case, vacate the stay of the Court of Appeals in the *Times* case and direct that it affirm the District Court.

The stays in these cases that have been in effect for more than a week constitute a flouting of the principles of the First Amendment as interpreted in *Near v. Minnesota.*

---

[1]See *Beauharnais v. Illinois,* 343 U.S. 250, 267 (dissenting opinion of Mr. Justice Black), 284 (my dissenting opinion); *Roth v. United States,* 354 U.S. 476, 508 (my dissenting opinion which Mr. Justice Black joined); *Yates v. United States,* 354 U.S. 298, 339 (separate opinion of Mr. Justice Black which I joined); *New York Times Co. v. Sullivan,* 376 U.S. 254, 293 (concurring opinion of Mr. Justice Black which I joined); *Garrison v. Louisiana,* 379 U.S. 64, 80 (my concurring opinion which Mr. Justice Black joined).

[2]These documents contain data concerning the communications system of the United States, the publication of which is made a crime. But the criminal sanction is not urged by the United States as the basis of equity power.

[3]There are numerous sets of this material in existence and they apparently are not under any controlled custody. Moreover, the President has sent a set to the Congress. We start then with a case where there already is rather wide distribution of the material that is destined for publicity, not secrecy. I have gone over the material listed in the *in camera* brief of the United States. It is all history, not future events. None of it is more recent than 1968.

Mr. Justice Brennan, concurring.

I

I write separately in these cases only to emphasize what should be apparent: that our judgments in the present cases may not be taken to indicate the propriety, in the future, of issuing temporary stays and restraining orders to block the publication of material sought to be suppressed by the Government. So far as I can determine, never before has the United States sought to enjoin a newspaper from publishing information in its possession. The relative novelty of the questions presented, the necessary haste with which decisions were reached, the magnitude of the interests asserted, and the fact that all the parties have concentrated their arguments upon the question whether permanent restraints were proper may have justified at least some of the restraints heretofore imposed in these cases. Certainly it is difficult to fault the several courts below for seeking to assure that the issues here involved were preserved for ultimate review by this Court. But even if it be assumed that some of the interim restraints were proper in the two cases before us, that assumption has no bearing upon the propriety of similar judicial action in the future. To begin with, there has now been ample time for reflection and judgment; whatever values there may be in the preservation of novel questions for appellate review may not support any restraints in the future. More important, the First Amendment stands as an absolute bar to the imposition of judicial restraints in circumstances of the kind presented by these cases.

II

The error that has pervaded these cases from the outset was the granting of any injunctive relief whatsoever, interim or otherwise. The entire thrust of the Government's claim throughout these cases has been that publication of the material sought to be enjoined "could," or "might," or "may" prejudice the national interest in various ways. But the First Amendment tolerates absolutely no prior judicial restraints of the press predicated upon surmise or conjecture that untoward consequences may result. Our cases, it is true, have indicated that there is a single, extremely narrow class of cases in which the First Amendment's ban on prior judicial restraint may be overridden. Our cases have thus far indicated that such cases may arise only when the Nation "is at war," *Schenck v. United States,* 249 U.S. 47, 52 (1919), during which times "[n]o one would question but that a government might prevent actual obstruction to its recruiting service or the publication of the sailing dates of transports or the number and location of troops." *Near v. Minnesota,* 283 U.S. 697, 716 (1931). Even if the present world situation were assumed to be tantamount to a time of war, or if the power of presently available armaments would justify even in peacetime the suppression of information that would set in motion a nuclear holocaust, in neither of these actions has the Government presented or even alleged that publication of items from or based upon the material at issue would cause the happening of an event of that nature. "[T]he chief purpose of [the First Amendment's] guaranty [is] to prevent previous restraints upon publication." *Near v. Minnesota, supra,* at 713. Thus, only governmental allegation and proof that publication must inevitably, directly, and immediately cause the occurrence of an event kindred to imperiling the safety of a transport already at sea can support even the issuance of an interim restraining order. In no event may mere conclusions be sufficient: for if the Executive Branch seeks judicial aid in preventing publication, it must inevitably submit the basis upon which that aid is sought to scrutiny by the judiciary. And therefore, every restraint issued in this case, whatever its form, has violated the First Amendment—and not less so because that restraint was justified as necessary to afford the courts an opportunity to examine the claim more thoroughly. Unless and until the Government has clearly made out its case, the First Amendment commands that no injunction may issue.

Mr. Justice Stewart, with whom Mr. Justice White joins, concurring.

In the governmental structure created by our Constitution, the Executive is endowed with enormous power in the two related areas of national defense and international relations. This power, largely unchecked by the Legislative[1] and Judicial[2] branches, has been pressed to the very hilt since the advent of the nuclear missile age. For better or for worse, the simple fact is that a President of the United States possesses vastly greater constitutional independence in these two vital areas of power than does, say, a prime minister of a country with a parliamentary form of government.

In the absence of the governmental checks and balances present in other areas of our national life, the only effective restraint upon executive policy and power in the areas of national defense and international affairs may lie in an enlightened citizenry—is an informed and critical public opinion which alone can here protect the values of democratic government. For this reason, it is perhaps here that a press that is alert, aware, and free most vitally serves the basic purpose of the First Amendment. For without an informed and free press there cannot be an enlightened people.

Yet it is elementary that the successful conduct of international diplomacy and the maintenance of an effective national defense require both confidentiality and secrecy. Other nations can hardly deal with this Nation in an atmosphere of mutual trust unless they can be assured that their confidences will be kept. And within our own executive departments, the development of considered and intelligent international policies would be impossible if those charged with their formulation could not communicate with each other freely, frankly, and in confidence. In the area of basic national defense the frequent need for absolute secrecy is, of course, self-evident.

I think there can be but one answer to this dilemma, if dilemma it be. The responsibility must be where the power is.[3] If the Constitution gives the Executive a large degree of unshared power in the conduct of foreign affairs and the maintenance of our national defense, then under the Constitution the Executive must have the largely unshared duty to determine and preserve the degree of internal security necessary to exercise that power successfully. It is an awesome responsibility, requiring judgment and wisdom of a high order. I should suppose that moral, political, and practical considerations would dictate that a very first principle of that wisdom would be an insistence upon avoiding secrecy for its own sake. For when everything is classified, then nothing is classified, and the system becomes one to be disregarded by the cynical or the careless, and to be manipulated by those intent on self-protection or self-promotion. I should suppose, in short, that the hallmark of a truly effective internal security system would be the maximum possible disclosure, recognizing that secrecy can best be preserved only when credibility is truly maintained. But be that as it may, it is clear to me that it is the constitutional duty of the Executive—as a matter of sovereign prerogative and not as a matter of law as the courts know law—through the promulgation and enforcement of executive regulations, to protect the confidentiality necessary to carry out its responsibilities in the fields of international relations and national defense.

This is not to say that Congress and the courts have no role to play. Undoubtedly Congress has the power to enact specific and appropriate criminal laws to protect government property and preserve government secrets. Congress has passed such laws, and several of them are of very colorable relevance to the apparent circumstances of these cases. And if a criminal prosecution is instituted, it will be the responsibility of the courts to decide the applicability of the criminal law under which the charge is brought. Moreover, if Congress should pass a specific law authorizing civil proceedings in this field, the courts would likewise have the duty to decide the constitutionality of such a law as well as its applicability to the facts proved.

But in the cases before us we are asked neither to construe specific regulations nor to apply specific laws. We are asked, instead, to perform a function that the Constitution gave to the Executive, not the Judiciary. We are asked, quite simply, to prevent the publication by two newspapers of material that the Executive Branch insists should not, in the national interest, be published. I am convinced that the Executive is correct with respect to some of the documents involved. But I cannot say that disclosure of any of them will surely result in direct, immediate, and irreparable damage to our Nation or its people. That being so, there can under the First Amendment be but one judicial resolution of the issues before us. I join the judgments of the Court.

---

[1]The President's power to make treaties and to appoint ambassadors is, of course, limited by the requirement of Art. II, § 2, of the Constitution that he obtain the advice and consent of the Senate. Article I, § 8, empowers Congress to "raise and support Armies," and "provide and maintain a Navy." And, of course, Congress alone can declare war. This power was last exercised almost 30 years ago at the inception of World War II. Since the end of that war in 1945, the Armed Forces of the United States have suffered approximately half a million casualties in various parts of the world.

[2]See *Chicago and Southern Air Lines v. Waterman S. S. Corp.*, 333 U.S. 103; *Hirabayashi v. United States*, 320 U.S. 81; *United States v. Curtiss-Wright Corp.*, 299 U.S. 304; cf. *Mora v. McNamara*, 128 U.S. App. D. C. 297, 387 F. 2d 862, cert. denied, 389 U.S. 934.

[3]"It is quite apparent that if, in the maintenance of our international relations, embarrassment—perhaps serious embarrassment—is to be avoided and success for our aims achieved, congressional legislation which is to be made effective through negotiation and inquiry within the international field must often accord to the President a degree of discretion and freedom from statutory restriction which would not be admissible were domestic affairs alone involved. Moreover, he, not Congress, has the better opportunity of knowing the conditions which prevail in foreign countries, and especially is this true in time of war. He has his confidential sources of information. He has his agents in the form of diplomatic, consular and other officials. Secrecy in respect of information gathered by them may be highly necessary, and the premature disclosure of it productive of harmful results. Indeed, so clearly is this true that the first President refused to accede to a request to lay before the House of Representatives the instructions, correspondence and documents relating to the negotiation of the Jay Treaty—a refusal the wisdom of which was recognized by the House itself and has never since been doubted. . . ." *United States v. Curtiss-Wright Corp.*, 299 U.S. 304, 320.

Mr. Justice White, with whom Mr. Justice Stewart joins, concurring.

I concur in today's judgments, but only because of the concededly extraordinary protection against prior restraints enjoyed by the press under our constitutional system. I do not say that in no circumstances would the First Amendment permit an injunction against publishing information about government plans or operations.[1] Nor, after examining the materials the Government characterizes as the most sensitive and destructive, can I deny that revelation of these documents will do substantial damage to public interests. Indeed, I am confident that their disclosure will have that result. But I nevertheless agree that the United States has not satisfied the very heavy burden that it must meet to warrant an injunction against publication in these cases, at least in the absence of express and appropriately limited congressional authorization for prior restraints in circumstances such as these.

The Government's position is simply stated: The responsibility of the Executive for the conduct of the foreign affairs and for the security of the Nation is so basic that the President is entitled to an injunction against publication of a newspaper story whenever he can convince a court that the information to be revealed threatens "grave and irreparable" injury to the public interest;[2] and the injunction should issue whether or not the material to be published is classified, whether or not publication would be lawful under relevant criminal statutes enacted by Congress, and regardless of the circumstances by which the newspaper came into possession of the information.

At least in the absence of legislation by Congress, based on its own investigations and findings, I am quite unable to agree that the inherent powers of the Executive and the courts reach so far as to authorize remedies having such sweeping potential for inhibiting publications by the press. Much of the difficulty inheres in the "grave and irreparable danger" standard suggested by the United States. If the United States were to have judgment under such a standard in these cases, our decision would be of little guidance to other courts in other cases, for the material at issue here would not be available from the Court's opinion or from public records, nor would it be published by the press. Indeed, even today where we hold that the United States has not met its burden, the material remains sealed in court records and it is properly not discussed in today's opinions. Moreover, because the material poses substantial dangers to national interests and because of the hazards of criminal sanctions, a responsible press may choose never to publish the more sensitive materials. To sustain the Government in these cases would start the courts down a long and hazardous road that I am not willing to travel, at least without congressional guidance and direction.

It is not easy to reject the proposition urged by the United States and to deny relief on its good-faith claims in these cases that publication will work serious damage to the country. But that discomfiture is considerably dispelled by the infrequency of prior-restraint cases. Normally, publication will occur and the damage be done before the Government has either opportunity or grounds for suppression. So here, publication has already begun and a substantial part of the threatened damage has already occurred. The fact of a massive breakdown in security is known, access to the documents by many unauthorized people is undeniable, and the efficacy of equitable relief against these or other newspapers to avert anticipated damage is doubtful at best.

What is more, terminating the ban on publication of the relatively few sensitive documents the Government now seeks to suppress does not mean that the law either requires or invites newspapers or others to publish them or that they will be immune from criminal action if they do. Prior restraints require an unusually heavy justification under the First Amendment; but failure by the Government to justify prior restraints does not measure its constitutional entitlement to a conviction for criminal publication. That the Government mistakenly chose to proceed by injunction does not mean that it could not successfully proceed in another way.

When the Espionage Act was under consideration in 1917, Congress eliminated from the bill a provision that would have given the President broad powers in time of war to proscribe, under threat of criminal penalty, the publication of various categories of information related to the national defense.[3] Congress at that time was unwilling to clothe the President with such far-reaching powers to monitor the press, and those opposed to this part of the legislation assumed that a necessary concomitant of such power was the power to "filter out the news to the people through some man." 55 Cong. Rec. 2008 (remarks of Sen. Ashurst). However, these same members of Congress appeared to have little doubt that newspapers would be subject to criminal prosecution if they insisted on publishing information of the type Congress had itself determined should not be revealed. Senator Ashurst, for example, was quite sure that the editor of such a newspaper "should be punished if he did publish information as to the movements of the fleet, the troops, the aircraft, the location of powder factories, the location of defense works, and all that sort of thing." *Id.*, at 2009.[4]

The Criminal Code contains numerous provisions potentially relevant to these cases. Section 797[5] makes it a crime to publish certain photographs or drawings of military installations. Section 798,[6] also in precise language, proscribes knowing and willful publication of any classified information concerning the cryptographic systems or communication intelligence activities of the United States as well as any information obtained from communication intelligence operations.[7] If any of the material here at issue is of this nature, the newspapers are presumably now on full notice of the position of the United States and must face the consequences if they publish. I would have no difficulty in sustaining convictions under these sections on facts that would not justify the intervention of equity and the imposition of a prior restraint.

The same would be true under those sections of the Criminal Code casting a wider net to protect the national defense. Section 793 (e)[8] makes it a criminal act for any unauthorized possessor of a document "relating to the national defense" either (1) willfully to communicate or cause to be communicated that document to any person not entitled to receive it or (2) willfully to retain the document and fail to deliver it to an officer of the United States entitled to receive it. The subsection was added in 1950 because pre-existing law provided no penalty for the unauthorized possessor unless demand for the documents was made.[9] "The dangers surrounding the unauthorized possession of such items are self-evident, and it is deemed advisable to require their surrender in such a case, regardless of demand, especially since their unauthorized possession may be unknown to the authorities who would otherwise make the demand." S. Rep. No. 2369, pt. 1, 81st Cong., 2d Sess., 9 (1950). Of course, in the cases before us, the unpublished documents have been demanded by the United States and their import has been made known at least to counsel for the newspapers involved. In *Gorin v. United States,* 312 U.S. 19, 28 (1941), the words "national defense" as used in a predecessor of § 793 were held by a unanimous Court to have "a well understood connotation"—a "generic concept of broad connotations, referring to the military and naval establishments and the related activities of national preparedness"—and to be "sufficiently definite to apprise the public of prohibited activities" and to be consonant with due process. 312 U.S., at 28. Also, as construed by the Court in *Gorin*, information "connected with the national defense" is obviously not limited to that threatening "grave and irreparable" injury to the United States.[10]

It is thus clear that Congress has addressed itself to the problems of protecting the security of the country and the national defense from unauthorized disclosure of potentially damaging information. Cf. *Youngstown Sheet & Tube Co. v. Sawyer*, 343 U.S. 579, 585-586 (1952); see also *id.*, at 593-628 (Frankfurter, J., concurring). It has not, however, authorized the injunctive remedy against threatened publication. It has apparently been satisfied to rely on criminal sanctions and their deterrent effect on the responsible as well as the irresponsible press. I am not, of course, saying that either of these newspapers has yet committed a crime or that either would commit a crime if it published all the material now in its possession. That matter must await resolution in the context of a criminal proceeding if one is instituted by the United States. In that event, the issue of guilt or innocence would be determined by procedures and standards quite different from those that have purported to govern these injunctive proceedings.

---

[1]The Congress has authorized a strain of prior restraints against private parties in certain instances. The National Labor Relations Board routinely issues cease-and-desist orders against employers who it finds have threatened or coerced employees in the exercise of protected rights. See 29 U. S. C. § 160 (c). Similarly, the Federal Trade Commission is empowered to impose cease-and-desist orders against unfair methods of competition. 15 U. S. C. § 45 (b). Such orders can, and quite often do, restrict what may be spoken or written under certain circumstances. See, *e.g., NLRB v. Gissel Packing Co.,* 395 U.S. 575, 616-620 (1969). Article I, § 8, of the Constitution authorizes Congress to secure the "exclusive right" of authors to their writings, and no one denies that a newspaper can properly be enjoined from publishing the copyrighted works of another. See *Westermann Co. v. Dispatch Co.,* 249 U.S. 100 (1919). Newspapers do themselves rely from time to time on the copyright as a means of protecting their accounts of important events. However, those enjoined under the statutes relating to the National Labor Relations Board and the Federal Trade Commission are private parties, not the press; and when the press is enjoined under the copyright laws the complainant is a private copyright holder enforcing a private right. These situations are quite distinct from the Government's request for an injunction against publishing information about the affairs of government, a request admittedly not based on any statute.

[2]The "grave and irreparable danger" standard is that asserted by the Government in this Court. In remanding to Judge Gurfein for further hearings in the *Times* litigation, five members of the Court of Appeals for the Second Circuit directed him to determine whether disclosure of certain items specified with particularity by the Government would "pose such grave and immediate danger to the security of the United States as to warrant their publication being enjoined."

[3]"Whoever, in time of war, in violation of reasonable regulations to be prescribed by the President, which he is hereby authorized to make and promulgate, shall publish any information with respect to the movement, numbers, description, condition, or disposition of any of the armed forces, ships, aircraft, or war materials of the United States, or with respect to the plans or conduct of any naval or military operations, or with respect to any works or measures undertaken for or connected with, or intended for the fortification or defense of any place, or any other information relating to the public defense calculated to be useful to the enemy, shall be punished by a fine . . . or by imprisonment. . . ." 55 Cong. Rec. 2100.

[4]Senator Ashurst also urged that " 'freedom of the press' means freedom from the restraints of a censor, means the absolute liberty and right to publish whatever you wish; but you take your chances of punishment in the courts of your country for the violation of the laws of libel, slander, and treason." 55 Cong. Rec. 2005.

[5]Title 18 U. S. C. § 797 provides:

"On and after thirty days from the date upon which the President defines any vital military or naval installation or equipment as being within the category contemplated under section 795 of this title, whoever reproduces, publishes, sells, or gives away any photograph, sketch, picture, drawing, map, or graphical representation of the vital military or naval installations or equipment so defined, without first obtaining permission of the commanding officer of the military or naval post, camp, or station concerned, or higher authority, unless such photograph, sketch, picture, drawing, map, or graphical representation has clearly indicated thereon that it has been censored by the proper military or naval authority, shall be fined not more than $1,000 or imprisoned not more than one year, or both."

[6]In relevant part 18 U. S. C. § 798 provides:

"(a) Whoever knowingly and willfully communicates, furnishes, transmits, or otherwise makes available to an unauthorized person, or publishes, or uses in any manner prejudicial to the safety or interest of the United States or for the benefit of any foreign government to the detriment of the United States any classified information—

"(1) concerning the nature, preparation, or use of any code, cipher, or cryptographic system of the United States or any foreign government; or

"(2) concerning the design, construction, use, maintenance, or repair of any device, apparatus, or appliance used or prepared or planned for use by the United States or any foreign government for cryptographic or communication intelligence purposes; or

"(3) concerning the communication intelligence activities of the United States or any foreign government; or

"(4) obtained by the process of communication intelligence from the communications of any foreign government, knowing the same to have been obtained by such processes—

"Shall be fined not more than $10,000 or imprisoned not more than ten years, or both."

[7]The purport of 18 U. S. C. § 798 is clear. Both the House and Senate Reports on the bill, in identical terms, speak of furthering the security of the United States by preventing disclosure of information concerning the cryptographic systems and the communication intelligence systems of the United States, and explaining that "[t]his bill makes it a crime to reveal the methods, techniques, and materiel used in the transmission by this Nation of enciphered or coded messages. . . . Further, it makes it a crime to reveal methods used by this Nation in breaking the secret codes of a foreign nation. It also prohibits under certain penalties the divulging of any information which may have come into this Government's hands as a result of such a code-breaking." H. R. Rep. No. 1895, 81st Cong., 2d Sess., 1 (1950). The narrow reach of the statute was explained as covering "only a small category of classified matter, a category which is both vital and vulnerable to an almost unique degree." *Id.*, at 2. Existing legislation was deemed inadequate.

"At present two other acts protect this information, but only in a limited way. These are the Espionage Act of 1917 (40 Stat. 217) and the act of June 10, 1933 (48 Stat. 122). Under the first, unauthorized revelation of information of this kind can be penalized only if it can be proved that the person making the revelation did so with an intent to injure the United States. Under the second, only diplomatic codes and messages transmitted in diplomatic codes are protected. The present bill is designed to protect against knowing and willful publication or any other revelation of all important information affecting the United States communication intelligence operations and all direct information about all United States codes and ciphers." *Ibid.*

Section 798 obviously was intended to cover publications by nonemployees of the Government and to ease the Government's burden in obtaining convictions. See H. R. Rep. No. 1895, *supra*, at 2-5. The identical Senate Report, not cited in parallel in the text of this footnote, is S. Rep. No. 111, 81st Cong., 1st Sess. (1949).

[8]Section 793 (e) of 18 U. S. C. provides that:

"(e) Whoever having unauthorized possession of, access to, or control over any document, writing, code book, signal book, sketch, photograph, photographic negative, blueprint, plan, map, model, instrument, appliance, or note relating to the national defense, or information relating to the national defense which information the possessor has reason to believe could be used to the injury of the United States or to the advantage of any foreign nation, willfully communicates, delivers, transmits or causes to be communicated, delivered, or transmitted, or attempts to communicate, deliver, transmit or cause to be communicated, delivered, or transmitted the same to any person not entitled to receive it, or willfully retains the same and fails to deliver it to the officer or employee of the United States entitled to receive it;"

is guilty of an offense punishable by 10 years in prison, a $10,000 fine, or both. It should also be noted that 18 U. .S. C. § 793 (g), added in 1950 (see 64 Stat. 1004; S. Rep. No. 2369, pt. 1, 81st Cong., 2d Sess., 9 (1950)), provides that "[i]f two or more persons conspire to violate any of the foregoing provisions of this section, and one or more of such persons do any act to effect the object of the conspiracy, each of the parties to such conspiracy shall be subject to the punishment provided for the offense which is the object of such conspiracy."

[9]The amendment of § 793 that added subsection (e) was part of the Subversive Activities Control Act of 1950, which was in turn Title I of the Internal Security Act of 1950. See 64 Stat. 987. The report of the Senate Judiciary Committee best explains the purposes of the amendment:

"Section 18 of the bill amends section 793 of title 18 of the United States Code (espionage statute). The several paragraphs of section 793 of title 18 are designated as subsections (a) through (g) for purposes of convenient reference. The significant changes which would be made in section 793 of title 18 are as follows:

"(1) Amends the fourth paragraph of section 793, title 18 (subsec. (d)), to cover the unlawful dissemination of 'information relating to the national defense which information the possessor has reason to believe could be used to the injury of the United States or to the advantage of any foreign nation.' *The phrase 'which information the possessor has reason to believe could be used to the injury of the United States or to the advantage of any foreign nation' would modify only 'information relating to the national defense' and not the other items enumerated in the subsection.* The fourth paragraph of section 793 is also amended to provide that only those with lawful possession of the items relating to national defense enumerated therein may retain them subject to demand therefor. Those who have unauthorized possession of such items are treated in a separated subsection.

"(2) Amends section 793, title 18 (subsec. (e)), to provide that unauthorized possessors of items enumerated in paragraph 4 of section 793 must surrender possession thereof to the proper authorities without demand. Existing law provides no penalty for the unauthorized possession of such items unless a demand for them is made by the person entitled to receive them. The dangers surrounding the unauthorized possession of such items are self-evident, and it is deemed advisable to require their surrender in such a case, regardless of demand, especially since their unauthorized possession may be unknown to the authorities who would otherwise make the demand. The only difference between subsection (d) and subsection (e) of section 793 is that a demand by the person entitled to receive the items would be a necessary element of an offense under subsection (d) where the possession is lawful, whereas such a demand would not be a necessary element of an offense under subsection (e) where the possession is unauthorized." S. Rep. No. 2369, pt. 1, 81st Cong., 2d Sess., 8-9 (1950) (emphasis added).

It seems clear from the foregoing, contrary to the intimations of the District Court for the Southern District of New York in this case, that in prosecuting for communicating or withholding a "document" as contrasted with similar action with respect to "information" the Government need not prove an intent to injure the United States or to benefit a foreign nation but only willful and knowing conduct. The District Court relied on *Gorin v. United States,* 312 U.S. 19 (1941). But that case arose under other parts of the predecessor to § 793, see 312 U.S., at 21-22—parts that imposed different intent standards not repeated in § 793 (d) or § 793 (e). Cf. 18 U. S. C. §§ 793 (a), (b), and (c). Also, from the face of subsection (e) and from the context of the Act of which it was a part, it seems undeniable that a newspaper, as well as other unconnected with the Government, are vulnerable to prosecution under § 793 (e) if they communicate or withhold the materials covered by that section. The District Court ruled that "communication" did not reach publication by a newspaper of documents relating to the national defense. I intimate no views on the correctness of that conclusion. But neither communication nor publication is necessary to violate the subsection.

[10]Also relevant is 18 U. S. C. § 794. Subsection (b) thereof forbids in time of war the collection or publication, with intent that it shall be communicated to the enemy, of any information with respect to the movements of military forces, "or with respect to the plans or conduct . . . of any naval or military operations . . . or any other information relating to the public defense, which might be useful to the enemy. . . ."

Mr. Justice Marshall, concurring.

The Government contends that the only issue in these cases is whether in a suit by the United States, "the First Amendment bars a court from prohibiting a newspaper from publishing material whose disclosure would pose a 'grave and immediate danger to the security of the United States.' " Brief for the United States 7. With all due respect, I believe the ultimate issue in these cases is even more basic than the one posed by the Solicitor General. The issue is whether this Court or the Congress has the power to make law.

In these cases there is no problem concerning the President's power to classify information as "secret" or "top secret." Congress has specifically recognized Presidential authority, which has been formally exercised in Exec. Order 10501 (1953), to classify documents and information. See, *e.g.,* 18 U. S. C. § 798; 50 U. S. C. § 783.[1] Nor is there any issue regarding the President's power as Chief Executive and Commander in Chief to protect national security by disciplining employees who disclose information and by taking precautions to prevent leaks.

The problem here is whether in these particular cases the Executive Branch has authority to invoke the equity jurisdiction of the courts to protect what it believes to be the national interest. See *In re Debs,* 158 U.S. 564, 584 (1895). The Government argues that in addition to the inherent power of any government to protect itself, the

President's power to conduct foreign affairs and his position as Commander in Chief give him authority to impose censorship on the press to protect his ability to deal effectively with foreign nations and to conduct the military affairs of the country. Of course, it is beyond cavil that the President has broad powers by virtue of his primary responsibility for the conduct of our foreign affairs and his position as Commander in Chief. *Chicago & Southern Air Lines v. Waterman S. S. Corp.*, 333 U.S. 103 (1948); *Hirabayashi v. United States,* 320 U.S. 81, 93 (1943); *United States v. Curtiss-Wright Corp.*, 299 U.S. 304 (1936).[2] And in some situations it may be that under whatever inherent powers the Government may have, as well as the implicit authority derived from the President's mandate to conduct foreign affairs and to act as Commander in Chief, there is a basis for the invocation of the equity jurisdiction of this Court as an aid to prevent the publication of material damaging to "national security," however that term may be defined.

It would, however, be utterly inconsistent with the concept of separation of powers for this Court to use its power of contempt to prevent behavior that Congress has specifically declined to prohibit. There would be a similar damage to the basic concept of these co-equal branches of Government if when the Executive Branch has adequate authority granted by Congress to protect "national security" it can choose instead to invoke the contempt power of a court to enjoin the threatened conduct. The Constitution provides that Congress shall make laws, the President execute laws, and courts interpret laws. *Youngstown Sheet & Tube Co. v. Sawyer*, 343 U.S. 579 (1952). It did not provide for government by injunction in which the courts and the Executive Branch can "make law" without regard to the action of Congress. It may be more convenient for the Executive Branch if it need only convince a judge to prohibit conduct rather than ask the Congress to pass a law, and it may be more convenient to enforce a contempt order than to seek a criminal conviction in a jury trial. Moreover, it may be considered politically wise to get a court to share the responsibility for arresting those who the Executive Branch has probable cause to believe are violating the law. But convenience and political considerations of the moment do not justify a basic departure from the principles of our system of government.

In these cases we are not faced with a situation where Congress has failed to provide the Executive with broad power to protect the Nation from disclosure of damaging state secrets. Congress has on several occasions given extensive consideration to the problem of protecting the military and strategic secrets of the United States. This consideration has resulted in the enactment of statutes making it a crime to receive, disclose, communicate, withhold, and publish certain documents, photographs, instruments, appliances, and information. The bulk of these statutes is found in chapter 37 of U. S. C., Title 18, entitled Espionage and Censorship.[3] In that chapter, Congress has provided penalties ranging from a $10,000 fine to death for violating the various statutes.

Thus it would seem that in order for this Court to issue an injunction it would require a showing that such an injunction would enhance the already existing power of the Government to act. See *Bennett v. Laman,* 277 N.Y. 368, 14 N. E. 2d 439 (1938). It is a traditional axiom of equity that a court of equity will not do a useless thing just as it is a traditional axiom that equity will not enjoin the commission of a crime. See Z. Chafee & E. Re, Equity 935-954 (5th ed. 1967); 1 H. Joyce, Injunctions §§ 58-60a (1909). Here there has been no attempt to make such a showing. The Solicitor General does not even mention in his brief whether the Government considers that there is probable cause to believe a crime has been committed or whether there is a conspiracy to commit future crimes.

If the Government had attempted to show that there was no effective remedy under traditional criminal law, it would have had to show that there is no arguably applicable statute. Of course, at this stage this Court could not and cannot determine whether there has been a violation of a particular statute or decide the constitutionality of any statute. Whether a good-faith prosecution could have been instituted under any statute could, however, be determined.

At least one of the many statutes in this area seems relevant to these cases. Congress has provided in 18 U. S. C. § 793 (e) that whoever "having unauthorized possession of, access to, or control over any document, writing, code book, signal book . . . or note relating to the national defense, or information relating to the national defense which information the possessor has reason to believe could be used to the injury of the United States or to the advantage of any foreign nation, willfully communicates, delivers, transmits . . . the same to any person not entitled to receive it, or willfully retains the same and fails to deliver it to the officer or employee of the United States entitled to receive it . . . [s]hall be fined not more than $10,000 or imprisoned not more than ten years, or both." Congress has also made it a crime to conspire to commit any of the offenses listed in 18 U. S. C. § 793 (e).

It is true that Judge Gurfein found that Congress had not made it a crime to publish the items and material specified in § 793 (e). He found that the words "communicates, delivers, transmits . . ." did not refer to publication of newspaper stories. And that view has some support in the legislative history and conforms with the past practice of using the statute only to prosecute those charged with ordinary espionage. But see 103 Cong. Rec. 10449 (remarks of Sen. Humphrey). Judge Gurfein's view of the statute is not, however, the only plausible construction that could be given. See my Brother White's concurring opinion.

Even if it is determined that the Government could not in good faith bring criminal prosecutions against the New York Times and the Washington Post, it is clear that Congress has specifically rejected passing legislation that would have clearly given the President the power he seeks here and made the current activity of the newspapers unlawful. When Congress specifically declines to make conduct unlawful it is not for this Court to redecide those issues—to overrule Congress. See *Youngstown Sheet & Tube Co. v. Sawyer,* 343 U.S. 579 (1952).

On at least two occasions Congress has refused to enact legislation that would have made the conduct engaged in here unlawful and given the President the power that he seeks in this case. In 1917 during the debate over the original Espionage Act, still the basic provisions of § 793, Congress rejected a proposal to give the President in time of war or threat of war authority to directly prohibit by proclamation the publication of information relating to national defense that might be useful to the enemy. The proposal provided that:

> "During any national emergency resulting from a war to which the United States is a party, or from threat of such a war, the President may, by proclamation, declare the existence of such emergency and, by proclamation, prohibit the publishing or communicating of, or the attempting to publish or communicate any information relating to the national defense which, in his judgment, is of such character that it is or might be useful to the enemy. Whoever violates any such prohibition shall be punished by a fine of not more than $10,000 or by imprisonment for not more than 10 years, or both: *Provided,* That nothing in this section shall be construed to limit or restrict any discussion, comment, or criticism of the acts or policies of the Government or its representatives or the publication of the same." 55 Cong. Rec. 1763.

Congress rejected this proposal after war against Germany had been declared even though many believed that there was a grave national emergency and that the threat of security leaks and espionage was serious. The Executive Branch has not gone to Congress and requested that the decision to provide such powered be reconsidered. Instead, the Executive Branch comes to this Court and asks that it be granted the power Congress refused to give.

In 1957 the United States Commission on Government Security found that "[a]irplane journals, scientific periodicals, and even the daily newspaper have featured articles containing information and other data which should have been deleted in whole or in part for security reasons." In response to this problem the Commission proposed that "Congress enact legislation making it a crime for any person willfully to disclose without proper authorization, for any purpose whatever, information classified 'secret' or 'top secret,' knowing, or having reasonable grounds to believe, such information to have been so classified." Report of Commission on Government Security 619-620 (1957). After substantial floor discussion on the proposal, it was rejected. See 103 Cong. Rec. 10447-10450. If the proposal that Sen. Cotton championed on the floor had been enacted, the publication of the documents involved here would certainly have been a crime. Congress refused, however, to make it a crime. The Government is here asking this Court to remake that decision. This Court has no such power.

Either the Government has the power under statutory grant to use traditional criminal law to protect the country or, if there is no basis for arguing that Congress has made the activity a crime, it is plain that Congress has specifically refused to grant the authority the Government seeks from this Court. In either case this Court does not have authority to grant the requested relief. It is not for this Court to fling itself into every breach perceived by some Government official nor is it for this Court to take on itself the burden of enacting law, especially a law that Congress has refused to pass.

I believe that the judgment of the United States Court of Appeals for the District of Columbia Circuit should be affirmed and the judgment of the United States Court of Appeals for the Second Circuit should be reversed insofar as it remands the case for further hearings.

---

[1]See n. 3, *infra.*

[2]But see *Kent v. Dulles,* 357 U.S. 116 (1958); *Youngstown Sheet & Tube Co. v. Sawyer,* 343 U.S. 579 (1952).

[3]There are several other statutory provisions prohibiting and punishing the dissemination of information, the disclosure of which Congress thought sufficiently imperiled national security to warrant that result. These include 42 U. S. C. §§ 2161 through 2166 relating to the authority of the Atomic Energy Commission to classify and declassify "Restricted Data" ["Restricted Data" is a term of art employed uniquely by the Atomic Energy Act]. Specifically, 42 U. S. C. § 2162 authorizes the Atomic Energy Commission to classify certain information. Title 42 U. S. C. § 2274, subsection (a), provides penalties for a person who "communicates, transmits, or discloses [restricted data]. . . with intent to injure the United States or with intent to secure an advantage to any foreign nation. . . ." Subsection (b) of § 2274 provides lesser penalties for one who "communicates, transmits, or discloses" such information "with reason to believe such data will be utilized to injure the United States or to secure an advantage to any foreign nation. . . ." Other sections of Title 42 of the United States Code dealing with atomic energy prohibit and punish acquisition, removal, concealment, tampering with, alteration, mutilation, or destruction of documents incorporating "Restricted Data" and provide penalties for employees and former employees of the Atomic Energy Commission, the armed services, contractors and licensees of the Atomic Energy Commission. Title 42 U. S. C. §§ 2276, 2277. Title 50 U. S. C. App. § 781, 56 Stat. 390, prohibits the making of any sketch or other representation of military installations or any military equipment located on any military

installation, as specified; and indeed Congress in the National Defense Act of 1940, 54 Stat. 676, as amended, 56 Stat. 179, conferred jurisdiction on federal district courts over civil actions "to enjoin any violation" thereof. 50 U. S. C. App. § 1152 (6). Title 50 U. S. C. § 783 (b) makes it unlawful for any officers or employees of the United States or any corporation which is owned by the United States to communicate material which has been "classified" by the President to any person who that governmental employee knows or has reason to believe is an agent or representative of any foreign government or any Communist organization.

Mr. Chief Justice Burger, dissenting. . . .

Mr. Justice Harlan, with whom the Chief Justice and Mr. Justice Blackman join, dissenting.

United States v. Marchetti

466 F.2d 1309 (1972)

Haynsworth, Chief Judge:

The question for decision is the enforceability of a secrecy agreement exacted by the government, in its capacity as employer, from an employee of the Central Intelligence Agency. Marchetti contends that his First Amendment rights foreclose any prior restraint upon him in carrying out his purpose to write and publish what he pleases about the Agency and its operations. Relying on a secrecy agreement signed by Marchetti when he became an employee of the Agency and on a secrecy oath signed by Marchetti when he resigned from the Agency, the District Court ordered Marchetti to submit to the Agency thirty days in advance of release to any person or corporation, any writing, fictional or non-fictional, relating to the Agency or to intelligence and ordering him not to release any writing relating to the Agency or to intelligence without prior authorization from the Director of Central Intelligence or from his designated representative. Marchetti was also ordered to return any writing or other property of the United States he had acquired while employed by the Agency.

We affirm the substance of the decision below, limiting the order, however to the language of the secrecy agreement Marchetti signed when he joined the Agency. We find the contract constitutional and otherwise reasonable and lawful.

This action was initiated on April 18, 1972, when the United States was granted an ex parte temporary restraining order against Marchetti by the District Court. A hearing was set for April 28, 1972, on the Government's motion for a preliminary injunction. On April 21, 1972, Marchetti moved to have the District Court dissolve the temporary restraining order. After that motion had been denied, an interlocutory appeal pursuant to 28 U.S.C. § 1292(b) was sought in this court. After oral argument, this panel denied the request for an interlocutory appeal and for writs of mandamus and prohibition, but directed the United States not to interfere with prospective witnesses for Marchetti. Counsel for Marchetti subsequently sought a postponement until May 14, 1972 of the hearing on the preliminary injunction. In granting this postponement, the District Court ordered the trial on the merits consolidated with the hearing on the motion for the preliminary injunction. The trial, held on May 15, was followed on May 19, 1972 by the District Court's

Memorandum Opinion and Order granting the injunction sought by the United States.

Marchetti was an employee of the Central Intelligence Agency from October 3, 1955 until he resigned effective September 5, 1969. The positions he held included the post of Executive Assistant to the Deputy Director. When he joined the Agency, he signed a secrecy agreement promising not to divulge in any way any classified information, intelligence or knowledge, except in the performance of his official duties, unless specifically authorized in writing by the Director or his authorized representative.[1] Marchetti also signed a secrecy oath when he resigned from the Agency in 1969.[2]

After his resignation, Marchetti published a novel, entitled *The Rope Dancer* concerning an agency called the "National Intelligence Agency." Marchetti has also published an article in the April 3, 1972 issue of the magazine, The Nation. Entitled "CIA: The President's Loyal Tool," the article criticized some policies and practices of the Agency. In March, 1972, Marchetti submitted to Esquire magazine and to six other publishers an article in which he reports some of his experiences as an agent. According to the United States, this article contains classified information concerning intelligence sources, methods and operations. Marchetti has appeared on television and radio shows and has given interviews to the press. He has submitted to a publishing house an outline of a book he proposes to write about his intelligence experiences.

I
Jurisdiction

[1, 2] Jurisdiction arises from the presence of the United States as a party. 28 U.S.C. § 1345. "The government can sue even if there is no specific authorization. In such cases, however, it must have some interest to be vindicated sufficient to give it standing." C. A Wright, Federal Courts 68 (2d ed. 1970), ch. 3, § 22. Standing arises from the government's interest in protecting the national security.[3]

II
The Freedom of Speech and of the Press are not Absolute

Marchetti claims that the present injunction is barred by the Supreme Court decision in the Pentagon Papers case because the Government has failed to meet the very heavy burden against any system of prior restraints on expression. New York Times Co. v. United States 403 U.S. 713, 714, 91 S.Ct. 2140, 29 L.Ed.2d 822.

[3, 4] We readily agree with Marchetti that the First Amendment limits the extent to which the United States, contractually or otherwise, may impose secrecy requirements upon its employees and enforce them with a system of prior censorship. It precludes such restraints with respect to information which is unclassified or officially disclosed, but we are here concerned with secret information touching upon the national defense and the conduct of foreign affairs, acquired by Marchetti while in a position of trust and confidence and contractually bound to respect it.

In order to protect freedom of speech and of the press, the First Amendment has been applied beyond its express terms, which were directed solely to Congress:

> "The first amendment provides that 'Congress shall make no law . . . abridging the freedom ... of the press,' and there has been common disposition to apply the amendment to the Executive and the courts as well. [Citing: Joing Anti-Fascist Refugee Comm. v. McGrath, 341 U.S. 123, 143 [-

144, 71 SCt. 624, 95 L.Ed. 817] (Black, J., concurring), 199 [, 71 S.Ct. 624] (Reed, J., dissenting) (1951); Watkins v. United States, 354 U.S. 178, 188 [, 77 S.Ct. 1173, 1 L.Ed.2d 1273] (1957); West Virginia [State] Bd. of Educ. v. Barnette, 319 U.S. 624, 642 [, 63 S.Ct. 1178, 87 L.Ed. 1628] (1943). *See also* Beauharnais v. Illinois, 343 U.S. 250, 386 [, 72 S. Ct. 725, 96 L.Ed. 919] (Douglas, J., dissenting) (1952); Reid v. Covert, 354 U.S. 1, 17 [, 77 S.Ct. 1222, 1 L.Ed.2d 1148] (1957).] But the import of the first amendment is as uncertain and undefined in regard to the freedom of the Press as to the other rights and freedoms that it protects, and, indeed, the courts have had far fewer occasions to define the freedom of the Press, than, say, freedom of speech." Henkin, The Right to Know and the Duty to Withhold: The Case of the Pentagon Papers, 120 U.Pa.L. Rev. 271, 277 (1971).

[5, 6] Nonetheless, "[f]ree speech is not so absolute or irrational a conception as to imply paralysis of the means for effective protection of all the freedoms secured by the Bill of Rights." Bridges v. California, 314 U.S. 252, 62 S.Ct. 190, 36 L.Ed. 192 (Frankfurter, J., dissenting).[4] In applying the First Amendment to actions taken by the judicial and executive branches, the Supreme Court has followed a flexible approach. As Mr. Justice Brennan wrote in Roth v. United States, 354 U.S. 476, 483, 77 S. Ct. 1304, 1308, 1 L.Ed.2d 1498, 1506:

> "[I]t is apparent that the unconditional phrasing of the First Amendment was not intended to protect every utterance. This phrasing did not prevent this Court from concluding that libelous utterances are not within the area of constitutionally protected speech. Beauharnais v. Ill., 343 U.S. 250, 266, 72 S.Ct. 725, 735, 96 L.Ed. 919. At the time of the adoption of the First Amendment, obscenity law was not as fully developed as libel law, but there is sufficiently contemporaneous evidence to show that obscenity, too, was outside the protection intended for speech and press."

[7] Threats and bribes are not protected simply because they are written or spoken; extortion is a crime although it is verbal. The Supreme Court has also upheld the Labor Board's attempt to protect employees from spoken coercion by employers. NLRB v. Gissel Packing Co., 395 U.S. 575, 616-619, 89 S.Ct. 1918, 23 L.Ed.2d 547. The "government might prevent actual obstruction to its recruiting service or the publication of the sailing dates of transports or the number and location of troops." Near v. Minnesota, 283 U.S. 697, 716, 51 S.Ct. 625, 631, 75 L.Ed. 1357, 1367. Cf. Pennsylvania v. Nelson, 350 U.S. 497, 76 S.Ct. 477, 100 L.Ed. 640. This flexible approach toward the executive and judicial branch is warranted not only because they are omitted from the express language of the First Amendment, but also because they lack legislative capacity to establish a pervasive system of censorship. This case itself illustrates the point that the executive and judicial branches proceed on a case by case basis, the executive branch being dependent on the judiciary to restrict unwarranted disclosures.

An earlier case upholding a government request to enjoin publication involved the Valachi papers, written while Valachi was in prison. The United States brought an action to obtain a permanent injunction requiring Maas, the editor of Valachi's manuscripts, to comply with a "Memorandum of Understanding" which required the approval of the manuscripts by the Department of Justice prior to publication or dissemination. The parties entered this agreement because the Attorney General had promulgated, pursuant to 18 U.S.C. §§ 4001, 4042, a regulation that no manuscript prepared by a federal prisoner should be approved for publication "if it deals with the life history or the criminal career of the writer." Valachi and his attorney had signed the Memorandum, but Maas had not, signing instead another agreement to which the Department of Justice was not a party. The District Court granted the United States a preliminary injunction which was upheld by the Court of Appeals based on the broad discretion of the District Court in considering preliminary injunctions. Maas v. United States, 125 U.S. App.D.C. 251, 371 F.2d 348.

This Court recently granted the government declaratory relief against a newspaper publisher who had published a racially discriminatory advertisement for the rental of a room in a private house, in violation of the 1968 Civil Rights Act. The Court denied the defendant's claim that freedom of the press was being abridged, concluding that the act affected the press only in a commercial context and not in the dissemination of ideas. United States v. Hunter, 4 Cir., 459 F.2d 205, 211-213.

III

The Government has a Right to Secrecy

[8, 9] Gathering intelligence information and the other activities of the Agency, including clandestine affairs against other nations, are all within the President's constitutional responsibility for the security of the Nation as the Chief Executive and as Commander in Chief of our Armed forces. Const., art. II, § 2. Citizens have the right to criticize the conduct of our foreign affairs, but the Government also has the right and the duty to strive for internal secrecy about the conduct of governmental affairs in areas in which disclosure may reasonably be thought to be inconsistent with the national interest.

The Supreme Court recognized the need for secrecy in government in United States v. Curtiss-Wright Export Corp., 299 U.S. 304, 320, 57 S.Ct. 216, 221, 81 L.Ed. 255, 263 where it said that the President

> "has his confidential sources of information. He has his agents in the form of diplomatic, consular and other officials. Secrecy in respect of information gathered by them may be highly necessary, and the premature disclosure of it productive of harmful results."

A similar view was expressed in Chicago & Southern Air Lines, Inc. v. Waterman Steamship Corp., 333 U.S. 103, 111, 68 S.Ct. 431, 436, 92 L.Ed. 568, 576:

> "The President, both as Commander-in-Chief and as the Nation's organ for foreign affairs, has available intelligence services whose reports are not and ought not to be published to the world."

In another case the government was granted an injunction to enforce an agreement with a private contractor who claimed the right to divulge the details of a torpedo to other potential customers. In E. W. Bliss Co. v. United States, 248 U.S. 37, 46, 39 S.Ct. 42, 45, 63 L.Ed. 112, 118, the Supreme Court quoted with approval from the opinion of the Second Circuit in that case:

> " 'The nature of the services rendered was such that secrecy might almost be implied. It is difficult to imagine a nation giving to one of its citizens contracts to manufacture implements necessary to the national defense and permitting that citizen to disclose the construction of such implement or sell it to another nation. The very nature of the service makes the construction urged by the defendant untenable.' "

[10] Although the First Amendment protects criticism of the government, nothing in the Constitution requires the government to divulge information:

"From our national beginnings, the Government of the United States has asserted the right to conceal and, therefore, in practical effect not to let the people know. Secrecy governed the deliberations in Philadelphia in 1787. Some need for secrecy was expressly recognized in the Constitution: in providing for publication of a journal of each House of Congress, it excepted 'such parts as may in their judgment require secrecy.' The occasional need for secrecy underlay some of the dispositions of the Constitution: the power to conduct foreign relations was given to the Executive rather than to Congress, and a part in making treaties to the less numerous Senate rather than to the House. Presidents from Washington to Nixon have asserted 'executive privilege' to withhold information from Congress. And Congresses and congressional committees have recognized the 'right,' the propriety, the need for some executive nondisclosure, even to them: since 1791 Congress, in requesting reports from Executive Departments, has asked the State Department to report only what in the President's judgment was 'not incompatible with the public interest.' Modern Congresses have recognized the Executive's classification system and provided for its enforcement, to some extent by criminal penalties. The Supreme Court, too, has repeatedly recognized the need for some secrecy in executive activities. For its own part, Congress has often claimed the need to conceal: the Senate in particular (especially in the executive session), and committees and subcommittees of both Houses, have often maintained secrecy. The courts, too, often insist on the confidentiality of deliberations in the jury room or in judicial chambers. The most confidential proceeding in all of government is probably the conference of the Justices of the Supreme Court." Henkin, The Right to Know and the Duty to Withhold: The Case of the Pentagon Papers, 120 U.Pa.L.Rev. 271, 273-74 (1971).[5]

IV
Secrecy Agreements with Employees Provide a Reasonable Means for Government Agencies to Protect Internal Secrets

[11] Congress has imposed on the Director of Central Intelligence the responsibility for protecting intelligence sources and methods. 50 U.S.C. § 403(d)(3). In attempting to comply with this duty, the Agency requires its employees as a condition of employment to sign a secrecy agreement, and such agreements are entirely appropriate to a program in implementation of the congressional direction of secrecy. Marchetti, of course, could have refused to sign, but then he would not have been employed, and he would not have been given access to the classified information he may now want to broadcast.

Confidentiality inheres in the situation and the relationship of the parties. Since information highly sensitive to the conduct of foreign affairs and the national defense was involved, the law would probably imply a secrecy agreement had there been no formally expressed agreement, but it certainly lends a high degree of reasonableness to the contract in its protection of classified information from unauthorized disclosure.

[12] Moreover, the Government's need for secrecy in this area lends justification to a system of prior restraint against disclosure by employees and former employees of classified information obtained during the course of employment. One may speculate that ordinary criminal sanctions might suffice to prevent unauthorized disclosure of such information, but the risk of harm from disclosure is so great and maintenance of the confidentiality of the information so necessary that greater and

more positive assurance is warranted. Some prior restraints in some circumstances are approvable of course. See Freedman v. Maryland, 380 U.S. 51, 85 S.Ct. 734, 13 L.Ed.2d 649.

V

Marchetti's Rights

[13-15] As we have said, however, Marchetti by accepting employment with the CIA and by signing a secrecy agreement did not surrender his First Amendment right of free speech. The agreement is enforceable only because it is not a violation of those rights. We would decline enforcement of the secrecy oath signed when he left the employment of the CIA to the extent that it purports to prevent disclosure of unclassified information, for, to that extent, the oath would be in contravention of his First Amendment rights.[6]

[16] Thus Marchetti retains the right to speak and write about the CIA and its operations, and to criticize it as any other citizen may, but he may not disclose classified information obtained by him during the course of his employment which is not already in the public domain.

[17] Because we are dealing with a prior restraint upon speech, we think that the CIA must act promptly to approve or disapprove any material which may be submitted to it by Marchetti. Undue delay would impair the reasonableness of the restraint, and that reasonableness is to be maintained if the restraint is to be enforced. We should think that, in all events, the maximum period for responding after the submission of material for approval should not exceed thirty days.

[18] Furthermore, since First Amendment rights are involved, we think Marchetti would be entitled to judicial review of any action by the CIA disapproving publication of the material. Some such review would seem essential to the enforcement of the prior restraint imposed upon Marchetti and other former employees. See Freedman v. Maryland, 380 U.S. 51, 85 S.Ct. 734, 13 L.Ed2d 649. Because of the sensitivity of the area and confidentiality of the relationship in which the information was obtained, however, we find no reason to impose the burden of obtaining judicial review upon the CIA. It ought to be on Marchetti.

Indeed, in most instances, there ought to be no practical reason for judicial review since, because of its limited nature, there would be only narrow areas for possible disagreement.

[19, 20] The Constitution in Article II § 2 confers broad powers upon the President in the conduct of relations with foreign states and in the conduct of the national defense. The CIA is one of the executive agencies whose activities are closely related to the conduct of foreign affairs and to the national defense. Its operations, generally, are an executive function beyond the control of the judicial power. If in the conduct of its operations the need for secrecy requires a system of classification of documents and information, the process of classification is part of the executive function beyond the scope of judicial review. See Oetjen v. Central Leather Co., 246 U.S. 297, 38 S.Ct. 309, 62 L.Ed. 726; United States v. Belmont, 301 U.S. 324, 57 S.Ct. 758, 81 L.Ed. 1134; Zemel v. Rusk, 381 U.S. 1, 85 S.Ct. 1271, 14 L.Ed.2d 179.

There is a practical reason for avoidance of judicial review of secrecy classifications. The significance of one item of information may frequently depend upon knowledge of many other items of information. What may seem trivial to the uninformed, may appear of great moment to one who has a broad view of the scene and may put the questioned item of information in its proper context. The courts, of course, are ill-equipped to become sufficiently steeped in foreign intelligence matters to serve effectively in the review of secrecy classifications in that area.

[21] Information, though classified, may have been publicly disclosed. If it has been, Marchetti should have as much right as anyone else to republish it. Rumor and speculation are not the equivalent of prior disclosure, however, and the presence of that kind of surmise should be no reason for avoidance of restraints upon confirmation from one in a position to know officially.

[22] The issues upon judicial review would seem to be simply whether or not the information was classified and, if so, whether or not, by prior disclosure, it had come into the public domain.

VI
Conclusion

For the stated reasons, our conclusion is that the secrecy agreement executed by Marchetti at the commencement of his employment was not in derogation of Marchetti's constitutional rights. Its provision for submission of material to the CIA for approval prior to publication is enforceable, provided the CIA acts promptly upon such submissions and withholds approval of publication only of information which is classified and which has not been placed in the public domain by prior disclosure.

Generally, therefore, we approve the injunctive order issued by the District Court. The case will be remanded, however, for the purpose of revising the order to limit its reach to classified information and for the conduct of such further proceedings as may be necessary if Marchetti contends that the CIA wrongfully withheld approval of the publication of any information under the standards we have laid down.

Affirmed and remanded.

Craven, Circuit Judge (concurring):

I agree that "[t]he conduct of the foreign relations of our government is committed by the Constitution to the executive and legislative—'the political'—departments of the government, and the propriety of what may be done in the exercise of this political power is not subject to judicial inquiry or decision." Oetjen v. Central Leather Co., 246 U.S. 297, 302, 38 S.Ct. 309, 311, 62 L.Ed. 726, 732 (1917).

I concur in the opinion of the court except for the statement that the classification of documents and information by the executive is not subject to judicial review. Because the national security may be involved and because of the expertise of the executive, I would resolve any doubt about the reasonableness of a classification in favor of the government. If the burden were put upon one who assails the classification, and surely it ought to be, much of the difficulty envisioned in the court's opinion would presumably disappear. Indeed, I would not object to a presumption of reasonableness, and a requirement that the assailant demonstrate by clear and convincing evidence that a classification is arbitrary and capricious before it may be invalidated.

But however difficult the adjudication of the reasonableness of a secrecy classification, I cannot subscribe to a flat rule that it may never be attempted. The "right to know" is in a period of gestation. I think that the people will increasingly insist upon knowing what their government is doing and that, because this knowledge is vital to government by the people, the "right to know" will grow. I am not yet ready to foreclose any inquiry into whether or not secrecy classifications are reasonable.

To protect those that are does not require that we also protect the frivolous and the absurd.

Other than my doubt about the insulation of a classification system from judicial review, I fully concur in the opinion of the court.

---

[1]The relevant provisions of the agreement are:

"Secrecy Agreement"

1. I, Victor L. Marchetti, understand that by virtue of my duties in the Central Intelligence Agency, I may be or have been the recipient of information and intelligence which concerns the present and future security of the United States. This information and intelligence, together with the methods of collecting and handling it, are classified according to security standards set by the United States Government. I have read and understand the provisions of the espionage laws, Act of June 25, 1948, as amended, concerning the disclosure of information relating to the National Defense and I am familiar with the penalties provided for violation thereof.

2. I acknowledge, that I do not now, nor shall I ever possess any right, interest, title or claim, in or to any of the information or intelligence or any method of collecting or handling it, which has come or shall come to my attention by virtue of my connection with the Central Intelligence Agency, but shall always recognize the property right of the United States of America, in and to such matters.

3. I do solemnly swear that I will never divulge, publish or reveal either by word, conduct, or by any other means, any classified information, intelligence or knowledge except in the performance of my official duties and in accordance with the laws of the United States, unless specifically authorized in writing, in each case, by the Director of Central Intelligence or his authorized representatives. . . ."

[2]The relevant provisions of the oath are:

"Secrecy Oath"

I, _______, am about to terminate my association with the Central Intelligence Agency. I realize that, by virtue of my duties with that Agency, I have been the recipient of information and intelligence which concerns the present and future security of the United States of America. I am aware that the unauthorized disclosure of such information is prohibited by the Espionage Laws (18 USC secs. 793 and 794), and by the National Security Act of 1947 which specifically requires the protection of intelligence sources and methods from unauthorized disclosure. Accordingly, I solemnly swear, without mental reservation or purpose of evasion, and in the absence of duress, as follows:

1. I will never divulge, publish, or reveal by writing, word, conduct, or otherwise, any information relating to the national defense and security and particularly information of this nature relating to intelligence sources, methods and operations, and specifically Central Intelligence Agency operations, sources, methods, personnel, fiscal data, or security measures to anyone, including but not limited to, any future governmental or private employer, private citizen, or other Government employee or official without the express written consent of the Director of Central Intelligence or his authorized representative.

* * *

3. I do not have any documents of materials in my possession, classified or unclassified, which are the property of, or in custodial responsibility of the Central Intelligence Agency, having come into my possession as a result of my duties with the Central Intelligence Agency, or otherwise. . . ."

[3]Cf. In re Debs, 158 U.S. 564, 584, 15 S.Ct. 900, 906, 39 L.Ed. 1092, 1102:

"Every government entrusted, by the very terms of its being, with powers and duties to be exercised and discharged for the general welfare, has a right to apply to its own courts for any proper assistance in the exercise of the one and the discharge of the other, and it is no sufficient answer to its appeal to one of those courts that it has no pecuniary interest in the matter. The obligations which it is under to promote the interest of all, and to prevent the wrongdoing of one resulting in injury to the general welfare, is often of itself sufficient to give it a standing in court."

"Because freedom of public expression alone assures the unfolding of truth, it is indispensable to the democratic process. But even that freedom is not an absolute and is not predetermined. By a doctrinaire overstatement of its scope and by giving it an illusory absolute appearance, there is danger of thwarting the free choice and the responsibility of exercising it which are basic to a democratic society."

* * *

[5]*Cf.* 5 U.S.C. § 552(b)(1) exempting from mandatory disclosure under the Freedom of Information Act "matters . . . specifically required by Executive Order to be kept secret in the interest of national defense or foreign policy. . . ." Executive Order 10501 has established a system of classifying

documents as "Top Secret", "Secret" or "Classified" depending on the effect of disclosure on the national defense and the conduct of the nation's affairs. Bridges v. California, 314 U.S. 252, 293, 62 S.Ct. 190, 268, 86 L.Ed. 192, 219 (Frankfurter, J., dissenting). *See also* Near v. Minnesota, 283 U.S. 697, 708, 51 S.Ct. 625, 628, 75 L.Ed. 1357, 1363, "Liberty of speech, and of press, is . . . not an absolute right, and the state may punish its abuse."

[6]There was no apparent consideration for the secrecy oath, so that it would be, generally, unenforceable on that ground. The oath has the support of the moral force underlying solemn oaths, but it added nothing to the Government's arsenal of legal rights in the context of this proceeding.

Environmental Protection Agency v. Mink

410 U.S. 73 (1973)

Mr. Justice White delivered the opinion of the Court.

The Freedom of Information Act of 1966, 5 U. S. C. § 552, provides that Government agencies shall make available to the public a broad spectrum of information, but exempts from its mandate certain specified categories of information, including matters that are "specifically required by Executive order to be kept secret in the interest of the national defense or foreign policy," § 552 (b)(1), or are "inter-agency or intra-agency memorandums or letters which would not be available by law to a party other than an agency in litigation with the agency," § 552 (b)(5). It is the construction and scope of these exemptions that are at issue here.

I

Respondents' lawsuit began with an article that appeared in a Washington, D.C., newspaper in late July 1971. The article indicated that the President had received conflicting recommendations on the advisability of the underground nuclear test scheduled for that coming fall and, in particular, noted that the "latest recommendations" were the product of "a departmental under-secretary committee named to investigate the controversy." Two days later, Congresswoman Patsy Mink, a respondent, sent a telegram to the President urgently requesting the "immediate release of recommendations and report by inter-departmental committee. . . ." When the request was denied, an action under the Freedom of Information Act was commenced by Congresswoman Mink and 32 of her colleagues in the House.[1]

Petitioners immediately moved for summary judgment on the ground that the materials sought were specifically exempted from disclosure under subsections (b)(1) and (b)(5) of the Act.[2] In support of the motion, petitioners filed an affidavit of John N. Irwin II, the Under Secretary of State. Briefly, the affidavit states that Mr. Irwin was appointed by President Nixon as Chairman of an "Under Secretaries Committee," which was a part of the National Security Council system organized by the President "so that he could use it as an instrument for obtaining advice on important questions relating to our national security." The Committee was directed by the President in 1969 "to review the annual underground nuclear test program and to encompass within this review requests for authorization of specific scheduled tests." Results of the Committee's reviews were to be transmitted to the President "in time to allow him to give them full consideration before the scheduled events." In ¶5 of the affidavit, Mr. Irwin stated that pursuant to "the foregoing directions from the President," the Under Secretaries Committee had prepared and transmitted to the President a report on the proposed underground nuclear test known as "Cannikin," scheduled to take place at Amchitka Island, Alaska. The report was said to have consisted of a covering memorandum from Mr. Irwin, the report of the Under Secretaries Committee, five documents attached to that report, and three additional letters separately sent to Mr. Irwin.[3] Of the total of 10 documents, one, an Environmental Impact Statement prepared by AEC, was publicly available and was not in dispute. Each of the other nine was claimed in the Irwin affidavit to have been

> "prepared and used solely for transmittal to the President as advice and recommendations and set forth the views and opinions of the individuals and agencies preparing the documents so that the President might be fully apprised of varying viewpoints and have been used for no other purpose."

In addition, at least eight (by now reduced to six) of the nine remaining documents were said to involve highly sensitive matter vital to the national defense and foreign policy and were described as having been classified Top Secret or Secret pursuant to Executive Order 10501.[4]

On the strength of this showing by petitioners, the District Court granted summary judgment in their favor on the ground that each of the nine documents sought was exempted from compelled disclosure by §§ (b)(1) and (b)(5) of the Act. The Court of Appeals reversed, concluding that subsection (b)(1) of the Act permits the withholding of only the secret portions of those documents bearing a separate classification under Executive Order 10501: "If the nonsecret components [of such documents] are separable from the secret remainder and may be read separately without distortion of meaning, they too should be disclosed." 150 U.S. App. D. C. 233, 237, 464 F. 2d 742, 746. The court instructed the District Judge to examine the classified documents "looking toward their possible separation for purposes of disclosure or nondisclosure." *Ibid.*

In addition, the Court of Appeals concluded that all nine contested documents fell within subsection (b)(5) of the Act, but construed that exemption as shielding only the "decisional processes" reflected in internal Government memoranda, not "factual information" unless that information is "inextricably intertwined with policymaking processes." The court then ordered the District Judge to examine the documents *in camera* (including, presumably, any "nonsecret components" of the six classified documents' to determine if "factual data" could be separated out and disclosed "without impinging on the policymaking decisional processes intended to be protected by this exemption." We granted certiorari, 405 U.S. 974, and now reverse the judgment of the Court of Appeals.

II

The Freedom of Information Act, 5 U. S. C. § 552,[5] is a revision of § 3, the public disclosure section, of the Administrative Procedure Act, 5 U. S. C. § 1002 (1964 ed.). Section 3 was generally recognized as falling far short of its disclosure goals and came to be looked upon more as a withholding statute than a disclosure statute. See S. Rep. No. 813, 89th Cong., 1st Sess., 5 (1965) (hereinafter S. Rep. No. 813); H. R. Rep. No. 1497, 89th Cong., 2d Sess., 5-6 (1966) (hereinafter H. R. Rep. No. 1497). The section was plagued with vague phrases, such as that exempting from disclosure "any function of the United States requiring secrecy in the public interest." Moreover, even "matters of official record" were only to be made available to "persons properly and directly concerned" with the information. And the section provided no remedy for wrongful withholding of information. The provisions of the Freedom of Information Act stand in sharp relief against those of § 3. The Act eliminates the "properly and directly concerned" test of access, stating repeatedly that official information shall be made available "to the public," "for public inspection." Subsection (b) of the Act creates nine exemptions from compelled disclosures. These exemptions are explicitly made exclusive, 5 U. S. C. § 552 (c), and are plainly intended to set up concrete, workable standards for determining whether particular material may be withheld or must be disclosed. Aggrieved citizens are given a speedy remedy in district courts, where "the court shall determine the matter de novo and the burden is on the agency to sustain its action." 5 U. S. C. § 552 (a)(3). Noncompliance with court orders may be punished by contempt. *Ibid.*

Without question, the Act is broadly conceived. It seeks to permit access to official information long shielded unnecessarily from public view and attempts to create a judicially enforceable public right to secure such information from possibly unwilling official hands. Subsection (b) is part of this scheme and represents the congressional determination of the types of information that the Executive Branch must have the option to keep confidential, if it so chooses. As the Senate Committee explained, it was not "an easy task to balance the opposing interests, but it is not an impossible one either. . . . Success lies in providing a workable formula which encompasses, balances, and protects all interests, yet places emphasis on the fullest responsible disclosure." S. Rep. No. 813, p. 3.[6]

It is in the context of the Act's attempt to provide a "workable formula" that "balances, and protects all interests," that the conflicting claims over the documents in this case must be considered.

A

Subsection (b)(1) of the Act exempts from forced disclosure matters "specifically required by Executive order to be kept secret in the interest of the national defense or foreign policy." According to the Irwin affidavit, the six documents for which Exemption 1 is now claimed were all duly classified Top Secret or Secret, pursuant to Executive Order 10501, 3 CFR 280 (Jan. 1, 1970). That order was promulgated under the authority of the President in 1953, 18 Fed. Reg. 7049, and, since that time, has served as the basis for the classification by the Executive Branch of information "which requires protection in the interests of national defense."[7] We do not believe that Exemption 1 permits compelled disclosure of documents, such as the six here that were classified pursuant to this Executive Order. Nor does the Exemption permit *in camera* inspection of such documents to sift out so-called "nonsecret components." Obviously, this test was not the only alternative available. But Congress chose to follow the Executive's determination in these matters and that choice must be honored.

The language of Exemption 1 was chosen with care. According to the Senate Committee, "[t]he change of standard from 'in the public interest' is made both to delimit more narrowly the exception and to give it a more precise definition. The phrase 'public interest' in section 3 (a) of the Administrative Procedure Act has been subject to conflicting interpretations, often colored by personal prejudices and predilections. It admits of no clear delineations." S. Rep. No. 813, p. 8. The House Committee similarly pointed out that Exemption 1 "both limits the present vague phrase, 'in the public interest,' and gives the area of necessary secrecy a more precise definition." H. R. Rep. No. 1497, p. 4. Manifestly, Exemption 1 was intended to dispel uncertainty with respect to public access to material affecting "national defense or foreign policy." Rather than some vague standard, the test was to be simply whether the President has determined by Executive Order that particular documents are to be kept secret. The language of the Act itself is sufficiently clear in this respect, but the legislative history disposes of any possible argument that Congress intended the Freedom of Information Act to subject executive security classifications to judicial review at the insistence of anyone who might seek to question them. Thus, the House Report stated with respect to subsection (b)(1) that "citizens both in and out of Government can agree to restrictions on categories of information which the President has determined must be kept secret to protect the national defense or to advance foreign policy, such as matters classified pursuant to Executive Order 10501." H. R. Rep. No. 1497, pp. 9-10.[8] Similarly, Representative Moss, Chairman of the House Subcommittee that considered the bill, stated that the exemption "was intended to specifically recognize that Executive order [No. 10501]" and was drafted "in conformity with that Executive order." Hearings on Federal Public Records Law before a Subcommittee of the House Committee on Government Operations, 89th Cong., 1st Sess., 52, 55 (1965) (hereinafter 1965 House Hearings). And a member of the Committee, Representative Gallagher, stated that the legislation and the Committee Report make it "crystal clear that the bill in no way affects categories of information which the President . . . has determined must be classified to protect the national defense or to advance foreign policy. These areas of information most generally are classified under Executive Order No. 10501." 112 Cong. Rec. 13659.

These same sources make untenable the argument that classification of material under Executive Order 10501 is somehow insufficient for Exemption 1 purposes, or that the exemption contemplates the issuance of orders, under some other authority, for each document the Executive may want protected from disclosure under the Act. Congress could certainly have provided that the Executive Branch adopt new procedures or it could have established its own procedures—subject only to whatever limitations the Executive privilege may be held to impose upon such congressional ordering. Cf. *United States v. Reynolds,* 345 U.S. 1 (1953). But Exemption 1 does neither. It states with the utmost directness that the Act exempts matters "specifically required by Executive order to be kept secret." Congress was well aware of the Order and obviously accepted determinations pursuant to that Order as qualifying for exempt status under § (b)(1). In this context it is patently unrealistic to argue that the "Order has nothing to do with the first exemption."[9]

What has been said thus far makes wholly untenable any claim that the Act intended to subject the soundness of executive security classifications to judicial review at the insistence of any objecting citizen. It also negates the proposition that Exemption 1 authorizes or permits *in camera* inspection of a contested document bearing a single classification so that the court may separate the secret from the supposedly nonsecret and order disclosure of the latter. The Court of Appeals was thus in error. The Irwin affidavit stated that each of the six documents for which Exemption 1 is now claimed "are and have been classified" Top Secret and Secret "pursuant to Executive Order No. 10501" and as involving "highly sensitive matter that is vital to our national defense and foreign policy." The fact of those classifications and the documents' characterizations have never been disputed by respondents. Accordingly, upon such a showing and in such circumstances, petitioners had met their burden of demonstrating that the documents were entitled to protection under Exemption 1, and the duty of the District Court under § 552 (a)(3) was therefore at an end.[10]

B

Disclosure of the three documents conceded to be "unclassified" is resisted solely on the basis of subsection (b)(5) of the Act (hereafter Exemption 5).[11] That Exemption was also invoked, alternatively, to support withholding the six documents for which Exemption 1 was claimed. It is beyond question that the Irwin affidavit, standing alone, is sufficient to establish that all of the documents involved in this litigation are "inter-agency or intra-agency" memoranda or "letters" that were used in the decisionmaking processes of the Executive Branch. By its terms, however, Exemption 5 creates an exemption for such documents only insofar as they "would not be available by law to a party . . . in litigation with the agency." This language clearly contemplates that the public is entitled to all such memoranda or letters that a private party could discover in litigation with the agency. Drawing such a line between what may be withheld and what must be disclosed is not without difficulties. In many important respects, the rules governing discovery in such litigation have remained uncertain from the very beginnings of the Republic.[12] Moreover, at best, the discovery rules can only be applied under Exemption 5 by way of rough analogies. For example, we do not know whether the Government is to be treated as though it were a prosecutor, a civil plaintiff, or a defendant.[13] Nor does the Act, by its terms, permit inquiry into particularized needs of the individual seeking the information, although such an inquiry would ordinarily be made of a private litigant. Still, the legislative history of Exemption 5 demonstrates that Congress intended to incorporate generally the recognized rule that "confidential intra-agency advisory opinions ... are privileged from inspection." *Kaiser Aluminum & Chemical Corp. v. United States,* 141 Ct. Cl. 38, 49, 157 F. Supp. 939, 946 (1958) (Reed, J.). As Mr. Justice Reed there stated:

> "There is a public policy involved in this claim of privilege for this advisory opinion—the policy of open, frank discussion between subordinate and chief concerning administrative action." *Id.,* at 48, 157 F. Supp., at 946.

The importance of this underlying policy was echoed again and again during legislative analysis and discussions of Exemption 5:

> "It was pointed out in the comments of many of the agencies that it would be impossible to have any frank discussion of legal or policy matters in writing if all such writings were to be subjected to public scrutiny. It was argued, and with merit, that efficiency of Government would be greatly hampered if, with respect to legal and policy matters, all Government agencies were prematurely forced to 'operate in a fishbowl.' The committee is convinced of the merits of this general proposition, but it has attempted to delimit the exception as narrowly as consistent with efficient Government operation." S. Rep. No. 813, p. 9.

See also H. R. Rep. No. 1497, p. 10. But the privilege that has been held to attach to intragovernmental memoranda clearly has finite limits, even in civil litigation. In each case, the question was whether production of the contested document would be "injurious to the consultative functions of government that the privilege of nondisclosure protects." *Kaiser Aluminum & Chemical Corp., supra.,* at 49, 157 F. Supp., at 946. Thus, in the absence of a claim that disclosure would jeopardize state secrets, see *United States v. Reynolds,* 345 U.S. 1 (1953), memoranda consisting only of compiled factual material or purely factual material contained in deliberative memoranda and severable from its context would generally be available for discovery by private parties in litigation with the Government.[14] Moreover, in applying the privilege, courts often were required to examine the disputed documents *in camera,* in order to determine which should be turned over or withheld.[15] We must assume, therefore, that Congress legislated against the backdrop of this case law, particularly since it expressly intended "to delimit the exception [5] as narrowly as consistent with efficient Government operation." S. Rep. No. 813, p. 9. See H. R. Rep. No. 1497, p. 10. Virtually all of the courts that have thus far applied Exemption 5 have recognized that it requires different treatment for materials reflecting deliberative or policymaking processes on the one hand, and purely factual, investigative matters on the other.[16]

Nothing in the legislative history of Exemption 5 is contrary to such a construction. When the bill that ultimately became the Freedom of Information Act, S. 1160, was introduced in the 89th Congress, it contained an exemption that excluded:

> "inter-agency or intra-agency memorandums or letters dealing solely with matters of law or policy."[17]

This formulation was designed to permit "[a]ll *factual* material in Government records . . . to be made available to the public." S. Rep. No. 1219, 88th Cong., 2d Sess., 7 (1964). (Emphasis in original.) The formulation was severely criticized, however, on the ground that it would permit compelled disclosure of an otherwise private document simply because the document did not deal "solely" with legal or policy matters. Documents dealing with mixed questions of fact, law, and policy would inevitably, under the proposed exemption, become available to the public.[18] As a result of this criticism, Exemption 5 was changed to substantially its present form. But plainly, the change cannot be read as suggesting that *all* factual material was to be rendered exempt from compelled disclosure. Congress sensibly discarded a wooden exemption that could have meant disclosure of manifestly private and confidential policy recommendations simply because the document containing them also happened to contain factual data. That decision should not be taken, however, to embrace an equally wooden exemption permitting the withholding of factual material otherwise available on discovery merely because it was placed in a memorandum with matters of law, policy, or opinion. It appears to us that Exemption 5 contemplates that the public's access to internal memoranda will be governed by the same flexible, commonsense approach that has long governed private parties' discovery of such documents involved in litigation with Government agencies. And, as noted, that approach extended and continues to extend to the discovery of purely factual material appearing in those documents in a form that is severable without compromising the private remainder of the documents.

Petitioners further argue that, although *in camera* inspection and disclosure of "low-level, routine, factual reports"[19] may be contemplated by Exemption 5, that type of document is not involved in this case. Rather, it is argued, the documents here were submitted directly to the President by top-level Government officials, involve matters of major significance, and contain, by their very nature, a blending of factual presentations and policy recommendations that are necessarily "inextricably intertwined with policymaking processes." 150 U.S. App. D.C., at 237, 464 F. 2d, at 746. For these reasons, the petitioners object both to disclosure of any portions of the documents and to *in camera* inspection by the District Court.

To some extent, this argument was answered by the Court of Appeals, for its remand expressly directed the District Judge to disclose only such factual material that is not "intertwined with policymaking processes" and that may safely be disclosed "without impinging on the policymaking decisional processes intended to be protected by this exemption." We have no reason to believe that, if petitioners' characterization of the documents is accurate, the District Judge would go beyond the limits of the remand and in any way compromise the confidentiality of deliberative information that is entitled to protection under Exemption 5.

We believe, however, that the remand now ordered by the Court of Appeals is unnecessarily rigid. The Freedom of Information Act may be invoked by any member of "the public"—without a showing of need—to compel disclosure of confidential Government documents. The unmistakable implication of the decision below is that any member of the public invoking the Act may require that otherwise confidential documents be brought forward and placed before the District Court for *in camera* inspection—no matter how little, if any, purely factual material may actually be contained therein. Exemption 5 mandates no such result. As was said in *Kaiser Aluminum & Chemical Corp.,* 141 Ct. Cl., at 50, 157 F. Supp., at 947: "It seems . . . obvious that the very purpose of the privilege, the encouragement of open expression of opinion as to governmental policy is somewhat impaired by a requirement to submit the evidence even [*in camera*]." Plainly, in some situations, *in camera* inspection will be necessary and appropriate. But it need not be automatic. An agency should be given the opportunity, by means of detailed affidavits or oral testimony, to establish to the satisfaction of the District Court that the documents sought fall clearly beyond the range of material that would be available to a private party in litigation with the agency. The burden is, of course, on the agency resisting disclosure, 5 U. S. C. § 552 (a)(3), and if it fails to meet its burden without *in camera* inspection, the District Court may order such inspection. But the agency may demonstrate, by surrounding circumstances, that particular documents are purely advisory and contain no separable, factual information. A representative document of those sought may be selected for *in camera* inspection. And, of course, the agency may itself disclose the factual portions of the contested documents and attempt to show, again by circumstances, that the excised portions constitute the barebones of protected matter. In short, *in camera* inspection of all documents is not a necessary or inevitable tool in every case. Others are available. Cf. *United States v. Reynolds,* 345 U.S. 1 (1953). In the present case, the petitioners proceeded on the theory that all of the nine documents were exempt from disclosure in their entirety under Exemption 5 by virtue of their use in the decisionmaking process. On remand, petitioners are entitled to attempt to demonstrate the propriety of withholding any documents, or portions thereof, by means short of submitting them for *in camera* inspection.

The judgment is reversed and the case is remanded for further proceedings consistent with this opinion.

It is so ordered.

Mr. Justice Rehnquist took no part in the consideration or decision of this case.

Mr. Justice Stewart, concurring.

* * *

Mr. Justice Brennan, with whom Mr. Justice Marshall joins, concurring in part and dissenting in part.

* * *

Mr. Justice Douglas, dissenting. . . .

[1]A separate action was brought to enjoin the test itself. *Committee for Nuclear Responsibility v. Seaborg* (DC, Civ. Action No. 1346-71). After adverse decisions below, plaintiffs in that case applied for an injunction in this Court. On November 6, 1971, we denied the application, *Committee for Nuclear Responsibility v. Schlesinger,* 404 U.S. 917, and the test was conducted that same day.

It should be noted that in the District Court respondents stated that they "have exhausted their administrative remedies [and] . . . have complied with all applicable regulations." Petitioners did not contest those assertions.

[2]Petitioners also moved for dismissal of the suit insofar as respondents sought disclosure of the documents in their official capacities as Members of Congress. The District Court granted this motion, but the Court of Appeals did not reach the issue. Accordingly, the issue is not before this Court.

[3]According to the Irwin affidavit, the report contained the following documents:

A. A covering memorandum from Mr. Irwin to the President, dated July 17, 1971. This memorandum is classified Top Secret pursuant to Executive Order 10501.

B. The Report of the Under Secretaries Committee. This report was also classified Top Secret. Attached to the report were additional documents:

1. A letter, classified Secret, from the Chairman of the Atomic Energy Commission (AEC) to Mr. Irwin.

2. A report, classified Top Secret, from the Defense Program Review Committee, of which Dr. Henry Kissinger was the Chairman.

3. The Environmental Impact Statement on the proposed Cannikin test, prepared by the AEC in 1971, pursuant to § 102 (C) of the National Environmental Policy Act of 1969, 83 Stat. 853, 42 U. S. C. § 4332 (C). This document had always been "publicly available" and a copy was attached to the Irwin affidavit.

4. A transcript of an oral briefing given by the AEC to the Committee. This document was classified Secret.

5. A memorandum from the Council on Environmental Quality to Mr. Irwin. This memorandum was separately unclassified.

C. In addition to the covering memorandum and the Committee's report (with attached documents), were three letters that had been transmitted to Mr. Irwin:

1. A letter from Mr. William Ruckelshaus, for the Environmental Protection Agency. This letter was classified Top Secret, but has now been declassified.

2. A letter from Mr. Russell Train, for the Council on Environmental Quality. Although the Irwin affidavit states that this letter was classified Top Secret, petitioners concede that it was so classified "only because it was to be attached to the Undersecretary's Report." Brief for Petitioners 6 n. 5.

3. A letter of Dr. Edward E. David, Jr., for the Office of Science and Technology. This letter is classified Top Secret.

[4]These eight documents were also described as having been classified as "Restricted Data . . . pursuant to the Atomic Energy Act of 1954, as amended. (42 U. S. C. [§§ 2014 (y)], 2161 and 2162.)" Petitioners have not asserted that these provisions, standing alone, would justify withholding the documents in this case. But see 5 U. S. C. § 552 (b)(3), relating to matters "specifically exempted from disclosure by statute."

[5]The Act was passed in 1966, 80 Stat. 383, and codified in its present form in 1967. 81 Stat. 54.

[6]The Report states (*ibid.*):

"It is the purpose of the present bill . . . to establish a general philosophy of full agency disclosure unless information is exempted under clearly delineated statutory language. . . .

"At the same time that a broad philosophy of 'freedom of information' is enacted into law, it is necessary to protect certain equally important rights of privacy with respect to certain information in Government files, such as medical and personnel records. It is also necessary for the very operation of our Government to allow it to keep confidential certain material, such as the investigatory files of the Federal Bureau of Investigation.

"It is not an easy task to balance the opposing interests, but it is not an impossible one either. It is not necessary to conclude that to protect one of the interests, the other must, of necessity, either be abrogated or substantially subordinated. Success lies in providing a workable formula which encompasses, balances, and protects all interests, yet places emphasis on the fullest responsible disclosure."

[7]Executive Order 10501 has been superseded, as of June 1, 1972, by Executive Order 11652, 37 Fed. Reg. 5209, which similarly provides for the classification of material "in the interest of the national defense or foreign relations."

Portions of two documents for which Exemption 1 is claimed were ordered disclosed in connection with the action brought to enjoin the test (see n. 1, *supra*). Petitioners seek no relief with respect to any matters already disclosed.

[8]The House Report, it is true, indicates that *the President* must determine that the exempted matter be kept secret. Clearly, however, Executive Order 10501 is based on presidential authority and specifically delegates that authority to "the departments, agencies, and other units of the executive branch *as hereinafter specified*." 3 CFR § 281 (Jan. 1, 1970) (emphasis added). One may disagree with the scope of the delegation or with how the delegated authority is exercised in particular cases, but the authority itself nevertheless remains the President's and it is his judgment that the first exemption was designed to respect.

[9]Brief for Respondents 18. Respondents note that the preamble of the new Executive Order 11652 (see n. 7, *supra*), specifies that material classified pursuant to its provisions "is expressly exempted from public disclosure by Section 552 (b)(1) of Title 5, United States Code." Executive Order 10501 has no comparable recital, but only the sheerest ritualism would distinguish the effect of the two orders on any such basis. Indeed, respondents' apparent acceptance of the new order as a justifiable ground for resisting disclosure under Exemption 1 points to the absurdity of maintaining that Executive Order 10501 is irrelevant to the Act.

[10]This conclusion is not undermined by the new Executive Order 11652, which calls for the separation of documents into classified and unclassified portions, where practicable. 37 Fed. Reg. 5212. On the contrary, that new order provides that the separating be done by the Executive, not the Judiciary, and, like its predecessor, permits declassification of material only in accordance with its procedures. More importantly, the very existence of the new order demonstrates that the Executive exercises a continuing responsibility for determining the need for secrecy in matters that affect national defense and foreign policy. Exemption 1 recognizes that responsibility by leaving to the Executive, under such orders as shall be developed, the decision of what may be disclosed and what must be kept secret.

[11]Title 5 U. S. C. § 552 reads in part as follows:

"(a) Each agency shall make available to the public information as follows:

* * *

"(b) This section does not apply to matters that are—

* * *

"(5) inter-agency or intra-agency memorandums or letters which would not be available by law to a party other than an agency in litigation with the agency."

The three documents are: the CEQ memorandum to Mr. Irwin, the Train letter, and the Ruckelshaus letter, which has now been declassified.

[12]See generally 4 J. Moore, Federal Practice ¶26.61 (1972) and authorities collected (*i.d.*, at ¶26.61 [1] n. 2) (hereinafter Moore); 8 J. Wigmore, Evidence §§ 2378, 2379 (McNaughton rev. 1961) (hereinafter Wigmore).

There were early disputes over the issue of Executive privilege. See Chief Justice Marshall's decisions in the trial of *United States v. Burr,* 25 F. Cas. 30 (No. 14,692d) and 25 F. Cas. 187, 191-192 (No. 14,694) (CCD Va. 1807), discussed in 8 Wigmore § 2371, pp. 739-741 (3d ed. 1940) and 4 Moore ¶26.61 [6.-4]. See also Wigmore § 2378, p. 805 and n. 21.

[13]Different rules have been held to apply in each situation. See, .*e.g., United States v. Andolschek,* 142 F. 2d 503, 506 (CA2 1944) (L. Hand, J.) (United States as prosecutor); *Bank line, Ltd. v. United States,* 76 F. Supp. 801 (SDNY 1948) (United States as defendant). Moreover, in actions under the Freedom of Information Act, courts are not given in option to impose alternative sanctions—short of compelled disclosure—such as striking a particular defense or dismissing the Government's action.

[14]See, *e.g., Machin v. Zuckert,* 114 U.S. App. D. C. 335, 316 F. 2d 336, cert. denied, 375 U.S. 896 (1963) (Air Force Aircraft Accident Investigation Report); *Boeing Airplane Co. v. Coggeshall,* 108 U.S. App. D. C. 106, 112-113, 280 F. 2d 654, 660-661 (1960) (Renegotiation Board documents); *Olson Rug Co. v. NLRB,* 291 F. 2d 655, 662 (CA7 1961) (no claim that NLRB documents are "exclusively policy recommendations"); *Carl Zeiss Stiftung v. V. E. B. Carl Zeiss, Jena,* 40 F. R. D. 318, 327 (DC 1966), aff'd, 128 U.S. App. D. C. 10, 384 F. 2d 979, cert. denied, 389 U.S. 952 (1967) (discovery denied because documents "wholly of opinions, recommendations and deliberations"); *McFadden v. Avco Corp.,* 278 F. Supp. 57, 59-60 (MD Ala. 1967), and cases cited therein.

In *United States v. Cotton Valley Operators Comm.,* 9 F. R. D. 719, 720 (WD La. 1949), aff'd by equally divided court, 339 U.S. 940 (1950), the United States offered to file "an abstract of factual information" contained in the contested documents (FBI reports).

[15]See, *e.g., Machin v. Zuckert, supra,* at 340, 316 F. 2d, at 341 (private tort action; discovery of Air Force Aircraft Accident Investigation Report); *Boeing Airplane Co. v. Coggeshall, supra,* at 114, 280 F. 2d,

at 662 (excess profits tax redetermination); *Olson Rug Co. v. NLRB, supra,* at 662 (discovery for use in defense against contempt proceedings); *O'Keefe v. Boeing Co.,* 38 F. R. D. 329, 336 (SDNY 1965) (private tort action; Air Force Investigation Reports); *Rosee v. Board of Trade,* 36 F. R. D. 684, 687-688 (ND Ill. 1965); *United States v. Cotton Valley Operators Comm., supra* (civil antitrust suit). Cf. *United States v. Procter & Gamble Co.,* 25 F. R. D. 485, 492 (NJ 1960) (criminal antitrust prosecution). See Wigmore § 2379, p. 812.

In *Kaiser Aluminum & Chemical Corp. v. United States,* 141 Ct. Cl. 38, 157 F. Supp. 939 (1958), where *in camera* inspection of a document was refused because of plaintiff's failure to make a definite showing of necessity, *id.,* at 50, 157 F. Supp., at 947, the "objective facts" contained in the disputed document were "otherwise available." *Id.,* at 48-49, 157 F. Supp., at 946.

[16]See, *e.g., Soucie v. David,* 145 U.S. App. D. C. 144, 448 F. 2d 1067 (1971); *Grumman Aircraft Eng. Corp. v. Renegotiation Bd.,* 138 U.S. App. D. C. 147, 151, 425 F. 2d 578, 582 (1970); *Bristol-Myers Co. v. FTC,* 138 U.S. App. D. C. 22, 424 F. 2d 935 (1970); *International Paper Co. v. FPC,* 438 F. 2d 1349, 1358-1359 (CA2), cert. denied, 404 U.S. 827 (1971); *General Services Admin. v. Benson,* 415 F. 2d 878 (CA9 1969), *aff'g* 289 F. Supp. 590 (WD Wash. 1968); *Long Island R. Co. v. United States,* 318 F. Supp. 490, 499 n. 9 (EDNY 1970); *Consumers Union v. Veterans Admin.,* 301 F. Supp. 796 (SDNY 1969), appeal dismissed as moot, 436 F. 2d 1363 (CA2 1971); *Olsen v. Camp,* 328 F. Supp. 728, 731 (ED Mich. 1970); *Reliable Transfer Co. v. United States,* 53 F. R. D. 24 (EDNY 1971).

The proposed Federal Rules of Evidence appear to recognize this construction of Exemption 5. Proposed Rule 509 (a)(2)(A) defines "official information" to include "intragovernmental opinions or recommendations submitted for consideration in the performance of decisional or policymaking functions." Rule 509 (c) further provides that "[i]n the case of privilege claimed for official information the court may require examination *in camera* of the information itself."

[17]Hearings on S. 1160, S. 1336, S. 1758, and S. 1879 before the Subcommittee on Administrative Practice and Procedure of the Senate Committee on the Judiciary, 89th Cong., 1st Sess., 7 (1965) (hereinafter 1965 Senate Hearings). This exemption itself had been broadened during its course through the Senate in the 88th Congress. The exemption originally applied only to internal memoranda "relating to the consideration and disposition of adjudicatory and rulemaking matters." Section 3 (c) of S. 1666, 88th Cong., 2d Sess. (1964), introduced in 110 Cong. Rec. 17086. That early formulation came under attack for not sufficiently protecting material dealing with general policy matters not directly related to adjudication or rulemaking. See Hearings on S. 1666 and S. 1663 before the Subcommittee on Administrative Practice and Procedure of the Senate Committee on the Judiciary, 88th Cong., 1st Sess., 202-203, 247 (1963).

[18]See 1965 Senate Hearings 36, 94-95, 112-113, 205, 236-237, 244, 366-367, 382-383, 402-403, 406-407, 417, 437, 445-446, 450, 490. See 1965 House Hearings 27-28, 49, 208, 220, 223-224, 229-230, 245-246, 255-257. Examples of these many statements are:

Federal Aviation Administration (1965 Senate Hearing 446):

"Few records would be entirely devoid of factual data, thus leaving papers on law and policy relatively unprotected. Staff working papers and reports prepared for use within the agency of the executive branch would not be protected by the proposed exemptions."

Department of Commerce (1965 Senate Hearings 406):

"Under this provision, internal memorandums dealing with *mixed questions of fact, law and policy* could well become public information." (Emphasis in original.)

[19]Tr. of Oral Arg. 23.

United States, Petitioner v. Richard M. Nixon, President of the United States, Petitioner

481 U.S. 683 (1974)

Mr. Chief Justice Burger delivered the opinion of the Court.

These cases present for review the denial of a motion, filed on behalf of the President of the United States, in the case of *United States v. Mitchell et al.* (D. C.

Crim. No. 74-110), to quash a third-party supboena *duces tecum* issued by the United States District Court for the District of Columbia, pursuant to Fed. Rule Crim. Proc. 17 (c). The subpoena directed the President to produce certain tape recordings and documents relating to his conversations with aides and advisers. The court rejected the President's claims of absolute executive privilege, of lack of jurisdiction, and of failure to satisfy the requirements of Rule 17 (c). The President appealed to the Court of Appeals. We granted the United States' petition for certiorari before judgment,[1] and also the President's responsive cross-petition for certiorari before judgment,[2] because of the public importance of the issues presented and the need for their prompt resolution. _____ U.S. _____, _____ (1974).

On March 1, 1974, a grand jury of the United States District Court for the District of Columbia returned an indictment charging seven named individuals[3] with various offenses, including conspiracy to defraud the United States and to an unindicted co-conspirator.[4] On April 18, 1974, upon motion of the Special Prosecutor, see n. 8, *infra,* a subpoena *duces tecum* was issued pursuant to Rule 17 (c) to the President by the United States District Court and made returnable on May 2, 1974. This subpoena required the production, in advance of the September 9 trial date, of certain tapes, memoranda, papers, transcripts, or other writings relating to certain precisely identified meetings between the President and others.[5] The Special Prosecutor was able to fix the time, place and persons present at these discussions because the White House daily logs and appointment records had been delivered to him. On April 30, the President publicly released edited transcripts of 43 conversations; portions of 20 conversations subject to subpoena in the present case were included. On May 1, 1974, the President's counsel, filed a "special appearance" and a motion to quash the subpoena, under Rule 17 (c). This motion was accompanied by a formal claim of privilege. At a subsequent hearing,[6] further motions to expunge the grand jury's action naming the President as an unindicted co-conspirator and for protective orders against the disclosure of that information were filed or raised orally by counsel for the President.

On May 20, 1974, the District Court denied the motion to quash and the motions to expunge and for protective orders. _____ F. Supp. _____ (1974). It further ordered "the President or any subordinate officer, official or employee with custody or control of the documents or objects subpoenaed," *id.,* at _____, to deliver to the District Court, on or before May 31, 1974, the originals of all subpoenaed items, as well as an index and analysis of those items, together with tape copies of those portions of the subpoenaed recordings for which transcripts had been released to the public by the President on April 30, The District Court rejected jurisdictional challenges based on a contention that the dispute was nonjusticiable because it was between the Special Prosecutor and the Chief Executive and hence "intra-executive" in character; it also rejected the contention that the judiciary was without authority to review an assertion of executive privilege by the President. The court's rejection of the first challenge was based on the authority and powers vested in the Special Prosecutor by the regulation promulgated by the Attorney General; the court concluded that a justiciable controversy was presented. The second challenge was held to be foreclosed by the decision in *Nixon v. Sirica,* _____ U.S. App. D.C. _____, 487 F. 2d 700 (1973).

The District Court held that the judiciary, not the President, was the final arbiter of a claim of executive privilege. The court concluded that, under the circumstances of this case, the presumptive privilege was overcome by the Special Prosecutor's prima facie "demonstration of need sufficiently compelling to warrant judicial examination in chambers. . . ." ______ F. Supp., at ______ The court held, finally, that the Special Prosecutor had satisfied the requirements of Rule 17 (c). The District Court stayed its order pending appellate review on condition that review was sought before 4 p. m., May 24. The court further provided that matters filed under seal remain under seal when transmitted as part of the record.

On May 24, 1974, the President filed a timely notice of appeal from the District Court order, and the certified record from the District Court was docketed in the United States Court of Appeals for the District of Columbia Circuit. On the same day, the President also filed a petition for writ of mandamus in the Court of Appeals seeking review of the District Court order.

Later on May 24, the Special Prosecutor also filed, in this Court, a petition for a writ of certiorari before judgment. On May 31, the petition was granted with an expedited briefing schedule. ______ U.S. ______ (1974). On June 6, the President filed, under seal, a cross-petition for writ of certiorari before judgment. This cross-petition was granted June 15, 1974, ______ U.S. ______ (1974), and the case was set for argument on July 8, 1974.

I. Jurisdiction

The threshold question presented is whether the May 20, 1974, order of the District Court was an appealable order and whether this case was properly "in," 28 U.S.C. § 1254, the United States Court of Appeals when the petition for certiorari was filed in this Court. Court of Appeals jurisdiction under 28 U.S.C. § 1291 encompasses only "final decisions of the district courts." Since the appeal was timely filed and all other procedural requirements were met, the petition is properly before this Court for consideration if the District Court order was final. 28 U.S.C. § 1254 (1); 28 U.S.C. § 2102 (e).

The finality requirement of 28 U.S.C. § 1291 embodies a strong congressional policy against piecemeal reviews, and against obstructing or impeding an ongoing judicial proceeding by interlocutory appeals. See, *e.g., Cobbledick v. United States,* 309 U.S. 323, 324-326 (1940). This requirement ordinarily promotes judicial efficiency and hastens the ultimate termination of litigation. In applying this principle to an order denying a motion to quash and requiring the production of evidence pursuant to a subpoena *duces tecum,* it is has been repeatedly held that the order is not final and hence not appealable. *United States v. Ryan,* 402 U.S. 530, 532 (1971); *Cobbledick v. United States,* 309 U.S. 322 (1940); *Alexander v. United States,* 201 U.S. 117 (1906). This Court has

> "consistently held that the necessity for expedition in the administration of the criminal law justifies putting one who seeks to resist the production of desired information to a choice between compliance with a trial court's order to produce prior to any review of that order, and resistance to that order with the concommitant possibility of an adjudication of contempt if his claims are rejected on appeal." *United States v. Ryan,* 402 U.S. 530, 533 (1971).

The requirement of submitting to contempt, however, is not without exception and in some instances the purposes underlying the finality rule require a different result. For example, in *Perlman v. United States,* 247 U.S. 7 (1918), a subpoena had been directed to a third party requesting certain exhibits; the appellant, who owned the exhibits, sought to raise a claim of privilege. The Court held an order compelling production was appealable because it was unlikely that the third party would risk a contempt citation in order to allow immediate review of the appellant's claim of privilege. *Id.,* at 12-13. That case fell within the "limited class of cases where denial of immediate review would render impossible any review whatsoever of an individual's claims." *United States v. Ryan, supra,* at 533.

Here too the traditional contempt avenue to immediate appeal is peculiarly inappropriate due to the unique setting in which the question arises. To require a President of the United States to place himself in the posture of disobeying an order of a court merely to trigger the procedural mechanism for review of the ruling would be unseemly, and present an unnecessary occasion for constitutional confrontation between two branches of the Government. Similarly, a federal judge should not be placed in the posture of issuing a citation to a President simply in order to invoke review. The issue whether a President can be cited for contempt could itself engender protracted litigation, and would further delay both review on the merits of his claim of privilege and the ultimate termination of the underlying criminal action for which his evidence is sought. These considerations lead us to conclude that the order of the District Court was an appealable order. The appeal from that order was therefore properly "in" the Court of Appeals, and the case is now properly before this Court on the writ of certiorari before judgment. 28 U.S.C. § 1254; 28 U.S.C. § 2101 (e). *Gay v. Ruff,* 292 U.S. 25, 30 (1934).[7]

II. Justiciability

In the District Court, the President's counsel argued that the court lacked jurisdiction to issue the subpoena because the matter was an intra-branch dispute between a subordinate and superior officer of the Executive Branch and hence not subject to judicial resolution. That argument has been renewed in this Court with emphasis on the contention that the dispute does not present a "case" or "controversy" which can be adjudicated in the federal courts. The President's counsel argues that the federal courts should not intrude into areas committed to the other branches of Government. He views the present dispute as essentially a "jurisdictional" dispute within the Executive Branch which he analogizes to a dispute between two congressional committees. Since the Executive Branch has exclusive authority and absolute discretion to decide whether to prosecute a case, *Confiscation Cases,* 7 Wall. 454 (1869), *United States v. Cox,* 342 F. 2d 167, 171 (CA5), cert. denied, 381 U.S. 935 (1965), it is contended that a President's decision is final in determining what evidence is to be used in a given criminal case. Although his counsel concedes the President has delegated certain specific powers to the Special Prosecutor, he has not "waived nor delegated to the Special Prosecutor the President's duty to claim privilege as to all materials . . . which fall within the President's inherent authority to refuse to disclose to any executive officer." Brief for the President 47. The Special Prosecutor's demand for the items therefore presents, in the view of the President's counsel, a political question under *Baker v. Carr,* 369 U.S. 186 (1962), since it involves a "textually demonstrable" grant of power under Art. II.

The mere assertion of a claim of an "intra-branch dispute," without more, has never operated to defeat federal jurisdiction; justiciability does not depend on such a surface inquiry. In *United States v. ICC,* 337 U.S. 426 (1949), the Court observed, "courts must look behind names that symbolize the parties to determine whether a justiciable case or controversy is presented." *Id.,* at 430. See also: *Powell v. McCormack,* 395 U.S. 486 (1969); *ICC v. Jersey City,* 322 U.S. 503 (1944); *United States ex rel. Chapman v. FPC,* 345 U.S. 153 (1953); *Secretary of Agriculture v. United States,* 347 U.S. 645 (1954); *FMB v. Isbrandsten Co.,* 356 U.S. 481, 482 n. 2 (1958); *United States v. Marine Bank Corp.,* _____ U.S. _____ (1974), and *United States v. Connecticut National Bank,* _____ U.S. _____ 1974.

Our starting point is the nature of the proceeding for which the evidence is sought—here a pending criminal prosecution. It is a judicial proceeding in a federal court alleging violation of federal laws and is brought in the name of the United States as sovereign. *Berger v. United States,* 295 U.S. 78, 88 (1935). Under the authority of Art. II § 2, Congress has vested in the Attorney General the power to conduct the criminal litigation of the United States Government. 28 U.S.C. § 516. It has also vested in him the power to appoint subordinate officers to assist him in the discharge of his duties. 28 U.S.C. §§ 509, 510, 515, 533. Acting pursuant to those statutes, the Attorney General has delegated the authority to represent the United States in these particular matters to a Special Prosecutor with unique authority and tenure.[8] The regulation gives the Special Prosecutor explicit power to contest the invocation of executive privilege in the process of seeking evidence deemed relevant to the performance of these specially delegated duties.[9] 38 Fed. Ref. 30739.

So long as this regulation is extant it has the force of law. In *Accardi v. Shaughnessy,* 347 U.S. 260 (1953), regulations of the Attorney General delegated certain of his discretionary powers to the Board of Immigration Appeals and required that Board to exercise its own discretion on appeals in deportation cases. The Court held that so long as the Attorney General's regulations remained operative, he denied himself the authority to exercise the discretion delegated to the Board even though the original authority was his and he could reassert it by amending the regulations. *Service v. Dulles,* 354 U.S. 363, 388, (1957), and *Vitarelli v. Seaton,* 359 U.S. 535 (1959), reaffirmed the basic holding of *Accardi.*

Here, as in *Accardi,* it is theoretically possible for the Attorney General to amend or revoke the regulation defining the Special Prosecutor's authority. But he has not done so.[10] So long as this regulation remains in force the Executive Branch is bound by it, and indeed the United States as the sovereign composed of the three branches is bound to respect and to enforce it. Moreover, the delegation of authority to the Special Prosecutor in this case is not an ordinary delegation by the Attorney General to a subordinate officer: with the authorization of the President, the Acting Attorney General provided in the regulation that the Special Prosecutor was not to be removed without the "consensus" of eight designated leaders of Congress. Note 8, *supra.*

The demands of and the resistance to the subpoena present an obvious controversy in the ordinary sense, but that alone is not sufficient to meet constitutional standards. In the constitutional sense, controversy means more than disagreement and conflict; rather it means the kind of controversy courts traditionally resolve. Here at issue is the production or nonproduction of specified evidence deemed by the Special Prosecutor to be relevant and admissible in a pending criminal case. It is sought by one official of the Government within the scope of his express authority; it is resisted by the Chief Executive on the ground of his duty to preserve the confidentiality of the communications of the President. Whatever the correct answer on the merits, these issues are "of a type which are traditionally justiciable." *United States v. ICC,* 337 U.S., at 430. The independent Special Prosecutor with his asserted need for the subpoenaed material in the underlying criminal prosecution is opposed by the President with his steadfast assertion of privilege against disclosure of the material. This setting assures there is "that concrete adverseness which sharpens the presentation of issues upon which the court so largely depends for illumination of difficult constitutional questions." *Baker v. Carr,* 369 U.S., at 204. Moreover, since the matter is one arising in the regular course of a federal criminal prosecution, it is within the traditional scope of Art. III power. *Id.,* at 198.

In light of the uniqueness of the setting in which the conflict arises, the fact that both parties are officers of the Executive Branch cannot be viewed as a barrier to justiciability. It would be inconsistent with the applicable law and regulation, and the unique facts of this case to conclude other than that the Special Prosecutor has standing to bring this action and that a justiciable controversy is presented for decision.

III. Rule 17 (c)

The subpoena *duces tecum* is challenged on the ground that the Special Prosecutor failed to satisfy the requirements of Fed. Rule Crim. Proc. 17 (c), which governs the issuance of subpoenas *duces tecum* in federal criminal proceedings. If we sustained this challenge, there would be no occasion to reach the claim of privilege asserted with respect to the subpoenaed material. Thus we turn to the question whether the requirements of Rule 17 (c) have been satisfied. See *Arkansas-Louisiana Gas Co. v. Dept. of Public Utilities,* 304 U.S. 61, 64 (1938); *Ashwander v. Tennessee Valley Authority,* 297 U.S. 288, 346-347 (1936). (Brandeis, J., concurring.)

Rule 17 (c) provides:

> "A subpoena may also command the person to whom it is directed to produce the books, papers, documents or other objects designated therein. The court on motion made promptly may quash or modify the subpoena if compliance would be unreasonable or oppressive. The court may direct that books, papers, documents or objects designated in the subpoena be produced before the court at a time prior to the trial or prior to the time when they are to be offered in evidence and may upon their production permit the books, papers, documents or objects or portions thereof to be inspected by the parties and their attorneys."

A subpoena for documents may be quashed if their production would be "unreasonable or oppressive," but not otherwise. The leading case in this Court interpreting this standard is *Bowman Dairy Co. v. United States,* 341 U.S. 214 (1950). This case recognized certain fundamental characteristics of the subpoena *duces tecum* in criminal cases: (1) it is not intended to provide a means of discovery for criminal cases. *Id.*, at 220; (2) its chief innovation was to expedite the trial by providing a time and place *before* trial for the inspection of subpoenaed materials.[11] Ibid. As both parties agree, cases decided in the wake of *Bowman* have generally followed Judge Weinfeld's formulation in *United States v. Iozia,* 13 F.R.D. 335, 338, (SDNY 1952), as to the required showing. Under this test, in order to require production prior to trial, the moving party must show: (1) that the documents are evidentiary[12] and relevant; (2) that they are not otherwise procurable reasonably in advance of trial by exercise of due diligence; (3) that the party cannot properly prepare for trial without such production and inspection in advance of trial and that the failure to obtain such inspection may tend unreasonably to delay the trial; (4) that the application is made in good faith and is not intended as a general "fishing expedition."

Against this background, the Special Prosecutor, in order to carry his burden, must clear three hurdles: (1) relevancy; (2) admissibility; (3) specificity. Our own review of the record necessarily affords a less comprehensive view of the total situation than was available to the trial judge and we are unwilling to conclude that the District Court erred in the evaluation of the Special Prosecutor's showing under Rule 17 (c). Our conclusion is based on the record before us, much of which is under seal. Of course, the contents of the subpoenaed tapes could not at that stage be described fully by the Special Prosecutor, but there was a sufficient likelihood that each of the tapes contains conversations relevant to the offenses charged in the indictment. *United States v. Gross,* 24 F.R.D. 138 (SDNY 1959). With respect to many of the tapes, the Special Prosecutor offered the sworn testimony or statements of one or more of the participants in the conversations as to what was said at the time. As for the remainder of the tapes, the identity of the participants and the time and place of the conversations, taken in their total context, permit a rational inference that at least part of the conversations relate to the offenses charged in the indictment.

We also conclude there was a sufficient preliminary showing that each of the subpoenaed tapes contains evidence admissible with respect to the offenses charged in the indictment. The most cogent objection to the admissibility of the taped conversations here at issue is that they are a collection of out-of-court statements by declarants who will not be subject to cross-examination and that the statements are therefore inadmissible hearsay. Here, however, most of the tapes apparently contain conversations to which one or more of the defendants named in the indictment were party. The hearsay rule does not automatically bar all out-of-court statements by a defendant in a criminal case.[13] Declarations by one defendant may also be admissible against other defendants upon a sufficient showing by independent evidence,[14] of a conspiracy among one or more other defendants and the declarant and if the declarations at issue were in furtherance of that conspiracy. The same is true of declarations of coconspirators who are not defendants in the case on trial. *Dutton v. Evans,* 400 U.S. 74, 81 (1970). Recorded conversations may also be admissible for the limited purpose of impeaching the credibility of any defendant who testifies or any other coconspirator who testifies. Generally, the need for evidence to impeach witnesses is insufficient to require its production in advance of trial. See, *e.g., United States v. Carter*, 15 F.R.D. 367, 371 (D.D.C. 1954). Here, however, there are other valid potential evidentiary uses for the same material and the analysis and possible transcription of the tapes may take a significant period of time. Accordingly, we cannot say that the District Court erred in authorizing the issuance of the subpoena *duces tecum.*

Enforcement of a pretrial subpoena *duces tecum* must necessarily be committed to the sound discretion of the trial court since the necessity for the subpoena most often turns upon a determination of factual issues. Without a determination of arbitrariness or that the trial court finding was without record support, an appellate court will not ordinarily disturb a finding that the applicant for a subpoena compiled with Rule 17 (c). See, *e.g., Sue v. Chicago Transit Authority*, 279 F. 2d 416, 419 (CA7 1960); *Shotkin v. Nelson*, 146 F. 2d 402 (CA 10 1944).

In a case such as this, however, where a subpoena is directed to a President of the United States, appellate review, in deference to a coordinate branch of government, should be particularly meticulous to ensure that the standards of Rule 17 (c) have been correctly applied. *United States v. Burr,* 25 Fed. Cas. 30, 34 (No. 14,692d) (1807). From our examination of the materials submitted by the Special Prosecutor to the District Court in support of his motion for the subpoena, we are persuaded that the District Court's denial of the President's motion to quash the subpoena was consistent with Rule 17 (c). We also conclude that the Special Prosecutor has made a sufficient showing to justify a subpoena for production *before* trial. The subpoenaed materials are not available from any other source, and their examination and processing should not await trial in the circumstances shown. *Bowman Dairy Co., supra; United States v. Iozia, supra.*

IV. The Claim of Privilege

A.

Having determined that the requirements of Rule 17 (c) were satisfied, we turn to the claim that the subpoena should be quashed because it demands "confidential conversations between a President and his close advisors that it would be inconsistent with the public interest to produce." App. 48a. The first contention is a broad claim that the separation of powers doctrine precludes judicial review of a President's claim of privilege. The second contention is that if he does not prevail on the claim of absolute privilege, the court should hold as a matter of constitutional law that the privilege prevails over the subpoena *duces tecum*.

In the performance of assigned constitutional duties each branch of the Government must initially interpret the Constitution, and the interpretation of its powers by any branch is due great respect from the others. The President's counsel, as we have noted, reads the Constitution as providing an absolute privilege of confidentiality for all presidential communications. Many decisions of this Court, however, have unequivocally reaffirmed the holding of *Marbury v. Madison*, 1 Cranch 137 (1803), that "it is emphatically the province and duty of the judicial department to say what the law is." *Id.*, at 177.

No holding of the Court has defined the scope of judicial power specifically relating to the enforcement of a subpoena for confidential presidential communications for use in a criminal prosecution, but other exercises of powers by the Executive Branch and the Legislative Branch have been found invalid as in conflict with the Constitution. *Powell v. McCormack, supra; Youngstown, supra.* In a series of cases, the Court interpreted the explicit immunity conferred by express provisions of the Constitution on Members of the House and Senate by the Speech or Debate Clause, U.S. Const. Art. I, § 6. *Doe v. McMillan*, 412 U.S. 306 (1973); *Gravel v. United States,* 408 U.S. 606 (1973); *United States v. Brewster,* 408 U.S. 501 (1972); *United States v. Johnson,* 383 U.S. 169 (1966). Since this Court has consistently exercised the power to construe and delineate claims arising under express powers, it must follow that the Court has authority to interpret claims with respect to powers alleged to derive from enumerated powers.

Our system of government "requires that federal courts on occasion interpret the Constitution in a manner at variance with the construction given the document by another branch." *Powell v. McCormack, supra,* 549. And in *Baker v. Carr,* 369 U.S. at 211, the Court stated:

> "[d]eciding whether a matter has in any measure been committed by the Constitution to another branch of government, or whether the action of that branch exceeds whatever authority has been committed, is itself a delicate exercise in constitutional interpretation, and is a responsibility of this Court as ultimate interpreter of the Constitution."

Notwithstanding the deference each branch must accord the others, the "judicial power of the United States" vested in the federal courts by Art. III, § 1 of the Constitution can no more be shared with the Executive Branch than the Chief Executive, for example, can share with the Judiciary the veto power, or the Congress share with the Judiciary the power to override a presidential veto. Any other conclusion would be contrary to the basic concept of separation of powers and the checks and balances that flow from the scheme of a tripartite government. The Federalist, No. 47, p. 313 (C. F. Mittel ed. 1938). We therefore reaffirm that it is "emphatically the province and the duty" of this Court "to say what the law is" with respect to the claim of privilege presented in this case. *Marbury v. Madison, supra,* at 177.

B.

In support of his claim of absolute privilege, the President's counsel urges two grounds one of which is common to all governments and one of which is peculiar to our system of separation of powers. The first ground is the valid need for protection of communications between high government officials and those who advise and assist them in the performance of their manifold duties; the important of this confidentiality is too plain to require further discussion. Human experience teaches that those who expect public dissemination of their remarks may well temper candor with a concern for appearances and for their own interests to the detriment of the decisionmaking process.[15] Whatever the nature of the privilege of confidentiality of presidential communications in the exercise of Art. II powers the privilege can be said to derive from the supremacy of each branch within its own assigned area of constitutional duties. Certain powers and privileges flow from the nature of enumerated powers;[16] the protection of the confidentiality of presidential communications has similar constitutional underpinnings.

The second ground asserted by the President's counsel in support of the claim of absolute privilege rests on the doctrine of separation of powers. Here it is argued that the independence of the Executive Branch within its own sphere, *Humphrey's Executor v. United States,* 295 U.S. 602, 629-630; *Kilbourn v. Thompson,* 103 U.S. 168, 190-191 (1880), insulates a president from a judicial subpoena in an ongoing criminal prosecution, and thereby protects confidential presidential communications.

However, neither the doctrine of separation of powers, nor the need for confidentiality of high level communications, without more, can sustain an absolute, unqualified presidential privilege of immunity from judicial process under all circumstances. The President's need for complete candor and objectivity from advisers calls for great deference from the courts. However, when the privilege depends solely on the broad, undifferentiated claim of public interest in the confidentiality of such conversations, a confrontation with other values arises. Absent a claim of need to protect military, diplomatic or sensitive national security secrets, we find it difficult to accept the argument that even the very important interest in confidentiality of presidential communications is significantly diminished by production of such material for *in camera* inspection with all the protection that a district court will be obliged to provide.

The impediment that an absolute, unqualified privilege would place in the way of the primary constitutional duty of the Judicial Branch to do justice in criminal prosecutions would plainly conflict with the function of the courts under Art. III. In designing the structure of our Government and dividing and allocating the sovereign power among three coequal branches, the Framers of the Constitution sought to provide a comprehensive system, but the separate powers were not intended to operate with absolute independence.

> "While the Constitution diffuses power the better to secure liberty, it also contemplates that practice will integrate the dispersed powers into a workable government. It enjoins upon its branches separateness but interdependence, autonomy but reciprocity." *Youngstown Sheet & Tube Co. v. Sawyer,* 343 U.S. 579, 635 (1952) (Jackson, J., concurring).

To read the Art. II powers of the President as providing an absolute privilege as against a subpoena essential to enforcement of criminal statutes on no more than a generalized claim of the public interest in confidentiality of nonmilitary and non-diplomatic discussions would upset the constitutional balance of "a workable government" and gravely impair the role of the courts under Art. III.

C.

Since we conclude that the legitimate needs of the judicial process may outweight presidential privilege, it is necessary to resolve those competing interests in a manner that preserves the essential functions of each branch. The right and indeed the duty to resolve that question does not free the judiciary from according high respect to the representations made on behalf of the President. *United States v. Burr,* 25 Fed. Cas. 187, 190 191-192 (No. 14,694) (1807).

The expectation of a President to the confidentiality of his conversations and correspondence, like the claim of confidentiality of judicial deliberations, for example, has all the values to which we accord deference for the privacy of all citizens and added to those values the necessity for protection of the public interest in candid, objective, and even blunt or harsh opinions in presidential decision making. A President and those who assist him must be free to explore alternatives in the process of shaping policies and making decisions and to do so in a way many would be unwilling to express except privately. These are the considerations justifying a presumptive privilege for presidential communications. The privilege is fundamental to the operation of government and inextricably rooted in the separation of powers under the Constitution.[17] In *Nixon v. Sirica,* ______ U.S. App. D.C. ______, 487 F. 2d 700 (1973), the Court of Appeals held that such presidential communications are "presumptively privileged," *id.,* at 717, and this position is accepted by both parties in the present litigation. We agree with Mr. Chief Justice Marshall's observation, therefore, that "in no case of this kind would a court be required to proceed against the President as against an ordinary individual." *United States v. Burr,* 25 Fed. Cas. 187, 191 (No. 14,694) (CCD Va. 1807).

But this presumptive privilege must be considered in light of our historic commitment to the rule of law. This is nowhere more profoundly manifest than in our view that "the twofold aim [of criminal justice] is that guilt shall not escape or innocence suffer." *Berger v. United States,* 295 U.S. 78, 88 (1935). We have elected to employ an adversary system of criminal justice in which the parties contest all issues before a court of law. The need to develop all relevant facts in the adversary system is both fundamental and comprehensive. The ends of criminal justice would be defeated if judgments were to be founded on a partial or speculative presentation of the facts. The very integrity of the judicial system and public confidence in the system depend on full disclosure of all the facts, within the framework of the rules of evidence. To ensure that justice is done, it is imperative to the function of courts that compulsory process be available for the production of evidence needed either by the prosecution or by the defense.

Only recently the Court restated the ancient proposition of law, albeit in the context of a grand jury inquiry rather than a trial,

> " 'that the public . . . has a right to every man's evidence' except for those persons protected by a constitutional, common law, or statutory privilege, *United States v. Bryan,* 339 U.S., at 331 (1949); *Blackmer v. United States,* 284 U.S. 421, 438; *Branzburg v. United States,* 408 U.S. 665, 688 (1973)."

The privileges referred to by the Court are designed to protect weighty and legitimate competing interests. Thus, the Fifth Amendment to the Constitution provides that no man "shall be compelled in any criminal case to be a witness against himself." And, generally, an attorney or a priest may not be required to disclose what has been revealed in professional confidence. These and other interests are recognized in law by privileges against forced disclosure, established in the Constitution, by statute, or at common law. Whatever their origins, these exceptions to the demand for every man's evidence are not lightly created nor expansively construed, for they are in derogation of the search for truth.[18]

In this case the President challenges a subpoena served on him as a third party requiring the production of materials for use in a criminal prosecution on the claim that he has a privilege against disclosure of confidential communications. He does not place his claim of privilege on the ground they are military or diplomatic secrets. As to these areas of Art. II duties the courts have traditionally shown the utmost deference to presidential responsibilities. In *C. & S. Air Lines v. Waterman Steamship Corp.*, 333 U.S. 103, 111 (1948), dealing with presidential authority involving foreign policy considerations, the Court said:

> "The President, both as Commander-in-Chief and as the Nation's organ for foreign affairs, has available intelligence services whose reports are not and ought not to be published to the world. It would be intolerable that courts, without the relevant information, should review and perhaps nullify actions of the Executive taken on information properly held secret." *Id.*, at 111.

In *United States v. Reynolds,* 345 U.S. 1 (1952), dealing with a claimant's demand for evidence in a damage case against the Government the Court said:

> "It may be possible to satisfy the court, from all the circumstances of the case, that there is a reasonable danger that compulsion of the evidence will expose military matters which, in the interest of national security, should not be divulged. When this is the case, the occasion for the privilege is appropriate, and the court should not jeopardize the security which the privilege is meant to protect by insisting upon an examination of the evidence, even by the judge alone, in chambers."

No case of the Court, however, has extended this high degree of deference to a President's generalized interest in confidentiality. Nowhere in the Constitution, as we have noted earlier, is there any explicit reference to a privilege of confidentiality, yet to the extent this interest relates to the effective discharge of a President's powers, it is constitutionally based.

The right to the production of all evidence at a criminal trial similarly has constitutional dimensions. The Sixth Amendment explicitly confers upon every defendant in a criminal trial the right "to be confronted with the witnesses against him" and "to have compulsory process for obtaining witnesses in his favor." Moreover, the Fifth Amendment also guarantees that no person shall be deprived of liberty without due process of law. It is the manifest duty of the courts to vindicate those guarantees and to accomplish that it is essential that all relevant and admissible evidence be produced.

In this case we must weigh the importance of the general privilege of confidentiality of presidential communications in performance of his responsibilities against the inroads of such a privilege on the fair administration of criminal justice.[19] The interest in preserving confidentiality is weighty indeed and entitled to great respect. However, we cannot conclude that advisers will be moved to temper the candor of their remarks by the infrequent occasions of disclosure because of the possibility that such conversations will be called for in the context of a criminal prosecution.[20]

On the other hand, the allowance of the privilege to withhold evidence that is demonstrably relevant in a criminal trial would cut deeply into the guarantee of due process of law and gravely impair the basic function of the courts. A President's acknowledged need for confidentiality in the communications of his office is general in nature, whereas the constitutional need for production of relevant evidence in a criminal proceeding is specific and central to the fair adjudication of a particular criminal case in the administration of justice. Without access to specific facts a criminal prosecution may be totally frustrated. The President's broad interest in confidentiality of communications will not be vitiated by disclosure of a limited number of conversations preliminarily shown to have some bearing on the pending criminal cases.

We conclude that when the ground for asserting privilege as to subpoenaed materials sought for use in a criminal trial is based only on the generalized interest in confidentiality, it cannot prevail over the fundamental demands of due process of law in the fair administration of criminal justice. The generalized assertion of privilege must yield to the demonstrated, specific need for evidence in a pending criminal trial.

D.

We have earlier determined that the District Court did not err in authorizing the issuance of the subpoena. If a president concludes that compliance with a subpoena would be injurious to the public interest he may properly, as was done here, invoke a claim of privilege on the return of the subpoena. Upon receiving a claim of privilege from the Chief Executive, it became the further duty of the District Court to treat the subpoenaed material as presumptively privileged and to require the Special Prosecutor to demonstrate that the presidential material was "essential to the justice of the [pending criminal] case." *United States v. Burr, supra,* at 192. Here the District Court treated the material as presumptively privileged, proceeded to find that the Special Prosecutor had made a sufficient showing to rebut the presumption and ordered an *in camera* examination of the subpoenaed material. On the basis of our examination of the record we are unable to conclude that the District Court erred in ordering the inspection. Accordingly we affirm the order of the District Court that subpoenaed materials be transmitted to that court. We now turn to the important question of the District Court's responsibilities in conducting the *in camera* examination of presidential materials or communications delivered under the compulsion of the subpoena *duces tecum.*

E.

Enforcement of the subpoena *duces tecum* was stayed pending this Court's resolution of the issues raised by the petitions for certiorari. Those issues now having been disposed of, the matter of implementation will rest with the District Court. "[T]he guard, furnished to [President] to protect him from being harassed by vexatious and unnecessary subpoenas, is to be looked for in the conduct of the [district] court after the subpoenas have issued; not in any circumstances which is to precede their being issued." *United States v. Burr, supra,* at 34. Statements that meet the test of admissibility and relevance must be isolated; all other material must be excised. At this stage the District Court is not limited to representations of the Special Prosecutor as to the evidence sought by the subpoena; the material will be available to the District Court. It is elementary that *in camera* inspection of evidence is always a procedure calling for scrupulous protection against any release or publication of material not found by the court, at that stage, probably admissible in evidence and relevant to the issues of the trial for which it is sought. That being true of an ordinary situation, it is obvious that the District Court has a very heavy responsibility to see to it that presidential conversations, which are either not relevant or not admissible, are accorded that high degree of respect due the President of the United States. Mr. Chief Justice Marshall sitting as a trial judge in the *Burr* case, *supra,* was extraordinarily careful to point out that:

> "[I]n no case of this kind would a Court be required to proceed against the President as against an ordinary individual." *United States v. Burr,* 25 Fed. Cases 187, 191 (No. 14,694).

Marshall's statement cannot be read to mean in any sense that a President is above the law, but relates to the singularly unique role under Art. II of a President's communications and activities, related to the performance of duties under that Article. Moreover, a President's communications and activities encompass a vastly wider range of sensitive material than would be true of any "ordinary individual." It is therefore necessary[21] in the public interest to afford presidential confidentiality the greatest protection consistent with the fair administration of justice. The need for confidentiality even as to idle conversations with associates in which casual reference might be made concerning political leaders within the country or foreign statesmen is too obvious to call for further treatment. We have no doubt that the District Judge will at all times accord to presidential records that high degree of deference suggested in *United States v. Burr, supra,* and will discharge his responsibility to see to it that until released to the Special Prosecutor no *in camera* material is revealed to anyone. This burden applies with even greater force to excised material; once the decision is made to excise, the material is restored to its privileged status and should be returned under seal to its lawful custodian.

Since this matter came before the Court during the pendency of a criminal prosecution, and on representations that time is of the essence, the mandate shall issue forthwith.

Affirmed.

Mr. Justice Rehnquist took no part in the consideration or decision of these cases.

---

[1]See 28 U.S.C. §§ 1254 (l) and 2101 (c) and our Rule 20. See, *e.g., Youngstown Sheet & Tube Co. v. Sawyer,* 343 U.S. 934, 579, 584 (1952); *United States v. United Mine Workers,* 329 U.S. 708, 709, 710 (1946); 330 U.S. 258, 269 (1947); *Carter v. Carter Coal Co.,* 298 U.S. 238 (1936); *Rickert Rice Mills v. Fontenot,* 294 U.S. 110 (1936); *Railroad Retirement Board v. Alton R. Co.,* 295 U.S. 330, 344 (1935); *United States v. Bankers Trust Co.,* 294 U.S. 240, 243 (1935).

[2]The Cross-petition in No. 73-1834 raised the issue whether the grand jury acted within its authority in naming the President as a coconspirator. Since we find resolution of this issue unnecessary to resolution of the question whether the claim of privilege is to prevail, the cross-petition for certiorari is dismissed as improvidently granted and the remainder of this opinion is concerned with the issues raised in No. 73-1766. On June 19, 1974, the President's counsel moved for disclosure and transmittal to this Court of all evidence presented to the grand jury relating to its action in naming the President as an unindicted coconspirator. Action on this motion was deferred pending oral argument of the case and is not denied.

[3]The seven defendants were John N. Mitchell, H. R. Haldeman, John D. Ehrlichman, Charles W. Colson, Robert C. Mardian, Kenneth W. Parkinson, and Gordon Strachan. Each had occupied either a position of responsibility on the White House staff or the Committee for the Re-Election of the President. Colson entered a guilty plea on another charge and is no longer a defendant.

[4]The President entered a special appearance in the District Court on June 6 and requested that court to lift its protective order regarding the naming of certain individuals as co-conspirators and to any

additional extent deemed appropriate by the Court. This motion of the President was based on the ground that the disclosures to the news media made the reasons for continuance of the protective order no longer meaningful. On June 7, the District Court removed its protective order and, on June 10, counsel for both parties jointly moved this Court to unseal those parts of the record which related to the action of the grand jury regarding the President. After receiving a statement in opposition from the defendants, this Court denied that motion on June 15, 1974, except for the grand jury's immediate finding relating to the status of the President as an unindicted co-conspirator. ______ U.S. ______ (1974).

[5]The specific meetings and conversations are enumerated in a schedule attached to the subpoena. 42a-46a of the App.

[6]At the joint suggestion of the Special Prosecutor and counsel for the President, and with the approval of counsel for the defendants, further proceedings in the District Court were held *in camera.*

[7]The parties have suggested this Court has jurisdiction on other grounds. In view of our conclusion that there is jurisdiction under 28 U.S.C. § 1254 (l) because the District Court's order was appealable, we need not decide whether other jurisdictional vehicles are available.

[8]The regulation issued by the Attorney General pursuant to his statutory authority, vests in the Special Prosecutor plenary authority to control the course of investigations and litigation related to "all offenses arising out of the 1972 Presidential Election for which the Special Prosecutor deems it necessary and appropriate to assume responsibility, allegations involving the President, members of the White House staff, or Presidential appointees, and any other matters which he consents to have assigned to him by the Attorney General." 38 Fed. Reg. 30739, as amended by 38 Fed. Reg. 32805. In particular, the Special Prosecutor was given full authority, *inter alia,* "to contest the assertion of 'Executive Privilege' . . . and handl[e] all aspects of any cases within his jurisdiction." *Ibid.* The regulations then go on to provide:

"In exercising this authority, the Special Prosecutor will have the greatest degree of independence that is consistent with the Attorney-General's statutory accountability for all matters falling within the jurisdiction of the Department of Justice. The Attorney General will not countermand or interfere with the Special Prosecutor's decisions or actions. The Special Prosecutor will determine whether and to what extent he will inform or consult with the Attorney General about the conduct of his duties and responsibilities. In accordance with assurances given by the President to the Attorney General that the President will not exercise his Constitutional powers to effect the discharge of the Special Prosecutor or to limit the independence he is hereby given, the Special Prosecutor will not be removed from his duties except for extraordinary improprieties on his part and without the President's first consulting the Majority and Minority Leaders and Chairman and ranking Minority Members of the Judiciary Committees of the Senate and House of Representatives and ascertaining that their consensus is in accord with his proposed action."

[9]That this was the understanding of Acting Attorney General Robert Bork, the author of the regulations establishing the independence of the Special Prosecutor, is shown by his testimony before the Senate Judiciary Committee:

"Although it is anticipated that Mr. Jaworski will receive cooperation from the White House in getting any evidence he feels he needs to conduct investigations and prosecutions, it is clear and understood on all sides that he has the power to use judicial processes to pursue evidence if disagreement should develop." Hearings before the Senate Judiciary Committee on the Special Prosecutor, 93d Cong., 1st Sess., pt. 2, at 470 (1973). Acting Attorney General Bork gave similar assurances to the House Subcommittee on Criminal Justice. Hearings before the House Judiciary Subcommittee on Criminal Justice on H. J. Res. 784 and H. R. 10937, 93d Cong., 1st Sess., 266 (1973). At his confirmation hearings, Attorney General William Saxbe testified that he shared Acting Attorney General Bork's views concerning the Special Prosecutor's authority to test any claim of executive privilege in the courts. Hearings before the Senate Judiciary Committee on the nomination of William B. Saxbe to be Attorney General, 93d Cong., 1st Sess. 9 (1973).

[10]At his confirmation hearings Attorney General William Saxbe testified that he agreed with the regulations adopted by Acting Attorney General Bork and would not remove the Special Prosecutor except for "gross impropriety." Hearings, Senate Judiciary Committee on the nomination of William B. Saxbe to be Attorney General, 93d Cong., 1st Sess., 5-6, 8-10 (1973). There is no contention here that the Special Prosecutor is guilty of any such impropriety.

[11]The Court quoted a statement of a member of the advisory committee that the purpose of the Rule was to bring documents into court "in advance of the time that they are offered in evidence, so that they may then be inspected in advance, for the purpose . . . of enabling the party to see whether he can use [them] or whether he wants to use [them]." 341 U.S., at 220 n. 5. The Manual for Complex and Multi-

district Litigation published by the Administrative Office of the United States Courts recommends that Rule 17 (c) be encouraged in complex criminal cases in order that each party may be compelled to produce its documentary evidence well in advance of trial and in advance of the time it is to be offered. P. 142, CCH Ed.

[12]The District Court found here that it was faced with "the more unusual situation . . . where the subpoena, rather than being directed to the government by the defendants, issues to what, as a practical matter, is a third party." *United States v. Mitchell*,______ F. Supp. ______(D.C. 1974). The Special Prosecutor suggested that the evidentiary requirement of *Bowman Diary Co.* and *Iozia* does not apply in its full vigor when the subpoena *duces tecum* is issued to third parties rather than to government prosecutors. Brief for the United States 128-129. We need not decide whether a lower standard exists because we are satisfied that the relevance and evidentiary nature of the subpoenaed tapes were sufficiently shown as a preliminary matter to warrant the District Court's refusal to quash the subpoena.

[13]Such statements are declarations by a party defendant that "would surmount all objections based on the hearsay rule . . ." and, at least as to the declarant himself "would be admissible for whatever inferences" might be reasonably drawn. *United States v. Matlock*, ______ U.S. ______(1974). On *Lee v. United States*, 343 U.S. 747, 757 (1953). See also McCormick on Evidence, § 270, at 651-652 (1972 ed).

[14]As a preliminary matter, there must be substantial, independent evidence of the conspiracy at least enough to take the question to the jury. *United States v. Vaught*, 385 F. 2d 320, 323 (CA4 1973); *United States v. Hoffa*, 349 F. 2d 20, 41-42 (CA6 1965), aff'd on other grounds, 385 U.S. 293 (1966); *United States v. Santos*, 385 F. 2d 43, 45 (CA7 1967), cert. denied, 390 U.S. 954 (1968); *United States v. Morton*, 483 F. 2d 573, 576 (CA8 1973); *The United States v. Spanos*, 462 F. 2d 1012, 1014 (CA9 1972); *Carbo v. United States*, 314 F. 2d 718, 737 (CA9 1963), cert. denied, 377 U.S. 953 (1964). Whether the standard has been satisfied is a question of *admissibility* of evidence to be decided by the trial judge.

[15]There is nothing novel about government confidentiality. The meetings of the Constitutional Convention in 1787 were conducted in complete privacy. 1 Farrand. The Records of the Federal Convention of 1787, xi-xxv (1911). Moreover, all records of those meetings were sealed for more than 30 years after the Convention. See 3 U.S. Stat. At Large, 15th Cong., 1st Sess., Res. 8 (1818). Most of the Framers acknowledged that without secrecy no constitution of the kind that was developed could have been written. Warren, *The Making of the Constitution*, 134-139 (1937).

[16]The Special Prosecutor argues that there is no provision in the Constitution for a presidential privilege as to his communications corresponding to the privilege of Members of Congress under the Speech or Debate Clause. But the silence of the Constitution on this score is not dispositive. "The rule of constitutional interpretation announced in *McCulloch v. Maryland*, 4 Wheat. 316, that that which was reasonably appropriate and relevant to the exercise of a granted power was considered as accompanying the grant, has been so universally applied it suffices merely to state it." *Marshall v. Gordon*, 243 U.S. 521, 537 (1917).

[17]Freedom of communication vital to fulfullment of wholesome relationships is obtained only by removing the specter of compelled disclosure . . . [G]overnment . . . needs open but protected channels for the kind of plain talk that is essential to the quality of its functioning." *Carl Zeiss Stiftung v. V. E. B. Carl Zeiss, Jena*, 40 F.R.D. 318, 325 (D.C. 1966). See *Nixon v. Sirica*, ______ U.S. App. D.C. ______, 487 F. 2d 700, 713 (1973); *Kaiser Aluminum & Chem. Corp. v. United States*, 157 F. Supp. 939 (Ct. Cl. 1958) (*per* Reed, J.); The Federalist No. 64 (S.F. Mittel ed. 1938).

[18]Because of the key role of the testimony of witnesses in the judicial process, courts have historically been cautions about privileges. Justice Frankfurter, dessenting in *Elkins v. United States*, 364 U.S. 206, 234 (1960), said of this: "Limitations are properly placed upon the operation of this general principle only to the very limited extent that permitting a refusal to testify or excluding relevant evidence has a public good transcending the normally predominant principle of utilizing all rational means for ascertaining truth."

[19]We are not here concerned with the balance between the President's generalized interest in confidentiality and the need for relevant evidence in civil litigation, nor with that between the confidentiality interest and congressional demands for information, nor with the President's interest in preserving state secrets. We address only the conflict between the President's assertion of a generalized privilege of confidentiality against the constitutional need for relevant evidence to criminal trials.

[20]Mr. Justice Cardozo made this point in an analogous context. Speaking for a unanimous Court in *Clark v. United States*, 289 U.S. 1 (1933), he emphasized the importance of maintaining the secrecy of

the deliberations of a petit jury in a criminal case. "Freedom of debate might be stifled and independence of thought checked if jurors were made to feel that their arguments and ballots were to be freely published in the world." *Id.*, at 13' Nonetheless, the Court also recognized that isolated inroads on confidentiality designed to serve the paramount need of the criminal law would not vitiate the interests served by secrecy:

"A juror of integrity and reasonably firmness will not fear to speak his mind if the confidences of debate bar barred to the ears of mere impertinence or malice. He will not expect to be shielded against the disclosure of his conduct in the event that there is evidence reflecting upon his honor. The chance that now and then there may be found some timid soul who will take counsel of his fears and give way to their repressive power is too remote and shadowly to shape the course of justice." *Id.*, at 16.

[21] When the subpoenaed material is delivered to the District Judge *in camera* questions may arise as to the excising of parts and it lies within the discretion of that court to seek the aid of the Special Prosecutor and the President's counsel for *in camera* consideration of the validity of particular excisions, whether the basis of excision is relevancy or admissibility or under such cases as *Reynolds, supra,* or *Waterman Steamship, supra.*

Knopf v. Colby

509 F.2d 1362 (4th Cir. 1975)

Haynsworth, Chief Judge:

This is a sequel to United States v. Marchetti, 4 Cir., 466 F.2d 1309 in which, because of a secrecy agreement he had executed, we upheld an injunction prohibiting Marchetti's public disclosure of classified information acquired by him during the course of his employment by the Central Intelligence Agency and requiring him to submit any material he intended to public to that agency for its review in advance of publication.

After our earlier decision, Marchetti, in collaboration with John Marks, a former employee of the State Department who had bound himself not to disclose classified information acquired by him during the course of his employment, prepared the manuscript of a book which the plaintiff, Alfred A. Knopf, Inc. intended to publish. After review in the CIA, a letter was written specifying the deletion of 339 items said to contain classified information. Later, after a conference with Marchetti and his lawyer, the CIA agreed to release 114 of the deletions. Later another 29 deletion items were released and still later another 57, leaving 168 deletion items upon which the CIA stood fast.

This action was filed by Alfred A. Knopf, Inc., Marchetti and Marks in the United States District Court for the Southern District of New York, seeking an order which would permit the publication of the then remaining deletion items. On motion of the defendants, the action was transferred to the Eastern District of Virginia where the *Marchetti* case had been tried and where it could come before the same judge who had tried *Marchetti.*

I.

At the trial, the four deputy directors of the CIA were presented as witnesses. Collectively they covered all of the 168 deletion items, each covering certain of them. Each testified, in effect, that the deletion item revealed information which was classified, that the information was classified from the inception of the program or from the time of the witness' first contact with it and was still classified. With respect to most, if not all of the items, however, the witness was unable to say who classified the information, for Executive Order No. 10501,[1] in effect in the relevant times, did not require the classifying officer to record his identity, as Executive Order No. 11652[2] now does. Nor were they certain about when a particular matter had been classified except certain of the items with respect to which the witness stated the information had been classified from the beginning or from the time of his first contact with it.

These witnesses were questioned about the manner in which they determined that particular items had been classified. Typically, the response was that the witness read the Marchetti-Marks manuscript, marked passages which he thought revealed classified information and then called upon members of the staff for research assistance. The witness indicated that he wished to be certain of his grounds and to make no mistake. The witness then reviewed classified documents produced by the staff, and, after consultation with staff assistants, made his determination or judgment that particular information was, indeed, classified. There were indications that the witness considered his own recollection, institutional history, reports of staff members and classified documents in deciding whether or not particular information was classified.

The District Judge was persuaded that information, which might be sensitive to our national defense or to our relations with foreign nations, is not classified until a classifying officer makes a conscious determination that the governmental interest in secrecy outweighs a general policy of disclosure and applies a label of "Top Secret" or "Secret" or "Confidential" to the information in question. The testimony of the deputy directors, with its imprecision and the generality of the considerations which they said underlaid their determinations seemed insufficient to persuade him that undisclosed individuals had gone through such conscious processes during the time of Marchetti's employment. It seemed to him that the deputy directors were making *ad hoc* classifications of material after having read the Marchetti-Marks manuscript, though he recognized that the deputy directors denied that they were doing any such thing.

Late in the trial, the United States offered a batch of documents, most of them bearing "Top Secret" stamps and collectively containing information relating to the deletion items. Some of these documents dealt with the actual classification of certain information. When a document, for instance, specified that certain information relating to a particular program should be classified as "Top Secret" while other information respecting that program should be classified as "Secret", the Judge accepted the document as showing that someone had gone through the conscious process of deciding whether, and in what degree, particular information should be classified. On this basis the District Judge found that the information embodied in 26 of the 168 items was classified during the time of Marchetti's employment. As to the remainder of the 168 deletion items, however, he found the submitted documents of no persuasive value. He was of that opinion because he had been told that a document properly classified as "Top Secret" may contain some bits of information which are not classifiable at all. His difficulty was compounded by the fact that many of the documents marked "Top Secret" had been reproduced with all of their contents blocked out except for one paragraph, sentence or message relating to a deletion item. He reasoned that only the classifying officer could say what information in a particular document led him to classify the entire document "Top Secret" and that a limited disclosure of something extracted from a document classified as "Top Secret" did not establish classification of that information as "Top Secret" or even as being classified in any degree. Recognizing that the deputy directors, at the very least, had testified that the disclosed information was classifiable, he still was of the view that the testimony and the documents in combination did not prove that the disclosed classifiable information had in fact been classified by the unidentified and possibly unidentifiable classifying officer. Though recognizing that some or much of the disclosed information, revealed in the deletion items, was "sensitive", the District Judge concluded that the United States had not shown that the remaining 142 deletion items had been classified. He felt, in short, since reasonableness of classification was proscribed, as we held in *Marchetti*, appropriate recognition of the first amendment rights of Marchetti and of Marks required strict proof of classification which he found wanting under the standards developed at the trial.

When writing in *Marchetti*, we did not foresee the problems as they developed in the district court. We had not envisioned any problem of identifying classified information embodied in a document produced from the files of such an agency as the CIA and marked "Top Secret", "Secret" or "Confidential". Of course, a document containing the results of tests of highly secret equipment may contain an incidental reference to the weather on a given day at a designated place in the United States, but we foresaw no particular problem in separating the grain from such chaff. With our strictures against inquiry into the reasonableness of any classification, however, we perhaps misled the District Judge into the imposition upon the United States of an unreasonable and improper burden of proof of classification.

When the earlier case was before us, we had supposed that all information in a classified document in the possession of the CIA, except rather obvious chaff of the sort we have mentioned, should be held to be classified and not subject to disclosure. We were influenced in substantial part by the principle that executive decisions respecting the classifying of information are not subject to judicial review. *See, e.g.,* EPA v. Mink, 410 U.S. 73, 93 S.Ct. 827, 35 L.Ed.2d 119 (1972). The October 1974 amendments[3] to the Freedom of Information Act introduced new considerations. Title 5, Section 552(b)(1) of the United States Code has been amended to provide for non-disclosure of matters that are "(A) specifically authorized under criteria established by an Executive order to be kept secret in the interest of national defense or foreign policy and (B) are in fact properly classified pursuant to such Executive order." Furthermore, a new subsection was introduced into Section 552(a), paragraph (B) of the new subsection now numbered (4) specifically providing for judicial review *de novo* and specifically providing that the judge "may examine the contents of such agency records in camera to determine whether such records or any part thereof shall be withheld under any of the exemptions set forth in subsection (b) of this section, and the burden is on the agency to sustain its action." The legislative history makes it clear that the Congress intended to overthrow the result of *Mink. See, e.g.,* Conference Report No. 93-1200, U.S. Code Cong. & Admin. News, 93rd Cong., 2d Sess. pp. 6221 at 6223, 6226. That history also discloses a congressional intention that the judge need not inspect the document *in camera* or require its production. He may act on the basis of testimony or affidavits but, in appropriate cases, he now has a right by virtue of the statute to require production of the document for his inspection *in camera.*

Since the Freedom of Information Act as now amended clearly provides for judicial review of questions of classifiability, any citizen now can compel the production of information actually classified if its classification was not authorized by the Executive Order.[4] These plaintiffs should not be denied the right to publish information which any citizen could compel the CIA to produce and, after production, could publish. We thus move to the conclusion that the deletion items should be suppressed only if they are found both to be classified and classifiable under the Executive Order.

We observed in *Marchetti* that the Congress has required the Director of the CIA to protect intelligence sources and methods from unauthorized disclosure.[5] In keeping with the Congressional directive, Executive Order No. 11652, Classification and Declassification of National Security Information and Material, as amended by Executive Order No. 11714[6] provides in § (1)(A) that information shall be classified "Top Secret" if its disclosure would disrupt "foreign relations vitally affecting the national security," would compromise "vital national defense plans . . . communications intelligence systems," would reveal "sensitive intelligence operations" or disclose "scientific or technological developments vital to national security." Subparagraph B provides that information shall be classified as "Secret" if it reveals "significant military plans or intelligence operations." This would encompass any significant intelligence operations not otherwise classifiable under Subparagraph A as "Top Secret." Subparagraph C requires the classification as "Confidential" of all other information the unauthorized disclosure of which might reasonably be expected to damage the national security.

The author of this opinion has examined some, but not all, of the 142 deletion items. The information in at least some of them does relate to sensitive intelligence operations and to scientific and technological developments useful, if not vital, to national security. Such items would seem clearly to be classifiable under the authorization of the Executive Order; others may relate to intelligence sources or methods, the protection of which Congress has decreed in the National Security Act of 1947[7] and classifiable under the Executive Order.

The statutory requirement is not directed to any procedure. It simply requires protection of intelligence sources and methods against unauthorized disclosure, and provision of such protection may require a variety of activity. One obviously appropriate tool in providing that protection, however, is a system of classification required under a succession of Executive orders. Under the statute and those orders, a classifying officer is required to classify a document containing classifiable information and to determine the degree under the guidelines of the current Executive order. Under Executive Order No. 10501, he performed his duty by affixing the appropriate stamp, "Top Secret", "Secret" or "Confidential."

There is a presumption of regularity in the performance by a public official of his public duty. "The presumption of regularity supports the official acts of public officers, and, in the absence of clear evidence to the contrary, courts presume that they have properly discharged their official duties." United States v. Chemical Foundation, Inc., 272 U.S. 1 at 14, 15, 47 S.Ct. 1 at 6, 71 L.Ed. 131. That presumption leaves no room for speculation that information which the district court can recognize as proper for top secret classification was not classified at all by the official who placed the "Top Secret" legend on the document. This is so whether or not the document contains or may contain other information which should have been classified in the same degree. Under the prevailing practice of classifying a document in accordance with the most sensitive information it contains, the presumption, in the absence of affirmative proof to the contrary, requires the conclusion that all information within it, required by the Executive Order to be classified, was classified when the legend was affixed to the document, even though the particular bit of relevant information, alone, may be properly classified only in a lower degree than the document's classification. In short, the government was required to show no more than that each deletion item disclosed information which was required to be classified in any degree and which was contained in a document bearing a classification stamp.

The presumption dispenses with another problem which bothered the District Judge, the time of classification. He took the view that the government must show that the document was classified before Marchetti left the service. We are dealing, however, with information acquired by Marchetti during his employment by the CIA. It simply cannot be supposed that no one performed the duty of classification until after his employment had terminated.

It would have been nice, of course, if, in each instance, the government could have identified and produced the classifying officer who, from other records or extraordinary memory, could have testified that he classified the document on a certain day and that, in doing so, he consciously intended to classify the relevant item of information. That was a practical impossibility, but, in light of the presumption, unnecessary. The office of the presumption, however, is supported by the testimony of the deputy directors that information was classified from the beginning of the operation to which it relates or from the time the Agency first received it.

Nor was it necessary for the government to disclose to lawyers, judges, court reporters, expert witnesses and others, perhaps, sensitive but irrelevant information in a classified document in order to prove that a particular item of information within it had been classified. It is not to slight judges, lawyers or anyone else to suggest that any such disclosure carries with it serious risk that highly sensitive information may be compromised. In our own chambers, we are ill equipped to provide the kind of security highly sensitive information should have. The national interest requires that the government withhold or delete unrelated items of sensitive information, as it did, in the absence of compelling necessity. It is enough, as we have said, that the particular item of information is classifiable and is shown to have been embodied in a classified document. This approach is consistent with the Freedom of Information Act which, as we have noticed, provides the judge only with discretionary authority even to require production of the document for his *in camera* inspection; he may find the information both classified and classifiable on the basis of testimony or affidavits.

It is said, however, that some classifiable information is not classified. Reference is made to disclosure of this country's development of Multiple Independently Targeted Reentry Vehicles and the release of information about North Vietnamese forces operating in South Vietnam, including the identity of units, their strength and the routes they took to reach their operating areas. These disclosures, however, were the result of high level executive decisions that disclosure was in the public interest, to counter popular and congressional pressure for more missiles, in the first instance, and, in the second instance, to bolster domestic support for our own military effort in South Vietnam. They are instances of declassification by official public disclosure. There has been no such disclosure of any of the information with which we are concerned, and there is nothing in the record to suggest that any of this classified information has, otherwise, been officially declassified. In the absence of declassification and of any countervailing evidence, the testimony of the deputy directors and the presumption of regularity compel a finding that information properly classified under the guidelines of the applicable Executive Order and embodied in a document bearing a classification stamp was classified at the time the information first came into the possession of the Agency or Department.

Moreover, if the documents in evidence, the testimony of the deputy directors and the presumptions compel a judicial finding that the material is both classifiable and classified, the plaintiffs are not without an avenue of relief within the Executive Branch. Under § 7 of Executive Order 11652, the National Security Council was given the responsibility of monitoring the implementation of the Order. To assist the Council, an Interagency Classification Review Committee was created. It is authorized to consider and act upon suggestions and complaint from persons within and without government. Composed of representatives of the Departments of State, Defense, and Justice, the Atomic Energy Commission, the Central Intelligence Agency and the Staff of the Security Council, it would not be expected to serve any parochial interest of a particular agency unless it coincided with the national interest. The members of the Review Committee, far more than any judge, have the background for making classification and declassification decisions. If, therefore, any of the items in dispute are thought to be properly declassifiable now, there appears to be an available administrative remedy which is far more effective than any the judiciary may provide, which can function without threat to the national security and which can act within the Executive's traditional sphere of autonomy.

For such reasons, we conclude that the burden of proof imposed upon the defendants to establish classification was far too stringent and that it is appropriate to vacate the judgment and remand for reconsideration and fresh findings imposing a burden of proof consistent with this opinion and including the additional element of classifiability.

II.

We decline to modify our previous holdings that the First Amendment is no bar against an injunction forbidding the disclosure of classifiable information within the guidelines of the Executive Orders when (1) the classified information was acquired, during the course of his employment, by an employee of a United States agency or department in which such information is handled and (2) its disclosure would violate a solemn agreement made by the employee at the commencement of his employment. With respect to such information, by his execution of the secrecy agreement and his entry into the confidential employment relationship, he effectively relinquished his First Amendment rights.

III.

The District Judge properly held that classified information obtained by the CIA or the State Department was not in the public domain unless there had been official disclosure of it. This we strongly intimated in our earlier opinion. Rumors and speculations circulate and sometimes get into print. It is one thing for a reporter or author to speculate or guess that a thing may be so or even, quoting undisclosed sources, to say that it is so; it is quite another thing for one in a position to know of it officially to say that it is so. The reading public is accustomed to treating reports from uncertain sources as being of uncertain reliability, but it would not be inclined to discredit reports of sensitive information revealed by an official of the United States in a position to know of what he spoke. The problem is highlighted and the appropriateness of the answer we reach emphasized by the fact that Marks, on Fifth Amendment grounds, on five different occasions declined to answer whether he was the undisclosed source of information contained in five magazine articles offered by the plaintiffs to show that the information was in the public domain. A public official in a confidential relationship surely may not leak information in violation of the confidence reposed in him and use the resulting publication as legitimating his own subsequent open and public disclosure of the same information. The same rule must apply though there be no basis for suspicion that one of the plaintiffs was the undisclosed source of the previously published information, for security of all official secrets would break down if speculative and unattributed reports were held to have removed all of their protection from them.

It is true that others may republish previously published material, but such republication by strangers to it lends no additional credence to it. Marchetti and Marks are quite different, for their republication of the material would lend credence to it, and, unlike strangers referring to earlier unattributed reports, they are bound by formal agreements not to disclose such information.

One may imagine situations in which information has been so widely circulated and is so generally believed to be true, that confirmation by one in a position to know would add nothing to its weight. However, appraisals of such situations by the judiciary would present a host of problems and obstacles. It may readily be done by the Interagency Classification Review Committee. If a particular item is held by the court to be not in the public domain because not officially disclosed, the Review Committee may still find that it has so far entered the public domain that it should be declassified. As long as it remains classified, however, there should be no further judicial inquiry.

IV.

On the basis of what the District Judge described as "an extremely subjective judgment" he found that seven of the deletion items contained information which was either learned by them outside of their employment or was learned both during their employment and afterwards and would have been learned afterwards "in any event." He concluded that they could publish the information contained in those items.

The agreement, of course, covers only information learned by them during their employment and in consequence of it. It does not cover information gathered by them outside of their employment or after its termination. They may not publish information first received by them during the course of their employment even though they later learned of it by communications which did not place the information in the public domain. In a sense, they may be said to have later learned all of the information contained in articles and other materials offered by them in an attempt to show that certain information was in the public domain, but that is not the kind of knowledge acquisition which places the material beyond the reach of the secrecy agreements. Information later received as a consequence of the indiscretion of overly trusting former associates is in the same category. In short, the individuals bound by the secrecy agreements may not disclose information, still classified, learned by them during their employments regardless of what they may learn or might learn thereafter.

Moreover, neither should be heard to say that he did not learn of information during the course of his employment if the information was in the Agency and he had access to it. At least, a substantial presumption should be raised against him in those circumstances. With whatever apparent sincerity a fallible recollection may be expressed, one in Marchetti's high position in the CIA should be presumed to have been informed of all important items of information to which he had access.

On remand the District Judge should review these general findings in light of this opinion, authorizing disclosure of those items of information only which first came to them unofficially after the termination of their employment.

V.

The judgment is affirmed in part, vacated in part and remanded for such further proceedings as may be necessary in accordance with this opinion.

Affirmed in part; vacated in part; remanded.

---

[1]November 10, 1953, 18 Fed. Reg. 7049.

[2]March 10, 1972 as amended April 26, 1973, 38 Fed. Reg. 10245.

[3]Pub. L. No. 93-502, 88 Stat. 1561.

[4]§ 552(b)(3) was not amended. It exempts matters "specifically exempted from disclosure by statute." The statutory direction to the Director to protect intelligence sources and methods from unauthorized disclosure may be such a statute, but such information is also clearly authorized to be classified by the Executive order. The problems that will arise therefore will be concerned with the application of (b)(1) rather than (b)(3).

[5]50 U.S.C.A. § 403(d)(3). See *Marchetti*, 466 F.2d 1309 at 1316.

[6]38 Fed. Reg. 10245.

[7]50 U.S.C.A. § 403(d)(3).

Punishing Release of Information

COMMENTARY

Espionage

The prohibition against prior restraint on publishing national security information, while not absolute, is very strong; the government has much broader latitude to punish publication or other unauthorized disclosure of national security information. This can be done under the various espionage laws. Until the Pentagon Papers were published, the laws had been used only in cases of alleged spying. In the Pentagon Papers criminal case they were used for the first time to seek to punish activity leading up to publication.

The current espionage laws are in a state of total confusion. They form no coherent structure, and each part of them poses many complicated problems of interpretation. Neither the intended meaning nor even the literal meaning of the terms of each statute is obvious.[1]

This situation is not only intellectually awkward, but it raises constitutional questions as well. Not even the strict, absolutist devotees of the First Amendment have been able to discern therein a right to convey weapons secrets to a foreign power. We may take it that a ban on spying as such is clearly valid. But an espionage law may run afoul of the Constitution if it is overbroad, that is, if it also clearly covers speech protected by the First Amendment, or if it is so vague that one cannot tell what kind of behavior is made illegal, so that a chilling effect is cast on public debate.

The scope of a law affecting speech must be tailored to the danger that justifies the law. If it covers speech that is constitutionally protected as well as what is properly punished, the law is invalid.[2] The due process doctrine known as void-for-vagueness states the elementary notion that it is unfair to punish one who, with the best of will, could not have determined with any certainty whether or not his conduct would be a crime. Especially where the law impinges on freedom of speech, one is entitled to clear notice of what is prohibited.[3] Such notice certainly is not provided by the simple act of reading the espionage laws.

Survey of Current Law

Until 1911, the United States had no espionage laws. It was in contemplation of American involvement in military conflict in Europe that a relatively simple law was passed in that year. In 1917, Congress passed the laws which are still, in virtually unchanged form, on the books today. In 1932 and in 1950, certain specialized laws were added, and in 1950 Congress made an important addition to the 1917 law.

The basic espionage law is contained in chapter 37, sections 793 and 794 of title 18, United States Code. Edgar and Schmidt have strongly argued that, except for the specific reference in 794(b) to wartime publication with intent, these provisions were not meant to apply to publication or acts preliminary thereto. Section 794, designed to deal with spies, makes it a crime to communicate directly or indirectly to a foreign agent information related to the national defense with intent, or reason to believe, that the information is to be used to the injury of the United States or to the advantage of a foreign power. Sections 793(a) and (b) are ancillary to section 794, in that they deal with copying or gathering national defense information with intent or reason to believe that the information is to be used to the injury of the United States or to the advantage of a foreign power. The remainder, and particularly subsections (d) and (e) of section 793, pose the greatest difficulties of interpretation or understanding. They prohibit the willful communication, to any person not entitled to receive it, of any writing relating to the national defense, or of information relating to the national defense which the possessor has reason to believe could be used to the injury of the United States or to the advantage of any foreign nation. Sections 793(d) and (3) do not require, on their face, any intent to injure the national defense; they appear to cover non-spies who release information to newspaper reporters or to other private citizens. Since these are the statutes under which Daniel Ellsberg and Anthony Russo were indicted, we will consider them in detail below.

Other statutes deal more specifically with particular kinds of information. Two statutes (18 U.S.C. sections 798 and 952) prohibit unauthorized release or use of information related to cryptography or other coded messages or materials. Similarly, the Atomic Energy Act (42 U.S.C. sections 2271-81) makes it a crime to release in an unauthorized way information related to atomic energy. This act is, relatively speaking, a model of clarity and precision: Congress has legislated a classification system, with graded penalties for unauthorized disclosure of information, and including provision for the release of information not classified under the act.

There is also a separate statute, discussed further below, which covers officers and employees of the federal government who pass to a foreign agent or a member of the communist party, information "of a kind which shall have been classified by the President . . . as affecting the security of the United States." This statute (50 U.S.C. section 783(b)), passed by Congress in 1950, is the only part of the espionage laws directly geared to the classification system. Finally, there is a series of so-called photographic statutes, which deal with unauthorized photographing of military installations or bases.[4] The remaining discussion will be directed essentially to the basic provisions of sections 793 and 794, except where otherwise indicated.[5]

There appears to be a great gap between what Congress intended in passing the espionage laws in 1917 and what it actually wrote into the law. On the one hand, Congress vehemently rejected a scheme of publication controls proposed by President Woodrow Wilson, which, in its view, would have interfered with public debate. The 1917 law referred expressly to publication only in the context of wartime publication of military information "with intent that the same shall be communicated to the enemy." Thus Congress clearly disclaimed any general purpose to interfere with the publication of information, merely because it might eventually be used by a foreign power to its advantage or to the injury of the national defense. Yet other portions of the law do proscribe information gathering and communication activities, such as might precede the publication of information related to the national defense, as well as its transmission directly to a foreign government. Moreover, portions of the law seem to apply to persons against whom the government can not allege any purpose of harming the national defense of the United States. In addition to the apparent gap between what Congress intended and what it actually enacted, in many cases the statutes defy any logical interpretation when examined closely and in relation to each other.

These ambiguities in the law have only recently been noticed. Until the Pentagon Papers episode, the laws had been used only in cases of spying, where information was actually passed to a foreign government.

The Understanding Prior to the Pentagon Papers Case

It was generally believed by officials of the United States government prior to 1971 that the espionage laws (sections 793 and 794) applied only to genuine spies, who sought to pass information to foreign agents with the intent, or at least reason to believe, that the information would be used by a foreign government to injure the United States or to aid that government.[6] Although this interpretation is not compelled by the language of the statutes, it was taken so seriously that the executive branch repeatedly declined to institute prosecution for leaks of classified information it regarded as serious. The government believed it could not indict, because there was not the requisite intent or reason to believe that the information would be used to injure the national defense.[7]

On several occasions Congress was asked by the executive branch for legislation to make criminal the release of any classified information by a present or former government official. These requests testify to the traditional belief inside the executive branch that leaking is not in general a violation of the espionage laws.

It is true that officials given access to classified information were routinely warned that unauthorized disclosure could be a criminal act. But in practice, violations of the classification system were punished by administrative action, not by criminal indictments.

The view of Congress was given in 1950, in the process of enacting a new criminal law protecting communications intelligence: "Under the Espionage Act of 1917, unauthorized revelation of information of this kind can be penalized only if it can be proven that the person making the revelation did so with an intent to injure the United States.[8]

This policy of Congress has been deliberate and consistent, and supported by self-interested as well as altruistic motives. For the extent of its own reliance on revelations by former officials has become quite apparent to Congress. There are frequent public hearings, as well as occasional ones in "executive" session, in which testimony is taken from former government officials.[9] This testimony has been of great importance to Congress in performing major responsibilities such as reviewing and developing alternatives on the defense budget. Moreover, congressional committees, individual Congressmen and Senators have recruited former officials for their staffs, intending to draw upon the information and experience they have acquired. Much of this information would be considered "classified" in the executive branch and/or could be said to "relate to the national defense."

The congressional attitude toward more narrowly focussed legislative proposals has been far more accepting. Congress has expressly made it a crime to publish classified information relating to atomic energy, communications intelligence, or codes. For example, in 1931 a former government official published a detailed account of American success in breaking Japanese diplomatic codes over the prior ten years. In 1933, it was learned that the same author was about to make further detailed revelations along these lines. Within a few weeks Congress passed legislation that made it a crime to publish cryptographic information; this quick response prevented the publication of the second book. According to the House Report accompanying a more recent cryptographic bill, it was the intent of the House "while carefully avoiding the infringement of civil liberties" to provide protection covering "only a small category of classified matter, a category which is both vital and vulnerable to an almost unique degree." The narrow scope of this legislation can scarcely be viewed as inadvertent.[10]

In the aftermath of the Pentagon Papers episode, Congress once again declined to act on an administration request for a broad Official Secrets Act. The publication of the Pentagon Papers indeed led to hearings, but these were not directed toward preventing the evil of leaking by former officials. Rather, the House Government Operations Committee and, later, three subcommittees of the Senate Judiciary and Government Operations Committees held hearings focussed on the evil of excessive classification of information. The weight of congressional sentiment was to the effect that the executive branch ought itself to have released the Pentagon Papers prior to their publication in *The New York Times.* Bowing to pressure from these committees, the executive branch did agree to the publication of most of the material contained in the Pentagon Papers.[11]

We think this record makes out an overwhelming case that Congress never intended the espionage laws to apply to leaks of nontechnical information.

The courts had no occasion prior to 1971 to express any opinion on the question before us. There have been, in fact, surprisingly few indictments even for actual spying. A few such indictments involving alleged German espionage agents occurred during the First and Second World Wars. After the Second World War, there were several indictments of alleged communist spies, the most notorious being those involving Julius and Ethel Rosenberg, Judith Coplon, and the Soviet spy Rudolf Abel. In all these cases, the facts alleged included clandestine transfer of information to agents or officials of foreign governments. The legal disputes turned mainly on Fourth and Fifth Amendment questions involving search and seizure of evidence, wiretaps, or the illegality of confessions. The only higher court opinions that dealt with fundamental constitutional issues of relevance here were those in the cases of *Gorin, Heine* and *Scarbeck.* Each of these cases will be discussed briefly in turn.

Gorin v. United States

The basic issue faced by the Supreme Court in *Gorin* was a challenge to the constitutionality of the law, directed specifically to the term, "relating to the national defense." Defendants argued that this term was fatally vague in meaning, unless construed as applying only to information about specific installations and objects mentioned elsewhere in the espionage laws, such as vessels, aircraft, forts, signal stations, and code books. The Court found no support in the legislative history for such a narrow construction, and instead accepted the broad definition of national defense suggested by the government: national defense is a "generic concept of broad connotations, referring to the military and naval establishments and the related activities of national preparedness."[12]

The Court went on to say that although this phrase might appear on its face to be excessively vague, the statute was saved by its separate *scienter* (state of mind) requirement. That is, the government was obliged to prove that defendants acted "with intent or reason to believe" that the information they were obtaining was "to be used to the injury of the United States or to the advantage of any foreign power." If one were proved to have acted with such intent, the Court reasoned, he must have known that he was engaging in conduct which violated the statute. Therefore, the phrase "relating to the national defense" was not fatally vague.

This flawed analysis left much to be desired. In general, each term of a criminal statute ought to be clear of such defects as overbreadth and vagueness. By sanctioning the construction it did, in effect the Court read the term "national defense" out of the statute; the result almost seems to permit a conviction for transmitting *any* information that might in *any* way advantage a foreign power.[13]

Moreover, the Court unwittingly aggravated the problem that would arise in applying other portions of the law to activities that clearly are not spying. In sections 793(d) and (e), there is no general requirement of "intent or reason to believe the information is to be used to injure the national defense"; here the mere transmitting to unauthorized persons of documents "relating to the national defense" is apparently made a crime. It is certainly arguable that in this unqualified context, the definition of "relating to the national defense" upheld in *Gorin* becomes so excessively vague and overbroad as to render the provisions unconstitutional.

United States v. Heine

In this Court of Appeals decision, authored by Judge Learned Hand, the main issue was whether collecting information from the public domain could be punished under the espionage statutes. As Judge Hand recognized, the term "relating to national defense" was to be broadly construed, and

> . . . so drastic a repression of the free exchange of information it is wise carefully to scrutinize, lest extravagant and absurd consequences result.
>
> It seems plain that the section cannot cover information about all those activities which become tributary to "the national defense" in time of war; for in modern war there are none which do not.

The Court found it possible, however, to avoid the impact of the holding in *Gorin* by addressing itself squarely to the question of criminal intent. From the *Gorin* decision, it was already clear that collection of information which the government had actually put into the public domain would not be punishable, because "where there is no occasion for secrecy . . . there can, of course, in all likelihood be no reasonable intent to give an advantage to a foreign government."[14] In *Heine,* the information had been gathered entirely from public sources and had never, in fact, been classified. Declining to distinguish information released by the government from that which was never secret, the Court concluded that the gathering of information entirely from public sources, as Heine had done, could not be a crime. Judge Hand wrote:

> The services must be trusted to determine what information may be broadcast without prejudice to the "national defense," and their consent to its dissemination is as much evidenced by what they do not seek to suppress, as by what they utter. Certainly it cannot be unlawful to spread such information within the United States; and, if so, it would be to the last degree fatuous to forbid its transmission to the citizens of a friendly foreign power.[15]

The court did not focus on the case of information which had once been held secret but has become public through processes other than formal release. This important question was to be presented in the Pentagon Papers trial.

United States v. Scarbeck

The special statute[16] under which Scarbeck was indicted makes it a crime for an official to transfer to a foreign or communist agent any classified information. This provision is the only portion of the espionage laws geared directly to the classification system. As such, it permits a trial in which the government need not disclose the nature and significance of the information alleged to have been transferred. In *Scarbeck,* there was oral testimony by the American Ambassador to Poland showing that the documents passed by Scarbeck to officials of the Polish government were marked with classification stamps, and that these stamps had been put on the documents by the Ambassador, who was authorized by Executive Order to classify documents. Nothing more, the court held, was required for a finding of guilt. Specifically, the propriety of the classification was not to be an issue in the case; and no showing of evil intent was required, beyond what could be inferred from the very identity of the recipients.

Scarbeck suggests the possibility of a similar procedure in trials under sections 793 and 794. That is, the government might propose to establish by simply asserting the mere fact of classification that the information is "related to the national defense"—without the need to reveal the secrets that are in issue or to prove anything about how harmful their release would be. As far as prosecutions for leaking information to the public are concerned, it is not clear that this innovation would materially ease the government's burden of proof. Unless stamped official documents had changed hands, it would be difficult to prove that the particular information was in fact classified, much less to prove it was *known* by the accused to be classified. Yet to presume such guilty knowledge on the part of a criminal defendant would fly in the face of the presumption of innocence. It would seem that such a procedure would be unconstitutional, despite the *Scarbeck* decision.

The application of Scarbeck procedures under the 1917 law seems precluded by the *Gorin* holding that it is for the jury to determine whether given information relates to the national defense. Thus instructions to the jury to ignore the classification markings on documents have been upheld in post-*Scarbeck* decisions.[17] The *Scarbeck* procedure has been accepted by the courts only in the context of a statute covering transfers of classified information to communist or foreign agents—a situation in which evil or reckless intent can plausibly be inferred even without a showing that the information was important. In the case of a statute that purported to punish all transfers of classified information without limitation as to the recipient, the danger of punishing truly innocent activity would be substantially greater. Such a law, we think, would meet constitutional requirements only if interpreted to require that the government prove not only the fact of classification, but the propriety of the classification and the defendant's intent to injure the United States as well. Even then, the result would be less than satisfactory. The fact that the present executive order permits an item to be classified is simply not of much relevance to the underlying question, whether the national security would be seriously jeopardized by its release.

These cases and the relatively few others decided under the espionage laws settled only a few issues of statutory interpretation and constitutional law. Others, such as the meaning of the cryptic terms "unauthorized possession" and "not entitled to receive," would surface only when the government, for the first time, sought to use sections 793(d) and (e) of the espionage statutes in a situation involving the public release of classified documents. It is to that case, the Pentagon Papers criminal trial, that we now turn.

The Pentagon Papers Criminal Trial

We are concerned here with the indictment of Daniel Ellsberg and Anthony Russo in connection with the alleged misuse of the Pentagon Papers.

The case in chief, known formally as *United States v. Russo and Ellsberg,* was dismissed by Judge Matthew Byrne in an unreported oral opinion because of government misconduct.[18] The proceedings terminated before the Judge came to definite and final conclusions about interpretation of the espionage law. Nevertheless, Judge Byrne did issue a tentative statement at the beginning of the trial, and later he gave a number of instructions to the jury which were consistent with, and covered most of the points raised in, his preliminary interpretation.

The indictment as handed down by the grand jury accused Ellsberg and Russo of violating either section 793(d) or section 793(e), which are virtually identical except that (d) deals with transmittals by a person in *authorized* possession of documents or information relating to the national defense, and (e) with acts done by one in *unauthorized* possession. At the trial, the judge directed the government to elect between proceeding under section (d) or (e); that is, to determine whether it regarded Ellsberg as an authorized possessor or not. The government, for reasons that were never explained, opted for section (e), thereby taking on the added burden of proving that Ellsberg was in unauthorized possession of the Pentagon Papers.

In an apparent effort to avoid directly confronting the problems involved in punishing the transfer of information to Congress or to the press, the indictment was limited to the period of xeroxing. Ellsberg's main offense thus appeared to consist of permitting Anthony Russo (a person "not entitled to receive") to assist him in xeroxing a copy of the Pentagon Papers.[20] The government alleged that Ellsberg was not authorized to take the volumes off the premises of the Rand Corporation, nor even to keep them in his own safe at Rand, rather than in Rand's Top Secret facility; and that he was not authorized to give them to Russo or to others. No evidence was presented at the trial respecting the reason for the xeroxing, or what was done with the xeroxed copies.

This was the first espionage indictment in American history that failed to allege that the defendants had the intent, or even the reason to believe, that the material would be used to the injury of the national defense or to the advantage of a foreign power. It was also the first case which did not involve the alleged transfer of information to foreign agents or spies.[21]

The Issues at Trial

Scienter: The Meaning of "Willfulness" and the *Gorin* Defense

The first defense attack on the indictment proceeded directly from the Supreme Court's decision in *Gorin.* There the Court had found that the phrase "relating to the national defense" in section 794(b) was not unconstitutionally vague, because of that section's *scienter* requirement. When a man intends to injure, the Supreme Court said, he cannot complain of insufficient warning that his conduct is a crime. But section 793(e), as it applies to the transfer of documents, does not require proof of "intent or reason to believe" that injury to the nation would follow. It requires only that communication be "willful."

As the government interpreted the term "willful," all it needed to show was that Ellsberg had deliberately given Russo the documents, as opposed to, say, carelessly leaving them on his desk where Russo had stumbled upon them. If Ellsberg had acted willfully, it was irrelevant whether he believed that the act was illegal, or whether he had any intent to injure the United States.

The defense argued, on the other hand, that under *Gorin* it would have to be proved that defendants intended to harm the national defense. Thus, if the court accepted the government's interpretation of "willful," it would be forced to find the act unconstitutional. Without a requirement of *scienter*, the defense argued, the phrase "relating to the national defense" becomes vague and overbroad. Alternatively, the court could read into the word "willful" the requirement of intent to injure the United States or benefit a foreign power. This would not be an insupportable reading, given the well-known prior interpretation of the law by administration officials. If he took this route, the Judge might find that the espionage counts of the indictment failed to state an offense, because no intent to injure was alleged. Or he might assume that the grant jury, in charging Ellsberg and Russo with "willful" conduct, meant to allege that they acted with intent; in this case the trial could proceed but the government would be obliged to prove intent. The defense was confident that the government would not be able to do so.

Judge Byrne was unwilling to follow the defense to a conclusion which, while it might have preserved the constitutionality of the act, did violence to the language of the statute and the congressional intent. For it seemed clear that the use of "intent" in one section of the law and "willful" in another was not accidental, but a deliberate congressional choice. Thus it was the court's tentative position that "willful" meant only that the defendant knew both that the information "related to the national defense," and that a person to whom he gave the information was "not entitled to receive it." Since section 793(e) lacked a *scienter* requirement, it could survive constitutional attack only if its other terms proved to have sufficient specificity: thus the *Gorin* issue needed reconsideration in the context of this provision.

The Nature of Protected Information: "Relating to the National Defense"; The *Heine* and *Scarbeck* Doctrines

The government stubbornly took the position that the broad *Gorin* definition of national defense was acceptable, even where the non-*scienter* provisions of the espionage statute were involved. Thus, defendants would be on fair notice of the criminality of their actions, if only they knew that the Pentagon Papers dealt with the Army, the Navy or the Air Force, or related to defense preparations in a broad sense.

Of course, the prosecution was implicitly bolstered by the fact that, as defendants knew, the study was classified, a circumstance overtly brought into the case only with respect to other issues discussed below. The court rejected the notion that any document known to be classified would automatically be "related to the national defense."[22] Instead, Judge Byrne resorted to the language of section 793(e) itself, which refers to "information relating to the national defense *which information the possessor has reason to believe could be used to the injury of the United States or to the advantage of any foreign nation.*" This qualification on its face appears to apply only to transfers of "information" and not of "documents"; moreover, it points to an "objective" quality of the documents themselves rather than to a defendant's actual state of mind. However, its application to the present case might save the constitutionality of the statute, while doing less violence to the legislative intent than the importing of a strict intent requirement. Thus Judge Byrne framed the issue as follows:

> Are the documents the type that require protection in the interests of national defense in that their disclosures could adversely affect or injure this nation or lead to the advantage of any foreign nation.[23]

It will be recalled that under Executive Order 10501, a document could be classified confidential if its disclosure "could be prejudicial to the defense interests of the United States." Thus the court's ruling came very close, in effect, to saying that information relates to the national defense if it is known to be classifiable. As we observed, however, the court did not by this intend to adopt the summary *Scarbeck* procedure, whereby the fact of classification is decisive of the outcome. Instead, proceeding from the Supreme Court holding in *Gorin* that the question of relation to the national defense was a factual determination for the jury to make, Judge Byrne ruled that the government was obliged to put into evidence the critical information alleged to meet the statutory test. Thus, the four negotiating volumes of the Pentagon Papers, which no one had made public prior to the trial, were put into evidence by the government and were available for reading and copying out by hand in the clerk's office.

At a number of stages during the presentation of evidence, Judge Byrne instructed the jury that it would be its job to determine from the documents and the testimony about them whether the information therein could have been used to injure the United States, or to give an advantage to a foreign power in connection with the defense of the United States. Under the circumstances the jury's task was a difficult one indeed. The government witnesses, principally Generals Paul Gorman and William DePuy, asserted that, as a whole, the information in the documents was such as could have been used to the injury of the United States or to the advantage of a foreign power. The prosecution stubbornly refused to commit itself, while giving examples now and then, as to which information in the documents could cause injury or give advantage, and, indeed, continued to advocate the unmodified *Gorin* position, that virtually all the material related to "the national defense," and that no more need be shown.

The defense, forbidden to make the "irrelevant" argument that the documents were given not to a foreign power but to a Senator, undertook to rebut the government's case by showing that there was no information in the volumes that could be used to the injury of the United States or to the advantage of a foreign power. Some of the defense witnesses testified about all of the volumes named in the indictment, and others about only one or two of them. They argued that neither the volumes as a whole nor any specific information in them could cause injury or give advantage.

The defense argued further that if any of the information could be viewed as relating to the national defense, still its release would not be culpable, for the information was already in the public domain. *Gorin* and *Heine* had approved this defense for the cases, respectively, of information released by the government and information which was at no time a secret.[24] But now, the court had to come to grips with a third situation: the documents in issue were indeed regarded as secret by the government; but the defense was prepared to show, for any given piece of information the government chose, that it might in fact have been found also, by a careful researcher, in documents of public record. The defense argued that if the information appeared in the public domain in any form, transmitting that information could not be espionage.

The government argued that as long as the information was obtained from documents which the government was keeping secret, there could be no public domain defense.

On this question, the court supported the position of the defense completely. The court permitted the introduction of a great deal of evidence from a variety of public sources, including newspaper articles, all offered to show that information in the documents, and particularly information to which the government witnesses had pointed as specifically related to the national defense, was already in the public domain. In some cases, the defense was able to show that the information had been put into the public domain by the government; in other cases, they could show only that it had been printed in publicly available documents.[25]

Status of the Transmitter and the Recipient: "Unauthorized Possession," "Not Entitled to Receive," and the Classification System

Section 793(e) of the espionage act contains still other exceedingly cryptic phrases: notably, "unauthorized possession" and "not entitled to receive." There is nothing in the statute, and not much in the legislative history or prior court decisions, to indicate how one would determine who was in "unauthorized possession" of a document related to the national defense, or who was "not entitled to receive" such a document.

In no earlier case had the government alleged unauthorized possession on the part of a government official or other person who had a security clearance; section 793(e) was used only if it seemed clear that the accused was not in authorized possession of the documents. But in this case there was testimony, uncontested by the government, that access was authorized for Ellsberg by the president and vice president of the Rand Corporation in accordance with Department of Defense procedures, as well as by those who had deposited the Pentagon Papers at Rand. The defense argued that this authorization disposed of the issue. The government contended that Ellsberg's possession of the documents, although initially authorized, had later become unauthorized by virtue of what he had done with them. The documents, the government argued, were classified, and hence were subject to the rules established by the President's Executive Order, as well as the rules found in documents known as the Industrial Security Manual and the Rand Corporation manual, both of which apply to officials and employees of the Rand Corporation.[26] Under these rules, Ellsberg was not authorized to take the documents out of Rand Corporation premises to xerox them, nor to show them to Russo. These actions, the government argued, made Ellsberg's possession of the documents unauthorized. In effect, proof of violation of the Manuals would ipso facto prove unauthorized possession of the documents.

The defense argued that the Executive Order and the Manuals could not fairly be used to interpret the criminal statute, since the statute itself gave no fair warning that its meaning was to be so interpreted. Likewise, the Executive Order on classification was designed to establish administrative procedures for the storage and handling of classified information within the government; it nowhere identified itself as implementing or interpreting the espionage statute. Nowhere in the Executive Order did it expressly define "unauthorized possession"; indeed, the only reference to criminal statutes in Executive Order 10501, in effect at the time, was a reference to marking documents sent outside the Executive Branch with the notation that release of the information might violate the espionage laws.[27]

This indefinite statement hardly amounts to explicit exercise by the President of an explicit congressional delegation of authority to set standards for applying a particular criminal law. Yet the espionage laws elsewhere do just that. Section 793(a) empowers the President in wartime to designate "prohibited places," which it will then be criminal to go upon. Exercise of such authority would properly take the form of a directive clearly identifying itself as issued pursuant to section 793(a).[28]

Even more decisive is the contrast with 50 U.S.C. section 783(b), the *Scarbeck* statute, which is expressly keyed to presidential definition of what constitutes information "affecting the security of the United States." That is why the criteria for classification may be legally decisive in prosecutions under this provision, passed in 1950. But Congress has refrained from amending the 1917 law to incorporate the same approach. Moreover, not only the inexplicitness of the supposed delegation in the present case left it open to attack: if the President or a department head can constitutionally be authorized to define what shall be a crime, it does not follow that the Rand Corporation can lawfully do so.

Judge Byrne's tentative analysis of this issue is difficult to characterize. In principle, he recognized a clear distinction between unauthorized use and unauthorized possession: "Even if his possession was originally authorized, had it at some point become unauthorized—not unauthorized in use, but, unauthorized in possession."[29] Yet over the strenuous objections of the defense, the court permitted the introduction of the Industrial Security Manual and the Rand Security Manual. It is not clear what instructions the court would ultimately have given the jury to help them to conclude from these whether or not Ellsberg's possession of the documents had become unauthorized. In admitting the Manuals, the court stressed to the jury that they did not define the espionage law or any of its terms as such; the rationale for admitting them was not made entirely clear.[30]

The Rand Security Manual, on which the government relied heavily, specifically distinguished between unauthorized possession and unauthorized use, but without clearly defining either. The most plausible reading of the manuals is that unauthorized possession would arise only if a demand for return of the documents were refused. Since Ellsberg had not been asked to give up the documents, the government could argue only that he would have been, had Rand officials been aware of the irregularities in his use of them. But nothing in the manuals suggests that improper use automatically forfeits authorized possession.

Moreover, such a suggestion directly contradicts the court's definition of the issue. Thus the introduction of the manuals does not seem to have enhanced the government's prospects for proving unauthorized possession in this case. On the other hand, the relevance of the classification system was recognized in principle, suggesting that in future cases unauthorized possession might be at least presumptively established by the absence of a clearance—a result the defense had sought to avoid. And of course, the fact of classification, once in the case, would doubtless affect also the jury's decision as to whether the information related to the national defense.

Any hopes that the government may have entertained, however, of introducing a *Scarbeck*-type procedure into prosecutions under section 793(e) were utterly shattered. The court issued a strict ruling to control the impact of the classification system on the case: he would require the government to prove that the documents were properly classified, both in a procedural and in a substantive sense. That is, if they wished to rely on the classification structure to prove unauthorized possession (or any other element of an offense), the government would have to show not only that the documents were classified by some one with authority to classify them, following the prescribed procedures, but also that the documents were "in fact classifiable—that is, at a minimum did they contain informational material, the unauthorized disclosure of which would be prejudicial to the defense interests of the United States."[31] Once again, this closely resembled the court's charge on the meaning of "relating to the national defense."

Here the court laid a heavy burden on the prosecution, a burden it never attempted directly to meet. In lieu of proving that prescribed classification procedures had been followed, the prosecution relied apparently on a presumption of administrative regularity. Nor did the prosecution offer any evidence that the documents were classifiable, beyond its attempt, discussed above, to prove that they could be of use to a foreign power. Defense witnesses, on the other hand, testified that the documents could not at the time of the alleged offenses have been properly classified "confidential."

The statute, when introduced in Congress in 1917, had specifically authorized the President to determine which individuals were "entitled to receive" material related to the national defense. Without explanation this provision was removed from the bill during the Senate-House conference; no substitute procedure was provided for determining who was "entitled to receive."[32] In the earlier cases this remarkable oversight had caused little difficulty. When Judith Coplon was accused of giving documents to an agent of the Soviet government, the defense conceded that the Soviet agent was a person "not entitled to receive" the documents within the meaning of the statute. In the present case, for this issue the government again straightforwardly relied upon the rules of the classification system: thus a person was "not entitled to receive" unless he had both a security clearance and an official duty in connection with the documents.

The defense argued that the only constitutionally acceptable definition of one "not entitled to receive," was a person who could be expected to use the information to injure the United States or to give advantage to a foreign power. Thus any loyal citizen, and certainly a member of Congress, is "entitled to receive information. The government's attempt to rely on the classification system here raised the gravest questions of overbreadth, as well as questions of improper delegation and lack of notice like those discussed above as to the term "unauthorized possession." The Executive Order does not even use the actual term, "not entitled to receive," and the security manuals use a contradictory assortment of terms. For example, while the Industrial Security Manual stresses heavily the "need to know" as a basis for access to documents, the Rand Manual indicates that, at least for classified materials that were not top secret, every Rand employee could be assumed to have a need to know.

The court again appeared to be willing to rely on the Executive Order, but probably not, in this instance, on the Industrial Security Manual and the Rand Manual; the government would be permitted to show that Anthony Russo and the other alleged co-conspirators did not hold appropriate clearances and did not have a need to see the documents by virtue of any official duties. Because the Court did not find it necessary to confront the grave constitutional ambiguities in the law, the dismissal left the government free to bring further prosecutions for the well-intended release of information to Congress or the public. An official or other citizen contemplating such action must now anticipate a trial focussing primarily on the single question of whether the information *could* be used to injure the United States or give advantage to a foreign power.

---

[1]For an exhaustive analysis of the espionage laws in relation to the publication of information, see Harold Edgar and Benno C. Schmidt, Jr., *The Espionage Statutes and the Publication of Defense Information,* 73 Columbia Law Review 930-1087 (May, 1973). Our discussion draws heavily on their analysis, which covers the origins and meaning of the law as it developed prior to the Pentagon Papers.

[2]See, *e.g., Aptheker v. Secretary of State,* 378 U.S. 500 (1954); *U.S. v. Robel,* 389 U.S. 258 (1967).

[3]See, *e.g., Musser v. Utah,* 333 U.S. 95 (1948); *Baggett v. Bullitt,* 377 U.S. 360 (1964).

[4]18 U.S.C. sections 795, 797 and 50 U.S.C. App. section 781.

[5]We do not deal here with "seditious" speech offenses involving advocacy of revolution, incitement of insubordination in the military, interference with the draft, and so on, found in 18 U.S.C. sections 2385-88 and elsewhere. See political crimes section for further discussion.

[6]See M. C. Miskovsky, *The Espionage Laws,* Office of General Counsel Monograph, CIA, 1961; Statement of Abram Chayes (Witness #8), former Legal Advisor, Department of Defense, at 21 of Affidavit of Goodell & Nesson, June 7, 1972, in support of Motion To Dismiss for Selective Prosecution, *United States v. Russo & Ellsberg,* No. 9373-WMB-CD (C.D. Cal. 1972); Brief for Petitioner at 52-53, *New York Times Co. v. United States,* 403 U.S. 713 (1971); and House of Representatives Report No. 1895, 81st Cong., 2d Sess. (1950).

[7]A further obstacle to indictment may have been the need to disclose the content and significance of the information, in order to persuade the jury that the information truly related to the national defense. This block against indictments has become particularly important in the post-Pentagon Papers era, when other restraints appear to have lost much of their potency.

[8]House of Representatives Report No. 1895, "Enhancing Further the Security of the United States by Preventing Disclosures of Information Concerning the Cryptographic Systems and the Communication Intelligence Activities of the United States," 81st Cong., 2d Sess. (1950).

[9]See, *e.g., Hearings on Strategic Arms Limitation Agreements* before the Senate Foreign Relations Committee, 92d Cong., 2d Sess. (July, 1972); and *Hearings on Tactical Nuclear Weapons in Europe* before the Subcommittee on Commitments of the Senate Foreign Relations Committee, 93d Cong., 2d Sess. (1975). The Foreign Relations Committees of both houses, the Government Operations Committees, and the Joint Economic Committee have ardently sought information obtained by former officials during their government employment.

[10]See House of Representatives Report No. 1895, "Enhancing Further the Security of the United States by Preventing Disclosures of Information Concerning the Cryptographic Systems and the Communication Intelligence Activities of the United States," 81st Cong., 2d Sess. (1950).

[11]See *Report on Executive Classification of Information—Security Classification Problems Involving Exemption (b)(1) of the Freedom of Information Act (5 U.S.C. 552),* House Committee on Government Operations, 93d Cong., 1st Sess. (1973); *Hearings on United States Government Information Policies and Practices—The Pentagon Papers,* before a Subcommittee of the House Committee on Government Operations, 92d Cong., 1st and 2d Sessions, 9 vols., (1971-1972); and *Hearings on Executive Privilege, Secrecy in Government, and Freedom of Information,* before the Subcommittee on Intergovernmental Relations of the Senate Committee on Government Operations and the Subcommittees on Separation of Powers and Administrative Practice and Procedure of the Senate Committee on the Judiciary, 93d Cong., 1st Sess., 3 vols., (1973).

[12]*Gorin v. United States,* 312 U.S. 19, 28 (1941).

[13]The Court did note that liability would not attach where the government had already released the information; see further discussion below.

[14]*Gorin v. United States,* 312 U.S. at 28.

[15]151 F.2d at 816.

[16]50 U.S.C. 783(b).

[17]*United States v. Drummond,* 354 F.2d 132 (2d Cir. 1965), *cert. denied,* 384 U.S. 1013 (1966).

[18]The text of Byrne's oral opinion is reprinted in the House Judicary Committee Impeachment Inquiry: *Hearings on House Resolution 803, Statement of Information,* 93d Cong., 2d Sess., Book VII, part 4, at 2076 (1974). The only aspects of the Pentagon Papers criminal trial to be officially reported were decisions involving a wiretapping of one of the lawyers in the case. See *Russo v. Byrne,* 409 U.S. 1013 (1972) (*cert. denied;* Douglas, J., dissenting); 409 U.S. 1219 (1972) (stay granted per Douglas, J.). A full set of the formal files and transcripts of the Pentagon Papers criminal trial is on file at the Harvard University Law Library.

[19]Ellsberg was also charged with one count under 793(c): obtaining documents related to the national defense with the intent to use them in violation of section (d) or (e). Both defendants, in addition, were charged with conspiracy to commit espionage.

[20]Lynda Sinay, the owner of the advertising agency whose xerox machine was used for the copying, and Vu Van Thai, a Vietnamese diplomat and former ambassador to the United States, were named as unindicted co-conspirators; and it was alleged that one or more volumes of the study had been "transferred" to Sinay and Thai as well as to Russo in that they helped to xerox those volumes.

[21]The indictment is printed as an appendix in Peter Schrag, *Test of Loyalty* (New York, 1974).

[22]He adopted the position that classification was not to be considered at all in determining whether information related to the national defense. Compare *United States v. Drummond,* 354 F.2d 132 (2d Cir. 1965), *cert. denied,* 384 U.S. 1013 (1966), approving jury instructions to the effect that "Whether any given document relates to the national defense is a question of fact for you to decide. It is not a question of how they were marked."

[23]Trial transcript, at 8219-20.

[24]The Court of Appeals in *Gorin* had remarked that a serious problem would have arisen had the defendants alleged that *all* the information listed in the indictment was available from public sources. *Gorin v. United States,* 111 F.2d at 722.

[25]This issue came up as well in the *Marchetti* prior restraint case, where the court reached a very different conclusion.

[26]The Industrial Security Manual is issued by the Defense Department and applies to defense industry generally; the Rand manual pertains to that organization only. The Industrial Security Manual is printed in the *Security and Loyalty Reporter,* published by the Bureau of National Affairs, at 25:10-1.

[27]The revised Executive Order includes a reference to the espionage laws in the form of a general stricture that "wrongful disclosure of such [classified] information or material is recognized in the Federal Criminal Code as providing a basis for prosecution." Executive Order 11652, Preamble, para. 3; see also sec. 13(B), instructing department heads to take administrative action against unauthorized disclosures, and to refer to the Justice Department cases "where a violation of criminal statutes may be involved."

[28]There might be valid constitutional objections even to such an explicit delegation; cf. *U.S. v. Robel,* 389 U.S. 258 (1967) (concurring opinion of Brennan, J.).

[29]Transcript, at 8218.

[30]Transcript at 12, 171 ff.

[31]Transcript, at 8221. Here, of course, the court was quoting from the definition of "confidential" in Executive Order 10501. A document is classifiable only if it could be said to meet this minimum standard.

[32]*Edgar and Schmidt,* 73 Columbia Law Review at 1051-52.

STATUTES

Espionage and Censorship

18 U.S.C. §792

Harboring or Concealing Persons

Whoever harbors or conceals any person who he knows, or has reasonable grounds to believe or suspect, has committed, or is about to commit, an offense under sections 793 or 794 of this title, shall be fined not more than $10,000 or imprisoned not more than ten years, or both.

18 U.S.C. §793

Gathering, Transmitting, or Losing Defense Information

(a) Whoever, for the purpose of obtaining information respecting the national defense with intent or reason to believe that the information is to be used to the injury of the United States, or to the advantage of any foreign nation, goes upon, enters, flies over, or otherwise obtains information concerning any vessel, aircraft, work of defense, navy yard, naval station, submarine base, fueling station, fort, battery, torpedo station, dockyard, canal, railroad, arsenal, camp, factory, mine, telegraph, telephone, wireless, or signal station, building, office, research laboratory or station or other place connected with the national defense owned or constructed, or in progress of construction by the United States or under the control of the United States, or of any of its officers, departments, or agencies, or within the exclusive jurisdiction of the United States, or any place in which any vessel, aircraft, arms, munitions, or other materials or instruments for use in time of war are being made, prepared, repaired, stored, or are the subject of research or development, under any contract or agreement with the United States, or any department or agency thereof, or with any person on behalf of the United States, or otherwise on behalf of the United States, or any prohibited place so designed by the President by proclamation in time of war or in case of national emergency in which anything for the use of the Army, Navy, or Air Force is being prepared or constructed or stored, information as to which prohibited place the President has determined would be prejudicial to the national defense; or

(b) Whoever, for the purpose aforesaid, and with like intent or reason to believe, copies, takes, makes, or obtains, or attempts to copy, take, make, or obtain, any sketch, photograph, photographic negative, blueprint, plan, map, model, instrument, appliance, document, writing, or note of anything connected with the national defense; or

(c) Whoever, for the purpose aforesaid, receives or obtains or agrees or attempts to receive or obtain from any person, or from any source whatever, any document, writing, code book, signal book, sketch, photograph, photographic negative, blueprint, plan, map, model, instrument, appliance, or note, of anything connected with the national defense, knowing or having reason to believe, at the time he receives or obtains, or agrees or attempts to receive or obtain it, that it has been or will be obtained, taken, made, or disposed of by any person contrary to the provisions of this chapter; or

(d) Whoever, lawfully having possession of, access to, control over, or being intrusted with any document, writing, code book, signal book, sketch, photograph, photographic negative, blueprint, plan, map, model, instrument, appliance, or note relating to the national defense, or information relating to the national defense which information the possessor has reason to believe could be used to the injury of the United States or to the advantage of any foreign nation, willfully communicates, delivers, transmits or causes to be communicated, delivered, or transmitted or attempts to communicate, deliver, transmit or cause to be communicated, delivered or transmitted the same to any person not entitled to receive it, or willfully retains the same and fails to deliver it on demand to the officer or employee of the United States entitled to receive it; or

(e) Whoever having unauthorized possession of, access to, or control over any document, writing, code book, signal book, sketch, photograph, photographic negative, blueprint, plan, map, model, instrument, appliance, or note relating to the national defense, or information relating to the national defense which information the possessor has reason to believe could be used to the injury of the United States or to the advantage of any foreign nation, willfully communicates, delivers, transmits or causes to be communicated, delivered, or transmitted, or attempts to communicate, deliver, transmit or cause to be communicated, delivered, or transmitted the same to any person not entitled to receive it, or willfully retains the same and fails to deliver it to the officer or employee of the United States entitled to receive it; or

(f) Whoever, being intrusted with or having lawful possession or control of any document, writing, code book, signal book, sketch, photograph, photographic negative, blueprint, plan, map, model, instrument, appliance, note, or information, relating to the national defense, (1) through gross negligence permits the same to be removed from its proper place of custody or delivered to anyone in violation of his trust, or to be lost, stolen, abstracted, or destroyed, or (2) having knowledge that the same has been illegally removed from its proper place of custody or delivered to anyone in violation of his trust, or lost, or stolen, abstracted, or destroyed, and fails to make prompt report of such loss, theft, abstraction, or destruction to his superior office—

Shall be fined not more than $10,000 or imprisoned not more than ten years, or both.

(g) If two or more persons conspire to violate any of the foregoing provisions of this section, and one or more of such persons do any act to effect the object of the consiracy, each of the parties to such conspiracy shall be subject to the punishment provided for the offense which is the object of such conspiracy.

As amended Sept. 23, 1950, c. 1024, § 18, 64 Stat. 1003.

18 U.S.C. §794

Gathering or Delivering Defense Information to Aid Foreign Government

(a) Whoever, with intent or reason to believe that it is to be used to the injury of the United States or to the advantage of a foreign nation, communicates, delivers, or transmits, or attempts to communicate, deliver, or transmit, to any foreign government, or to any faction or party or military or naval force within a foreign country, whether recognized or unrecognized by the United States, or to any representative, officer, agent, employee, subject, or citizen thereof, either directly or indirectly, any document, writing, code book, signal book, sketch, photograph, photographic negative, blueprint, plan, map, model, note, instrument, appliance, or information relating to the national defense, shall be punished by death or by imprisonment for any term of years or for life.

(b) Whoever, in time of war, with intent that the same shall be communicated to the enemy, collects, records, publishes, or communicates, or attempts to elicit any information with respect to the movement, numbers, description, condition, or disposition of any of the Armed Forces, ships, aircraft, or war materials of the United States, or with respect to the plans or conduct, or supposed plans or conduct of any naval or military operations, or with respect to any works or measures undertaken for or connected with, or intended for the fortification or defense of any place, or any other information relating to the public defense, which might be useful to the enemy, shall be punished by death or by imprisonment for any term of years or for life.

(c) If two or more persons conspire to violate this section, and one or more of such persons do any act to effect the object of the conspiracy, each of the parties to such conspiracy shall be subject to the punishment provided for the offense which is the object of such conspiracy.

As amended Sept. 3, 1954, c. 1261, Title II, § 201, 68 Stat. 1219.

18 U.S.C. §795

Photographing and Sketching Defense Installations

(a) Whenever, in the interests of national defense, the President defines certain vital military and naval installations or equipment as requiring protection against the general dissemination of information relative thereto, it shall be unlawful to make any photograph, sketch, picture, drawing, map, or graphical representation of such vital military and naval installations or equipment without first obtaining permission of the commanding officer of the military or naval post, camp, or station, or naval vessels, military and naval aircraft, and any separate military or naval command concerned, or higher authority, and promptly submitting the product obtained to such commanding officer or higher authority for censorship or such other action as he may deem necessary.

(b) Whoever violates this section shall be fined not more than $1,000 or imprisoned not more than one year, or both.

18 U.S.C. §796

Use of Aircraft for Photographing Defense Installations

Whoever uses or permits the use of an aircraft or any contrivance used, or designed for navigation or flight in the air, for the purpose of making a photograph, sketch, picture, drawing, map, or graphical representation of vital military or naval installations or equipment, in violation of section 795 of this title, shall be fined not more than $1,000 or imprisoned not more than one year, or both.

18 U.S.C. §797

Publication and Sale of Photographs of Defense Installations

On and after thirty days from the date upon which the President defines any vital military or naval installation or equipment as being within the category contemplated under section 795 of this title, whoever reproduces, publishes, sells, or gives away any photograph, sketch, picture, drawing, map, or graphical representation of the vital military or naval installations or equipment so defined, without first obtaining permission of the commanding officer of the military or naval post, camp, or station concerned, or higher authority, unless such photograph, sketch, picture, drawing, map, or graphical representation has clearly indicated thereon that it has been censored by the proper military or naval authority, shall be fined not more than $1,000 or imprisoned not more than one year, or both.

18 U.S.C. §798

Disclosure of Classified Information

(a) Whoever knowingly and willfully communicates, furnishes, transmits, or otherwise makes available to an unauthorized person, or publishes, or uses in any manner prejudicial to the safety or interest of the United States or for the benefit of any foreign government to the detriment of the United States any classified information—

(1) concerning the nature, preparation, or use of any code, cipher, or cryptographic system of the United States or any foreign government, or

(2) concerning the design, construction, use, maintenance, or repair of any device, apparatus, or appliance used or prepared or planned for use by the United States or any foreign government for cryptographic or communication intelligence purposes; or

(3) concerning the communication intelligence activities of the United States or any foreign government; or

(4) obtained by the processes of communication intelligence from the communications of any foreign government, knowing the same to have been obtained by such processes—

Shall be fined not more than $10,000 or imprisoned not more than ten years, or both.

(b) as used in subsection (a) of this section—

The term "classified information" means information which, at the time of a violation of this section, is, for reasons of national security, specifically designated by a United States Government Agency for limited or restricted dissemination or distribution;

The terms "code," "cipher," and "cryptographic system" include in their meanings, in addition to their usual meanings, any method of secret writing and any mechanical or electrical device or method used for the purpose of disguising or concealing the contents, significance, or meanings of communications;

The term "foreign government" includes in its meaning any person or persons acting or purporting to act for or on behalf of any faction, party, department, agency, bureau, or military force of or within a foreign country, or for or on behalf of any government or any person or persons purporting to act as a government within a foreign country, whether or not such government is recognized by the United States;

The term "communication intelligence" means all procedures and methods used in the interception of communications and the obtaining of information from such communications by other than the intended recipients;

The term "unauthorized person" means any person who, or agency which, is not authorized to receive information of the categories set forth in subsection (a) of this section, by the President, or by the head of a department or agency of the United States Government which is expressly designated by the President to engage in communication intelligence activities for the United States.

(c) Nothing in this section shall prohibit the furnishing, upon lawful demand, of information to any regularly constituted committee of the Senate or House of Representatives of the United States of America, or joint committee thereof.

Added Oct. 31, 1951, c. 655, § 24(a), 65 Stat. 719.

18 U.S.C. §798

Temporary Extension of Section 794

The provisions of section 794 of this title, as amended and extended by section 1(a) (29) of the Emergency Powers Continuation Act (66 Stat. 333), as further amended by Public Law 12, Eighty-third Congress, in addition to coming into full force and effect in time of war shall remain in full force and effect until six months after the termination of the national emergency proclaimed by the President on December 16, 1950 (Proc. 2912, 3 C.F.R., 1950 Supp., p. 71), or such earlier date as may be prescribed by concurrent resolution of the Congress, and acts which would give rise to legal consequences and penalties under section 794 when performed during a state of war shall give rise to the same legal consequences and penalties when they are performed during the period above provided for.

Added June 30, 1953, c. 175, § 4, 67 Stat. 134.

18 U.S.C. §799

Violation of Regulations of National Aeronautics and Space Administration

Whoever willfully shall violate, attempt to violate, or conspire to violate any regulation or order promulgated by the Administrator of the National Aeronautics and Space Administration for the protection or security of any laboratory, station, base or other facility, or part thereof, or any aircraft, missile, spacecraft, or similar vehicle, or part thereof, or other property or equipment in the custody of the Administration, or any real or personal property or equipment in the custody of any contractor under any contract with the Administration or any subcontractor of any such contractor, shall be fined not more than $5,000, or imprisoned not more than one year, or both.

Added Pub.L. 85-568, Title III, § 304(c) (1), July 29, 1958, 72 Stat. 434.

18 U.S.C. §952

Diplomatic Codes and Correspondence

Whoever, by virtue of his employment by the United States, obtains from another or has or has had custody of or access to, any official diplomatic code or any matter prepared in any such code, or which purports to have been prepared in any such code, and without authorization or competent authority, willfully publishes or furnishes to another any such code or matter, or any matter which was obtained while in the process of transmission between any foreign government and its diplomatic mission in the United States, shall be fined not more than $10,000 or imprisoned not more than ten years, or both.

June 25, 1948, c. 645, 62 Stat. 734.

50 U.S.C. §783(b)

It shall be unlawful for any officer or employee of the United States or of any department or agency thereof, or of any corporation the stock of which is owned in whole or in major part by the United States or any department or agency thereof, to communicate in any manner or by any means, to any other person whom such officer or employee knows or has reason to believe to be an agent or representative of any foreign government or an officer or member of any Communist organization as defined in paragraph (5) of section 782 of this title, any information of a kind which shall have been classified by the President (or by the head of any such department, agency, or corporation with the approval of the President) as affecting the security of the United States, knowing or having reason to know that such information has been so classified, unless such officer or employee shall have been specifically authorized by the President, or by the head of the department, agency, or corporation by which this officer or employee is employed, to make such disclosure of such information.

18 U.S.C. §2071

Concealment, Removal, or Mutilation Generally

(a) Whoever willfully and unlawfully conceals, removes, mutilates, obliterates, or destroys, or attempts to do so, or, with intent to do so takes and carries away any record, proceeding, map, book, paper, document, or other thing, filed or deposited with any clerk or officer of any court of the United States, or in any public office, or with any judicial or public officer of the Unites States, shall be fined not more than $2,000 or imprisoned not more than three years, or both.

(b) Whoever, having the custody of any such record, proceeding, map, book, document, paper, or other thing, willfully and unlawfully conceals, removes, mutilates, obliterates, falsifies, or destroys the same, shall be fined not more than $2,000 or imprisoned not more than three years, or both; and shall forfeit his office and be disqualified from holding any office under the United States.

18 U.S.C. §641

Public Money, Property or Records

Whoever embezzles, steals, purloins, or knowingly converts to his use or the use of another, or without authority, sells, conveys or disposes of any record, voucher, money, or thing of value of the United States or of any department or agency thereof, or any property made or being made under contract for the United States or any department or agency thereof; or

Whoever receives, conceals, or retains the same with intent to convert it to his use or gain, knowing it to have been embezzled, stolen, purloined or converted—

Shall be fined not more than $10,000 or imprisoned not more than ten years, or both; but if the value of such property does not exceed the sum of $100, he shall be fined not more than $1,000 or imprisoned not more than one year, or both.

18 U.S.C. §371

Conspiracy to Commit Offense or to Defraud United States

If two or more persons conspire either to commit any offense against the United States, or to defraud the United States, or any agency thereof in any manner or for any purpose, and one or more of such persons do any act to effect the object of the conspiracy, each shall be fined not more than $10,000 or imprisoned not more than five years, or both.

If, however, the offense, the commission of which is the object of the conspiracy, is a misdemeanor only, the punishment for such conspiracy shall not exceed the maximum punishment provided for such misdemeanor.

Atomic Energy Act Statutes

42 U.S.C. §2271

General Provisions

(a) To protect against the unlawful dissemination of Restricted Data and to safeguard facilities, equipment, materials, and other property of the Commission, the President shall have authority to utilize the services of any Government agency to the extent he may deem necessary or desirable.

(b) The Federal Bureau of Investigation of the Department of Justice shall investigate all alleged or suspected criminal violations of this chapter.

(c) No action shall be brought against any individual or person for any violation under this chapter unless and until the Attorney General of the United States has advised the Commission with respect to such action and no such action shall be commenced except by the Attorney General of the United States: *Provided, however,* That no action shall be brought under section 2272, 2273, 2274, 2275, or 2276 of this title except by the express direction of the Attorney General: *And provided further,* That nothing in this subsection shall be construed as applying to administrative action taken by the Commission.

Aug. 1, 1946, c. 724, § 221, as added Aug. 30, 1954, c. 1073, § 1, 68 Stat. 958, and amended Dec. 24, 1969, Pub.L. 91-161, § 5, 83 Stat. 445.

42 U.S.C. §2272

Violation of Specific Sections

Whoever willfully violates, attempts to violate, or conspires to violate, any provision of sections 2077, 2122, or 2131 of this title, or whoever unlawfully interferes, attempts to interfere, or conspires to interfere with any recapture or entry under section 2138 of this title, shall, upon conviction thereof, be punished by a fine of not more than $10,000 or by imprisonment for not more than ten years, or both, except that whoever commits such an offense with intent to injure the United States or with intent to secure an advantage to any foreign nation shall, upon conviction thereof, be punished by imprisonment for life, or by imprisonment for any term of years or a fine of not more than $20,000 of both.

Aug. 1, 1946, c. 724, § 222, as added Aug. 30, 1954, c. 1073, § 1, 68 Stat. 958, and amended Dec. 24, 1969, Pub.L. 91-161, §§ 2, 3(a), 83 Stat. 444.

42 U.S.C. §2273

Violation of Sections Generally

Whoever willfully violates, attempts to violate, or conspires to violate, any provision of this chapter for which no criminal penalty is specifically provided or of any regulation or order prescribed or issued under section 2095 or 2201(b), (i), or (o) of this title shall, upon conviction thereof, be punished by a fine of not more than $5,000 or by imprisonment for not more than two years, or both, except that whoever commits such an offense with intent to injure the United States or with intent to secure an advantage to any foreign nation, shall, upon conviction thereof, be punished by a fine of not more than $20,000 or by imprisonment for not more than twenty years, or both.

Aug. 1, 1946, c. 724, § 223, as added Aug. 30, 1954, c. 1073, § 1, 68 Stat. 958, and amended Dec. 14, 1967, Pub.L. 90-190, § 12, 81 Stat. 578; Dec. 24, 1969, Pub.L. 91-161, § 6, 83 Stat. 445.

42 U.S.C. §2274

Communication of Restricted Data

Whoever, lawfully or unlawfully, having possession of, access to, control over, or being entrusted with any document, writing, sketch, photograph, plan, model, instrument, appliance, note, or information involving or incorporating Restricted Data—

(a) communicates, transmits, or discloses the same to any individual or person, or attempts or conspires to do any of the foregoing, with intent to injure the United States or with intent to secure an advantage to any foreign nation, upon conviction thereof, shall be punished by imprisonment for life, or by imprisonment for any term of years or a fine of not more than $20,000 or both;

(b) communicates, transmits, or discloses the same to any individual or person, or attempts or conspires to do any of the foregoing, with reason to believe such data will be utilized to injure the United States or to secure an advantage to any foreign nation, shall, upon conviction, be punished by a fine of not more than $10,000 or imprisonment for not more than ten years, or both.

Aug. 1, 1946, c. 724, § 224, as added Aug. 30, 1954, c. 1073, § 1, 68 Stat. 958, and amended Dec. 24, 1969, Pub.L. 91-161, § 3(b), 83 Stat. 444.

42 U.S.C. §2275

Receipt of Restricted Data

Whoever, with intent to injure the United States or with intent to secure an advantage to any foreign nation, acquires, or attempts or conspires to acquire any document, writing, sketch, photograph, plan, model, instrument, appliance, note, or information involving or incorporating Restricted Data shall, upon conviction thereof, be punished by imprisonment for life, or by imprisonment for any term of years or a fine of not more than $20,000 or both.

Aug. 1, 1946, c. 724, § 225, as added Aug. 30, 1954, c. 1073, § 1, 68 Stat. 959, and amended Dec. 24, 1969, Pub.L. 91-161, § 3(c), 83 Stat. 444.

42 U.S.C. §2276

Tampering with Restricted Data

Whoever, with intent to injure the United States or with intent to secure an advantage to any foreign nation, removes, conceals, tampers with, alters, mutilates, or destroys any document, writing, sketch, photograph, plan, model, instrument, appliance, or note involving or incorporating Restricted Data and used by an individual or person in connection with the production of special nuclear material, or research or development relating to atomic energy, conducted by the United States, or financed in whole or in part by Federal funds, or conducted with the aid of special nuclear material, shall be punished by imprisonment for life, or by imprisonment for any term of years or a fine of not more than $20,000 or both.

Aug. 1, 1946, c. 724, § 226, as added Aug. 30, 1954, c. 1073, § 1, 68 Stat. 959, and amended Dec. 24, 1969, Pub.L. 91-161, § 3(b), 83 Stat. 444.

42 U.S.C. §2277

Disclosure of Restricted Data

Whoever, being or having been an employee or member of the Commission, a member of the Armed Forces, an employee of any agency of the United States, or being or having been a contractor of the Commission or of an agency of the United States, or being or having been an employee of a contractor of the Commission or of an agency of the United States, or being or having been a licensee of the Commission, or being or having been an employee of a lincensee of the Commission, knowingly communicates, or whoever conspires to communicate or to receive, any Restricted Data, knowing or having reason to believe that such data is Restricted Data, to any person not authorized to receive Restricted Data pursuant to the provisions of this chapter or under rule or regulation of the Commission issued pursuant thereto, knowing or having reason to believe such person is not so authorized to receive Restricted Data shall, upon conviction thereof, be punishable by a fine of not more than $2,500.

Aug. 1, 1946, c. 724, § 227, as added Aug. 30, 1954, c. 1073, § 1, 68 Stat. 959.

42 U.S.C. §2278

Statute of Limitations

Except for a capital offense, no individual or person shall be prosecuted, tried, or punished for any offense prescribed or defined in sections 2274 to 2276 of this title unless the indictment is found or the information is instituted within ten years next after such offense shall have been committed.

Aug. 1, 1946, c. 724, § 228, as added Aug. 30, 1954, c 1073, § 1, 68 Stat. 959.

42 U.S.C. §2278a

Trespass Upon Commission Installations; Issuance and Posting of Regulations; Penalties for Violation

(a) The Commission is authorized to issue regulations relating to the entry upon or carrying, transporting, or otherwise introducing or causing to be introduced any dangerous weapon, explosive, or other dangerous instrument or material likely to produce substantial injury or damage to persons or property, into or upon any facility, installation, or real property subject to the jurisdiction, administration, or in the custody of the Commission. Every such regulation of the Commission shall be posted conspicuously at the location involved.

(b) Whoever shall willfully violate any regulation of the Commission issued pursuant to subsection (a) of this section shall, upon conviction thereof, be punishable by a fine of not more than $1,000.

(c) Whoever shall willfully violate any regulation of the Commission issued pursuant to subsection (a) of this section with respect to any installation or other property which is enclosed by a fence, wall, floor, roof, or other structural barrier shall be guilty of a misdemeanor and upon conviction thereof shall be punished by a fine of not to exceed $5,000 or to imprisonment for not more than one year, or both.

Aug. 1, 1946, c. 724, § 229, as added Aug. 6, 1956, c 1015, § 6, 70 Stat. 1070.

42 U.S.C. §2278b

Photographing, etc., of Commission Installations; Penalty

It shall be an offense, punishable by a fine of not more than $1,000 or imprisonment for not more than one year, or both—

(1) to make any photograph, sketch, picture, drawing, map or graphical representation, while present on property subject to the jurisdiction, administration or in the custody of the Commission, of any installations or equipment designated by the President as requiring protection against the general dissemination of information relative thereto, in the interest of the

common defense and security, without first obtaining the permission of the Commission, and promptly submitting the product obtained to the Commission for inspection or such other action as may be deemed necessary; or

(2) to use or permit the use of an aircraft or any contrivance used, or designed for navigation or flight in air, for the purpose of making a photograph, sketch, picture, drawing, map or graphical representation of any installation or equipment designated by the President as provided in the preceding paragraph, unless authorized by the Commission.

Aug. 1, 1946, c. 724, § 230, as added Aug. 6, 1956, c. 1015, § 6, 70 Stat. 1070.

42 U.S.C. §2279

Applicability of Other Laws

Sections 2274 to 2278b of this title shall not exclude the applicable provisions of any other laws.

Aug. 1, 1946, c. 724, § 231, and formerly 229, as added Aug. 30, 1954, c. 1073, § 1, 68 Stat. 959, renumbered and amended Aug. 6, 1956, c. 1015, §§ 6, 7, 70 Stat. 1070.

Photographic Statutes

50 U.S.C. App. §781

Whoever, except in performance of duty or employment in connection with the national defense, shall knowingly and willfully make any sketch, photograph, photographic negative, blueprint, plan, map, model, copy, or other representation of any navy yard, naval station, or of any military post, fort, camp, station, arsenal, airfield, or other military or naval reservation, or place used for national defense purposes by the Departments of the Army or the Navy, or of any vessel, aircraft, installation, equipment, or other property whatsoever, located within any such post, fort, camp, arsenal, airfield, yard, station, reservation or place, or in the waters adjacent thereto, or in any defensive sea area established in accordance with law; or whoever, except in performance of duty or employment in connection with the national defense, shall knowingly and willfully make any sketch, photograph, photographic negative, blueprint, plan, map, model, copy, or other representation of any vessel, aircraft, installation, equipment, or other property relating to the national defense being manufactured or under construction or repair for or awaiting delivery to the Departments of the Army or the Navy or the government of any country whose defense the President deems vital to the defense of the United States under any contract or agreement with the United States or such country or otherwise on behalf of the United States or such country, located at the factory, plant, yard, storehouse, or other place of business of any contractor, subcontractor, or other person, or in the waters adjacent to any such place, shall be punished as provided herein.

18 U.S.C. §795

(a) Whenever, in the interests of national defense, the President defines certain vital military and naval installations or equipment as requiring protection against the general dissemination of information relative thereto, it shall be unlawful to make any photograph, sketch, picture, drawing, map, or graphical representation of such vital military and naval installations or equipment without first obtaining permission of the commanding officer of the military or naval post, camp, or station, or naval vessels, military and naval aircraft, and any separate military or naval command concerned, or higher authority, and promptly submitting the product obtained to such commanding officer or higher authority for censorship or such other action as he may deem necessary.

(b) Whoever violates this section shall be fined not more than $1,000 or imprisoned not more than one year, or both.

18 U.S.C. §797

On and after thirty days from the date upon which the President defines any vital military or naval installation or equipment as being within the category contemplated under section 795 of this title, whoever reproduces, publishes, sells, or gives away any photograph, sketch, picture, drawing, map, or graphical representation of the vital military or naval installations or equipment so defined, without first obtaining permission of the commanding officer of the military or naval post, camp, or station concerned, or higher authority, unless such photograph, sketch, picture, drawing, map, or graphical representation has clearly indicated thereon that it has been censored by the proper military or naval authority, shall be fined not more than $1,000 or imprisoned not more than one year, or both.

CASES

Gorin v. United States

312 U.S. 19 (1941)

Argued Dec. 19, 1940.
Decided Jan. 13, 1941.
Rehearing Denied Feb. 10, 1941.
See 312 U.S. 713, 61 S.Ct. 617, 618,
85 L.Ed. ______

Mr. Justice Reed delivered the opinion of the Court.

This certiorari brings here a judgment of the Circuit Court of Appeals affirming the sentences of the two petitioners who were convicted of violation of the Espionage Act of June 15, 1917, 50 U.S.C.A. § 31 et seq., 9 Cir., 111 F.2d 712. As the affirmance turned upon a determination of the scope of the Act and its constitutionality as construed, the petition was allowed because of the questions, important in enforcing this criminal statute.

The joint indictment in three counts charged in the first count violation of section 1(b) by allegations in the words of the statute of obtaining documents "connected with the national defense"; in the second count violation of section 2(a) in delivering and inducing the delivery of these documents to the petitioner, Gorin, the agent of a foreign nation; and in the third count of section 4 by conspiracy to deliver them to a foreign government and its agent, just named. The pertinent statutory provisions appear below.[1] A third party, the wife of Gorin, was joined in and acquitted on all three counts. The petitioners were found guilty on each count and sentenced to various terms of imprisonment to run concurrently and fines of $10,000 each. The longest term of Gorin is six years and of Salich four years.

The proof indicated that Gorin, a citizen of the Union of Soviet Socialist Republics, acted as its agent in gathering information. He sought and obtained from Salich for substantial pay the contents of over fifty reports relating chiefly to Japanese activities in the United States. These reports were in the files of the Naval Intelligence branch office at San Pedro, California. Salich, a naturalized, Russian-born citizen, had free access to the records as he was a civilian investigator for that office. Speaking broadly the reports detailed the coming and going on the west coast of Japanese military and civil officials as well as private citizens whose actions were deemed of possible interest to the Intelligence Office. Some statements appear as to the movements of fishing boats, suspected of espionage and as to the taking of photographs of American war vessels.

Petitioners object to the convictions principally on the grounds (1) that the prohibitions of the act are limited to obtaining and delivering information concerning the specifically described places and things set out in the act, such as a vessel, aircraft, fort, signal station, code or signal book; and (2) that an interpretation which put within the statute the furnishing of any other information connected with or relating to the national defense than that concerning these specifically described places and things would make the act unconstitutional as violative of due process because of indefiniteness.

The philosophy behind the insistence that the prohibitions of sections 1(b) and 2(a), upon which the indictment is based, are limited to the places and things which are specifically set out in section 1(a) relies upon the traditional freedom of discussion of matters connected with national defense which is permitted in this country. It would require, urge petitioners, the clearest sort of declaration by the Congress to bring under the statute the obtaining and delivering to a foreign government for its advantage of reports generally published and available which deal with food production, the advances of civil aeronautics, reserves of raw materials or other similar matters not directly connected with and yet of the greatest importance to national defense. The possibility of such an interpretation of the terms "connected with" or "relating to" national defense is to be avoided by construing the act so as "to make it a crime only to obtain information as to places and things specifically listed in section 1 as connected with or related to the national defense." Petitioners argue that the statute should not be construed so as to leave to a jury to determine whether an innocuous report on a crop yield is "connected" with the national defense.

Petitioners rely upon the legislative history to support this position.[2] The passage of the Espionage Act[3] during the World War year of 1917 attracted the close scrutiny of Congress and resulted in different bills in the two Houses which were reconciled only after a second conference report. Nothing more definite appears in this history as to the Congressional intention in regard to limiting the act's prohibitions upon which this indictment depends to the places and things in section 1(a), than that a House definition of "national defense" which gave it a broad meaning was stricken out[4] and the conference report stated as to the final form of the present act: "Section 1 sets out the places connected with the national defense to which the prohibitions of the section apply." Neither change seems significant on this inquiry. The House bill had not specified the places under surveillance. The Conference change made them definite. The fact that the clause "or other place connected with the national defense" is also included in section 1(a) is not an unusual manner of protecting enactments against inadvertent omissions. With this specific designation of prohibited places, the broad definition of section 1202 of the House was stricken as no longer apt and, as stated in Conference Report No. 69, section 6 of the act was therefore adopted. Obviously the purpose was to give flexibility to the designated places.[5] We see nothing in this legislative history to affect our conclusion which is drawn from the meaning of the entire act.[6]

[1] An examination of the words of the statute satisfies us that the meaning of national defense in sections 1(b) and 2(a) cannot be limited to the places and things specified in section 1(a). Certainly there is no such express limitation in the later sections. Section 1(a) lays down the test of purpose and intent and then defines the crime as going upon or otherwise obtaining information as to named things and places connected with the national defense. Section 1(b) adopts the same purpose and intent of 1(a) and then defines the crime as copying, taking or picturing certain articles such as models, appliances, documents, and so forth of anything connected with the national defense. None of the articles specified in 1(b) are the same as the things specified in 1(a). Apparently the draftsmen of the act first set out the places to be protected, and included in that connotation ships and planes and then in 1(b) covered much of the contents of such places in the nature of plans and documents. Section 2(a), it will be observed, covers in much the same way the delivery of these movable articles or information to a foreign nation or its agent. If a government model of a new weapon were obtained or delivered there seems to be little logic in making its transfer a crime only when it is connected in some undefined way with the places catalogued under 1(a). It is our view that it is a crime to obtain or deliver, in violation of the intent and purposes specified, the things described in sections 1(b) and 2(a) without regard to their connection with the places and things of 1(a).

[2] In each of these sections the document or other thing protected is required also to be "connected with" or "relating to" the national defense. The sections are not simple prohibitions against obtaining or delivering to foreign powers information which a jury may consider relating to national defense. If this were the language, it would need to be tested by the inquiry as to whether it had double meaning[7] or forced anyone, at his peril, to speculate as to whether certain actions violated the statute.[8] This Court has frequently held criminal laws deemed to violate these tests invalid. United States v. Cohen Grocery Company,[9] urged as a precedent by petitioners, points out that the statute there under consideration forbade no specific act,[10] that it really punished acts "detrimental to the public interest when unjust and unreasonable" in a jury's view. In Lanzetta v. New Jersey[11] the statute was equally vague. "Any person not engaged in any lawful occupation, known to be a member of any gang, . . . who has been convicted at least three times of being a disorderly person or who has been convicted of any crime in this or in any other

State, is declared to be a gangster. . . ." We there said that the statute "condemns no act or omission"; that the vagueness is such as to violate due process.[12]

[3-5] But we find no uncertainty in this statute which deprives a person of the ability to predetermine whether a contemplated action is criminal under the provisions of this law.[13] The obvious delimiting words in the statute are those requiring "intent or reason to believe that the information to be obtained is to be used to the injury of the United States, or to the advantage of any foreign nation." This requires those prosecuted to have acted in bad faith. The sanctions apply only when scienter is established.[14] Where there is no occasion for secrecy, as with reports relating to national defense, published by authority of Congress or the military departments, there can, of course, in all likelihood be no reasonable intent to give an advantage to a foreign government. Finally, we are of the view that the use of the words "national defense" has given them, as here employed, a well understood connotation. They were used in the Defense Secrets Act of 1911.[15] The traditional concept of war as a struggle between nations is not changed by the intensity of support given to the armed forces by civilians or the extension of the combat area. National defense, the Government maintains, "is a generic concept of broad connotations, referring to the military and naval establishments and the related activities of national preparedness." We agree that the words "national defense" in the Espionage Act carry that meaning. Whether a document or report is covered by sections 1(b) or 2(a) depends upon their relation to the national defense, as so defined, not upon their connection with places specified in section 1(a). The language employed appears sufficiently definite to apprise the public of prohibited activities and is consonant with due process.

At the conclusion of all the evidence petitioners sought a directed verdict of acquittal because (1) the innocuous character of the evidence forbade a conclusion that petitioners had intent or reason to believe that the information was to be used to the injury of the United States or the advantage of a foreign nation and (2) the evidence failed to disclose that any of the reports related to or was connected with the national defense. As a corollary to this second contention, reversal is sought on the ground that the trial court overruled the petitioners' objection that as a matter of law none of the reports dealt with national defense. That is, as the trial court stated the objection, that "the jury has no privilege in determining whether or no any of these reports have to do with the national defense, that that is a matter for the Court and not for the jury, as a matter of law."

To justify a court's refusing to permit a jury to consider a defendant's intent in obtaining and delivering these reports, one would be compelled to conclude that nothing in them could be violative of the law. As they gave a detailed picture of the counter-espionage work of the Naval Intelligence, drawn from its own files, they must be considered as dealing with activities of the military forces. A foreign government in possession of this information would be in a position to use it either for itself, in following the movements of the agents reported upon, or as a check upon this country's efficiency in ferreting out foreign espionage. It could use the reports to advise the state of the persons involved of the surveillance exercised by the United States over the movements of these foreign citizens. The reports, in short, are a part of this nation's plan for armed defense. The part relating to espionage and counter-espionage cannot be viewed as separated from the whole.

[6] Nor do we think it necessary to prove that the information obtained was to be used to the injury of the United States. The statute is explicit in phrasing the crime of espionage as an act of obtaining information relating to the national defense "to be

used . . . to the advantage of any foreign nation." No distinction is made between friend or enemy. Unhappily the status of a foreign government may change. The evil which the statute punishes is the obtaining or furnishing of this guarded information, either to our hurt or another's gain. If we accept petitioners' contention that "advantage" means advantage as against the United States, it would be a useless addition, as no advantage could be given our competitor or opponent in that sense without injury to us.

An examination of the instructions convinces us that no injustice was done petitioners by their content. Weighed by the test previously outlined of relation to the military establishments, they are favorable to petitioners' contentions. A few excerpts will make this clear:

"You are instructed that the term 'national defense' includes all matters directly and reasonably connected with the defense of our nation against its enemies. . . . As you will note, the statute specifically mentions the places and things connected with or comprising the first line of defense when it mentions vessels, aircraft, works of defense, fort or battery and torpedo stations. You will note, also, that the statute specifically mentions by name certain other places or things relating to what we may call the secondary line of national defense. Thus some at least of the storage of reserves of men and materials is ordinarily done at naval stations, submarine bases, coaling stations, dock yards, arsenals and camps; all of which are specifically designated in the statute. . . . You are instructed in the first place that for purposes of prosecution under these statutes, the information, documents, plans, maps, etc.; connected with these places or things must directly relate to the efficiency and effectiveness of the operation of said places or things as instruments for defending our nation. . . . You are instructed that in the second place the information, documents or notes must relate to those angles or phases of the instrumentality, place or thing which relates to the defense of our nation; thus if a place or thing has one use in peacetime and another use in wartime, you are to distinguish between information relating to the one or the other use. . . .

"The information, document or note might also relate to the possession of such information by another nation and as such might also come within the possible scope of this statute. . . . For from the standpoint of military or naval strategy it might not only be dangerous to use for a foreign power to know our weaknesses and our limitations, but it might also be dangerous to us when such a foreign power knows that we know that they know of our limitations.

"You are, then, to remember that the information, documents or notes, which are alleged to have been connected with the national defense, may relate or pertain to the usefulness, efficiency or availability of any of the above places, instrumentalities or things for the defense of the United States of America. The connection must not be a strained one nor an arbitrary one. The relationship must be reasonable and direct."

Petitioners' objection, however, is that after having given these instructions, the court instead of determining whether the reports were or were not connected with national defense, left this question to the jury in these words:

"Whether or not the information, obtained by any defendant in this case, concerned, regarded or was connected with the national defense is a question of fact solely for the determination of this jury, under these instructions."

[7-10] These quotations show that the trial court undertook to give to the jury the tests by which they were to determine whether the acts of the petitioners were connected with or related to the national defense. We are of the opinion this was

properly left to the jury. If we assume, as we must here after our earlier discussion as to the definiteness of the statute, that the words of the statute are sufficiently specific to advise the ordinary man of its scope, we think it follows that the words of the instructions given adequate definition to "connected with" or "relating to" national defense. The inquiry directed at the instructions is whether the jury is given sufficient guidance to enable it to determine whether the acts of the petitioners were within the prohibitions. These instructions set out the definition of national defense in a manner favorable and unobjectionable to petitioners. When they refer to facts connected with or related to defense, however, petitioners urge that the connection should be determined by the court. Instructions can, of course, go no farther than to say the connection must be reasonable, direct and natural. Further elaboration would not clarify. The function of the court is to instruct as to the kind of information which is violative of the statute and of the jury to decide whether the information secured is of the defined kind. It is not the function of the court, where reasonable men may differ, to determine whether the acts do or do not come within the ambit of the statute. The question of the connection of the information with national defense is a question of fact to be determined by the jury as negligence upon undisputed facts is determined.[16]

In a trial under an indictment for violation of section 3[17] of this same Espionage Act, this Court had occasion to consider a similar question as to the function of the jury. A pamphlet was introduced as evidence of making false statements with the intent to cause insubordination. To the objection that the pamphlet could not legitimately be construed as tending to produce the prohibited consequences this Court said: "What interpretation ought to be placed upon the pamphlet, what would be the probable effect of distributing it in the mode adopted, and what were defendants' motives in doing this, were questions for the jury, not the court, to decide. . . . Whether the printed words would in fact produce as a proximate result a material interference with the recruiting or enlistment service, or the operation or success of the forces of the United States, was a question for the jury to decide in view of all the circumstances of the time and considering the place and manner of distribution."[18]

Viewing the instructions as a whole, we find no objection sufficient to justify reversal.

The Circuit Court of Appeals properly refused to consider the errors alleged with respect to the conspiracy count.[19]

Affirmed.

Mr. Justice Murphy took no part in the consideration or decision of this case.

[1]Espionage Act of June 15, 1917, c. 30, 40 Stat. 217:

"Title 1. Espionage. Section 1. That (a) whoever, for the purpose of obtaining information respecting the national defense with intent or reason to believe that the information to be obtained is to be used to the injury of the United States, or to the advantage of any foreign nation, goes upon, enters, flies over, or otherwise obtains information concerning any vessel, aircraft, work of defense, navy yard, naval station, submarine base, coaling station, fort, battery, torpedo station, dockyard, canal, railroad, arsenal, camp, factory, mine, telegraph, telephone, wireless, or signal station, building, office, or other place connected with the national defense, . . . or any place in which any vessel, aircraft, arms, munitions, or other materials or instruments for use in time of war are being made, prepared, repaired, or stored; . . . or (b) whoever for the purpose aforesaid, and with like intent or reason to believe, copies, takes, makes, or obtains, or attempts, or induces or aids another to copy, take, make, or obtain, any sketch, photograph, photographic negative, blue print, plan, map, model, instrument, appliance, document, writing, or note of anything connected with the national defense; . . . shall be punished by a fine of not more than $10,000, or by imprisonment for not more than two years, or both.

"Sec. 2. (a) Whoever, with intent or reason to believe that it is to be used to the injury of the United States or to the advantage of a foreign nation, communicates, delivers, or transmits, or attempts to, or aids or induces another to, communicate, deliver, or transmit, to any foreign government, or to any faction or party or military or naval force within a foreign country, whether recognized or unrecognized by the United States, or to any representative, officer, agent, employee, subject, or citizen thereof, either directly or indirectly, any document, writing, code book, signal book, sketch, photograph, photographic negative, blue print, plan, map, model, note, instrument, appliance, or information relating to the national defense, shall be punished by imprisonment for not more than twenty years: *Provided,* That whoever shall violate the provisions of subsection (a) of this section in time of war shall be punished by death or by imprisonment for not more than thirty years; and (b) whoever, in time or war, with intent that the same shall be communicated to the enemy, shall collect, record, publish, or communicate, or attempt to elicit any information with respect to the movement, numbers, description, condition, or disposition of any of the armed forces, ships, aircraft, or war materials of the United States, or with respect to the plans or conduct, or supposed plans or conduct of any naval or military operations, or with respect to any works or measures undertaken for or connected with, or intended for the fortification or defense of any place, or any other information relating to the public defense, which might be useful to the enemy, shall be punished by death or by imprisonment for not more than thirty years.

* * *

"Sec. 4. If two or more persons conspire to violate the provisions of sections two or three of this title, and one or more of such persons does any act to effect the object of the conspiracy, each of the parties to such conspiracy shall be punished as in said sections provided in the case of the doing of the act the accomplishment of which is the object of such conspiracy. . . ."

[2]H.R. 201, 65th Cong., 1st Sess.; Conference Report No. 69, 55 Cong. Rec. 3301.

[3]Other titles such as neutrality, foreign commerce and at one time censorship, 55 Cong. Rec. 2097; 2102; 2109-2111; 2262; 2265; 3145; 3259; 3266, added to the difficulties.

[4]That definition read: "Section 1202. The term 'national defense' as used herein shall include any person, place, or thing in anywise having to do with the preparation for or the consideration or execution of any military or naval plans, expeditions, orders, supplies, or warfare for the advantage, defense, or security of the United States of America."

[5]55 Cong. Rec. 3306. Subsequent legislation relating to the protection of national defense information is not important. The act of January 12, 1938, 52 Stat. 3, 50 U.S.C.A. § 45 et seq., is to protect against innocent disclosures. S.Rep. 108, 75th Cong., 2d Sess.

Public No. 443, 76th Cong., 3d Sess., 54 Stat. 79, is merely an increase of penalties.

[6]Cf. United States v. American Trucking Ass'ns, 310 U.S. 534, 543, 60 S.Ct. 1059, 1063, 84 L.Ed. 1345.

[7]United States v. Reese, 92 U.S. 214, 23 L.Ed. 563.

[8]Lanzetta v. New Jersey, 306 U.S. 451, 59 S.Ct. 618, 83 L.Ed. 888.

[9]255 U.S. 81, 89, 41 S.Ct. 298, 300, 65 L.Ed. 516, 14 A.L.R. 1045.

[10]"That it is hereby made unlawful for any person willfully . . . to make any unjust or unreasonable rate or charge in handling or dealing in or with any necessaries." Act of October 22, 1919, c. 80, § 2, 41 Stat. 297.

[11]306 U.S. 451, 59 S.Ct. 618, 621, 83 L.Ed. 888.

[12]Criminal statutes deemed vague: International Harvester Co. v. Kentucky, 234 U.S. 216, 221-224, 34 S.Ct. 853, 854-856, 58 L.Ed. 1284 (raising prices above "market value under fair competition, and under normal market conditions"); Collins v. Kentucky, 234 U.S. 634, 34 S.Ct. 924, 58 L.Ed. 1510 (same); Weeds, Inc. v. United States, 255 U.S. 109, 41 S.Ct. 306, 307, 65 L.Ed. 537 (exacting "excessive prices for necessaries"); Stromberg v. California, 283 U.S. 350, 369, 51 S.Ct. 532, 535, 75 L.Ed. 1117, 73 A.L.R. 1484 (displaying any "symbol or emblem of opposition to organized government"); Smith v. Cahoon, 283 U.S. 553, 564, 565, 51 S.Ct. 582, 586, 75 L.Ed. 1264 (such provisions regulating common carriers as could constitutionally be applied to private carriers); Herndon v. Lowry, 301 U.S. 242, 261-264, 57 S.Ct. 732, 740-742, 81 L.Ed. 1066 (distribution of pamphlets intended at any time in the future to lead to forcible resistance to law).

[13]Cf. Adequately definite criminal statutes: State of Ohio ex rel. Lloyd v. Dollison, 194 U.S. 445, 450, 24 S.Ct. 703, 705, 48 L.Ed. 1062 (liquor restrictions varying according to sale at "wholesale" or "retail"); Waters-Pierce Oil Co. v. Texas (No. 1), 212 U.S. 86, 108-111, 29 S.Ct. 220, 225-227, 53 L.Ed. 417

(contracts "reasonably calculated" or which "tend" to fix prices); Nash v. United States, 229 U.S. 373, 376-378, 33 S.Ct. 780, 781, 782, 57 L.Ed. 1232 (unreasonable or undue restraints of trade); Omaechevarria v. Idaho, 246 U.S. 343, 345, 348, 38 S.Ct. 323, 324, 325, 62 L.Ed. 763 ("any cattle range previously . . . or . . . usually occupied by any cattle grower"); Ilygrade Provision Co. v. Sherman, 266 U.S. 497, 501-503, 45 S.Ct. 141, 142, 143, 69 L.Ed. 402 (meat represented to be "kosher"); Miller v. Oregon, 273 U.S. 657, 47 S.Ct. 344, 71 L.Ed. 825 (dangerous rate of speed; see Cline v. Frink Dairy Co., 274 U.S. 415, at 464, 465, 47 S.Ct. 681, 687, 71 L.Ed. 1146); United States v. Alford, 274 U.S. 264, 267, 47 S.Ct. 597, 598, 71 L.Ed. 1040 (building fires "near" any forest or inflammable material); United States v. Wurzbach, 280 U.S. 396, 399, 50 S.Ct. 167, 168, 74 L.Ed. 508 (receiving contributions for "any political purpose whatever"); United States v. Shreveport Grain & Elevator Co., 287 U.S. 77, 81, 82, 53 S.Ct. 42, 43, 77 L.Ed. 175 ("reasonable variations" in weight or measure); Kay v. United States, 303 U.S. 1, 8, 9, 58 S.Ct. 468, 472, 82 L.Ed. 607 ("ordinary fees . . . for services actually rendered").

[14]Cf. Hygrade Provision Co. v. Sherman, 266 U.S. 497, 501, 45 S.Ct. 141, 142, 69 L.Ed. 402.

[15]36 Stat. 1084: "That whoever, for the purpose of obtaining information respecting the national defense, to which he is not lawfully entitled, goes upon any vessel, or enters any navy yard, naval station, fort, battery, torpedo station, arsenal, camp, factory, building, office, or other place connected with the national defense, owned or constructed or in process of construction by the United States. . . ."

[16]Grand Trunk Ry. v. Ives, 144 U.S. 408, 417, 12 S.Ct. 679, 682, 36 L.Ed. 485; Gunning v. Cooley, 281 U.S. 90, 94, 50 S.Ct. 231, 233, 74 L.Ed. 720. Cf Dunlop v. United States, 165 U.S. 486, 500, 501, 17 S.Ct. 375, 380, 41 L.Ed. 799.

[17]40 Stat. 217, 219, c. 30, 50 U.S.C.A. § 33:

"Sec. 3. Whoever, when the United States is at war, shall willfully make or convey false reports or false statements with intent to interfere with the operation or success of the military or naval forces of the United States or to promote the success of its enemies and whoever, when the United States is at war, shall willfully cause or attempt to cause insubordination, disloyalty, mutiny, or refusal of duty, in the military or naval forces of the United States, or shall willfully obstruct the recruiting or enlistment service of the United States, to the injury of the service or of the United States, shall be punished by a fine of not more than $10,000 or imprisonment for not more than twenty years, or both."

[18]Pierce v. United States, 252 U.S. 239, 250, 40 S.Ct. 205, 209, 64 L.Ed. 542. Justices Brandeis and Holmes dissented, largely on the ground that the jury should not be left to decide whether statements in the pamphlet were facts or conclusions. Id., 252 U.S. page 269, 40 S.Ct. page 216, 64 L.Ed. 542.

[19]Brooks v. United States, 267 U.S. 432, 441, 45 S.Ct. 345, 347, 69 L.Ed. 699, 37 A.L.R. 1407.

United States v. Heine

151 F.2d 813 (1945)

L. Hand, Circuit Judge.

Heine was indicted with thirty-two other defendants, under an indictment in two counts. The first count (under § 88 of Title 18, U.S.C.A.), was for a conspiracy to violate § 233 of Title 22, U.S.C.A.: which makes it a crime not to register with the Secretary of State, if one is acting as an agent for a foreign government. The second count under § 34 of Title 50, U.S.C.A., was for a conspiracy to violate § 32 of that title, the relevant language of which is set forth in the margin.* The most important point raised upon this appeal, and the only one which we find it necessary to discuss, is the sufficiency of the evidence to sustain a verdict. We will consider the two counts in inverse order, for the second is much the more important; especially as the defendant has already served the term for which he was sentenced under the first.

Heine was a native-born German, fifty years old at the time of the trial (November and December, 1941), who came to this country in June, 1914. Although he had had some business experience, his first job in the United States was as a mechanic in the Packard Motorcar Company in Detroit, where he lived with his brother. In January, 1918, he went into the employ of the Ford Motor Company, and was sent to the West Indies in 1919. Upon his return in 1920, the company sent him to South America, where he worked in Brazil, Argentine, Uruguay and other countries. He was naturalized in 1920, was married in January, 1922; and in August, 1922, returned to this country. Later he went to England, and after that to Italy, the Balkans, and Barcelona. He came back again to this country in 1925; but on January 1, 1926, he was sent to Berlin as assistant manager of the Ford assembly plant, and in August, 1928, he became a manager of the business. Late in 1930 or early in 1931, he went to Cologne to superintend a new manufacturing plant which had been built there. In 1935 he returned to Detroit, and in May of that year he left the Ford Company for good, and took a position with the Chrysler Corporation, for which he worked in Spain, Portugal and North Africa.

In 1939 and 1939 a German automobile corporation, known as the Volkswagenwerke, suggested that a position might be open to him; but this he was unwilling, however, to consider, because, as he swore, the American consul at Munich told him that he must go home, if he wished to keep his citizenship. Whatever the reason, he did return to the United States in May, 1940, with authority from the Volkswagenwerke to recover some deposits paid to local companies which they had received upon contracts that the companies had abandoned. The Volkswagenwerke also asked him to find out what he could about the automobile and aviation industries in this country. A few weeks after his return he began to send back reports about the aviation industry which constitute the gravamen of the charge against him. These he continued to send until August, 1940, and perhaps later, though not after December 7, 1941. At the direction of the Volkswagenwerke he did not send these direct, but posted them to addresses in New York and Lima, Peru, from which they were to be forwarded to Germany. The evidence permitted the jury to find that this course was surreptitiously adopted in order to escape detection.

The information which Heine collected was from various sources: ordinary magazines, books and newspapers; technical catalogues, handbooks and journals; correspondence with airplane manufacturers; consultation with one, Aldrich, who was already familiar with the industry; talks with one or two employees in airplane factories; exhibits, and talks with attendants, at the World's Fair in New York in the summer of 1940. This material he condensed and arranged in his reports, so as to disclose in compressed form the kinds and numbers of the planes—military and commercial—which were being produced and which it was proposed to produce; the location and capacity of the factories; the number of their employees; and everything else, of which he could get hold, that would contribute to as full a conspectus as possible of the airplane industry. All of this information came from sources that were lawfully accessible to anyone who was willing to take the pains to find, sift and collate it; no public authorities, naval, military or other, had ordered, or indeed suggested, that the manufacturers of airplanes—even including those made for the services—should withhold any facts which they were personally willing to give out. The question which the second count raises is whether § 32 of Title 50, U.S.C.A. covers such activities as we have described.

[1] The evidence as a whole supported a finding that Heine was engaged in collecting all available information about our production of airplanes, so that the Reich should be advised of our defense in the event of war. That would not however serve, unless § 32 would have equally condemned what he did, if he had sent his reports to a friendly power in a time of unthreatened peace. This follows from the

fact that the section covers, not only information intended to be used "to the injury of the United States," but that intended to be used "to the advantage of a foreign nation." When the bill left the House it did not have the second clause; and it does not appear at what stage it was amended by adding the alternative, which greatly enlarged its scope; for while it is true that it is somewhat hard to imagine instances in which anyone would be likely to transmit information "relating to the national defense," which would be injurious to the United States, and yet not advantageous to a foreign power, it is possible to think of many cases where information might be advantageous to another power, and yet not injurious to the United States. The section as enacted necessarily implies that there are some kinds of information "relating to the national defense" which must not be given to a friendly power, not even to an ally, no matter how innocent, or even commendable, the purpose of the sender may be. Obviously, so drastic a repression of the free exchange of information it is wise carefully to scrutinize, lest extravagant and absurd consequences result.

It seems plain that the section cannot cover information about all those activities which become tributary to "the national defense" in time of war; for in modern war there are none which do not. The amount of iron smelted, of steel forged, of parts fabricated; the number of arable acres, their average yield; engineering schools, scientific schools, medical schools, their staffs, their students, their curriculums, their laboratories; metal deposits; technical publications of all kinds; such non-technical publications as disclose the pacific or belligerent temper of the people, or their discontent with the government: every part in short of the national economy and everything tending to disclose the national mind are important in time of war, and will then "relate to the national defense." If the words mean that, it would be criminal to send to a subject of Britain or to a citizen of France a railway map, a list of merchant ships, a description of automobile assembly technique, an account of the latest discoveries in antisepsis, or in plant or animal breeding, or even a work upon modern physics, provided only the sender had reason to believe that the information might reach the government, and be helpful to it in any of its activities. Nor would this become tolerable, though we limited the phrase to what would be advantageous to those countries in their own national defense, because that is as all-embracing as our own. Such an assertion of national isolationism is certainly not to be imputed to Congress.

[2, 3] A less impossible interpretation would be to confine the clause to information about things adapted only for the national defense, and things of ambiguous use which have been already collected, or prepared, for the supply of the armed services. The first would include airplanes, cannon, small arms and munitions of war, warships, forts, and the like: the second, coal, food, clothing or other supplies accumulated for the army and navy. In that interpretation the clause would cover those military planes, though made by private companies, which Heine's reports included. Even so, there might be doubt whether the judge's charge to the jury should not have distinguished betweeen military and commercial planes; but we need not consider that question because we think that it was lawful for him to include information about both kinds of planes. As declared in Gorin v. United States, 312 U.S. 19, 28, 61 S.Ct. 429, 85 L.Ed. 488, and as the judge himself charged, it is obviously lawful to transmit any information about weapons and munitions of war which the services had themselves made public; and if that be true, we can see no warrant for making a distinction between such information, and information which the services have never thought it necessary to withhold at all. There can, for

example, be no rational difference between information about a factory which is turning out bombers, and to which the army allows access to all comers, and information about the same bombers, contained in an official report, or procured by a magazine through interviews with officers. The services must be trusted to determine what information may be broadcast without prejudice to the "national defense," and their consent to its dissemination is as much evidenced by what they do not seek to suppress, as by what they utter. Certainly it cannot be unlawful to spread such information within the United States; and, if so, it would be to the last degree fatuous to forbid its transmission to the citizens of a friendly foreign power. "Information relating to the national defense," whatever else it means, cannot therefore include that kind of information, and so far as Heine's reports contained it, they were not within the section.

[4-6] There is independently reason to suppose that this was the meaning which the House at least had in mind when the bill was before it during the First War—1917. It is true that the debates on the floor of both Houses do not tell much, but at the hearings before the Judiciary Committee a number of the witnesses expressed concern at the possible suppression of information as the bill read even before its scope had been enlarged by the amendment. Possibly it was to allay these fears that the Committee, in reporting to the House, used the following words in connection with § 4 as it then was: "This section of the bill has been carefully and patiently considered by the Committee. The Committee realizes that the section as recommended gives the President broad power, but it must be admitted by all patriotic persons anxious for the success of our armies in times like these through which we are now going, it is important that the Commander-in-Chief shall have authority to prevent the publication of national defense secrets which would be useful to the enemy, and, therefore, harmful to the United States." Section 4, about which this language was used, gave the President power to declare a national emergency, and to "prohibit the publication or communication of . . . any information relating to the national defense which in his judgment is of such a character that it is, or might be, useful to the enemy." It is most unlikely that the words in § 4 had a meaning different from the same words then in § 2 of the bill, and now in § 32 of Title 50. At least the Judiciary Committee of the House supposed that the act was directed at "secrets." It is not necessary for us to go so far; and in any event "secrets" is an equivocal word whose definition might prove treacherous. It is enough in the case at bar to hold, as we do, that whatever it was lawful to broadcast throughout the country it was lawful to send abroad; and that it was lawful to prepare and publish domestically all that Heine put in his reports. We do not forget that there was evidence that in his letters and in his talks he misled his correspondents as to his motive in asking for information; but that is not relevant to the second count. Whatever the wrong done to his correspondents, that motive did not make the spread of information criminal, which it would not have been criminal to spread, if he had got it fairly. Nor did it make a difference that Heine did not transmit to the Volkswagenwerke the information as he got it; but combed it out, arranged it and compressed it into convenient form. The section is aimed at the substance of the proscribed information, not at the act of making it more readily available for use.

Gorin v. United States, supra (312 U.S. 19, 61 S.Ct. 429, 85 L.Ed. 488), contains nothing to the contrary of what we are holding. It is true that the court (312 U.S. 28, 61 S.Ct. 434) there accepted the following definition of the phrase, "relating to the national defense" taken from the prosecution's brief: "a generic concept of broad connotations, referring to the military and naval establishments and the related activities of national preparedness." The words, "related activities of national preparedness," do indeed create a penumbra of some uncertainty; but it cannot comprise such information as is here in question, as appears from what immediately preceded the language we have quoted: "Where there is no occasion for secrecy, as with reports relating to national defense, published by authority of Congress or the military departments, there can, of course, in all likelihood be no reasonable intent to give an advantage to a foreign government." Obviously, this could not mean that it may not be to the advantage of a foreign government to have possession of such information; it can only mean that, when the information has once been made public, and has thus become available in one way or another to any foreign government, the "advantage" intended by the section cannot reside in facilitating its use by condensing and arranging it.

[7] As to the first count, in spite of the absence of any direct evidence showing the connection of the Volkswagenwerke with the Reich, there was ample in Heine's history and conduct to support a verdict based upon the finding that he was acting as an agent for the Reich, and the jury was of course not bound to accept his own explanation. The Volkswagenwerke had never made airplanes; and, so far as appears, they did not propose to make military planes anyway. Why should they wish accounts of the industry in this country as complete as possible? What good would it do them to learn the amount of our production, all of which at the time was for our own use? Moreover, although it is true that in the summer of 1940, war was not imminent, everyone knew that it was not impossible. France had fallen; Russia was apparently neutral, and had overrun part of Poland in conjunction with Germany; Britian stood alone, with every prospect of herself going down. We were already embarked upon our belated preparation, and that could be directed only against the Reich. If a jury was not permitted in such a setting to infer that the collection and transmission of such information by such means as Heine employed, was for the Reich, and not for the Volkswagenwerke, there is an end to circumstantial proof. Nobody but a simpleton could fail to detect the hall-marks of the principal in whose interest the whole web of chicane and evasion had been woven.

Conviction on the first count affirmed.

Conviction on the second count reversed.

---

*"§ 32. Unlawfully disclosing information affecting national defense. Whoever, with intent or reason to believe that it is to be used to the injury of the United States or to the advantage of a foreign nation, communicates, delivers, or transmits, or attempts to, or aids or induces another to, communicate, deliver, or transmit, to any foreign government, or to any faction or party or military or naval force within a foreign country, whether recognized or unrecognized by the United States, or to any representative, officer, agent, employee, subject, or citizen thereof, either directly or indirectly, any document, writing, code book, signal book, sketch, photograph, photographic negative, blue print, plan, map, model, note, instrument, appliance, or information relating to the national defense, shall be punished by imprisonment for not more than twenty years."

Scarbeck v. United States

317 F.2d 546 (1963)
cert denied 374 U.S. 856 (1963)

Washington, Circuit Judge.

Appellant Irvin C. Scarbeck was tried in the District Court on an indictment which charged him in three counts with communicating classified information to representatives of the Polish Government, in violation of 50 U.S.C. § 783(b), and in a fourth count with removing a document on file at the United States Embassy in Warsaw, Poland, in violation of 18 U.S.C. § 2071. After a jury trial, Scarbeck was found guilty on the first three counts, and not guilty on the fourth. He was sentenced to ten years imprisonment on each of the first three counts, to be served consecutively. Appeal was taken from the judgment of conviction. During its pendency, a motion for a new trial was made in the District Court. This was denied, and an appeal was taken from the denial. The two appeals were consolidated by order of this court.

The Government's evidence, the substance, was that appellant Scarbeck was employed in the United States Embassy in Warsaw from December 1958 until June 1961, serving as Second Secretary and General Services Officer. In September 1959 he met and thereafter became involved with Miss Urzsula Maria Discher, a Polish national. He maintained an apartment for her, and visited her there almost nightly when he was in Warsaw. On the night of December 22-23, 1960, when appellant and Miss Discher were undressed and in bed together, the door was opened and several men entered—one in the uniform of the Polish militia. One of the men had a camera and took compromising pictures. Miss Discher was then taken to the police station, where she was interrogated by Polish security police (known as the "U.B.") and threatened with expulsion from Warsaw, imprisonment for black market dealings, and forced service as a prostitute.

The facts following are derived largely (but not wholly) from appellant's statements to a security officer of the State Department and to agents of the Federal Bureau of Investigation, which were received in evidence over appellant's objection.

The appellant remained in the apartment and conversed with two other men who arrived to interview him. He was told that Miss Discher would be imprisoned, that his activities with her would have to be reported to the United States Embassy, and that his career would be finished. The men suggested, however, that if appellant furnished information and documents from the Embassy to them, they might be able to quash the report to the Embassy concerning his activities and to procure the release of Miss Discher. Appellant disclaimed having any knowledge of classified matters and stated that he would not under any circumstances give them any information which would endanger the security of the United States. He agreed, however, to meet with them again. Miss Discher was then returned to her apartment from the police station.

Appellant thereafter met with the men, whom he believed to be Polish security policemen, once a week or once in two weeks until about April 11, 1961. He first gave them unclassified documents and information obtained from unclassified material, but the men became insistent that he provide them with more important documents and information. According to appellant's statements, about five or six weeks after his first meeting with them he took to them Despatch No. 344, a document prepared by the Ambassador of the United States and classified and marked as "Secret." The men photographed and returned this document to him in about fifteen minutes. He also provided them on other occasions with information contained in Despatch No. 518 classified and marked "Secret," and in Despatch No. 444 classified and marked "Confidential."

During his talks with the U.B. men, appellant had asked their assistance in obtaining a Polish passport for Miss Discher. Early in April 1961 Miss Discher obtained the passport and used it immediately to go to Germany. Appellant had previously arranged for the issuance of a West German visa to her, permitting her entry, and had arranged accommodations for her in Frankfurt. He paid her transportation to Germany. Before she left Warsaw, appellant mentioned to the two U.B. men his worries about her lack of funds and accepted 1600 German marks (then about $400) which they offered him. Appellant stated to them that it was a loan which he would repay. He had refused previous offers of money made by these men.

Appellant joined Miss Discher in Frankfurt about the middle of April and remained until the first week of May, when he returned to Warsaw. He was then under suspicion by his superiors, and was ordered to report on June 5, 1961, to the United States Embassy in Bonn, Germany, to attend a conference. Later that day (June 5) he was interviewed by a security official of the Department of State and signed an inculpatory statement detailing some of the facts outlined above. He returned to the United States where he was questioned by agents of the F.B.I., and where he signed three more inculpatory statements. He was arrested, indicted and tried, resulting in the conviction now under review.

I.

Appellant's initial contention raises the question of the proper interpretation of the statute under which he was convicted, 50 U.S.C. § 783(b) (1958), incorporating Section 4(b) of the Internal Security Act of 1950, 64 Stat. 991. This section provides, in pertinent part:

> "It shall be unlawful for any officer or employee of the United States or of any department or agency thereof, or of any corporation the stock of which is owned in whole or in major part by the United States or any department or agency thereof, to communicate in any manner or by any means, to any other person whom such officer or employee knows or has reason to believe to be an agent or representative of any foreign government . . . *any information of a kind which shall have been classified by the President (or by the head of any such department,* agency, or corporation *with the approval of the President) as affecting the security of the United States,* knowing or having reason to know that such information has been so classified, unless such officer or employee shall have been specifically authorized by the President, or by the head of the department, agency, or corporation by which this officer or employee is employed, to make such disclosure of such information." (Emphasis supplied.)

As we have seen, appellant Scarbeck was an employee of the State Department, stationed in Warsaw, Poland, from December 1958 until June 1961. He was found guilty of having communicated to Polish government agents Foreign Service Despatches numbered 344, 518 and 444 (or information contained in them); the first two Despatches had been classified and certified "Secret," and the last Despatch had been classified and certified "Confidential," by the United States Ambassador to Poland. The Ambassador testified that these classifications were security classifications applied to information which should be protected in the interst of the national defense of the United States; and that his authority for the classifications was the President's Executive Order 10501, as amended by Executive Order 10901, and the Foreign Service Regulations based on the Executive Order.

Appellant's contention is that his conviction under Section 783(b) cannot stand because there was no showing that he had communicated the contents of any document which had been classified *personally* by the President as "affecting the security of the United States," or one that had been so classified *personally* by the Secretary of State with the approval of the President.[1]

At the outset, we note that the construction of the statute urged by appellant would largely reduce it to a dead letter. With the pressures of more urgent business, the President and the Secretary of State of necessity could personally classify very few documents or items of information. In the normal course of events a subordinate Government employee or official labels his own materials with whatever classification he deems appropriate, within the scope of his authority, and his superiors reviewing those material later re-classify or de-classify as they may judge necessary or desirable. But in this process the great mass of documents in the State Department never will reach the Secretary of State or the President. Executive Order 10501 of November 5, 1953, 18 Fed.Reg. 7049, as amended by Executive Order 10901 of January 9, 1961, 26 Fed.Reg. 217, fully recognizes this; after defining classification categories, it provides that the authority to classify under the order may be exercised, as to the Department of State, by the head (Secretary) "or by such responsible officers or employees as he, or his representative, may designate for that purpose."

We note further that security and defense information has long been "classified" against disclosure and that the term classified by, or with the approval of, the President or a department head, had a well understood connotation on September 23, 1950, when Section 783(b) was enacted by Congress.[2] For example, Executive Order 8381 of March 22, 1940, 5 Fed.Reg. 1147, defines "vital military and naval installations or equipment . . . requiring protection against the general dissemination of information relative thereto" within the meaning of the Act of January 12, 1938, 52 Stat. 3, 18 U.S.C. § 795, as:

> "1. All military or naval installations and equipment which are *now classified, designated, and marked under the authority or at the direction of* the Secretary of War or the Secretary of the Navy as 'secret', 'confidential', or 'restricted'. . . ." (Emphasis supplied.)

Executive Order 10104 of February 1, 1950, 15 Fed.Reg. 597, superseded Order 8381, and contained three numbered paragraphs defining vital military and naval installations and equipment under the 1938 Act. Most pertinent here is the following:

> "3. All official military, naval, or air force books, pamphlets, documents, reports, maps, charts, plans, designs, models, drawings, photographs, contracts, or specifications *which are now marked under the authority or at the direction of* the President, the Secretary of Defense, the Secretary of the Army, the Secretary of the Navy, or the Secretary of the Air Force as 'top secret', 'secret', 'confidential' or 'restricted' and all such articles or equipment *which may hereafter be so marked with the approval or at the direction of* the President." (Emphasis supplied).

Congress itself in the Act of May 13, 1950, passed only a few months prior to the statute here involved, made it a crime to communicate knowingly certain types of classified information (see 50 U.S.C. § 46a) and defined the term "classified information" as "information which, at the time of a violation under this chapter, is, for reasons of national security, *specifically designated by a United States Government agency* for limited or restricted dissemination or distribution." (Emphasis supplied.) 50 U.S.C. § 46.[3]

It could hardly be supposed that in enacting Section 783(b) Congress was not aware of this background and of the necessity for, and the existing practice of, delegation to others by the President and department heads of the authority to classify security and other defense information. It seems highly unlikely that

Congress would have intended to provide a penalty for disclosure only of such information as had personally been classified by the President or the head of a department—necessarily a fairly rare occurrence. And the legislative history of Section 783(b) bears this out.

The language of Section 783(b) in the respect now pertinent, i.e., "of a kind which shall have been classified by the President (or by the head of any such department, agency, or corporation with the approval of the President) as affecting the security of the United States," was contained in identical form in Section 4(b) of the original congressional bill, S. 1194, introduced by Senator Mundt on March 8, 1949; the Section 4(b) of the second 1949 bill, S. 2311, introduced by Senator Mundt on July 22, 1949;[4] in Section 4(b) of S. 4037 introduced by Senator McCarran on August 10, 1950; and in Section 4(a) of H.R. 9490 introduced by Representative Wood in the House on August 21, 1950. This latter bill became the Internal Security Act of 1950 over the President's veto, and the pertinent section was incorporated in 50 U.S.C. § 783(b), which is now before us:

At the Senate Hearings on S. 1194, Senator Mundt pointed out that Section 4(b) of the bill grew "directly out of the experience we had in the House Committee on Un-American Activities last fall in investigation of the so-called pumpkin papers case, the espionage activities in the Chambers-Hiss case, the Bentley case, and others."[5] When S. 4037 was reported favorably on August 17, 1950 the Senate Report (S. Rep. No. 2369, 81st Cong., 2d Sess.) stated:

> "Section 4(b) makes it unlawful, except with special authorization, for any officer or employee of the United States or of any Federal agency to communicate with any representative of a foreign government or to any officer or member of a Communist organization, *information of a kind* which he knows or has reason to know has been *classified by or with the approval of the President* as affecting the security of the United States." (Emphasis supplied).

The language emphasized indicates stronly that personal classification by the President was not required.

The debate in the Senate relative to Section 4(b) of S. 4037 centered about its possible application to employees of corporations only partly owned by the United States, and to representatives of friendly governments. Senator Kefauver considered the bill to be too broad in these respects.[6] Senators McCarran, Mundt and Ferguson replied to his criticisms. Portions of the debate are following:

> "Mr. Ferguson. . . .
>
> "First, we must know what we are trying to prevent. The purpose of this part of the bill is to prevent Government employees and those working for Government agencies and those who are serving in capacities in which they are likely to receive very vital information which has been classified by the President as being security information, from knowingly and willfully giving such information to foreign agents or to persons who belong to Communist organizations. 96 Cong.Rec. 14615.
>
> * * *
>
> "The only persons who are entitled to receive such secret information are those whom the President of the United States or the heads of the departments allow to have such information. That is as it should be. Ibid.
>
> * * *
>
> "Mr. Kefauver. The Senator from Michigan knows that in all the departments, practically all documents are marked 'confidential' or 'restricted.' Under such circumstances, it would be impossible for anyone to have a full appreciation of what might be marked 'restricted.'

"This measure does not mean that anyone who might be so charged would have to have seen what was so marked. On the contrary, if such a person should pass on such information third hand, and if subsequently it should turn out to have been marked 'restricted,' that person would be guilty, because the amendment does not provide that the person passing on the information must have seen it.

"Mr. Ferguson. Mr. President, that is not a fact. The amendment provides that such a person must know that the material is restricted or must have reason to believe that it is restricted. How would that situation develop? It would develop in this way: If certain information is classified by the President or by the head of any Department or agency, with the approval of the President, then if any person knows that a certain paper or certain information has been *classified by the President or, on his authority, by someone else* as affecting the security of the United States, such person should not give the information to any foreign agent or any foreign government; it should be a crime for anyone to do so. . . ." (Emphasis supplied.) Ibid.

"Mr. Kefauver. This subsection says it shall be unlawful to communicate in any way any information that has been *classified by the President or any division of the Government with the approval of the President.* That is paraphrasing it. . . ." (Emphasis supplied.) 96 Cong.Rec. 15198.

"Mr. Kefauver. . . . I was at the Department of Justice late this afternoon. They told me, for instance, that they mark things confidential that a third or fourth assistant can read, which the President in the White House also marks confidential. We have some material marked confidential by the President which a third or fourth assistant from the top also marks confidential.

"Mr. Mundt. I am not sure of the pertinence of the Senator's question. I do not think it has anything to do with the colloquy now in progress. *So far as marking matters confidential, under this legislation it must be done by the President or someone authorized by him to do it.* I do not want to get into all of these details. . . ." (Emphasis supplied.) 96 Cong.Rec. 15253.

Pertinent also are certain of the colloquies which occurred at the Senate hearings on S. 1194, the original bill on this subject introduced by Senator Mundt on March 8, 1949. As indicated, that bill was, and the intervening bills were, in all respect now relevant, identical with the final legislation. These colloquies are set out in the margin.[7]

These passages in the debates and hearings indicate, in our view, that the speakers understood that the President would take ultimate responsibility for the protection and classification of security documents and information, but that the actual marking of documents and the safeguarding of information would be delegated to others. There can be little doubt, in view of the legislative history taken in the light of the existing background, that Congress intended to enact a broad and effective statute, prohibiting the transfer of all documents officially classified as affecting the national security, whether or not the President or the head of a department had personally marked them as such. The question is whether the statutory language can fairly be construed to accomplish that result. We think it can.

In the first place, the statute does not read "classified by the President." It says "*of a kind*" classified by the President (or a department head). Those words must mean that the President (or the head of an approved department) is to establish the kinds or categories of documents and information which are to be classified by appropriate authority. This requirement has been fulfilled in the instant case, through the issuance by the President of Executive Orders, stated to be "in the best interests of the national security," and the promulgation by the Secretary of State of the regulations contained in the Foreign Service Manual. Executive Order 10501, as amended by Executive Order 10901, describes the "categories" of information which shall be classifed as "Top Secret," "Secret," and "Confidential." The "Secret" category, for example, is authorized, "by appropriate authority, only for defense information or material the unauthorized disclosure of which could result in serious damage to the Nation, such as by jeopardizing the international relations of the United States, endangering the effectiveness of a program or policy of vital importance to the national defense, or compromising important military or defense plans, scientific or technological developments important to national defense, or information revealing important intelligence operations." Any information of this character is "of a kind" described by the President by Executive Order as being suitable for classification as "Secret." Similarly, the Executive Order authorizes use of the classification "Confidential," "by appropriate authority, only for defense information or material the unauthorized disclosure of which could be prejudicial to the defense interests of the nation."[8]

The Executive Order goes on to select certain documents as "having primary responsibility for matters pertaining to national defense," one of which is the Department of State,[9] and provides as follows with respect to them:

> ". . . the authority for original classification of information or material under this order may be exercised by the head of the department, agency, or Governmental unit concerned or by such responsible officers or employees as he, or his representative, may designate for that purpose. The delegation of such authority to classify shall be limited as severely as is consistent with the orderly and expeditious transaction of Government business."

Thus express authority for, and "approval of the President" of, the delegation by the Secretary of State to selected responsible officers and employees of his power to assign an original classification is given in the Executive Order. It is implicit, of course, that the original classification will be subject to review by superior officers and the Secretary.

Since the Secretary's power to delegate his authority to classify originally is established, the Ambassador's authority to classify and to certify the classification of the three Despatches in question is not debatable. He was clearly authorized as the "originator" of Despatch 344 to give the original and appropriate classification to it, and as principal officer of the Embassy, his power to certify (or to change if deemed appropriate) the original classification given by others to Despatches 518 and 444 is also plain. See the Regulations contained in the Foreign Service Manual, Part II, §§ 912.1, 913.1, and 913.2.[10] And it is equally clear that his classifications were made with the approval and under the authority of the President and the Secretary of State.

We conclude that Ambassador Beam had authority to classify Despatches 344, 518, and 444 by virtue of the provisions of the Executive Order and the Foreign Service Manual; and that the Despatches as classified and certified by him are within the scope of Section 783(b).

Appellant also urges that since criminal statutes must be strictly construed, no meaning can be given to Section 783(b) beyond the narrowest interpretation of its words. He quotes from Connally v. General Construction Co., 269 U.S. 385, 391, 46 S.Ct. 126, 70 L.Ed. 322 (1926), where the Supreme Court said:

> "That the terms of a penal statute creating a new offense must be

sufficiently explicit to inform those who are subject to it what conduct on their part will render them liable to its penalties, is a well-recognized requirement, consonant alike with ordinary notions of fair play and the settled rules of law. And a statute which either forbids or requires the doing of an act in terms so vague that men of common intelligence must necessarily guess at its meaning and differ as to its application, violates the first essential of due process of law. International Harvester Co. V. Kentucky, 234 U.S. 216, 221, [34 S.Ct. 853, 58 L.Ed. 1284]; Collins v. Kentucky, 234 U.S. 634, 638 [34 S.Ct. 924, 58 L.Ed. 1510]."

[3, 4] The general principle just stated is of course well settled. But it is not to be applied in derogation of common sense, especially where the statute deals with a limited class of persons, so situated as to have special knowledge concerning the acts prohibited, and where punishment is to be imposed only on those who have scienter. See Gorin v. United States, 312 U.S. 19 at 27-28, 61 S.Ct. 429, 85 L.Ed. 488 (1941). Here the scienter requirement is explicit: Section 783(b) says that the accused must be in the posture of "knowing or having reason to know that such information has been so classified." And here the class to which the statute applies is a relatively small group—employees of the Federal Government. This group is not only a limited one: it is a well-informed one. Federal employees are subject to the orders of their superiors, and are informed by statutes, regulations, other published directives, and oral instructions, as to what they shall or shall not do in connection with their Government employment. Employees of the State Department were told, by Section 783(b) and by the regulations set out in the Foreign Service Manual, which incorporates the directives of Executive Order 10501, as amended, that they are not to communicate to representatives of a foreign government information known by them to have been classified as "Secret" or "Confidential" by officials authorized to classify them. As Mr. Justice Holmes said in a highly pertinent case, involving prohibitions against Government officials receiving or soliciting funds for political purposes:

> "It is argued at some length that the statute, if extended beyond the political purposes under the control of Congress, is too vague to be valid. The objection to uncertainty concerning the persons embraced need not trouble us now. . . . The other objection is to the meaning of 'political purposes.' This would be open even if we accepted the limitations that would make the law satisfactory to the respondent's counsel. But we imagine that no one not in search of trouble would feel any [trouble]. Whenever the law draws a line there will be cases very near each other on opposite sides. The precise course of the line may be uncertain, but no one can come near it without knowing that he does so, if he thinks, and if he does so it is familiar to the criminal law to make him take the risk." United States v. Wurzbach, 280 U.S. 396 at 399, 50 S.Ct. 167, 74 L.Ed. 508 (1930).[11]

We think a like view must be taken here.

II.

Appellant further urges that even if his construction of the statute—that the classification of documents must be made personally by the President or the Secretary of State—is rejected, then the Government was required to prove at the trial that the documents involved were properly classified "as affecting the security of the United States." He argues that "This would present an insurmountable hurdle since, as is obvious, the standards set forth in E.O. 10501 relate to the protection of information involving the 'national defense' and not to 'the security of the United States,' the criterion set forth in 783(b)."

But the Executive Order itself negates this. Its preamble recites that the President deems his order "necessary in the best interests of the national security." It is quite true that the classification categories set up in the Order relate to what is referred to as "defense information," but the definitions of material appropriate for classification can as well be described as relating to the national security. (See Part I of this opinion.) Appellant has not undertaken to show that "defense information," as described in the Executive Order, is not of necessity "information . . . affecting the security of the United States," within the meaning of Section 783(b). Common sense tells us that it is: defense is one aspect of security and indeed in their broad senses the two terms have a very similar connotation. The legislative history, as we have seen, shows that Congress must have equated the two terms.[12] Furthermore, Ambassador Beam, who was primarily responsible for the classifications involved here, testified that the classifications "Top Secret," "Secret" and "Confidential" were security classifications applying to information which should be protected in the interest of national defense. And the definition of "Defense Information" contained in Section 911.2 of the regulations in the Foreign Service Manual is phrased in terms which include protection of the national security, both internal and external, in every aspect; it is not limited to protection against physical attack.[13]

We think, therefore, that documents classified as "Secret" or "Confidential" pursuant to the Executive Order and the Foreign Service Manual are "classified . . . as affecting the security of the United States," within the meaning of Section 783(b). The remaining inquiry is whether the prosecution was required to show that they were properly so classified. In our view, the answer to this question must be in the negative.

There is no suggestion in the language of Section 783(b), by specific requirement or otherwise, that the information must properly have been classified as affecting the security of the United States. The essence of the offense described by Section 783(b) is the communication—by a United States employee to agents of a foreign government—of information of a kind which has been classified by designated officials as affecting the security of the United States, knowing or having reason to know that it has been so classified. The important elements for present purposes are the security classification of the material by an official authorized to do so and the transmission of the classified material by the employee with the knowledge that the material has been so classified. Indeed, we think that the inclusion of the requirement for scienter on the part of the employee is a clear indication of the congressional intent[14] to make the superior's classification binding on the employee, once he knows of it.[15] Cf. Gorin v. United States, 312 U.S. 19, 27-28, 61 S.Ct. 429, 85 L.Ed. 488 (1941). The excerpts from the Senate Hearings set out above in footnote 7, supra, confirm this.

Gorin v. United States, supra, involved a prosecution under Sections 1(b) and 2 of the Espionage Act of 1917, for obtaining any information connected with or relating to the national defense and delivering it to an agent of a foreign country with an intent, or reason to believe, that it is to be used to the injury of the United States or the advantage of a foreign nation. The Supreme Court held that the statute embraced everything connected with or related to national defense in its well understood connotation (312 U.S. at 28, 61 S.Ct. at 434), and that, once properly instructed as to the meaning of national defense as used in the statute, it was for the jury to determine whether the documents involved were in fact connected with the national defense.[16] Here, similarly, the function of the court was to instruct as to the meaning of "classified" information, the disclosure of which would be violative of Section 783(b), and the function of the jury was to decide whether the information revealed was classified information in that sense.

The Gorin case does not support the proposition that in a prosecution under Section 783(b) the jury must be permitted to determine not only the question whether the document was classified but also whether it affected the security of the United States. The Espionage Act of 1917, involved in Gorin, covered the entire population: it forbade any person to obtain and deliver documents connected with the national defense, irrespective of whether they had been so classified or marked, and the factual determination whether they were so connected had to be resolved in each case. However, as we have noted, Section 783(b) was aimed at a small group—employees of the Federal Government. Under the Foreign Service Regulations, see footnote 10, supra, only the originator of a document is authorized to assign the original classification, and only certain other officers are authorized to certify the classification and to review or change it. As already shown, this procedure is in accord with the Executive Order and has the approval of the President. Once the classification has been given and certified, every employee must respect it until an official authorized to change the classification has done so. In the meantime, if a Foreign Service employee sees a document marked "Secret" or "Confidential" and has legitimate reasons for thinking that the security interests of the Government would be better served by treating the document as unclassified, he may apply to his superiors, give those reasons, and have the point decided. But certainly an employee of the State Department could not bring an action in the courts to remove the label "Secret" attached by his superiors to a particular document, simply because he was being blackmailed and wished to be able to offer the document to his blackmailers without criminal consequences. Merely to describe such a litigation is enough to show its absurdity. Yet appellant is urging that after such an employee has obtained and delivered a classified document to an agent of a foreign power, knowing the document to be classified, he can present proof that his superior officer had no justification for classifying the document, and can obtain an instruction from the court to the jury that one of their duties is to determine whether the document, admittedly classified, was of such a nature that the superior was justified in classifying it. The trial of the employee would be converted into a trial of the superior. The Government might well be compelled either to withdraw the prosecution or to reveal policies and information going far beyond the scope of the classified documents transferred by the employee. The embarrassments and hazards of such a proceeding could soon render Section 783(b) an entirely useless statute.

We conclude that it is the intent of the statute to make the superior's classification binding on the employee. In this case, if the Government's evidence be believed, appellant knew perfectly well what he was about: the Polish agents were demanding classified (i.e., valuable and secret) information, and he tried to satisfy their demands. He cannot now claim that the Government is required to prove that the documents he gave were in fact properly classified.[17] The factual determination required for purposes of Section 783(b) is whether the information has been classified and whether the employee knew or had reason to know that it was classified. Neither the employee nor the jury is permitted to ignore the classification given under Presidential authority.

III.

We turn to appellant's contention that it was error to admit in evidence the four inculpatory statements given by him under circumstances now to be related.

* * *

For the reasons given, the judgment of conviction, and the order denying a new trial, will be affirmed. However, in view of the extent of appellant's cooperation with the authorities during the investigation, we think the District Court should seriously consider exercising its power, under Fed.R.Crim.P. 35, to reduce the sentences which have been imposed, as for example, by making them run concurrently. See Kaplan v. United States, 241 F.2d 521, 523 (5th Cir.), cert. denied, 354 U.S. 941, 77 S.Ct. 1406, 1 L.Ed.2d 1539 (1957).

Affirmed.

---

[1]This contention goes to the sufficiency of the indictment, which charges the appellant with having communicated, with respect to each of the three Despatches in question, "information the defendant had reason to know had been classified, under the authority of the President of the United States and the Secretary of State, as affecting the security of the United States." It is irrelevant that this point may not have been made at the trial; it may be raised at any time. Fed.R.Crim.P. 12(b); see United States v. Manuszak, 234 F.2d 421, 422 (3d Cir., 1956); Johnson v. United States, 206 F.2d 806, 808, 14 Alaska 380 (9th Cir., 1953).

[2]Section 783(b), of course, does not purport to be an enabling act; the power of the Executive branch to protect secret documents affecting the national defense and security has been exercised from the beginning, and is in no way limited or extended by Section 783(b).

[3]50 U.S.C. §§ 46, 46a, and 46b were superseded by Section 24(a) of the Act of October 31, 1951, 18 U.S.C. § 798, which continued in Section 798(b) the same definition of classified information as is found in 50 U.S.C. § 46.

[4]On March 21, 1950, S. 2311 was reported favorably by the Senate Committee on the Judiciary, with amendments designed to make the prohibitions of the bill "operative whether or not the classified information was obtained within or without the scope of the official duties or employment," and to add the requirement of scienter. The words "obtained in the course of his official duties or employment," were omitted and the words "knowing or having reason to know that such information has been so classified" were added. See S.Rep. No. 1358, 81st Cong., 2d Sess., March 21, 1950.

[5]It is a matter of common knowledge that many if not most of the documents involved in these cases were not documents personally classified or described by the President or a department head as secret or not to be disclosed. The quoted language is found at page 31 of the Hearings, cited infra at footnote 7.

[6]See, for example, 96 Cong.Rec. 14240 et seq. (September 6, 1950).

[7]"*Senator Ferguson.* What kind of papers do you have in mind that it would be a crime to deliver to allies?

"*Senator Mundt.* That is spelled out in definition. It is any paper which has been—

"*Senator O'Conor.* Classified.

"*Senator Mundt.* Yes; classified as affecting the security of the United States, all classified information.

"As the Senator understands, one time a thing is classified and at another time it is not.

"*Senator Ferguson.* I understand that, but the word 'classified' is not always under a directive of the President.

"*Senator Mundt.* By the President or by somebody acting for him.

"*Senator O'Conor.* The head of any department, agency, or corporation.

"*Senator Ferguson.* Then this goes so far as to allow an administrative officer to classify anything, and the transfer of that would be criminal under your act.

"*Senator Mundt.* It permits him to transfer anything provided he has the approval of the President so to do, but it keeps the responsibility on the President. It says with the approval of the President.

* * *

"*Senator Ferguson.* Has this anything to do with the national defense?

"*Senator Mundt.* This is very definitely a part of the national defense.

"*Senator Ferguson.* I mean the papers we are talking about. If it is marked 'Secret' because it is for the national defense, that is one thing, but suppose it is just marked 'Secret' and it has nothing to do with the national defense.

"*Senator Mundt.* That is covered in the definition as affecting the security of the United States. It is spelled out.

"*Senator O'Conor.* In line 12 of the bill the requirement is that the classification would be of those papers which affect the security of the United States.

"*Senator Ferguson.* That was what I wanted to get at.

"*Senator Mundt.* That is right. That is definite.

"*Senator Ferguson.* What about the person knowing, or believing or having reason to believe that it would affect the security?

"*Senator Mundt.* From the standpoint of the person against whom the statute runs he can determine that by whether it is marked 'Classified' or not. The man who does the classifying acts in his responsible capacity as the representative of the President.

"*Senator Ferguson.* All right. What you do, then, is to use the word 'classified' to be the determining feature. Suppose it is not marked?

"*Senator Mundt.* If it is classified it is marked or it is supposed to be marked.

"*Senator Ferguson.* Suppose he gets the knowledge from a classified paper and then gives it orally?

"*Senator Mundt.* If he knows or has reason to believe that it is classified, he is guilty." Hearings before a Sub-Committee of the Committee on the Judiciary, United States Senate, 81st Cong., 1st Sess., on S. 1194 and S. 1196 (1949), at 32-33.

[8]The definitions of material to be classified as Secret and Confidential as set out in the regulations contained in the Foreign Service Manual are patterned on, and appear to be identical with, the definitions of those terms in the Executive Order. See §§ 911.32 and 911.33 thereof.

[9]Under Section 783(b), one of the President's functions is recognized to be this process of selection. This, it seems to us, is the meaning of the words "with the approval of the President" as used in the phrase "classified by the President (or by the head of any such department, agency, or corporation with the approval of the President)." The "approval of the President" is to be given by authorizing the heads of selected agencies to institute a plan of classifying their protected documents. Appellant appears in substance to agree. His brief says:

"The 'approval of the President' refers to heads of a department, agency, or corporation, and is intended to limit the authority to classify under the statute to only *certain heads* of a department, agency, or corporation actually those having a direct responsibility for national defense or security."

[10]These are as follows:

"912 *Principles of Classification and Control*

"912.1 *Assigning Classification or Control Designation*

"The originator of a document shall be responsible for the original assignment of its classification or control designation. . . .

"913 *Authority to Certify Classifications or Control Designations*

"913.1 *General*

"The final signature or approval of a document bearing a classification or administrative control designation constitutes a certification by the signing or approving officer that the classification or control designation assigned is appropriate. The officer who signs or approves such a document is called the 'certifying officer' with respect to the classification or control designation of the document. Thus, authorization to sign a document automatically confers authority to certify its classification or control designation unless a prohibition is specifically included in the authorization to sign.

"913.2 *Designation of Certifying Officers*

"Any officer at a post authorized to sign correspondence in accordance with 1 FSM II 121 is authorized to certify the classification or administrative control designation of any document which he signs, except that the Top Secret classification shall be certified only by the principal officer or his designee. The authority to certify classifications or control designations should not be confused with the responsibility for initial assignment of a classification or control designation. Any employee who originates a classified or administratively controlled document has the responsibility for assigning the appropriate classification or administrative control designation at the time the document is prepared. The classification or control designation so assigned may be changed or eliminated by the certifying officer or by intermediate reviewing officers." Foreign Service Manual, Part II, §§ 912.1, 913.1, 913.2.

[11]See also Hygrade Provision Co. v. Sherman, 266 U.S. 497 at 501-502, 45 S.Ct. 141, 69 L.Ed. 402 (1925):

"By engaging in the business of selling kosher products they [appellant meat dealers] in effect assert an honest purpose to distinguish to the best of their judgment between what is and what is not kosher. The statutes require no more." Similarly, the United States v. Hood, 343 U.S. 148 at 151, 72 S.Ct. 568, 96 L.Ed. 846 (1952), it is said:

"This Act penalized corruption. . . .

". . . The picture of the unsuspecting influence merchant, steering a careful course between violation of the statute on the one hand and obtaining money by false pretenses on the other by confining himself to the sale of non-existent but plausible offices, entrapped by the dubieties of this statute, is not one to commend itself to reason."

[12]See, for example, the colloquy in fn. 7, supra, between Senators Ferguson and Mundt.

[13]"911.2 *Defense Information*

"The Department was informed by the Attorney General of the United States on April 17, 1954, that defense classifications may be interpreted by the Department, in proper instances, to include the safeguarding of information and material developed in the course of conduct of foreign relations of the United States whenever it appears that the effect of the unauthorized disclosure of such information or material upon international relations or upon policies being pursued through diplomatic channels could result in serious damage to the Nation. The Attorney General further noted that it is a fact that there exists an interrelation between the foreign relations of the United States and the national defense of the United States, which fact is recognized in section 1 of Executive Order 10501. Accordingly, defense information shall be interpreted as including information or material which, if disclosed to unauthorized individuals, may result in a break in diplomatic relations affecting the defense of the United States; may cause an armed attack to be launched against the United States or its allies; may reduce the ability of the United States to defend itself against attack; may increase the enemy's ability to wage war against the United States; may compromise military or defense plans, intelligence operations, or technological developments vital to national defense; may jeopardize the international relations of the United States; or may endanger the effectiveness of a program or policy of vital importance to the national defense or otherwise be prejudicial to defense interests. Illustrative examples of such information which may require classification include:

"a. Information and material relating to cryptographic devices and systems;

"b. Information pertaining to vital defense or diplomatic programs or operations;

"c. Intelligence or information relating to intelligence operations which will assist the United States to be better prepared to defend itself against attack or to conduct foreign relations;

"d. Information pertaining to national stockpiles, requirements for strategic materials, critical products, technological development, or testing activities vital to national defense;

"e. Investigative reports which contain information relating to subversive activities affecting the internal security of the United States;

"f. Political and economic reports containing information, the unauthorized disclosure of which may jeopardize the international relations of the United States or may otherwise affect the national defense; or

"g. Information received in confidence from officials of a foreign government whenever it appears that the breach of such confidence might have serious consequences affecting the national defense."

[14]The following passage from the Senate debate is of interest here:

"*Mr. Ferguson.* It says 'information which has been classified.'

"*Mr. Kefauver.* That is correct; but it does not mean that the individual must actually seize the document to come within the terms of the bill.

"*Mr. Ferguson.* The person would have to know the information contained in the document is classified.

"*Mr. Kefauver.* Or have reason to believe that it is confidential.

"*Mr. Ferguson.* Or to be told that it is." 96 Cong.Rec. 14242.

[15]There can of course be no contention, and there is none, that appellant was not aware that the Despatches involved here were classified as affecting the security of the United States. Each page of each Despatch was marked at top and bottom with its classification. And appellant as a foreign service officer was charged with knowledge of the regulations applicable to such officers, relating to classified material.

[16]The Supreme Court said:

"The function of the court is to instruct as to the kind of information which is violative of the statute, and of the jury to decide whether the information secured is of the defined kind. It is not the function of the court, where reasonable men may differ, to determine whether the acts do or do not come within the ambit of the statute. The question of the connection of the information with national defense is a question of fact to be determined by the jury as negligence upon undisputed facts is determined." 312 U.S. at 32, 61 S.Ct. at 436.

[17]His counsel seems to have agreed to this at the trial, as indicated by the following colloquy in the trial court:

"The Court: The question that we have to determine is did this defendant take a document that was on the face of it listed as Top Secret, Secret or Confidential, the document itself. Then we are going to start in to evaluate what the State Department should have considered—

"Mr. Klein [counsel for defendant, now appellant] (interposing):—which we are not going to do. What I am going to relate to another exhibit which shows when a document should have been classified as Secret and show there was over-classification. I think I have a right to do that.

"Of course he has the authority to classify anything he wants Secret or Top Secret.

"The Court: But my only point is, that once he does classify it, it is not for an employee to determine that it is mis-classified.

"Mr. Klein: Yes.

"The Court: Do you get my point?

"Mr. Klein: Yes, of course.

"The Court: Now don't you agree?

"Mr. Klein: Yes, I agree."

LIMITS ON THE RIGHTS OF AMERICANS

LIMITS ON THE RIGHTS OF AMERICANS

Surveillance

COMMENTARY

There has been surprisingly little effort to establish the rights and limits of the power of the President in gathering information on national security matters from American citizens. The courts have had surprisingly little to say about the basis of the claimed right of the President to conduct such surveillance, whether or not closely connected to the gathering of information about criminal activity—and even less about the limits which the Bill of Rights may put on such surveillance. Most of what the courts have had to say has pertained to the applicability of the warrant requirement of the Fourth Amendment to wiretaps when claimed to be justified on national security grounds. Congress has passed no laws at all authorizing national security-related surveillance or prohibiting or regulating it. The sections of the Safe Streets Act of 1968 dealing with wiretaps (18 U.S.C. 2510-20) specifically decline to specify or limit presidential power where national security is concerned. The FBI had until the post-Watergate period relied on a press release of President Franklin Roosevelt to justify its vast program of domestic surveillance; and the other intelligence agencies, including the CIA, had relied on secret directives issued by various Presidents and referred to as National Security Council Intelligence Directives (NSCIDs). In 1976, President Gerald Ford issued an Executive Order, No. 11905, which defines the authority of foreign intelligence agencies to gather information (inter alia) from American citizens at home and abroad; and Attorney General Edward Levi issued two directives authorizing and limiting FBI domestic intelligence investigations and investigations directed at those believed to be agents of foreign powers. These directives taken together authorize one or more agencies to freely gather information about the political activities of Americans when necessary for national security purposes, subject only to the limitations imposed by the criminal laws (*e.g.*, the statute prohibiting the opening of first class mail without a warrant) and by the Fourth Amendment.

To determine what those limitations may entail, we discuss briefly the general question of the applicability of the Fourth Amendment to surveillances justified on national security grounds, then consider the specific issue of wiretaps, and finally discuss the First Amendment issues.

Fourth Amendment

Until Watergate it appeared to be well settled that the Fourth Amendment applies with full force, even when the national security of the United States is involved. This means that even national security-motivated searches and seizures (1) require a judicial warrant and (2) must be reasonable. The matter appears to have reached the Supreme Court only once, in the celebrated case of Col. Rudolph Ivanovich Abel, a KGB agent illegally in the United States to run an espionage ring. The full applicability of the Fourth Amendment in this case, even though there could be no question of the bonafides of the national security claim, was taken for granted by the Court, as is evident from the parenthetical remark of Justice Frankfurther that:

> (Of course the nature of the case, the fact that it was a prosecution for espionage, has no bearing whatever upon the legal considerations relevant to the admissibility of evidence.)[1]

Thus, the Fourth Amendment applied with the same force to a KGB agent illegally in the United States as it did to any other person. If the government had violated the Constitution in seizing evidence, it could not be used to convict Abel. Nowhere in the Court's opinion or the dissents is there a suggestion that the Fourth Amendment did not apply or applied differently because the national security was involved.[2]

Such a contention arose for the first, and perhaps the last time, in connection with the break-in into the office of one Dr. Fielding, now well-known as the psychiatrist of Daniel Ellsberg. President Richard Nixon sought to keep information about the burglary secret on grounds that it was a national security matter, and when it became public sought to justify it on the same grounds. The indictment of several officials for the burglary provoked a Justice Department amicus brief, arguing on behalf of the United States government that warrantless searches under the Fourth Amendment could be constitutional when foreign intelligence or espionage are involved, where the intrusion is kept to a minimum and where the intrusion was authorized by the President or the Attorney General. The Court of Appeals, in affirming defendants' conviction, held only that if there was any right to search without a warrant on national security grounds it rested with the President and the Attorney General. Since there was no allegation that either had authorized the burglary, there was no reason to inquire into the President's power.[3]

In a concurring opinion, Judge Leventhal did examine the claim of the right of the President to proceed without a warrant in national security cases, and showed that it had no basis in prior decisions or in the Constitution. The only conceivable basis for a contrary conclusion would have been an analogy—which Judge Leventhal firmly rejected—to the case of wiretaps. Wiretaps have had a unique role in the development of Fourth Amendment doctrine; the current confusion of the law on wiretaps need not and should not be extended to other forms of surveillance. It is to those wiretap cases that we now turn.

The invention of the telephone and then the technology to intercept messages using telephone wires were both, of course, totally unanticipated by the founding fathers. These developments raised the question for the Court of whether or not such interceptions were violations of the Fourth Amendment if conducted without appropriate warrant procedures. Initially, the Supreme Court (in *Olmstead v. United States,* 277 U.S. 438 (1928)) took the position that the Fourth Amendment related strictly to trespassing onto the property of an individual as that term was defined in the common law. Thus, if a wiretap or other electronic surveillance were accomplished without any trespass onto the actual property of an individual, the Court held that it did not violate the Fourth Amendment.[4]

The Supreme Court however, became increasingly unhappy with its decision in *Olmstead,* holding that wiretaps did not violate the Fourth Amendment, and finally moved to overrule it. In *Berger v. New York,* 388 U.S. 41 (1967) and *Katz v. United States,* 389 U.S. 347 (1967), the Supreme Court held for the first time that wiretaps were fully subject to the Fourth Amendment. In a famous phrase it stated that "the Fourth Amendment protects people, not places" and that therefore it would provide protection for any conversation conducted with a reasonable expectation of privacy. This, the Courts said specifically, included conversations carried over telephone wires.

Despite the mystique that surrounds Supreme Court decisions and the notion that they somehow emerge from the Court as inevitable interpretations of the Constitution, it is clear that a great deal of negotiation and compromise often is necessary to secure a Supreme Court majority. To obtain a majority holding that wiretaps violated the Fourth Amendment three compromises were necessary.

The first involved the question of general warrants. Many civil libertarians have argued not only that wiretaps were covered by the Fourth Amendment but also that telephone surveillances by their nature violated the Fourth Amendment since they were general searches intercepting all conversations. The Katz Court rejected that argument, stating that Congress could constitutionally authorize wiretaps with a warrant under specified circumstances. These included: (1) specifying what conversations were to be overheard, (2) avoiding the interception of other conversations, and (3) limiting the time period of the surveillance.

The second compromise involved retroactivity. The Court later held that it would not apply its decision to wiretaps which took place before the decision was handed down.

The third compromise directly relates to national security. The Supreme Court for the first time suggested that the Fourth Amendment warrant requirement, at least as it related to wiretaps, might be different in national security cases. The Court did not reach this position. It merely left open the possibility. It did so by noting in a footnote:

> Whether safeguards other than prior authorization by a magistrate would satisfy the Fourth Amendment in a situation involving the national security is a question not presented by this case.[5]

Several members of the Supreme Court had served in the Justice Department and were aware of embassy taps. It appears that these surveillances were at the core of the concern of the justices who desired to leave this question open, but the Court's opinion made no effort to define national security. Justice Byron White, who had served as deputy attorney general in the Kennedy Administration, stated in a concurring opinion his view that national security wiretaps should not require a warrant. He offered no further definition of the term, nor did Justices Douglas and Brennan who, in another concurring opinion, expressed the view that the Fourth Amendment warrant requirement must be the same for all cases, including those involving national security. Justice Douglas did note that "spies and saboteurs are as entitled to the protection of the Fourth Amendment as suspected gamblers." Two actions, one by the Supreme Court and one by the Congress, would, however, within the next few years force the Courts to come to grips with the question of a national security exemption.

The action by the Supreme Court flowed from its rule that evidence obtained in violation of a constitutional right cannot be used in a criminal prosecution. The Court has interpreted this rule to mean that the evidence obtained from an unconstitutional search cannot be used as the basis for obtaining admissible evidence. If an accused person has been the subject of an illegal search, the Court must be satisfied that none of the evidence has been tainted by the search.

Wiretaps pose unusual problems in this regard since many conversations may be overheard which provide leads and because the individual does not know if his conversations have been overheard. The Supreme Court in *Alderman v. United States,* 394 U.S. 165 (1968), laid down the rules for dealing with possible unconstitutional wiretaps occurring after its Katz decision. The Court held that anyone indicted (or called before a grand jury) could demand to know if he or she had been overheard on an electronic surveillance. If so, the Court would be provided with the rationale for the surveillance and the procedures followed and would determine if the surveillance were legal. If it were not, then the logs of the conversations would have to be turned over to the defendant for a taint hearing. The Court would not by itself determine if evidence introduced at the trial had been derived from the unconstitutional surveillance.[6]

The *Alderman* decision meant that any time an individual was indicted, he could demand a search of the wiretap files of the government. If it were revealed that he had been overheard on a warrantless "national security" electronic surveillance, the Court would have to determine if the surveillance were illegal. This requirement has led to a number of Court decisions on the legality of various kinds of "national security" wiretaps.

The second event which has triggered extensive litigation on the question of warrantless "national security" wiretaps was the passage by Congress in 1968 of the so-called Safe Streets Act which for the first time provided a procedure for wiretaps under warrants by federal officials. That act basically held that all wiretaps were illegal except if conducted under the provisions of the Safe Streets Act itself. Responding to the Court's invitation in *Katz* and *Berger,* the act specified procedures designed to insure that the search was reasonable and that it did not amount to a general warrant. At the same time, in order to discourage illegal wiretaps, the act provided that anyone whose phone was tapped in violation of the Safe Streets Act could sue for civil damages and would be entitled to damages at the rate of $100 a day for each day of illegal interception, use, or transfer of information from an illegal interception.

In passing the legislation, the Congress explicitly left open the question of whether wiretaps without a warrant would be premitted in certain national security situations. The relevant portions of the Safe Streets Act read as follows:

> Nothing contained in this chapter or in section 605 of the Communications Act of 1934 (48 Stat. 1103; 47 U.S.C. §605) shall limit the constitutional power of the President to take such measures as he deems necessary to protect the Nation against actual or potential attack or other hostile acts of a foreign power, to obtain foreign intelligence information deemed essential to the security of the United States, or to protect national security information against foreign intelligence activities. *Nor shall anything contained in this*

> *chapter be deemed to limit the constitutional power of the President to take such measures as he deems necessary to protect the United States against the overthrow of the Government by force or other unlawful means, or against any other clear and present danger to the structure or existence of the Government.* The contents of any wire or oral communication intercepted by authority of the President in the exercise of the foregoing powers may be received in evidence in any trial, hearing, or other proceeding only where such interception was reasonable, and shall not be otherwise used or disclosed except as is necessary to implement that power. (Emphasis supplied.)[7]

We can best understand the Court decisions which have followed as a result of *Alderman* and the Safe Streets Act by pausing to consider how practice has evolved in the executive branch. With the passage of Section 605 of the Federal Communications Act, most wiretapping by the Federal government appears to have ceased except for that connected with national security. In 1940, President Franklin Roosevelt sent a directive to his Attorney General indicating that he did not interpret a Court decision holding that Section 605 required the suppression of evidence obtained from wiretaps to prohibit wiretaps against enemy agents, and authorized electronic surveillance "of persons suspected of subversive activities against the government of the United States, including suspected spies." Roosevelt's memorandum concluded: "You are requested further to limit these investigations so conducted to a minimum and to limit them insofar as possible to aliens."

This directive was in 1946 renewed by President Harry Truman in a slightly broadened form which omitted the directive to minimize the use of surveillance.

Under Roosevelt the surveillances apparently focused on suspected Nazi and Japanese sympathizers, although pacifist and other antiwar groups may also have been subject to electronic surveillance. Under Truman, the Communist Party and other Communist and front groups were the subjects of surveillance and the use of this technique seems to have spread to other groups. Indeed, little is known about the criteria employed by the FBI and the Justice Department in approving electronic surveillances under Truman, Eisenhower or Kennedy.

President Lyndon B. Johnson moved to regularize procedures in 1965 by directing that all national security wiretaps in the United States should be conducted by the FBI with the approval of the Attorney General.[8] The criteria employed appear to have been quite loose, since a surveillance against Martin Luther King was continued based on the allegation that he was in contact with a communist agent.

During the Nixon Administration, the claimed right to engage in warrantless electronic surveillance was greatly broadened to include antiwar groups and other "dissident" groups and individuals. The coverage of such groups was greatly expanded, leading to a number of situations in which an indicted individual either had been the subject of a surveillance or had been overheard.[9] In such cases, the Courts were compelled to decide if a warrantless national security wiretap was legal. The Supreme Court in one such case held that, in cases involving domestic security, warrants were required. In that case, commonly known as *Keith,* [*United States v. United States District Court,* 407, U.S. 297 (1972)], the Supreme Court, without dissent, rejected the government's argument that the Courts were not capable of evaluating the rationale for an electronic surveillance. Justice Powell put it this way:

> We cannot accept the Government's argument that internal security matters are too subtle and complex for judicial evaluation. Courts regularly

> deal with the most difficult issues of our society. There is no reason to believe that federal judges will be insensitive to or uncomprehending of the issues involved in domestic security cases. Certainly courts can recognize that domestic security surveillance involves different considerations from the surveillance of ordinary crime. If the threat is too subtle or complex for our senior law enforcement officers to convey its significance to a court, one may question whether there is probable cause for surveillance.[10]

The Supreme Court declined to decide the entire issue. It emphasized the limited nature of its decision and that it was asserting no opinion on whether other national security wiretaps would require a warrant. It explicitly left open the question of whether warrants would be required in cases involving foreign powers or their agents.

Subsequent criminal cases have apparently involved surveillances directed against foreign powers or their agents. Here most Courts, including two Circuit Courts of Appeals, have held that the President may tap foreign powers or their agents without a warrant without violating the Fourth Amendment.[11]

The Appeals Court for the District of Columbia has declined to make such a finding and, in a case of surveillance of the Jewish Defense League, held that even when national security was involved a warrant was required.[12] The plurality opinion of four judges held that "a warrant must be obtained before a wiretap is installed on a domestic organization that is neither the agent of nor acting in collaboration with a foreign power, even if surveillance is installed under presidential directive in the name of foreign intelligence gathering for protection of the national security." The opinion intimated that warrants should be required in all circumstances, even if there were a link with a foreign power: "Nobody in the intelligence community has seen any civil-liberties question involved in such surveillance despite the fact that they must routinely overhear hundreds if not thousands of conversations of American citizens each year."

First Amendment Issues

Although a number of the surveillance decisions discussed above make reference to the First Amendment, none rest their holding on a First Amendment right to be free of government surveillance.

The right to private political association has been frequently confirmed by the Supreme Court.[13] Thus, statutes which compel the disclosure of information, such as membership lists, which might be used to harass a political organization are unconstitutional. It would appear to follow that the government cannot obtain by surreptitious means, such as the use of informants, information which it could not compel an organization to release. However, no Court has yet so held.

The Supreme Court has often held statutes regulating speech to be unconstitutional because their over-breadth could be said to cast a chilling effect on protected political activity.[14] However, the Supreme Court has seldom dealt with the issue in the specific context of political surveillance. In *Laird v. Tatum,* 408 U.S. 1 (1972) the Court accepted the principle that political surveillance could be unconstitutional if it produced in fact a direct chilling effect on the exercise of First Amendment rights. However, the Court at the same time accepted the government's right to gather information about the political activities of Americans, provided the intelligence gathering did not violate the Fourth Amendment or the criminal laws and did not cast a chilling effect on political activity.[15]

The Supreme Court in the *Keith* case also explicitly upheld the right of the

President to gather information about political activity, at least when it was relevant to preventing violence. Justice Powell, writing for the Court without dissent, noted that:

> We recognize that domestic security surveillances may involve different policy and practical considerations from the surveillance of "ordinary crime." The gathering of security intelligence is often long range and involves the interrelation of various sources and types of information. The exact targets of such surveillance may be more difficult to identify than in surveillance operations against many types of crimes specified in Title III. Often, too, the emphasis of domestic intelligence gathering is on the prevention of unlawful activity of the enhancement of the Government's preparedness for some possible future crisis or emergency. Thus the focus of domestic surveillance may be less precise than that directed against more conventional types of crime.[16]

In the same opinion, Justice Powell recognized the special problems arising under the First Amendment when the government was intruding on political activity:

> National security cases, moreover, often reflect a convergence of First and Fourth Amendment values not present in cases of "ordinary" crime. Though the investigative duty of the executive may be stronger in such cases, so also is there greater jeopardy to constitutionally protected speech. . . .
>
> The price of lawful dissent must not be a dread of subjection to an unchecked surveillance power. Nor must the fear of unauthorized official eavesdropping deter vigorous citizen dissent and discussion of Government action in private conversations. For private dissent, no less than open public discourse, is essential to our free society.[17]

The Court's opinion actually decided the matter purely on Fourth Amendment grounds, holding that there was no occasion to invoke or to create an exception to the warrant requirement. However, Justice Powell has elsewhere suggested that the First Amendment might intervene to prohibit politically sensitive searches and seizures that the Fourth Amendment would otherwise permit.[18] One of the many surveillance cases now in the Courts as a result of the relevations of Watergate and the activities of the intelligence agencies could lead to such a holding.

---

[1]*Abel v. United States,* 362 U.S. 217, 220 (1960).

[2]The Sixth Amendment fight to counsel has also been held to apply equally to national security matters. See *United States v. Coplon,* 185 F.2d 165 (1950).

[3]*United States v. Ehrlichman,* 546 F.2d 910 (D.C. Cir. 1976).

[4]No court has questioned Congress' power to ban all wiretaps including those justified on national security grounds. However, the question of whether Section 605 of the Federal Communications Act was meant by the Congress to apply to national security cases is a long and tangled one. The early courts held that it did, and more recently several circuit courts have held that Congress did not intend to limit the President's ability to wiretap in the interest of national security in Section 605 of the Federal Communications Act. In 1968, in passing the Safe Streets Act, Congress specifically exempted both that act and Section 605 from limiting any presidential power to wiretap in the interest of national security. Since this controversy is now moot, we will not attempt to deal with this tangled debate about statutory construction. On this issue, see, for example, the varying opinions in *United States v. Butenko,* 494 F.2d 593 (1974).

[5]389 U.S. 358 n.23. The wording of the amendment made it clear that the "reasonableness" requirements of the Fourth Amendment would apply even if no warrant were required. See *Halperin v. Kissinger,* 424 F.Supp. 838 (D.D.C. 1976).

[6]This decision in the closing days of the Johnson Administration was greeted with great concern by John Mitchell and his associates in the Justice Department. According to later press accounts, they sent a department official to talk with several members of the Supreme Court to get them to reconsider the decision. While there was no reconsideration, in a concurring opinion in a future case Justice Stewart stressed that wiretap logs would be turned over to defendants only after the court found the wiretaps to be illegal. He emphasized that the Supreme Court had not yet stated any opinion on warrantless national security wiretaps. *Giordano v. United States,* 394 U.S. 310, 313 (1969), Justice Stewart, concurring.

[7]18 U.S.C. 2511 (3).

[8]This memorandum appears to have brought a halt to most taps by other agencies within the United States although both the CIA and the Secret Service are known to have conducted at least one surveillance since the memorandum was issued. Neither the National Security Agency's surveillance of international communications nor the army's overseas electronic surveillance programs was affected by this memorandum. Both programs continue.

[9]The number of electronic surveillances did not go up appreciably during the Nixon Administration's early years. Nor did it go down following the court decisions described below. Although there may well have been some juggling of rationales to conform to the changing law, the basic explanation for the relatively constant number appears to be bureaucratic. The units conducting the surveillances have a fixed number of lines leased from the telephone company and act to keep them all in use; also, they struggle to keep their share of the budget.

[10]*United States v. United States District Court,* 407 U.S. 1320.

[11]*United States v. Brown,* 484 F.2d 418 (5th Cir 1973) *United States v. Butenko,* 494 F.2d 593 (3rd Cir 1974) (en banc) cert. denied, 419 U.S. 881 (1974).

[12]*Zweibon v. Mitchell,* 516 F.2d 594 (D.C.Cir. 1975).

[13]*E.g., NAACP v. Button,* 357 U.S. 449 (1958); *Buckley v. Valeo,* 424 U.S. 1 (1976).

[14]*E.g., Keyishian v. Board of Regents,* 385 U.S. 589 (1967).

[15]The Court dismissed the case on standing grounds.

[16]407 U.S. 296.

[17]407 U.S. 314.

[18]*E.g., United States v. Miller,* 425 U.S. 435, 444 n. 6 (1976); *California Bankers Assn. v. Shultz,* 416 U.S. 21 (1974) at 78-79 (Powell, J. concurring).

STATUTES

Title III, Omnibus Crime Control and Safe Streets Act of 1968

18 U.S.C. §2510

Definitions

As used in this chapter—

(1) "wire communication" means any communication made in whole or in part through the use of facilities for the transmission of communications by the aid of wire, cable, or other like connection between the point of origin and the point of reception furnished or operated by any person engaged as a common carrier in providing or operating such facilities for the transmission of interstate or foreign communications;

(2) "oral communication" means any oral communication uttered by a person exhibiting an expectation that such communication is not subject to interception under circumstances justifying such expectation;

(3) "State" means any State of the United States, the District of Columbia, the Commonwealth of Puerto Rico, and any territory or possession of the United States;

(4) "intercept" means the aural acquisition of the contents of any wire or oral communication through the use of any electronic, mechanical, or other device.

(5) "electronic, mechanical, or other device" means any device or apparatus which can be used to intercept a wire or oral communication other than—

(a) any telephone or telegraph instrument, equipment or facility, or any component thereof, (i) furnished to the subscriber or user by a communications common carrier in the ordinary course of its business and being used by the subscriber or user in the ordinary course of its business; or (ii) being used by a communications common carrier in the ordinary course of its business, or by an investigative or law enforcement officer in the ordinary course of his duties;

(b) a hearing aid or similar device being used to correct subnormal hearing to not better than normal;

(6) "person" means any employee, or agent of the United States or any State or political subdivision thereof, and any individual, partnership, association, joint stock company, trust, or corporation;

(7) "Investigative or law enforcement officer" means any officer of the United States or of a State or political subdivision thereof, who is empowered by law to conduct investigations of or to make arrests for offenses enumerated in this chapter, and any attorney authorized by law to prosecute or participate in the prosecurtion of such offenses;

(8) "contents", when used with respect to any wire or oral communication, includes any information concerning the identity of the parties to such communication or the existence, substance, purport, or meaning of that communication;

(9) "Judge of competent jurisdiction" means—

(a) a judge of a United States district court or a United States court of appeals; and

(b) a judge of any court of general criminal jurisdiction of a State who is authorized by a statute of that State to enter orders authorizing interceptions of wire or oral communications;

(10) "communication common carrier" shall have the same meaning which is given the term "common carrier" by section 153(h) of title 47 of the United States Code; and

18 U.S.C. §2511

Interception and Disclosure of Wire or Oral Communications Prohibited

(1) Except as otherwise specifically provided in this chapter any person who—

(a) willfully intercepts, endeavors to intercept, or procures any other person to intercept or endeavor to intercept, any wire or oral communication;

(b) willfully uses, endeavors to use, or procures any other person to use or endeavor to use any electronic, mechanical, or other device to intercept any oral communication when—

(i) such device is affixed to, or otherwise transmits a signal through, a wire, cable, or other like connection used in wire communication; or

(ii) such device transmits communications by radio, or interferes with the transmission of such communication; or

(iii) such person knows, or has reason to know, that such device or any component thereof has been sent through the mail or transported in interstate or foreign commerce; or

(iv) such use or endeavor to use (A) takes place on the premises of any business or other commercial establishment the operations of which affect interstate or foreign commerce; or (B) obtains or is for the purpose of obtaining information relating to the operations of any business or other commercial establishment the operations of which affect interstate or foreign commerce; or

(v) such person acts in the District of Columbia, the Commonwealth of Puerto Rico, or any territory or possession of the United States;

(c) willfully discloses, or endeavors to disclose, to any other person the contents of any wire or oral communication, knowing or having reason to know that the information was obtained through the interception of a wire or oral communication in violation of this subsection; or

(d) willfully uses, or endeavors to use, the contents of any wire or oral communication, knowing or having reason to know that the information was obtained through the interception of a wire or oral communication in violation of this subsection;

shall be fined not more than $10,000 or imprisoned not more than five years, or both.

(2) (a) (i) It shall not be unlawful under this chapter for an operator of a switchboard, or an officer, employee, or agent of any communication common carrier, whose facilities are used in the transmission of a wire communication, to intercept, disclose, or use that communication in the normal course of his employment while engaged in any activity which is a necessary incident to the rendition of his service or to the protection of the rights or property of the carrier of such communication: *Provided,* That said communication common carriers shall not utilize service observing or random monitoring except for mechanical or service quality control checks.

(ii) It shall not be unlawful under this chapter for an officer, employee, or agent of any communication common carrier to provide information, facilities, or technical assistance to an investigative or law enforcement officer who, pursuant to this chapter, is authorized to intercept a wire or oral communication.

(b) It shall not be unlawful under this chapter for an officer, employee, or agent of the Federal Communications Commission, in the normal course of his employment and in discharge of the monitoring responsibilities exercised by the Commission in the enforcement of chapter 5 of title 47 of the United States Code, to intercept a wire communication, or oral communication transmitted by radio, or to disclose or use the information thereby obtained.

(c) It shall not be unlawful under this chapter for a person acting under color of law to intercept a wire or oral communication, where such person is a party to the communication or one of the parties to the communication has given prior consent to such interception.

(d) It shall not be unlawful under this chapter for a person not acting under color of law to intercept a wire or oral communication where such person is a party to the communication or where one of the parties to the communication has given prior consent to such interception unless such communication is intercepted for the purpose of committing any criminal or tortious act in violation of the Constitution or laws of the United States or of any State or for the purpose of committing any other injurious act.

(3) Nothing contained in this chapter or in section 605 of the Communications Act of 1934 (48 Stat. 1143; 47 U.S.C. 605) shall limit the constitutional power of the President to take such measures as he deems necessary to protect the Nation against actual or potential attack or other hostile acts of a foreign power, to obtain foreign intelligence information deemed essential to the security of the United States, or to protect national security information against foreign intelligence activities. Nor shall anything contained in this chapter be deemed to limit the constitutional power of the President to take such measures as he deems necessary to protect the United States against the overthrow of the Government by force or other unlawful means, or against any other clear and present danger to the structure or existence of the Government. The contents of any wire or oral communication intercepted by authority of the President in the exercise of the foregoing powers may be received in evidence in any trial hearing, or other proceeding only where such interception was reasonable, and shall not be otherwise used or disclosed except as is necessary to implement that power.

Added Pub.L. 90-351, Title III, § 802, June 19, 1968, 82 Stat. 213. As amended Pub.L. 91-358, Title II, § 211(a), July 29, 1970, 84 Stat. 654.

18 U.S.C. §2515

Prohibition of Use As Evidence of Intercepted Wire or Oral Communications

Whenever any wire or oral communications has been intercepted, no part of the contents of such communication and no evidence derived therefrom may be received in evidence in any trial, hearing, or other proceeding in or before any court, grand jury, department, officer, agency, regulatory body, legislative committee, or other authority of the United States, a State, or a political subdivision thereof if the disclosure of that information would be in violation of this chapter.

Added Pub.L. 90-351, Title III, § 802, June 19, 1968, 82 Stat. 216.

18 U.S.C. §2516

Authorization for Interception of Wire or Oral Communications

(1) The Attorney General, or any Assistant Attorney General specially designated by the Attorney General, may authorize an application to a Federal

judge of competent jurisdiction for, and such judge may grant in conformity with section 2518 of this chapter an order authorizing or approving the interception of wire or oral communication by the Federal Bureau of Investigation, or a Federal agency having responsibility for the investigation of the offense as to which the application is made, when such interception may provide or has provided evidence of—

(a) any offense punishable by death or by imprisonment for more than one year under sections 2274 through 2277 of title 42 of the United States Code (relating to the enforcement of the Atomic Energy Act of 1954), or under the following chapters of this title: chapter 37 (relating to espionage), chapter 105 (relating to sabotage), chapter 115 (relating to treason), or chapter 102 (relating to riots);

(b) a violation of section 186 or section 501(c) of title 29, United States Code (dealing with restrictions on payments and loans to labor organizations), or any offense which involves murder, kidnapping, robbery, or extortion, and which is punishable under this title;

(c) any offense which is punishable under the following sections of this title: section 201 (bribery of public officials and witnesses), section 224 (bribery in sporting contests), subsection (d), (e), (f), (g), (h) or (i) of section 844 (unlawful use of explosives), section 1084 (transmission of wagering information), section 1503 (influencing or injuring an officer, juror, or witness generally), section 1510 (obstruction of criminal investigations), section 1511 (obstruction of State or local law enforcement), section 1751 (Presidential assassinations, kidnapping, and assault), section 1951 (interference with commerce by threats or violence), section 1952 (interstate and foreign travel or transportation in aid of racketeering enterprises), section 1954 (offer, acceptance, or solicitation to influence operations of employee benefit plan), section 1955 (prohibition of business enterprises of gambling), section 659 (theft from interstate shipment), section 664 (embezzlement from pension and welfare funds), sections 2314 and 2315 (interstate transportation of stolen property), section 1963 (violations with respect to racketeer influenced and corrupt organizations or section 351 (violations with respect to congressional assassination, kidnapping and assault);

(d) any offense involving counterfeiting punishable under section 471, 472, or 473 or this title;

(e) any offense involving bankruptcy fraud or the manufacture, importation, receiving, concealment, buying, selling, or otherwise dealing in narcotic drugs, marihuana, or other dangerous drugs, punishable under any law of the United States;

(f) any offense including extortionate credit transactions under sections 892, 893, or 894 of this title; or

(g) any conspiracy to commit any of the foregoing offenses.

(2) The principal prosecuting attorney of any State, or the principal prosecuting attorney of any political subdivision thereof, if such attorney is authorized by a statute of that State to make application to a State court judge of competent jurisdiction for an order authorizing or approving the interception of wire or oral communications, may apply to such judge for, and such judge may grant in conformity with section 2518 of this chapter and with the applicable State statute an order authorizing, or approving the interception of wire or oral communications by investigative or law enforcement officers having responsibility for the investigation of the offense as to which the application is made, when such interception may

provide or has provided evidence of the commission of the offense of murder, kidnapping, gambling, robbery bribery, extortion, or dealing in narcotic drugs, marihuana or other dangerous drugs, or other crime dangerous to life, limb, or property, and punishable by imprisonment for more than one year, designated in any applicable State statute authorizing such interception, or any conspiracy to commit any of the foregoing offenses.

Added Pub.L. 90-351, Title III, § 802, June 19, 1968, 82 Stat. 216. As amended Pub.L. 91-452, Title VIII, § 810, Title IX, § 902(a), Title XI, § 1103, Oct. 15, 1970, 84 Stat. 940, 947, 959; Pub.L. 91-644, Title IV, § 16, Jan. 2, 1971, 84 Stat. 1891.

18 U.S.C. §2517

Authorization for Disclosure and Use of Intercepted Wire or Oral Communications

(1) Any investigative or law enforcement officer who, by any means authorizedby this chapter, has obtained knowledge of the contents of any wire or oral communication, or evidence derived therefrom, may disclose such contents to another investigative or law enforcement officer to the extent that such disclosure is appropriate to the proper performance of the official duties of the officer making or receiving the disclosure.

(2) Any investigative or law enforcement officer who, by any means authorized by this chapter, has obtained knowledge of the contents of any wire or oral communication or evidence derived therefrom may use such contents to the extent such use is appropriate to the proper performance of his official duties.

(3) Any person who has received, by any means authorized by this chapter, any information concerning a wire or oral communication, or evidence derived therefrom intercepted in accordance with the provisions of this chapter may disclose the contents of that communication or such derivative evidence while giving testimony under oath or affirmation in any proceeding held under the authority of the United States or of any State or political subdivision thereof.

(4) No otherwise privileged wire or oral communication intercepted in accordance with, or in violation of, the provisions of this chapter shall lose its privileged character.

(5) When an investigative or law enforcement officer, while engaged in intercepting wire or oral communications in the manner authorized herein, intercepts wire or oral communications relating to offenses other than those specified in the order of authorization or approval, the contents thereof, and evidence derived therefrom, may be disclosed or used as provided in subsections (1) and (2) of this section. Such contents and any evidence derived therefrom may be used under subsection (3) of this section when authorized or approved by a judge of competent jurisdiction where such judge finds on subsequent application that the contents were otherwise intercepted in accordance with the provisions of this chapter. Such application shall be made as soon as practicable.

Added Pub.L. 90-351, Title III, § 802, June 19, 1968, 82 Stat. 217. As amended Pub.L. 91-452, Title IX, § 902(b), Oct. 15, 1970, 84 Stat. 947.

18 U.S.C. §2518

Procedure for Interception of Wire or Oral Communications

(1) Each application for an order authorizing or approving the interception of a wire or oral communication shall be made in writing upon oath or affirmation to a judge of competent jurisdiction and shall state the applicant's authority to make such application. Each application shall include the following information:

(a) the identity of the investigative or law enforcement officer making the application, and the officer authorizing the application;

(b) a full and complete statement of the facts and circumstances relied upon by the applicant, to justify his belief that an order should be issued, including (i) details as to the particular offense that has been, is being, or is about to be committed, (ii) a particular description of the nature and location of the facilities from which or the place where the communication is to be intercepted, (iii) a particular description of the type of communications sought to be intercepted, (iv) the identity of the person, if known, committing the offense and whose communications are to be intercepted;

(c) a full and complete statement as to whether or not other investigative procedures have been tried and failed or why they reasonably appear to be unlikely to succeed if tried or to be too dangerous;

(d) a statement of the period of time for which the interception is required to be maintained. If the nature of the investigation is such that the authorization for interception should not automatically terminate when the described type of communication has been first obtained, a particular description of facts establishing probable cause to believe that additional communications of the same type will occur thereafter;

(e) a full and complete statement of the facts concerning all previous applications known to the individual authorizing and making the application, made to any judge for authorization to intercept, or for approval of interceptions of, wire or oral communications involving any of the same persons, facilities or places specified in the application, and the action taken by the judge on each such application; and

(f) where the application is for the extension of an order, a statement setting forth the results thus far obtained from the interception, or a reasonable explanation of the failure to obtain such results.

(2) The judge may require the applicant to furnish additional testimony or documentary evidence in support of the application.

(3) Upon such application the judge may enter an ex parte order, as requested or as modified, authorizing or approving interception of wire or oral communications within the territorial jurisdiction of the court in which the judge is sitting, if the judge determines on the basis of the facts submitted by the applicant that—

(a) there is probable cause for belief that an individual is committing, has committed, or is about to commit a particular offense enumerated in section 2516 of this chapter;

(b) there is probable cause for belief that particular communications concerning that offense will be obtained through such interception;

(c) normal investigative procedures have been tried and have failed or reasonably appear to be unlikely to succeed if tried or to be too dangerous;

(d) there is probable cause for belief that the facilities from which, or the place where, the wire or oral communications are to be intercepted are being used, or are about to be used, in connection with the commission of such offense, or are leased to, listed in the name of, or commonly used by such person.

(4) Each order authorizing or approving the interception of any wire or oral communication shall specify—

(a) the identity of the person, if known, whose communications are to be intercepted;

(b) the nature and location of the communications facilities as to which, or the place where, authority to intercept is granted;

(c) a particular description of the type of communication sought to be intercepted, and a statement of the particular offense to which it relates;

(d) the identity of the agency authorized to intercept the communications, and of the person authorizing the application; and

(e) the period of time during which such interception is authorized, including a statement as to whether or not the interception shall automatically terminate when the described communication has been first obtained.

An order authorizing the interception of a wire or oral communication shall, upon request of the applicant, direct that a communication common carrier, landlord, custodian or other person shall furnish the applicant forthwith all information, facilities, and technical assistance necessary to accomplish the interception unobstrusively and with a minimum of interference with the services that such carrier, landlord, custodian, or person is according the person whose communications are to be intercepted. Any communication common carrier, landlord, custodian or other person furnishing such facilities or technical assistance shall be compensated therefor by the applicant at the prevailing rates.

(5) No order entered under this section may authorize or approve the interception of any wire or oral communication for any period longer than is necessary to achieve the objective of the authorization, nor in any event longer than thirty days. Extensions of an order may be granted, but only upon application for an extension made in accordance with subsection (1) of this section and the court making the findings required by subsection (3) of this section. The period of extension shall be no longer than the authorizing judge deems necessary to achieve the purposes for which it was granted and in no event for longer than thirty days. Every order and extension thereof shall contain a provision that the authorization to intercept shall be executed as soon as practicable, shall be conducted in such a way as to minimizc the interception of communications not otherwise subject to interception under this chapter, and must terminate upon attainment of the authorized objective, or in any event in thirty days.

(6) Whenever an order authorizing interception is entered pursuant to this chapter, the order may require reports to be made to the judge who issued the order showing what progress has been made toward achievement of the authorized objective and the need for continued interception. Such reports shall be made at such intervals as the judge may require.

(7) Notwithstanding any other provision of this chapter, any investigative or law enforcement officer, specially designated by the Attorney General or by the principal prosecuting attorney of any State or subdivision thereof acting pursuant to a statute of that State, who reasonably determines that—

(a) an emergency situation exists with respect to conspiratorial activities threatening the national security interest or to conspiratorial activities characteristic of organized crime that requires a wire or oral communication to be intercepted before an order authorizing such interception can with due diligence be obtained, and

(b) there are grounds upon which an order could be entered under this chapter to authorize such interception,

may intercept such wire or oral communication if an application for an order approving the interception is made in accordance with this section within forty-eight hours after the interception has occurred, or begins to occur. In the absence of an order, such interception shall immediately terminate when the communication sought is obtained or when the application for the order is denied, whichever is earlier. In the event such application for approval is denied, or in any other case where the interception is terminated without an order having been issued, the contents of any wire or oral communication intercepted shall be treated as having been obtained in violation of this chapter, and an inventory shall be served as provided for in subsection (d) of this section on the person named in the application.

(8) (a) The contents of any wire or oral communication intercepted by any means authorized by this chapter shall, if possible, be recorded on tape or wire or other comparable device. The recording of the contents of any wire or oral communication under this subsection shall be done in such way as will protect the recording from editing or other alterations. Immediately upon the expiration of the period of the order, or extensions thereof, such recordings shall be made available to the judge issuing such order and sealed under his directions. Custody of the recordings shall be wherever the judge orders. They shall not be destroyed except upon an order of the issuing or denying judge and in any event shall be kept for ten years. Duplicate recordings may be made for use or disclosure pursuant to the provisions of subsections (1) and (2) of section 2517 of this chapter for investigations. The presence of the seal provided for by this subsection, or a satisfactory explanation for the absence thereof, shall be a prerequisite for the use or disclosure of the contents of any wire or oral communication or evidence derived therefrom under subsection (3) of section 2517.

(b) Applications made and orders granted under this chapter shall be sealed by the judge. Custody of the applications and orders shall be wherever the judge directs. Such applications and orders shall be disclosed only upon a showing of good cause before a judge of competent jurisdiction and shall not be destroyed except on order of the issuing or denying judge, and in any event shall be kept for ten years.

(c) Any violation of the provisions of this subsection may be punished as contempt of the issuing or denying judge.

(d) Within a reasonable time but not later than ninety days after the filing of an application for an order of approval under section 2518(7)(b) which is denied or the termination of the period of an order or extensions thereof, the issuing or denying judge shall cause to be served, on the persons named in the order or the application, and such other parties to intercepted communications as the judge may determine in his discretion that is in the interest of justice, an inventory which shall include notice of—

(1) the fact of the entry of the order or the application;

(2) the date of the entry and the period of authorized, approved or disapproved interception, or the denial of the application; and

(3) the fact that during the period wire or oral communications were or were not intercepted.

The judge, upon the filing of a motion, may in his discretion make available to such person or his counsel for inspection such portions of the intercepted communications, applications and orders as the judge determines to be in the interest of justice. On an ex parte showing of good cause to a judge of competent jurisdiction the serving of the inventory required by this subsection may be postponed.

(9) The contents of any intercepted wire or oral communication or evidence derived therefrom shall not be received in evidence or otherwise disclosed in any trial, hearing, or other proceeding in a Federal or State court unless each party, not less than ten days before the trial, hearing, or proceeding, has been furnished with a copy of the court order, and accompanying application, under which the interception was authorized or approved. This ten-day period may be waived by the judge if he finds that it was not possible to furnish the party with the above information ten days before the trial, hearing, or proceeding and that the party will not be prejudiced by the delay in receiving such information.

(10) (a) Any aggrieved person in any trial, hearing, or proceeding in or before any court, department, officer, agency, regulatory body, or other authority of the United States, a State, or a political subdivision thereof, may move to suppress the contents of any intercepted wire or oral communication, or evidence derived therefrom, on the grounds that—

(i) the communication was unlawfully intercepted;

(ii) the order of authorization or approval under which it was intercepted is insufficient on its face; or

(iii) the interception was not made in conformity with the order of authorization or approval.

Such motion shall be made before the trial, hearing, or proceeding unless there was no opportunity to make such motion or the person was not aware of the grounds of the motion. If the motion is granted, the contents of the intercepted wire or oral communication, or evidence derived therefrom, shall be treated as having been obtained in violation of this chapter. The judge, upon the filing of such motion by the aggrieved person may in his discretion make available to the aggrieved person or his counsel for inspection such portions of the intercepted communication or evidence derived therefrom as the judge determines to be in the interests of justice.

(b) In addition to any other right to appeal, the United States shall have the right to appeal from an order granting a motion to suppress made under paragraph (a) of this subsection, or the denial of an application for an order of approval, if the United States attorney shall certify to the judge or other official granting such motion or denying such application that the appeal is not taken for purposes of delay. Such appeal shall be taken within thirty days after the date the order was entered and shall be diligently prosecuted.

Added Pub.L. 90-351, Title III, § 802, June 19, 1968, 82 Stat. 218. As amended Pub.L. 91-358, Title II, § 211(b), July 29, 1970, 84 Stat. 654.

18 U.S.C. §2519

Reports Concerning Intercepted Wire or Oral Communications

(1) Within thirty days after the expiration of an order (or each extension thereof)

entered under section 2518, or the denial of an order approving an interception, the issuing or denying judge shall report to the Administrative Officer of the United States Courts—

(a) the fact that an order or extension was applied for;

(b) the kind of order or extension applied for;

(c) the fact that the order or extension was granted as applied for, was modified, or was denied;

(d) the period of interceptions authorized by the order, and the number and duration of any extensions of the order;

(e) the offense specified in the order or application, or extension of an order;

(f) the identity of the applying investigative or law enforcement officer and agency making the application and the person authorizing the application; and

(g) the nature of the facilities from which or the place where communications were to be intercepted.

(2) In January of each year the Attorney General, an Assistant Attorney General specially designated by the Attorney General, or the principal prosecuting attorney of a State, or the principal prosecuting attorney for any political subdivision of a State, shall report to the Administrative Office of the United States Courts—

(a) the information required by paragraphs (a) through (g) of subsection (1) of this section with respect to each application for an order or extension made during the preceding calendar year;

(b) a general description of the interceptions made under such order or extension, including (i) the approximate nature and frequency of incriminating communications intercepted, (ii) the approximate nature and frequency of other communications intercepted, (iii) the approximate number of persons whose communications were intercepted, and (iv) the approximate nature, amount, and cost of the manpower and other resources used in the interceptions;

(c) the number of arrests resulting from interceptions made under such order or extension, and the offenses for which arrests were made;

(d) the number of trials resulting from such interceptions;

(e) the number of motions to suppress made with respect to such interceptions, and the number granted or denied;

(f) the number of convictions resulting from such interceptions and the offenses for which the convictions were obtained and a general assessment of the importance of the interceptions; and

(g) the information required by paragraphs (b) through (f) of this subsection with respect to orders or extensions obtained in a preceding calendar year.

(3) In April of each year the Director of the Administrative Office of the United States Courts shall transmit to the Congress a full and complete report concerning the number of applications for orders authorizing or approving the interception of wire or oral communications and the number of orders and extensions granted or denied during the preceding calendar year. Such report shall include a summary and analysis of the data required to be filed with the Administrative Office by subsections (1) and (2) of this section. The Director of the Administrative Office of the United States Courts is authorized to issue binding regulations dealing with the

content and form of the reports required to be filed by subsections (1) and (2) of this section.

Added Pub.L. 90-351, Title III, § 802, June 19, 1968, 82 Stat. 222.

18 U.S.C. §2520

Recovery of Civil Damages Authorized

Any person whose wire or oral communication is intercepted, disclosed, or used in violation of this chapter shall (1) have a civil cause of action against any person who intercepts, discloses, or uses, or procures any other person to intercept, disclose, or use such communications, and (2) be entitled to recover from any such person—

(a) actual damages but not less than liquidated damages computed at the rate of $100 a day for each day of violation or $1,000, whichever is higher;

(b) punitive damages; and

(c) a reasonable attorney's fee and other litigation costs reasonably incurred.

A good faith reliance on a court order or legislative authorization shall constitute a complete defense to any civil or criminal action brought under this chapter or under any other law.

As amended Pub.L. 91-358, Title II, § 211(c), July 29, 1970, 84 Stat. 654.

Federal Communications Act of 1934

48 Stat. 1103

Sec. 605. No person receiving or assisting in receiving, or transmitting, or assisting in transmitting, any interstate or foreign communication by wire or radio shall divulge or publish the existence, contents, substance, purport, effect, or meaning thereof, except through authorized channels of transmission or reception, to any person other than the addressee, his agent, or attorney, or to a person employed or authorized to forward such communication to its destination, or to proper accounting or distributing officers of the various communicating centers over which the communication may be passed, or to the master of a ship under whom he is serving, or in response to a subpena issued by a court of competent jurisdiction, or on demand of other lawful authority; and no person not being authorized by the sender shall intercept any communication and divulge or publish the existence, contents, substance, purport, effect, or meaning of such intercepted communication to any person; and no person not being entitled thereto shall receive or assist in receiving any interstate or foreign communication by wire or radio and use the same or any information therein contained for his own benefit or for the benefit of another not entitled thereto; and no person having received such intercepted communication or having become acquainted with the contents, substance, purport, effect, or meaning of the same or any part thereof, knowing that such information was so obtained, shall divulge or publish the existence, contents, substance, purport, effect, or meaning of the same or any part thereof, or use the same or any information therein contained for his own benefit or for the benefit of another not entitled thereto: *Provided,* That this section shall not apply to the receiving, divulging, publishing, or utilizing the contents of any radio communication broadcast, or transmitted by amateurs or others for the use of the general public, or relating to ships in distress.

United States Foreign Intelligence Activities

Executive Order 11905
41 Federal Register 7703 (1976)

By virtue of the authority vested in me by the Constitution and statutes of the United States, including the National Security Act of 1947, as amended, and as President of the United States of America, it is hereby ordered as follows:

Section 1. *Purpose.* The purpose of this Order is to establish policies to improve the quality of intelligence needed for national security, to clarify the authority and responsibilities of the intelligence departments and agencies, and to establish effective oversight to assure compliance with law in the management and direction of intelligence agencies and departments of the national government.

Sec. 2. *Definitions.* For the purpose of this Order, unless otherwise indicated, the following terms shall have these meanings:

(a) *Intelligence* means:

(1) *Foreign intelligence* which means information, other than foreign counterintelligence, on the capabilities, intentions and activities of foreign powers, organizations or their agents; and

(2) *Foreign counterintelligence* which means activities conducted to protect the United States and United States citizens from foreign espionage, sabotage, subversion, assassination or terrorism.

(b) *Intelligence Community* refers to the following organizations:

(1) Central Intelligence Agency;

(2) National Security Agency;

(3) Defense Intelligence Agency;

(4) Special offices within the Department of Defense for the collection of specialized intelligence through reconnaissance programs;

(5) Intelligence elements of the military services;

(6) Intelligence element of the Federal Bureau of Investigation;

(7) Intelligence element of the Department of State;

(8) Intelligence element of the Department of the Treasury; and

(9) Intelligence element of the Energy Research and Development Administration.

(c) *Special activities in support of national foreign policy objectives* means activities, other than the collection and production of intelligence and related support functions, designed to further official United States programs and policies abroad which are planned and executed so that the role of the United States Government is not apparent or publicly acknowledged.

(d) *National Foreign Intelligence Program* means the programs of the Central Intelligence Agency and the special offices within the Department of Defense for the collection of specialized intelligence through reconnaissance programs, the Consolidated Cryptologic Program, and those elements of the General Defense Intelligence Program and other programs of the departments and agencies, not including tactical intelligence, designated by the Committee on Foreign Intelligence as part of the Program.

Sec. 3. *Control and Direction of National Intelligence Organizations.*

(a) *National Security Council.*

(1) The National Security Council was established by the National Security Act of 1947 to advise the President with respect to the integration of domestic, foreign, and military policies relating to the national security. Statutory members of the National Security Council are the President, the Vice President, the Secretary of State, and the Secretary of Defense.

(2) Among its responsibilities, the National Security Council shall provide guidance and direction to the development and formulation of national intelligence activities.

(3) The National Security Council shall conduct a semi-annual review of intelligence policies and of ongoing special activities in support of national Foreign policy objectives. These reviews shall consider the needs of users of intelligence and the timeliness and quality of intelligence products and the continued appropriateness of special activities in support of national Foreign policy objectives. The National Security Council shall consult with the Secretary of the Treasury and such other users of intelligence as designated by the President as part of these reviews.

(b) *Committee on Foreign Intelligence.*

(1) There is established the Committee on Foreign Intelligence (hereinafter referred to as the CFI), which shall be composed of the Director of Central Intelligence, hereinafter referred to as the DCI, who shall be the Chairman; the Deputy Secretary of Defense for Intelligence; and the Deputy Assistant to the President for National Security Affairs. The CFI shall report directly to the National Security Council.

(2) The CFI shall (i) control budget preparation and resource allocation for the National Foreign Intelligence Program.

(A) The CFI shall, prior to submission to the office of Management and Budget, review, and amend as it deems appropriate, the budget for the National Foreign Intelligence Program.

(B) The CFI shall also adopt rules governing the reprogramming of funds within this budget. Such rules may require that reprogrammings of certain types or amounts be given prior approval by the CFI.

(ii) Establish policy priorities for the collection and production of national intelligence.

(iii) Establish policy for the management of the National Foreign Intelligence Program.

(iv) Provide guidance on the relationship between tactical and national intelligence, however, neither the DCI nor the CFI shall have responsibility for tactical intelligence.

(v) Provide continuing guidance to the Intelligence Community in order to ensure compliance with policy directions of the NSC.

(3) The CFI shall be supported by the Intelligence Community staff headed by the Deputy to the Director of Central Intelligence for the Intelligence Community.

(4) The CFI shall establish such subcommittees as it deems appropriate to ensure consultation with members of the Intelligence Community on policies and guidance issued by the CFI.

(5) Decisions of the CFI may be reviewed by the National Security Council upon appeal by the Director of Central Intelligence or any member of the National Security Council.

(c) *The Operations Advisory Group.*

(1) There is established the Operations Advisory Group (hereinafter referred to as the Operations Group), which shall be composed of the Assistant to the President for National Security Affairs; the Secretaries of State and Defense; the Chairman of the Joint Chiefs of Staff; and the Director of Central Intelligence. The Chairman shall be designed by the President. The Attorney General and the Director of the Office of Management and Budget or their representatives, and others who may be designated by the President, shall attend all meetings as observers.

(2) The Operations Group shall (i) consider and develop a policy recommendation, including any dissents, for the President prior to his decision on each special activity in support of national foreign policy objectives.

(ii) Conduct periodic reviews of programs previously considered by the Operations Group.

(iii) Give approval for specific sensitive intelligence collection operations as designed by the Operations Group.

(iv) Conduct periodic reviews of ongoing sensitive intelligence collection operations.

(3) The Operations Group shall discharge the responsibilities assigned by subparagraphs (c) (2) (i) and (c) (2) (iii) of this section only after consideration in a formal meeting attended by all members and observers; or, in unusual circumstances when any member or observer is unavailable, when a designated representative of the member or observer attends.

(4) The staff of the National Security Council shall provide support to the Operations Group.

(d) *Director of Central Intelligence.*

(1) The Director of Central Intelligence, pursuant to the National Security Act of 1947, shall be responsible directly to the National Security Council and the President. He shall:

(i) Chair the CFI.

(ii) Act as executive head of the CIA and Intelligence Community staff.

(iii) Ensure the development and submission of a budget for the National Foreign Intelligence Program to the CFI.

(iv) Act as the President's primary adviser on foreign intelligence and provide him and other officials in the Executive branch with foreign intelligence, including National Intelligence Estimates; develop national intelligence requirements and priorities; and supervise production and dissemination of national intelligence.

(v) Ensure appropriate implementation of special activities in support of national foreign policy objectives.

(vi) Establish procedures to ensure the propriety of requests, and responses thereto, from the White House Staff or other Executive departments and agencies to the Intelligence Community.

(vii) Ensure that appropriate programs are developed which properly protect intelligence sources, methods and analytical procedures. His responsibility within the United States shall be limited to:

(A) Protection by lawful means against disclosure by present or former employees of the Central Intelligence Agency or persons, or employees of persons or organizations, presently or formerly under contract with the Agency;

(B) providing leadership, guidance and technical assistance to other government departments and agencies performing foreign intelligence activities; and

(C) in cases involving serious or continuing security violations, recommending to the Attorney General that the case be referred to the Federal Bureau of Investigation for further investigation.

(viii) Establish a vigorous program to downgrade and declassify foreign intelligence information as appropriate and consistent with Executive Order No. 11652.

(ix) Ensure the existence of strong Inspector General capabilities in all elements of the Intelligence Community and that each Inspector General submits quarterly to the Intelligence Oversight Board a report which sets forth any questionable activities in which that intelligence organization has engaged or is engaged.

(x) Ensure the establishment, by the Intelligence Community, of common security standards for managing and handling foreign intelligence systems, information and products, and for granting access thereto.

(xi) Act as the principal spokesman to the Congress for the Intelligence Community and facilitate the use of foreign intelligence products by Congress.

(xii) Promote the development and maintenance by the Central Intelligence Agency of services of common concern to the Intelligence Community organizations, including multi-discipline analysis, national level intelligence products, and a national level current intelligence publication.

(xiii) Establish uniform criteria for the identification, selection, and designation of relative priorities for the transmission of critical intelligence, and provide the Secretary of Defense with continuing guidance as to the communications requirements of the Intelligence Community for the transmission of such intelligence.

(xiv) Establish such committees of collectors, producers and users of intelligence to assist in his conduct of his responsibilities as he deems appropriate.

(xv) Consult with users and producers of intelligence, including the Departments of State, Treasury, and Defense, the military services, the Federal Bureau of Investigation, the Energy Research and Development Administration, and the Council of Economic Advisors, to ensure the timeliness, relevancy and quality of the intelligence product.

(2) To assist the Director of Central Intelligence in the supervision and direction of the Intelligence Community, the position of Deputy to the Director of Central Intelligence for the Intelligence Community is hereby established (Committee on Foreign Intelligence).

(3) To assist the Director of Central Intelligence in the supervision and direction of the Central Intelligence Agency, the Director of Central Intelligence shall, to the extent consistent with his statutory responsibilities, delegate the day-to-day operation of the Central Intelligence Agency to the Deputy Director of Central Intelligence (50 U.S.C. 403(a)).

(4) To assist the DCI in the fulfillment of his responsibilities, the heads of all departments and agencies shall give him access to all information relevant to the foreign intelligence needs of the United States. Relevant information requested by

the DCI shall be provided, and the DCI shall take appropriate steps to maintain its confidentiality.

Sec. 4. *Responsibilities and Duties of the Intelligence Community. Purpose.* The rules of operation prescribed by this section of the Order relate to the activities of our foreign intelligence agencies. In some instances, detailed implementation of this Executive Order will be contained in classified documents because of the sensitivity of the information and its relation to national security. All such classified instructions will be consistent with this Order. Unless otherwise specified within this section, its provisions apply to activities both inside and outside the United States, and all references to law are to applicable laws of the United States. Nothing in this section of this Order shall be construed to interfere with any law-enforcement responsibility of any department or agency.

(a) *Senior Officials of the Intelligence Community.* The senior officials of the CIA, Departments of State, Treasury and Defense, ERDA and the FBI shall ensure that, in discharging the duties and responsibilities enumerated for their organizations which relate to foreign intelligence, they are responsive to the needs of the President, the National Security Council and other elements of the Government. In carrying out their duties and responsibilities, senior officials shall ensure that all policies and directives relating to intelligence activities are carried out in accordance with law and this Order, including Section 5, and shall:

(1) Make appropriate use of the capabilities of the other elements of the Intelligence Community in order to achieve maximum efficiency.

(2) Contribute in areas of his responsibility to the national intelligence products produced under auspices of the Director of Central Intelligence.

(3) Establish internal policies and guidelines governing employee conduct and ensuring that such are made known to, and acknowledged by, each employee.

(4) Provide for a strong and independent organization for identification and inspection of, and reporting on, unauthorized activity.

(5) Report to the Attorney General that information which relates to detection or prevention of possible violations of law by any person, including an employee of the senior official's department or agency.

(6) Furnish to the Director of Central Intelligence, the CFI, the Operations Group, the President's Foreign Intelligence Advisory Board, and the Intelligence Oversight Board all of the information required for the performance of their respective duties.

(7) Participate, as appropriate, in the provision of services of common concern as directed by the Director of Central Intelligence and provide other departments and agencies with such mutual assistance as may be within his capabilities and as may be required in the interests of the Intelligence Community for reasons of economy, effectiveness, or operational necessity.

(8) Protect intelligence and intelligence sources and methods within his department or agency, consistent with policies and guidance of the Director of Central Intelligence.

(9) Conduct a continuing review of all classified material originating within his organization and promptly declassifying such material consistent with Executive Order No. 11652, as amended.

(10) Provide administrative and support functions required by his department or agency.

(b) *The Central Intelligence Agency.* All duties and responsibilities of the Central Intelligence Agency shall be related to the foreign intelligence functions outlined below. As authorized by the National Security Act of 1947, as amended, the CIA Act of 1949, as amended, and other laws, regulations, and directives, the Central Intelligence Agency shall:

(1) Produce and disseminate foreign intelligence relating to the national security, including foreign political, economic, scientific, technical, military, sociological, and geographic intelligence, to meet the needs of the President, the National Security Council, and other elements of the United States Government.

(2) Develop and conduct programs to collect political, economic, scientific, technical, military, geographic, and sociological information, not otherwise obtainable, relating to foreign intelligence, in accordance with directives of the National Security Council.

(3) Collect and produce intelligence on foreign aspects of international terrorist activities and traffic in narcotics.

(4) Conduct foreign counterintelligence activities outside the United States and when in the United States in coordination with the FBI subject to the approval of the Attorney General.

(5) Carry out such other special activities in support of national foreign policy objectives as may be directed by the President or the National Security Council and which are within the limits of applicable law.

(6) Conduct, for the Intelligence Community, services of common concern as directed by the National Security Council, such as monitoring of foreign public radio and television broadcasts and foreign press services, collection of foreign intelligence information from cooperating sources in the United States, acquisition and translation of foreign publications and photographic interpretation.

(7) Carry out or contract for research, development and procurement of technical systems and devices relating to the functions authorized in this subsection.

(8) Protect the security of its installations, activities, information and personnel. In order to maintain this security, the CIA shall conduct such investigations of applicants, employees, and other persons with similar associations with the CIA as are necessary.

(9) Conduct administrative, technical and support activities in the United States or abroad as may be necessary to perform the functions described in paragraphs (1) through (8) above, including procurement, maintenance and transport; communications and data processing; recruitment and training; the provision of personnel, financial and medical services; development of essential cover and proprietary arrangements; entering into contracts and arrangements with appropriate private companies and institutions to provide classified or unclassified research, analytical and developmental services and specialized expertise; and entering into similar arrangements with academic institutions, *provided* CIA sponsorship is known to the appropriate senior officials of the academic institutions and to senior project officials.

(c) *The Department of State.* The Secretary of State shall:

(1) Collect, overtly, foreign political, political-military, sociological, economic, scientific, technical and associated biographic information.

(2) Produce and disseminate foreign intelligence relating to United States foreign policy as required for the execution of his responsibilities and in support of policy-makers involved in foreign relations within the United States Government.

(3) Disseminate within the United States Government, as appropriate, reports received from United States diplomatic missions abroad.

(4) Coordinate with the Director of Central Intelligence to ensure that United

States intelligence activities and programs are useful for and consistent with United States foreign policy.

(5) Transmit reporting requirements of the Intelligence Community to our Chiefs of Missions abroad and provide guidance for their collection effort.

(6) Contribute to the Intelligence Community guidance for its collection of intelligence based on the needs of those responsible for foreign policy decisions.

(7) Support Chiefs of Missions in discharging their responsibilities to direct and coordinate the activities of all elements of their missions.

(d) *The Department of the Treasury.* The Secretary of the Treasury shall:

(1) Collect, overtly, foreign financial and monetary information.

(2) Participate with the Department of State in the overt collection of general foreign economic information.

(3) Produce that intelligence required for the execution of the Secretary's interdepartmental responsibilities and the mission of the Department of the Treasury.

(4) Contribute intelligence and guidance required for the development of national intelligence.

(5) Disseminate within the United States Government, as appropriate, foreign intelligence information acquired.

(e) *Department of Defense.*

(1) The Secretary of Defense shall:

(i) Collect foreign military intelligence information as well as military-related foreign intelligence information, including scientific, technical, political and economic information as required for the execution of his responsibilities.

(ii) Produce and disseminate, as appropriate, intelligence emphasizing foreign military capabilities and intentions and scientific, technical and economic developments pertinent to his responsibilities.

(iii) Conduct such programs and missions necessary to fulfill national intelligence requirements as determined by the CFI.

(iv) Direct, fund and operate the National Security Agency, and national, defense and military intelligence and reconnaissance entities as required.

(v) Conduct, as the executive agent of the United States Government, signals intelligence activities and communications security, except as otherwise approved by the CFI.

(vi) Provide for the timely transmission of critical intelligence, as defined by the Director of Central Intelligence, within the United States Government.

(2) In carrying out these assigned responsibilities, the Secretary of Defense is authorized to utilize the following:

(i) The Defense Intelligence Agency (whose functions, authorities and responsibilities are currently publicly assigned by Department of Defense Directive No. 5105.21) to:

(A) Produce or provide military intelligence for the Secretary of Defense, the Joint Chiefs of Staff, other Defense components, and, as appropriate, non-Defense agencies.

(B) Coordinate all Department of Defense intelligence collection requirements and manage the Defense Attache system.

(C) Establish substantive intelligence priority goals and objectives for the Department of Defense and provide guidance on substantive intelligence matters to all major Defense intelligence activities.

(D) Review and maintain cognizance over all plans, policies and procedures for noncryptologic intelligence functions of the Department of Defense.

(E) Provide intelligence staff support as directed by the Joint Chiefs of Staff.

(ii) The National Security Agency, whose functions, authorities and responsibilities shall include:

(A) Establishment and operation of an effective unified organization for the signals intelligence activities of the United States Government, except for certain operations which are normally exercised through appropriate elements of the military command structure, or by the CIA.

(B) Exercise control over signals intelligence collection and processing activities of the Government, delegating to an appropriate agent specified resources for such periods and tasks as required for the direct support of military commanders.

(C) Collection, processing and dissemination of signals intelligence in accordance with objectives, requirements, and priorities established by the Director of Central Intelligence.

(D) Dissemination of signals intelligence to all authorized elements of the Government, including the Armed Services, as requested.

(E) Serving under the Secretary of Defense as the central communications security authority of the United States Government.

(F) Conduct of research and development to meet the needs of the United States for signals intelligence and communications security.

(iii) Special offices for the collection of specialized intelligence through reconnaissance programs, whose functions, authorities, and responsibilities shall include:

(A) Carrying out consolidated programs for reconnaissance.

(B) Assigning responsibility to the various departments and agencies of the Government, according to their capabilities, for the research, development, procurement, operations and control of designated means of collection.

(iv) Such other offices within the Department of Defense as shall be deemed appropriate for conduct of the intelligence missions and responsibilities assigned to the Secretary of Defense.

(f) *Energy Research and Development Administration.* The Administrator of the Energy Research and Development Administration shall:

(1) Produce intelligence required for the execution of his responsibilities and the mission of the Energy Research and Development Administration, hereinafter referred to as ERDA, including the area of nuclear and atomic energy.

(2) Disseminate such intelligence and provide technical and analytical expertise to other Intelligence Community organizations and be responsive to the guidance of the Director of Central Intelligence and the Committee on Foreign Intelligence.

(3) Participate with other Intelligence Community agencies and departments in formulating collection requirements where its special technical expertise can contribute to such collection requirements.

(g) *The Federal Bureau of Investigation.* Under the supervision of the Attorney General and pursuant to such regulations as the Attorney General may establish, the Director of the FBI shall:

(1) Detect and prevent espionage, sabotage, subversion, and other unlawful activities by or on behalf of foreign powers through such lawful counterintelligence operations within the United States, including electronic surveillance, as are necessary or useful for such purposes.

(2) Conduct within the United States and its territories, when requested by officials of the Intelligence Community designated by the President, those lawful activities, including electronic surveillance, authorized by the President and specifically approved by the Attorney General, to be undertaken in support of foreign intelligence collection requirements of other intelligence agencies.

(3) Collect foreign intelligence by lawful means within the United States and its

territories when requested by officials of the Intelligence Community designated by the President to make such requests.

(4) Disseminate, as appropriate, foreign intelligence and counterintelligence information which it acquires to appropriate Federal agencies, State and local law enforcement agencies and cooperating foreign governments.

(5) Carry out or contract for research, development and procurement of technical systems and devices relating to the functions authorized above.

Sec. 5. *Restrictions on Intelligence Activities.* Information about the capabilities, intentions and activities of other governments is essential to informed decision-making in the field of national defense and foreign relations. The measures employed to acquire such information should be responsive to the legitimate needs of our Government and must be conducted in a manner which preserves and respects our established concepts of privacy and our civil liberties.

Recent events have clearly indicated the desirability of government-wide direction which will ensure a proper balancing of these interests. This section of this Order does not authorize any activity not previously authorized and does not provide exemption from any restrictions otherwise applicable. Unless otherwise specified, the provisions of this section apply to activities both inside and outside the United States. References to law are to applicable laws of the United States.

(a) *Definitions.* As used in this section of this Order, the following terms shall have the meanings ascribed to them below:

(1) "Collection" means any one or more of the gathering, analysis, dissemination or storage of non-publicly available information without the informed express consent of the subject of the information.

(2) "Counterintelligence" means information concerning the protection of foreign intelligence or of national security information and its collection from detection or disclosure.

(3) "Electronic surveillance" means acquisition of a non-public communication by electronic means, without the consent of a person who is a party to, or, in the case of a non-electronic communication, visibly present at, the communication.

(4) "Employee" means a person employed by, assigned or detailed to, or acting for a United States foreign intelligence agency.

(5) "Foreign intelligence" means information concerning the capabilities, intentions and activities of any foreign power, or of any non-United States person, whether within or outside the Unites States, or concerning areas outside the United States.

(6) "Foreign intelligence agency" means the Central Intelligence Agency, National Security Agency, and Defense Intelligence Agency; and further includes any other department or agency of the United States Government or component thereof while it is engaged in the collection of foreign intelligence or counterintelligence, but shall not include any such department, agency or component thereof to the extent that it is engaged in its authorized civil or criminal law enforcement functions; nor shall it include in any case the Federal Bureau of Investigation.

(7) "National security information" has the meaning ascribed to it in Executive Order No. 11652, as amended.

(8) "Physical surveillance" means continuing visual observation by any means; or acquisition of a non-public communication by a person not a party thereto or visibly present threat through any means which does not involve electronic surveillance.

(9) "United States person" means United States citizens, aliens admitted to the United States for permanent residence and corporations or other organizations incorporated or organized in the United States.

(b) *Restrictions on Collection.* Foreign intelligence agencies shall not engage in any of the following activities:

(1) Physical surveillance directed against a United States person, unless it is a lawful surveillance conducted pursuant to procedures approved by the head of the foreign intelligence agency and directed against any of the following:

(i) A present or former employee of such agency, its present or former contractors or their present or former employees, for the purpose of protecting foreign intelligence or counterintelligence sources or methods or national security information from unauthorized disclosure; or

(ii) a United States person, who is in contact with either such a present or former contractor or employee or with a non-United States person who is the subject of a foreign intelligence or counterintelligence inquiry, but only to the extent necessary to identify such United States person; or

(iii) a United States person outside the United States who is reasonably believed to be acting on behalf of a foreign power or engaging in international terrorist or narcotics activities or activities threatening the national security.

(2) Electronic surveillance to intercept a communication which is made from, or is intended by the sender to be received in, the United States, or directed against United States persons abroad, except lawful electronic surveillance under procedures approved by the Attorney General; *provided,* that the Central Intelligence Agency shall not perform electronic surveillance within the United States, except for the purpose of testing equipment under procedures approved by the Attorney General consistent with law.

(3) Unconsented physical searches within the United States; or unconsented physical searches directed against United States persons abroad, except lawful searches under procedures approved by the Attorney General.

(4) Opening of mail or examination of envelopes of mail in United States postal channels except in accordance with applicable statutes and regulations.

(5) Examination of Federal tax returns or tax information except in accordance with applicable statutes and regulations.

(6) Infiltration or undisclosed participation within the United States in any organization for the purpose of reporting on or influencing its activities or members; except such infiltration or participation with respect to an organization composed primarily of non-United States persons which is reasonably believed to be acting on behalf of a foreign power.

(7) Collection of information, however acquired, concerning the domestic activities of United States persons except:

(i) Information concerning corporations or other commercial organizations which constitutes foreign intelligence or counterintelligence.

(ii) Information concerning present or former employees, present or former contractors or their present or former employees, or applicants for any such employment or contracting, necessary to protect foreign intelligence or counterintelligence sources or methods or national security information from unauthorized disclosure; and the identity of persons in contact with the foregoing or with a non-United States person who is the subject of a foreign intelligence or counterintelligence inquiry.

(iii) Information concerning persons who are reasonably believed to be potential sources or contacts, but only for the purpose of determining the suitability or credibility of such persons.

(iv) Foreign intelligence or counterintelligence gathered abroad or from electronic surveillance conducted in compliance with Section 5(b) (2); or foreign intelligence acquired from cooperating sources in the United States.

(v) Information about a United States person who is reasonably believed to be acting on behalf of a foreign power or engaging in international terrorist or narcotics activities.

(vi) Information concerning persons or activities that pose a clear threat to foreign intelligence agency facilities or personnel, *provided,* that such information is retained only by the foreign intelligence agency threatened and that proper coordination with the Federal Bureau of Investigation is accomplished.

(c) *Dissemination and Storage.* Nothing in this section of this Order shall prohibit:

(1) Lawful dissemination to the appropriate law enforcement agencies of incidentally gathered information indicating involvement in activities which may be in violation of law.

(2) Storage of information required by law to be retained.

(3) Dissemination to foreign intelligence agencies of information of the subject matter types listed in Section 5(b) (7).

(d) *Restrictions on Experimentation.* Foreign intelligence agencies shall not engage in experimentation with drugs on human subjects, except with the informed consent, in writing and witnessed by a disinterested third party, of each such human subject and in accordance with the guidelines issued by the National Commission for the Protection of Human Subjects for Biomedical and Behavioral Research.

(e) *Assistance to Law Enforcement Authorities.*

(1) No foreign intelligence agency shall, except as expressly authorized by law (i) provide services, equipment, personnel or facilities to the Law Enforcement Assistance Administration or to State or local police organizations of the United States or (ii) participate in or fund any law enforcement activity within the United States.

(2) These prohibitions shall not, however, preclude: (i) cooperation between a foreign intelligence agency and appropriate law enforcement agencies for the purpose of protecting the personnel and facilities of the foreign intelligence agency or preventing espionage or other criminal activity related to foreign intelligence or counterintelligence or (ii) provision of specialized equipment or technical knowledge for use by any other Federal department or agency.

(f) *Assignment of Personnel.* An employee of a foreign intelligence agency detailed elsewhere within the Federal Government shall be responsible to the host agency and shall not report to such employee's parent agency on the affairs of the host agency, except as may be directed by the latter. The head of the host agency, and any successor, shall be informed of the detailee's association with the parent agency.

(g) *Prohibition of Assassination.* No employee of the United States Government shall engage in, or conspire to engage in, political assassination.

(h) *Implementation.*

(1) This section of this Order shall be effective on March 1, 1976. Each department and agency affected by this section of this Order shall promptly issue internal

directives to implement this section with respect to its foreign intelligence and counterintelligence operations.

(2) The Attorney General shall, within ninety days of the effective date of this section of this Order, issue guidelines relating to activities of the Federal Bureau of Investigation in the areas of foreign intelligence and counterintelligence.

Sec. 6. *Oversight of Intelligence Organizations.*

(a) There is hereby established an Intelligence Oversight Board, hereinafter referred to as the Oversight Board.

(1) The Oversight Board shall have three members who shall be appointed by the President and who shall be from outside the Government and be qualified on the basis of ability, knowledge, diversity of background and experience. The members of the Oversight Board may also serve on the President's Foreign Intelligence Advisory Board (Executive Order No. 11460 of March 20, 1969). No member of the Oversight Board shall have any personal contractual relationship with any agency or department of the Intelligence Community.

(2) One member of the Oversight Board shall be designated by the President as its Chairman.

(3) The Oversight Board shall:

(i) Receive and consider reports by Inspectors General and General Counsels of the Intelligence Community concerning activities that raise questions of legality or propriety.

(ii) Review periodically the practices and procedures of the Inspectors General and General Counsels of the Intelligence Community designed to discover and report to the Oversight Board activities that raise questions of legality or propriety.

(iii) Review periodically with each member of the Intelligence Community their internal guidelines to ensure their adequacy.

(iv) Report periodically, at least quarterly, to the Attorney General and the President on its findings.

(v) Report in a timely manner to the Attorney General and to the President any activities that raise serious questions about legality.

(vi) Report in a timely manner to the President any activities that raise serious questions about propriety.

(b) Inspectors General and General Counsels within the Intelligence Community shall:

(1) Transmit to the Oversight Board reports of any activities that come to their attention that raise questions of legality or propriety.

(2) Report periodically, at least quarterly, to the Oversight Board on its findings concerning questionable activities, if any.

(3) Provide to the Oversight Board all information requested about activities within their respective departments or agencies.

(4) Report to the Oversight Board any occasion on which they were directed not to report any activity to the Oversight Board by their agency or department heads.

(5) Formulate practices and procedures designed to discover and report to the Oversight Board activities that raise questions of legality or propriety.

(c) Heads of intelligence agencies or departments shall:

(1) Report periodically to the Oversight Board on any activities of their organizations that raise questions of legality or propriety.

(2) Instruct their employees to cooperate fully with the Oversight Board.

(3) Ensure that Inspectors General and General Counsels of their agencies have

access to any information necessary to perform their duties assigned by paragraph (4) of this section.

(d) The Attorney General shall:

(1) Receive and consider reports from the Oversight Board.

(2) Report periodically, at least quarterly, to the President with respect to activities of the Intelligence Community, if any, which raise questions of legality.

(e) The Oversight Board shall receive staff support. No person who serves on the staff of the Oversight Board shall have any contractual or employment relationship with any department or agency in the Intelligence Community.

(f) The President's Foreign Intelligence Advisory Board established by Executive Order No. 11460 of March 20, 1969, remains in effect.

Sec. 7. *Secrecy Protection.*

(a) In order to improve the protection of sources and methods of intelligence, all members of the Executive branch and its contractors given access to information containing sources or methods of intelligence shall, as a condition of obtaining access, sign an agreement that they will not disclose that information to persons not authorized to receive it.

(b) In the event of any unauthorized disclosure of information concerning sources or methods of intelligence, the names of any persons found to have made unauthorized disclosure shall be forwarded (1) to the head of applicable departments or agencies for appropriate disciplinary action; and (2) to the Attorney General for appropriate legal action.

(c) In the event of any threatened unauthorized disclosure of information concerning sources or methods of intelligence by a person who has agreed not to make such disclosure, the details of the threatened disclosure shall be transmitted to the Attorney General for appropriate legal action, including the seeking of a judicial order to prevent such disclosure.

(d) In further pursuit of the need to provide protection for other significant areas of intelligence, the Director of Central Intelligence is authorized to promulgate rules and regulations to expand the scope of agreements secured from those persons who, as an aspect of their relationship with the United States Government, have access to classified intelligence material.

Sec. 8. *Enabling Data.*

(a) The Committee on Foreign Intelligence and the Director of Central Intelligence shall provide for detailed implementation of this Order by issuing appropriate directives.

(b) All existing National Security Council and Director of Central Intelligence directives shall be amended to be consistent with this Order within ninety days of its effective date.

(c) This Order shall supersede the Presidential Memorandum of November 5, 1971, on the "Organization and Management of the U.S. Foreign Intelligence Community."

(d) Heads of departments and agencies within the Intelligence Community shall issue supplementary directives to their organizations consistent with this Order within ninety days of its effective date.

(e) This Order will be implemented within current manning authorizations of the Intelligence Community. To this end, the Director of the Office of Management and Budget will facilitate the required realignment of personnel positions. The

Director of the Office of Management and Budget will also assist in the allocation of appropriate facilities.

Gerald R. Ford

The White House,
February 18, 1976.

Guidelines by Attorney General Edward Levi on Domestic Intelligence

Domestic Security Investigations

I. Bases of Investigation

A. Domestic security investigations are conducted, when authorized under Section II(C), II(F), or II(I), to ascertain information on the activities of individuals, or the activities of groups, which involve or will involve the use of force or violence and which involve or will involve the violation of federal law, for the purpose of:

(1) overthrowing the government of the United States or the government of a State;

(2) substantially interfering, in the United States, with the activities of a foreign government or its authorized representatives;

(3) substantially impairing for the purpose of influencing U.S. government policies or decisions:

(a) the functioning of the government of the United States;

(b) the functioning of the government of a State; or

(c) interstate commerce.

(4) depriving persons of their civil rights under the Constitution, laws, or treaties of the United States.

II. Initiation and Scope of Investigations

A. Domestic security investigations are conducted at three levels—preliminary investigations, limited investigations, and full investigations—differing in scope and in investigative techniques which may be used.

B. All investigations undertaken through these guidelines shall be designed and conducted so as not to limit the full exercise of rights protected by the Constitution and laws of the United States.

Preliminary Investigations

C. Preliminary investigations may be undertaken on the basis of allegations or other information that an individual or a group may be engaged in activities which involve or will involve the use of force or violence and which involve or will involve the violation of federal law for one or more of the purposes enumerated in IA(1)-IA(4). These investigations shall be confined to determining whether there is a factual basis for opening a full investigation.

D. Information gathered by the FBI during preliminary investigations shall be pertinent to verifying or refuting the allegations or information concerning activities described in paragraph IA.

E. FBI field offices may, on their own initiative, undertake preliminary investigations limited to:

1. examination of FBI indices and files;

2. examination of public records and other public sources of information;

3. examination of federal, state, and local records;

4. inquiry of existing sources of information and use of previously established informants; and

5. physical surveillance and interviews or persons not mentioned in E(1)-E(4) for the limited purpose of identifying the subject of an investigation.

Limited Investigations

F. A limited investigation must be authorized in writing by a Special Agent in Charge or FBI Headquarters when the techniques listed in paragraph E are inadequate to determine if there is a factual basis for a full investigation. In addition to the techniques set forth in E(1)-E(4) the following techniques also may be used in a limited investigation:

1. physical surveillance for purposes other than identifying the subject of the investigation;

2. interviews of persons not mentioned in E(1)-E(4) for purposes other than identifying the subject of the investigation, but only when authorized by the Special Agent in Charge after full consideration of such factors as the seriousness of the allegation, the need for the interview, and the consequences of using the technique. When there is a question whether an interview should be undertaken, the Special Agent in Charge shall seek approval of FBI Headquarters.

G. Techniques such as recruitment or placement of informants in groups, "mail covers," or electronic surveillance, may not be used as part of a preliminary or a limited investigation.

H. All preliminary and limited investigations shall be closed within 90 days of the date upon which the preliminary investigation was initiated. However, FBI Headquarters may authorize in writing extension of a preliminary or limited investigation for periods of not more than 90 days when facts or information obtained in the original period justify such an extension. The authorization shall include a statement of the circumstances justifying the extension.

Full Investigation

I. Full investigations must be authorized by FBI Headquarters. They may only be authorized on the basis of specific and articulable facts giving reason to believe that an individual or a group is or may be engaged in activities which involve the use of force or violence and which involve or will involve the violation of federal law for one or more of the purposes enumerated in IA(1)-IA(4). The following factors must be considered in determining whether a full investigation should be undertaken:

(1) the magnitude of the threatened harm;

(2) the likelihood it will occur;

(3) the immediacy of the threat; and

(4) the danger to privacy and free expression posed by a full investigation.

Investigative Techniques

J. Whenever use of the following investigative techniques are permitted by these guidelines, they shall be implemented as limited herein:

(1) use of informants to gather information, when approved by FBI Headquarters, and subject to review at intervals not longer than 180 days; provided,

(a) when persons have been arrested or charged with a crime, and criminal proceedings are still pending, informants shall not be used to gather information concerning that crime from the person(s) charged; and

(b) informants shall not be used to obtain privileged information; and where such information is obtained by an informant on his own initiative no record or use shall be made of the information.

(2) "mail covers," pursuant to postal regulations, when approved by the Attorney General or his designee, initially or upon request for extension; and

(3) electronic surveillance in accordance with the requirement of Title III of the Omnibus Crime Control and Safe Streets Act of 1968.

Provided that whenever it becomes known that person(s) under surveillance are engaged in privileged conversation (e.g., with attorney), interception equipment shall be immediately shut off and the Justice Department advised as soon as practicable. Where such a conversation is recorded it shall not be transcribed, and a Department attorney shall determine if such conversation is privileged.

NOTE: These techniques have been the subject of strong concern. The committee is not yet satisfied that all sensitive areas have been covered (e.g., inquiries made under "pretext;" "trash covers," photographic or other surveillance techniques.)

III. Terminating Investigations

A. Preliminary, limited, and full investigations may be terminated at any time by the Attorney General, his designee, or FBI Headquarters.

B. FBI Headquarters shall periodically review the results of full investigations, and at such time as it appears that the standard for a full investigation under II(I) can no longer be satisfied and all logical leads have been exhausted or are not likely to be productive, FBI Headquarters shall terminate the full investigation.

C. The Department of Justice shall review the results of full domestic intelligence investigations at least annually, and shall determine in writing whether continued investigation is warranted. Full investigations shall not continue beyond one year without the written approval of the Department. However, in the absence of such notification the investigation may continue for an additional 30 day period pending response by the Department.

IV. Reporting, Dissemination, and Retention

A. Reporting

1. Preliminary investigations which involve a 90-day extension under IIH and limited investigations under IIF, shall be reported periodically to the Department of Justice. Reports of preliminary and limited investigations shall include the identity of the subject of the investigation, the identity of the person interviewed or the person or place surveilled, and shall indicate which investigations involved a 90-day extension. FBI Headquarters shall maintain, and provide to the Department of Justice upon request, statistics on the number of preliminary investigations instituted by each field office, the number of limited investigations under IIF, the number of preliminary investigations that involved 90-day extensions under IIH, and the number of preliminary or limited investigations that resulted in the opening of a full investigation.

2. Upon opening a full domestic security investigation the FBI shall, within one week, advice the Attorney General or his designee thereof, setting forth the basis for undertaking the investigation.

3. The FBI shall report the progress of full domestic security investigations to the Department of Justice not later than 90 days after the initiation thereof, and the results at the end of each year the investigation continues.

4. Where the identity of the source of information is not disclosed in a domestic security report, an assessment of the reliability of the source shall be provided.

B. Dissemination

1. *Other Federal Authorities*

The FBI may disseminate facts or information obtained during a domestic security investigation to other federal authorities when such information:

(a) falls within their investigative jurisdiction;

(b) may assist in preventing the use of force or violence; or

(c) may be required by statute, interagency agreement approved by the Attorney General, or Presidential directive. All such agreements and directives shall be published in the *Federal Register.*

2. *State and Local Authorities*

The FBI may disseminate facts or information relative to activities described in paragraph IB to state and local law enforcement authorities when such information:

(a) falls within their investigative jurisdiction;

(b) may assist in preventing the use of force or violence; or

(c) may protect the integrity of a law enforcement agency.

3. When information relating to serious crimes not covered by paragraph IA is obtained during a domestic security investigation, the FBI shall promptly refer the information to the appropriate lawful authorities if it is within the jurisdiction of state and local agencies.

4. Nothing in these guidelines shall limit the authority of the FBI to inform any individual(s) whose safety or property is directly threatened by planned force or violence, so that they may take appropriate protective safeguards.

5. The FBI shall maintain records, as required by law, of all disseminations made outside the Department of Justice, of information obtained during domestic security investigations.

C. Retention

1. The FBI shall, in accordance with a Records Retention Plan approved by the National Archives and Records Service, within ______ years after closing domestic service investigations, destroy all information obtained during the investigation, as well as all index references thereto, or transfer all information and index references to the National Archives and Records Service.

NOTE: We are not yet certain whether empirical data exists to help define a period of retention for information gathered in preliminary or full investigations. Whatever period is determined should take into account the retention period for other categories of information (e.g., general criminal, organized crime, and background checks); since we have not yet considered these areas we cannot fix a period for retention at this time.

NOTE: It may also be possible to establish a sealing procedure to preserve investigative records for an interim period prior to destruction. After being sealed, access would be permitted only under controlled conditions.

2. Information relating to activities not covered by paragraph IA obtained during domestic security investigations, which may be maintained by the FBI under other parts of these guidelines, shall be retained in accordance with such other provisions.

3. The provisions of paragraphs one (1), and two (2) above apply to all domestic security investigations completed after the promulgation of these guidelines, and apply to investigations completed prior to promulgation of these guidelines when use of these files serves to identify them as subject to destruction or transfer to the National Archives and Records Service.

4. When an individual's request pursuant to law for access to FBI records identifies the records as being subject to destruction or transfer under paragraph one (1), the individual shall be furnished all information to which he is entitled prior to destruction or transfer.

CASES

Katz v. United States

389 U.S. 347 (1967)

Mr. Justice Stewart delivered the opinion of the Court.

* * *

The Government does not question these basic principles. Rather, it urges the creation f a new exception to cover this case.[23] It argues that surveillance of a telephone booth should be exempted from the usual requirement of advance authorization by a magistrate upon a showing of probable cause. We cannot agree. Omission of such authorization

> "bypasses the safeguards provided by an objective predetermination of probable cause, and substitutes instead the far less reliable procedure of an after-the-event justification for the ... search, too likely to be subtly influenced by the familiar shortcomings of hindsight judgment." *Beck v. Ohio,* 379 U.S. 89, 96.

And bypassing a neutral predetermination of the *scope* of a search leaves individuals secure from Fourth Amendment violations "only in the discretion of the police." *Id.,* at 97.

Mr. Justice Douglas, with whom Mr. Justice Brennan joins, concurring.

While I join the opinion of the Court, I feel compelled to reply to the separate concurring opinion of my Brother White, which I view as a wholly unwarranted green light for the Executive Branch to resort to electronic eavesdropping without a warrant in cases which the Executive Branch itself labels "national security" matters.

Neither the President nor the Attorney General is a magistrate. In matters where they believe national security may be involved they are not detached, disinterested, and neutral as a court or magistrate must be. Under the separation of powers created by the Constitution, the Executive Branch is not supposed to be neutral and disinterested. Rather it should vigorously investigate and prevent breaches of national security and prosecute those who violate the pertinent federal laws. The President and Attorney General are properly interested parties, cast in the role of adversary, in national security cases. They may even be the intended victims of subversive action. Since spies and saboteurs are as entitled to the protection of the Fourth Amendment as suspected gamblers like petitioner, I cannot agree that where spies and saboteurs are involved adequate protection of Fourth Amendment rights is assured when the President and Attorney General assume both the position of adversary-and-prosecutor and disinterested, neutral magistrate.

There is, so far as I understand constitutional history, no distinction under the Fourth Amendment between types of crimes. Article III, § 3, gives "treason" a very narrow definition and puts restrictions on its proof. But the Fourth Amendment draws no lines between various substantive offenses. The arrests in cases of "hot pursuit" and the arrests on visible or other evidence of probable cause cut across the board and are not peculiar to any kind of crime.

I would respect the present lines of distinction and not improvise because a particular crime seems particularly heinous. When the Framers took that step, as they did with treason, the worst crime of all, they made their purpose manifest.

Mr. Justice White, concurring.

I agree that the official surveillance of petitioner's telephone conversations in a public booth must be subjected to the test of reasonableness under the Fourth Amendment and that on the record now before us the particular surveillance undertaken was unreasonable absent a warrant properly authorizing it. This application of the Fourth Amendment need not interfere with legitimate needs of law enforcement.*

In joining the Court's opinion, I note the Court's acknowledgment that there are circumstances in which it is reasonable to search without a warrant. In this connection, in footnote 23 the Court points out that today's decision does not reach national security cases. Wiretapping to protect the security of the Nation has been authorized by successive Presidents. The present Administration would apparently save national security cases from restrictions against wiretapping. See *Berger v. New York,* 388 U.S. 41, 112-118 (1967) (White, J., dissenting). We should not require the warrant procedure and the magistrate's judgment if the President of the United States or his chief legal officer, the Attorney General, has considered the requirements of national security and authorized electronic surveillance as reasonable.

---

[23]Whether safeguards other than prior authorization by a magistrate would satisfy the Fourth Amendment in a situation involving the national security is a question not presented by this case.

*In previous cases, which are undisturbed by today's decision, the Court has upheld, as reasonable under the Fourth Amendment, admission at trial of evidence obtained (1) by an undercover police agent to whom a defendant speaks without knowledge that he is in the employ of the police, *Hoffa v. United States,* 385 U.S. 293 (1966); (2) by a recording device hidden on the person of such an informant, *Lopez v. United States,* 373 U.S. 427 (1963); *Osborn v. United States,* 385 U.S. 323 (1966); and (3) by a policeman listening to the secret micro-wave transmissions of an agent conversing with the defendant in another location, *On Lee v. United States,* 343 U.S. 747 (1952). When one man speaks to another he takes all the risks ordinarily inherent in so doing, including the risk that the man to whom he speaks will make public what he has heard. The Fourth Amendment does not protect against unreliable (or law-abiding) associates. *Hoffa v. United States, supra.* It is but a logical and reasonable extension of this principle that a man take the risk that his hearer, free to memorize what he hears for later verbatim repetitions, is instead recording it or transmitting it to another. The present case deals with an entirely different situation, for as the Court emphasizes the petitioner "sought to exclude . . . the uninvited ear," and spoke under circumstances in which a reasonable person would assume that uninvited ears were not listening.

Giordano v. United States

394 U.S. 310 (1969)

Mr. Justice Stewart, concurring.

A few words in amplification of this *per curiam* opinion may help to avoid misunderstanding on the part of the litigants, and of the District Courts to which these cases are remanded.

As we made explicit in *Alderman, Butenko,* and *Ivanov,* the requirement that certain products of governmental electronic surveillance be turned over to defense counsel was expressly limited to situations where the surveillance had violated the Fourth Amendment. We did not decide in those cases, and we do not decide in these, that any of the surveillances *did* violate the Fourth Amendment.[1] Instead, we have left the threshold question for the District Courts to decide in all these case.

Moreover, we did not in *Alderman, Butenko,* or *Ivanov,* and we do not today, specify the procedure that the District Courts are to follow in making this preliminary determination. We have nowhere indicated that this determination cannot appropriately be made in *ex parte, in camera* proceedings. "Nothing in *Alderman v. United States, Ivanov v. United States,* or *Butenko v. United States, ante,* p. 165, requires an adversary proceeding and full disclosure for resolution of every issue raised by an electronic surveillance." *Taglianetti v. United States, post,* p. 316.

Finally, the Court has not in any of these cases addressed itself to the standards governing the constitutionality of electronic surveillance relating to the gathering of foreign intelligence information—necessary for the conduct of international affairs, and for the protection of national defense secrets and installations from foreign espionage and sabotage. Mr. Justice White has elsewhere made clear his view that such surveillance does not violate the Fourth Amendment, "if the President of the United States or his chief legal officer, the Attorney General, has considered the requirements of national security and authorized electronic surveillance as reasonable."[2] While two members of the Court have indicated disagreement with that view,[3] the issue remains open.[4]

One might suppose that all of this should be entirely clear to any careful reader of the Court's opinion in *Alderman, Butenko,* and *Ivanov.* Perhaps so, and perhaps, therefore, what I have said is quite unnecessary. But 10 years of experience here have taught me that the most carefully written opinions are not always carefully read—even by those most directly concerned.

[1]In oral argument of the *Butenko* and *Ivanov* cases, the Solicitor General, mystifyingly, sought to concede that the surveillances there *were* in fact unconstitutional, although he was repeatedly invited

to argue that they were not. The following colloquies during oral argument of the *Ivanov* case are illustrative:

"Q. Are you asking us to decide here or to leave open on remand the question as to whether this violates, this bugging in this particular case, violates the Fourth Amendment?

"A. Our position would be the same had it or not. We are not arguing that it did not violate the Fourth Amendment.

* * *

"Q. In other words, the premise in which you are proceeding here is that you admit for the purposes of this case that this was illegal bugging?

"A. Yes, Mr. Justice.

* * *

"Q. And you are going to remain free to argue to the district judge that there was no violation?

"A. No, sir."

In deciding those cases, the Court declined to accept the Solicitor General's proffered concession.

[2]*Katz v. United States,* 389 U.S. 347, 364 (White, J., concurring).

[3]*Id.,* at 359 (Douglas, J., concurring).

[4]See *id.,* at 358, n. 23.

United States v. United States District Court

407 U.S. 297 (1972)

Mr. Justice Powell delivered the opinion of the Court.

The issue before us is an important one for the people of our country and their Government. It involves the delicate question of the President's power, acting through the Attorney General, to authorize electronic surveillance in internal security matters without prior judicial approval. Successive Presidents for more than one-quarter of a century have authorized such surveillance in varying degrees,[1] without guidance from the Congress or a definitive decision of this Court. This case brings the issue here for the first time. Its resolution is a matter of national concern, requiring sensitivity both to the Government's right to protect itself from unlawful subversion and attack and to the citizen's right to be secure in his privacy against unreasonable Government intrusion.

This case arises from a criminal proceeding in the United States District Court for the Eastern District of Michigan, in which the United States charged three defendants with conspiracy to destroy Government property in violation of 18 U. S. C. § 371. One of the defendants, Plamondon, was charged with the dynamite bombing of an office of the Central Intelligence Agency in Ann Arbor, Michigan.

During pretrial proceedings, the defendants moved to compel the United States to disclose certain electronic surveillance information and to conduct a hearing to determine whether this information "tainted" the evidence on which the indictment was based or which the Government intended to offer at trial. In response, the Government filed an affidavit of the Attorney General, acknowledging that its agents had overheard conversations in which Plamondon had participated. The affidavit also stated that the Attorney General approved the wiretaps "to gather intelligence information deemed necessary to protect the nation from attempts of domestic organizations to attack and subvert the existing structure of the Government."[2] The logs of the surveillance were filed in a sealed exhibit for *in camera* inspection by the District Court.

On the basis of the Attorney General's affidavit and the sealed exhibit, the Government asserted that the surveillance was lawful, though conducted without prior judicial approval, as a reasonable exercise of the President's power (exercised through the Attorney General) to protect the national security. The District Court held that the surveillance violated the Fourth Amendment, and ordered the Government to make full disclosure to Plamondon of his overheard conversations. 321 F. Supp. 1074 (ED Mich. 1971).

The Government then filed in the Court of Appeals for the Sixth Circuit a petition for a writ of mandamus to set aside the District Court order, which was stayed pending final disposition of the case. After concluding that it had jurisdiction,[3] that court held that the surveillance was unlawful and that the District Court had properly required disclosure of the overheard conversations, 444 F. 2d 651 (1971). We granted certiorari, 403 U.S. 930.

I

Title III of the Omnibus Crime Control and Safe Streets Act, 18 U. S. C. §§ 2510-2520, authorizes the use of electronic surveillance for classes of crimes carefully specified in 18 U. S. C. § 2516. Such surveillance is subject to prior court order. Section 2518 sets forth the detailed and particularized application necessary to obtain such an order as well as carefully circumscribed conditions for its use. The Act represents a comprehensive attempt by Congress to promote more effective control of crime while protecting the privacy of individual thought and expression. Much of Title III was drawn to meet the constitutional requirements for electronic surveillance enunciated by this Court in *Berger v. New York,* 388 U.S. 41 (1967), and *Katz v. United States,* 389 U.S. 347 (1967).

Together with the elaborate surveillance requirements in Title III, there is the following proviso, 18 U. S. C. § 2511 (3):

> "Nothing contained in this chapter or in section 605 of the Communications Act of 1934 48 Stat. 1143; 47 U. S. C. 605) shall limit the constitutional power of the President to take such measures as he deems necessary to protect the Nation against actual or potential attack or other hostile acts of a foreign power, to obtain foreign intelligence information deemed essential to the security of the United States, or to protect national security information against foreign intelligence activities. *Nor shall anything contained in this chapter be deemed to limit the constitutional power of the President to take such measures as he deems necessary to protect the United States against the overthrow of the Government by force or other unlawful means, or against any other clear and present danger to the structure or existence of the Government.* The contents of any wire or oral communication intercepted by authority of the President in the exercise of the foregoing powers may be received in evidence in any trial hearing, or other proceeding only where such interception was reasonable, and shall not be otherwise used or disclosed except as is necessary to implement that power." (Emphasis supplied.)

The Government relies on § 2511 (3). It argues that "in excepting national security surveillances from the Act's warrant requirement Congress recognized the President's authority to conduct such surveillances without prior judicial approval." Brief for United States 7, 28. The section thus is viewed as a recognition or affirmance of a constitutional authority in the President to conduct warrantless domestic security surveillance such as that involved in this case.

We think the language of § 2511 (3), as well as the legislative history of the statute, refutes this interpretation. The relevant language is that:

> "Nothing contained in this chapter . . . shall limit the constitutional power of the President to take such measures as he deems necessary to protect . . ."

against the dangers specified. At most, this is an implicit recognition that the President does have certain powers in the specified areas. Few would doubt this, as the section refers—among other things—to protection "against actual or potential attack or other hostile acts of a foreign power." But so far as the use of the President's electronic surveillance power is concerned, the language is essentially neutral.

Section 2511 (3) certainly confers no power, as the language is wholly inappropriate for such a purpose. It merely provides that the Act shall not be interpreted to limit or disturb such power as the President may have under the Constitution. In short, Congress simply left presidential powers where it found them. This view is reinforced by the general context of Title III. Section 2511 (1) broadly prohibits the use of electronic surveillance "[e]xcept as otherwise specifically provided in this chapter." Subsection (2) thereof contains four specific exceptions. In each of the specified exceptions, the statutory language is as follows:

> "It shall not be unlawful . . . to intercept" the particular type of communication described.[4]

The language of subsection (3), here involved, is to be contrasted with the language of the exceptions set forth in the preceding subsection. Rather than stating that warrantless presidential uses of electronic surveillance "shall not be unlawful" and thus employing the standard language of exception, subsection (3) merely disclaims any intention to "limit the constitutional power of the President."

The express grant of authority to conduct surveillances is found in § 2516, which authorizes the Attorney General to make application to a federal judge when surveillance may provide evidence of certain offenses. These offenses are described with meticulous care and specificity.

Where the Act authorizes surveillance, the procedure to be followed is specified in § 2518. Subsection (1) thereof requires application to a judge of competent jurisdiction for a prior order of approval, and states in detail the information required in such application.[5] Subsection (3) prescribes the necessary elements of probable cause which the judge must find before issuing an order authorizing an interception. Subsection (4) sets forth the required contents of such an order. Subsection (5) sets strict time limits on an order. Provision is made in subsection (7) for "an emergency situation" found to exist by the Attorney General (or by the principal prosecuting attorney of a State) "with respect to conspiratorial activities threatening the national security interest." In such a situation, emergency surveillance may be conducted "if an application for an order approving the interception is made . . . within forty-eight hours." If such an order is not obtained, or the application therefor is denied, the interception is deemed to be a violation of the Act.

In view of these and other interrelated provisions delineating permissible interceptions of particular criminal activity upon carefully specified conditions, it would have been incongruous for Congress to have legislated with respect to the important and complex area of national security in a single brief and nebulous paragraph. This would not comport with the sensitivity of the problem involved or with the extraordinary care Congress exercised in drafting other sections of the Act. We therefore think the conclusion inescapable that Congress only intended to make clear that the Act simply did not legislate with respect to national security surveillances.[6]

The legislative history of § 2511 (3) supports this interpretation. Most relevant is the colloquy between Senators Hart, Holland, and McClellan on the Senate floor:

> "Mr. Holland.... The section [2511 (3)] from which the Senator [Hart] has read does not affirmatively give any power.... *We are not affirmatively conferring any power upon the President.* We are simply saying that nothing herein shall limit such power as the President has under the Constitution.... We certainly do not grant him a thing.
>
> "There is nothing affirmative in this statement.
>
> "Mr. McClellan. Mr. President, *we make it understood that we are not trying to take anything away from him.*
>
> "Mr. Holland. The Senator is correct.
>
> "Mr. Hart. Mr. President, there is no intention here to expand by this language a constitutional power. Clearly we could not do so.
>
> "Mr. McClellan. Even though intended, we could not do so.
>
> "Mr. Hart. . . . However, we are agreed that this language should not be regarded as intending to grant any authority, including authority to put a bug on, that the President does not have now.
>
> "In addition, Mr. President, *as I think our exchange makes clear, nothing in section 2511 (3) even attempts to define the limits of the President's national security power under present law, which I have always found extremely vague. . . . Section 2511 (3) merely says that if the President has such a power, then its exercise is in no way affected by title III.*"[7] (Emphasis supplied.)

One could hardly expect a clearer expression of congressional neutrality. The debate above explicitly indicates that nothing in § 2511 (3) was intended to *expand* or to *contract* or to *define* whatever presidential surveillance powers existed in matters affecting the national security. It we could accept the Government's characterization of § 2511 (3) as a congressionally prescribed exception to the general requirement of a warrant, it would be necessary to consider the question of whether the surveillance in this case came within the exception and, if so, whether the statutory exception was itself constitutionally valid. But viewing § 2511 (3) as a congressional disclaimer and expression of neutrality, we hold that the statute is not the measure of the executive authority asserted in this case. Rather, we must look to the constitutional powers of the President.

II

It is important at the outset to emphasize the limited nature of the question before the Court. This case raises no constitutional challenge to electronic surveillance as specifically authorized by Title III of the Omnibus Crime Control and Safe Streets Act of 1968. Nor is there any question or doubt as to the necessity of obtaining a warrant in the surveillance of crimes unrelated to the national security interest. *Katz v. United States,* 389 U.S. 347 (1967); *Berger v. New York,* 388 U.S. 41 (1967). Further, the instant case requires no judgment on the scope of the President's surveillance power with respect to the activities of foreign powers, within or without this country. The Attorney General's affidavit in this case states that the surveillances were "deemed necessary to protect the nation from attempts of *domestic organizations* to attack and subvert the existing structure of Government" (emphasis supplied). There is no evidence of any involvement, directly or indirectly, of a foreign power.[8]

Our present inquiry, though important, is therefore a narrow one. It addresses a question left open by *Katz, supra,* at 358 n. 23:

> "Whether safeguards other than prior authorization by a magistrate would satisfy the Fourth Amendment in a situation involving the national security. . . ."

The determination of this question requires the essential Fourth Amendment inquiry into the "reasonableness" of the search and seizure in question, and the way in which that "reasonableness" derives content and meaning through reference to the warrant clause. *Coolidge v. New Hampshire,* 403 U.S. 443, 473-484 (1971).

We begin the inquiry by noting that the President of the United States has the fundamental duty, under Art. II, § 1, of the Constitution, to "preserve, protect and defend the Constitution of the United States." Implicit in that duty is the power to protect our Government against those who would subvert or overthrow it by unlawful means. In the discharge of this duty, the President—through the Attorney General—may find it necessary to employ electronic surveillance to obtain intelligence information on the plans of those who plot unlawful acts against the Government.[9] The use of such surveillance in internal security cases has been sanctioned more or less continuously by various Presidents and Attorneys General since July 1946.[10] Herbert Brownell, Attorney General under President Eisenhower, urged the use of electronic surveillance both in internal and international security matters on the grounds that those acting against the Government

> "turn to the telephone to carry on their intrigue. The success of their plans frequently rests upon piecing together shreds of information received from many sources and many nests. The participants in the conspiracy are often dispersed and stationed in various strategic positions in government and industry throughout the country."[11]

Though the Government and respondents debate their seriousness and magnitude, threats and acts of sabotage against the Government exist in sufficent number to justify investigative powers with respect to them.[12] The covertness and complexity of potential unlawful conduct against the Government and the necessary dependency of many conspirators upon the telephone make electronic surveillance an effective investigatory instrument in certain circumstances. The marked acceleration in technological developments and sophistication in their use have resulted in new techniques for the planning, commission, and concealment of criminal activities. It would be contrary to the public interst for Government to deny to itself the prudent and lawful employment of those very techniques which are employed against the Government and its law-abiding citizens.

It has been said that "[t]he most basic function of any government is to provide for the security of the individual and of his property." *Miranda v. Arizona,* 384 U.S. 436, 539 (1966) (White, J., dissenting). And unless Government safeguards its own capacity to function and to preserve the security of its people, society itself could become so disordered that all rights and liberties would be endangered. As Chief Justice Hughes reminded us in *Cox v. New Hampshire,* 312 U.S. 569, 574 (1941):

> "Civil liberties, as guaranteed by the Constitution, imply the existence of an organized society maintaining public order without which liberty itself would be lost in the excesses of unrestrained abuses."

But a recognition of these elementary truths does not make the employment by Government of electronic surveillance a welcome development—even when employed with restraint and under judicial supervision. There is, understandably, a deep-seated uneasiness and apprehension that this capability will be used to intrude upon cherished privacy of law-abiding citizens.[13] We look to the Bill of Rights to safeguard this privacy. Though physical entry of the home is the chief evil against which the wording of the Fourth Amendment is directed, its broader spirit now shields private speech from unreasonable surveillance. *Katz v. United States, supra; Berger v. New York, supra; Silverman v. United States,* 365 U.S. 505 (1961). Our decision in *Katz* refused to lock the Fourth Amendment into instances of actual physical trespass. Rather, the Amendment governs "not only the seizure of tangible items, but extends as well to the recording of oral statements . . . without any 'technical trespass under . . . local property law.' " *Katz, supra,* at 353. That decision implicitly recognized that the broad and unsuspected governmental incursions into conversational privacy which electronic surveillance entails[14] necessitate the application of Fourth Amendment safeguards.

National security cases, moreover, often reflect a convergence of First and Fourth Amendment values not present in cases of "ordinary" crime. Though the investigative duty of the executive may be stronger in such cases, so also is there greater jeopardy to constitutionally protected speech. "Historically the struggle for freedom of speech and press in England was bound up with the issue of the scope of the search and seizure power," *Marcus v. Search Warrant,* 367 U.S. 717, 724 (1961). History abundantly documents the tendency of Government—however benevolent and benign its motives—to view with suspicion those who most frequently dispute its policies. Fourth Amendment protections become the more necessary when the targets of official surveillance may be those suspected of unorthodoxy in their political beliefs. The danger to political dissent is acute where the Government attempts to act under so vague a concept as the power to protect "domestic security." Given the difficulty of defining the domestic security interest, the danger of abuse in acting to protect that interest becomes apparent. Senator Hart addressed this dilemma in the floor debate on § 2511 (3):

> "As I read it—and this is my fear—we are saying that the President, on his motion, could declare—name your favorite poison—draft dodgers, Black Muslims, the Ku Klux Klan, or civil rights activists to be a clear and present danger to the structure or existence of the Government."[15]

The price of lawful public dissent must not be a dread of subjection to an unchecked surveillance power. Nor must the fear of unauthorized official eavesdropping deter vigorous citizen dissent and discussion of Government action in private conversation. For private dissent, no less than open public discourse, is essential to our free society.

III

As the Fourth Amendment is not absolute in its terms, our task is to examine and balance the basic values at stake in this case: the duty of Government to protect the domestic security, and the potential danger posed by unreasonable surveillance to individual privacy and free expression. If the legitimate need of Government to safeguard domestic security requires the use of electronic surveillance, the question is whether the needs of citizens for privacy and free expression may not be better protected by requiring a warrant before such surveillance is undertaken. We must also ask whether a warrant requirement would unduly frustrate the efforts of Government to protect itself from acts of subversion and overthrow directed against it.

Though the Fourth Amendment speaks broadly of "unreasonable searches and seizures," the definition of "reasonableness" turns, at least in part, on the more specific commands of the warrant clause. Some have argued that "[t]he relevant test is not whether it is reasonable to procure a search warrant, but whether the search was reasonable," *United States v. Rabinowitz,* 339 U.S. 56, 66 (1950).[16] This view, however, overlooks the second clause of the Amendment. The warrant clause of the Fourth Amendment is not dead language. Rather, it has been

> "a valued part of our constitutional law for decades, and it has determined the result in scores and scores of cases in courts all over this country. It is not an inconvenience to be somehow 'weighed' against the claims of police efficiency. It is, or should be, an important working part of our machinery of government, operating as a matter of course to check the 'well-intentioned but mistakenly overzealous executive officers' who are a part of any system of law enforcement." *Coolidge v. New Hampshire,* 403 U.S., at 481.

See also *United States v. Rabinowitz, supra,* at 68 (Frankfurter, J., dissenting); *Davis v. United States,* 328 U.S. 582, 604 (1946) (Frankfurter, J., dissenting).

Over two centuries ago, Lord Mansfield held that common-law principles prohibited warrants that ordered the arrest of unnamed individuals who the *officer* might conclude were guilty of seditious libel. "It is not fit," said Mansfield, "that the receiving or judging of the information should be left to the discretion of the officer. The magistrate ought to judge; and should give certain directions to the officer." *Leach v. Three of the King's Messengers,* 19 How. St. Tr. 1001, 1027 (1765).

Lord Mansfield's formulation touches the very heart of the Fourth Amendment directive: that, where practical, a governmental search and seizure should represent both the efforts of the officer to gather evidence of wrongful acts and the judgment of the magistrate that the collected evidence is sufficient to justify invasion of a citizen's private premises or conversation. Inherent in the concept of a warrant is its issuance by a "neutral and detached magistrate." *Coolidge v. New Hampshire, supra,* at 453; *Katz v. United States, supra,* at 356. The further requirement of "probable cause" instructs the magistrate that baseless searches shall not proceed.

These Fourth Amendment freedoms cannot properly be guaranteed if domestic security surveillances may be conducted solely within the discretion of the Executive Branch. The Fourth Amendment does not contemplate the executive officers of Government as neutral and disinterested magistrates. Their duty and responsibility are to enfore the laws, to investigate, and to prosecute. *Katz v. United States, supra,* at 359-360 (Douglas, J., concurring). But those charged with this investigative and prosecutorial duty should not be the sole judges of when to utilize constitutionally sensitive means in pursuing their tasks. The historical judgment, which the Fourth Amendment accepts, is that unreviewed executive discretion may yield too readily to pressures to obtain incriminating evidence and overlook potential invasions of privacy and protected speech.[17]

It may well be that, in the instant case, the Government's surveillance of Plamondon's conversations was a reasonable one which readily would have gained prior judicial approval. But this Court "has never sustained a search upon the sole ground that officers reasonably expected to find evidence of a particular crime and voluntarily confined their activities to the least intrusive means consistent with the end." *Katz, supra,* at 356-357. The Fourth Amendment contemplates a prior judicial judgment,[18] not the risk that executive discretion may be reasonably exercised. This judicial role accords with our basic constitutional doctrine that individual freedoms will best be preserved through a separation of powers and division of functions among the different branches and levels of Government.

Harlan, Thoughts at a Dedication: Keeping the Judicial Function in Balance, 49 A. B. A. J. 943-944 (1963). The independent check upon executive discretion is not satisfied, as the Government argues, by "extremely limited" post-surveillance judicial review.[19] Indeed, post-surveillance review would never reach the surveillances which failed to result in prosecutions. Prior review by a neutral and detached magistrate is the time-tested means of effectuating Fourth Amendment rights. *Beck v. Ohio,* 379 U.S. 89, 96, (1964).

It is true that there have been some exceptions to the warrant requirement. *Chimel v. California,* 395 U.S. 752 (1969); *Terry v. Ohio,* 392 U.S. 1 (1968); *McDonald v. United States,* 335 U.S. 451 (1948); *Carroll v. United States,* 267 U.S. 132 (1925). But those exceptions are few in number and carefully delineated, *Katz, supra,* at 357; in general, they serve the legitimate needs of law enforcement officers to protect their own well-being and preserve evidence from destruction. Even while carving out those exceptions, the Court has reaffirmed the principle that the "police must, whenever practicable, obtain advance judicial approval of searches and seizures through the warrant procedure," *Terry v. Ohio, supra,* at 20; *Chimel v. California, supra,* at 762.

The Government argues that the special circumstances applicable to domestic security surveillances necessitate a further exception to the warrant requirement. It is urged that the requirement of prior judicial review would obstruct the President in the discharge of his constitutional duty to protect domestic security. We are told further that these surveillances are directed primarily to the collecting and maintaining of intelligence with respect to subversive forces, and are not an attempt to gather evidence for specific criminal prosecutions. It is said that this type of surveillance should not be subject to traditional warrant requirements which were established to govern investigation of criminal activity, not ongoing intelligence gathering. Brief for United States 15-16, 23-24; Reply Brief for United States 2-3.

The Government further insists that courts "as a practical matter would have neither the knowledge nor the techniques necessary to determine whether there was probable cause to believe that surveillance was necessary to protect national security." These security problems, the Government contends, involve "a large number of complex and subtle factors" beyond the competence of courts to evaluate. Reply Brief for United States 4.

As a final reason for exemption from a warrant requirement, the Government believes that disclosure to a magistrate of all or even a significant portion of the information involved in domestic security surveillances "would create serious potential dangers to the national security and to the lives of informants and agents. . . . Secrecy is the essential ingredient in intelligence gathering; requiring prior judicial authorization would create a greater 'danger of leaks, . . . because in addition to the judge, you have the clerk, the stenographer and some other officer like a law assistant or bailiff who may be apprised of the nature' of the surveillance." Brief for United States 24-25.

These contentions in behalf of a complete exemption from the warrant requirement, when urged on behalf of the President and the national security in its domestic implications, merit the most careful consideration. We certainly do not reject them lightly, especially at a time of worldwide ferment and when civil disorders in this country are more prevalent than in the less turbulent periods of our history. There is, no doubt, pragmatic force to the Government's position.

But we do not think a case has been made for the requested departure from Fourth Amendment standards. The circumstances described do not justify complete exemption of domestic security surveillance from prior judicial scrutiny. Official surveillance, whether its purpose be criminal investigation or ongoing intelligence gathering, risks infringement of constitutionally protected privacy of speech. Security surveillances are especially sensitive because of the inherent vagueness of the domestic security concept, the necessarily broad and continuing nature of intelligence gathering, and the temptation to utilize such surveillances to oversee political dissent. We recognize, as we have before, the constitutional basis of the President's domestic security role, but we think it must be exercised in a manner compatible with the Fourth Amendment. In this case we hold that this requires an appropriate prior warrant procedure.

We cannot accept the Government's argument that internal security matters are too subtle and complex for judicial evaluation. Courts regularly deal with the most difficult issues of our society. There is no reason to believe that federal judges will be insensitive to or uncomprehending of the issues involved in domestic security cases. Certainly courts can recognize that domestic security surveillance involves different considerations from the surveillance of "ordinary crime." If the threat is too subtle or complex for our senior law enforcement officers to convey its significance to a court, one may question whether there is probable cause for surveillance.

Nor do we believe prior judicial approval will fracture the secrecy essential to official intelligence gathering. The investigation of criminal activity has long involved imparting sensitive information to judicial officers who have respected the confidentialities involved. Judges may be counted upon to be especially conscious of security requirements in national security cases. Title III of the Omnibus Crime Control and Safe Streets Act already has imposed this responsibility on the judiciary in connection with such crimes as espionage, sabotage, and treason, §§ 2516 (1) (a) and (c), each of which may involve domestic as well as foreign security threats. Moreover, a warrant application involves no public or adversary proceedings: it is an *ex parte* request before a magistrate or judge. Whatever security dangers clerical and secretarial personnel may pose can be minimized by proper administrative measures, possibly to the point of allowing the Government itself to provide the necessary clerical assistance.

Thus, we conclude that the Government's concerns do not justify departure in this case from the customary Fourth Amendment requirement of judicial approval prior to initiation of a search or surveillance. Although some added burden will be imposed upon the Attorney General, this inconvenience is justified in a free society to protect constitutional values. Nor do we think the Government's domestic surveillance powers will be impaired to any significant degree. A prior warrant establishes presumptive validity of the surveillance and will minimize the burden of justification in post-surveillance judicial review. By no means of least importance will be the reassurance of the public generally that indiscriminate wiretapping and bugging of law-abiding citizens cannot occur.

IV

We emphasize, before concluding this opinion, the scope of our decision. As stated at the outset, this case involves only the domestic aspects of national security. We have not addressed, and express no opinion as to, the issues which may be involved with respect to activities of foreign powers or their agents.[20] Nor does our decision rest on the language of § 2511 (3) or any other section of Title III of the Omnibus Crime Control and Safe Streets Act of 1968. That act does not attempt to define or delineate the powers of the President to meet domestic threats to the national security.

Moreover, we do not hold that the same type of standards and procedures prescribed by Title III are necessarily applicable to this case. We recognize that domestic security surveillance may involve different policy and practical considerations from the surveillance of "ordinary crime." The gathering of security intelligence is often long range and involves the interrelation of various sources and types of information. The exact targets of such surveillance may be more difficult to identify than in surveillance operations against many types of crime specified in Title III. Often, too, the emphasis of domestic intelligence gathering is on the prevention of unlawful activity or the enhancement of the Government's preparedness for some possible future crisis or emergency. Thus, the focus of domestic surveillance may be less precise than that directed against more conventional types of crime.

Given these potential distinctions between Title III criminal surveillance and those involving the domestic security, Congress may wish to consider protective standards for the latter which differ from those already prescribed for specified crimes in Title III. Different standards may be compatible with the Fourth Amendment if they are reasonable both in relation to the legitimate need of Government for intelligence information and the protected rights of our citizens. For the warrant application may vary according to the governmental interest to be enforced and the nature of citizen rights deserving protection. As the Court said in *Camara v. Municipal Court,* 387 U.S. 523, 534-535 (1967):

> "In cases in which the Fourth Amendment requires that a warrant to search be obtained, 'probable cause' is the standard by which a particular decision to search is tested against the constitutional mandate of reasonableness. . . . In determining whether a particular inspection is reasonable—and thus in determining whether there is probable cause to issue a warrant for that inspection—the need for the inspection must be weighed in terms of these reasonable goals of code enforcement."

It may be that Congress, for example, would judge that the application and affidavit showing probable cause need not follow the exact requirements of § 2518 but should allege other circumstances more appropriate to domestic security cases; that the request for prior court authorization could, in sensitive cases, be made to any member of a specially designated court (*e.g.,* the District Court for the District of Columbia or the Court of Appeals for the District of Columbia Circuit); and that the time and reporting requirements need not be so strict as those in § 2518.

The above paragraph does not, of course, attempt to guide the congressional judgment but rather to delineate the present scope of our own opinion. We do not attempt to detail the precise standards for domestic security warrants any more than our decision in *Katz* sought to set the refined requirements for the specified criminal surveillances which now constitute Title III. We do hold, however, that prior judicial approval is required for the type of domestic security surveillance involved in this case and that such approval may be made in accordance with such reasonable standards as the Congress may prescribe.

V

As the surveillance of Plamondon's conversations was unlawful, because conducted without prior judicial approval, the courts below correctly held that *Alderman v. United States,* 394 U.S. 165 (1969), is controlling and that it requires disclosure to the accused of his own impermissibly intercepted conversations. As stated in *Alderman,* "the trial court can and should, where appropriate, place a defendant and his counsel under enforceable orders against unwarranted disclosure of the materials which they may be entitled to inspect." 394 U.S., at 185.[21]

The judgment of the Court of Appeals is hereby

Affirmed.

The Chief Justice concurs in the result.

Mr. Justice Rehnquist took no part in the consideration or decision of this case.

Mr. Justice White, concurring. . . .

---

[1]See n. 10, *infra.*

[2]The Attorney General's affidavit reads as follows:

"John N. Mitchell being duly sworn deposes and says:

"1. I am the Attorney General of the United States.

"2. This affidavit is submitted in connection with the Government's opposition to the disclosure to the defendant Plamondon of information concerning the overhearing of his conversations which occurred during the course of electronic surveillances which the Government contends were legal.

"3. The defendant Plamondon has participated in conversations which were overheard by Government agents who were monitoring wiretaps which were being employed to gather intelligence information deemed necessary to protect the nation from attempts of domestic organizations to attack and subvert the existing structure of the Government. The records of the Department of Justice reflect the installation of these wiretaps had been expressly approved by the Attorney General.

"4. Submitted with this affidavit is a sealed exhibit containing the records of the intercepted conversations, a description of the premises that were the subjects of surveillances, and copies of the memoranda reflecting the Attorney General's express approval of the installation of the surveillances.

"5. I certify that it would prejudice the national interest to disclose the particular facts concerning these surveillances other than to the court *in camera.* Accordingly, the sealed exhibit referred to herein is being submitted solely for the court's *in camera* inspection and a copy of the sealed exhibit is not being furnished to the defendants. I would request the court, at the conclusion of its hearing on this matter, to place the sealed exhibit in a sealed envelope and return it to the Department of Justice where it will be retained under seal so that it may be submitted to any appellate court that may review this matter."

[3]Jurisdiction was challenged before the Court of Appeals on the ground that the District Court's order was interlocutory and not appealable under 28 U. S. C. § 1291. On this issue, the court correctly held that it did have jurisdiction, relying upon the All Writs Act, 28 U. S. C. § 1651, and cases cited in its opinion, 444 F. 2d, at 655-656. No attack was made in this Court as to the appropriateness of the writ of mandamus procedure.

[4]These exceptions relate to certain activities of communication common carriers and the Federal Communications Commission, and to specified situations where a party to the communication has consented to the interception.

[5]Title 18 U. S. C. § 2518, subsection (1), reads as follows:

"§ 2518. Procedure for interception of wire or oral communications

"'(1) Each application for an order authorizing or approving the interception of a wire or oral communication shall be made in writing upon oath or affirmation to a judge of competent jurisdiction and shall state the applicant's authority to make such application. Each application shall include the following information:

"(a) the identity of the investigative or law enforcement officer making the application, and the officer authorizing the application;

"(b) a full and complete statement of the facts and circumstances relied upon by the applicant, to justify his belief that an order should be issued, including (i) details as to the particular offense that has been, is being, or is about to be committed, (ii) a particular description of the nature and location of the facilities from which or the place where the communication is to be intercepted, (iii) a particular description of the type of communications sought to be intercepted, (iv) the identity of the person, if known, committing the offense and whose communications are to be intercepted;

"(c) a full and complete statement as to whether or not other investigative procedures have been tried and failed or why they reasonably appear to be unlikely to succeed if tried or to be too dangerous;

"(d) a statement of the period of time for which the interception is required to be maintained. If the nature of the investigation is such that the authorization for interception should not automatically terminate when the described type of communication has been first obtained, a particular description of facts establishing probable cause to believe that additional communications of the same type will occur thereafter;

"(e) a full and complete statement of the facts concerning all previous applications known to the individual authorizing and making the application, made to any judge for authorization to intercept, or for approval of interceptions of, wire or oral communications involving any of the same persons, facilities or places specified in the application, and the action taken by the judge on each such application; and

"(f) where the application is for the extension of an order, a statement setting forth the results thus far obtained from the interception, or a reasonable explanation of the failure to obtain such results."

[6]The final sentence of § 2511 (3) states that the contents of an interception "by authority of the President in the exercise of the foregoing powers may be received in evidence . . . only where such interception was reasonable. . . ." This sentence seems intended to assure that when the President conducts lawful surveillance—pursuant to whatever power he may possess—the evidence is admissible.

[7]114 Cong. Rec. 14751. Senator McClellan was the sponsor of the bill. The above exchange constitutes the only time that § 2511 (3) was expressly debated on the Senate or House floor. The Report of the Senate Judiciary Committee is not so explicit as the exchange on the floor, but it appears to recognize that under § 2511 (3) the national security power of the President—whatever it may be—"is not to be deemed disturbed." S. Rep. No. 1097, 90th Cong., 2d Sess., 94 (1968). See also The "National Security Wiretap": Presidential Prerogative or Judicial Responsibility, where the author concludes that in § 2511 (3) "Congress took what amounted to a position of neutral noninterference on the question of the constitutionality of warrantless national security wiretaps authorized by the President." 45 S. Cal. L. Rev. 888, 889 (1972).

[8]Section 2511 (3) refers to "the constitutional power of the President" in two types of situations: (i) where necessary to protect against attack, other hostile acts or intelligence activities of a "foreign power"; or (ii) where necessary to protect against the overthrow of the Government or other clear and present danger to the structure or existence of the Government. Although both of the specified situations are sometimes referred to as "national security" threats, the term "national security" is used only in the first sentence of § 2511 (3) with respect to the activities of foreign powers. This case involves only the second sentence of § 2511 (3), with the threat emanating—according to the Attorney General's affidavit—from "domestic organizations." Although we attempt no precise definition, we use the term "domestic organization" in this opinion to mean a group or organization (whether formally or informally constituted) composed of citizens of the United States and which has no significant connection with a foreign power, its agents or agencies. No doubt there are cases where it will be difficult to distinguish between "domestic" and "foreign" unlawful activities directed against the Government of the United States where there is collaboration in varying degrees between domestic groups or organizations and agents or agencies of foreign powers. But this is not such a case.

[9]Enactment of Title III reflects congressional recognition of the importance of such surveillance in combatting various types of crime. Frank S. Hogan, District Attorney for New York County for over 25 years, described telephonic interception, pursuant to court order, as "the single most valuable weapon in law enforcement's fight against organized crime." 117 Cong. Rec. 14051. The "Crime Commission" appointed by President Johnson noted that "[t]he great majority of law enforcement officials believe that the evidence necessary to bring criminal sanctions to bear consistently on the higher echelons of organized crime will not be obtained without the aid of electronic surveillance techniques. They maintain these techniques are indispensable to develop adequate strategic intelligence concerning organized crime, to set up specific investigations, to develop witnesses, to corroborate their testimony, and to serve as substitutes for them—each a necessary step in the evidence-gathering process in organized crime investigations and prosecutions." Report by the President's Commission on Law Enforcement and Administration of Justice, The Challenge of Crime in a Free Society 201 (1967).

[10]In that month Attorney General Tom Clark advised President Truman of the necessity of using wiretaps "in cases vitally affecting the domestic security." In May 1940 President Roosevelt had authorized Attorney General Jackson to utilize wiretapping in matters "involving the defense of the nation," but it is questionable whether this language was meant to apply to solely domestic subversion. The nature and extent of wiretapping apparently varied under different administrations and

Attorneys General, but, except for the sharp curtailment under Attorney General Ramsey Clark in the latter years of the Johnson administration, electronic surveillance has been used both against organized crime and in domestic security cases at least since the 1946 memorandum from Clark to Truman. Brief for United States 16-18; Brief for Respondents 51-56; 117 Cong. Rec. 14056.

[11]Brownell, The Public Security and Wire Tapping, 39 Cornell L. Q. 195, 202 (1954). See also Rogers, The Case For Wire Tapping, 63 Yale L. J. 792 (1954).

[12]The Government asserts that there were 1,562 bombing incidents in the United States from January 1, 1971, to July 1, 1971, most of which involved Government related facilities. Respondents dispute these statistics as incorporating many frivolous incidents as well as bombings against nongovernmental facilities. The precise level of this activity, however, is not relevant to the disposition of this case. Brief for United States 18; Brief for Respondents 26-29; Reply Brief for United States 13.

[13]Professor Alan Westin has written on the likely course of future conflict between the value of privacy and the "new technology" of law enforcement. Much of the book details techniques of physical and electronic surveillance and such possible threats to personal privacy as psychological and personality testing and electronic information storage and retrieval. Not all of the contemporary threats to privacy emanate directly from the pressures of crime control. Privacy and Freedom (1967).

[14]Though the total number of intercepts authorized by state and federal judges pursuant to Tit. III of the 1968 Omnibus Crime Control and Safe Streets Act was 597 in 1970, each surveillance may involve interception of hundreds of different conversations. The average intercept in 1970 involved 44 people and 655 conversations, of which 295 or 45% were incriminating. 117 Cong. Rec. 14052.

[15]114 Cong. Rec. 14750. The subsequent assurances, quoted in part I of the opinion, that § 2511 (3) implied no statutory grant, contraction, or definition of presidential power eased the Senator's misgivings.

[16]This view has not been accepted. In *Chimel v. California,* 395 U.S. 752 (1969), the Court considered the Government's contention that the search be judged on a general "reasonableness" standard without reference to the warrant clause. The Court concluded that argument was "founded on little more than a subjective view regarding the acceptability of certain sorts of police conduct, and not on considerations relevant to Fourth Amendment interests. Under such an unconfined analysis, Fourth Amendment protection in this area would approach the evaporation point." *Id.,* at 764-765.

[17]N. Lasson, The History and Development of the Fourth Amendment to the United States Constitution 79-105 (1937).

[18]We use the word "judicial" to connote the traditional Fourth Amendment requirement of a neutral and detached magistrate.

[19]The Government argues that domestic security wiretaps should be upheld by courts in post-surveillance review "[u]nless it appears that the Attorney General's determination that the proposed surveillance relates to a national security matter is arbitrary and capricious, *i.e.,* that it constitutes a clear abuse of the broad discretion that the Attorney General has to obtain all information that will be helpful to the President in protecting the Government . . ." against the various unlawful acts in § 2511 (3). Brief for United States 22.

[20]See n. 8, *supra.* For the view that warrantless surveillance, though impermissible in domestic security cases, may be constitutional where foreign powers are involved, see *United States v. Smith,* 321 F. Supp. 424, 425-426 (CD Cal. 1971); and American Bar Association Project on Standards for Criminal Justice, Electronic Surveillance 120, 121 (Approved Draft 1971, and Feb. 1971 Supp. 11). See also *United States v. Clay,* 430 F. 2d 165 (CA5 1970).

[21]We think it unnecessary at this time and on the facts of this case to consider the arguments advanced by the Government for a re-examination of the basis and scope of the Court's decision in *Alderman.*

The Right To Speak

COMMENTARY

Invoking claims of national security, the government has from time to time sought to punish speech based on the assertion that it had the potential to interfere with an ongoing military campaign or with defense preparations. The government has also sought to punish speech that was said to threaten the very existence of the government.

A very special case is the law of treason, the only crime specified in the Constitution, where it is bounded by procedural and substantive safeguards designed in part to protect free speech.

It is difficult to find another area of the law where the Supreme Court has so utterly failed to establish well-defined principles, viable both in periods of turmoil and of tranquility. Existing precedents scarcely provide a consistent basis for determining when the First Amendment will permit restrictions on speech because of overriding national security interests. The earliest test was announced in 1919 in *Schenck v. United States,* 249 U.S. 47 (1919). Justice Holmes, writing for the Court, stated that:

> The question in every case is whether the words used are used in such circumstances and are of such a nature as to create a clear and present danger that they will bring about the substantive evils that Congress has a right to prevent. It is a question of proximity and degree. When a nation is at war many things that might be said in peace are of such hindrance to its effort that their utterance will not be endured so long as men fight and that no Court could regard them as protected by any constitutional right.

In other cases the Court has upheld limitations on speech where the danger was neither clear nor present but was nevertheless felt to be substantial. In 1951, in *Dennis v. United States,* 341 U.S. 494, the Court sustained convictions of Communist Party members under the Smith Act for advocating the violent overthrow of the government. The Court adopted the formulations by Judge Learned Hand in the court below that "In each case (courts) must ask whether the gravity of the evil discounted by its improbability, justifies such invasion of free speech as is necessary to avoid the danger."[1]

The Court also indicated that in weighing these factors it would be inclined to defer to the judgments of the "political branches" of the government as to the degree of risk. The essence of the Court's position appears to be that when the nation feels itself at war or under seige, it is not prudent for the courts to compel the government to tolerate speech that might interfere with the war effort. In times viewed as less threatening the Court has been willing to expand the limits of permissible speech, for example by distinguishing between abstract, ideological speech and personal committment to violence, or by invoking procedural doctrines such as vagueness and overbreadth.[2]

Special problems arise when speech is combined with non-speech in a single symbolic action. In *United States v. O'Brien,* 391 U.S. 367 (1968), the Court summarized the position it had taken:

> A government regulation is sufficiently justified if it is within the constitutional power of the Government; if it furthers an important or substantial government interest; if the governmental interest is unrelated to the suppression of free expression; and if the incidental restriction on alleged First Amendment freedoms is no greater than is essential to the furtherance of that interest.

In *O'Brien,* the application of these principles led the Court to uphold a draft card burning conviction; yet in 1974 the Court, ostensibly on the same principles, overturned a conviction based on abuse of the flag.[3] The distinction offered by the Court, that card-burning could interfere with the draft, was perhaps less germane than the change in political climate in the intervening years.

In its effort to curb dissent to the Vietnam War, the government did not rely on the speech-crime statutes that were used and abused during the McCarthy period, but instead resorted to a more recent statute which makes it a crime to counsel others to avoid the draft, 18 U.S.C. 462(a).[4] A group of anti-war activists, including famous pediatrician Benjamin Spock, was indicted and convicted of conspiracy to violate this statute. In reversing the conviction and ordering a new trial, the Court of Appeals established new and more stringent criteria for conspiracy convictions when First Amendment activity is involved.[5]

In the leading case on treason, *Cramer v. United States,* 325 U.S. 1 (1945) the Court overturned the conviction of an American who collaborated with Nazi saboteurs. In their discussion, both majority and dissenting opinions pointed to the desire of the founding fathers to prevent the abuse of treason charges to curb legitimate debate. The Court did not stop to inquire whether the Framers of the Constitution meant to leave the government free to punish nonconformist speech provided that the offense is not labelled as treason. Such attempts, of course, raise questions about the scope of First Amendment protection for speech that is alleged to threaten the national security.

---

[1] 188, F.2d at 212.

[2] For a discussion of the various techniques used by the courts to sustain or over-rule convictions for speech crimes, see "Judicial Standards and Techniques in the Resolution of First Amendment Cases," in Emerson, Haber and Dorsen, *Political and Civil Rights in the United States* (Fourth Edition), 51-59.

[3] *Spence v. Washington,* 418 U.S. 405 (1974).

[4] 18 U.S.C. 462(a).

[5] *United States v. Spock,* 461 F.2d 165 (1st Cir. 1969).

STATUTES

U.S. Constitution, Article III

Section 3. [1] Treason against the United States, shall consist only in levying War against them, or, in adhering to their Enemies, giving them Aid and Comfort.

No Person shall be convicted of Treason unless on the Testimony of two Witnesses to the same overt Act, or on Confession in open Court.

Alien and Sedition Acts

1 Stat. 570 (1798)

Chap. LVIII.—An Act Concerning Aliens.

Section 1. Be it enacted by the Senate and House of Representatives of the United States of America in Congres assembled, that it shall be lawful for the President of the United States at any time during the continuance of this act, to *order* all such *aliens* as he shall judge dangerous to the peace and safety of the United States, or shall have reasonable grounds to suspect are concerned in any treasonable or secret machinations against the government thereof, to depart out of the territory of the United States, within such time as shall be expressed in such order, which order shall be served on such alien by delivering him a copy thereof, or leaving the same at his usual abode, and returned to the office of the Secretary of State, by the marshal or other person to whom the same shall be directed. And in case any alien, so ordered to depart, shall be found at large within the United States after the time limited in such order for his departure, and not having obtained a *license* from the President to reside therein, or having obtained such *license* shall not have conformed thereto, every such alien shall, on conviction thereof, be imprisoned for a term not exceeding three years, and shall never after be admitted to become a citizen of the United States. *Provided always, and be it further enacted,* that if any alien so ordered to depart shall prove to the satisfaction of the President, by evidence to be taken before such person or persons as the President shall direct, who are for that purpose hereby authorized to administer oaths, that no injury or danger to the United States will arise from suffering such alien to reside therein, the President may grant a *license* to such alien to remain within the United States for such time as he shall judge proper, and at such place as he may designate. And the President may also require of such alien to enter into a bond to the United States, in such penal sum as he may direct, with one or more sufficient sureties to the satisfaction of the person authorized by the President to take the same, conditioned for the good behavior of such alien during his residence in the United States, and not violating his license, which license the President may revoke, whenever he shall think proper.

Sec. 2. *And be it further enacted,* That it shall be lawful for the President of the United States, whenever he may deem it necessary for the public safety, to order to be removed out of the territory thereof, any alien who may or shall be in prison in pursuance of this act; and to cause to be arrested and sent out of the United States such of those aliens as shall have been ordered to depart therefrom and shall not have obtained a license as aforesaid, in all cases where, in the opinion of the President, the public safety requires a speedy removal. And if any alien so removed or sent out of the United States by the President shall voluntarily return thereto, unless by permission of the President of the United States, such alien on conviction thereof, shall be imprisoned so long as, in the opinion of the President, the public safety may require.

Sec. 3. *And be it further enacted,* That every master or commander of any ship or vessel which shall come into any port of the United States after the first day of July next, shall immediately on his arrival make report in writing to the collector or other chief officer of the customs of such port, of all aliens, if any, on board his vessel, specifying their names, age, the place of nativity, the country from which they shall have come, the nation to which they belong and owe allegiance, their occupation and a description of their persons, as far as he shall be informed thereof, and on failure, every such master and commander shall forfeit and pay three hundred dollars, for the payment whereof on default of such master or commander, such vessel shall also be holden, and may by such collector or other officer of the customs be detained. And it shall be the duty of such collector or other officer of the customs, forthwith to transmit to the office of the department of state true copies of all such returns.

Sec. 4. *And be it further enacted,* That the circuit and district courts of the United States, shall respectively have cognizance of all crimes and offences against this act. And all marshals and other officers of the United States are required to execute all precepts and orders of the President of the United States issued in pursuance or by virtue of this act.

Sec. 5. *And be it further enacted,* That it shall be lawful for any alien who may be ordered to be removed from the United States, by virtue of this act, to take with him such part of his goods, chattels, or other property, as he may find convenient; and all property left in the United States by any alien, who may be removed, as aforesaid, shall be, and remain subject to his order and disposal, in the same manner as if this act had not been passed.

Sec. 6 *And be it further enacted,* That this act shall continue and be in force for and during the term of two years from the passing thereof.

Approved, June 25, 1798.

Chap. LXVI.—An Act Respecting Alien Enemies.(a)

Section 1. *Be it enacted by the Senate and House of Representatives of the United States of America in Congress assembled,* That whenever there shall be a declared war between the United States and any foreign nation or government, or any invasion or predatory incursion shall be perpetrated, attempted, or threatened against the territory of the United States, by any foreign nation or government, and the President of the United States shall make public proclamation of the event, all natives, citizens, denizens, or subjects of the hostile nation or government, being males of the age of fourteen years and upwards, who shall be within the United States, and not actually naturalized, shall be liable to be apprehended, restrained, secured and removed, as alien enemies. And the President of the United States shall be, and he is hereby authorized, in any event, as aforesaid, by his proclamation thereof, or other public act, to direct the conduct to be observed, on the part of the United States, towards the aliens who shall become liable, as aforesaid; the manner and degree of the restraint to which they shall be subject, and in what cases, and upon what security their residence shall be permitted, and to provide for the removal of those, who, not being permitted to reside within the United States, shall refuse or neglect to depart therefrom; and to establish any other regulations which shall be found necessary in the premises and for the public safety: Provided, that aliens resident within the United States, who shall become liable as enemies, in the manner aforesaid, and who shall not be chargeable with actual hostility, or other crime against the public safety, shall be allowed, for the recovery, disposal, and removal of their goods and effects, and for their departure, the full time which is, or shall be stipulated by any treaty, where any shall have been between the United States, and the hostile nation or government, of which they shall be natives, citizens, denizens or subjects: and where no such treaty shall have existed, the President of the United States may ascertain and declare such reasonable time as may be consistent with the public safety, and according to the dictates of humanity and national hospitality.

Sec. 2. *And be it further enacted,* That after any proclamation shall be made as aforesaid, it shall be the duty of the several courts of the United States, and of each state, having criminal jurisdiction, and of the several judges and justices of the courts of the United States, and they shall be, and are hereby respectively, authorized upon complaint, against any alien or alien enemies, as aforesaid, who shall be resident and at large within such jurisdiction or district, to the danger of the public peace or safety, and contrary to the tenor or intent of such proclamation, or other regulations which the President of the United States shall and may establish in the premises, to cause such alien or aliens to be duly apprehended and convened before such court, judge or justice; and after a full examination and hearing on such complaint, and sufficient cause therefor appearing, shall and may order such alien or aliens to be removed out of the territory of the United States, or to give sureties of their good behaviour, or to be otherwise restrained, conformably to the proclamation or regulations which shall and may be established as aforesaid, and may imprison, or otherwise secure such alien or aliens, until the order which shall and may be made, as aforesaid, shall be preformed.

Sec. 3. *And be it further enacted,* That it shall be the duty of the marshal of the district in which any alien enemy shall be apprehended, who by the President of the United States, or by order of any court, judge or justice, as aforesaid, shall be required to depart, and to be removed, as aforesaid, to provide therefor, and to execute such order, by himself or his deputy, or other discreet person or persons to be employed by him, by causing a removal of such alien out of the territory of the United States; and for such removal the marshal shall have the warrant of the President of the United States, or of the court, judge or justice ordering the same, as the case may be.

Approved, July 6, 1798.

Chap. LXXIV.—An Act in Addition to the Act, Entitled "An Act for the Punishment of Certain Crimes Against the United States."

Section 1. *Be it enacted by the Senate and House of Representatives of the United States of America, in Congress assembled,* That if any persons shall unlawfully combine or conspire together, with intent to oppose any measure or measures of the government of the United States, which are or shall be directed by proper authority, or to impede the operation of any law of the United States, or to intimidate or prevent any person holding a place or office in or under the government of the United States, from undertaking, performing or executing his trust or duty; and if any person or persons, with intent as aforesaid, shall counsel, advise or attempt to procure any insurrection, riot, unlawful assembly, or combination, whether such conspiracy, threatening, counsel, advice, or attempt shall have the proposed effect or not, he or they shall be deemed guilty of a high misdemeanor, and on conviction, before any court of the United States having jurisdiction thereof, shall be punished by a fine not exceeding five thousand dollars, and by imprisonment during a term not less than six months nor exceeding five years; and further, at the discretion of the court may be holden to find sureties for his good behaviour in such sum, and for such time, as the said court may direct.

Sec. 2. *And be it further enacted,* That if any person shall write, print, utter or publish, or shall cause or procure to be written, printed, uttered or published, or shall knowingly and willingly assist or aid in writing, printing, uttering or publishing any false, scandalous and malicious writing or writings against the government of the United States, or either house of the Congress of the United States, or the President of the United States, with intent to defame the said government, or either house of the said Congress, or the said President, or to bring them, or either of them, into contempt or disrepute; or to excite against them, or either or any of them, the hatred of the good people of the United States, or to stir up sedition within the United States, or to excite any unlawful combinations therein, for opposing or resisting any law of the United States, or any act of the President of the United States, done in pursuance of any such law, or of the powers in him vested by the constitution of the United States, or to resist, oppose, or defeat any such law or act, or to aid, encourage or abet any hostile designs of any foreign nation against the United States, their people or government, then such person, being thereof convicted before any court of the United States having jurisdiction thereof, shall be punished by a fine not exceeding two thousand dollars, and by imprisonment not exceeding two years.

Sec. 3. *And be it further enacted and declared,* That if any person shall be prosecuted under this act, for the writing or publishing any libel aforesaid, it shall be lawful for the defendant, upon the trial of the cause, to give in evidence in his defence, the truth of the matter contained in the publication charged as a libel. And the jury who shall try the cause, shall have a right to determine the law and the fact, under the direction of the court, as in other cases.

Sec. 4. *And be it further enacted,* That this act shall continue and be in force until the third day of March, one thousand eight hundred and one, and no longer: *Provided,* that the expiration of the act shall not prevent or defeat a prosecution and punishment of any offence against the law, during the time it shall be in force.

Approved, July 14, 1798.

Logan Act

1 Stat. 613 (1799)

Statute III.

Chapter I.—An Act for the Punishment of Certain Crimes Therein Specified.

Be it enacted by the Senate and House of Representatives of the United States of America in Congress assembled, That if any person, being a citizen of the United

States, whether he be actually resident, or abiding within the United States, or in any foreign country, shall, without the permission or authority of the government of the United States, directly or indirectly, commence, or carry on, any verbal or written correspondence or intercourse with any foreign government, or any officer or agent thereof, with an intent to influence the measures or conduct of any foreign government, or of any officer or agent thereof, in relation to any disputes or controversies with the United States, or defeat the measures of the government of the United States; or if any person, being a citizen of, or resident within the United States, and not duly authorized, shall counsel, advise, aid or assist in any such correspondence, with intent, as aforesaid, he or they shall be deemed guilty of a high misdemeanor, and on conviction before any court of the United States having jurisdiction thereof, shall be punished by a fine not exceeding five thousand dollars, and by imprisonment during a term not less than six months, nor exceeding three years: *Provided always,* that nothing in this act contained shall be construed to abridge the right of individual citizens of the United States to apply, by themselves, or their lawful agents, to any foreign government, or the agents thereof, for the redress of any injuries in relation to person or property which such individuals may have sustained from such government, or any of its agents, citizens or subjects.

Approved, January 30, 1799.

Espionage Act of 1918

40 Stat. 553

Chap. 75.—An Act To amend section three, title one, of the Act entitled "An Act to punish acts of interference with the foreign relations, the neutrality, and the foreign commerce of the United States, to punish espionage, and better to enforce the criminal laws of the United States, and for other purposes," approved June fifteenth, nineteen hundred and seventeen, and for other purposes.

Be it enacted by the Senate and House of Representatives of the United States of America in Congress assembled, That section three of title one of the Act entitled "An Act to punish acts of interference with the foreign relations, the neutrality, and the foreign commerce of the United States, to punish espionage, and better to enforce the criminal laws of the United States, and for other purposes," approved June fifteenth, nineteen hundred and seventeen, be, and the same is hereby, amended so as to read as follows:

"Sec. 3. Whoever, when the United States is at war, shall willfully make or convey false reports or false statements with intent to interfere with the operation or success of the military or naval forces of the United States, or to promote the success of its enemies, or shall willfully make or convey false reports or false statements, or say or do anything except by way of bona fide and not disloyal advice to an investor or investors, with intent to obstruct the sale by the United States of bonds or other securities of the United States or the making of loans by or to the United States, and whoever, when the United States is at war, shall willfully cause or attempt to cause, or incite or attempt to incite, insubordination, disloyalty, mutiny, or refusal of duty, in the military or naval forces of the United States, or shall willfully obstruct or attempt to obstruct the recruiting or enlistment service of the United States, and whoever, when the United States is at war, shall willfully utter, print, write, or publish any disloyal, profane, scurrilous, or abusive language about the form of government of the United States, or the Constitution of the United States, or the military or naval forces of the United States, or the flag of the United States, or the uniform of the Army or Navy of the United States, or any language intended to bring the form of government of the United States, or the Constitution of the United States, or the military or naval forces of the United States, or the flag of the United States, or the uniform of the Army or Navy of the United States into contempt, scorn, contumely, or disrepute, or shall willfully utter, print, write, or publish any language intended to incite, provoke, or encourage resistance to the United States, or to promote the cause of its enemies, or shall willfully display the flag of any foreign enemy, or shall willfully by utterance, writing, printing, publication, or language spoken, urge, incite, or advocate any curtailment of production in this country of any thing or things, product or products, necessary or essential to the prosecution of the war in which the United States may be engaged, with intent by such curtailment to cripple or hinder the United States in the prosecution of the war, and whoever shall willfully advocate, teach, defend, or suggest the doing of any of the acts or things in this section enumerated, and whoever shall by word or act support or favor the cause of any country with which the United States is at war or by word or act oppose the cause of the United States therein, shall be punished by a fine of not more than $10,000 or imprisonment for not more than twenty years, or both: *Provided,* That any employee or official of the United States Government who commits any disloyal act or utters any unpatriotic or disloyal language, or who, in an abusive and violent manner criticizes the Army or Navy or the flag of the United States shall be at once dismissed from the service. Any such employee shall be dismissed by the head of the department in which the employee may be engaged, and any such official shall be dismissed by the authority having power to appoint a successor to the dismissed official."

Sec. 2. That section one of Title XII and all other provisions of the Act entitled "An Act to punish acts of interference with the foreign relations, the neutrality, and the foreign commerce of the United States, to punish espionage, and better to enforce the criminal laws of the United States, and for other purposes," approved June fifteenth, nineteen hundred and seventeen, which apply to section three of Title I thereof shall apply with equal force and effect to said section three as amended.

Title XII of the said Act of June fifteenth, nineteen hundred and seventeen, be, and the same is hereby, amended by adding thereto the following section:

"Sec. 4. When the United States is at war, the Postmaster General may, upon evidence satisfactory to him that any person or concern is using the mails in violation of any of the provisions of this Act, instruct the postmaster at any post office at which mail is received addressed to such person or concern to return to the postmaster at the office at which they were originally mailed all letters or other matter so addressed, with the words 'Mail to this address undeliverable under Espionage Act' plainly written or stamped upon the outside thereof, and all such letters or other matter so returned to such postmasters shall be by them returned to the senders thereof under such regulations as the Postmaster General may prescribe."

Approved, May 16, 1918.

Foreign Agents Registration Act

52 Stat. 631 (1938)

An Act

To require the registration of certain persons employed by agencies to disseminate propaganda in the United States and for other purposes.

Be it enacted by the Senate and House of Representatives of the United States of America in Congress assembled,

That as used in this Act—

(a) The term "person" means an individual, partnership, association, or corporation;

(b) The term "United States" includes the United States and any place subject to the jurisdiction thereof;

(c) The term "foreign principal" means the government of a foreign country, a political party of a foreign country, a person domiciled abroad, or any foreign business, partnership, association, corporation, or political organization;

(d) The term "agent of a foreign principal" means any person who acts or engages or agrees to act as a public-relations counsel, publicity agent, or as agent, servant, representative, or attorney for a foreign principal or for any domestic organization subsidized directly or indirectly in whole or in part by a foreign principal. Such term shall not include a duly accredited diplomatic or consular officer of a foreign government who is so recognized by the Department of State of the United States, nor a person, other than a public-relations counsel, or publicity agent, performing only private, non-political, financial, mercantile, or other activities in furtherance of the bona fide trade or commerce of such foreign principal;

(e) The term "Secretary" means the Secretary of State of the United States.

Sec. 2. Every person who is now an agent of a foreign principal shall, within thirty days after this Act takes effect, and every person who shall hereafter become an agent of a foreign principal shall forthwith file with the Secretary a registration statement, under oath, on a form prescribed by the Secretary which shall set forth—

(a) The name, business address, and residence address of the registrant;

(b) The name of the foreign principal or other person or organization for which such person is acting as agent;

(c) A copy of all contracts of employment under which such person acts or agrees to act as such agent, if written, or a full statement of the terms and conditions thereof, if oral;

(d) The date when each such contract was made, the date of commencement of activity thereunder, and the period during which such contract is to be in effect;

(e) The compensation to be paid, if any, and the form and time of payment, under such contract;

(f) The name of every foreign principal, or other person or organization which has contributed or which has promise to contribute to the compensation provided in such contract; and

(g) If the registrant be a partnership, association, or corporation, a true and complete copy of its charter, articles of incorporation, copartnership, association, constitution, and bylaws, and any other instrument or instruments relating to its organization, powers, and purposes.

Sec. 3. Every person who has filed a registration statement required by section 2 shall, within thirty days after the expiration of such period of six months succeeding the first filing, file with the Secretary a statement, under oath, on a form prescribed by the Secretary, which shall set forth with respect to such preceding six months' period—

(a) Such facts as may be necessary to make the information required under section 2 hereof accurate and current with respect to such period;

(b) The amount and form of compensation received by such person for acting as agent for a foreign principal which has been received during such six months' period either directly or indirectly from any foreign principal; and

(c) A statement containing such details required under this Act as the Secretary shall fix, of the activities of such persons as agent of a foreign principal during such six months' period.

Sec. 4. The Secretary shall retain in permanent form all statements filed under this Act, and such statements shall be public records and open to public examination and inspection at all reasonable hours, under such rules and regulations as the Secretary may prescribe.

Sec. 5. Any person who willfully fails to file any statement required to be filed under this Act, or in complying with the provisions of this Act, makes a false statement of a material fact, or willfully omits to state any material fact required to be stated therein shall, on conviction thereof, be punished by a fine of not more than $1,000 or imprisonment for not more than two years, or both.

Sec. 6. The Secretary is authorized and directed to prescribe such rules, regulations, and forms as may be necessary to carry out this Act.

Sec. 7. This Act shall take effect on the ninetieth day after the date of its enactment.

Approved, June 8, 1938.

Alien Registration Act

54 Stat. 670 (1940)

An Act

To prohibit certain subversive activities; to amend certain provisions of law with respect to the admission and deportation of aliens; to require the fingerprinting and registration of aliens; and for other purposes.

Be it enacted by the Senate and House of Representatives of the United States of America in Congress assembled,

Title I

Section 1. (a) It shall be unlawful for any person, with intent to interfere with, impair, or influence the loyalty, morale, or discipline of the military or naval forces of the United States—

(1) to advise, counsel, urge, or in any manner cause insubordination, disloyalty, mutiny, or refusal of duty by any member of the military or naval forces of the United States; or

(2) to distribute any written or printed matter which advises, counsels, or urges insubordination, disloyalty, mutiny, or refusal of duty by any member of the military or naval forces of the United States.

(b) For the purposes of this section, the term "military or naval forces of the United States" includes the Army of the United States, as defined in section 1 of the National Defense Act of June 3, 1916, as amended (48 Stat. 153; U. S. C., title 10, sec. 2), the Navy, Marine Corps, Coast Guard, Naval Reserve, and Marine Corps Reserve of the United States; and, when any merchant vessel is commissioned in the Navy or is in the service of the Army or the Navy, includes the master, officers, and crew of such vessel.

Sec. 2 (a) It shall be unlawful for any person—

(1) to knowingly or willfully advocate, abet, advise, or teach the duty, necessity, desirability, or propriety of overthrowing or destroying any government in the United States by force or violence, or by the assassination of any officer of any such government;

(2) with the intent to cause the overthrow or destruction of any government in the United States, to print, publish, edit, issue, circulate, sell, distribute, or publicly display any written or printed matter advocating, advising, or teaching the duty, necessity, desirability, or propriety of overthrowing or destroying any government in the United States by force or violence;

(3) to organize or help to organize any society, group, or assembly of persons who teach, advocate, or encourage the overthrow or destruction of any government in the United States by force or violence; or to be or become a member of, or affiliate with, any such society, group, or assembly of persons, knowing the purposes thereof.

(b) For the purposes of this section, the term "government in the United States" means the Government of the United States, the government of any State, Territory, or possession of the United States, the government of the District of Columbia, or the government of any political subdivision of any of them.

Sec. 3. It shall be unlawful for any person to attempt to commit, or to conspire to commit, any of the acts prohibited by the provisions of this title.

Sec. 4. Any written or printed matter of the character described in section 1 or section 2 of this Act, which is intended for use in violation of this Act, may be taken from any house or other place in which it may be found, or from any person in whose possession it may be, under a search warrant issued pursuant to the provisions of title XI of the Act entitled "An Act to punish acts of interference with the foreign relations, the neutrality and the foreign commerce of the United States, to punish espionage, and better to enforce the criminal laws of the United States, and for other purposes", approved June 15, 1917 (40 Stat. 228; U. S. C., title 18, ch. 18).

Sec. 5. (a) Any person who violates any of the provisions of this title shall, upon conviction thereof, be fined not more than $10,000 or imprisoned for not more than ten years, or both.

(b) No person convicted of violating any of the provisions of this title shall, during the five years next following his conviction, be eligible for employment by the United States, or by any department or agency thereof (including any corporation the stock of which is wholly owned by the United States).

Title II

Sec. 20. Section 19 of the Immigration Act of February 5, 1917 (39 Stat. 889; U. S. C., title 8, sec. 155), as amended, is amended by inserting, after "Sec. 19.", the letter "(a)", and by adding at the end of such section the following new subsections:

"(b) Any alien of any of the classes specified in this subsection, in addition to aliens who are deportable under other provisions of law, shall, upon warrant of the Attorney General, be taken into custody and deported:

"(1) Any alien who, at any time within five years after entry, shall have, knowingly and for gain, encouraged, induced, assisted, abetted, or aided any other alien to enter or to try to enter the United States in violation of law.

"(2) Any alien who, at any time after entry, shall have on more than one occasion, knowingly and for gain, encouraged, induced, assisted, abetted, or aided any other alien or aliens to enter or to try to enter the United States in violation of law.

"(3) Any alien who, at any time after entry, shall have been convicted of possessing or carrying in violation of any law any weapon which shoots or is designed to shoot automatically or semi-automatically more than one shot without manual reloading, by a single function of the trigger, or a weapon commonly called a sawed-off shotgun.

"(4) Any alien who, at any time within five years after entry, shall have been convicted of violating the provisions of title I of the Alien Registration Act, 1940.

"(5) Any alien who, at any time after entry, shall have been convicted more than once of violating the provisions of title I of the Alien Registration Act, 1940.

No alien who is deportable under the provisions of paragraph (3), (4), or (5) of this subsection shall be deported until the termination of his imprisonment or the entry of an order releasing him on probation or parole.

"(c) In the case of any alien (other than one to whom subsection (d) is applicable) who is deportable under any law of the United States and who has proved good moral character for the preceding five years, the Attorney General may (1) permit such alien to depart the United States to any country of his choice at his own expense, in lieu of deportation, or (2) suspend deportation of such alien if not racially inadmissible or ineligible to naturalization in the United States if he finds that such deportation would result in serious economic detriment to a citizen or legally resident alien who is the spouse, parent, or minor child of such deportable alien. If the deportation of any alien is suspended under the provisions of this subsection for more than six months, all of the facts and pertinent provisions of law in the case shall be reported to the Congress within ten days after the beginning of its next regular session, with the reasons for such suspension. The Clerk of the House shall have such report printed as a public document. If during that session the two Houses pass a concurrent resolution stating in substance that the Congress does not favor the suspension of such deportation, the Attorney General shall thereupon deport such alien in the manner provided by law. If during that session the two Houses do not pass such a resolution, the Attorney General shall cancel deportation proceedings upon the termination of such session, except that such proceedings shall not be canceled in the case of any alien who was not legally admitted for permanent residence at the time of his last entry into the United States, unless such alien pays to the Commissioner of Immigration and Naturalization a fee of $18 (which fee shall be deposited in the Treasury of the United States as miscellaneous receipts). Upon the cancelation of such proceedings in any case in which such fee has been paid, the Commissioner shall record the alien's admission for permanent residence as of the date of his last entry into the United States and the Secretary of State shall, if the alien was a quota immigrant at the time of entry and was not charged to the appropriate quota, reduce by one the immigration quota of the country of the alien's nationality as defined in section 12 of the Act of May 26, 1924 (U. S. C., title 8, sec. 212), for the fiscal year then current or next following.

"(d) The provisions of subsection (c) shall not be applicable in the case of any alien who is deportable under (1) the Act of October 16, 1918 (40 Stat. 1008; U. S. C., title 8, sec. 137), entitled 'An Act to exclude and expel from the United States aliens who are members of the anarchist and similar classes', as amended; (2) the Act of May 26, 1922, entitled 'An Act to amend the Act entitled "An Act to prohibit the importation and use of opium for other than medicinal purposes", approved February 9, 1909, as amended' (42 Stat. 596; U. S. C., title 21, sec. 175); (3) the Act of February 18, 1931, entitled 'An Act to provide for the deportation of aliens convicted and sentenced for violation of any law regulating traffic in narcotics', as amended (46 Stat. 1171; U. S. C., title 8, sec. 156a); (4) any of the provisions of so much of subsection (a) of this section as relates to criminals, prostitutes, procurers, or other immoral persons, the mentally and physically deficient, anarchists, and similar classes; or (5) subsection (b) of this section."

Sec. 21. The Act entitled "An Act to provide for the deportation of aliens convicted and sentenced for violation of any law regulating traffic in narcotics", approved February 18, 1931, is amended—

(1) By striking out the words "and sentenced";

(2) By inserting after the words "any statute of the United States" the following: "or of any State, Territory, possession, or of the District of Columbia,"; and

(3) By inserting after the word "heroin" a comma and the word "marihuana".

Sec. 22. No alien shall be deportable by reason of the amendments made by section 20 or 21 on account of any act committed prior to the date of enactment of this Act.

Sec. 23. (a) The first paragraph of section 1 of the Act entitled "An Act to exclude and expel from the United States aliens who are members of the anarchistic and similar classes", approved October 16, 1918, as amended, is amended to read as follows:

"That any alien who, at any time, shall be or shall have been a member of any one of the following classes shall be excluded from admission into the United States:".

(b) Section 2 of such Act of October 16, 1918, as amended, is amended to read as follows:

"Sec. 2. Any alien who was at the time of entering the United States, or has been at any time thereafter, a member of any one of the classes of aliens enumerated in section 1 of this Act, shall, upon the warrant of the Attorney General, be taken into custody and deported in the manner provided in the Immigration Act of February

5, 1917. The provisions of this section shall be applicable to the classes of aliens mentioned in this Act, irrespective of the time of their entry into the United States."

Title III

Sec. 30. No visa shall hereafter be issued to any alien seeking to enter the United States unless said alien has been registered and fingerprinted in duplicate. One copy of the registration and fingerprint record shall be retained by the consul. The second copy shall be attached to the alien's visa and shall be taken up by the examining immigrant inspector at the port of arrival of the alien in the United States and forwarded to the Department of Justice, at Washington, District of Columbia.

Any alien seeking to enter the United States who does not present a visa (except in emergency cases defined by the Secretary of State), a reentry permit, or a border-crossing identification card shall be excluded from admission to the United States.

Sec. 31. (a) It shall be the duty of every alien now or hereafter in the United States, who (1) is fourteen years of age or older, (2) has not been registered and fingerprinted under section 30, and (3) remains in the United States for thirty days or longer, to apply for registration and to be fingerprinted before the expiration of such thirty days.

(b) It shall be the duty of every parent or legal guardian of any alien now or hereafter in the United States, who (1) is less than fourteen years of age, (2) has not been registered under section 30, and (3) remains in the United States for thirty days or longer, to apply for the registration of such alien before the expiration of such thirty days. Whenever any alien attains his fourteenth birthday in the United States he shall, within thirty days thereafter, apply in person for registration and to be fingerprinted.

Sec. 32. Notwithstanding the provisions of sections 30 and 31—

(a) The application for the registration and fingerprinting, or for the registration, of any alien who is in the United States on the effective date of such sections may be made at any time within four months after such date.

(b) No foreign government official, or member of his family, shall be required to be registered or fingerprinted under this title.

(c) The Commissioner is authorized to prescribe, with the approval of the Attorney General, special regulations for the registration and fingerprinting of (1) alien seamen, (2) holders of border-crossing identification cards, (3) aliens confined in institutions within the United States, (4) aliens under order of deportation, and (5) aliens of any other class not lawfully admitted to the United States for permanent residence.

Sec. 33. (a) All applications for registration and fingerprinting under section 31 shall be made at post offices or such other places as may be designated by the Commissioner.

(b) It shall be the duty of every postmaster, with such assistance as shall be provided by the Commissioner, to register and fingerprint any applicant for registration and fingerprinting under such section, and for such purposes to designate appropriate space in the local post office for such registration and fingerprinting. Every postmaster shall forward promptly to the Department of Justice, at Washington, District of Columbia, the registration and fingerprint record of every alien registered and fingerprinted by him. The Commissioner may designate such other places for registration and fingerprinting as may be necessary for carrying out the provisions of this Act, and provide for registration and fingerprinting of aliens at such places by officers or employees of the Immigration and Naturalization Service designated by the Commissioner. The duties imposed upon any postmaster under this Act shall also be performed by any employees at the post office of such postmaster who are designated by the postmaster for such purpose.

Sec. 34 (a) The Commissioner is authorized and directed to prepare forms for the registration and fingerprinting of aliens under this title. Such forms shall contain inquiries with respect to (1) the date and place of entry of the alien into the United States; (2) activities in which he has been and intends to be engaged; (3) the length of time he expects to remain in the United States; (4) the criminal record, if any, of such alien; and (5) such additional matters as may be prescribed by the Commissioner, with the approval of the Attorney General.

(b) All registration and fingerprint records made under the provisions of this title shall be secret and confidential, and shall be made available only to such persons or agencies as may be designated by the Commissioner, with the approval of the Attorney General.

(c) Every person required to apply for the registration of himself or another under this title shall submit under oath the information required for such registration. Any person authorized to register aliens under this title shall be authorized to administer oaths for such purpose.

Sec. 35. Any alien required to be registered under this title who is a resident of the United States shall notify the Commissioner in writing of each change of residence and new address within five days from the date of such change. Any other alien required to be registered under this title shall notify the Commissioner in writing of his address at the expiration of each three months' period of residence in the United States. In the case of an alien for whom a parent or legal guardian is required to apply for registration, the notices required by this section shall be given by such parent or legal guardian.

Sec. 36. (a) Any alien required to apply for registration and to be fingerprinted who willfully fails or refuses to make such application or to be fingerprinted, and any parent or legal guardian required to apply for the registration of any alien who willfully fails or refuses to file application for the registration of such alien shall, upon conviction thereof be fined not to exceed $1,000 or be imprisoned not more than six months, or both.

(b) Any alien, or any parent or legal guardian of any alien, who fails to give written notice to the Commissioner of change of address as required by section 35 of this Act shall, upon conviction thereof, be fined not to exceed $100, or be imprisoned not more than thirty days, or both.

(c) Any alien or any parent or legal guardian of any alien, who files an application for registration containing statements known by him to be false, or who procures or attempts to procure registration of himself or another person through fraud, shall, upon conviction thereof, be fined not to exceed $1,000, or be imprisoned not more than six months, or both; and any alien so convicted within five years after entry into the United States shall, upon the warrant of the Attorney General, be taken into custody and be deported in the manner provided in sections 19 and 20 of the Immigration Act of February 5, 1917, as amended.

Sec. 37. (a) The Commissioner, with the approval of the Attorney General, is authorized and empowered to make and prescribe, and from time to time to change and amend, such rules and regulations not in conflict with this Act as he may deem necessary and proper in aid of the administration and enforcement of this title (including provisions for the identification of aliens registered under this title); except that all such rules and regulations, insofar as they relate to the performance of functions by consular officers or officers or employees in the Postal Service, shall be prescribed by the Secretary of State and the Postmaster General, respectively, upon recommendation of the Attorney General. The powers conferred upon the Attorney General by this Act and all other powers of the Attorney General relating to the administration of the Immigration and Naturalization Service may be exercised by the Attorney General through such officers of the Department of Justice, including officers of the Immigration and Naturalization Service, attorneys, special attorneys, and special assistants to the Attorney General, as he may designate specifically for such purposes.

(b) The Commissioner is authorized to make such expenditures, to employ such additional temporary and permanent employees, and to rent such quarters outside the District of Columbia as may be necessary for carrying out the provisions of this title.

Sec. 38. (a) For the purposes of this title—

(1) the term "United States", when used in a geographical sense, means the States, the Territories of Alaska and Hawaii, the District of Columbia, Puerto Rico, and the Virgin Islands;

(2) the term "Commissioner" means the Commissioner of Immigration and Naturalization.

(b) The provisions of this title shall take effect upon the date of enactment of this Act; except that sections 30 and 31 shall take effect sixty days after the date of its enactment.

Sec. 39. The President is authorized to provide, by Executive order, for the registration and fingerprinting, in a manner as nearly similar to that provided in this title as he deems practicable, of aliens in the Panama Canal Zone.

Title IV

Sec. 40. If any provision of this Act, or the application thereof to any person or circumstance, is held invalid, the remainder of the Act, and the application of such provision to other persons or circumstances, shall not be affected thereby.

Sec. 41. This Act may be cited as the "Alien Registration Act, 1940".

Approved, June 28, 1940.

Smith Act

54 Stat. 1201 (1940)

An Act

To require the registration of certain organizations carrying on activities within the United States, and for other purposes.

Be it enacted by the Senate and House of Representatives of the United States of America in Congress assembled, That for the purposes of this Act—

(a) The term "Attorney General" means the Attorney General of the United States;

(b) The term "organization" means any group, club, league, society, committee, association, political party, or combination of individuals, whether incorporated or otherwise, but such term shall not include any corporation, association, community chest, fund or foundation, organized and operated exclusively for religious, charitable, scientific, literary, or educational purposes;

(c) The term "political activity" means any activity the purpose or aim of which, or one of the purposes or aims of which, is the control by force or overthrow of the Government of the United States or a political subdivision thereof, or any State or political subdivision thereof;

(d) An organization shall be deemed to be engaged in "civilian military activity" if (1) it gives instruction to, or prescribes instruction for, its members in the use of firearms or other weapons or any substitute therefor, or military or naval science, or (2) it receives from any other organization or from any individual instruction in military or naval science, or (3) it engages in any military or naval maneuvers or activities, or (4) it engages, either with or without arms, in drills or parades of a military or naval character, or (5) it engages in any other form of organized activity which in the opinion of the Attorney General constitutes preparation for military action; and

(e) An organization shall be deemed "subject to foreign control" if (1) it solicits or accepts financial contributions, loans, or support of any kind, directly, or indirectly, from, or is affiliated directly or indirectly with, a foreign government or a political subdivision thereof, or an agent, agency, or instrumentality of a foreign government or political subdivision thereof, or a political party in a foreign country, or an international political organization, or (2) its policies, or any of them, are determined by or at the suggestion of, or in collaboration with, a foreign government or political subdivision thereof, or an agent, agency, or instrumentality of a foreign government or a political subdivision thereof, or a political party in a foreign country, or an international political organization.

Sec. 2. (a) The following organizations shall be required to register with the Attorney General as hereinafter provided:

(1) Every organization subject to foreign control which engages in political activity;

(2) Every organization which engages both in civilian military activity and in political activity;

(3) Every organization subject to foreign control which engages in civilian military activity; and

(4) Every organization, the purpose or aim of which, or one of the purposes or aims of which, is the establishment, control, conduct, seizure, or overthrow of a government or subdivision thereof by the use of force, violence, military measures, or threats of any one or more of the foregoing.

Every such organization shall register by filing with the Attorney General, on such forms and in such detail as the Attorney General may by rules and regulations prescribe, a registration statement containing the information and documents prescribed in subsection (c) and shall within thirty days after the expiration of each period of six months succeeding the filing of such registration statement, file with the Attorney General, on such forms and in such detail as the Attorney General may by rules and regulations prescribe, a supplemental statement containing such information and documents as may be necessary to make the information and documents previously filed under this section accurate and current with respect to such preceding six months' period. Every statement required to be filed by this section shall be subscribed, under oath, by all of the officers of the organization.

(b) Nothing in subsection (a) shall be deemed to require registration or the filing of any statement with the Attorney General by (1) the armed forces of the United States, or (2) the organized militia or National Guard of any States, Territory, District, or possession of the United States, or (3) any law-enforcement agency of the United States or of any Territory, District, or possession thereof, or of any State or political subdivision of a State, or of any agency or instrumentality of one or more States, or (4) any duly established diplomatic mission or consular office of a foreign government which is so recognized by the Department of State, or (5) any nationally recognized organization of persons who are veterans of the armed forces of the United States, or affiliates of such organizations.

(c) Every registration statement required by subsection (a) to be filed by any organization shall contain the following information and documents:

(1) The name and post-office address of the organization in the United States, and the names and addresses of all branches, chapters, and affiliates of such organization;

(2) The name, address, and nationality of each officer, and of each person who performs the functions of an officer, of the organization, and of each branch, chapter, and affiliate of the organization;

(3) The qualifications for membership in the organization;

(4) The existing and proposed aims and purposes of the organization, and all the means by which these aims or purposes are being attained or are to be attained;

(5) The address or addresses of meeting places of the organization, and of each branch, chapter, or affiliate of the organization, and the times of meetings;

(6) The name and address of each person who has contributed any money, dues, property, or other thing ov value to the organization or to any branch, chapter, or affiliate of the organization;

(7) A detailed statement of the assets of the organization, and of each branch, chapter, and affiliate of the organization, the manner in which such assets were acquired, and a detailed statement of the liabilities and income of the organization and of each branch, chapter, and affiliate of the organization;

(8) A detailed description of the activities of the organization, and of each chapter, branch, and affiliate of the organization;

(9) A description of the uniforms, badges, insignia, or other means of identification prescribed by the organization, and worn or carried by its officers or members, or any of such officers or members;

(10) A copy of each book, pamphlet, leaflet, or other publication or item of written, printed, or graphic matter issued or distributed directly or indirectly by the organization, or by any chapter, branch, or affiliate of the organization, or by any of the members of the organization under its authority or within its knowledge, together with the name of its author or authors and the name and address of the publisher;

(11) A description of all firearms or other weapons owned by the organization, or by any chapter, branch, or affiliate of the organization, identified by the manufacturer's number thereon;

(12) In case the organization is subject to foreign control, the manner in which it is so subject;

(13) A copy of the charter, articles of association, constitution, bylaws, rules, regulations, agreements, resolutions, and all other instruments

relating to the organization, powers, and purposes of the organization and to the powers of the officers of the organization and of each chapter, branch, and affiliate of the organization; and

(14) Such other information and documents pertinent to the purposes of this Act as the Attorney General may from time to time require.

All statements filed under this section shall be public records and open to public examination and inspection at all reasonable hours under such rules and regulations as the Attorney General may prescribe.

Sec. 3. The Attorney General is authorized at any time to make, amend, and rescind such rules and regulations as may be necessary to carry out the provisions of this Act, including rules and regulations governing the statements required to be filed by this Act.

Sec. 4. Any violation of any of the provisions of this Act shall be punishable by a fine of not more than $10,000 or by imprisonment for not more than five years, or both. Whoever in a statement filed pursuant to section 2 willfully makes any false statement or willfully omits to state any fact which is required to be stated, or which is necessary to make the statements made not misleading, shall, upon conviction, be subject to a fine of not more than $2,000 or to imprisonment for not more than five years, or both.

Sec. 5. If any provisions of this Act, or the application thereof to any person or circumstances, is held invalid, the remainder of the Act, and the application of such provisions to other persions or circumstances, shall not be affected thereby.

Sec. 6. This Act shall take effect on the ninetieth day after the date of its enactment, except that prior to such ninetieth day the Attorney General may make, amend, or rescind such rules and regulations as may be necessary to carry out the provisions of this Act.

Approved, October 17, 1940.

Internal Security Act of 1950

64 Stat. 987 (1950)

An Act

To protect the United States against certain un-American and subversive activities by requiring registration of Communist organizations, and for other purposes.

Be it enacted by the Senate and House of Representatives of the United States of America in Congress assembled, That this Act may be cited as the "Internal Security Act of 1950".

Title I—Subversive Activities Control

Section 1. (a) This title may be cited as the "Subversive Activities Control Act of 1950".

(b) Nothing in this Act shall be construed to authorize, require, or establish military or civilian censorship or in any way to limit or infringe upon freedom of the press or of speech as guaranteed by the Constitution of the United States and no regulation shall be promulgated hereunder having that effect.

Necessity for Legislation

Sec. 2. As a result of evidence adduced before various committees of the Senate and House of Representatives, the Congress hereby finds that—

(1) There exists a world Communist movement which, in its origins, its development, and its present practice, is a world-wide revolutionary movement whose purpose it is, by treachery, deceit, infiltration into other groups (governmental and otherwise), espionage, sabotage, terrorism, and any other means deemed necessary, to establish a Communist totalitarian dictatorship in the countries throughout the world through the medium of a world-wide Communist organization.

(2) The establishment of a totalitarian dictatorship in any country results in the suppression of all opposition to the party in power, the subordination of the rights of individuals to the state, the denial of fundamental rights and liberties which are characteristic of a representative form of government, such as freedom of speech, of the press, of assembly, and of religious worship, and results in the maintenance of control over the people through fear, terrorism, and brutality.

(3) The system of government known as a totalitarian dictatorship is characterized by the existence of a single political party, organized on a dictatorial basis, and by substantial identity between such party and its policies and the government and governmental policies of the country in which it exists.

(4) The direction and control of the world Communist movement is vested in and exercised by the Communist dictatorship of a foreign country.

(5) The Communist dictatorship of such foreign country, in exercising such direction and control and in furthering the purposes of the world Communist movement, establishes or causes the establishment of, and utilizes, in various countries, action organizations which are not free and independent organizations, but are sections of a world-wide Communist organization and are controlled, directed, and subject to the discipline of the Communist dictatorship of such foreign country.

(6) The Communist action organizations so established and utilized in various countries, acting under such control, direction, and discipline, endeavor to carry out the objectives of the world Communist movement by bringing about the overthrow of existing governments by any available means, including force if necessary, and setting up Communist totalitarian dictatorships which will be subservient to the most powerful existing Communist totalitarian dictatorship. Although such organizations usually designate themselves as political parties, they are in fact constituent elements of the world-wide Communist movement and promote the objectives of such movement by conspiratorial and coercive tactics, instead of through the democratic processes of a free elective system or through the freedom-preserving means employed by a political party which operates as an agency by which people govern themselves.

(7) In carrying on the activities referred to in paragraph (6), such Communist organizations in various countries are organized on a secret, conspiratorial basis and operate to a substantial extent through organizations, commonly known as "Communist fronts", which in most instances are created and maintained, or used, in such manner as to conceal the facts as to their true character and purposes and their membership. One result of this

method of operation is that such affiliated organizations are able to obtain financial and other support from persons who would not extend such support if they knew the true purposes of, and the actual nature of the control and influence exerted upon, such "Communist fronts".

(8) Due to the nature and scope of the world Communist movement, with the existence of affiliated constituent elements working toward common objectives in various countries of the world, travel of Communist members, representatives, and agents from country to country facilitates communication and is a prerequisite for the carrying on of activities to further the purposes of the Communist movement.

(9) In the United States those individuals who knowingly and willfully participate in the world Communist movement, when they so participate, in effect repudiate their allegiance to the United States, and in effect transfer their allegiance to the foreign country in which is vested the direction and control of the world Communist movement.

(10) In pursuance of communism's stated objectives, the most powerful existing Communist dictatorship has, by the methods referred to above, already caused the establishment in numerous foreign countries of Communist totalitarian dictatorships, and threatens to establish similar dictatorships in still other countries.

(11) The agents of communism have devised clever and ruthless espionage and sabotage tactics which are carried out in many instances in form or manner successfully evasive of existing law.

(12) The Communist network in the United States is inspired and controlled in large part by foreign agents who are sent into the United States ostensibly as attaches of foreign legations, affiliates of international organizations, members of trading commissions, and in similar capacities, but who use their diplomatic or semidiplomatic status as a shield behind which to engage in activities prejudicial to the public security.

(13) There are, under our present immigration laws, numerous aliens who have been found to be deportable, many of whom are in the subversive, criminal, or immoral classes who are free to roam the country at will without supervision or control.

(14) One device for infiltration by Communists is by procuring naturalization for disloyal aliens who use their citizenship as a badge for admission into the fabric of our society.

(15) The Communist movement in the United States is an organization numbering thousands of adherents, rigidly and ruthlessly disciplined. Awaiting and seeking to advance a moment when the United States may be so far extended by foreign engagements, so far divided in counsel, or so far in industrial or financial straits, that overthrow of the Government of the United States by force and violence may seem possible of achievement, it seeks converts far and wide by an extensive system of schooling and indoctrination. Such preparations by Communist organizations in other countries have aided in supplanting existing governments. The Communist organization in the United States, pursuing its stated objectives, the recent successes of Communist methods in other countries, and the nature and control of the world Communist movement itself, present a clear and present danger to the security of the United States and to the existence of free American institutions, and make it necessary that Congress, in order to provide for the common defense, to preserve the sovereignty of the United

States as an independent nation, and to guarantee to each State a republican form of government, enact appropriate legislation recognizing the existence of such world-wide conspiracy and designed to prevent it from accomplishing its purpose in the United States.

Definitions

Sec. 3. For the purposes of this title—

(1) The term "person" means an individual or an organization.

(2) The term "organization" means an organization, corporation, company, partnership, association, trust, foundation, or fund; and includes a group of persons, whether or not incorporated, permanently or temporarily associated together for joint action on any subject or subjects.

(3) The term "Communist-action organization" means—

(a) any organization in the United States (other than a diplomatic representative or mission of a foreign government accredited as such by the Department of State) which (i) is substantially directed, dominated, or controlled by the foreign government or foreign organization controlling the world Communist movement referred to in section 2 of this title, and (ii) operates primarily to advance the objectives of such world Communist movement as referred to in section 2 of this title; and

(b) any section, branch, fraction, or cell of any organization defined in subparagraph (a) of this paragraph which has not complied with the registration requirements of this title.

(4) The term "Communist-front organization" means any organization in the United States (other than a Communist-action organization as defined in paragraph (3) of this section) which (A) is substantially directed, dominated, or controlled by a Communist-action organization, and (B) is primarily operated for the purpose of giving aid and support to a Communist-action organization, a Communist foreign government, or the world Communist movement referred to in section 2 of this title.

(5) The term "Communist organization" means a Communist-action organization or a Communist-front organization.

(6) The term "to contribute funds or services" includes the rendering of any personal service and the making of any gift, subscription, loan, advance, or deposit, of money or of anything of value, and also the making of any contract, promise, or agreement to contribute funds or services, whether or not legally enforcible.

(7) The term "facility" means any plant, factory or other manufacturing, producing or service establishment, airport, airport facility, vessel, pier, water-front facility, mine, railroad, public utility, laboratory, station, or other establishment or facility, or any part, division, or department of any of the foregoing. The term "defense facility" means any facility designated and proclaimed by the Secretary of Defense pursuant to section 5 (b) of this title and included on the list published and currently in effect under such subsection, and which is in compliance with the provisions of such subsection respecting the posting of notice of such designation.

(8) The term "publication" means any circular, newspaper, periodical, pamphlet, book, letter, post card, leaflet, or other publication.

(9) The term "United States", when used in a geographical sense, includes the several States, Territories, and possessions of the United States, the District of Columbia, and the Canal Zone.

(10) The term "interstate or foreign commerce" means trade, traffice, commerce,

transportation, or communication (A) between any State, Territory, or possession of the United States (including the Canal Zone), or the District of Columbia, and any place outside thereof, or (B) within any Territory or possession of the United States (including the Canal Zone), or within the District of Columbia.

(11) The term "Board" means the Subversive Activities Control Board created by section 12 of this title.

(12) The term "final order of the Board" means an order issued by the Board under section 13 of this title, which has become final as provided in section 14 of this title.

(13) The term "advocates" includes advises, recommends, furthers by overt act, and admits belief in; and the giving, loaning, or promising of support or of money or anything of value to be used for advocating any doctrine shall be deemed to constitute the advocating of such doctrine.

(14) The term "world communism" means a revolutionary movement, the purpose of which is to establish eventually a Communist totalitarian dictatorship in any or all the countries of the world through the medium of an internationally coordinated Communist movement.

(15) The terms "totalitarian dictatorship" and "totalitarianism" mean and refer to systems of government not representative in fact, characterized by (A) the existence of a single political party, organized on a dictatorial basis, with so close an identity between such party and its policies and the governmental policies of the country in which it exists, that the party and the government constitute an indistinguishable unit, and (B) the forcible suppression of opposition to such party.

(16) The term "doctrine" includes, but is not limited to, policies, practices, purposes, aims, or procedures.

(17) The giving, loaning, or promising of support or of money or any other thing of value for any purpose to any organization shall be conclusively presumed to constitute affiliation therewith; but nothing in this paragraph shall be construed as an exclusive definition of affiliation.

(18) "Advocating the economic, international, and governmental doctrines of world communism" means advocating the establishment of a totalitarian Communist dictatorship in any or all of the countries of the world through the medium of an internationally coordinated Communist movement.

(19) "Advocating the economic and governmental doctrines of any other form of totalitarianism" means advocating the establishment of totalitarianism (other than world communism) and includes, but is not limited to, advocating the economic and governmental doctrines of fascism and nazism.

Certain Prohibited Acts

Sec. 4. (a) It shall be unlawful for any person knowingly to combine, conspire, or agree with any other person to perform any act which would substantially contribute to the establishment within the United States of a totalitarian dictatorship, as defined in paragraph (15) of section 3 of this title, the direction and control of which is to be vested in, or exercised by or under the domination or control of, any foreign government, foreign organization, or foreign individual: *Provided, however,* That this subsection shall not apply to the proposal of a constitutional amendment.

(b) It shall be unlawful for any officer or employee of the United States or of any department or agency thereof, or of any corporation the stock of which is owned in whole or in major part by the United States or any department or agency thereof, to communicate in any manner or by any means, to any other person whom such officer or employee knows or has reason to believe to be an agent or representative of any foreign government or an officer or member of any Communist organization as defined in paragraph (5) of section 3 of this title, any information of a kind which shall have been classified by the President (or by the head of any such department, agency, or corporation with the approval of the President) as affecting the security of the United States, knowing or having reason to know that such information has been so classified, unless such officer or employees shall have been specifically authorized by the President, or by the head of the department, agency, or corporation by which this officer or employee is employed, to make such disclosure of such information.

(c) It shall be unlawful for any agent or representative of any foreign government, or any officer or member of any Communist organization as defined in paragraph (5) of section 3 of this title, knowingly to obtain or receive, or attempt to obtain or receive, directly or indirectly, from any officer or employee of the United States or of any department or agency thereof or of any corporation the stock of which is owned in whole or in major part by the United States or any department or agency thereof, any information of a kind which shall have been classified by the President (or by the head of any such department, agency, or corporation with the approval of the President) as affecting the security of the United States, unless special authorization for such communication shall first have been obtained from the head of the department, agency, or corporation having custody of or control over such information.

(d) Any person who violates any provision of this section shall, upon conviction thereof, be punished by a fine of not more than $10,000, or imprisonment for not more than ten years, or by both such fine and such imprisonment, and shall, moreover, be thereafter ineligible to hold any office, or place of honor, profit, or trust created by the Constitution or laws of the United States.

(e) Any person may be prosecuted, tried, and punished for any violation of this section at any time within ten years after the commission of such offense, notwithstanding the provisions of any other statute of limitations: *Provided,* That if at the time of the commission of the offense such person is an officer or employee of the United States or of any department or agency thereof, or of any corporation the stock of which is owned in whole or in major part by the United States or any department or agency thereof, such person may be prosecuted, tried, and punished for any violation of this section at any time within ten years after such person has ceased to be employed as such officer or employee.

(f) Neither the holding of office nor membership in any Communist organization by any person shall constitute per se a violation of subsection (a) or subsection (c) of this section or of any other criminal statute. The fact of the registration of any person under section 7 or section 8 of this title as an officer or member of any Communist organization shall not be received in evidence against such person in any prosecution for any alleged violation of subsection (a) or subsection (c) of this section or for any alleged violation of any other criminal statute.

Employment of Members of Communist Organizations

Sec. 5. (a) When a Communist organization, as defined in paragraph (5) of section 3 of this title, is registered or there is in effect a final order of the Board requiring such organization to register, it shall be unlawful—

(1) For any member of such organization, with knowledge or notice that such organization is so registered or that such order has become final—

(A) in seeking, accepting, or holding any nonelective office or employment under the United States, to conceal or fail to disclose the fact that he is a member of such organization; or

(B) to hold any nonelective office or employment under the United States; or

(C) in seeking, accepting, or holding employment in any defense facility, to conceal or fail to disclose the fact that he is a member of such organization; or

(D) if such organization is a Communist-action organization, to engage in any employment in any defense facility.

(2) For any officer or employee of the United States or of any defense facility, with knowledge or notice that such organization is so registered or that such order has become final—

(A) to contribute funds or services to such organization; or

(B) to advise, counsel or urge any person, with knowledge or notice that such person is a member of such organization, to perform, or to omit to perform, any act if such act or omission would constitute a violation of any provision of subparagraph (1) of this subsection.

(b) The Secretary of Defense is authorized and directed to designate and proclaim, and from time to time revise, a list of facilities, as defined in paragraph (7) of section 3 of this title, with respect to the operation of which he finds and determines that the security of the United States requires the application of the provisions of subsection (a) of this section. The Secretary shall cause such list as designated and proclaimed, or any revision thereof, to be promptly published in the Federal Register, and shall promptly notify the management of any facility so listed; whereupon such management shall immediately post conspicuously, and thereafter while so listed keep posted, notice of such designation in such form and in such place or places as to give reasonable notice thereof to all employees of, and to all applicants for employment in, such facility.

(c) As used in this section, the term "member" shall not include any individual whose name has not been made public because of the prohibition contained in section 9 (b) of this title.

Denial of Passports to Members of Communist Organizations

Sec. 6. (a) When a Communist organization as defined in paragraph (5) of section 3 of this title is registered, or there is in effect a final order of the Board requiring such organization to register, it shall be unlawful for any member of such organization, with knowledge or notice that such organization is so registered or that such order has become final—

(1) to make application for a passport, or the renewal of a passport, to be issued or renewed by or under the authority of the United States; or

(2) to use or attempt to use any such passport.

(b) When an organization is registered, or there is in effect a final order of the Board requiring an organization to register, as a Communist-action organization, it shall be unlawful for any officer or employee of the United States to issue a passport to, or renew the passport of, any individual knowing or having reason to believe that such individual is a member of such organization.

(c) As used in this section, the term "member" shall not include any individual whose name has not been made public because of the prohibition contained in section 9 (b) of this title.

Registration and Annual Reports of Communist Organizations

Sec. 7. (a) Each Communist-action organization (including any organization required, by a final order of the Board, to register as a Communist-action organization) shall, within the time specified in subsection (c) of this section, register with the Attorney General, on a form prescribed by him by regulations, as a Communist-action organization.

(b) Each Communist-front organization (including any organization required, by a final order of the Board, to register as a Communist-front organization) shall, within the time specified in subsection (c) of this section, register with the Attorney General, on a form prescribed by him by regulations, as a Communist-front organization.

(c) The registration required by subsection (a) or (b) shall be made—

(1) in the case of an organization which is a Communist-action organization or a Communist-front organization on the date of the enactment of this title, within thirty days after such date;

(2) in the case of an organization becoming a Communist-action organization or a Communist-front organization after the date of the enactment of this title, within thirty days after such organization becomes a Communist-action organization or a Communist-front organization, as the case may be; and

(3) in the case of an organization which by a final order of the Board is required to register, within thirty days after such order becomes final.

(d) The registration made under subsection (a) or (b) shall be accompanied by a registration statement, to be prepared and filed in such manner and form as the Attorney General shall by regulations prescribe, containing the following information:

(1) The name of the organization and the address of its principal office.

(2) The name and last-known address of each individual who is at the time of filing of such registration statement, and of each individual who was at any time during the period of twelve full calendar months next preceding the filing of such statement, an officer of the organization, with the designation or title of the office so held, and with a brief statement of the duties and functions of such individual as such officer.

(3) An accounting, in such form and detail as the Attorney General shall by regulations prescribe, of all moneys received and expended (including the sources from which received and the purposes for which expended) by the organization during the period of twelve full calendar months next preceding the filing of such statement.

(4) In the case of a Communist-action organization, the name and last-known address of each individual who was a member of the organization at any time during the period of twelve full calendar months preceding the filing of such statement.

(5) In the case of any officer or member whose name is required to be shown in such statement, and who uses or has used or who is or has been

known by more than one name, each name which such officer or member uses or has used or by which he is shown or has been known.

(e) It shall be the duty of each organization registered under this section to file with the Attorney General on or before February 1 of the year following the year in which it registers, and on or before February 1 of each succeeding year, an annual report, prepared and filed in such manner and form as the Attorney General shall by regulations prescribe, containing the same information which by subsection (d) is required to be included in a registration statement, except that the information required with respect to the twelve-month period referred to in paragraph (2), (3), or (4) of such subsection shall, in such annual report, be given with respect to the calendar year preceding the February 1 on or before which such annual report must be filed.

(f) (1) It shall be the duty of each organization registered under this section to keep, in such manner and form as the Attorney General shall by regulations prescribe, accurate records and accounts of moneys received and expended (including the sources from which received and purposes for which expended) by such organization.

(2) It shall be the duty of each Communist-action organization registered under this section to keep, in such manner and form as the Attorney General shall by regulations prescribe, accurate records of the names and addresses of the members of such organization and of persons who actively participate in the activities of such organization.

(g) It shall be the duty of the Attorney General to send to each individual listed in any registration statement or annual report, filed under this section, as an officer or member of the organization in respect of which such registration statement or annual report was filed, a notification in writing that such individual is so listed; and such notification shall be sent at the earliest practicable time after the filing of such registration statement or annual report. Upon written request of any individual so notified who denies that he holds any office or membership (as the case may be) in such organization, the Attorney General shall forthwith initiate and conclude at the earliest practicable time an appropriate investigation to determine the truth or falsity of such denial, and, if the Attorney General shall be satisfied that such denial is correct, he shall thereupon strike from such registration statement or annual report the name of such individual. If the Attorney General shall decline or fail to strike the name of such individual from such registration statement or annual report within five months after receipt of such written request, such individual may file with the Board a petition for relief pursuant to section 13 (b) of this title.

(h) In the case of failure on the part of any organization to register or to file any registration statement or annual report as required by this section, it shall be the duty of the executive officer (or individual performing the ordinary and usual duties of an executive officer) and of the secretary (or individual performing the ordinary and usual duties of a secretary) of such organization, and of such officer or officers of such organization as the Attorney General shall by regulations prescribe, to register for such organization, to file such registration statement, or to file such annual report, as the case may be.

Registration of Members of Communist-Action Organizations

Sec. 8. (a) Any individual who is or becomes a member of any organization concerning which (1) there is in effect a final order of the Board requiring such organization to register under section 7 (a) of this title as a Communist-action organization, (2) more than thirty days have elapsed since such order has become final, and (3) such organization is not registered under section 7 of this title as a Communist-action organization, shall within sixty days after said order has become final, or within thirty days after becoming a member of such organization, whichever is later, register with the Attorney General as a member of such organization.

(b) Each individual who is or becomes a member of any organization which he knows to be registered as a Communist-action organization under section 7 (a) of this title, but to have failed to include his name upon the list of members thereof filed with the Attorney General, pursuant to the provisions of subsections (d) and (e) of section 7 of this title, shall, within sixty days after he shall have obtained such knowledge, register with the Attorney General as a member of such organization.

(c) The registration made by any individual under subsection (a) or (b) of this section shall be accompanied by a registration statement to be prepared and filed in such manner and form, and containing such information, as the Attorney General shall by regulations prescribe.

Keeping of Registers; Public Inspection; Reports to President and Congress

Sec. 9. (a) The Attorney General shall keep and maintain separately in the Department of Justice—

(1) a "Register of Communist-Action Organizations", which shall include (A) the names and addresses of all Communist-action organizations registered under section 7, (B) the registration statements and annual reports filed by such organizations thereunder, and (C) the registration statements filed by individuals under section 8; and

(2) a "Register of Communist-Front Organizations", which shall include (A) the names and addresses of all Communist-front organizations registered under section 7, and (B) the registration statements and annual reports filed by such organizations thereunder.

(b) Such registers shall be kept and maintained in such manner as to be open for public inspection: *Provided,* That the Attorney General shall not make public the name of any individual listed in either such register as an officer or member of any Communist organization until sixty days shall have elapsed after the transmittal of the notification required by section 7 (g) to be sent to such individual, and if prior to the end of such period such individual shall make written request to the Attorney General for the removal of his name from any such list, the Attorney General shall not make public the name of such individual until six months shall have elapsed after receipt of such request by the Attorney General, or until thirty days shall have elapsed after the Attorney General shall have denied such request and shall have transmitted to such individual notice of such denial, whichever is earlier.

(c) The Attorney General shall submit to the President and to the Congress on or before June 1 of each year (and at any other time when requested by either House by resolution) a report with respect to the carrying out of the provisions of this title, including the names and addresses of the organizations listed in such registers and (except to the extent prohibited by subsection (b) of this section) the names and addresses of the individuals listed as members of such organizations.

(d) Upon the registration of each Communist organization under the provisions of this title, the Attorney General shall publish in the Federal Register the fact that such organization has registered as a Communist-action organization, or as a Communist-front organization, as the case may be, and the publication thereof shall constitute notice to all members of such organization that such organization has so registered.

Use of the Mails and Instrumentalities of Interstate or Foreign Commerce

Sec. 10. It shall be unlawful for any organization which is registered under section 7, or for any organization with respect to which there is in effect a final order of the Board requiring it to register under section 7, or for any person acting for or on behalf of any such organization—

(1) to transmit or cause to be transmitted, through the United States mails or by any means or instrumentality of interstate or foreign commerce, any publication which is intended to be, or which it is reasonable to believe is intended to be, circulated or disseminated among two or more persons, unless such publication, and any envelope, wrapper, or other container in which it is mailed or otherwise circulated or transmitted, bears the following, printed in such manner as may be provided in regulations prescribed by the Attorney General, with the name of the organization appearing in lieu of the blank: "Disseminated by ______, a Communist organization"; or

(2) to broadcast or cause to be broadcast any matter over any radio or television station in the United States, unless such matter is preceded by the following statement, with the name of the organization being stated in place of the blank: "The following program is sponsored by ______, a Communist organization".

Denial of Tax Deductions and Exemptions

Sec. 11. (a) Notwithstanding any other provision of law, no deduction for Federal income-tax purposes shall be allowed in the case of a contribution to or for the use of any organization if at the time of the making of such contribution (1) such organization is registered under section 7, or (2) there is in effect a final order of the Board requiring such organization to register under section 7.

(b) No organization shall be entitled to exemption from Federal income tax, under section 101 of the Internal Revenue Code, for any taxable year if at any time during such taxable year (1) such organization is registered under section 7, or (2) there is in effect a final order of the Board requiring such organization to register under section 7.

Subversive Activities Control Board

Sec. 12. (a) There is hereby established a board, to be known as the Subversive Activities Control Board, which shall be composed of five members, who shall be appointed by the President, by and with the advice and consent of the Senate. Not more than three members of the Board shall be members of the same political party. Two of the original members shall be appointed for a term of one year, two for a term of two years, and one for a term of three years, but their successors shall be appointed for terms of three years each, except that any individual chosen to fill a vacancy shall be appointed only for the unexpired term of the member whom he shall succeed. The President shall designate one member to serve as Chairman of the Board. Any member of the Board may be removed by the President, upon notice and hearing, for neglect of duty or malfeasance in office, but for no other cause.

(b) A vacancy in the Board shall not impair the right of the remaining members to exercise all the powers of the Board, and three members of the Board shall, at all times, constitute a quorum. The Board shall have an official seal which shall be judicially noticed.

(c) The Board shall at the close of each fiscal year make a report in writing to the Congress and to the President stating in detail the cases it has heard, the decisions it has rendered, the names, salaries, and duties of all employees of the Board, and an account of all moneys it has disbursed.

(d) Each member of the Board shall receive a salary of $12,500 a year, shall be eligible for reappointment, and shall not engage in any other business, vocation, or employment.

(e) It shall be the duty of the Board—

(1) upon application made by the Attorney General under section 13 (a) of this title, or by any organization under section 13 (b) of this title, to determine whether any organization is a "Communist-action organization" within the meaning of paragraph (3) of section 3 of this title, or a "Communist-front organization" within the meaning of paragraph (4) of section 3 of this title; and

(2) upon application made by the Attorney General under section 13 (a) of this title, or by any individual under section 13 (b) of this title, to determine whether any individual is a member of any Communist-action organization registered, or by final order of the Board required to be registered, under section 7 (a) of this title.

(f) Subject to the civil-service laws and Classification Act of 1949, the Board may appoint and fix the compensation of a chief clerk and such examiners and other personnel as may be necessary for the performance of its functions.

(g) The Board may make such rules and regulations, not inconsistent with the provisions of this title, as may be necessary for the performance of its duties.

(h) There are hereby authorized to be appropriated to the Board such sums as may be necessary to carry out its functions.

Sec. 13. (a) Whenever the Attorney General shall have reason to believe that any organization which has not registered under subsection (a) or subsection (b) of section 7 of this title is in fact an organization of a kind required to be registered under such subsection, or that any individual who has not registered under section 8 of this title is in fact required to register under such section, he shall file with the Board and serve upon such organization or individual a petition for an order requiring such organization or individual to register pursuant to such subsection or section, as the case may be. Each such petition shall be verified under oath, and shall contain a statement of the facts upon which the Attorney General relies in support of his prayer for the issuance of such order.

(b) Any organization registered under subsection (a) or subsection (b) of section 7 of this title, and any individual registered under section 8 of this title, may, not oftener than once in each calendar year, make application to the Attorney General for the cancellation of such registration and (in the case of such organization) for relief from obligation to make further annual reports. Within sixty days after the denial of any such application by the Attorney General, the organization or individual concerned may file with the Board and serve upon the Attorney General a petition for an order requiring the cancellation of such registration and (in the case of such organization) relieving such organization of obligation to make further annual reports. Any individual authorized by section 7 (g) of this title to file a petition for relief may file with the Board and serve upon the Attorney General a petition for an order requiring the Attorney General to strike his name from the registration statement or annual report upon which it appears.

(c) Upon the filing of any petition pursuant to subsection (a) or subsection (b) of this section, the Board (or any member thereof or any examiner designated thereby) may hold hearings, administer oaths and affirmations, may examine witnesses and receive evidence at any place in the United States, and may require by subpena the attendance and testimony of witnesses and the production of books, papers, correspondence, memoranda, and other records deemed relevant, to the matter under inquiry. Subpenas may be signed and issued by any member of the Board or any duly authorized examiner. Subpenas shall be issued on behalf of the organization or the individual who is a party to the proceeding upon request and upon a statement or showing of general relevance and reasonable scope of the evidence sought. Such attendance of witnesses and the production of such documentary evidence may be required from any place in the United States at any designated place of hearing. Witnesses summoned shall be paid the same fees and mileage paid witnesses in the district courts of the United States. In case of disobedience to a subpena, the Board may invoke the aid of any court of the United States in requiring the attendance and testimony of witnesses and the production of documentary evidence. Any of the district courts of the United States within the jurisdiction of which such inquiry is carried on may, in case of contumacy or refusal to obey a subpena issued to any person, issue an order requiring such person to appear (and to produce documentary evidence if so ordered) and give evidence relating to the matter in question; and any failure to obey such order of the court may be punished by such court as a contempt thereof. All process in any such case may be served in the judicial district whereof such person is an inhabitant or wherever he may be found. No person shall be held liable in any action in any court, State or Federal, for any damages resulting from (1) his production of any documentary evidence in any proceeding before the Board if he is required, by a subpena issued under this subsection, to produce the evidence; or (2) any statement under oath he makes in answer to a question he is asked while testifying before the Board in response to a subpena issued under this subsection, if the statement is pertinent to the question.

(d) (1) All hearings conducted under this section shall be public. Each party to such proceeding shall have the right to present its case with the assistance of counsel, to offer oral or documentary evidence, to submit rebuttal evidence, and to conduct such cross-examination as may be required for a full and true disclosure of the facts. An accurate stenographic record shall be taken of the testimony of each witness, and a transcript of such testimony shall be filed in the office of the Board.

(2) Where an organization or individual declines or fails to appear at a hearing accorded to such organization or individual by the Board pursuant to this section, the Board may, without further proceedings and without the introduction of any evidence, enter an order requiring such organization or individual to register or denying the application of such organization or individual, as the case may be. Where in the course of any hearing before the Board or any examiner thereof a party or counsel is guilty of misbehavior which obstructs the hearing, such party or counsel may be excluded from further participation in the hearing.

(e) In determining whether any organization is a "Communist-action organization", the Board shall take into consideration—

(1) the extent to which its policies are formulated and carried out and its activities performed, pursuant to directives or to effectuate the policies of the

foreign government or foreign organization in which is vested, or under the domination or control of which is exercised, the direction and control of the world Communist movement referred to in section 2 of this title; and

(2) the extent to which its views and policies do not deviate from those of such foreign government or foreign organization; and

(3) the extent to which it receives financial or other aid, directly or indirectly, from or at the direction of such foreign government or foreign organization; and

(4) the extent to which it sends members or representatives to any foreign country for instruction or training in the principles, policies, strategy, or tactics of such world Communist movement; and

(5) the extent to which it reports to such foreign government or foreign organization or to its representatives; and

(6) the extent to which its principal leaders or a substantial number of its members are subject to or recognize the disciplinary power of such foreign government or foreign organization or its representatives; and

(7) the extent to which, for the purpose of concealing foreign direction, domination, or control, or of expediting or promoting its objectives, (i) it fails to disclose, or resists efforts to obtain information as to, its membership (by keeping membership lists in code, by instructing members to refuse to acknowledge membership, or by any other method); (ii) its members refuse to acknowledge membership therein; (iii) it fails to disclose, or resists efforts to obtain information as to, records other than membership lists; (iv) its meetings are secret; and (v) it otherwise operates on a secret basis; and

(8) the extent to which its principal leaders or a substantial number of its members consider the allegiance they owe to the United States as subordinate to their obligations to such foreign government or foreign organization.

(f) In determining whether any organization is a "Communist-front organization", the Board shall take into consideration—

(1) the extent to which persons who are active in its management, direction, or supervision, whether or not holding office therein, are active in the management, direction, or supervision of, or as representatives of, any Communist-action organization, Communist foreign government, or the world Communist movement referred to in section 2; and

(2) the extent to which its support, financial or otherwise, is derived from any Communist-action organization, Communist foreign government, or the world Communist movement referred to in section 2; and

(3) the extent to which its funds, resources, or personnel are used to further or promote the objectives of any Communist-action organization, Communist foreign government, or the world Communist movement referred to in section 2; and

(4) the extent to which the positions taken or advanced by it from time to time on matters of policy do not deviate from those of any Communist-action organization, Communist foreign government, or the world Communist movement referred to in section 2.

(g) If, after hearing upon a petition filed under subsection (a) of this section, the Board determines—

(1) that an organization is a Communist-action organization or a Communist-front organization, as the case may be, it shall make a report in

writing in which it shall state its findings as to the facts and shall issue and cause to be served on such organization an order requiring such organization to register as such under section 7 of this title; or

(2) that an individual is a member of a Communist-action organization (including an organization required by final order of the Board to register under section 7 (a)), it shall make a report in writing in which it shall state its findings as to the facts and shall issue and cause to be served on such individual an order requiring him to register as such under section 8 of this title.

(h) If, after hearing upon a petition filed under subsection (a) of this section, the Board determines—

(1) that an organization is not a Communist-action organization or a Communist-front organization, as the case may be, it shall make a report in writing in which it shall state its findings as to the facts; issue and cause to be served upon the Attorney General an order denying his petition for an order requiring such organization to register as such under section 7 of this title; and send a copy of such order to such organization; or

(2) that an individual is not a member of any Communist-action organization, it shall make a report in writing in which it shall state its findings as to the facts; issue and cause to be served upon the Attorney General an order denying his petition for an order requiring such individual to register as such member under section 8 of this title; and send a copy of such order to such individual.

(i) If, after hearing upon a petition filed under subsection (b) of this section, the Board determines—

(1) that an organization is not a Communist-action organization or a Communist-front organization, as the case may be, it shall make a report in writing in which it shall state its findings as to the facts; issue and cause to be served upon the Attorney General an order requiring him to cancel the registration of such organization and relieve it from the requirement of further annual reports; and send a copy of such order to such organization; or

(2) that an individual is not a member of any Communist-action organization, or (in the case of an individual listed as an officer of a Communist-front organization) that an individual is not an officer of a Communist-front organization, it shall make a report in writing in which it shall state its findings as to the facts; issue and cause to be served upon the Attorney General an order requiring him to (A) strike the name of such individual from the registration statement or annual report upon which it appears or (B) cancel the registration of such individual under section 8, as may be appropriate; and send a copy of such order to such individual.

(j) If, after hearing upon a petition filed under subsection (b) of this section, the Board determines—

(1) that an organization is a Communist-action organization or a Communist-front organization, as the case may be, it shall make a report in writing in which it shall state its findings as to the facts and shall issue and cause to be served on such organization an order denying its petition for the cancellation of its registration and for relief from the requirement of further annual reports; or

(2) that an individual is a member of a Communist-action organization,

or (in the case of an individual listed as a officer of a Communist-front organization) that an individual is an officer of a Communist-front organization, it shall make a report in writing in which it shall state it findings as to the facts and shall issue and cause to be served on such individual an order denying his petition for an order requiring the Attorney General (A) to strike his name from any registration statement or annual report on which it appears or (B) to cancel the registration of such individual under section 8, as the case may be.

(k) When any order of the Board requiring registration of a Communist organization becomes final under the provisions of section 14 (b) of this title, the Board shall publish in the Federal Register the fact that such order has become final, and publication thereof shall constitute notice to all members of such organization that such order has become final.

Judicial Review

Sec. 14. (a) The party aggrieved by any order entered by the Board under subsection (g), (h), (i), or (j) of section 13 may obtain a review of such order by filing in the United States Court of Appeals for the District of Columbia, within sixty days from the date of service upon it of such order, a written petition praying that the order of the Board be set aside. A copy of such petition shall be forthwith served upon the Board, and thereupon the Board shall certify and file in the court a transcript of the entire record in the proceeding, including all evidence taken and the report and order of the Board. Thereupon the court shall have jurisdiction of the proceeding and shall have power to affirm or set aside the order of the Board; but the court may in its discretion and upon its own motion transfer any action so commenced to the United States Court of Appeals for the circuit wherein the petitioner resides. The findings of the Board as to the facts, if supported by the preponderance of the evidence, shall be conclusive. If either party shall apply to the court for leave to adduce additional evidence, and shall show to the satisfaction of the court that such additional evidence is material, the court may order such additional evidence to be taken before the Board and to be adduced upon the proceeding in such manner and upon such terms and conditions as to the court may seem proper. The Board may modify its findings as to the facts, by reason of the additional evidence so taken, and it shall file such modified or new findings, which, if supported by the preponderance of the evidence shall be conclusive, and its recommendations, if any, with respect to action in the matter under consideration. If the court shall set aside an order issued under subsection (j) of section 13 it may, in the case of an organization, enter a judgment canceling the registration of such organization and relieving it from the requirement of further annual reports, or in the case of an individual, enter a judgment requiring the Attorney General (A) to strike the name of such individual from the registration statement or annual report on which it appears, or (B) cancel the registration of such individual under section 8, as may be appropriate. The judgment and decree of the court shall be final, except that the same shall be subject to review by the Supreme Court upon certiorari, as provided in title 28, United States Code, section 1254.

(b) Any order of the Board issued under section 13 shall become final—

(1) upon the expiration of the time allowed for filing a petition for review, if no such petition has been duly filed within such time; or

(2) upon the expiration of the time allowed for filing a petition for certiorari, if the order of the Board has been affirmed or the petition for

review dismissed by a United States Court of Appeals, and no petition for certiorari has been duly filed; or

(3) upon the denial of a petition for certiorari, if the order of the Board has been affirmed or the petition for review dismissed by a United States Court of Appeals; or

(4) upon the expiration of ten days from the date of issuance of the mandate of the Supreme Court, if such Court directs that the order of the Board be affirmed or the petition for review dismissed.

Penalties

Sec. 15. (a) If there is in effect with respect to any organization or individual a final order of the Board requiring registration under section 7 or section 8 of this title—

(1) such organization shall, upon conviction of failure to register, to file any registration statement or annual report, or to keep records as required by section 7, be punished for each such offense by a fine of not more than $10,000, and

(2) each individual having a duty under subsection (h) of section 7 to register or to file any registration statement or annual report on behalf of such organization, and each individual having a duty to register under section 8, shall, upon conviction of failure to so register or to file any such registration statement or annual report, be punished for each such offense by a fine of not more than $10,000, or imprisonment for not more than five years, or by both such fine and imprisonment.

For the purposes of this subsection, each day of failure to register, whether on the part of the organization or any individual, shall constitute a separate offense.

(b) Any individual who, in a registration statement or annual report filed under section 7 or section 8, willfully makes any false statement or willfully omits to state any fact which is required to be stated, or which is necessary to make the statements made or information given not misleading, shall upon conviction thereof be punished for each such offense by a fine of not more than $10,000, or by imprisonment for not more than five years, or by both such fine and imprisonment. For the purposes of this subsection—

(1) each false statement willfully made, and each willful omission to state any fact which is required to be stated, or which is necessary to make the statements made or information given not misleading, shall constitute a separate offense; and

(2) each listing of the name or address of any one individual shall be deemed to be a separate statement.

(c) Any organization which violates any provision of section 10 of this title shall, upon conviction thereof, be punished for each such violation by a fine of not more than $10,000. Any individual who violates any provision of section 5, 6, or 10 of this title shall, upon conviction thereof, be punished for each such violation by a fine of not more than $10,000 or by imprisonment for not more than five years, or by both such fine and imprisonment.

Applicability of Administrative Procedure Act

Sec. 16. Nothing in this title shall be held to make the provisions of the Administrative Procedure Act inapplicable to the exercise of functions, or the conduct of proceedings, by the Board under this title.

Existing Criminal Statutes

Sec. 17. The foregoing provisions of this title shall be construed as being in addition to and not in modification of existing criminal statutes.

Amending Title 18, Section 793, United States Code

Sec. 18. Title 18, United States Code, section 793, be and the same is hereby, amended to read as follows:

"§ 793. Gathering, transmitting, or losing defense information

"(a) Whoever, for the purpose of obtaining information respecting the national defense with intent or reason to believe that the information is to be used to the injury of the United States, or to the advantage of any foreign nation, goes upon, enters, flies over, or otherwise obtains information concerning any vessel, aircraft, work of defense, navy yard, naval station, submarine base, fueling station, fort, battery, torpedo station, dockyard, canal, railroad, arsenal, camp, factory, mine, telegraph, telephone, wireless, or signal station, building, office, research laboratory or station or other place connected with the national defense owned or constructed, or in progress of construction by the United States or under the control of the United States or of any of its officers, departments, or agencies, or within the exclusive jurisdiction of the United States, or any place in which any vessel, aircraft, arms, munitions, or other materials or instruments for use in time of war are being made, prepared, repaired, stored, or are the subject of research or development, under any contract or agreement with the United States, or any department or agency thereof, or with any person on behalf of the United States, or otherwise on behalf of the United States, or any prohibited place so designated by the President by proclamation in time of war or in case of national emergency in which anything for the use of the Army, Navy, or Air Force is being prepared or constructed or stored, information as to which prohibited place the President has determined would be prejudicial to the national defense; or

"(b) Whoever, for the purpose aforesaid, and with like intent or reason to believe, copies, takes, makes, or obtains, or attempts to copy, take, make, or obtain, any sketch, photograph, photographic negative, blueprint, plan, map, model, instrument, appliance, document, writing, or note of anything connected with the national defense; or

"(c) Whoever, for the purpose aforesaid, receives or obtains or agrees or attempts to receive or obtain from any person, or from any source whatever, any document, writing, code book, signal book, sketch, photograph, photographic negative, blueprint, plan, map, model, instrument, appliance, or note, of anything connected with the national defense, knowing or having reason to believe, at the time he receives or obtains, or agrees or attempts to receive or obtain it, that it has been or will be obtained, taken, made, or disposed of by any person contrary to the provisions of this chapter; or

"(d) Whoever, lawfully having possession of, access to, control over, or being entrusted with any document, writing, code book, signal book, sketch, photograph, photographic negative, blueprint, plan, map, model, instrument, appliance, or note relating to the national defense, or information relating to the national defense which information the possessor has reason to believe could be used to the injury of the United States or to the advantage of any foreign nation, willfully communicates, delivers, transmits or causes to be communicated, delivered, or transmitted or attempts to communicate, deliver, transmit or cause to be communicated, delivered or transmitted the same to any person not entitled to receive it, or willfully retains the same and fails to deliver it on demand to the officer or employee of the United States entitled to receive it; or

"(e) Whoever having unauthorized possession of, access to, or control over any document, writing, code book, signal book, sketch, photograph, photographic negative, blueprint, plan, map, model, instrument, appliance, or note relating to the national defense, or information relating to the national defense which information the possessor has reason to believe could be used to the injury of the United States or to the advantage of any foreign nation, willfully communicates, delivers, transmits or causes to be communicated, delivered, or transmitted, or attempts to communicate, deliver, transmit or cause to be communicated, delivered, or transmitted the same to any person not entitled to receive it, or willfully retains the same and fails to deliver it to the officer or employee of the United States entitled to receive it; or

"(f) Whoever, being entrusted with or having lawful possession or control of any document, writing, code book, signal book, sketch, photograph, photographic negative, blueprint, plan, map, model, instrument, appliance, note, or information, relating to the national defense, (1) through gross negligence permits the same to be removed from its proper place of custody or delivered to anyone in violation of his trust, or to be lost, stolen, abstracted, or destroyed, or (2) having knowledge that the same has been illegally removed from its proper place of custody or delivered to anyone in violation of his trust, or lost, or stolen, abstracted, or destroyed, and fails to make prompt report of such loss, theft, abstraction, or destruction to his superior officer—

"Shall be fined not more than $10,000 or imprisoned not more than ten years, or both.

"(g) If two or more persons conspire to violate any of the foregoing provisions of this section, and one or more of such persons do any act to effect the object of the conspiracy, each of the parties to such conspiracy shall be subject to the punishment provided for the offense which is the object of such conspiracy."

Period of Limitation

Sec. 19. An indictment for any violation of title 18, United States Code, section 792, 793, or 794, other than a violation constituting a capital offense, may be found at any time within ten years next after such violation shall have been committed. This section shall not authorize prosecution, trial, or punishment for any offense now barred by the provisions of existing law.

Amending Act of June 18, 1938

Sec. 20. The Act of June 8, 1938 (52 Stat. 631; 22 U. S. C. 611-621), entitled "An Act to require the registration of certain persons employed by agencies to disseminate propaganda in the United States, and for other purposes", as amended, is hereby further amended as follows:

(a) Strike out the word "and" at the end of section 1 (c) (3), insert the word "and" at the end of section 1 (c) (4), and add the following paragraph immediately after section 1 (c) (4):

> "(5) any person who has knowledge of or has received instruction or assignment in the espionage, counterespionage, or sabotage service or tactics of a government of a foreign country or of a foreign political party, unless such knowledge, instruction, or assignment has been acquired by reason of

civilian, military, or police service with the United States Government, the governments of the several States, their political subdivisions, the District of Columbia, the Territories, the Canal Zone, or the insular possessions, or unless such knowledge has been acquired solely by reason of academic or personal interest not under the supervision of or in preparation for service with the government of a foreign country or a foreign political party or unless, by reason of employment at any time by an agency of the United States Government having responsibilities in the field of intelligence, such person has made full written disclosure of such knowledge or instruction to officials within such agency, such disclosure has been made a matter of record in the files of such agency, and a written determination has been made by the Attorney General or the Director of Central Intelligence that registration would not be in the interest of national security;".

(b) Add the following subsection immediately after section 8 (d):

"(e) Failure to file any such registration statement or supplements thereto as is required by either section 2 (a) or section 2 (b) shall be considered a continuing offense for as long as such failure exists, notwithstanding any statute of limitation or other statute to the contrary."

Security Regulations and Orders and Penalty for Violation Thereof

Sec. 21. (a) Whoever willfully shall violate any such regulation or order as, pursuant to lawful authority, shall be or has been promulgated or approved by the Secretary of Defense, or by any military commander designated by the Secretary of Defense, or by the Director of the National Advisory Committee for Aeronautics, for the protection or security of military or naval aircraft, airports, airport facilities, vessels, harbors, ports, piers, water-front facilities, bases, forts, posts, laboratories, stations, vehicles, equipment, explosives, or other property or places subject to the jurisdiction, administration, or in the custody of the Department of Defense, any Department or agency of which said Department consists, or any officer or employee of said Department or agency, or of the National Advisory Committee for Aeronautics or any officer or employee thereof, relating to fire hazards, fire protection, lighting, machinery, guard service, disrepair, disuse or other unsatisfactory conditions thereon, or the ingress thereto or egress or removal of persons therefrom, or otherwise providing for safeguarding the same against destruction, loss, or injury by accident or by enemy action, sabotage or other subversive actions, shall be guilty of a misdemeanor and upon conviction thereof shall be liable to a fine of not to exceed $5,000 or to imprisonment for not more than one year, or both.

(b) Every such regulation or order shall be posted in conspicuous and appropriate places.

Amending Act of October 16, 1918

Sec. 22. The Act of October 16, 1918, as amended (40 Stat. 1012, 41 Stat. 1008, 54 Stat. 673; 8 U. .S. C. 137), be, and the same is hereby, amended to read as follows: "That any alien who is a member of any one of the following classes shall be excluded from admission into the United States:

"(1) Aliens who seek to enter the United States whether solely, principally, or incidentally, to engage in activities which would be prejudicial to the public interest, or would endanger the welfare or safety of the United States;

"(2) Aliens who, at any time, shall be or shall have been members of any of the following classes:

"(A) Aliens who are anarchists;

"(B) Aliens who advocate or teach, or who are members of or affiliated with any organization that advocates or teaches, opposition to all organized government;

"(C) Aliens who are members of or affiliated with (i) the Communist Party of the United States, (ii) any other totalitarian party of the United States' (iii) the Communist Political Association, (iv) the Communist or other totalitarian party of any State of the United States, of any foreign state, or of any political or geographical subdivision of any foreign state; (v) any section, subsidiary, branch, affiliate, or subdivision of any such association or party; or (vi) the direct predecessors or successors of any such association or party, regardless of what name such group or organization may have used, may now bear, or may hereafter adopt;

"(D) Aliens not within any of the other provisions of this paragraph (2) who advocate the economic, international, and governmental doctrines of world communism or the economic and governmental doctrines of any other form of totalitarianism, or who are members of or affiliated with any organization that advocates the economic, international, and governmental doctrines of world communism, or the economic and governmental doctrines of any other form of totalitarianism, either through its own utterances or through any written or printed publications issued or published by or with the permission or consent of or under the authority of such organization or paid for by the funds of such organization:

"(E) Aliens not within any of the other provisions of this paragraph (2), who are members of or affiliated with any organization which is registered or required to be registered under section 7 of the Subversive Activities Control Act of 1950, unless such aliens establish that they did not know or have reason to believe at the time they became members of or affiliated with such an organization (and did not thereafter and prior to the date upon which such organization was so registered or so required to be registered acquire such knowledge or belief) that such organization was a Communist organization.

"(F) Aliens who advocate or teach or who are members of or affiliated with any organization that advocates or teaches (i) the overthrow by force or violence of other unconstitutional means of the Government of the United States or of all forms of law; or (ii) the duty, necessity, or propriety of the unlawful assaulting or killing of any officer or officers (either of specific individuals or of officers generally) of the Government of the United States or of any other organized government, because of his or their official character; or (iii) the unlawful damage, injury, or destruction of property; or (iv) sabotage;

"(G) Aliens who write or publish, or cause to be written or published, or who knowingly circulate, distribute, print, or display, or knowingly cause to be circulated, distributed, printed, published, or displayed, or who knowingly have in their possession for the purpose of circulation, publication, or display, any written or printed matter, advocating or teaching opposition to all organized government, or advocating (i) the overthrow by force or violence or other unconstitutional means of the Government of the United States or of all forms of law; or (ii) the duty, necessity, or propriety of the unlawful assaulting or killing of any officer or officers (either of specific individuals or of officers generally) of the Government of the United States or of any other organized government; or (iii) the unlawful damage, injury, or destruction of property; or (iv) sabotage; or (v) the economic, international, and governmental doctrines of world communism or the economic and governmental doctrines of any other form of totalitarianism.

"(H) Aliens who are members of or affiliated with any organization that writes, circulates, distributes, prints, publishes, or displays, or causes to be written, circulated, distributed, printed, published, or displayed, or that has in its possession for the purpose of circulation, distribution, publication, issue, or display, any written or printed matter of the character described in subparagraph (G).

"(3) Aliens with respect to whom there is reason to believe that such aliens would, after entry, be likely to (A) engage in activities which would be prohibited by the laws of the United States relating to espionage, sabotage, public disorder, or in other activity subversive to the national security; (B) engage in any activity a purpose of which is the opposition to, or the control or overthrow of, the Government of the United States by force, violence, or other unconstitutional means; or (C) organize, join, affiliate with, or participate in the activities of any organization which is registered or required to be registered under section 7 of the Subversive Activities Control Act of 1950.

"Sec. 2. The provision of paragraph (2) of section 1 shall not be applicable to any alien who is seeking to enter the United States temporarily as a nonimmigrant under section 3 (1) or 3 (7) of the Immigration Act of 1924, as amended (43 Stat. 153; 8 U. S. C. 201).

"Sec. 3. No visa or other documentation shall be issued to any alien who seeks to enter the United States either as an immigrant or as a nonimmigrant if the consular officer knows or has reason to believe that such alien is inadmissible to the United States under this Act. The case of an alien within any of the categories enumerated in section 1 shall not be defined as an emergency case within the meaning of section 30 of the Alien Registration Act of 1940 (54 Stat. 673; 8 U. S. C. 451).

"Sec. 4. (a) Any alien who was at the time of entering the United States, or has been at any time thereafter, a member of any one of the classes of aliens enumerated in section 1 (1) or section 1 (3) of this Act or (except in the case of an alien who is legally in the United States temporarily as a nonimmigrant under section 3 (1) or 3 (7) of the Immigration Act of 1924, as amended) a member of any one of the classes of aliens enumerated in section 1 (2) of this Act, shall, upon the warrant of the Attorney General, be taken into custody and deported in the manner provided in the Immigration Act of February 5, 1917. The provisions of this section shall be applicable to the classes of aliens mentioned in this Act, irrespective of the time of their entry into the United States.

"(b) The Attorney General shall, in like manner as provided in subsection (a) of this section, take into custody and deport from the United States any alien who at any time, whether before or after the effective date of this Act, has engaged, or has had a purpose to engage, in any of the activities described in paragraph (1) or in any of the subparagraphs of paragraph (3) of section 1, unless the Attorney General is satisfied, in the case of any alien who engaged in any activity within category (C) of paragraph (3) of section 1 that such alien did not know or have reason to believe at the time such alien became a member of or affiliated with the organization referred to in category (C) or paragraph (3) of section 1 (and did not thereafter and prior to the date upon which such organization was registered or required to be registered under section 7 of the Subversive Activities Control Act of 1950 acquire such knowledge or belief) that such organization was a Communist organization.

"Sec. 5. Notwithstanding the provisions of sections 16 and 17 of the Immigration Act of February 5, 1917, as amended (39 Stat. 885-887; 8 U. S. C. 152, 153), which relate to boards of special inquiry and to appeal from the decisions of such boards, any alien who may appear to the examining immigration officer at the port of arrival to be excludable under section 1 shall be temporarily excluded, and no further inquiry by a board of special inquiry shall be conducted until after the case is reported to the Attorney General and such an inquiry is directed by the Attorney General. If the Attorney General is satisfied that the alien is excludable under section 1 on the basis of information of a confidential nature, the disclosure of which would be prejudicial to the public interest, safety, or security, he may deny any further inquiry by a board of special inquiry and order such alien to be excluded and deported.

"Sec. 6. (a) The provisions of the seventh proviso to section 3 of the Immigration Act of February 5, 1917, as amended (39 Stat. 875; 8 U. S. C. 136), relating to the admission of aliens to the United States, shall have no application to cases falling within the purview of section 1 of this Act.

"(b) The provisions of the ninth proviso to section 3 of the Immigration Act of February 5, 1917, as amended (39 Stat. 875; 8 U. S. C. 136), relating to the temporary admission of aliens to the United States, shall have no application to cases falling within the purview of section 1 (1) and 1 (3) of this Act. The Attorney General shall make a detailed report to Congress in any case where the authority granted in the ninth proviso above is exercised on behalf of any alien excludible under section 1 (2).

"(c) Notwithstanding the provisions of the tenth proviso to section 3 of the Immigration Act of February 5, 1917, as amended (39 Stat. 875; 8 U. S. C. 136), or any other law—

"(1) the provisions of section 1 (1) and 1 (3) shall be applicable to any alien within the purview of section 3 (1) of the Immigration Act of 1924, as amended (43 Stat. 153; 8 U. S. C. 201), except ambassadors, public ministers, and career diplomatic and consular officers who have been accredited by a foreign government recognized de jure by the United States and who are accepted by the President or the Secretary of State, and the members of the immediate families of such aliens, who shall be subject to exclusion under the provisions of section 1 (1) only pursuant to such rules and regulations as the President may deem to be necessary; and

"(2) the provisions of section 1 (1) shall be applicable to any alien within the purview of section 3 (7) of the Immigration Act of 1924, as amended (43 Stat. 153; 8 U. S. C. 201); the provisions of section 1 (3) shall be applicable to any such alien except a designated principal resident representative of a foreign government member of an international organization entitled to enjoy privileges, exemptions, and immunities as an international organization under the International Organizations Immunities Act (59 Stat. 669), accredited resident members of the staff of such representative, and members of his immediate family.

"(d) The proviso to section 15 of the Immigration Act of 1924, as amended (43

Stat. 153; 8 U. S. C. 201), relating to the departure of any alien who has failed to maintain status under section 3 (1) or 3 (7) of said Act shall not be applicable in the case of any alien who would be subject to exclusion under the provisions of section 1 of this Act if he were applying for admission.

"Sec. 7. Upon the notification by the Attorney General that any country upon request denies or unduly delays acceptance of the return of any alien who is a national, citizen, subject or resident thereof, the Secretary of State shall instruct consular officers performing their duties in the territory of such country to discontinue the issuance of immigration visas to nationals, citizens, subjects, or residents of such country, until such time as the Attorney General shall inform the Secretary of State that such country has accepted such alien.

"Sec. 8. (a) Any person who knowingly aids or assists any alien excludable under section 1 to enter the United States, or who connives or conspires with any person or persons to allow, procure, or permit any such alien to enter the United States, shall be guilty of a felony, and upon conviction thereof shall be punished by a fine of not more than $5,000 or by imprisonment for not more than five years, or both.

"(b) Any alien who shall, after he has been excluded and deported or arrested and deported in pursuance of the provisions of this Act, thereafter and without the express authorization of the Attorney General return to or enter the United States or attempt to return to or to enter the United States shall be deemed guilty of a felony, and upon conviction thereof shall be punished by imprisonment for a term of not more than five years; and shall, upon the termination of such imprisonment, be taken into custody, upon the warrant of the Attorney General, and deported in the manner provided in the Immigration Act of February 5, 1917.

"Sec. 9. Any statute or other authority or provision having the force or effect of law, to the extent that it is inconsistent with any of the provisions of this Act, is hereby expressly declared to be inapplicable to any alien whose case is within the purview of this Act.

"Sec. 10. If any provision of this Act, or the application thereof to any person or circumstances, is held invalid, the remaining provisions of this Act, or the application of such provisions to other persons or circumstances, shall not be affected thereby."

Amending Section 20 of Immigration Act of February 5, 1917

Sec. 23. Section 20 of the Immigration Act of February 5, 1917, as amended (39 Stat. 890; 57 Stat. 553; 8 U. S. C. 156), is hereby amended to read as follows:

"Sec. 20. (a) That the deportation of aliens provided for in this Act and all other immigration laws of the United States shall be directed by the Attorney General to the country specified by the alien, if it is willing to accept him into its territory; otherwise such deportation shall be directed by the Attorney General within his discretion and without priority of preference because of their order as herein set forth, either to the country from which such alien last entered the United States; or to the country in which is located the foreign port at which such alien embarked for the United States or for foreign contiguous territory; or to any country in which he resided prior to entering the country from which he entered the United States; or to the country which had sovereignty over the birthplace of the alien at the time of his birth; or to any country of which such an alien is a subject, national, or citizen; or to the country in which he was born; or to the country in which the place of his birth is situated at the time he is ordered deported; or, if deportation to any of the said foregoing places or countries is impracticable, inadvisable, or impossible, then to any country which is willing to accept such alien into its territory. If the United States is at war and the deportation, in accordance with the preceding provisions of this section, of any alien who is deportable under any law of the United States, shall be found by the Attorney General to be impracticable or inconvenient because of enemy occupation of the country whence such alien came or wherein is located the foreign port at which he embarked for the United States or because of other reasons connected with the war, such alien may, at the option of the Attorney General, be deported (1) if such alien is a citizen or subject of a country whose recognized government is in exile, to the country wherein is located that government in exile, if that country will permit him to enter its territory; or (2) if such alien is a citizen or subject of a country whose recognized government is not in exile, then, to a country or any political or territorial subdivision thereof which is approximate to the country of which the alien is a citizen or subject, or with the consent of the country of which the alien is a citizen or subject, to any other country. No alien shall be deported under any provisions of this Act to any country in which the Attorney General shall find that such alien would be subjected to physical persecution. If deportation proceedings are instituted at any time within five years after the entry of the alien, such deportation, including one-half of the entire cost of removal to the port of deportation, shall be at the expense of the contractor, procurer, or other person by whom the alien was unlawfully induced to enter the United States or, if that cannot be done, then the cost of removal to the port of deportation shall be at the expense of the appropriation for the enforcement of this Act, and the deportation from such port shall be at the expense of the owner or owners of such vessels or transportation lines by which such aliens respectively came, or, if that is not practicable, at the expense of the appropriation for the enforcement of this Act. If deportation proceedings are instituted later than five years after the entry of the alien, or, if the deportation is made by reason of causes arising subsequent to entry, the cost thereof shall be payable from the appropriation for the enforcement of this Act. A failure or refusal on the part of the masters, agents, owners, or consignees of vessels to comply with the order of the Attorney General to take on board, guard safely, and transport to the destination specified any alien ordered to be deported under the provisions of this Act shall be punished by the imposition of the penalties prescribed in section 18 of this Act: *Provided,* That when in the opinion of the Attorney General the mental or physical condition of such alien is such as to require personal care and attendance, the said Attorney General shall when necessary employ a suitable person for that purpose, who shall accompany such alien to his or her final destination, and the expense incident to such service shall be defrayed in the same manner as the expense of deporting the accompanied alien is defrayed. Pending final determination of the deportability of any alien taken into custody under warrant of the Attorney General, such alien may, in the discretion of the Attorney General (1) be continued in custody; or (2) be released under bond in the amount of not less than $500, with security approved by the Attorney General; or (3) be released on conditional parole. It shall be among the conditions of any such bond, or of the terms of release on parole, that the alien shall be produced, or will produce himself, when required to do so for the purpose of defending himself against the charge or charges under which he was taken into custody and any other charges which subsequently are lodged against him, and for deportation if an order for his deportation has been made. When such an order of deportation has been made against any alien, the Attorney General shall have a period of six months from the date of such order within which to effect the alien's departure from the United States, during which period, at the Attorney General's discretion, the alien may be detained, released on conditional parole, or upon bond in an amount and specifying such conditions for surrender of the alien to the Immigration and Naturalization Service as may be determined by the Attorney General. If deportation has not been practicable, advisable, or possible, or departure of the alien from the United States has not been effected, within six months from the date of the order of deportation the alien shall become subject to such further supervision and detention pending eventual deportation as is authorized hereinafter in this section. The Attorney General is hereby authorized and directed to arrange for appropriate places of detention for those aliens whom he shall take into custody and detain.

"(b) Any alien, against whom an order of deportation, heretofore or hereafter issued, has been outstanding for more than six months shall, pending eventual deportation, be subject to supervision under regulations prescribed by the Attorney General. Such regulations shall require any alien subject to supervision (1) to appear from time to time at specified times or intervals before an officer of the Immigration and Naturalization Service for identification; (2) to submit, if necessary, to medical and psychiatric examination at the expense of the United States; (3) to give information under oath as to his nationality, circumstances, habits, associations, and activities, and such other information whether or not related to the foregoing as the Attorney General may deem fit and proper; and (4) to conform to such reasonable written restrictions on his conduct or activities as are prescribed by the Attorney General in his case. Any alien who shall willfully fail to comply with such regulations, or willfully fail to appear or to give information or submit to medical or psychiatric examination if required, or knowingly give false information in relation to the requirements of such regulations, or knowingly violate a reasonable restriction imposed upon his conduct or activity, shall upon conviction be guilty of a felony, and shall be fined not more than $1,000 or shall be imprisoned not more than one year, or both.

"(c) Any alien against whom an order of deportation is outstanding under (1) the Act of October 16, 1918, as amended (40 Stat. 1012, 41 Stat. 1008, 54 Stat. 673; 8 U. S. C. 137); (2) the Act of February 9, 1909, as amended (35 Stat. 614, 42 Stat. 596; 21 U. S. C. 171, 174-175); (3) the Act of February 18, 1931, as amended (46 Stat. 1171, 54 Stat. 673; 8 U. S. C. 156a); or (4) so much of section 19 of the Immigration Act of 1917, as amended (39 Stat. 889-890; 54 Stat. 671-673, 56 Stat. 1044; 8 U. S. C. 155) as relates to criminals, prostitutes, procurers or other immoral persons, anarchists, subversives and similar classes, who shall willfully fail or refuse to depart from the United States within a period of six months from the date of such order of deportation, or from the date of the enactment of the Subversive Activities Control Act of 1950, whichever is the later, or shall willfully fail or refuse to make timely application in good faith for travel or other documents necessary to his departure, or who shall connive or conspire, or take any other action, designed to prevent or hamper or with the purpose of preventing or hampering his departure pursuant to such order of deportation, or who shall willfully fail or refuse to present himself for deportation at the time and place required by the Attorney General pursuant to such order of deportation, shall upon conviction be guilty of a felony, and shall be imprisoned not more than ten years: *Provided,* That this subsection shall not make it illegal for any alien to take any proper steps for the purpose of securing cancellation of or exemption from such order of deportation or for the purpose of securing his release from incarceration or custody: *Provided further,*

That the court may for good cause suspend the sentence of such alien and order his release under such conditions as the court may prescribe. In determining whether good cause has been shown to justify releasing the alien, the court shall take into account such factors as (1) the age, health, and period of detention of the alien; (2) the effect upon the national security and public peace or safety; (3) the likelihood of the alien's following a course of conduct which made or would make him deportable; (4) the character of the efforts made by such alien himself and by representatives of the country or countries to which his deportation is directed to expedite the alien's departure from the United States; (5) the reason for the inability of the Government of the United States to secure passports, other travel documents, or deportation facilities from the country or countries to which the alien has been ordered deported; and (6) the eligibility of the alien for discretionary relife under the immigration laws.

"(d) Should any alien subject to the provisions of subsection (c) unlawfully return to the United States after having been released for departure or deported pursuant to this section, the previous warrant of deportation against him shall be considered as reinstated from its original date of issuance.

"(e) If any alien subject to this section is able to depart from the United States, except that he is financially unable to pay his passage, the expense of such passage to the country to which he is destined may be paid from the appropriation for the enforcement of this Act, unless such payment is otherwise provided for under this Act."

Amending Alien Registration Act of 1940

Sec. 24. (a) Section 35 of the Alien Registration Act of 1940, approved June 28, 1940 (54 Stat. 675; 8 U. S. C. 456), is hereby amended to read as follows:

"Sec. 35. Any alien required to be registered under this title who is an alien resident of the United States on January 1, 1951, and on January 1 of any succeeding year, shall, within ten days following such dates, notify the Commissioner in writing of his current address. In the case of an alien for whom a parent or legal guardian is required to apply for registration, the notice required by this section shall be given by such parent or legal guardian."

(b) Subsection (b) of section 36 of the said Act is hereby amended to read as follows:

"(b) Any alien, or any parent or legal guardian of any alien, who fails to give written notice to the Commissioner, as required by section 35 of this Act, shall, upon conviction thereof, be fined not to exceed $100 or imprisoned not more than thirty days, or both."

Amending Section 305 of Nationality Act of 1940

Sec. 25. Section 305 of the Nationality Act of 1940, as amended, is hereby amended to read as follows:

"Sec. 305. (a) No person shall hereafter be naturalized as a citizen of the United States—

> "(1) who advocates or teaches, or who is a member of or affiliated with any organization that advocates or teaches, opposition to all organized government; or
>
> "(2) who is a member of or affiliated with any Communist action organization that is registered or required to be registered under the provisions of section 7 of the Subversive Activities Control Act of 1950; or

"(3) who, while not within any of the other provisions of this section, advocates the economic, international, and governmental doctrines of world communism or the economic or governmental doctrines of any other form of totalitarianism, or who is a member of or affiliated with any organization that advocates the economic, international, and governmental doctrines of world communism, or the economic and governmental doctrines of any other form of totalitarianism, either through its own utterances or through any written or printed publications issued or published by or with the permission or consent of or under authority of such organization or paid for by the funds of such organization; or

"(4) who advocates or teaches or who is a member of or affiliated with any organization that advocates or teaches (i) the overthrow by force or violence or other unconstitutional means of the Government of the United States or of all forms of law; or (ii) the duty, necessity, or propriety of the unlawful assaulting or killing of any officer or officers (either of specific individuals or of officers generally) of the Government of the United States or of any other organized government because of his or their official character; or (iii) the unlawful damage, injury, or destruction of property; or (iv) sabotage; or

"(5) who writes or publishes or causes to be written or published, or who knowingly circulates, distributes, prints, or displays, or knowingly causes to be circulated, distributed, printed, published, or displayed, or who knowingly has in his possession for the purpose of circulation, publication, or display, any written or printed matter, advocating or teaching opposition to all organized government, or advocating (i) the overthrow by force, violence, or other unconstitutional means of the Government of the United States or of all forms of law; or (ii) the duty, necessity, or propriety of the unlawful assaulting or killing of any officer or officers (either of specific individuals or of officers generally) of the Government of the United States or of any other organized government; or (iii) the unlawful damage, injury, or destruction of property; or (iv) sabotage; or (v) the economic, international, and governmental doctrines of world communism or the economic and governmental doctrines of any other form of totalitarianism; or

"(6) who is a member of or affiliated with any organization that writes, circulates, distributes, prints, publishes, or displays, or causes to be written, circulated, distributed, printed, published, or displayed, or that has in its possession for the purpose of circulation, distribution, publication, issue, or display, any written or printed matter of the character described in subparagraph (5).

"(b) The provisions of this section or of any other section of this Act shall not be construed as declaring that any of the organizations referred to in this section or in any other section of this Act do not advocate the overthrow of the Government of the United States by force, violence, or other unconstitutional means.

"(c) The provisions of this section shall be applicable to any applicant for naturalization who at any time within a period of ten years immediately preceding the filing of the petition for naturalization is, or has been found to be, within any of the classes enumerated within this section, notwithstanding that at the time petition is filed he may not be included within such classes.

"(d) If a person who shall have been naturalized after January 1, 1951, shall within five years next following such naturalization—

"(1) become a member of or affiliated with any organization, membership in or affiliation with which at the time of naturalization would have precluded such person from naturalization under the provisions of this section; or

"(2) become a member of any organization, membership in which at the time of naturalization would have raised the presumption that such person was not attached to the principles of the Constitution of the United States and not well disposed to the good order and happiness of the United States, under the provisions of this section

it shall be considered prima facie evidence that such person was not attached to the principles of the Constitution of the United States and was not well disposed to the good order and happiness of the United States at the time of naturalization, and, in the absence of countervailing evidence, it shall be sufficient in the proper proceeding to authorize the revocation and setting aside of the order admitting such person to citizenship and the cancellation of the certificate of naturalization as having been obtained by fraud or illegal procurement.

"(e) Any alien who has been at any time within ten years next preceding the filing of his petition for naturalization, or is at the time of filing such petition, or has been at any time between such filing and the time of taking of the final oath of citizenship, a member of or affiliated with any Communist-front organization which is registered or required to be registered under section 7 of the Subversive Activities Control Act of 1950, shall be presumed to be a person not attached to the principles of the Constitution of the United States and not well disposed to the good order and happiness of the United States, and unless he shall rebut such presumption he shall not be naturalized as a citizen of the United States: *Provided,* That the provisions of this section shall not apply to any person who shall be a member of or affiliated with any such Communist-front organization who shall, within three months from the date upon which such organization was so registered or so required to be registered, renounce, withdraw from, and utterly abandon such membership or affiliation, and who thereafter ceases entirely to be affiliated with such organization."

Amending Section 325 of Nationality Act of 1940

Sec. 26. Section 325 of the Nationality Act of 1940, as amended, is hereby amended to read:

"Sec. 325. (a) Any periods of time during all of which an alien who was previously lawfully admitted for permanent residence has served honorably or with good conduct, in any capacity other than as a member of the armed forces of the United States, (1) on board a vessel operated by the United States, or an agency thereof, the full legal and equitable title to which is in the United States; or (2) on board a vessel whose home port is in the United States, and (A) which is registered under the laws of the United States, or (B) the full legal and equitable title to which is in a citizen of the United States, or a corporation organized under the laws of any of the several States of the United States, shall be deemed residence within the United States within the meaning of section 307 (a) of this Act, if such service occurred within five years immediately preceding the date such alien shall file a petition for naturalization. Service with good conduct on vessels described in clause (1) of this subsection shall be proved by duly authenticated copies of the records of the executive departments or agency having custody of the records of such service. Service with good conduct on vessels described in clause (2) of this subsection may be proved by certificates from the masters of such vessels.

"(b) Any alien who (1) was excepted from certain requirements of the naturalization laws under the provisions of this section prior to this amendment, and (2) has filed a petition for naturalization under this section prior to the date of approval of this amendment may, if such petition is pending on the date of approval of this section as amended, be naturalized upon compliance with the applicable provisions of the naturalization laws in effect upon the date such petition was filed."

Amending Section 329 of Nationality Act of 1940

Sec. 27. Section 329 of the Nationality Act of 1940, as amended, is hereby amended by adding a new subsection (c), as follows:

"(c) Except as otherwise provided in this Act, no person shall be naturalized unless he has been lawfully admitted to the United States for permanent residence in accordance with all applicable provisions of this Act and of the immigration laws. The burden of proof shall be upon such person to show that he entered the United States lawfully, and the time, place, and manner of such entry into the United States, but in presenting such proof he shall be entitled to the production of his immigration visa, if any, or of other documents concerning such entry, in the custody of the Commissioner. No person shall be naturalized against whom there is outstanding a final finding of deportability, and no petition for naturalization shall be finally heard by a naturalization court if there is pending against the petitioner a deportation proceeding pursuant to a warrant of arrest issued under the provisions of this or any other Act: *Provided,* That the findings of the Commissioner in terminating deportation proceedings or in suspending the deportation of an alien pursuant to law, shall not be deemed binding in any way upon the naturalization court with respect to the question of whether such person has established his eligibility for naturalization as required by this Act."

Amending Sections 333 and 334 (b) of Nationality Act of 1940

Sec. 28. (a) Section 333 of the Nationality Act of 1940, as amended, is hereby amended to read:

"Sec. 333. (a) The Commissioner or a Deputy Commissioner shall designate employees of the Service to conduct preliminary examinations upon petitions for naturalization to any naturalization court and to make recommendations thereon to such court. For such purposes any such employee so designated is hereby authorized to take testimony concerning any matter touching or in any way affecting the admissibility of any petitioner for naturalization, to administer oaths, and to require by subpena the attendance and testimony of witnesses, including petitioner, before such employee so designated and the production of relevant books, papers, and documents, and to that end may invoke the aid of any court exercising naturalization jurisdiction as specified in section 301 of this Act; and any such court wherein the petition is filed may, in the event of neglect or refusal to respond to a subpena issued by any such employee so designated or refusal to testify before such employee so designated, issue an order requiring such person to appear before such employee so designated, produce relevant books, papers, and documents if demanded, and testify; and any failure to obey such order of the court may be punished by the court as a contempt thereof. The record of the preliminary examination authorized by this subsection shall be admissible as evidence in any final hearing conducted by a naturalization court designated in section 301 of this Act.

"(b) The record of the preliminary examination upon any petition for naturalization may be transmitted to the Commissioner and the recommendation with respect thereto of the employee designated to conduct such preliminary examination shall when made also be transmitted to the Commissioner.

"(c) The recommendation of the employee designated to conduct any such preliminary examination shall be submitted to the court at the hearing upon the petition and shall include a recommendation that the petition be granted, or denied, or continued, with reasons therefor. In any case in which the recommendation of the Commissioner does not agree with that of the employee designated to conduct such preliminary examination, the recommendations of both such employee and the Commissioner shall be submitted to the court at the hearing upon the petition, and the officer of the Service in attendance at such hearing shall, at the request of the court, present both the views of such employee and those of the Commissioner with respect to such petition to the court. The recommendations of such employee and of the Commissioner shall be accompanied by duplicate lists containing the names of the petitioners, classified according to the character of the recommendations, and signed by such employee or the Commissioner, as the case may be. The judge to whom such recommendations are submitted shall, if he approve such recommendations, enter a written order with such exceptions as the judge may deem proper, by subscribing his name to each such list when corrected to conform to his conclusions upon such recommendations. One of each such lists shall thereafter be filed permanently of record in such court and the duplicate of each such list shall be sent by the clerk of such court to the Commissioner.

"(d) After the petition for naturalization has been filed in the office of the clerk of the naturalization court, the petitioner shall not be permitted to withdraw his petition, except with the consent of the Commissioner. In cases where the Commissioner does not consent to withdrawal of the petition, the court shall determine the petition on its merits and enter a final order accordingly. In cases where the petitioner fails to prosecute his petition, the petition shall be decided upon its merits unless the Commissioner moves that the petition be dismissed for lack of prosecution."

(b) Section 334 (b) of the Nationality Act of 1940, as amended, is amended to read as follows:

"(b) The requirement of subsection (a) of this Section for the examination of the petitioner and witnesses under oath before the court and in the presence of the court shall not apply in any case where a designated examiner has conducted the preliminary examination authorized by subsection (a) of Section 333; except that the court may, in its discretion, and shall, upon the demand of the petitioner, require the examination of the petitioner and the witnesses under oath before the court and in the presence of the court. If the petitioner is prevented by sickness or other disability from being in open court for the final hearing upon petition for naturalization, such final hearing may be had by a judge or judges at such place as may be designated by the court."

Amending Section 335 of Nationality Act of 1940

Sec. 29. Section 335 of the Nationality Act of 1940, as amended, is amended to read:

"Sec. 335. (a) A person who has petitioned for naturalization shall, before being admitted to citizenship, take in open court one of the oaths set forth in subsection (b) of this section (1) to support the Constitution of the United States; (2) to renounce and abjure absolutely and entirely all allegiance and fidelity to any foreign prince, potentate, state, or sovereignty of whom or which the petitioner was before a subject or citizen; (3) to support and defend the Constitution and the laws of the United States against all enemies, foreign and domestic; (4) to bear true faith and allegiance to the same; and (5) to bear arms on behalf of the United States when required by law, or to perform noncombatant service in the Armed Forces of the United States when required by law: *Provided,* That any such person shall be required to take the oath prescribed in subsection (b) (1) of this section unless by clear and convincing evidence he can show to the satisfaction of the naturalization court that he is opposed to the bearing of arms or the performance of noncombantant service in the Armed Forces of the United States by reason of religious training and belief: *Provided further,* That in the case of the naturalization of a child under the provisions of section 315 or 316 of this Act the naturalization court may waive the taking of either of such oaths if in the opinion of the court the child is unable to understand their meaning.

"(b) As provided in subsection (a) of this section, the petitioner for naturalization shall take one of the following oaths:

"(1) I hereby declare, on oath, that I absolutely and entirely renounce and abjure all allegiance and fidelity to any foreign prince, potentate, state, or sovereignty of whom or which I have heretofore been a subject or citizen; that I will support and defend the Constitution and laws of the United States of America against all enemies, foreign and domestic; that I will bear true faith and allegiance to the same; that I will bear arms on behalf of the United States or perform noncombatant service in the Armed Forces of the United States when required by law; and that I take this obligation freely without any mental reservation or purpose of evasion: So help me God. In acknowledgment whereof I have hereunto affixed my signature; or

"(2) I hereby declare, on oath, that I absolutely and entirely renounce and abjure all allegiance and fidelity to any foreign prince, potentate, state, or sovereignty of whom or which I have heretofore been a subject or citizen; that I will support and defend the Constitution and laws of the United States of America against all enemies, foreign and domestic; that I will bear true faith and allegiance to the same; and that I take this obligation freely and without any mental reservation or purpose of evasion: So help me God. In acknowledgment whereof I have hereunto affixed my signature.

"(c) In case the person petitioning for naturalization has borne any hereditary title, or has been of any of the orders of nobility in any foreign state, the petitioner shall in addition to complying with the requirements of subsections (a) and (b) of this section, make under oath in open court to which the petition for naturalization is made, an express renunciation of such title or order of nobility, and such renunciation shall be recorded in the court as a part of such proceedings.

"(d) If the petitioner is prevented by sickness or other disability from being in open court, the oath required to be taken by subsection (a) of this section may be taken before a judge of the court at such place as may be designated by the court."

Amending Section 304 of Nationality Act of 1940

Sec. 30. Section 304 of the Nationality Act of 1940, as amended, is hereby amended to read as follows:

"Sec. 304. No person except as otherwise provided in this Act shall hereafter be naturalized as a citizen of the United States upon his own petition who cannot demonstrate—

"(1) an understanding of the English language, including an ability to read, write, and speak words in ordinary usage in the English language: *Provided,* That this requirement shall not apply to any person physically unable to comply therewith, if otherwise qualified to be naturalized, or to any person who, on the date of approval of this amendment, is over fifty years of age and has been legally residing in the United States for twenty years: *Provided further,* That the requirements of this section relating to ability to read and write shall be met if the applicant can read or write simple words and phrases to the end that a reasonable test of his literacy shall be made and that no extraordinary or unreasonable conditions shall be imposed upon the applicant; and

"(2) a knowledge and understanding of the fundamentals of the history, and the principles and form of government, of the United States."

Amending Chapter 73, Title 18, United States Code

Sec. 31. (a) Chapter 73 of title 18, United States Code, is amended by inserting, immediately following section 1506 of such chapter, a new section, to be designated as section 1507, and to read as follows:

"§ 1507. Picketing or parading.

"Whoever, with the intent of interfering with, obstructing, or impeding the administration of justice, or with the intent of influencing any judge, juror, witness, or court officer, in the discharge of his duty, pickets or parades in or near a building housing a court of the United States, or in or near a building or residence occupied or used by such judge, juror, witness, or court officer, or with such intent uses any sound-truck or similar device or resorts to any other demonstration in or near any such building or residence, shall be fined not more than $5,000 or imprisoned not more than one year, or both.

"Nothing in this section shall interfere with or prevent the exercise by any court of the United States of its power to punish for contempt."

(b) The analysis of such chapter is amended by inserting, immediately after and underneath item 1506, as contained in such analysis, the following new item: "1507. Picketing or parading."

Separability of Provisions

Sec. 32. If any provision of this title, or the application thereof to any person or circumstances, is held invalid, the remaining provisions of this title, or the application of such provision to other persons or circumstances, shall not be affected thereby.

Communist Control Act of 1954

68 Stat. 775 (1954)

An Act

To outlaw the Communist Party, to prohibit members of Communist organizations from serving in certain representative capacities, and for other purposes.

Be it enacted by the Senate and House of Representatives of the United States of America in Congress assembled, That this Act may be cited as the "Communist Control Act of 1954".

Findings of Fact

Sec. 2. The Congress hereby finds and declares that the Communist Party of the United States, although purportedly a political party, is in fact an instrumentality of a conspiracy to overthrow the Government of the United States. It constitutes an authoritarian dictatorship within a republic, demanding for itself the rights and privileges accorded to political parties, but denying to all others the liberties guaranteed by the Constitution. Unlike political parties, which evolve their policies and programs through public means, by the reconciliation of a wide variety of individual views, and submit those policies and programs to the electorate at large for approval or disapproval, the policies and programs of the Communist Party are secretly prescribed for it by the foreign leaders of the world Communist movement. Its members have no part in determining its goals, and are not permitted to voice dissent to party objectives. Unlike members of political parties, members of the Communist Party are recruited for indoctrination with respect to its objectives and methods, and are organized, instructed, and disciplined to carry into action slavishly the assignments given them by their hierarchical chieftains. Unlike political parties, the Communist Party acknowledges no constitutional or statutory limitations upon its conduct or upon that of its members. The Communist Party is relatively small numerically, and gives scant indication of capacity ever to attain its ends by lawful political means. The peril inherent in its operation arises not from its numbers, but from its failure to acknowledge any limitation as to the nature of its activities, and its dedication to the proposition that the present constitutional Government of the United States ultimately must be brought to ruin by any available means, including resort to force and violence. Holding that doctrine, its role as the agency of a hostile foreign power renders its existence a clear present and continuing danger to the security of the United States. It is the means whereby individuals are seduced into the service of the world Communist movement, trained to do its bidding, and directed and controlled in the conspiratorial performance of their revolutionary services. Therefore, the Communist Party should be outlawed.

Proscribed Organizations

Sec. 3. The Communist Party of the United States, or any successors of such party regardless of the assumed name, whose object or purpose is to overthrow the Government of the United States, or the government of any State, Territory, District, or possession thereof, or the government of any political subdivision therein by force and violence, are not entitled to any of the rights, privileges, and immunities attendant upon legal bodies created under the jurisdiction of the laws of the United States or any political subdivision thereof; and whatever rights, privileges, and immunities which have heretofore been granted to said party or any subsidiary organizations by reason of the laws of the United States or any political subdivision thereof, are hereby terminated: *Provided, however,* That nothing in this section shall be construed as amending the Internal Security Act of 1950, as amended.

Sec. 4. Whoever knowingly and willfully becomes or remains a member of (1) the Communist Party, or (2) any other organization having for one of its purposes or objectives the establishment, control, conduct, seizure, or overthrow of the Government of the United States, or the government of any State or political subdivision thereof, by the use of force or violence, with knowledge of the purpose or objective of such organization shall be subject to all the provisions and penalties of the Internal Security Act of 1950, as amended, as a member of a "Communist-action" organization.

(b) For the purposes of this section, the term "Communist Party" means the organization now known as the Communist Party of the United States of America, the Communist Party of any State or subdivision thereof, and any unit or subdivision of any such organization, whether or not any change is hereafter made in the name thereof.

Sec. 5. In determining membership or participation in the Communist Party or any other organization defined in this Act, or knowledge of the purpose or objective of such party or organization, the jury, under instructions from the court, shall consider evidence, if presented, as to whether the accused person:

(1) Has been listed to his knowledge as a member in any book or any of the lists, records, correspondence, or any other document of the organization;

(2) Has made financial contribution to the organization in dues, assessments, loans, or in any other form;

(3) Has made himself subject to the discipline of the organization in any form whatsoever;

(4) Has executed orders, plans, or directives of any kind of the organization;

(5) Has acted as an agent, courier, messenger, correspondent, organizer, or in any other capacity in behalf of the organization;

(6) Has conferred with officers or other members of the organization in behalf of any plan or enterprise of the organization;

(7) Has been accepted to his knowledge as an officer or member of the organization or as one to be called upon for services by other officers or members of the organization;

(8) Has written, spoken or in any other way communicated by signal, semaphore, sign, or in any other form of communication orders, directives, or plans of the organization;

(9) Has prepared documents, pamphlets, leaflets, books, or any other type of publication in behalf of the objectives and purposes of the organization;

(10) Has mailed, shipped, circulated, distributed, delivered, or in any other way sent or delivered to others material or propaganda of any kind in behalf of the organization;

(11) Has advised, counseled or in any other way imparted information, suggestions, recommendations to officers or members of the organization or to anyone else in behalf of the objectives of the organization;

(12) Has indicated by word, action, conduct, writing or in any other way a will-

ingness to carry out in any manner and to any degree the plans, designs, objectives, or purposes of the organization;

(13) Has in any other way participated in the activities, planning, actions, objectives, or purposes of the organization;

(14) The enumeration of the above subjects of evidence on membership or participation in the Communist Party or any other organization as above defined, shall not limit the inquiry into and consideration of any other subject of evidence on membership and participation as herein stated.

Subversive Activities Control Act Amendment

Sec. 6. Subsection 5 (a) (1) of the Subversive Activities Control Act of 1950 (50 U. S. C. 784) is amended by striking out the period at the end thereof and inserting in lieu thereof a semicolon and the following: "or

"(E) to hold office or employment with any labor organization, as that term is defined in section 2 (5) of the National Labor Relations Act, as amended (29 U. S. C. 152), or to represent any employer in any matter or proceeding arising or pending under that Act."

Sec. 7. (a) Section 3 of the Subversive Activities Control Act of 1950 (50 U. S. C. 782) is amended by inserting, immediately after paragraph (4) thereof, the following new paragraph:

"(4A) The term 'Communist-infiltrated organization' means any organization in the United States (other than a Communist-action organization or a Communist-front organization) which (A) is substantially directed, dominated, or controlled by an individual or individuals who are, or who within three years have been actively engaged in, giving aid or support to a Communist-action organization, a Communist foreign government, or the world Communist movement referred to in section 2 of this title, and (B) is serving, or within three years has served, as a means for (i) the giving of aid or support to any such organization, government, or movement, or (ii) the impairment of the military strength of the United States or its industrial capacity to furnish logistical or other material support required by its Armed Forces: *Provided, however,* That any labor organization which is an affiliate in good standing of a national federation or other labor organization whose policies and activities have been directed to opposing Communist organizations, any Communist foreign government, or the world Communist movement, shall be presumed prima facie not to be a 'Communist-infiltrated organization'."

(b) Paragraph (5) of such section is amended to read as follows:

"(5) The term 'Communist organization' means any Communist-action organization, Communist-front organization, or Communist-infiltrated organization."

(c) Subsections 5 (c) and 6 (c) of such Act are repealed.

Sec. 8. (a) Section 10 of such Act (50 U. S. C. 789) is amended by inserting, immediately after the words "final order of the Board requiring it to register under section 7", the words "or determining that it is a Communist-infiltrated organization".

(b) Subsections (a) and (b) of section 11 of such Act (50 U. S. C. 790) are amended by inserting immediately preceding the period at the end of each such subsection, the following: "or determining that it is a Communist-infiltrated organization".

Sec. 9. (a) Subsection 12 (e) of such Act (50 U. S. C. 791) is amended by—

(1) striking out the period at the end thereof and inserting in lieu thereof a semicolon and the word "and"; and

(2) inserting at the end thereof the following new paragraph:

"(3) upon any application made under subsection (a) or subsection (b) of section 13A of this title, to determine whether any organization is a Communist-infiltrated organization."

(b) The section caption to section 13 of such Act (50 U. S. C. 792) is amended to read as follows: "Registration Proceedings Before the Board".

Sec. 10. Such Act is amended by inserting, immediately after section 13 thereof, the following new section:

"Proceedings with Respect to Communist-Infiltrated Organizations

"Sec. 13A. (a) Whenever the Attorney General has reason to believe that any organization is a Communist-infiltrated organization, he may file with the Board and serve upon such organization a petition for a determination that such organization is a Communist-infiltrated organization. In any proceeding so instituted, two or more affiliated organizations may be named as joint respondents. Whenever any such petition is accompanied by a certificate of the Attorney General to the effect that the proceeding so instituted is one of exceptional public importance, such proceeding shall be set for hearing at the earliest possible time and all proceedings therein before the Board or any court shall be expedited to the greatest practicable extent.

"(b) Any organization which has been determined under this section to be a Communist-infiltrated organization may, within six months after such determination, file with the Board and serve upon the Attorney General a petition for a determination that such organization no longer is a Communist-infiltrated organization.

"c) Each such petition shall be verified under oath, and shall contain a statement of the facts relied upon in support thereof. Upon the filing of any such petition, the Board shall serve upon each party to such proceeding a notice specifying the time and place for hearing upon such petition. No such hearing shall be conducted within twenty days after the service of such notice.

"(d) The provisions of subsections (c) and (d) of section 13 shall apply to hearings conducted under this section, except that upon the failure of any organization named as a party in any petition filed by or duly served upon it pursuant to this section to appear at any hearing upon such petition, the Board may conduct such hearing in the absence of such organization and may enter such order under this section as the Board shall determine to be warranted by evidence presented at such hearing.

"(e) In determining whether any organization is a Communist-infiltrated organization, the Board shall consider—

"(1) to what extent, if any, the effective management of the affairs of such organization is conducted by one or more individuals who are, or within two years have been, (A) members, agents, or representatives of any Communist organization, and Communist foreign government, or the world Communist movement referred to in section 2 of this title, with knowledge of the nature and purpose thereof, or (B) engaged in giving aid or support to any such organization, government, or movement with knowledge of the nature and purpose thereof;

"(2) to what extent, if any, the policies of such organization are, or within three years have been, formulated and carried out pursuant to the direction or advice of any member, agent, or representative of any such organization, government, or movement;

"(3) to what extent, if any, the personnel and resources of such organization are, or within three years have been, used to further or promote the objectives of any such Communist organization, government, or movement;

"(4) to what extent, if any, such organization within three years has received from, or furnished to or for the use of, any such Communist organization, government, or movement any funds or other material assistance;

"(5) to what extent, if any, such organization is, or within three years has been, affiliated in any way with any such Communist organization, government, or movement;

"(6) to what extent, if any, the affiliation of such organization, or of any individual or individuals who are members thereof or who manage it affairs, with any such Communist organization, government, or movement is concealed from or is not disclosed to the membership of such organization; and

"(7) to what extent, if any, such organization or any of its members or managers are, or within three years have been, knowingly engaged—

"(A) in any conduct punishable under section 4 or 15 of this Act or under chapter 37, 105, or 115 of title 18 of the United States Code; or

"(B) with intent to impair the military strength of the United States or its industrial capacity to furnish logistical or other support required by its armed forces, in any activity resulting in or contributing to any such impairment.

"(f) After hearing upon any petition filed under this section, the Board shall (1) make a report in writing in which it shall state its findings as to the facts and its conclusions with respect to the issues presented by such petition, (2) enter its order granting or denying the determination sought by such petition, and (3) serve upon each party to the proceeding a copy of such order. Any order granting any determination on the question whether any organization is a Communist-infiltrated organization shall become final as provided in section 14 (b) of this Act.

"(g) When any order has been entered by the Board under this section with respect to any labor organization or employer (as these terms are defined by section 2 of the National Labor Relations Act, as amended, and which are organizations within the meaning of section 3 of the Subversive Activities Control Act of 1950), the Board shall serve a true and correct copy of such order upon the National Labor Relations Board and shall publish in the Federal Register a statement of the substance of such order and its effective date.

"(h) When there is in effect a final order of the Board determining that any such labor organization is a Communist-action organization, a Communist-front organization, or a Communist-infiltrated organization, such labor organization shall be ineligible to—

"(1) act as representative of any employee within the meaning or for the purposes of section 7 of the National Labor Relations Act, as amended (29 U. S. C. 157);

"(2) serve as an exclusive representative of employees of any bargaining unit under section 9 of such Act, as amended (29 U. S. C. 159);

"(3) make, or obtain any hearing upon, any charge under section 10 of such Act (29 U. S. C. 160); or

"(4) exercise any other right or privilege, or receive any other benefit, substantive or procedural, provided by such Act for labor organizations.

"(i) When an order of the Board determining that any such labor organization is a Communist-infiltrated organization has become final, and such labor organization theretofore has been certified under the National Labor Relations Act, as amended, as a representative of employees in any bargaining unit—

"(1) a question of representation affecting commerce, within the meaning of section 9 (c) of such Act, shall be deemed to exist with respect to such bargaining unit; and

"(2) the National Labor Relations Board, upon petition of not less than 20 per centum of the employees in such bargaining unit or any person or persons acting in their behalf, shall under section 9 of such Act (notwithstanding any limitation of time contained therein) direct elections in such bargaining unit or any subdivision thereof (A) for the selection of a representative thereof for collective bargaining purposes, and (B) to determine whether the employees thereof desire to rescind any authority previously granted to such labor organization to enter into any agreement with their employer pursuant to section 8 (a) (3) (ii) of such Act.

"(j) When there is in effect a final order of the Board determining that any such employer is a Communist-infiltrated organization, such employer shall be ineligible to—

"(1) file any petition for an election under section 9 of the National Labor Relations Act, as amended (29 U. S. C. 157), or participate in any proceeding under such section; or

"(2) make or obtain any hearing upon any charge under section 10 of such Act (29 U. S. C. 160); or

"(3) exercise any other right or privilege or receive any other benefit, substantive or procedural, provided by such Act for employers."

Sec. 11. Subsections (a) and (b) of section 14 of such Act (50 U. S. C. 793) are amended by inserting in each such subsection, immediately after the words "section 13", a comma and the following: "or subsection (f) of section 13A,"

Sec. 12. If any provision of this title or the application thereof to any person or circumstances is held invalid, the remainder of the title, and the application of such provisions to other persons or circumstances, shall not be affected thereby.

Approved August 24, 1954, 9:40 a.m., M.S.T.

Treason, Sedition, and Subversive Activities

18 U.S.C. §2381

Treason

Whoever, owing allegiance to the United States, levies war against them or adheres to their enemies, giving them aid and comfort within the United States or elsewhere, is guilty of treason and shall suffer death, or shall be imprisoned not less than five years and fined not less than $10,000; and shall be incapable of holding any office under the United States.

18 U.S.C. §2382

Misprision of Treason

Whoever, owing allegiance to the United States and having knowledge of the commission of any treason against them, conceals and does not, as soon as may be, disclose and make known the same to the President or to some judge of the United States, or to the governor or to some judge or justice of a particular State, is guilty of misprision of treason and shall be fined not more than $1,000 or imprisoned not more than seven years, or both.

18 U.S.C. §2383

Rebellion or Insurrection

Whoever incites, sets on foot, assists, or engages in any rebellion or insurrection against the authority of the United States or the laws thereof, or gives aid or comfort thereto, shall be fined not more than $10,000 or imprisoned not more than ten years, or both; and shall be incapable of holding any office under the United States.

18 U.S.C. §2384

Seditious Conspiracy

If two or more persons in any State or Territory, or in any place subject to the jurisdiction of the United States, conspire to overthrow, put down, or to destroy by force the Government of the United States, or to levy war against them, or to oppose by force the authority thereof, or by force to prevent, hinder, or delay the execution of any law of the United States, or by force to seize, take, or possess any property of the United States contrary to the authority thereof, they shall each be fined not more than $20,000 or imprisoned not more than twenty years, or both.

As amended July 24, 1956, c. 678, § 1, 70 Stat. 623.

18 U.S.C. §2385

Advocating Overthrow of Government

Whoever knowingly or willfully advocates, abets, advises, or teaches the duty, necessity, desirability, or propriety of overthrowing or destroying the government of the United States or the government of any State, Territory, District or Possession thereof, or the government of any political subdivision therein, by force or violence, or by the assassination of any officer of any such government; or

Whoever, with intent to cause the overthrow or destruction of any such government, prints, publishes, edits, issues, circulates, sells, distributes, or publicly displays any written or printed matter advocating, advising, or teaching the duty, necessity, desirability, or propriety of overthrowing or destroying any government in the United States by force or violence or attempts to do so; or

Whoever organizes or helps or attempts to organize any society, group, or assembly of persons who teach, advocate, or encourage the overthrow or destruction of any such government by force or violence; or becomes or is a member of, or affiliates with, any such society, group, or assembly of persons, knowing the purposes thereof—

Shall be fined not more than $20,000 or imprisoned not more than twenty years, or both, and shall be ineligible for employment by the United States or any department or agency thereof, for the five years next following his conviction.

If two or more persons conspire to commit any offense named in this section, each shall be fined not more than $20,000 or imprisoned not more than twenty years, or both, and shall be ineligible for employment by the United States or any department or agency thereof, for the five years next following his conviction.

As used in this section, the terms "organizes" and "organize", with respect to any society, group, or assembly of persons, include the recruiting of new members, the forming of new units, and the regrouping or expansion of existing clubs, classes, and other units of such society, group, or assembly of persons.

As amended July 24, 1956, c. 678, § 2, 70 Stat. 623;
June 19, 1962, Pub.L. 87-486, 76 Stat. 103.

18 U.S.C. §2386

Registration of Certain Organizations

(A) For the purposes of this section:

"Attorney General" means the Attorney General of the United States;

"Organization" means any group, club, league, society, committee, association, political party, or combination of individuals, whether incorporated or otherwise, but such term shall not include any corporation, association, community chest, fund, or foundation, organized and operated exclusively for religious, charitable, scientific, literary, or educational purposes;

"Political activity" means any activity the purpose or aim of which, or one of the purposes or aims of which, is the control by force or overthrow of the Government of the United States or a political subdivision thereof, or any State or political subdivision thereof;

An organization is engaged in "civilian military activity" if:

(1) it gives instruction to, or prescribes instruction for, its members in the use of firearms or other weapons or any substitute therefor, or military or naval science; or

(2) it receives from any other organization or from any individual instruction in military or naval science; or

(3) it engages in any military or naval maneuvers or activities; or

(4) it engages, either with or without arms, in drills or parades of a military or naval character; or

(5) it engages in any other form of organized activity which in the opinion of the Attorney General constitutes preparation for military action;

An organization is "subject to foreign control" if:

(a) it solicits or accepts financial contributions, loans, or support of any kind, directly or indirectly, from, or is affiliated directly or indirectly with, a foreign government or a political subdivision thereof, or an agent, agency, or instrumentality of a foreign government or political subdivision thereof, or a political party in a foreign country, or an international political organization; or

(b) its policies, or any of them, are determined by or at the suggestion of, or in collaboration with, a foreign government or political subdivision thereof, or an agent, agency, or instrumentality of a foreign government or a political subdivision thereof, or a political party in a foreign country, or an international political organization.

(B) (1) The following organizations shall be required to register with the Attorney General:

Every organization subject to foreign control which engages in political activity;

Every organization which engages both in civilian military activity and in political activity;

Every organization subject to foreign control which engages in civilian military activity; and

Every organization, the purpose or aim of which, or one of the purposes or aims of which, is the establishment, control, conduct, seizure, or overthrow of a government or subdivision thereof by the use of force, violence, military measures, or threats of any one or more of the foregoing.

Every such organization shall register by filing with the Attorney General, on such forms and in such detail as the Attorney General may by rules and regulations prescribe, a registration statement containing the information and documents prescribed in subsection (B) (3) and shall within thirty days after the expiration of each period of six months succeeding the filing of such registration statement, file with the Attorney General, on such forms and in such detail as the Attorney General may by rules and regulations prescribe, a supplemental statement containing such information and documents as may be necessary to make the information and documents previously filed under this section accurate and current with respect to such preceding six months' period. Every statement required to be filed by this section shall be subscribed, under oath, by all of the officers of the organization.

(2) This section shall not require registration or the filing of any statement with the Attorney General by:

(a) The armed forces of the United States; or

(b) The organized militia or National Guard of any State, Territory, District, or possession of the United States; or

(c) Any law-enforcement agency of the United States or of any Territory, District or possession thereof, or of any State or political subdivision of a State, or of any agency or instrumentality of one or more States; or

(d) Any duly established diplomatic mission or consular office of a foreign government which is so recognized by the Department of State; or

(e) Any national recognized organization of persons who are veterans of the armed forces of the United States, or affiliates of such organizations.

(3) Every registration statement required to be filed by any organization shall contain the following information and documents:

(a) The name and post-office address of the organization in the United States, and the names and addresses of all branches, chapters, and affiliates of such organization;

(b) The name, address, and nationality of each officer, and of each person who performs the functions of an officer, of the organization, and of each branch, chapter, and affiliate of the organization;

(c) The qualifications for membership in the organization;

(d) The existing and proposed aims and purposes of the organization, and all the means by which these aims or purposes are being attained or are to be attained;

(e) The address or addresses of meeting places of the organization, and of each branch, chapter, or affiliate of the organization, and the times of meetings;

(f) The name and address of each person who has contributed any money, dues, property, or other thing of value to the organization or to any branch, chapter, or affiliate of the organization;

(g) A detailed statement of the assets of the organization, and of each branch, chapter, and affiliate of the organization, the manner in which such assets were acquired, and a detailed statement of the liabilities and income of the organization and of each branch, chapter, and affiliate of the organization;

(h) A detailed description of the activities of the organization, and of each chapter, branch, and affiliate of the organization;

(i) A description of the uniforms, badges, insignia, or other means of identification prescribed by the organization, and worn or carried by its officers or members, or any of such officers or members;

(j) A copy of each book, pamphlet, leaflet, or other publication or item of written, printed, or graphic matter issued or distributed directly or indirectly by the organization, or by any chapter, branch, or affiliate of the organization, or by any of the members of the organization under its authority or within its knowledge, together with the name of its author or authors and the name and address of the publisher;

(k) A description of all firearms or other weapons owned by the organization, or by any chapter, branch, or affiliate of the organization, identified by the manufacturer's number thereon;

(l) In case the organization is subject to foreign control, the manner in which it is so subject;

(m) A copy of the charter, articles of association, constitution, bylaws, rules, regulations, agreements, resolutions, and all other instruments relating to the organization, powers, and purposes of the organization and to the powers of the officers of the organization and of each chapter, branch, and affiliate of the organization; and

(n) Such other information and documents pertinent to the purposes of this section as the Attorney General may from time to time require.

All statements filed under this section shall be public records and open to public examination and inspection at all reasonable hours under such rules and regulations as the Attorney General may prescribe.

(C) The Attorney General is authorized at any time to make, amend, and rescind such rules and regulations as may be necessary to carry out this section, including rules and regulations governing the statements required to be filed.

(D) Whoever violates any of the provisions of this section shall be fined not more than $10,000 or imprisoned not more than five years, or both.

Whoever in a statement filed pursuant to this section willfully makes any false statement or willfully omits to state any fact which is required to be stated, or which is necessary to make the statements made not misleading, shall be fined not more than $2,000 or imprisoned not more than five years, or both.

18 U.S.C. §2387

Activities Affecting Armed Forces Generally

(a) Whoever, with intent to interfere with, impair, or influence the loyalty, morale, or discipline of the military or naval forces of the United States:

(1) advises, counsels, urges, or in any manner causes or attempts to cause insubordination, disloyalty, mutiny, or refusal of duty by any member of the military or naval forces of the United States; or

(2) distributes or attempts to distribute any written or printed matter which advises, counsels, or urges insubordination, disloyalty, mutiny, or refusal of duty by any member of the military or naval forces of the United States—

Shall be fined not more than $10,000 or imprisoned not more than ten years, or both, and shall be ineligible for employment by the United States or any department or agency thereof, for the five years next following his conviction.

(b) For the purposes of this section, the term "military or naval forces of the United States" includes the Army of the United States, the Navy, Air Force, Marine Corps, Coast Guard, Naval Reserve, Marine Corps Reserve, and Coast Guard Reserve of the United States; and, when any merchant vessel is commissioned in the Navy or is in the service of the Army or the Navy, includes the master, officers, and crew of such vessel.

As amended May 24, 1949, c. 139, § 46, 68 Stat. 96.

18 U.S.C. §2388

Activities Affecting Armed Forces During War

(a) Whoever, when the United States is at war, willfully makes or conveys false reports or false statements with intent to interfere with the operation or success of the military or naval forces of the United States or to promote the success of its enemies; or

Whoever, when the United States is at war, willfully causes or attempts to cause insubordiniation, disloyalty, mutiny, or refusal of duty, in the military or naval forces of the United States, or willfully obstructs the recruiting or enlistment service of the United States, to the injury of the service or the United States, or attempts to do so—

Shall be fined not more than $10,000 or imprisoned not more than twenty years, or both.

(b) If two or more persons conspire to violate subsection (a) of this section and one or more such persons do any act to effect the object of the conspiracy, each of the parties to such conspiracy shall be punished as provided in said subsection (a).

(c) Whoever harbors or conceals any person who he knows, or has reasonable grounds to believe or suspect, has committed, or is about to commit, an offense under this section, shall be fined not more than $10,000 or imprisoned not more than ten years, or both.

(d) This section shall apply within the admiralty and maritime jurisdiction of the United States, and on the high seas, as well as within the United States.

18 U.S.C. §2389

Recruiting for Service Against United States

Whoever recruits soldiers or sailors within the United States, or in any place subject to the jurisdiction thereof, to engage in armed hostility against the same; or

Whoever opens within the United States, or in any place subject to the jurisdiction thereof, a recruiting station for the enlistment of such soldiers or sailors to serve in any manner in armed hostility against the United States—

Shall be fined not more than $1,000 or imprisoned not more than five years, or both.

18 U.S.C. §2390

Enlistment to Serve Against United States

Whoever enlists or is engaged within the United States or in any place subject to the jurisdiction thereof, with intent to serve in armed hostility against the United States, shall be fined $100 or imprisoned not more than three years, or both.

18 U.S.C. §2391

Temporary Extension of Section 2388

The provisions of section 2388 of this title, as amended and extended by section 1(a) (29) of the Emergency Powers Continuation Act (66 Stat. 333), as further amended by Public Law 12, Eighty-third Congress, in addition to coming into full force and effect in time of war shall remain in full force and effect until six months after the termination of the national emergency proclaimed by the President on December 16, 1950 (Proc. 2912, 3 C.F.R., 1950 Supp., p. 71), or such earlier date as may be prescribed by concurrent resolution of the Congress, and acts which would give rise to legal consequences and penalties under section 2388 when performed during a state of war shall give rise to the same legal consequences and penalties when they are performed during the period above provided for.

Added June 30, 1953, c. 175, § 6, 67 Stat. 134.

Conspiracy Against Civil Rights

18 U.S.C. §9241

Conspiracy Against Rights of Citizens

If two or more persons conspire to injure, oppress, threaten, or intimidate any citizen in the free exercise or enjoyment of any right or privilege secured to him by the Constitution or laws of the United States, or because of his having so exercised the same; or

If two or more persons go in disguise on the highway, or on the premises of another, with intent to prevent or hinder his free exercise or enjoyment of any right or privilege so secured—

They shall be fined not more than $10,000 or imprisoned not more than ten years, or both; and if death results, they shall be subject to imprisonment for any term of years or for life.

As amended Apr. 11, 1968, Pub.L. 90-284, Title I, § 103(a), 82 Stat. 75.

Anti-Riot Act

18 U.S.C. §2101

Riots

(a) (1) Whoever travels in interstate or foreign commerce or uses any facility of interstate or foreign commerce, including, but not limited to, the mail, telegraph, telephone, radio, or television, with intent—

(A) to incite a riot; or

(B) to organize, promote, encourage, participate in, or carry on a riot; or

(C) to commit any act of violence in furtherance of a riot; or

(D) to aid or abet any person in inciting or participating in or carrying on a riot or committing any act of violence in furtherance of a riot;

and who either during the course of any such travel or use or thereafter performs or attempts to perform any other overt act for any purpose specified in subparagraph (A), (B), (C), or (D) of this paragraph—

Shall be fined not more than $10,000, or imprisoned not more than five years, or both.

(b) In any prosecution under this section, proof that a defendant engaged or attempted to engage in one or more of the overt acts described in subparagraph (A), (B), (C), or (D) of paragraph (1) of subsection (a) and (1) has traveled in interstate or foreign commerce, or (2) has use of or used any facility of interstate or foreign commerce, including but not limited to, mail, telegraph, telephone, radio, or television, to communicate with or broadcast to any person or group of persons prior to such overt acts, such travel or use shall be admissible proof to establish that such defendant traveled in or used such facility of interstate or foreign commerce.

(c) A judgment of conviction or acquittal on the merits under the laws of any State shall be a bar to any prosecution hereunder for the same act or acts.

(d) Whenever, in the opinion of the Attorney General or of the appropriate officer of the Department of Justice charged by law or under the instructions of the Attorney General with authority to act, any person shall have violated this chapter, the Department shall proceed as speedily as possible with a prosecution of such person hereunder and with any appeal which may lie from any decision adverse to the Government resulting from such prosecution; or in the alternative shall report in writing, to the respective Houses of the Congress, the Department's reason for not so proceeding.

(e) Nothing contained in this section shall be construed to make it unlawful for any person to travel in, or use any facility of, interstate or foreign commerce for the purpose of pursuing the legitimate objectives of organized labor, through orderly and lawful means.

(f) Nothing in this section shall be construed as indicating an intent on the part of Congress to prevent any State, any possession or Commonwealth of the United States, or the District of Columbia, from exercising jurisdiction over any offense over which it would have jurisdiction in the absence of this section; nor shall anything in this section be construed as depriving State and local law enforcement authorities of responsibility for prosecuting acts that may be violations of this section and that are violations of State and local law.

Added Pub.L. 90-284, Title I, § 104(a), Apr. 11, 1968, 82 Stat. 75.

White Slave Traffic

18 U.S.C. §2421

Transportation Generally

Whoever knowingly transports in interstate or foreign commerce, or in the District of Columbia or in any Territory or Possession of the United States, any woman or girl for the purpose of prostitution or debauchery, or for any other immoral purpose, or with the intent and purpose to induce, entice, or compel such woman or girl to become a prostitute or to give herself up to debauchery, or to engage in any other immoral practice; or

Whoever knowingly procures or obtains any ticket or tickets, or any form of transportation or evidence of the right thereto, to be used by any woman or girl in interstate or foreign commerce, or in the District of Columbia or any Territory or Possession of the United States, in going to any place for the purpose of prostitution or debauchery, or for any other immoral purpose, or with the intent or purpose on the part of such person to induce, entice, or compel her to give herself up to the practice of prostitution, or to give herself up to debauchery, or any other immoral practice, whereby any such woman or girl shall be transported in interstate or foreign commerce, or in the District of Columbia or any Territory or Possession of the United States—

Shall be fined not more than $5,000 or imprisoned not more than five years, or both.

As amended May 24, 1949, c. 139, § 47, 63 Stat. 96.

18 U.S.C. §2422

Coercion or Enticement of Female

Whoever knowingly persuades, induces, entices, or coerces any woman or girl to go from one place to another in interstate or foreign commerce, or in the District of Columbia or in any Territory or Possession of the United States, for the purpose of prostitution or debauchery, or for any other immoral purpose, or with the intent and purpose on the part of such person that such woman or girl shall engage in the practice of prostitution or debauchery, or any other immoral practice, whether with or without her consent, and thereby knowingly causes such woman or girl to go and to be carried or transported as a passenger upon the line or route of any common carrier or carriers in interstate or foreign commerce, or in the District of Columbia or in any Territory or Possession of the United States, shall be fined not more than $5,000 or imprisoned not more than five years, or both.

18 U.S.C. §2423

Coercion or Enticement of Minor Female

Whoever knowingly persuades, induces, entices, or coerces any woman or girl who has not attained her eighteenth birthday, to go from one place to another by common carrier, in interstate commerce or within the District of Columbia or any Territory or Possession of the United States, with intent that she be induced or coerced to engage in prostitution, debauchery or other immoral practice, shall be fined not more than $10,000 or imprisoned not more than ten years, or both.

18 U.S.C. §2424

Filing Factual Statement About Alien Female

(a) Whoever keeps, maintains, controls, supports, or harbors in any house or place for the purpose of prostitution, or for any other immoral purpose, any alien woman or girl within three years after she has entered the United States from any country, party to the arrangement adopted July 25, 1902, for the suppression of the white-slave traffic, shall file with the Commissioner of Immigration and Naturalization a statement in writing setting forth the name of such alien woman or girl, the place at which she is kept, and all facts as to the date of her entry into the United States, the port through which she entered, her age, nationality, and parentage, and concerning her procuration to come to this country within the knowledge of such person; and

Whoever fails within thirty days after commencing to keep, maintain, control, support, or harbor in any house or place for the purpose of prostitution, or for any other immoral purpose, any alien woman or girl within three years after she has entered the United States from any country, party to the said arrangement for the suppression of the white-slave traffic, to file such statement concerning such alien woman or girl with the Commissioner of Immigration and Naturalization; or

Whoever knowingly and willfully states falsely or fails to disclose in such statement any fact within his knowledge or belief with reference to the age, nationality, or parentage of any such alien woman or girl, or concerning her procuration to come to this country—

Shall be fined not more than $2,000 or imprisoned not more than two years, or both.

(b) In any prosecution brought under this section, if it appears that any such statement required is not on file in the office of the Commissioner of Immigration and Naturalization, the person whose duty it is to file such statement shall be presumed to have failed to file said statement, unless such person or persons shall prove otherwise. No person shall be excused from furnishing the statement, as requied by this section, on the ground or for the reason that the statement so required by him, or the information therein contained, might tend to criminate him or subject him to a penalty or forfeiture, but no person shall be prosecuted or subjected to any penalty or forfeiture under any law of the United States for or on account of any transaction, matter, or thing, concerning which he may truthfully report in such statement.

Conspiracy

18 U.S.C. §9371

Conspiracy to Commit Offense or to Defraud United States

If two or more persons conspire either to commit any offense against the United States, or to defraud the United States, or any agency thereof in any manner or for any purpose, and one or more of such persons do any act to effect the object of the conspiracy, each shall be fined not more than $10,000 or imprisoned not more than five years, or both.

If, however, the offense, the commission of which is the object of the conspiracy, is a misdemeanor only, the punishment for such conspiracy shall not exceed the maximum punishment provided for such misdemeanor.

Nonmailable Letters

18 U.S.C. §1717

Letters and Writings as Nonmailable; Opening Letters

(a) Every letter, writing, circular, postal card, picture, print, engraving, photograph, newspaper, pamphlet, book, or other publication, matter or thing, in violation of sections 499, 506, 793, 794, 915, 954, 956, 957, 960, 964, 1017, 1542, 1543, 1544 or 2388 of this title or which contains any matter advocating or urging treason, insurrection, or forcible resistance to any law of the United States is nonmailable and shall not be conveyed in the mails or delivered from any post office or by any letter carrier.

(b) Whoever uses or attempts to use the mails or Postal Service of the United States for the transmission of any matter declared by this section to be nonmailable, shall be fined not more than $5,000 or imprisoned not more than ten years or both.

As amended Sept. 2, 1960, Pub.L. 86-682, § 12(b), 74 Stat. 708.

Importing Immoral Material

19 U.S.C. §1305

Immoral Articles; Prohibition of Importation

(a) All persons are prohibited from importing into the United States from any foreign country any book, pamphlet, paper, writing, advertisement, circular, print, picture, or drawing containing any matter advocating or urging treason or insurrection against the United States, or forcible resistance to any law of the United States, or containing any threat to take the life of or inflict bodily harm upon any person in the United States, or any obscene book, pamphlet, paper, writing, advertisement, circular, print, picture, drawing, or other representation, figure, or image on or of paper or other material, or any cast, instrument, or other article which is obscene or immoral, or any drug or medicine or any article whatever for the prevention of conception or for causing unlawful abortion, or any lottery ticket, or any printed paper that may be used as a lottery ticket, or any advertisement of any lottery. No such articles whether imported separately or contained in packages with other goods entitled to entry, shall be admitted to entry; and all such articles and, unless it appears to the satisfaction of the collector that the obscene or other prohibited articles contained in the package were inclosed therein without the knowledge or consent of the importer, owner, agent, or consignee, the entire contents of the package in which such articles are contained, shall be subject to seizure and forfeiture as hereinafter provided: *Provided,* That the drugs hereinbefore mentioned, when imported in bulk and not put up for any of the purposes hereinbefore specified, are excepted from the operation of this subdivision: *Provided further,* That the Secretary of the Treasury may, in his discretion, admit the so-called classics or books or recognized and established literary or scientific merit, but may, in his discretion, admit such classic or books only when imported for non-commercial purposes.

Upon the appearance of any such book or matter at any customs office, the same shall be seized and held by the collector to await the judgment of the district court as hereinafter provided; and no protest shall be taken to the United States Customs Court from the decision of the collector. Upon the seizure of such book or matter the collector shall transmit information thereof to the district attorney of the district in which is situated the office at which such seizure has taken place, who shall institute proceedings in the district court for the forfeiture, confiscation, and destruction of the book or matter seized. Upon the adjudication that such book or matter thus seized is of the character the entry of which is by this section prohibited, it shall be ordered destroyed and shall be destroyed. Upon adjudication that such book or matter thus seized is not of the character the entry of which is by this section prohibited, it shall not be excluded from entry under the provisions of this section.

In any such proceeding any party in interest may upon demand have the facts at issue determined by a jury and any party may have an appeal or the right of review as in the case of ordinary actions or suits.

(b) Repealed. June 25, 1948, c. 645, § 21, 62 Stat. 862.

June 17, 1930, c. 497, Title III, § 305, 46 Stat. 688; June 25, 1948, c. 645, § 21, 62 Stat. 862.

Registration of Foreign Propagandists

22 U.S.C. §611

Definitions

As used in and for the purposes of this subchapter—

(a) The term "person" includes an individual, partnership, association, corporation, organization, or any other combination of individuals;

(b) The term "foreign principal" includes—

(1) a government of a foreign country and a foreign political party;

(2) a person outside of the United States, unless it is established that such person is an individual and a citizen of and domiciled within the United States, or that such person is not an individual and is organized under or created by the laws of the United States or of any State or other place subject to the jurisdiction of the United States and has its principal place of business within the United States; and

(3) a partnership, association, corporation, organization, or other combination of persons organized under the laws of or having its principal place of business in a foreign country.

(c) Expect as provided in subsection (d) of this section, the term "agent of a foreign principal" means—

(1) any person who acts as an agent, representative, employee, or servant, or any person who acts in any other capacity at the order, request, or under the direction or control, or a foreign principal or of a person any of whose activities are directly or indirectly supervised, directed, controlled, financed, or subsidized in whole or in major part by a foreign principal, and who directly or through any other person—

(i) engages within the United States in political activities for or in the interests of such foreign principal;

(ii) acts within the United States as a public relations counsel, publicity agent, information-service employee or political consultant for or in the interests of such foreign principal;

(iii) within the United States solicits, collects, disburses, or dispenses contributions, loans, money, or other things of value for or in the interest of such foreign principal; or

(iv) within the United States represents the interests of such foreign principal before any agency or official of the Government of the United States; and

(2) any person who agrees, consents, assumes or purports to act as, or who is or holds himself out to be, whether or not pursuant to contractual relationship, an agent of a foreign principal as defined in clause (1) of this subsection.

(d) The term "agent of a foreign principal" does not include any news or press service or association organized under the laws of the United States or of any State or other place subject to the jurisdiction of the United States, or any newspaper, magazine, periodical, or other publication for which there is on file with the United States Postal Service information in compliance with section 3611 of Title 39, published in the United States, solely by virtue of any bona fide news or journalistic activities, including the solicitation or acceptance of advertisements, subscriptions, or other compensation therefor, so long as it is at least 80 per centum beneficially owned by, and its officers and directors, if any, are citizens of the United States, and such news or press service or association, newspaper, magazine, periodical, or other publication, is not owned, directed, supervised, controlled, subsidized, or financed, and none of its policies are determined by any foreign principal defined in subsection (b) of this section, or by any agent of a foreign principal required to register under this subchapter;

(e) The term "government of a foreign country" includes any person or groups of persons exercising sovereign de facto or de jure political jurisdiction over any country, other than the United States, or over any part of such country, and includes any subdivision of any such group and any group or agency to which such sovereign de facto or de jure authority or functions are directly or indirectly delegated. Such term shall include any faction or body of insurgents within a country assuming to exercise governmental authority whether such faction or body of insurgents has or has not been recognized by the United States;

(f) The term "foreign political party" includes any organization or any other combination of individuals in a country other than the United States, or any unit or branch thereof, having for an aim or purpose, or which is engaged in any activity devoted in whole or in part to, the establishment, administration, control, or acquisition of administration or control, of a government of a foreign country or a subdivision thereof, or the furtherance or influencing of the political or public interests, policies, or relations of a government of a foreign country or a subdivision thereof;

(g) The term "public-relations counsel" includes any person who engages directly or indirectly in informing, advising, or in any way representing a principal in any public relations matter pertaining to political or public interests, policies, or relations of such principal;

(h) The term "publicity agent" includes any person who engages directly or indirectly in the publication or dissemination of oral, visual, graphic, written, or pictorial information or matter of any kind, including publication by means of advertising, books, periodicals, newspapers, lectures, broadcasts, motion pictures, or otherwise;

(i) The term "information-service employee" includes any person who is engaged in furnishing, disseminating, or publishing accounts, descriptions, information, or data with respect to the political, industrial, employment, economic, social, cultural, or other benefits, advantages, facts, or conditions of any country other than the United States or of any government of a foreign country or of a foreign political party or of a partnership, association, corporation, organization, or other combination of individuals organized under the laws of, or having its principal place of business in, a foreign country;

(j) The term "political propaganda" includes any oral, visual, graphic, written, pictorial, or other communication or expression by any person (1) which is reasonably adapted to, or which the person disseminating the same believes will, or which he intends to, prevail upon, indoctrinate, convert, induce, or in any other way influence a recipient or any section of the public within the United States with reference to the political or public interests, policies, or relations of a government of a foreign country or a foreign political party or with reference to the foreign policies of the United States or promote in the United States racial, religious, or social dissensions, or (2) which advocates, advises, instigates, or promotes any racial, social, political, or religious disorder, civil riot, or other conflict involving the use of force or violence in any other American republic or the overthrow of any government or political subdivision of any other American republic by any means involving the use of force or violence. As used in this subsection the term "disseminating" includes transmitting or causing to be transmitted in the United States mails or by any means or instrumentality of interstate or foreign commerce or offering or causing to be offered in the United States mails;

(k) The term "registration statement" means the registration statement required to be filed with the Attorney General under section 612(a) of this title, and any supplements thereto required to be filed under section 612(b) of this title, and includes all documents and papers required to be filed therewith or amendatory thereof or supplemental thereto, whether attached thereto or incorporated therein by reference;

(l) The term "American republic" includes any of the states which were signatory to the Final Act of the Second Meeting of the Ministers of Foreign Affairs of the American Republics of Habana, Cuba, July 30, 1940;

(m) The term "United States", when used in a geographical sense, includes the several States, the District of Columbia, the Territories, the Canal Zone, the insular possessions, and all other places now or hereafter subject to the civil or military jurisdiction of the United States;

(n) The term "prints" means newspapers and periodicals, books, pamphlets, sheet music, visiting cards, address cards, printing proofs, engravings, photographs, pictures, drawings, plans, maps, patterns to be cut out, catalogs, prospectuses, advertisements, and printed, engraved, lithographed, or autographed notices of various kinds, and, in general, all impressions or reproductions obtained on paper or other material assimilable to paper, on parchment or on cardboard, by means of printing, engraving, lithography, autography, or any other easily recognizable mechanical process, with the exception of the copying press, stamps with movable or immovable type, and the typewriter;

(o) The term "political activities" means the dissemination of political propaganda and any other activity which the person engaging therein believes will, or which he intends to, prevail upon, indoctrinate, convert, induce, persuade, or in any other way influence any agency or official of the Government of the United States or any section of the public within the United States with reference to formulating, adopting, or changing the domestic or foreign policies of the United States or with reference to the political or public interests, policies, or relations of a government of a foreign country or a foreign political party;

(p) The term "political consultant" means any person who engages in informing or advising any other person with reference to the domestic or foreign policies of the United States or the political or public interest, policies, or relations of a foreign country or of a foreign political party;

(q) For the purpose of section 613(d) of this title, activities in furtherance of the bona fide commercial, industrial or financial interests of a domestic person engaged in substantial commercial, industrial or financial operations in the United States shall not be deemed to serve predominantly a foreign interest because such activities also benefit the interests of a foreign person engaged in bona fide trade or commerce which is owned or controlled by, or which owns or controls, such domestic person: *Provided,* That (i) such foreign person is not, and such activities are not directly or indirectly supervised, directed, controlled, financed or subsidized in whole or in substantial part by, a government of a foreign country or a foreign political party, (ii) the identity of such foreign person is disclosed to the agency or official of the United States with whom such activities are conducted, and (iii) whenever such foreign person owns or controls such domestic person, such activities are substantially in furtherance of the bona fide commercial, industrial or financial interests of such domestic person. As amended July 4, 1966, Pub.L. 89-486, § 1, 80 Stat. 244; Aug. 12, 1970, Pub.L. 91-375, § 6(k), 84 Stat. 782.

22 U.S.C. §612

Registration Statement; Filing; Contents

(a) No person shall act as an agent of a foreign principal unless he has filed with the Attorney General a true and complete registration statement and supplements thereto as required by this section and subsection (b) of this section or unless he is exempt from registration under the provisions of this subchapter. Except as hereinafter provided, every person who becomes an agent of a foreign principal shall, within ten days thereafter, file with the Attorney General, in duplicate, a registration statement, under oath on a form prescribed by the Attorney General. The obligation of an agent of a foreign principal to file a registration statement shall, after the tenth day of his becoming such agent, continue from day to day, and termination of such status shall not relieve such agent from his obligation to file a registration statement for the period during which he was an agent of a foreign principal. The registration statement shall include the following, which shall be regarded as material for the purposes of this subchapter:

(1) Registrant's name, principal business address, and all other business addresses in the United States or elsewhere, and all residence addresses, if any;

(2) Status of the registrant; if an individual, nationality; if a partnership, name, residence addresses, and nationality of each partner and a true and complete copy of its articles of copartnership; if an association, corporation, organization, or any other combination of individuals, the name, residence addresses, and nationality of each director and officer and of each person performing the functions of a director or officer and a true and complete copy of its charter, articles of incorporation, association, constitution, and bylaws, and amendments thereto; a copy of every other instrument or document and a statement of the terms and conditions of every oral agreement relating to its organization, powers, and purposes; and a statement of its ownership and control;

(3) A comprehensive statement of the nature of registrant's business; a complete list of registrant's employees and a statement of the nature of the work of each; the name and address of every foreign principal for whom the registrant is acting, assuming or purporting to act or has agreed to act; the character of the business or other activities of every such foreign principal, and, if any such foreign principal be other than a natural person, a statement of the ownership and control of each; and the extent, if any, to which each such foreign principal is supervised, directed, owned, controlled, financed, or subsidized, in whole or in part, by any government of a foreign country or foreign political party, or by any other foreign principal;

(4) Copies of each written agreement and the terms and conditions of each oral agreement, including all modifications of such agreements, or, where no contract exists, a full statement of all the circumstances, by reason of which the registrant is an agent of a foreign principal; a comprehensive statement of the nature and method of performance of each such contract, and of the existing and proposed activity or activities engaged in or to be engaged in by the registrant as agent of a foreign principal for each such foreign principal, including a detailed statement of any such activity which is a political activity;

(5) The nature and amount of contributions, income, money, or thing of value, if any, that the registrant has received within the preceding sixty days from each such foreign principal, either as compensation or for disbursement or otherwise, and the form and time of each such payment and from whom received;

(6) A detailed statement of every activity which the registrant is performing or is assuming or purporting or has agreed to perform for himself or any other person other than a foreign principal and which requires his registration hereunder, including a detailed statement of any such activity which is a political activity;

(7) The name, business, and residence addresses, and if an individual, the nationality, of any person other than a foreign principal for whom the registrant is acting, assuming or purporting to act or has agreed to act under such circumstances as require his registration hereunder; the extent to which each such person is supervised, directed, owned, controlled, financed, or subsidized, in whole or in part, by any government of a foreign country or foreign political party or by any other foreign principal; and the nature and

amount of contributions, income, money, or thing of value, if any, that the registrant has received during the preceding sixty days from each such person in connection with any of the activities referred to in clause (6) of this subsection, either as compensation or for disbursement or otherwise, and the form and time of each such payment and from whom received;

(8) A detailed statement of the money and other things of value spent or disposed of by the registrant during the preceding sixty days in furtherance of or in connection with activities which require his registration hereunder and which have been undertaken by him either as an agent of a foreign principal or for himself or any other person or in conection with any activities relating to his becoming an agent of such principal, and a detailed statement of any contributions of money or other things of value made by him during the preceding sixty days (other than contributions the making of which is prohibited under the terms of section 613 of Title 18) in connection with an election to any political office or in connection with any primary election, convention, or caucus held to select candidates for any political office;

(9) Copies of each written agreement and the terms and conditions of each oral agreement, including all modifications of such agreements, or, where no contract exists, a full statement of all the circumstances, by reason of which the registrant is performing or assuming or purporting or has agreed to perform for himself or for a foreign principal or for any person other than a foreign principal any activities which require his registration hereunder;

(10) Such other statements, information, or documents pertinent to the purposes of this subchapter as the Attorney General, having due regard for the national security and the public interest, may from time to time require;

(11) Such further statements and such further copies of documents as are necessary to make the statements made in the registration statement and supplements thereto, and the copies of documents furnished therewith, not misleading.

(b) Every agent of a foreign principal who has filed a registration statement required by subsection (a) of this section shall, within thirty days after the expiration of each period of six months succeeding such filing, file with the Attorney General a supplement thereto under oath, on a form prescribed by the Attorney General, which shall set forth with respect to such preceding six months' period such facts as the Attorney General, having due regard for the national security and the public interest, may deem necessary to make the information required under this section accurate, complete, and current with respect to such period. In connection with the information furnished under clauses (3), (4), (6), and (9) of subsection (a) of this section, the registrant shall give notice to the Attorney General of any changes therein within ten days after such changes occur. If the Attorney General, having due regard for the national security and the public interest, determines that it is necessary to carry out the purposes of this subchapter, he may, in any particular case, require supplements to the registration statement to be filed at more frequent intervals in respect to all or particular items of information to be furnished.

(c) The registration statement and supplements thereto shall be executed under oath as follows: If the registrant is an individual, by him; if the registrant is a partnership, by the majority of the members thereof; if the registrant is a person other than an individual or a partnership, by a majority of the officers thereof or persons performing the functions of officers or by a majority of the board of directors thereof or person performing the functions of directors, if any.

(d) The fact that a registration statement or supplement thereto has been filed shall not necessarily be deemed a full compliance with this subchapter and the regulations thereunder on the part of the registrant; nor shall it indicate that the Attorney General has in any way passed upon the merits of such registration statement or supplement thereto; nor shall it preclude prosecution, as provided for in this subchapter, for willful failure to file a registration statement or supplement thereto when due or for a willful false statement of a material fact therein or the willful omission of a material fact required to be stated therein or the willful omission of a material fact or copy of a material document necessary to make the statements made in a registration statement and supplements thereto, and the copies of documents furnished therewith, not misleading.

(e) If any agent of a foreign principal, required to register under the provisions of this subchapter, has previously thereto registered with the Attorney General under the provisions of sections 14-17 of Title 18, the Attorney General, in order to eliminate inappropriate duplication, may permit the incorporation by reference in the registration statement or supplements thereto filed hereunder of any information or documents previously filed by such agent of a foreign principal under the provisions of said sections. June 8, 1938, c. 327, § 2, 52 Stat. 632; Apr. 29, 1942, c. 263, § 2, 56 Stat. 251; Aug. 3, 1950, c. 524, § 1, 64 Stat. 399.

(f) The Attorney General may, by regulation, provide for the exemption—

(1) from registration, or from the requirement of furnishing any of the information required by this section, of any person who is listed as a partner, officer, director, or employee in the registration statement filed by an agent of a foreign principal under this subchapter, and

(2) from the requirement of furnishing any of the information required by this section of any agent of a foreign principal,

where by reason of the nature of the functions or activities of such person the Attorney General, having due regard for the national security and the public interest, determines that such registration, or the furnishing of such information, as the case may be, is not necessary to carry out the purposes of this subchapter. As amended July 4, 1966, Pub.L. 89-486, § 2, 80 Stat. 245.

22 U.S.C. §613

Exemptions

The requirements of section 612(a) of this title shall not apply to the following agents of foreign principals:

(a) A duly accredited diplomatic or consular officer of a foreign government who is so recognized by the Department of State, while said officer is engaged exclusively in activities which are recognized by the Department of State as being within the scope of the functions of such officer;

(b) Any official of a foreign government, if such government is recognized by the United States, who is not a public-relations counsel, publicity agent, information-service employee, or a citizen of the United States, whose name and status and the character of whose duties as such official are of public record in the Department of

State, while said official is engaged exclusively in activities which are recognized by the Department of State as being within the scope of the functions of such official;

(c) Any member of the staff of, or any person employed by, a duly accredited diplomatic or consular officer of a foreign government who is so recognized by the Department of State, other than a public-relations counsel, publicity agent, or information-service employee, whose name and status and the character of whose duties as such member or employee are of public record in the Department of State, while said member or employee is engaged exclusively in the performance of activities which are recognized by the Department of State as being within the scope of the functions of such member or employee;

(d) Any person engaging or agreeing to engage only (1) in private and nonpolitical activities in furtherance of the bona fide trade or commerce of such foreign principal; or (2) in other activities not serving predominantly a foreign interest; or (3) in the soliciting or collecting of funds and contributions within the United States to be used only for medical aid and assistance, or for food and clothing to relieve human suffering, if such solicitation or collection of funds and contributions is in accordance with and subject to the provisions of sections 441, 444, 445 and 447-457 of this title, and such rules and regulations as may be prescribed thereunder;

(e) Any person engaging or agreeing to engage only in activities in furtherance of bona fide religious, scholastic, academic, or scientific pursuits or of the fine arts;

(f) Any person, or employee of such person, whose foreign principal is a government of a foreign country the defense of which the President deems vital to the defense of the United States while, (1) such person or employee engages only in activities which are in furtherance of the policies, public interest, or national defense both of such government and of the Government of the United States, and are not intended to conflict with any of the domestic or foreign policies of the Government of the United States, (2) each communication or expression by such person or employee which he intends to, or has reason to believe will, be published, disseminated, or circulated among any section of the public, or portion thereof, within the United States, is a part of such activities and is believed by such person to be truthful and accurate and the identity of such person as an agent of such foreign principal is disclosed therein, and (3) such government of a foreign country furnishes to the Secretary of State for transmittal to, and retention for the duration of this subchapter by, the Attorney General such information as to the identity and activities of such person or employee at such times as the Attorney General may require. Upon notice to the Government of which such person is an agent or to such person or employee, the Attorney General, having due regard for the public interest and national defense, may, with the approval of the Secretary of State, and shall, at the request of the Secretary of State, terminate in whole or in part the exemption herein of any such person or employee;

(g) Any person qualified to practice law, insofar as he engages or agrees to engage in the legal representation of a disclosed foreign principal before any court of law or any agency of the Government of the United States: *Provided,* That for tne purposes of this subsection legal representation does not include attempts to influence or persuade agency personnel or officials other than in the course of established agency proceedings, whether formal or informal. As amended July 4, 1966, Pub.L. 89-486, § 3, 80 Stat. 246.

22 U.S.C. §614

Filing and Labeling of Political Propaganda

(a) Every person within the United States who is an agent of a foreign principal and required to register under the provisions of this subchapter and who transmits or causes to be transmitted in the United States mails or by any means or instrumentality of interstate or foreign commerce any political propaganda for or in the interests of such foreign principal (i) in the form of prints, or (ii) in any other form which is reasonably adapted to being, or which he believes will be, or which he intends to be, disseminated or circulated among two or more persons shall, not later than forty-eight hours after the beginning of the transmittal thereof, file with the Attorney General two copies thereof and a statement, duly signed by or on behalf of such agent, setting forth full information as to the places, times, and extent of such transmittal.

(b) It shall be unlawful for any person within the United States who is an agent of a foreign principal and required to register under the provisions of this subchapter to transmit or cause to be transmitted in the United States mails or by any means or instrumentality of interstate or foreign commerce any political propaganda for or in the interests of such foreign principal (i) in the form of prints, or (ii) in any other form which is reasonably adapted to being, or which he believes will be or which he intends to be, disseminated or circulated among two or more persons, unless such political propaganda is conspicuously marked at its beginning with, or prefaced or accompanied by, a true and accurate statement in the language or languages used in such political propaganda, setting forth the relationship or connection between the person transmitting the political propaganda or causing it to be transmitted and such propaganda; that the person transmitting such political propaganda or causing it to be transmitted is registered under this subchapter with the Department of Justice, Washington, District of Columbia, as an agent of a foreign principal, together with the name and address of such agent of a foreign principal and of such foreign principal; that, as required by this subchapter, his registration statement is available for inspection at and copies of such political propaganda are being filed with the Department of Justice; and that registration of agents of foreign principals required by the subchapter does not indicate approval by the United States Government of the contents of their political propaganda. The Attorney General, having due regard for the national security and the public interest, may by regulation prescribe the language or languages and the manner and form in which such statement shall be made and require the inclusion of such other information contained in the registration statement identifying such agent of a foreign principal and such political propaganda and its sources as may be appropriate.

(c) The copies of political propaganda required by this subchapter to be filed with the Attorney General shall be available for public inspection under such regulations as he may prescribe.

(d) For purposes of the Library of Congress, other than for public distribution, the Secretary of the Treasury and the Postmaster General are authorized, upon the request of the Librarian of Congress, to forward to the Library of Congress fifty copies, or as many fewer thereof as are available, of all foreign prints determined to be prohibited entry under the provisions of section 1305 of Title 19 and of all foreign prints excluded from the mails under authority of section 343 of Title 18.

Notwithstanding the provisions of section 1305 of Title 19 and of section 343 of Title 18, the Secretary of the Treasury is authorized to permit the entry and the Postmaster General is authorized to permit the transmittal in the mails of foreign prints imported for governmental purposes by authority or for the use of the United States or for the use of the Library of Congress.

(e) It shall be unlawful for any person within the United States who is an agent of a foreign principal required to register under the provisions of this subchapter to transmit, convey, or otherwise furnish to any agency or official of the Government (including a Member or committee of either House of Congress) for or in the interests of such foreign principal any political propaganda or to request from any such agency or official for or in the interests of such foreign principal any information or advice with respect to any matter pertaining to the political or public interests, policies or relations of a foreign country or of a political party or pertaining to the foreign or domestic policies of the United States unless the propaganda or the request is prefaced or accompanied by a true and accurate statement to the effect that such person is registered as an agent of such foreign principal under this subchapter.

(f) Whenever any agent of a foreign principal required to register under this subchapter appears before any committee of Congress to testify for or in the interests of such foreign principal, he shall, at the time of such appearance, furnish the committee with a copy of his most recent registration statement filed with the Department of Justice as an agent of such foreign principal for inclusion in the records of the committee as part of his testimony. As amended July 4, 1966, Pub.L. 89-486, § 4, 80 Stat. 246.

22 U.S.C. §615

Books and Records

Every agent of a foreign principal registered under this subchapter shall keep and preserve while he is an agent of a foreign principal such books of account and other records with respect to all his activities, the disclosure of which is required under the provisions of this subchapter, in accordance with such business and accounting practices, as the Attorney General, having due regard for the national security and the public interest, may by regulation prescribe as necessary or appropriate for the enforcement of the provisions of this subchapter and shall preserve the same for a period of three years following the termination of such status. Until regulations are in effect under this section every agent of a foreign principal shall keep books of account and shall preserve all written records with respect to his activities. Such books and records shall be open at all reasonable times to the inspection of any official charged with the enforcement of this subchapter. It shall be unlawful for any person willfully to conceal, destroy, obliterate, mutilate, or falsify, or to cause to be concealed, destroyed, obliterated, mutilated or falsified, any books or records required to be kept under the provisions of this section. As amended July 4, 1966, Pub.L. 89-486, § 5, 80 Stat. 247.

22 U.S.C. §616

Public Examination of Official Records; Transmittal of Records and Information

(a) The Attorney General shall retain in permanent form one copy of all registration statements and all statements concerning the distribution of political propaganda furnished under this subchapter, and the same shall be public records and open to public examination and inspection at such reasonable hours, under such regulations, as the Attorney General may prescribe, and copies of the same shall be furnished to every applicant at such reasonable fee as the Attorney General may prescribe. The Attorney General may withdraw from public examination the registration statement and other statements of any agent of a foreign principal whose activities have ceased to be of a character which requires registration under the provisions of this subchapter.

(b) The Attorney General shall, promptly upon receipt, transmit one copy of every registration statement filed hereunder and one copy of every amendment or supplement thereto, and one copy of every item of political propaganda filed hereunder, to the Secretary of State for such comment and use as the Secretary of State may determine to be appropriate from the point of view of the foreign relations of the United States. Failure of the Attorney General so to transmit such copy shall not be a bar to prosecution under this subchapter.

(c) The Attorney General is authorized to furnish to departments and agencies in the executive branch and committees of the Congress such information obtained by him in the administration of this subchapter, including the names of registrants under this subchapter, copies of registration statements, or parts thereof, copies of political propaganda, or other documents or information filed under this subchapter, as may be appropriate in the light of the purposes of this subchapter. As amended July 4, 1966, Pub.L. 89-486, § 6, 80 Stat. 247.

22 U.S.C. §617

Liability of Officers

Each officer, or person performing the functions of an officer, and each director, or person performing the functions of a director, of an agent of a foreign principal which is not an individual shall be under obligation to cause such agent to execute and file a registration statement and supplements thereto as and when such filing is required under subsections (a) and (b) of section 612 of this title and shall also be under obligation to cause such agent to comply with all the requirements of sections 614(a) and (b) and 615 of this title and all other requirements of this subchapter. Dissolution of any organization acting as an agent of a foreign principal shall not relieve any officer, or person performing the functions of an officer, or any director, or person performing the functions of a director, from complying with the provisions of this section. In case of failure of any such agent of a foreign principal to comply with any of the requirements of this subchapter, each of its officers, or persons performing the functions of officers, and each of its directors, or persons performing the functions of directors, shall be subject to prosecution therefor. June

8, 1938, c. 327, § 7, 52 Stat. 633; Apr. 29, 1942, c. 263, § 1, 56 Stat. 256; Aug. 3, 1950, c. 524, § 2, 64 Stat. 400.

22 U.S.C. §618

Enforcement and Penalties—Violations; False Statements and Willful Omissions

(a) Any person who—

(1) willfully violates any provision of this subchapter or any regulation thereunder, or

(2) in any registration statement or supplement thereto or in any statement under section 614(a) of this title concerning the distribution of political propaganda or in any other document filed with or furnished to the Attorney General under the provisions of this subchapter willfully makes a false statement of a material fact or willfully omits any material fact required to be stated therein or willfully omits a material fact or a copy of a material document necessary to make the statements therein and the copies of documents furnished therewith not misleading, shall, upon conviction thereof be punished by a fine of not more than $10,000 or by imprisonment for not more than five years, or both, except that in the case of a violation of subsection (b), (e), or (f) of section 614 of this title or of subsection (g) or (h) of this section the punishment shall be a fine of not more than $5,000 or imprisonment for not more than six months, or both.

Proof of Identity of Foreign Principal

(b) In any proceeding under this subchapter in which it is charged that a person is an agent of a foreign principal with respect to a foreign principal outside of the United States, proof of the specific identity of the foreign principal shall be permissible but not necessary.

Deportation

(c) Any alien who shall be convicted of a violation of, or a conspiracy to violate, any provision of this subchapter or any regulation thereunder shall be subject to deportation in the manner provided by sections 1251-1253 of Title 8.

Nonmailable Matter

(d) The Postmaster General may declare to be nonmailable any communication or expression falling within clause (2) of section 611(j) of this title in the fom of prints or in any other form reasonably adapted to, or reasonably appearing to be intended for, dissemination or circulation among two or more persons, which is offered or caused to be offered for transmittal in the United States mails to any person or persons in any other American republic by any agent of a foreign principal, if the Postmaster General is informed in writing by the Secretary of State that the duly accredited diplomatic representative of such American republic has made written representation to the Department of State that the admission or circulation of such communication or expression in such American republic is prohibited by the laws thereof and has requested in writing that its transmittal thereto be stopped.

Continuing Offense

(e) Failure to file any such registration statement or supplements thereto as is required by either section 612(a) or section 612(b) of this title shall be considered a continuing offense for as long as such failure exists, notwithstanding any statue of limitation or other statute to the contrary.

Injunctive Remedy; Jurisdiction of District Court; Expedition of Proceedings

(f) Whenever in the judgment of the Attorney General any person is engaged in or about to engage in any acts which constitute or will constitute a violation of any provision of this subchapter, or regulations issued thereunder, or whenever any agent of a foreign principal fails to comply with any of the provisions of this subchapter or the regulations issued thereunder, or otherwise is in violation of the subchapter, the Attorney General may make application to the appropriate United States district court for an order enjoining such acts or enjoining such person from continuing to act as an agent of such foreign principal, or for an order requiring compliance with any appropriate provision of the subchapter or regulation thereunder. The district court shall have jurisdiction and authority to issue a temporary or permanent injunction, restraining order or such other order which it may deem proper. The proceedings shall be made a preferred cause and shall be expedited in every way.

Deficient Registration Statement

(g) If the Attorney General determines that a registration statement does not comply with the requirements of this subchapter or the regulations issued thereunder, he shall so notify the registrant in writing, specifying in what respects the statement is deficient. It shall be unlawful for any person to act as an agent of a foreign principal at any time ten days or more after receipt of such notification without filing an amended registration statement in full compliance with the requirements of this subchapter and the regulations issued thereunder.

Contingent Fee Arrangement

(h) It shall be unlawful for any agent of a foreign principal required to register under this subchapter to be a party to any contract, agreement, or understanding, either express or implied, with such foreign principal pursuant to which the amount or payment of the compensation, fee, or other remuneration of such agent is contingent in whole or in part upon the success of any political activities carried on by such agent. As amended July 4, 1966, Pub.L. 89-486, § 7, 80 Stat. 248.

22 U.S.C. §619

Territorial Applicability of Subchapter

This subchapter shall be applicable in the several States, the District of Columbia, the Territories, the Canal Zone, the insular possessions, and all other places now or hereafter subject to the civil or military jurisdiction of the United States. June 8, 1938, c. 327, § 9, as added Apr. 29, 1942, c. 263, § 1, 56 Stat. 257, and amended Proc. No. 2695, July 4, 1946, 11 F.R. 7517, 60 Stat. 1352.

22 U.S.C. §620

Rules and Regulations

The Attorney General may at any time make, prescribe, amend, and rescind such rules, regulations, and forms as he may deem necessary to carry out the provisions of this subchapter. June 8, 1938, c. 327, § 10, as added Apr. 29, 1942, c. 263, § 1, 56 Stat. 257.

22 U.S.C. §621

Reports to Congress

The Attorney General shall, from time to time, make a report to the Congress concerning the administration of this subchapter, including the nature, sources, and content of political propaganda disseminated or distributed. June 8, 1938, c. 327, § 11, as added Apr. 29, 1942, c. 263, § 1, 56 Stat. 258.

Control of Subversive Activities

50 U.S.C. §781

Congressional Finding of Necessity

As a result of evidence adduced before various committees of the Senate and House of Representatives, the Congress finds that—

(1) There exists a world Communist movement which, in its origins, its development, and its present practice, is a world-wide revolutionary movement whose purpose it is, by treachery, deceit, infiltration into other groups (governmental and otherwise), espionage, sabotage, terrorism, and any other means deemed necessary, to establish a Communist totalitarian dictatorship in the countries throughout the world through the medium of a world-wide Communist organization.

(2) The establishment of a totalitarian dictatorship in any country results in the suppression of all opposition to the party in power, the subordination of the rights of individuals to the state, the denial of fundamental rights and liberties which are characteristic of a representative form of government, such as freedom of speech, of the press, of assembly, and of religious worship, and results in the maintenance of control over the people through fear, terrorism, and brutality.

(3) The system of government known as a totalitarian dictatorship is characterized by the existence of a single political party, organized on a dictatorial basis, and by substantial identity between such party and its policies and the government and governmental policies of the country in which it exists.

(4) The direction and control of the world Communist movement is vested in and exercised by the Communist dictatorship of a foreign country.

(5) The Communist dictatorship of such foreign country, in exercising such direction and control and in furthering the purposes of the world Communist move-

ment, establishes or causes the establishment of, and utilizes, in various countries, action organizations which are not free and independent organizations, but are sections of a world-wide Communist organization and are controlled, directed, and subject to the discipline of the Communist dictatorship of such foreign country.

(6) The Communist action organizations so established and utilized in various countries, acting under such control, direction, and discipline, endeavor to carry out the objectives of the world Communist movement by bringing about the overthrow of existing governments by any available means, including force if necessary, and setting up Communist totalitarian dictatorships which will be subservient to the most powerful existing Communist totalitarian dictatorship. Although such organizations usually designate themselves as political parties, they are in fact constituent elements of the world-wide Communist movement and promote the objectives of such movement by conspiratorial and coercive tactics, instead of through the democratic processes of a free elective system or through the freedom-preserving means employed by a political party which operates as an agency by which people govern themselves.

(7) In carrying on the activities referred to in paragraph (6) of this section, such Communist organizations in various countries are organized on a secret, conspiratorial basis and operate to a substantial extent through organizations, commonly known as "Communist fronts", which in most instances are created and maintained, or used, in such manner as to conceal the facts as to their true character and purposes and their membership. One result of this method of operation is that such affiliated organizations are able to obtain financial and other support from persons who would not extend such support if they knew the true purposes of, and the actual nature of the control and influence exerted upon, such "Communist fronts".

(8) Due to the nature and scope of the world Communist movement, with the existence of affiliated constituent elements working toward common objectives in various countries of the world, travel of Communist members, representatives, and agents from country to country facilitates communication and is a prerequisite for the carrying on of activities to further the purposes of the Communist movement.

(9) In the United States those individuals who knowingly and willfully participate in the world Communist movement, when they so participate, in effect repudiate their allegiance to the United States, and in effect transfer their allegiance to the foreign country in which is vested the direction and control of the world Communist movement.

(10) In pursuance of communism's stated objectives, the most powerful existing Communist dictatorship has, by the methods referred to above, already caused the establishment in numerous foreign countries of Communist totalitarian dictatorships, and threatens to establish similar dictatorships in still other countries.

(11) The agents of communism have devised clever and ruthless espionage and sabotage tactics which are carried out in many instances in form or manner successfully evasive of existing law.

(12) The Communist network in the United States is inspired and controlled in large part by foreign agents who are sent into the United States ostensibly as attachés of foreign legations, affiliates of international organizations, members of trading commissions, and in similar capacities, but who use their diplomatic or semidiplomatic status as a shield behind which to engage in activities prejudicial to the public security.

(13) There are, under our present immigration laws, numerous aliens who have

been found to be deportable, many of whom are in the subversive, criminal, or immoral classes who are free to roam the country at will without supervision or control.

(14) One device for infiltration by Communists is by procuring naturalization for disloyal aliens who use their citizenship as a badge for admission into the fabric of our society.

(15) The Communist movement in the United States is an organization numbering thousands of adherents, rigidly and ruthlessly disciplined. Awaiting and seeking to advance a moment when the United States may be so far extended by foreign engagements, so far divided in counsel, or so far in industrial or financial straits, that overthrow of the Government of the United States by force and violence may seem possible of achievement, it seeks converts far and wide by an extensive system of schooling and indoctrination. Such preparations by Communist organizations in other countrics havc aidcd in supplanting existing governments. The Communist organization in the United States, pursuing its stated objectives, the recent successes of Communist methods in other countries, and the nature and control of the world Communist movement itself, present a clear and present danger to the security of the United States and to the existence of free American institutions, and make it necessary that Congress, in order to provide for the common defense, to preserve the sovereignty of the United States as an independent nation, and to guarantee to each State a republican form of government, enact appropriate legislation recognizing the existence of such world-wide conspiracy and designed to prevent it from accomplishing its purpose in the United States. Sept. 23, 1950, c. 1024, Title I, § 2, 64 Stat. 987.

(16) The findings of fact contained in paragraphs (1) through (15) of this section are reiterated. Recent court decisions involving the registration provisions of this subchapter make it necessary to enact legislation to accomplish the purposes of such subchapter without the requirements of registration. Disclosure of Communist organizations and of the members of Communist-action organizations as provided in this subchapter is essential to the protection of the national welfare. As amended Jan. 2, 1968, Pub.L. 90-237, § 1, 81 Stat. 765.

50 U.S.C. §782

Definitions

For the purposes of this subchapter, sections 137 to 137-8, 156, 456, 457(b), 704, 705, 725, 729(c), 733, 734(b) and 735 of Title 8, sections 793 and 1507 of Title 18, and sections 611(c) (5) and 618(e) of Title 22—

(1) The term "person" means an individual or an organization.

(2) The term "organization" means an organization, corporation, company, partnership, association, trust, foundation, or fund; and includes a group of persons, whether or not incorporated, permanently or temporarily associated together for joint action on any subject or subjects.

(3) The term "Communist-action organization" means any organization in the United States (other than a diplomatic representative or mission of a foreign government accredited as such by the Department of State) which (i) is substantially directed, dominated, or controlled by the foreign government or foreign organization controlling the world Communist movement referred to in section 781 of this

title, and (ii) operates primarily to advance the objectives of such world Communist movement referred to in section 781 of this title.

(4) The term "Communist-front organization" means any organization in the United States (other than a Communist-action organization as defined in paragraph (3) of this section) which (A) is substantially directed, dominated, or controlled by a Communist-action organization, or (B) is substantially directed, dominated, or controlled by one or more members of a Communist-action organization, and (C) is primarily operated for the purpose of giving aid and support to a Communist-action organization, a Communist foreign government, or the world Communist movement referred to in section 781 of this title.

(4A) The term "Communist-infiltrated organization" means any organization in the United States (other than a Communist-action organization or a Communist-front organization) which (A) is substantially directed, dominated, or controlled by an individual or individuals who are, or who within three years have been actively engaged in, giving aid or support to a Communist-action organization, a Communist foreign government, or the world Communist movement referred to in section 781 of this title, and (B) is serving, or within three years has served, as a means for (i) the giving of aid or support to any such organization, government, or movement, or (ii) the impairment of the military strength of the United States or its industrial capacity to furnish logistical or other material support required by its Armed Forces: *Provided, however,* That any labor organization which is an affiliate in good standing of a national federation or other labor organization whose policies and activities have been directed to opposing Communist organizations, any Communist foreign government, or the world Communist movement, shall be presumed prima facie not to be a "Communist-infiltrated organization".

(5) The term "Communist organization" means any Communist-action organization, Communist-front organization, or Communist-infiltrated organization.

(6) The term "to contribute funds or services" includes the rendering of any personal service and the making of any gift, subscription, loan, advance, or deposit, of money or of anything of value, and also the making of any contract, promise, or agreement to contribute funds or services, whether or not legally enforcible.

(7) The term "facility" means any plant, factory or other manufacturing, producing or service establishment, airport, airport facility, vessel, pier, water-front facility, mine, railroad, public utility, laboratory, station, or other establishment or facility, or any part, division, or department of any of the foregoing. The term "defense facility" means any facility designated by the Secretary of Defense pursuant to section 784(b) of this title and which is in compliance with the provisions of such subsection respecting the posting of notice of such designation.

(8) The term "publication" means any circular, newspaper, periodical, pamphlet, book, letter, post card, leaflet, or other publication.

(9) The term "United States", when used in a geographical sense, includes the several States, Territories, and possessions of the United States, the District of Columbia, and the Canal Zone.

(10) The term "interstate or foreign commerce" means trade, traffic, commerce, transportation, or communication (A) between any State, Territory, or possession of the United States (including the Canal Zone), or the District of Columbia, and any place outside thereof, or (B) within any Territory or possession of the United States (including the Canal Zone), or within the District of Columbia.

(11) The term "Board" means the Subversive Activities Control Board created by section 791 of this title.

(12) The term "final order of the Board" means an order issued by the Board under section 792 of this title, which has become final as provided in section 793 of this title.

(13) The term "advocates" includes, advises, recommends, furthers by overt act, and admits belief in; and the giving, loaning, or promising of support or of money or anything of value to be used for advocating any doctrine shall be deemed to constitute the advocating of such doctrine.

(14) The term "world communism" means a revolutionary movement, the purpose of which is to establish eventually a Communist totalitarian dictatorship in any or all the countries of the world through the medium of an internationally coordinated Communist movement.

(15) The terms "totalitarian dictatorship" and "totalitarianism" mean and refer to systems of government not representative in fact, characterized by (A) the existence of a single political party, organized on a dictatorial basis, with so close an identity between such party and its policies and the governmental policies of the country in which it exists, that the party and the government constitute an indistinguishable unit, and (B) the forcible suppression of opposition to such party.

(16) The term "doctrine" includes, but is not limited to, policies, practices, purposes, aims, or procedures.

(17) The giving, loaning, or promising of support or of money or any other thing of value for any purpose to any organization shall be conclusively presumed to constitute affiliation therewith; but nothing in this paragraph shall be construed as an exclusive definition of affiliation.

(18) "Advocating the economic, international, and governmental doctrines of world communism" means advocating the establishment of a totalitarian Communist dictatorship in any or all of the countries of the world through the medium of an internationally coordinated Communist movement.

(19) "Advocating the economic and governmental doctrines of any other form of totalitarianism" means advocating the establishment of totalitarianism (other than world communism) and includes, but is not limited to, advocating the economic and governmental doctrines of fascism and nazism. Sept. 23, 1950, c. 1024, Title I, § 3, 64 Stat. 989.

As amended Aug. 24, 1954, c. 886, § 7(a), (b), 68 Stat. 777; May 31, 1962, Pub.L. 87-474, § 1(a), 76 Stat. 91; Jan. 2, 1968, Pub.L. 90-237, § 2, 81 Stat. 765.

50 U.S.C. §783

Offenses—(a) Conspiracy or Attempt to Establish Totalitarian Dictatorship

It shall be unlawful for any person knowingly to combine, conspire, or agree with any other person to perform any act which would substantially contribute to the establishment within the United States of a totalitarian dictatorship, as defined in paragraph (15) of section 782 of this title, the direction and control of which is to be vested in, or exercised by or under the domination or control of, any foreign government, foreign organization, or foreign individual: *Provided, however,* That this subsection shall not apply to the proposal of a constitutional amendment.

Communication of Classified Information by Government Officer or Employee

(b) It shall be unlawful for any officer or employee of the United States or of any department or agency thereof, or of any corporation the stock of which is owned in whole or in major part by the United States or any department or agency thereof, to communicate in any manner or by any means, to any other person whom such officer or employee knows or has reason to believe to be an agent or representative of any foreign government or an officer or member of any Communist organization as defined in paragraph (5) of section 782 of this title, any information of a kind which shall have been classified by the President (or by the head of any such department, agency, or corporation with the approval of the President) as affecting the security of the United States, knowing or having reason to know that such information has been so classified, unless such officer or employee shall have been specifically authorized by the President, or by the head of the department, agency, or corporation by which this officer or employee is employed, to make such disclosure of such information.

Receipt of, or Attempt to Receive, by Foreign Agent or Member of Communist Organization, Classified Information

(c) It shall be unlawful for any agent or representative of any foreign government, or any officer or member of any Communist organization as defined in paragraph (5) of section 782 of this title, knowingly to obtain or receive, or attempt to obtain or receive, directly or indirectly, from any officer or employee of the United States or of any department or agency thereof or of any corporation the stock of which is owned in whole or in major part by the United States or any department or agency thereof, any information of a kind which shall have been classified by the President (or by the head of any such department, agency, or corporation with the approval of the President) as affecting the security of the United States, unless special authorization for such communication shall first have been obtained from the head of the department, agency, or corporation having custody of or control over such information.

Penalties for Violation

(d) Any person who violates any provision of this section shall, upon conviction thereof, be punished by a fine of not more than $10,000, or imprisonment for not more than ten years, or by both such fine and such imprisonment, and shall, moreover, be thereafter ineligible to hold any office, or place of honor, profit, or trust created by the Constitution or laws of the United States.

Limitation Period

(e) Any person may be prosecuted, tried, and punished for any violation of this section at any time within ten years after the commission of such offense, notwithstanding the provisions of any other statute of limitations: *Provided,* That if at the time of the commission of the offense such person is an officer or employee of the United States or of any department or agency thereof, or of any corporation the stock of which is owned in whole or in major part by the United States or any department or agency thereof, such person may be prosecuted, tried, and punished for any violation of this section at any time within ten years after such person has ceased to be employed as such officer or employee.

Membership as Not Violation Per Se

(f) Neither the holding of office nor membership in any Communist organization by any person shall constitute per se a violation of subsection (a) or subsection (c) of this section or of any other criminal statute. As amended Jan. 2, 1968, Pub.L. 90-237, § 3, 81 Stat. 765.

50 U.S.C. §784

Employment of Members of Communist Organizations—Failure to Disclose Membership; Defense Facilities; Contribution of Funds, Services or Advice by Government Personnel

(a) When there is in effect a final order of the Board determining any organization to be a Communist-action organization or a Communist-front organization, it shall be unlawful—

(1) For any member of such organization, with knowledge or notice of such final order of the Board—

(A) in seeking, accepting, or holding any nonelective office or employment under the United States, to conceal or fail to disclose the fact that he is a member of such organization; or

(B) to hold any nonelective office or employment under the United States; or

(C) in seeking, accepting, or holding employment in any defense facility, to conceal or fail to disclose the fact that he is a member of such organization; or

(D) if such organization is a Communist-action organization, to engage in any employment in any defense facility; or

(E) to hold office or employment with any labor organization, as that term is defined in section 2(5) of the National Labor Relations Act, as amended, or to represent any employer in any matter or proceeding arising or pending under that act.

(2) For any officer or employee of the United States or of any defense facility, with knowledge or notice of such final order of the Board—

(A) to contribute funds or services ro such organization; or

(B) to advise, counsel or urge any person, with knowledge or notice that such person is a member of such organization, to perform, or to omit to perform, any act if such act or omission would constitute a violation of any provision of paragraph (1) of this subsection.

Designation of Defense Facilities by Secretary of Defense; Posting by Management and Sufficiency Thereof as Notice; Employee's Statement of Knowledge of Designation

(b) The Secretary of Defense is authorized and directed to designate facilities, as defined in paragraph (7) of section 782 of this title, with respect to the operation of which he finds and determines that the security of the United States requires the application of the provisions of subsection (a) of this section. The Secretary shall promptly notify the management of any facility so designated, whereupon such management shall immediately post conspicuously notice of such designation in such form and in such place or places as to give notice thereof to all employees of, and to all applicants for employment in, such facility. Such posting shall be sufficient to give notice of such designation to any person subject thereto or affected thereby. Upon the request of the Secretary, the management of any facility so designated shall require each employee of the facility, or any part thereof, to sign a statement that he knows that the facility has, for the purposes of this subchapter, been designated by the Secretary under this subsection.

(c) Repealed. Aug. 24, 1954, c. 886, § 7(c), 68 Stat. 778.

As amended Aug. 24, 1954, c. 886, §§ 6, 7(c), 68 Stat. 777, 778; May 31, 1962, Pub.L. 87-474, § 1(b), 76 Stat. 91; Jan. 2, 1968, Pub.L. 90-237, § 4, 81 Stat. 765.

50 U.S.C. §785

Denial of Passports to Members of Communist Organizations

(a) When a Communist organization as defined in paragraph (5) of section 782 of this title is registered, or there is in effect a final order of the Board requiring such organization to register, it shall be unlawful for any member of such organization, with knowledge or notice that such organization is so registered or that such order has become final—

(1) to make application for a passport, or the renewal of a passport, to be issued or renewed by or under the authority of the United States; or

(2) to use or attempt to use any such passport.

(b) When an organization is registered, or there is in effect a final order of the Board requiring an organization to register, as a Communist-action organization, it shall be unlawful for any officer or employee of the United States to issue a passport to, or renew the passport of, any individual knowing or having reason to believe that such individual is a member of such organization.

(c) Repealed. Aug. 24, 1954, c. 886, § 7(c), 68 Stat. 778.

As amended Aug. 24, 1954, c. 886, § 7(c), 68 Stat. 778.

50 U.S.C. §787

Registration and Statements of Members of Communist-action Organizations

(a) Any individual who is or becomes a member of any organization concerning which (1) there is in effect a final order of the Board requiring such organization to register under section 786(a) of this title as a Communist-action organization, (2) more than thirty days have elapsed since such order has become final, and (3) such organization is not registered under section 786 of this title as a Communist-action organization, shall within sixty days after said order has become final, or within thirty days after becoming a member of such organization, whichever is later, register with the Attorney General as a member of such organization.

(b) Each individual who is or becomes a member of any organization which he knows to be registered as a Communist-action organization under section 786(a) of this title, but to have failed to include his name upon the list of members thereof filed with the Attorney General, pursuant to the provisions of subsections (d) and (e) of section 786 of this title, shall, within sixty days after he shall have obtained such knowledge, register with the Attorney General as a member of such organization.

(c) The registration made by any individual under subsection (a) or (b) of this section shall be accompanied by a registration statement to be prepared and filed in such manner and form, and containing such information, as the Attorney General shall by regulations prescribe. Sept. 28, 1950, c. 1024, Title I, § 8, 64 Stat. 995.

50 U.S.C. §788

Records of Final Orders of Board; Public Inspection; Reports to President and Congress

(a) The Board shall keep and maintain records, which shall be open to public inspection, giving the names and addresses of all organizations as to which, and individuals as to whom, there are in effect final orders of the Board issued pursuant to any of the provisions of subsections (g) through (j), inclusive, of section 792 of this title, or subsection (f) of section 792a of this title.

(b) Copies of all public proceedings and hearings before the Board, including the reports and orders of the Board, shall be furnished by the Board to any person upon request and upon the payment of the reasonable costs thereof as then currently fixed by the Board.

(c) The Board shall submit to the President and to the Congress on or before June 1 of each year (and at any other time when requested by either House by resolution) a report giving the names and addresses of all Communist-action, Communist-front, or Communist-infiltrated organizations as to which, and all individual members of Communist-action organizations as to whom, there are in effect such final orders of the Board.

As amended Jan. 2, 1968, Pub.L. 90-237, § 6, 81 Stat. 766.

50 U.S.C. §789

Use of Mails and Instrumentalities of Interstate or Foreign Commerce

It shall be unlawful for any organization with respect to which there is in effect a final order of the Board determining it to be a Communist organization as defined in paragraph (5) of section 782 of this title, or for any person with knowledge or notice of such final order acting for or on behalf of any such organization—

(1) to transmit or cause to be transmitted, through the United States

mails or by any means or instrumentality of interstate or foreign commerce, any publication which is intended to be, or which it is reasonable to believe is intended to be, circulated or disseminated among two or more persons, unless such publication, and any envelope, wrapper, or other container in which it is mailed or otherwise circulated or transmitted, bears the following, printed in such manner as may be provided in regulations prescribed by the Attorney General: "Disseminated by   ," (with the name of the organization in lieu of the blank) "an organization determined by final order of the Subversive Activities Control Board to be a Communist-   organization" (setting forth in lieu of the blank whether action, front, or infiltrated, as the case may be); or

(2) to broadcast or cause to be broadcast any matter over any radio or television station in the United States, unless such matter is preceded by the following statement: "The following program is sponsored by   ," (with the name of the organization in lieu of the blank) "an organization determined by final order of the Subversive Activities Control Board to be a Communist-   organization" (setting forth in lieu of the blank whether action, front, or infiltrated, as the case may be); or

(3) to use the United States mails or any means, facility, or instrumentality of interstate or foreign commerce, including but not limited to radio and television broadcasts, to solicit any money, property, thing, or service, unless such solicitation if made orally is preceded by the following statement, and if made in writing or in print is preceded by the following written or printed statement: "This solicitation is made for or on behalf of   ," (with the name of the organization in lieu of the blank) "an organization determined by final orders of the Subversive Activities Control Board to be a Communist-   organization" (setting forth in lieu of the blank whether action, front, or infiltrated, as the case may be).

As amended Aug. 24, 1954, c. 886, § 8(a), 68 Stat. 778;
Jan. 2, 1968, Pub.L. 90-237, § 7, 81 Stat. 766.

50 U.S.C. §790

Denial of Tax Deductions and Exemptions

(a) Notwithstanding any other provision of law, no deduction for Federal income tax purposes shall be allowed in the case of a contribution to or for the use of any organization if at the time of the making of such contribution there is in effect a final order of the Board determining such organization to be a Communist-action, Communist-front, or Communist-infiltrated organization.

(b) No organization shall be entitled to exemption from Federal income tax, under section 501 of Title 26, for any taxable year if at any time during such taxable year there is in effect a final order of the Board determining such organization to be a Communist-action, Communist-front, or Communist-infiltrated organization.

As amended Aug. 24, 1954, c. 886, § 8(b), 68 Stat. 778;
Jan. 2, 1968, Pub.L. 90-237, § 8, 81 Stat. 767.

50 U.S.C. §791

Subversive Activities Control Board—Creation; Membership; Designation of Chairman; Removal

(a) There is established a board, to be kown as the Subversive Activities Control Board, which shall be composed of five members, who shall be appointed by the President, by and with the advice and consent of the Senate. Not more than three members of the Board shall be members of the same political party. The terms of office of the members of the Board in office on August 5, 1955 shall expire at the time they would have expired if such Act had not been enacted. The term of office of each member of the Board appointed after August 5, 1955 shall be for five years from the date of expiration of the term of his predecessor, except that (1) the term of office of that member of the Board who is designated by the President and is appointed to succeed one of the two members of the Board whose terms expire on August 9, 1955, shall be for four years from the date of expiration of the term of his predecessor, and (2) the term of office of any member appointed to fill a vacancy occurring prior to the expiration of the term for which his predecessor was appointed shall be for the remainder of the term of his predecessor. Upon the expiration of his term of office a member of the Board shall continue to serve until his successor shall have been appointed and shall have qualified. The President shall designate one member to serve as Chairman of the Board. Any member of the Board may be removed by the President, upon notice and hearing, for neglect of duty or malfeasance in office, but for no other cause.

Vacancies; Powers of Remaining Members; Quorum; Official Seal; Judicial Notice

(b) A vacancy in the Board shall not impair the right of the remaining members to exercise all the powers of the Board, and three members of the Board shall, at all times, constitute a quorum. The Board shall have an official seal which shall be judicially noticed.

Reports to Congress and President

(c) The Board shall at the close of each fiscal year make a report in writing to the Congress and to the President stating in detail the cases it has heard, the decisions it has rendered, the names, salaries, and duties of all employees of the Board, and an account of all moneys it has disbursed.

Right of Reappointment; Ineligibility to Engage in Other Business

(d) Each member of the Board shall be eligible for reappointment, and shall not engage in any other business, vocation, or employment.

Duties of Board

(e) It shall be the duty of the Board—

(1) upon application made by the Attorney General under section 792(a) of this title, or by any organization under section 792(b) of this title, to determine whether any organization is a "Communist-action organization" within the meaning of paragraph (3) of section 782 of this title, or a "Communist-front organization" within the meaning of paragraph (4) of section 782 of this title; and

(2) upon application made by the Attorney General under section 792(a) of this title, or by any individual under section 792(b) of this title, to determine whether any individual is a member of any organization as to which there is in effect a final order of the Board determining such organization to be a Communist-action organization; and

(3) upon any application made under subsection (a) or subsection (b) of section 792a of this title, to determine whether any organization is a Communist-infiltrated organization.

(2) upon application made by the Attorney General under section 792(a) of this title, or by any individual under section 792(b) of this title, to determine whether any individual is a member of any Communist-action organization registered, or by final order of the Board required to be registered, under section 786(a) of this title.

Appointment and Compensation of Personnel

(f) Subject to the civil-service laws and Classification Act of 1949, the Board may appoint and fix the compensation of a chief clerk and such examiners and other personnel as may be necessary for the performance of its functions.

Rules and Regulations

(g) The Board may make such rules and regulations, not inconsistent with the provisions of this subchapter, sections 137 to 137-8, 156, 456, 457(b), 704, 705, 725, 729(c), 733, 734(b) and 735 of Title 8, sections 793 and 1057 of Title 18, and sections 611(c) (5) and 618(e) of Title 22, as may be necessary for the performance of its duties.

Authorization for Appropriations

(h) There are authorized to be appropriated to the Board such sums as may be necessary to carry out its functions. Sept. 23, 1950, c. 1024, Title I, § 12, 64 Stat. 997.

Termination of Existence; Reports to Congress

(i) The Board shall cease to exist on June 30, 1969, unless in the period beginning on January 2, 1968, and ending on December 31, 1968, a proceeding under this subchapter shall have been instituted before the Board and a hearing under this subchapter shall have been conducted by the Board. On or before June 30, 1968, the Attorney General shall report to the Congress on the proceedings he has instituted before the Board under this subchapter during the period from January 2, 1968, to the date of the report, and the Board shall report on the progress it has made in conducting hearings under the subchapter during such period. If no proceedings have been instituted before the Board by the Attorney General, the Attorney General shall report his reasons for not having done so. If no hearings have been conducted, the Board shall report the reasons for not having done so. Similar reports shall be filed by the Attorney General and the Board on or before January 10, 1969, and each year thereafter, to cover the immediately preceding calendar year.

As amended July 12, 1952, c. 69, 66 Stat. 590; Aug. 24, 1954, c. 886, § 9(a), 68 Stat. 778; Aug. 5, 1955, c. 580, § 1, 69 Stat. 539; July 31, 1956, c. 804, Title I, § 106(a), 70 Stat. 739; Jan. 2, 1968, Pub.L. 90-237, § 9, 81 Stat. 767.

50 U.S.C. §792

Board Proceedings with Respect to Communist-action or Communist-front Organizations—Petition by Attorney General for Determination; Verification; Contents; Joinder of Respondents; Dissolution of Organization Subsequent to Filing

(a) Whenever the Attorney General shall have reason to believe that any organization is a Communist-action organization or a Communist-front organization, or that any individual is a member of an organization which has been determined by final order of the Board to be a Communist-action organization, he shall file with the Board and serve upon such organization or individual, as the case may be, a petition for a determination that such organization is a Communist-action or Communist-front organization, or determining that such individual is a member of such Communist-action organization. Each such petition shall be verified under oath, and shall contain a statement of the facts upon which the Attorney General relies in support thereof. Two or more such individual members of a Communist-action organization or of any section, branch, fraction, cell, board, committee, commission, or unit thereof, may be joined as respondents in one petition for an order determining each of such individuals to be a member of such organization. A dissolution of any organization subsequent to the date of the filing of any petition for a determination that such organization is a Communist-action or Communist-front organization shall not moot or abate the proceedings, but the Board shall receive evidence and proceed to a determination of the issues: *Provided, however,* That if the Board shall find such organization to be a Communist-action or Communist-front organization as of the time of the filing of such petition and prior to its alleged dissolution, and shall find that a dissolution of the organization has in fact occurred, the Board shall enter an order determining such organization to be a Communist-action or Communist-front organization, as the case may be, and the Board shall include it as such in the appropriate records maintained pursuant to section 788 of this title, together with a notation of its dissolution.

Petition by Organization or Individual for Determination; Verification; Contents; Notice and Time of Hearing

(b) Any organization as to which there is in effect a final order of the Board determining it to be a Communist-action or Communist-front organization, and any individual as to whom there is in effect a final order of the Board determining such individual to be a member of a Communist-action organization may, not more often than once in each calendar year, file with the Board and serve upon the Attorney General a petition for a determination that such organization no longer is a Communist-action or Communist-front organization, or that such individual no longer is a member of a Communist-action organization, as the case may be. Each petition filed under this subsection shall be verified under oath, and shall contain a statement of the facts relied upon in support thereof. Upon the filing of any such petition, the Board shall serve upon each party to such proceeding a notice specifying the time and place for hearing upon such petition. No such hearing shall be conducted within twenty days after the service of such notice.

Hearings; Oaths, Examination, Evidence, and Subpoenas; Aid of Courts; Contempt; Process; Exemption from Liability

(c) Upon the filing of any petition pursuant to subsection (a) or subsection (b) of this section, the Board (or any member thereof or any examiner designated thereby) may hold hearings, administer oaths and affirmations, may examine witnesses and receive evidence at any place in the United States, and may require by subpoena the attendance and testimony of witnesses and the production of books, papers, correspondence, memoranda, and other records deemed relevant, to the matter under inquiry. Subpoenas may be signed and issued by any member of the Board or any duly authorized examiner. Subpoenas shall be issued on behalf of the organization or the individual who is a party to the proceeding upon request and upon a statement or showing of general relevance and reasonable scope of the evidence sought. Such attendance of witnesses and the production of such documentary evidence may be required from any place in the United States at any designated place of hearing. Witnesses summoned shall be paid the same fees and mileage paid witnesses in the district courts of the United States. In case of disobedience to a subpoena, the Board may invoke the aid of any court of the United States in requiring the attendance and testimony of witnesses and the production of documentary evidence. Any of the district courts of the United States within the jurisdiction of which such inquiry is carried on may, in case of contumacy or refusal to obey a subpoena issued to any person, issue an order requiring such person to appear (and to produce documentary evidence if so ordered) and give evidence relating to the matter in question; and any failure to obey such order of the court may be punished by such court as a contempt thereof. All process in any such case may be served in the judicial district whereof such person is an inhabitant or wherever he may be found. No person shall be held liable in any action in any court, State or Federal, for any damages resulting from (1) his production of any documentary evidence in any proceeding before the Board if he is required, by a subpoena issued under this subsection, to produce the evidence; or (2) any statement under oath he makes in answer to a question he is asked while testifying before the Board in response to a subpoena issued under this subsection, if the statement is pertinent to the question.

Hearings Open to Public; Rights of Parties; Record and Transcript of Testimony; Failure to Appear; Penalty for Misbehavior; Jurisdiction of Courts

(d) (1) All hearings conducted under this section shall be public. Each party to such proceeding shall have the right to present its case with the assistance of counsel, to offer oral or documentary evidence, to submit rebuttal evidence, and to conduct such cross-examination as may be required for a full and true disclosure of the facts. An accurate stenographic record shall be taken of the testimony of each witness, and a transcript of such testimony shall be filed in the office of the Board.

(2) Where an organization or individual declines or fails to appear at a hearing accorded to such organization or individual by the Board in proceedings initiated pursuant to subsection (a) of this section, the Board shall, nevertheless, proceed to receive evidence, make a determination of the

issues, and enter such order as shall be just and appropriate. Upon failure of an organization or individual to appear at a hearing accorded to such organization or individual in proceedings under subsection (b) of this section the Board may forthwith and without further proceedings enter an order dismissing the petition of such organization or individual.

(3) Any person who, in the course of any hearing before the Board or any member thereof or any examiner designated thereby, shall misbehave in their presence or so near thereto as to obstruct the hearing or the administration of the provisions of this subchapter, shall be guilty of an offense and upon conviction thereof by a court of competent jurisdiction shall be punished by a fine of not less than $500 nor more than $5,000, or by imprisonment for not more than one year, or by both such fine and imprisonment. Whenever a statement of fact constituting such misbehavior is reported by the Board to the appropriate United States attorney, it shall be his duty to bring the matter before the grand jury for its action.

(4) The authority, function, practice, or process of the Attorney General or Board in conducting any proceeding pursuant to the provisions of this subchapter shall not be questioned in any court of the United States, nor shall any such court, or judge or justice thereof, have jurisdiction of any action, suit, petition, or proceeding, whether for declaratory judgment, injunction, or otherwise, to question such authority, function, practice, or process, except on review in the court or courts having jurisdiction of the actions and orders of the Board pursuant to the provisions of section 793 of this title, or when such authority, function, practice, or process, is appropriately called into question by the accused or respondent, as the case may be, in the court or courts having jurisdiction of his prosecution or other proceeding (or the review thereof) for any contempt or any offense charged against him pursuant to the provisions of this subchapter.

Determination of Communist-action Organization; Matters Considered

(e) In determining whether any organization is a "Communist-action organization", the Board shall take into consideration—

(1) the extent to which its policies are formulated and carried out and its activities performed, pursuant to directives or to effectuate the policies of the foreign government or foreign organization in which is vested, or under the domination or control of which is exercised, the direction and control of the world Communist movement referred to in section 781 of this title; and

(2) the extent to which its views and policies do not deviate from those of such foreign government or foreign organization; and

(3) the extent to which it receives financial or other aid, directly or indirectly, from or at the direction of such foreign government or foreign organization; and

(4) the extent to which it sends members or representatives to any foreign country for instruction or training in the principles, policies, strategy, or tactics of such world Communist movement; and

(5) the extent to which it reports to such foreign government or foreign organization or to its representatives; and

(6) the extent to which its principal leaders or a substantial number of its members are subject to or recognize the disciplinary power of such foreign government or foreign organization or its representatives; and

(7) the extent to which, for the purpose of concealing foreign direction, domination, or control, or of expediting or promoting its objectives, (i) it fails to disclose, or resists efforts to obtain information as to, its membership (by keeping membership lists in code, by instructing members to refuse to acknowledge membership, or by any other method), (ii) its members refuse to acknowledge membership therein; (iii) it fails to disclose, or resists efforts to obtain information as to, records other than membership lists; (iv) its meetings are secret; and (v) it otherwise operates on a secret basis; and

(8) the extent to which its principal leaders or a substantial number of its members consider the allegiance they owe to the United States as subordinate to their obligations to such foreign government or foreign organization.

Determination of Communist-front Organization; Matters Considered

(f) In determining whether any organization is a "Communist-front organization", the Board shall take into consideration—

(1) the extent to which persons who are active in its management, direction, or supervision, whether or not holding office therein, are active in the management, direction, or supervision of, or as representatives or members of, any Communist-action organization, Communist foreign government, or the world Communist movement referred to in section 781 of this title; and

(2) the extent to which its support, financial or otherwise, is derived from any Communist-action organization, Communist foreign government, or the world Communist movement referred to in section 781 of this title; and

(3) the extent to which its funds, resources, or personnel are used to further or promote the objectives of any Communist-action organization, Communist foreign government, or the world Communist movement referred to in section 781 of this title; and

(4) the extent to which the positions taken or advanced by it from time to time on matters of policy do not deviate from those of any Communist-action organization, Communist foreign government, or the world Communist movement referred to in section 781 of this title.

Written Report of Findings; Issuance and Service of Orders Granting Determination Sought by Petition of Attorney General

(g) If, after hearing upon a petition filed under subsection (a) of this section the Board determines—

(1) that an organization is a Communist-action organization or a Communist-front organization, as the case may be, it shall make a report in writing in which it shall state its findings as to the facts and shall issue and cause to be served on such organization an order determining the organization to be a Communist-action organization or a Communist-front organization as the case may be; or

(2) that an individual is a member of a Communist-action organization it shall make a report in writing in which it shall state its findings as to the facts and shall issue and cause to be served on such individual an order determining such individual to be a member of a Communist-action organization.

Written Report of Findings; Issuance and Service of Orders Denying Determination Sought by Petition of Attorney General

(h) If, after hearing upon a petition filed under subsection (a) of this section, the Board determines—

(1) that an organization is not a Communist-action organization or a Communist-front organization, as the case may be, it shall make a report in writing in which it shall state its findings as to the facts and shall issue and cause to be served upon the Attorney General an order denying the determination sought by his petition, and shall send a copy of such order to such organization; or

(2) that an individual is not a member of any Communist-action organization, it shall make a report in writing in which it shall state its findings as to the facts and shall issue and cause to be served upon the Attorney General an order denying the determination sought by his petition, and shall send a copy of such order to such individual.

Written Report of Findings; Issuance and Service of Orders Granting Determination Sought by Petition of Organization or Individual

(i) If, after hearing upon a petition filed under subsection (b) of this section, the Board determines—

(1) that an organization no longer is a Communist-action organization or a Communist-front organization, as the case may be, it shall make a report in writing in which it shall state its findings as to the facts and shall issue and cause to be served upon the Attorney General and such organization an order determining that the organization no longer is a Communist-action organization or Communist-front organization as the case may be; or

(2) that an individual no longer is a member of any Communist-action organization, it shall make a report in writing in which it shall state its findings as to the facts and shall issue and cause to be served upon the Attorney General and such individual an order determining that such individual no longer is a member of a Communist-action organization.

Written Report of Findings; Issuance and Service of Orders Denying Determination Sought by Petition of Organization or Individual

(j) If, after hearing upon a petition filed under subsection (b) of this section, the Board determines—

(1) that an organization is a Communist-action organization or a Communist-front organization, as the case may be, it shall make a report in writing in which it shall state its findings as to the facts and shall issue and cause to be served on such organization an order denying its petition for a determination that the organization no longer is a Communist-action organization or a Communist-front organization as the case may be; or

(2) that an individual is a member of a Communist-action organization, it shall make a report in writing in which it shall state its findings as to the facts and shall issue and cause to be served upon such individual an order

denying his petition for a determination that the individual no longer is a member of a Communist-action organization.

Publication in Federal Register of Fact of Finality of Order; Publication as Notice

(k) When any order of the Board issued under subsection (g), (h), (i), or (j) of this section becomes final under the provisions of section 793(b) of this title, the Board shall publish in the Federal Register the fact that such order has become final, and publication thereof shall constitute notice to all persons that such order has become final.

As amended Aug. 24, 1954, c. 886, § 9(b), 68 Stat. 778; Jan. 2, 1968, Pub.L. 90-237, § 10(b)-(f), 81 Stat. 768, 769; Oct. 15, 1970, Pub.L. 91-452, Title II, § 247, 84 Stat. 931.

50 U.S.C. §792a

Board Proceedings with Respect to Communist-infiltrated Organizations—Petition by Attorney General for Determination; Joint Respondents; Expedition of Proceedings

(a) Whenever the Attorney General has reason to believe that any organization is a Communist-infiltrated organization, he may file with the Board and serve upon such organization a petition for a determination that such organization is a Communist-infiltrated organization. In any proceeding so instituted, two or more affiliated organizations may be named as joint respondents. A dissolution of such organization subsequent to the date of the filing of any petition for a determination that it is Communist-infiltrated, shall not moot or abate the proceedings, but the Board shall receive evidence and proceed to a determination of the issues: *Provided, however,* That if the Board shall determine such organization to be a Communist-infiltrated organization as of the time of the filing of such petition and prior to its alleged dissolution, and shall find that a dissolution of the organization has in fact occurred, the Board shall enter an order determining such organization to be a Communist-infiltrated organization and the Board shall include it as such in the appropriate records maintained pursuant to section 788 of this title, together with a notation of its dissolution. Whenever any such petition is accompanied by a certificate of the Attorney General to the effect that the proceeding so instituted is one of exceptional public importance, such proceeding shall be set for hearing at the earliest possible time and all proceedings therein before the Board or any court shall be expedited to the greatest practicable extent.

Petition by Organization Affected After Determination in the Affirmative

(b) Any organization which has been determined under this section to be a Communist-infiltrated organization may, within six months after such determination, file with the Board and serve upon the Attorney General a petition for a determination that such organization no longer is a Communist-infiltrated organization.

Verification of Petitions; Notice of Hearing; Minimum Time Period Before Hearing

(c) Each such petition shall be verified under oath, and shall contain a statement of the facts relied upon in support thereof. Upon the filing of any such petition, the Board shall serve upon each party to such proceeding a notice specifying the time and place for hearing upon such petition. No such hearing shall be conducted within twenty days after the service of such notice.

Applicability of Section 792(c), (d)

(d) The provisions of subsections (c) and (d) of section 792 of this title shall apply to hearings conducted under this section.

Evidence Considered in Making Determination

(e) In determining whether any organization is a Communist-infiltrated organization, the Board shall consider—

(1) to what extent, if any, the effective management of the affairs of such organization is conducted by one or more individuals who are, or within three years have been, (A) members, agent, or representatives of any Communist organization, any Communist foreign government, or the world Communist movement referred to in section 781 of this title, with knowledge of the nature and purpose thereof, or (B) engaged in giving aid or support to any such organization, government, or movement with knowledge of the nature and purpose thereof;

(2) to what extent, if any, the policies of such organization are, or within three years have been, formulated and carried out pursuant to the direction or advice of any member, agent, or representative of any such organization, government, or movement;

(3) to what extent, if any, the personnel and resources of such organization are, or within three years have been, used to further or promote the objectives of any such Communist organization, government, or movement;

(4) to what extent, if any, such organization within three years has received from, or furnished to or for the use of, any such Communist organization, government, or movement any funds or other material assistance;

(5) to what extent, if any, such organization is, or within three years has been, affiliated in any way with any such Communist organization, government, or movement;

(6) to what extent, if any, the affiliation of such organization, or of any individual or individuals who are members thereof or who manage its affairs, with any such Communist organization, government, or movement is concealed from or is not disclosed to the membership of such organization; and

(7) to what extent, if any, such organization or any of its members or managers are, or within three years have been, knowingly engaged—

(A) in any conduct punishable under section 783 or 794 of this title or under chapter 37, 105, or 115 of Title 18; or

(B) with intent to impair the military strength of the United States or its industrial capacity to furnish logistical or other support required by its armed forces, in any activity resulting in or contributing to any such impairment.

Written Report of Findings; Grant or Denial, Service, and Finality, of Order

(f) After hearing upon any petition filed under this section, the Board shall (1) make a report in writing in which it shall state its findings as to the facts and its conclusions with respect to the issues presented by such petition, (2) enter its order granting or denying the determination sought by such petition, and (3) serve upon each party to the proceeding a copy of such order. Any order granting any determination on the question whether any organization is a Communist-infiltrated organization shall become final as provided in section 793(b) of this title.

Orders Regarding Labor Organizations or Employers Which are Organizations Within Meaning of Section 782; Service Upon National Labor Relations Board; Publication in Federal Register

(g) When any order has been entered by the Board under this section with respect to any labor organization or employer (as these terms are defined by section 152 of title 29, and which are organizations within the meaning of section 782 of this title), the Board shall serve a true and correct copy of such order upon the National Labor Relations Board and shall publish in the Federal Register a statement of the substance of such order and its effective date.

Effect on Labor Organization of Order Making Determination in Affirmative

(h) When there is in effect a final order of the Board determining that any such labor organization is a Communist-action organization, a Communist-front organization, or a Communist-infiltrated organization, such labor organization shall be ineligible to—

(1) act as representative of any employee within the meaning or for the purposes of section 157 of Title 29;

(2) serve as an exclusive representative of employees of any bargaining unit under section 159 of Title 29;

(3) make, or obtain any hearing upon, any charge under section 160 of Title 29; or

(4) exercise any other right or privilege, or receive any other benefit, substantive or procedural, provided by the National Labor Relations Act, as amended, for labor organizations.

Effect on Employer of Order Making Determination in Affirmative

(j) When there is in effect a final order of the Board determining that any such employer is a Communist-infiltrated organization, such employer shall be ineligible to—

(1) file any petition for an election under section 159 of Title 29, or participate in any proceeding under such section; or

(2) make or obtain any hearing upon any charge under section 160 of Title 29; or

(3) exercise any other right or privilege or receive any other benefit, substantive or procedural, provided by the National Labor Relations Act, as amended, for employers.

Sept. 23, 1950, c. 1024, Title I, § 13 A, as added Aug. 24, 1954, c. 886, § 10, 68 Stat. 778, and amended July 26, 1955, c. 381, 69 Stat. 375; Jan. 2, 1968, Pub.L. 90-237, § 11, 81 Stat. 771.

50 U.S.C. §793

Judicial Review—Courts of Appeals; Petition; Place; Record; Transfer; Conclusiveness of Board's Findings; Additional Evidence; Modification by Board; Judgment; Finality

(a) The party aggrieved by any order entered by the Board under subsections (g), (h), (i), or (j) of section 792 of this title, or subsection (f) of section 792a of this title, may obtain a review of such order by filing in the United States Court of Appeals for the District of Columbia, within sixty days from the date of service upon it of such order, a written petition praying that the order of the Board be set aside. A copy of such petition shall be forthwith transmitted by the clerk of the court to the Board, and thereupon the Board shall file in the court the record in the proceeding, as provided in section 2112 of Title 28. Upon the filing of such petition the court shall have jurisdiction of the proceeding and shall have power to affirm or set aside the order of the Board; but the court may in its discretion and upon its own motion transfer any action so commenced to the United States Court of Appeals for the circuit wherein the petitioner resides. The findings of the Board as to the facts, if supported by the preponderance of the evidence, shall be conclusive. If either party shall apply to the court for leave to adduce additional evidence, and shall show to the satisfaction of the court that such additional evidence is material, the court may order such additional evidence to be taken before the Board and to be adduced upon the proceeding in such manner and upon such terms and conditions as to the court may seem proper. The Board may modify its findings as to the facts, by reason of the additional evidence so taken, and it shall file such modified or new findings, which, if supported by the preponderance of the evidence shall be conclusive, and its recommendations, if any, with respect to action in the matter under consideration. If the court shall set aside an order issued under subsection (j) of section 792 of this title, or under subsection (f) of section 792a of this title, it may, in the case of an organization, enter a judgment requiring the Board to issue an order determining that such organization no longer is a Communist-action organization, Communist-front organization, or a Communist-infiltrated organization, as the case may be, or in the case of an individual, enter a judgment requiring the Board to issue an order determining that such individual no longer is a member of a Communist-action organization. The judgment and decree of the court shall be final, except that the same shall be subject to review by the Supreme Court upon certiorari, as provided in section 1254 of Title 28.

Time of Finality of Board's Orders

(b) Any order of the Board issued under section 792 of this title, or subsection (f) of section 792a of this title, shall become final—

(1) upon the expiration of the time allowed for filing a petition for review, if no such petition has been duly filed within such time; or

(2) upon the expiration of the time allowed for filing a petition for certiorari, if the order of the Board has been affirmed or the petition for review dismissed by a United States Court of Appeals, and no petition for certiorari has been duly filed; or

(3) upon the denial of a petition for certiorari, if the order of the Board has been affirmed or the petition for review dismissed by a United States Court of Appeals; or

(4) upon the expiration of ten days from the date of issuance of the mandate of the Supreme Court, if such Court directs that the order of the Board be affirmed or the petition for review dismissed.

As amended Aug. 24, 1954, c. 886, § 11, 68 Stat. 780; Aug. 28, 1958, Pub.L. 85-791, § 29, 72 Stat. 950; Jan. 2, 1968, Pub.L. 90-237, § 12, 81 Stat. 771.

50 U.S.C. §794

Penalties

Any organization which violates any provision of section 789 of this title shall, upon conviction thereof, be punished for each such violation by a fine of not more than $10,000. Any individual who violates any provision of section 784 or 789 of this title shall, upon conviction thereof, be punished for each such violation by a fine of not more than $10,000 or by imprisonment for not more than five years, or by both such fine and imprisonment.

As amended Jan. 2, 1968, Pub.L. 90-237, § 13, 81 Stat. 771.

50 U.S.C. §795

Applicability of Administrative Procedure Act

Nothing in this subchapter, sections 137 to 137-8, 156, 456, 457(b), 704, 705, 725, 729(c), 733, 734(b) and 735 of Title 8, sections 793 and 1507 of Title 18, and sections 611(c) (5) and 618(e) of Title 22 shall be held to make the provisions of the Administrative Procedure Act inapplicable to the exercise of functions, or the conduct of proceedings, by the Board under this subchapter and said sections. Sept. 23, 1950, c. 1024, Title I, § 16, 64 Stat. 1003.

50 U.S.C. §796

Effect of Subchapter on Other Criminal Laws

The foregoing provisions of this subchapter shall be construed as being in addition to and not in modification of existing criminal statutes. Sept. 23, 1950, c. 1024, Title I, § 17, 64 Stat. 1003.

50 U.S.C. §797

Security Regulations and Orders; Penalty for Violation

(a) Whoever willfully shall violate any such regulation or order as, pursuant to lawful authority, shall be or has been promulgated or approved by the Secretary of Defense, or by any military commander designated by the Secretary of Defense, or by the Director of the National Advisory Committee for Aeronautics, for the protection or security of military or naval aircraft, airports, airport facilities, vessels, harbors, ports, piers, water-front facilities, bases, forts, posts, laboratories, stations, vehicles, equipment, explosives, or other property or places subject to the jurisdiction, administration, or in the custody of the Department of Defense, any Department or agency of which said Department consists, or any officer or employee of said Department or agency, or of the National Advisory Committee for Aeronautics or any officer or employee thereof, relating to fire hazards, fire protection, lighting, machinery, guard service, disrepair, disuse or other unsatisfactory conditions thereon, or the ingress thereto or egress or removal of persons therefrom, or otherwise providing for safeguarding the same against destruction, loss, or injury by accident or by enemy action, sabotage or other subversive actions, shall be guilty of a misdemeanor and upon conviction thereof shall be liable to a fine of not to exceed $5,000 or to imprisonment for not more than one year, or both.

(b) Every such regulation or order shall be posted in conspicuous and appropriate places. Sept. 23, 1950, c. 1024, Title I, § 21, 64 Stat. 1005.

50 U.S.C. §798

Preservation of Certain Rights

Nothing in this chapter, sections 137 to 137-8, 156, 456, 457(b), 704, 705, 725, 729, 733, 734(b) and 735 of Title 8, sections 793 and 1507 of Title 18, and sections 611(c) (5) and 618(e) of Title 22 shall be construed to authorize, require, or establish military or civilian censorship or in any way to limit or infringe upon freedom of the press or of speech as guaranteed by the Constitution of the United States and no regulation shall be promulgated under said subchapter and sections having that effect. Sept. 23, 1950, Title I, § 1(b), 64 Stat. 787.

Sabotage

18 U.S.C. §2151

Definitions

As used in this chapter:

The words "war material" include arms, armament, ammunition, livestock, forage, forest products and standing timber, stores of clothing, air, water, food, foodstuffs, fuel, supplies, munitions, and all articles, parts or ingredients, intended for, adapted to, or suitable for the use of the United States or any associate nation, in connection with the conduct of war or defense activities.

The words "war premises" include all buildings, grounds, mines, or other places wherein such war material is being produced, manufactured, repaired, stored, mined, extracted, distributed, loaded, unloaded, or transported, together with all machinery and appliances therein contained; and all forts, arsenals, navy yards, camps, prisons, or other installations of the Armed Forces of the United States, or any associate nation.

The words "war utilities" include all railroads, railways, electric lines, roads of whatever description, any railroad or railway fixture, canal, lock, dam, wharf, pier, dock, bridge, building, structure, engine, machine, mechanical contrivance, car, vehicle, boat, aircraft, airfields, air lanes, and fixtures or appurtenances thereof, or any other means of transportation whatsoever, whereon or whereby such war material or any troops of the United States, or of any associate nation, are being or may be transported either within the limits of the United States or upon the high seas or elsewhere; and all air-conditioning systems, dams, reservoirs, aqueducts, water and gas mains and pipes, structures and buildings, whereby or in connection with which air, water or gas is being furnished, or may be furnished, to any war premises or to the Armed Forces of the United States, or any associate nation, and all electric light and power, steam or pneumatic power, telephone and telegraph plants, poles, wires, and fixtures, and wireless stations, and the buildings connected with the maintenance and operation thereof used to supply air, water, light, heat, power, or facilities of communication to any war premises or to the Armed Forces of the United States, or any associate nation.

The words "associate nation" mean any nation at war with any nation with which the United States is at war.

The words "national-defense material" include arms, armament, ammunition, livestock, forage, forest products and standing timber, stores of clothing, air, water, food, foodstuffs, fuel, supplies, munitions, and all other articles of whatever description and any part or ingredient thereof, intended for, adapted to, or suitable for the use of the United States in connection with the national defense or for use in or in connection with the producing, manufacturing, repairing, storing, mining, extracting, distributing, loading, unloading, or transporting of any of the materials or other articles hereinbefore mentioned or any part or ingredient thereof.

The words "national-defense premises" include all buildings, grounds, mines, or other places wherein such national-defense material is being produced, manufactured, repaired, stored, mined, extracted, distributed, loaded, unloaded, or transported, together with all machinery and appliances therein contained; and all forts, arsenals, navy yards, camps, prisons, or other installations of the Armed Forces of the United States.

The words "national-defense utilities" include all railroads, railways, electric lines, roads of whatever description, railroad or railway fixture, canal, lock, dam, wharf, pier, dock, bridge, building, structure, engine, machine, mechanical contrivance, car, vehicle, boat, aircraft, airfields, air lanes, and fixtures or appurtenances thereof, or any other means of transportation whatsoever, whereon or whereby such national-defense material, or any troops of the United States, are being or may be transported either within the limits of the United States or upon the high seas or elsewhere; and all air-conditioning systems, dams, reservoirs, aqueducts, water and gas mains and pipes, structures, and buildings, whereby or in connection with which air, water, or gas may be furnished to any national-defense premises or to the Armed Forces of the United States, and all electric light and power, steam or pneumatic power, telephone and telegraph plants, poles, wires, and fixtures and wireless stations, and the buildings connected with the maintenance and operation thereof used to supply air, water, light, heat, power, or facilities of communication to any national-defense premises or to the Armed Forces of the United States.

As amended June 30, 1953, c. 175, §§ 2, 7, 67 Stat. 133, 134; Sept. 3, 1954, c. 1261, Title I, § 101, 68 Stat. 1216.

18 U.S.C. §2152

Fortifications, Harbor Defenses, or Defensive Sea Areas

Whoever willfully trespasses upon, injures, or destroys any of the works or property or material of any submarine mine or torpedo or fortification or harbor-defense system owned or constructed or in process of construction by the United States; or

Whoever willfully interferes with the operation or use of any such submarine mine, torpedo, fortification, or harbor-defense system; or

Whoever knowingly, willfully, or wantonly violates any duly authorized and promulgated order or regulation of the President governing persons or vessels within the limits of defensive sea areas, which the President, for purposes of national defense, may from time to time establish by executive order—

Shall be fined not more than $5,000 or imprisoned not more than five years, or both.

18 U.S.C. §2153

Destruction of War Material, War Premises, or War Utilities

(a) Whoever, when the United States is at war, or in times of national emergency as declared by the President or by the Congress, with intent to injure, interfere with, or obstruct the United States or any associate nation in preparing for or carrying on the war or defense activities, or, with reason to believe that his act may injure, interfere with, or obstruct the United States or any associate nation in preparing for or carrying on the war or defense activities, willfully injures, destroys, contaminates or infects, or attempts to so injure, destroy, contaminate or infect any war material, war premises, or war utilities, shall be fined not more than $10,000 or imprisoned not more than thirty years, or both.

(b) If two or more persons conspire to violate this section, and one or more of such persons do any act to effect the object of the conspiracy, each of the parties to such conspiracy shall be punished as provided in subsection (a) of this section.

As amended June 30, 1953, c. 175, §§ 2, 7, 67 Stat. 133, 134; Sept. 3, 1954, c. 1261, Title I, § 102, 68 Stat. 1217.

18 U.S.C. §2154

Production of Defective War Material, War Premises, or War Utilities

(a) Whoever, when the United States is at war, or in times of national emergency as declared by the President or by the Congress, with intent to injure, interfere with, or obstruct the United States or any associate nation in preparing for or carrying on the war or defense activities, or, with reason to believe that his act may injure, interfere with, or obstruct the United States or any associate nation in preparing for or carrying on the war or defense activities, willfully makes, constructs, or causes to be made or constructed in a defective manner, or attempts to make, construct, or cause to be made or constructed in a defective manner any war material, war premises or war utilities, or any tool, implement, machine, utensil, or receptacle used or employed in making, producing, manufacturing, or repairing any such war material, war premises or war utilities, shall be fined not more than $10,000 or imprisoned not more than thirty years, or both.

(b) If two or more persons conspire to violate this section, and one or more of such persons do any act to effect the object of the conspiracy, each of the parties to such conspiracy shall be punished as provided in subsection (a) of this section.

As amended June 30, 1953, c. 175, §§ 2, 7, 67 Stat. 133, 134; Sept. 3, 1954, c. 1261, Title I, § 103, 68 Stat. 1218.

18 U.S.C. §2155

Destruction of National-Defense Materials, National-Defense Premises or National-Defense Utilities

(a) Whoever, with intent to injure, interfere with, or obstruct the national defense of the United States, willfully injures, destroys, contaminates or infects, or attempts to so injure, destroy, contaiminate or infect any national-defense material, national-defense premises, or national-defense utilities, shall be fined not more than $10,000 or imprisoned not more than ten years, or both.

(b) If two or more persons conspire to violate this section, and one or more of such persons do any act to effect the object of the conspiracy, each of the parties to such conspiracy shall be punished as provided in subsection (a) of this section.

As amended Sept. 3, 1954, c. 1261, Title I, § 104, 68 Stat. 1218.

18 U.S.C. § 2156

Production of Defective National-Defense Material, National-Defense Premises or National-Defense Utilities

(a) Whoever, with intent to injure, interfere with, or obstruct the national defense of the United States, willfully makes, constructs, or attempts to make or construct in a defective manner, any national-defense material, national-defense premises or national-defense utilities, or any tool, implement, machine, utensil, or receptacle used or employed in making, producing, manufacturing, or repairing any such national-defense material, national-defense premises or national-defense utilities, shall be fined not more than $10,000 or imprisoned not more than ten years, or both.

(b) If two or more persons conspire to violate this section, and one or more of such persons do any act to effect the object of the conspiracy, each of the parties to such conspiracy shall be punished as provided in subsection (a) of this section.

As amended Sept. 3, 1954, c. 1261, Title I, § 105, 68 Stat. 1218.

18 U.S.C. §2157

Temporary Extension of Sections 2153 and 2154

(a) The provisions of sections 2153 and 2154 of this title, as amended and extended by section 1(a) (29) of the Emergency Powers Continuation Act (66 Stat. 333), s further amended by Public Law 12, Eighty-third Congress, in addition to coming into full force and effect in time of war shall remain in full force and effect until six months after the termination of the national emergency proclaimed by the President on December 16, 1950 (Proc. 2912, 3 C.F.R., 1950 Supp., p. 71), or such earlier date as may be prescribed by concurrent resolution of the Congress, and acts which would give rise to legal consequences and penalties under any of these provisions when performed during a state of war shall give rise to the same legal consequences and penalties when they are performed during the period above provided for.

(b) Effective in each case for the period above provided for, title 18, United States Code, section 2151, as amended by inserting the words "or defense activities" immediately before the period at the end of the definition of "war material", and said sections 2153 and 2154 are amended by inserting the words "or defense activities" immediately after the words "carrying on the war" wherever they appear therein.

Added June 30, 1953, c. 175, § 2, 67 Stat. 133.

CASES

Schenck v. United States

249 U.S. 47 (1919)

Mr. Justice Holmes delivered the opinion of the court.

This is an indictment in three counts. The first charges a conspiracy to violate the

Espionage Act of June 15, 1917, c. 30, § 3, 40 Stat. 217, 219, by causing and attempting to cause insubordination, &c., in the military and naval forces of the United States, and to obstruct the recruiting and enlistment service of the United States, when the United States was at war with the German Empire, to-wit, that the defendants wilfully conspired to have printed and circulated to men who had been called and accepted for military service under the Act of May 18, 1917, a document set forth and alleged to be calculated to cause such insubordination and obstruction. The count alleges overt acts in pursuance of the conspiracy, ending in the distribution of the document set forth. The second count alleges a conspiracy to commit an offence against the United States, to-wit, to use the mails for the transmission of matter declared to be non-mailable by Title XII, § 2 of the Act of June 15, 1917, to-wit, the above mentioned document, with an averment of the same overt acts. The third count charges an unlawful use of the mails for the transmission of the same matter and otherwise as above. The defendants were found guilty on all the counts. They set up the First Amendment to the Constitution forbidding Congress to make any law abridging the freedom of speech, or of the press, and bringing the case here on that ground have argued some other points also of which we must dispose.

It is argued that the evidence, if admissible, was not sufficient to prove that the defendant Schenck was concerned in sending the documents. According to the testimony Schenck said he was general secretary of the Socialist party and had charge of the Socialist headquarters from which the documents were sent. He identified a book found there as the minutes of the Executive Committee of the party. The book showed a resolution of August 13, 1917, that 15,000 leaflets should be printed on the other side of one of them in use, to be mailed to men who had passed exemption boards, and for distribution. Schenck personally attended to the printing. On August 20 the general secretary's report said "Obtained new leaflets from printer and started work addressing envelopes" &c.; and there was a resolve that Comrade Schenck be allowed $125 for sending leaflets through the mail. He said that he had about fifteen or sixteen thousand printed. There were files of the circular in question in the inner office which he said were printed on the other side of the one sided circular and were there for distribution. Other copies were proved to have been sent through the mails to drafted men. Without going into confirmatory details that were proved, no reasonable man could doubt that the defendant Schenck was largely instrumental in sending the circulars about. As to the defendant Baer there was evidence that she was a member of the Executive Board and that the minutes of its transactions were hers. The argument as to the sufficiency of the evidence that the defendants conspired to send the documents only impairs the seriousness of the real defence.

It is objected that the documentary evidence was not admissible because obtained upon a search warrant, valid so far as appears. The contrary is established. *Adams v. New York,* 192 U.S. 585; *Weeks v. United States,* 232 U.S. 383, 395, 396. The search warrant did not issue against the defendant but against the Socialist headquarters at 1326 Arch Street and it would seem that the documents technically were not even in the defendants' possession. See *Johnson v. United States,* 228 U.S. 457. Notwithstanding some protest in argument the notion that evidence even directly proceeding from the defendant in a criminal proceeding is excluded in all cases by the Fifth Amendment is plainly unsound. *Holt v. United States,* 218 U.S. 245, 252, 253.

The document in question upon its first printed side recited the first section of the Thirteenth Amendment, said that the idea embodied in it was violated by the

Conscription Act and that a conscript is little better than a convict. In impassioned language it intimated that conscription was despotism in its worst form and a monstrous wrong against humanity in the interest of Wall Street's chosen few. It said "Do not submit to intimidation," but in form at least confined itself to peaceful measures such as a petition for the repeal of the act. The other and later printed side of the sheet was headed "Assert Your Rights." It stated reasons for alleging that any one violated the Constitution when he refused to recognize "your right to assert your opposition to the draft," and went on "If you do not assert and support your rights, you are helping to deny or disparage rights which it is the solemn duty of all citizens and residents of the United States to retain." It described the arguments on the other side as coming from cunning politicans and a mercenary capitalist press, and even silent consent to the conscription law as helping to support an infamous conspiracy. It denied the power to send our citizens away to foreign shores to shoot up the people of other lands, and added that words could not express the condemnation such cold-blooded ruthlessness deserves, &c., &c., winding up "You must do your share to maintain, support and uphold the rights of the people of this country." Of course the document would not have been sent unless it had been intended to have some effect, and we do not see what effect it could be expected to have upon persons subject to the draft except to influence them to obstruct the carrying of it out. The defendants do not deny that the jury might find against them on this point.

But it is said, suppose that that was the tendency of this circular, it is protected by the First Amendment to the Constitution. Two of the strongest expressions are said to be quoted respectively from well-known public men. It well may be that the prohibition of laws abridging the freedom of speech is not confined to previous restraints, although to prevent them may have been the main purpose, as intimated in *Patterson v. Colorado,* 205 U.S. 454, 462. We admit that in many places and in ordinary times the defendants in saying all that was said in the circular would have been within their constitutional rights. But the character of every act depends upon the circumstances in which it is done. *Aikens v. Wisconsin,* 195 U.S. 194, 205, 206. The most stringent protection of free speech would not protect a man in falsely shouting fire in a theatre and causing a panic. It does not even protect a man from an injunction against uttering words that may have all the effect of force. *Gompers v. Bucks Stove & Range Co.,* 221 U.S. 418, 439. The question in every case is whether the words used are used in such circumstances and are of such a nature as to create a clear and present danger that they will bring about the substantive evils that Congress has a right to prevent. It is a question of proximity and degree. When a nation is at war many things that might be said in time of peace are such a hindrance to its effort that their utterance will not be endured so long as men fight and that no Court could regard them as protected by any constitutional right. It seems to be admitted that if an actual obstruction of the recruiting service were proved, liability for words that produced that effect might be enforced. The statute of 1917 in § 4 punishes conspiracies to obstruct as well as actual obstruction. If the act, (speaking, or circulating a paper,) its tendency and the intent with which it is done are the same, we perceive no ground for saying that success alone warrant making the act a crime. *Goldman v. United States,* 245 U.S. 474, 477. Indeed that case might be said to dispose of the present contention if the precedent covers all *media concludendi.* But as the right to free speech was not referred to specially, we have thought fit to add a few words.

It was not argued that a conspiracy to obstruct the draft was not within the words of the Act of 1917. The words are "obstruct the recruiting or enlistment service," and it might be suggested that they refer only to making it hard to get volunteers. Recruiting heretofore usually having been accomplished by getting volunteers the word is apt to call up that method only in our minds. But recruiting is gaining fresh supplies for the forces, as well by draft as otherwise. It is put as an alternative to enlistment or voluntary enrollment in this act. The fact that the Act of 1917 was enlarged by the amending Act of May 16, 1918, c. 75, 40 Stat. 553, of course, does not affect the present indictment and would not, even if the former act had been repealed. Rev. Stats., § 13.

Judgments affirmed.

United States v. O'Brien

391 U.S. 367 (1968)

Mr. Chief Justice Warren delivered the opinion of the Court.

On the morning of March 31, 1966, David Paul O'Brien and three companions burned their Selective Service registration certificates on the steps of the South Boston Courthouse. A sizable crowd, including several agents of the Federal Bureau of Investigation, witnessed the event.[1] Immediately after the burning, members of the crowd began attacking O'Brien and his companions. An FBI agent ushered O'Brien to safety inside the courthouse. After he was advised of his right to counsel and to silence, O'Brien stated to FBI agents that he had burned his registration certificate because of his beliefs, knowing that he was violating federal law. He produced the charred remains of the certificate, which, with his consent, were photographed.

For this act, O'Brien was indicted, tried, convicted, and sentenced in the United States District Court for the District of Massachusetts.[2] He did not contest the fact that he had burned the certificate. He stated in argument to the jury that he burned the certificate publicly to influence others to adopt his antiwar beliefs, as he put it, "so that other people would reevaluate their positions with Selective Service, with the armed forces, and reevaluate their place in the culture of today, to hopefully consider my position."

The indictment upon which he was tried charged that he "willfully and knowingly did mutilate, destroy, and change by burning . . . [his] Registration Certificate (Selective Service System Form No. 2); in violation of Title 50, App., United States Code, Section 462(b)." Section 462(b) is part of the Universal Military Training and Service Act of 1948. Section 462(b)(3), one of six numbered subdivisions of § 462(b), was amended by Congress in 1965, 79 Stat. 586 (adding the words italicized below), so that at the time O'Brien burned his certificate an offense was commited by any person,

> "who forges, alters, *knowingly destroys, knowingly mutilates,* or in any manner changes any such certificate. . . ." (Italics supplied.)

In the District Court, O'Brien argued that the 1965 Amendment prohibiting the knowing destruction or mutilation of certificates was unconstitutional because it was enacted to abridge free speech, and because it served no legitimate legislative purpose.[3] The District Court rejected these arguments, holding that the statute on its face did not abridge First Amendment rights, that the court was not competent to inquire into the motives of Congress in enacting the 1965 Amendment, and that the Amendment was a reasonable exercise of the power of Congress to raise armies.

On appeal, the Court of Appeals for the First Circuit held the 1965 Amendment unconstitutional as a law abridging freedom of speech.[4] At the time the Amendment was enacted, a regulation of the Selective Service System required registrants to keep their registration certificates in their "personal possession at all times." 32 CFR § 1617.1 (1962).[5] Wilful violations of regulations promulgated pursuant to the Universal Military Training and Service Act were made criminal by statute. 50 U. S. C. App. § 462(b)(6). The Court of Appeals, therefore, was of the opinion that conduct punishable under the 1965 Amendment was already punishable under the nonpossession regulation, and consequently that the Amendment served no valid purpose; further, that in light of the prior regulation, the Amendment must have been "directed at public as distinguished from private destruction." On this basis, the court concluded that the 1965 Amendment ran afoul of the First Amendment by singling out persons engaged in protests for special treatment. The court ruled, however, that O'Brien's conviction should be affirmed under the statutory provision, 50 U. S. C. App. § 462(b)(6), which in its view made violation of the nonpossession regulation a crime, because it regarded such violation to be a lesser included offense of the crime defined by the 1965 Amendment.[6]

The Government petitioned for certiorari in No. 232, arguing that the Court of Appeals erred in holding the statute unconstitutional, and that its decision conflicted with decisions by the Courts of Appeals for the Second[7] and Eighth Circuits[8] upholding the 1965 Amendment against identical constitutional challenges. O'Brien cross-petitioned for certiorari in No. 233, arguing that the Court of Appeals erred in sustaining his conviction on the basis of a crime of which he was neither charged nor tried. We granted the Government's petition to resolve the conflict in the circuits, and we also granted O'Brien's cross-petition. We hold that the 1965 Amendment is constitutional both as enacted and as applied. We therefore vacate the judgment of the Court of Appeals and reinstate the judgment and sentence of the District Court without reaching the issue raised by O'Brien in No. 233.

I.

When a male reaches the age of 18, he is required by the Universal Military Training and Service Act to register with a local draft board.[9] He is assigned a Selective Service number,[10] and within five days he is issued a registration certificate (SSS Form No. 2).[11] Subsequently, and based on a questionnaire completed by the registrant,[12] he is assigned a classification denoting his eligibility for induction,[13] and "[a]s soon as practicable" thereafter he is issued a Notice of Classification (SSS Form No. 110).[14] This initial classification is not necessarily permanent,[15] and if in the interim before induction the registrant's status changes in some relevant way, he may be reclassified.[16] After such a reclassification, the local board "as soon as practicable" issues to the registrant a new Notice of Classification.[17]

Both the registration and classification certificates are small white cards, approximately 2 by 3 inches. The registration certificate specifies the name of the registrant, the date of registration, and the number and address of the local board with which he is registered. Also inscribed upon it are the date and place of the registrant's birth, his residence at registration, his physical description, his signature, and his Selective Service number. The Selective Service number itself indicates his State of registration, his local board, his year of birth, and his chronological position in the local board's classification record.[18]

The classification certificate shows the registrant's name, Selective Service number, signature, and eligibility classification. It specifies whether he was so classified by his local board, an appeal board, or the President. It contains the address of his local board and the date the certificate was mailed.

Both the registration and classification certificates bear notices that the registrant must notify his local board in writing of every change in address, physical condition, and occupational, marital, family, dependency, and military status, and of any other fact which might change his classification. Both also contain a notice that the registrant's Selective Service number should appear on all communications to his local board.

Congress demonstrated its concern that certificates issued by the Selective Service System might be abused well before the 1965 Amendment here challenged. The 1948 Act, 62 Stat. 604, itself prohibited many different abuses involving "any registration certificate, . . . or any other certificate issued pursuant to or prescribed by the provisions of this title, or rules or regulations promulgated hereunder. . . ." 62 Stat. 622. Under §§ 12(b)(1)-(5) of the 1948 Act, it was unlawful (1) to transfer a certificate to aid a person in making false identification; (2) to possess a certificate not duly issued with the intent of using it for false identification; (3) to forge, alter, "or in any manner" change a certificate or any notation validly inscribed thereon; (4) to photograph or make an imitation of a certificate for the purpose of false identification; and (5) to possess a counterfeited or altered certificate. 62 Stat. 622. In addition, as previously mentioned, regulations of the Selective Service System required registrants to keep both their registration and classification certificates in their personal possession at all times. 32 CFR § 1617.1 (1962) (Registration Certificates);[19] 32 CFR § 1623.5 (1962) (Classification Certificates).[20] And § 12(b)(6) of the Act, 62 Stat. 622, made knowing violation of any provision of the Act or rules and regulations promulgated pursuant thereto a felony.

By the 1965 Amendment, Congress added to § 12(b)(3) of the 1948 Act the provision here at issue, subjecting to criminal liability not only one who "forges, alters, or in any manner changes" but also one who "knowingly destroys, [or] knowingly mutilates" a certificate. We note at the outset that the 1965 Amendment plainly does not abridge free speech on its face, and we do not understand O'Brien to argue otherwise. Amended § 12(b)(3) on its face deals with conduct having no connection with speech. It prohibits the knowing destruction of certificates issued by the Selective Service System, and there is nothing necessarily expressive about such conduct. The Amendment does not distinguish between public and private destruction, and it does not punish only destruction engaged in for the purpose of expressing views. Compare *Stromberg v. California,* 283 U.S. 359 (1931).[21] A law prohibiting destruction of Selective Service certificates no more abridges free speech on its face than a motor vehicle law prohibiting the destruction of drivers' licenses, or a tax law prohibiting the destruction of books and records.

O'Brien nonetheless argues that the 1965 Amendment is unconstitutional in its application to him, and is unconstitutional as enacted because what he calls the "purpose" of Congress was "to suppress freedom of speech." We consider these arguments separately.

II.

O'Brien first argues that the 1965 Amendment is unconstitutional as applied to him because his act of burning his registration certificate was protected "symbolic speech" within the First Amendment. His argument is that the freedom of expression which the First Amendment guarantees includes all modes of "communication of ideas by conduct," and that his conduct is within this definition because he did it in "demonstration against the war and against the draft."

We cannot accept the view that an apparently limitless variety of conduct can be labeled "speech" whenever the person engaging in the conduct intends thereby to express an idea. However, even on the assumption that the alleged communicative element in O'Brien's conduct is sufficient to bring into play the First Amendment, it does not necessarily follow that the destruction of a registration certificate is constitutionally protected activity. This Court has held that when "speech" and "nonspeech" elements are combined in the same course of conduct, a sufficiently important governmental interest in regulating the nonspeech element can justify incidental limitations on First Amendment freedoms. To characterize the quality of the governmental interest which must appear, the Court has employed a variety of descriptive terms: compelling;[22] substantial;[23] subordinating;[24] paramount;[25] cogent; [26] strong.[27]. Whatever imprecision inheres in these terms, we think it clear that a government regulation is sufficiently justified if it is within the constitutional power of the Government; if it furthers an important or substantial governmental interest; if the governmental interest is unrelated to the suppression of free expression; and if the incidental restriction on alleged First Amendment freedoms is no greater than is essential to the furtherance of that interest. We find that the 1965 Amendment to § 12(b)(3) of the Universal Military Training and Service Act meets all of these requirements, and consequently that O'Brien can be constitutionally convicted for violating it.

The constitutional power of Congress to raise and support armies and to make all laws necessary and proper to that end is broad and sweeping. *Lichter v. United States,* 334 U.S. 742, 755-758 (1948); *Selective Draft Law Cases,* 245 U.S. 366 (1918); see also *Ex parte Quirin,* 317 U.S. 1, 25-26 (1942). The power of Congress to classify and conscript manpower for military service is "beyond question." *Lichter v. United States, supra,* at 756; *Selective Draft Law Cases, supra.* Pursuant to this power, Congress may establish a system of registration for individuals liable for training and service, and may require such individuals within reason to cooperate in the registration system. The issuance of certificates indicating the registration and eligibility classification of individuals is a legitimate and substantial administrative aid in the functioning of this system. And legislation to insure the continuing availability of issued certificates serves a legitimate and substantial purpose in the system's administration.

O'Brien's argument to the contrary is necessarily premised upon his unrealistic characterization of Selective Service certificates. He essentially adopts the position that such certificates are so many pieces of paper designed to notify registrants of their registration or classification, to be retained or tossed in the wastebasket according to the convenience or taste of the registrant. Once the registrant has received notification, according to this view, there is no reason for him to retain the certificates. O'Brien notes that most of the information on a registration certificate serves no notification purpose at all; the registrant hardly needs to be told his address and physical characteristics. We agree that the registration certificate contains much information of which the registrant needs no notification. This circumstance, however, does not lead to the conclusion that the certificate serves no purpose, but that, like the classification certificate, it serves purposes in addition to initial notification. Many of these purposes would be defeated by the certificates' destruction or mutilation. Among these are:

1. The registration certificate serves as proof that the individual described thereon has registered for the draft. The classification certificate shows the eligibility classification of a named but undescribed individual. Voluntarily displaying the two certificates is an easy and painless way for a young man to dispel a question as to whether he might be delinquent in his Selective Service obligations. Correspondingly, the availability of the certificates for such display relieves the Selective Service System of the administrative burden it would otherwise have in veryifying the registration and classification of all suspected delinquents. Further, since both certificates are in the nature of "receipts" attesting that the registrant has done what the law requires, it is in the interest of the just and efficient administration of the system that they be continually available, in the event, for example, of a mix-up in the registrant's file. Additionally, in a time of national crisis, reasonable availability to each registrant of the two small cards assures a rapid and uncomplicated means for determining his fitness for immediate induction, no matter how distant in our mobile society he may be from his local board.

2. The information supplied on the certificates facilitates communication between registrants and local boards, simplifying the system and benefiting all concerned. To begin with, each certificate bears the address of the registrant's local board, an item unlikely to be committed to memory. Further, each card bears the registrant's Selective Service number, and a registrant who has his number readily available so that he can communicate it to his local board when he supplies or requests information can make simpler the board's task in locating his file. Finally, a registrant's inquiry, particularly through a local board other than his own, concerning his eligibility status is frequently answerable simply on the basis of his classification certificate; whereas, if the certificate were not reasonably available and the registrant were uncertain of his classification, the task of answering his questions would be considerably complicated.

3. Both certificates carry continual reminders that the registrant must notify his local board of any change of address, and other specified changes in his status. The smooth functioning of the system requires that local boards be continually aware of the status and whereabouts of registrants, and the destruction of certificates deprives the system of a potentially useful notice device.

4. The regulatory scheme involving Selective Service certificates includes clearly valid prohibitions against the alteration, forgery, or similar deceptive misuse of certificates. The destruction or mutilation of certificates obviously increases the difficulty of detecting and tracing abuses such as these. Further, a mutilated certificate might itself be used for deceptive purposes.

The many functions performed by Selective Service certificates establish beyond doubt that Congress has a legitimate and substantial interest in preventing their wanton and unrestrained destruction and assuring their continuing availability by punishing people who knowingly and wilfully destroy or mutilate them. And we are unpersuaded that the pre-existence of the nonpossession regulations in any way negates this interest.

In the absence of a question as to multiple punishment, it has never been suggested that there is anything improper in Congress' providing alternative statutory avenues of prosecution to assure the effective protection of one and the same interest. Compare the majority and dissenting opinions in *Gore v. United States,* 357 U.S. 386 (1958).[28] Here, the pre-existing avenue of prosecution was not even statutory. Regulations may be modified or revoked from time to time by administrative discretion. Certainly, the Congress may change or supplement a regulation.

Equally important, a comparison of the regulations with the 1965 Amendment indicates that they protect overlapping but not identical governmental interests, and that they reach somewhat different classes of wrongdoers.[29] The gravamen of the offense defined by the statute is the deliberate rendering of certificates unavailable for the various purposes which they may serve. Whether registrants keep their certificates in their personal possession at all times, as required by the regulations, is of no particular concern under the 1965 Amendment, as long as they do not mutilate or destroy the certificates so as to render them unavailable. Although as we note below we are not concerned here with the nonpossession regulations, it is not inappropriate to observe that the essential elements of nonpossession are not identical with those of mutilation or destruction. Finally, the 1965 Amendment, like § 12(b) which it amended, is concerned with abuses involving *any* issued Selective Service certificates, not only with the registrant's own certificates. The knowing destruction or mutilation of someone else's certificates would therefore violate the statute but not the nonpossession regulations.

We think it apparent that the continuing availability to each registrant of his Selective Service certificates substantially furthers the smooth and proper functioning of the system that Congress has established to raise armies. We think it also apparent that the Nation has a vital interest in having a system for raising armies that functions with maximum efficiency and is capable of easily and quickly responding to continually changing circumstances. For these reasons, the Government has a substantial interest in assuring the continuing availability of issued Selective Service certificates.

It is equally clear that the 1965 Amendment specifically protects this substantial governmental interest. We perceive no alternative means that would more precisely and narrowly assure the continuing availability of issued Selective Service certificates than a law which prohibits their wilful mutilation or destruction. Compare *Sherbert v. Verner,* 374 U.S. 398, 407-408 (1963), and the cases cited therein. The 1965 Amendment prohibits such conduct and does nothing more. In other words, both the governmental interest and the operation of the 1965 Amendment are limited to the noncommunicative aspect of O'Brien's conduct. The governmental interest and the scope of the 1965 Amendment are limited to preventing harm to the smooth and efficient functioning of the Selective Service System. When O'Brien deliberately rendered unavailable his registration certificate, he wilfully frustrated this governmental interest. For this noncommunicative impact of his conduct, and for nothing else, he was convicted.

The case at bar is therefore unlike one where the alleged governmental interest in regulating conduct arises in some measure because the communication allegedly integral to the conduct is itself thought to be harmful. In *Stromberg v. California,* 283 U.S. 359 (1931), for example, this Court struck down a statutory phrase which punished people who expressed their "opposition to organized government" by displaying "any flag, badge, banner, or device." Since the statute there was aimed at suppressing communication it could not be sustained as a regulation of noncommunicative conduct. See also, *NLRB v. Fruit & Vegetable Packers Union,* 377 U.S. 58, 79 (1964) (concurring opinion).

In conclusion, we find that because of the Government's substantial interest in assuring the continuing availability of issued Selective Service certificates, because amended § 462(b) is an appropriately narrow means of protecting this interest and condemns only the independent noncommunicative impact of conduct within its reach, and because the noncommunicative impact of O'Brien's act of burning his registration certificate frustrated the Government's interest, a sufficient governmental interest has been shown to justify O'Brien's conviction.

III.

O'Brien finally argues that the 1965 Amendment is unconstitutional as enacted because what he calls the "purpose" of Congress was "to suppress freedom of speech." We reject this argument because under settled principles the purpose of Congress, as O'Brien uses that term, is not a basis for declaring this legislation unconstitutional.

It is a familiar principle of constitutional law that this Court will not strike down an otherwise constitutional statute on the basis of an alleged illicit legislative motive. As the Court long ago stated:

> "The decisions of this court from the beginning lend no support whatever to the assumption that the judiciary may restrain the exercise of lawful power on the assumption that a wrongful purpose or motive has caused the power to be exerted." *McCray v. United States,* 195 U.S. 27, 56 (1904).

This fundamental principle of constitutional adjudication was reaffirmed and the many cases were collected by Mr. Justice Brandeis for the Court in *Arizona v. California,* 283 U.S. 423, 455 (1931).

Inquiries into congressional motives or purposes are a hazardous matter. When the issue is simply the interpretation of legislation, the Court will look to statements by legislators for guidance as to the purpose of the legislature,[30] because the benefit to sound decision-making in this circumstance is thought sufficient to risk the possibility of misreading Congress' purpose. It is entirely a different matter when we are asked to void a statute that is, under well-settled criteria, constitutional on its face, on the basis of what fewer than a handful of Congressmen said about it. What motivates one legislator to make a speech about a statute is not necessarily what motivates scores of others to enact it, and the stakes are sufficiently high for us to eschew guesswork. We decline to void essentially on the ground that it is unwise legislation which Congress had the undoubted power to enact and which could be reenacted in its exact form if the same or another legislator made a "wiser" speech about it.

O'Brien's position, and to some extent that of the court below, rest upon a misunderstanding of *Grosjean v. American Press Co.,* 297 U.S. 233 (1936), and *Gomillion v. Lightfoot,* 364 U.S. 339 (1960). These cases stand, not for the proposition that legislative motive is a proper basis for declaring a statute unconstitutional, but that the inevitable effect of a statute on its face may render it unconstitutional. Thus, in *Grosjean* the Court, having concluded that the right of publications to be free from certain kinds of taxes was a freedom of the press protected by the First Amendment, struck down a statute which on its face did nothing other than impose just such a tax. Similarly, in *Gomillion,* the Court sustained a complaint which, if true, established that the "inevitable effect," 364

U.S., at 341, of the redrawing of municipal boundaries was to deprive the petitioners of their right to vote for no reason other than that they were Negro. In these cases, the purpose of the legislation was irrelevant, because the inevitable effect—the "necessary scope and operation," *McCray v. United States,* 195 U.S. 27, 59 (1904)—abridged constitutional rights. The statute attacked in the instant case has no such inevitable unconstitutional effect, since the destruction of Selective Service certificates is in no respect inevitably or necessarily expressive. Accordingly, the statute itself is constitutional.

We think it not amiss, in passing, to comment upon O'Brien's legislative-purpose argument. There was little floor debate on this legislation in either House. Only Senator Thurmond commented on its substantive features in the Senate. 111 Cong. Rec. 19746, 20433. After his brief statement, and without any additional substantive comments, the bill, H. R. 10306, passed the Senate. 111 Cong. Rec. 20434. In the House debate only two Congressmen addressed themselves to the Amendment—Congressmen Rivers and Bray. 111 Cong. Rec. 19871, 19872. The bill was passed after their statements without any further debate by a vote of 393 to 1. It is principally on the basis of the statements by these three Congressmen that O'Brien makes his congressional-"purpose" argument. We note that if we were to examine legislative purpose in the instant case, we would be obliged to consider not only these statements but also the more authoritative reports of the Senate and House Armed Services Committees. The portions of those reports explaining the purpose of the Amendment are reproduced in the Appendix in their entirety. While both reports make clear a concern with the "defiant" destruction of so-called "draft cards" and with "open" encouragement to others to destroy their cards, both reports also indicate that this concern stemmed from an apprehension that unrestrained destruction of cards would disrupt the smooth functioning of the Selective Service System.

IV.

Since the 1965 Amendment to § 12(b)(3) of the Universal Military Training and Service Act is constitutional as enacted and as applied, the Court of Appeals should have affirmed the judgment of conviction entered by the District Court. Accordingly, we vacate the judgment of the Court of Appeals, and reinstate the judgment and sentence of the District Court. This disposition makes unnecessary consideration of O'Brien's claim that the Court of Appeals erred in affirming his conviction on the basis of the nonpossession regulation.[31]

It is so ordered.

Mr. Justice Marshall took no part in the consideration or decision of these cases.

Mr. Justice Douglas, dissenting. . . .

---

[1]At the time of the burning, the agents knew only that O'Brien and his three companions had burned small white cards. They later discovered that the card O'Brien burned was his registration certificate, and the undisputed assumption is that the same is true of his companions.

[2]He was sentenced under the Youth Corrections Act, 18 U. S. C. § 5010 (b), to the custody of the Attorney General for a maximum period of six years for supervision and treatment.

[3]The issue of the constitutionality of the 1965 Amendment was raised by counsel representing O'Brien in a pretrial motion to dismiss the indictment. At trial and upon sentencing, O'Brien chose to represent himself. He was represented by counsel on his appeal to the Court of Appeals.

[4]*O'Brien v. United States,* 376 F. 2d 538 (C. A. 1st Cir. 1967).

[5]The portion of 32 CFR relevant to the instant case was revised as of January 1, 1967. Citations in this opinion are to the 1962 edition which was in effect when O'Brien committed the crime, and when Congress enacted the 1965 Amendment.

[6]The Court of Appeals nevertheless remanded the case to the District Court to vacate the sentence and resentence O'Brien. In the court's view, the district judge might have considered the violation of the 1965 Amendment as an aggravating circumstance in imposing sentence. The Court of Appeals subsequently denied O'Brien's petition for a rehearing, in which he argued that he had not been charged, tried, or convicted for nonpossession, and that nonpossession was not a lesser included offense of mutilation or destruction. *O'Brien v. United States,* 376 F. 2d 538, 542 (C. A. 1st Cir. 1967).

[7]*United States v. Miller,* 367 F. 2d 72 (C. A. 2d Cir. 1966), cert. denied, 386 U.S. 911 (1967).

[8]*Smith v. United States,* 368 F. 2d 529 (C. A. 8th Cir. 1966).

[9]See 62 Stat. 605, as amended, 65 Stat. 76, 50 U. S. C. App. § 453; 32 CFR § 1613.1 (1962).

[10]32 CFR § 1621.2 (1962).

[11]32 CFR § 1613.43a (1962).

[12]32 CFR §§ 1621.9, 1623.1 (1962).

[13]32 CFR §§ 1623.1, 1623.2 (1962).

[14]32 CFR § 1623.4 (1962).

[15]32 CFR § 1625.1 (1962).

[16]32 CFR §§ 1625.1, 1625.2, 1625.3, 1625.4, and 1625.11 (1962).

[17]32 CFR § 1625.12 (1962).

[18]32 CFR § 1621.2 (1962).

[19]32 CFR § 1617.1 (1962), provides, in relevant part:

"Every person required to present himself for and submit to registration must, after he is registered, have in his personal possession at all times his Registration Certificate (SSS Form No. 2) prepared by his local board which has not been altered and on which no notation duly and validly inscribed thereon has been changed in any manner after its preparation by the local board. The failure of any person to have his Registration Certificate (SSS Form No. 2) in his personal possession shall be prima facie evidence of his failure to register."

[20]32 CFR § 1623.5 (1962), provides, in relevant part:

"Every person who has been classified by a local board must have in his personal possession at all times, in addition to his Registration Certificate (SSS Form No. 2), a valid Notice of Classification (SSS Form No. 110) issued to him showing his current classification."

[21]See text, *infra,* at 382.

[22]*NAACP v. Button,* 371 U.S. 415, 438 (1963); see also *Sherbert v. Verner,* 374 U.S. 398, 403 (1963).

[23]*NAACP v. Button,* 371 U.S. 415, 444 (1963); *NAACP v. Alabama ex rel. Patterson,* 357 U.S. 449, 464 (1958).

[24]*Bates v. Little Rock,* 361 U.S. 516, 524 (1960).

[25]*Thomas v. Collins,* 323 U.S. 516, 530 (1945); see also *Sherbert v. Verner,* 374 U.S. 398, 406 (1963).

[26]*Bates v. Little Rock,* 361 U.S. 516, 524 (1960).

[27]*Sherbert v. Verner,* 374 U.S. 398, 408 (1963).

[28]Cf. *Milanovich v. United States,* 365 U.S. 551 (1961); *Heflin v. United States,* 358 U.S. 415 (1959); *Prince v. United States,* 352 U.S. 322 (1957).

[29]Cf. *Milanovich v. United States,* 365 U.S. 551 (1961); *Heflin v. United States,* 358 U.S. 415 (1959); *Prince v. United States,* 352 U.S. 322 (1957).

[30]The Court may make the same assumption in a very limited and well-defined class of cases where the very nature of the constitutional question requires an inquiry into legislative purpose. The principal class of cases is readily apparent—those in which statutes have been challenged as bills of attainder. This Court's decisions have defined a bill of attainder as a legislative Act which inflicts punishment on named individuals or members of an easily ascertainable group without a judicial trial. In determining whether a particular statute is a bill of attainder, the analysis necessarily requires an inquiry into whether the three definitional elements—specificity in identification, punishment, and lack of a judicial trial—are contained in the statute. The inquiry into whether the challenged statute contains the necessary element of punishment has on occasion led the Court to examine the legislative motive in enacting the statute. See, *e.g., United States v. Lovett,* 328 U.S. 303 (1946). Two

other decisions not involving a bill of attainder analysis contain an inquiry into legislative purpose or motive of the type that O'Brien suggests we engage in in this case. *Kennedy v. Mendoza-Martinez,* 372 U.S. 144, 169-184 (1963); *Trop v. Dulles,* 356 U.S. 86, 95-97 (1958). The inquiry into legislative purpose or motive in *Kennedy* and *Trop,* however, was for the same limited purpose as in the bill of attainder decisions—*i.e.,* to determine whether the statutes under review were punitive in nature. We face no such inquiry in this case. The 1965 Amendment to § 462(b) was clearly penal in nature, designed to impose criminal punishment for designated acts.

Brandenburg v. Ohio

395 U.S. 444 (1969)

Per Curiam.

The appellant, a leader of a Ku Klux Klan group, was convicted under the Ohio Criminal Syndicalism statute for "advocat[ing] . . . the duty, necessity, or propriety of crime, sabotage, violence, or unlawful methods of terrorism as a means of accomplishing industrial or political reform" and for "voluntarily assembl[ing] with any society, group, or assemblage of persons formed to teach or advocate the doctrines of criminal syndicalism." Ohio Rev. Code Ann. § 2923.13. He was fined $1,000 and sentenced to one to 10 years' imprisonment. The appellant challenged the constitutionality of the criminal syndicalism statute under the First and Fourteenth Amendments to the United States Constitution, but the intermediate appellate court of Ohio affirmed his conviction without opinion. The Supreme Court of Ohio dismissed his appeal, *sua sponte,* "for the reason that no substantial constitutional question exists herein." It did not file an opinion or explain its conclusions. Appeal was taken to this Court, and we noted probable jurisdiction. 393 U.S. 948 (1968). We reverse.

The records shows that a man, identified at trial as the appellant, telephoned an announcer-reporter on the staff of a Cincinnati television station and invited him to come to a Ku Klux Klan "rally" to be held at a farm in Hamilton County. With the cooperation of the organizers, the reporter and a cameraman attended the meeting and filmed the events. Portions of the films were later broadcast on the local station and on a national network.

The prosecution's case rested on the films and on testimony identifying the appellant as the person who communicated with the reporter and who spoke at the rally. The State also introduced into evidence several articles appearing in the film, including a pistol, a rifle, a shotgun, ammunition, a Bible, and a red hood worn by the speaker in the films.

One film showed 12 hooded figures, some of whom carried firearms. They were gathered around a large wooden cross, which they burned. No one was present other than the participants and the newsmen who made the film. Most of the words uttered during the scene were incomprehensible when the film was projected, but scattered phrases could be understood that were derogatory of Negroes and, in one instance, of Jews. Another scene on the same film showed the appellant, in Klan regalia, making a speech. The speech, in full, was as follows:

> "This is an organizers' meeting. We have had quite a few members here today which are—we have hundreds, hundreds of members throughout the State of Ohio. I can quote from a newspaper clipping from the Columbus, Ohio Dispatch, five weeks ago Sunday morning. The Klan has more members

> in the State of Ohio than does any other organization. We're not a revengent organization, but if our President, our Congress, our Supreme Court, continues to suppress the white, Caucasian race, it's possible that there might have to be some revengeance taken.
>
> "We are marching on Congress July the Fourth, four hundred thousand strong. From there we are dividing into two groups, one group to march on St. Augustine, Florida, the other group to march into Mississippi. Thank you."

The second film showed six hooded figures one of whom, later identified as the appellant, repeated a speech very similar to that recorded on the first film. The reference to the possibility of "revengeance" was omitted, and one sentence was added: "Personally, I believe the nigger should be returned to Africa, the Jew returned to Israel." Though some of the figures in the films carried weapons, the speaker did not.

The Ohio Criminal Syndicalism Statute was enacted in 1919. From 1917 to 1920, identical or quite similar laws were adopted by 20 States and two territories. E. Dowell, A History of Criminal Syndicalism Legislation in the United States 21 (1939). In 1927, this Court sustained the constitutionality of California's Criminal Syndicalism Act, Cal. Penal Code §§ 11400-11402, the text of which is quite similar to that of the laws of Ohio. *Whitney v. California,* 274 U.S. 357 (1927). The Court upheld the statute on the ground that, without more, "advocating" violent means to effect political and economic change involves such danger to the security of the State that the State may outlaw it. Cf. *Fiske v. Kansas,* 274 U.S. 380 (1927). But *Whitney* has been thoroughly discredited by later decisions. See *Dennis v. United States,* 341 U.S. 494, at 507 (1951). These later decisions have fashioned the principle that the constitutional guarantees of free speech and free press do not permit a State to forbid or proscribe advocacy of the use of force or of law violation except where such advocacy is directed to inciting or producing imminent lawless action and is likely to incite or produce such action. As we said in *Noto v. United States,* 367 U.S. 290, 297-298 (1961), "the mere abstract teaching . . . of the moral propriety or even moral necessity for a resort to force and violence, is not the same as preparing a group for violent action and steeling it to such action." See also *Herndon v. Lowry,* 301 U.S. 242, 259-261 (1937); *Bond v. Floyd,* 385 U.S. 116, 134 (1966). A statute which fails to draw this distinction impermissibly intrudes upon the freedoms guaranteed by the First and Fourteenth Amendments. It sweeps within its condemnation speech which our Constitution has immunized from governmental control. Cf. *Yates v. United States,* 354 U.S. 298 (1957); *De Jonge v. Oregon,* 299 U.S. 353 (1937); *Stromberg v. California,* 283 U.S. 359 (1931). See also *United States v. Robel,* 389 U.S. 258 (1967); *Keyishian v. Board of Regents,* 385 U.S. 589 (1967); *Elfbrandt v. Russell,* 384 U.S. 11 (1966); *Aphtheker v. Secretary of State,* 378 U.S. 500 (1964); *Baggett v. Bullitt,* 377 U.S. 360 (1964).

Measured by this test, Ohio's Criminal Syndicalism Act cannot be sustained. The Act punishes persons who "advocate or teach the duty, necessity, or propriety" of violence "as a means of accomplishing industrial or political reform"; or who publish or circulate or display any book or paper containing such advocacy; or who "justify" the commission of violent acts "with intent to exemplify, spread or advocate the propriety of the doctrines of criminal syndicalism"; or who "voluntarily assemble" with a group formed "to teach or advocate the doctrines of criminal syndicalism." Neither the indictment nor the trial judge's instructions to the jury in any way refined the statute's bald definition of the crime in terms of mere advocacy not distinguished from incitement to imminent lawless action.

Accordingly, we are here confronted with a statute which, by its own words and as applied, purports to punish mere advocacy and to forbid, on pain of criminal punishment, assembly with others merely to advocate the described type of action. Such a statute falls within the condemnation of the First and Fourteenth Amendments. The contrary teaching of *Whitney v. California, supra,* cannot be supported, and that decision is therefore overruled.

Reversed.

United States v. Spock

416 F.2d 165 (1st Cir. 1969)

Aldrich, Chief Judge.

These are appeals by four defendants[1] convicted under a single count indictment for conspiracy. We reverse.

As is well known, the war in Vietnam and the draft to support it have engendered considerable animosity and frustration. In August 1967 a number of academic, clerical, and professional persons discussed the need of more vigorous opposition to governmental policies. From their eventually consolidated efforts came a document entitled "A Call to Resist Illegitimate Authority" (hereinafter the Call) and a cover letter requesting signatures and support. The letter was signed by defendant Dr. Benjamin Spock and defendant Rev. William Sloane Coffin, Jr., and two other persons. The Call was originally signed by them, numerous others, and eventually by hundreds. The defendant Mitchell Goodman had been preparing a somewhat similar statement against the war and the draft. In mid-September he learned of the Call, which he also signed. He, Coffin, Spock and others spoke on October 2 at a press conference in New York City to launch the Call. It was there announced by Goodman that further activities were contemplated, including a nationwide collection of draft cards and a ceremonial surrender thereof to the Attorney General. On October 16 a draft card burning and turn-in took place at the Arlington Street Church in Boston, arranged by the defendant Michael Ferber, and participated in by Coffin. Four days afterwards all four defendants attended a demonstration in Washington, in the course of which an unsuccessful attempt was made to present the fruits of that collection and similar gatherings to the Attorney General.[2] The details of these matters will be discussed later.

[1] The indictment was framed under section 12 of the Military Selective Service Act of 1967, 50 App. U.S.C. § 462(a). It charged that defendants, and others known and unknown, conspired to "counsel, aid and abet diverse Selective Service registrants to . . . neglect, fail, refuse and evade service in the armed forces of the United States and all other duties required of registrants under the Universal Military Training and Service Act . . . and the rules, regulations and directions duly made pursuant to said Act . . . to . . . fail and refuse to have in their personal possession at all times their registration certificates [and] . . . valid notices of classification[3] [and conspired to] . . . unlawfully, willfully and knowingly hinder and interfere, by any means, with the administration of the Universal Military Training and Service Act."[4] The case was tried to a jury, which answered special

questions framed by the court, most answers being unfavorable to the defendants, and returned general verdicts of guilty. On this appeal defendants raise a number of issues, the most basic of which is their asserted right to directed acquittals, either because of constitutional immunity or because the government failed in its proof. We consider these contentions in that order.

I

[2] Inseparable from the question of the sufficiency of the evidence to convict are the rights of the defendants, and others,[5] under the First Amendment. We approach the constitutional problem on the assumption, which we will later support, that the ultimate objective of defendants' alleged agreement, viz., the expression of opposition to the war and the draft, was legal, but that the means or intermediate objectives encompassed both legal and illegal activity without any clear indication, initially, as to who intended what. This intertwining of legal and illegal aspects, the public setting of the agreement and its political purposes, and the loose confederation of possibly innocent and possibly guilty participants raise the most serious First Amendment problems. Indeed our Brother Coffin, in dissent,[6] admits to a temptation "to say that the law should recognize no overt conspiracy in the sensitive area of public opinion." This temptation leads him down paths that we cannot follow, but which, nevertheless, we must consider.

As the defendants point out, most conspiracies are secret. To argue from this, however, that illegality presupposes secrecy is to confuse means with ends. Illegality normally seeks cover, but conspirators may act openly or not, as best suits their purpose. Here the defendants' primary object was publicity, and their conduct was designedly open. No one before has suggested that this fact, or the concomitant warning to the government of impending danger, requires that the government's hand be stayed until the substantive offense is committed.[7] Contrary to the defendants' position, many "public" conspiracies have been successfully prosecuted. A case remarkably similar is Fraina v. United States, 2 Cir., 1918, 255 F. 28. There two defendants were charged with conspiring, together with persons unknown, to aid, abet and counsel divers unknown persons to evade and neglect the requirements of the then Selective Service Act. The overt acts alleged were the organizing of a mass meeting and the distribution of pamphlets entitled "Conscientious Objectors" (who proved to be "nonreligious conscientious objectors" whose "idealism compels them to decline all forms of military service.") The opinion affirming the convictions touches many aspects of the case at bar in addition to the matter of publicity.[8]

[3] That openness does not immunize an agreement may be demonstrated by an example. A group of vigilantes agreeing in the town square to solicit cohorts to call out a lynch mob would not be absolved because their agreement was open. Nor should their agreement be protected by the First Amendment if, at the same time, they were engaging in free speech on the evils of their victim's alleged offense; nor, indeed, because their principal object was the proper one of deterring such offenses. The dissent's finding the present agreement pasteurized because it was exposed to the light is in effect granting a right to public association which is not given free speech itself. Cox v. Louisiana, 1965, 379 U.S. 559, 563-564, 85 S.Ct. 476, 13 L.Ed.2d 487; Giboney v. Empire Storage & Ice Co., 1949, 336 U.S. 490, 501-502, 69 S.Ct. 684, 93 L.Ed. 834. Lack of arcana cannot be determinative.[9]

Admittedly, the First Amendment rights of free speech and free association, *see, e.g.*, Elfbrandt v. Russell, 1966, 384 U.S. 11, 86 S.Ct. 1238, 16 L.Ed.2d 321; NAACP

v. Alabama, 1958, 357 U.S. 449, 460, 78 S.Ct. 1163, 2 L.Ed.2d 1488, are of such importance that they must prevail if the government's interest in deterring substantive crimes before they take place.[10] is insubstantial, or there is a "less restrictive alternative" by which the substantive evil may be prevented. United States v. Robel, 1967, 389 U.S. 258, 265-268, 88 S.Ct. 419, 19 L.Ed.2d 508; Aptheker v. Secretary of State, 1964, 378 U.S. 500, 512-514, 84 S.Ct. 1659, 12 L.Ed.2d 992; Shelton v. Tucker, 1960, 364 U.S. 479, 488-489, 81 S.Ct. 247, 5 L.Ed.2d 231. This calls for a weighing. In *Aptheker* the Court struck down the broad Congressional proscription against issuing passports to Communists only after considering the availability and adequacy of other security measures, one actually proposed by the President. In defendants' much emphasized case of New York Times Co. v. Sullivan, 1964, 376 U.S. 254, 279-283, 84 S.Ct. 710, 11 L.Ed.2d 686, not all public discussion was held protected; immunity was denied speakers motivated by "actual malice."

In comparing the present private and public interests we start with the assumption that the defendants were not to be prevented from vigorous criticism of the government's program merely because the natural consequences might be to interfere with it, or even to lead to unlawful action.[11] Thus Bond v. Floyd, 1966, 385 U.S. 116, 87 S.Ct. 339, 17 L.Ed.2d 235, held that the First Amendment protected an expression of "sympathy . . . and support [for] the men in this country who are unwilling to respond to a military draft." The Court said, with specific reference to section 462(a), "[T]his statement alone cannot be interpreted as a call to unlawful refusal to be drafted." Id. at 133, 87 S.Ct. at 348. The defendants here are not charged, however, with expressions of sympathy and moral support, but with conspiring to counsel, aid and abet Selective Service registrants to disobey various duties imposed by the Selective Service Act. The maintenance of an army in peacetime is a valid, in fact vital, governmental function. United States v. O'Brien, 1968, 391 U.S. 367, 377-378, 88 S.Ct. 1673, 20 L.Ed.2d 672. If a registrant may be convicted for violation of the draft laws, surely "[a] man may be punished for encouraging the commission of [the] crime." Cox v. Louisiana, *supra,* at 563, 85 S.Ct. at 480; Fox v. Washington, 1915, 236 U.S. 273, 35 S.Ct. 383, 59 L.Ed. 573.

[4] The government's ability to deter and punish those who increase the likelihood of crime by concerted action has long been established. *See* Developments in the Law—Criminal Conspiracy, 72 Harv.L.Rev. 920, 923-25 (1959). Restricting it to punishment of substantive violations ignores the potency of conspiratorial conduct;[12] to wait for the substantive offense may be to wait too long. Congress has a right to prefer registrants to felons. However attractive the dissent's conclusion may be to those of liberal First Amendment views, it sets its own stage by asking "whether there is reason or authority which *compels* the application [here] of the conspiracy sanction." (emphasis in orig.) The authority is an act of Congress. We do not read the "less restrictive alternative" cases as placing such a burden upon the government.[13]

Nor is the government's interest diminished in this case by defendants' claim that their conduct did not involve "incitement" and their reliance upon Bond v. Floyd's pronouncement that an expression of "sympathy and support" for those who resisted the draft did not violate section 462(a). The defendants do not quote all of *Bond.* The Court regarded Bond's first remarks as "opaque." Accordingly, it considered a second statement,[14] which it viewed as a "clarification" demonstrating that Bond was not in fact "advocating" a violation of law. It concluded that an expression of " 'sympathy . . . and support' . . . *alone* cannot be interpreted as a call to unlawful refusal." (emphasis suppl.) The implication is apparent.

In the early Smith Act cases, in considering the defendants' conduct in teaching the doctrines of revolution and advocacy of violence, substantial questions arose as to imminency of accomplishment. Dennis v. United States, 1951, 341 U.S. 494, 71 S.Ct. 857, 95 L.Ed. 1137; Yates v. Unites States, 1957, 354 U.S. 298, 77 S.Ct. 1064, 1 L.Ed.2d 1356. In the case at bar the defendants were concerned with the present. Their objective did not relate to some future war, but was a call for immediate action to thwart the one at hand. *See* Thomas v. Collins, 1945, 323 U.S. 516, 529-538, 65 S.Ct. 315, 89 L.Ed. 430. *See also* De Jonge v. Oregon, 1937, 299 U.S. 353, 365, 57 S.Ct. 255, 81 L.Ed. 278. What is effective persuasion must depend on the circumstances.[15] The existence of a large number of young men, perhaps impressionable, and in any event oriented in defendants' direction by natural self-interest, adequately distinguishes this case from Wood v. Georgia, 1962, 370 U.S. 375, 82 S.Ct. 1364, 8 L.Ed.2d 569, and Bridges v. California, 1941, 314 U.S. 252, 62 S.Ct. 190, 86 L.Ed. 192. In this context the "soft sell" may be the most telling.[16]

[5] Despite the validity of the government's present interest, the defendants were entitled under the cases to certain protections before they could be convicted of conspiracy in what we might call a bifarious undertaking, involving both legal and illegal conduct. This matter was considered by Mr. Justice Harlan, speaking for the Court in Scales v. United States, 1961, 367 U.S. 203, 81 S.Ct. 1469, 6 L.Ed.2d 782. The question there was whether convicting "active" members of the Communist party would interfere with the freedom of inactive, or legal, members. In the course of discussing this question he spoke of such groups as not being a "technical conspiracy" because of their mixed motives, and recognized the impropriety of a "blanket prohibition of association with a group having both legal and illegal aims." It did not follow, however, that distinction could not be effected. Indeed, this is the substantive purpose of all conspiracy law, which is directed only at those who have intentionally agreed to further the illegal object.[17] The First Amendment cases merely present a more difficult problem of insuring that the government does not use its procedural advantages to expand the strict elements of the offense.

[6] In *Scales* the Court held that protection for the innocent could be adequately accomplished by requiring that the defendants' specific illegal intent be proved to the degree demanded in Noto v. United States, 1961, 367 U.S. 290, 81 S.Ct. 1517, 6 L.Ed.2d 836. "[C]riminal intent . . . must be judged *strictissimi juris,* for otherwise there is a danger that one in sympathy with the legitimate aims of such an organization, but not specifically intending to accomplish them by resort to violence, might be punished for his adherence to lawful and constitutionally protected purposes, because of other and unprotected purposes which he does not necessarily share." Noto v. United States, at 299-300, 81 S.Ct. at 1522.[18] When the alleged agreement is both bifarious and political within the shadow of the First Amendment, we hold that an individual's specific intent to adhere to the illegal portions may be shown in one of three ways: by the individual defendant's prior or subsequent unambiguous statements; by the individual defendant's subsequent commission of the very illegal act contemplated by the agreement; or by the individual defendant's subsequent legal act if that act is "clearly undertaken for the specific purpose of rendering effective the later illegal activity which is advocated." Scales v. United States, 367 U.S. at 234, 81 S.Ct. at 1488.[19]

Application of such a standard should forcefully answer the defendant's protests that conviction of any of them would establish criminal responsibility of all of the many hundreds of persons who signed the Call. Even if the Call included illegal objectives, there is a wide gap between signing a document such as the Call and demonstrating one's personal attachment to illegality. Of greater importance, it responds to the legitimate apprehension of the amicus that the evil must be separable from the good without inhibiting legitimate association in an orderly society.

[7-12] At the same time, this principle demonstrates a fundamental error in the government's approach. Adopting the panoply of rules applicable to a conspiracy having purely illegal purposes, the government introduced numerous statements of third parties alleged to be co-conspirators. This was improper. The specific intent of one defendant in a case such as this is not ascertained by reference to the conduct or statements of another even though he has knowledge thereof. *Cf.* United States v. Silverman, 2 Cir., 1957, 248 F.2d 671; Enfield v. United States, 8 Cir., 1919, 261 F. 141, 143-144. The metastatic rules of ordinary conspiracy are at direct variance with the principle of *strictissimi juris.*[20] We need not determine, however, to what extent, because of a failure to recognize this principle, there may have been prejudicial error requiring a new trial. For reasons that we will come to (Point III, *infra*,) a new trial is required in any event. What we do determine is that the First Amendment does not, per se, require acquittal.

II

In this section we consider whether, on the review of the record which is required by Yates v. United States, *supra,* and Dennis v. United States, *supra,* the evidence was sufficient to take the defendants to the jury. We divide this consideration into three parts. First, whether there was evidence of an agreement; second, whether the agreement contemplated or included illegal activity; third, whether the defendants individually adhered to that illegality.

The Evidence of Agreement

The government's claim of agreement looks basically to the Call, the cover letter, and the subsequent press conference.[21] Spock participated in drafting the Call and, as has been stated, he and Coffin were two of the four persons who signed the cover letter. Goodman signed the Call, and was an active participant in the launching press conference which was chaired by Coffin and at which Spock appeared. Ferber did not sign the Call. The Call was addressed "To the young men of America, to the whole of the American people, and to all men of good will everywhere."[22] It observed there was a "growing number of young American men" who, because of their moral and religious beliefs could not contribute to the war in Vietnam in any way. After setting forth at some length the signers' belief that the war was unconstitutional and illegal, it stated, "[W]e believe on all these grounds that every free man has a legal right and a moral duty to exert every effort to end this war, to avoid collusion with it, and to encourage others to do the same." There followed a recital of the forms of resistance that young men were exercising, the detail of which we will return to, and an assertion of the signers' belief that "each of these forms of resistance . . . is courageous and justified. . . . We will continue to lend our support to those who undertake resistance to this war. We will raise funds to organize draft resistance unions, to supply legal defense and bail, to support families and otherwise aid resistance to the war in whatever ways may seem appropriate. . . . We call upon all men of good will to join us in this confrontation with immoral authority. . . . Now is the time to resist."

The cover letter, requesting signatures and other response to the Call, stated that the signers of the Call "have pledged themselves to extend material and moral support to young men who are directly resisting the war." There followed a "box" containing requests for further signatures of "endorsement," contributions of "$______ to support the work of RESIST. (Please make checks payable to RESIST.)," and volunteers interested in organizing or joining local groups "to support young men directly resisting the war." A similar "box" appeared in the Call itself, when printed.

At the press conference, in addition to discussing the Call, Goodman advanced his own paper, signed also by Coffin, along strikingly similar lines, entitled "Civil Disobedience Against the War" (hereinafter Civil Disobedience). It announced that the purpose of the signers was to "take away from the government the support and bodies it needs" and contained the following:

> "The draft law commands that we shall not aid, abet or counsel men to refuse the draft. But as a group of the clergy has recently said, . . . when young men refuse to allow their conscience to be violated by an unjust law and a criminal war, then it is necessary for their elders—their teachers, ministers, friends—to make clear their commitment, in conscience, to *aid, abet and counsel* them against conscription. Most of us have already done this privately. Now publicly we will demonstrate, side by side with these young men, our determination to continue to do so." (emphasis in orig.)

Goodman described the Call as a first step, and said that further activity was to follow. He announced a demonstration to be held in Washington on October 20, as an act of "direct creative resistance," at which time draft cards surrendered at turn-ins that had been planned for October 16 would be delivered to the Attorney General. This announcement, as both conceded, was the result of a prearrangement with Coffin.

[13] Spock argues that there was no "agreement among leaders of an integrated political group. . . . [T]his case presents no more than the publicly expressed coincidence of views on public affairs." No merit, however, lies in the suggestion that there must be a cohesiveness in the group beyond the confines of the agreement itself. *See* Direct Sales Co. v. United States, *supra* n. 7, at 713, 63 S.Ct. 1265; *cf.* United States v. Falcone, 1940, 311 U.S. 205, 61 S.Ct. 204, 85 L.Ed. 128.[23] In the light of all the circumstances the jury was not obliged, in considering the question of agreement, to find a mere coincidence in the appearance of several speakers on the same platform. *See* Fraina v. United States, *supra*. *Cf.* United States v. Kompinski, 2 Cir., 1967, 373 F.2d 429, 434.[24]

[14] The Call was not what is known in law as an integrated document, limited to the four corners of the instrument. The jury could properly infer that it could not occur in the abstract, with no parents, and no active participants in a joint undertaking. We hold that they could look to Spock as one of the drafters, and to Spock and Coffin as two of the four signers of the solicitation letter, and in the light of the press conference held to publicize the Call in which Goodman took a prominent part, they could find that Goodman included himself as an active member. The evidence disclosed more than parallel conduct, *see* United States v. Bufalino, 2 Cir., 1960, 285 F.2d 408, 414-415; rather there are several instances of concerted activity from which the jury could infer an agreement.[25] Whether the defendants' intended participation was unlawful is another matter.

The Evidence of Illegal Purpose

The defendants contend that nothing in the record would justify a finding of unlawful purpose in their agreement. Spock puts this succinctly: "There is nothing in the Call to Resist . . . which suggests the objective of counseling, aiding and abetting anyone to resist induction." Rather, he contends the only action contemplated was "simply moral support and financial aid for young men and their families who in good conscience are unable to participate in the war." Coffin argues further, "[D]raft 'resistance' is not a crime; the statute forbids only 'evasion' and 'refusal.' "

Examination of the Call shows nothing suggesting it sought to distinguish between "resistance" and "refusal." It was addressed to laymen, and is to be given a common sense and not a legalistic interpretation. We look, as indeed with any document, to its own clues as to what its subscribers may have intended the words to mean. So doing, we believe a jury would be amply justified in finding that "resist" included that type of resistance which the signers recognized, to use the words of Bond v. Floyd, *supra,* as "a call to unlawful refusal." Hence the whole concept of "illegitimate" authority. "[R]efusing to be inducted" must imply an order of induction to be refused. Hence the "heavy penalty" for "resisting openly." Hence the "need to support families," since families would not need support if the registrants' conduct met legal standards. "[S]anctuary in other countries" scaracely suggests travel authorized by the registrant's draft board.[26]

Nor was this a mere factual recital of what others were doing. "Now is the time to resist." It was at least open to the jury to find that these illicit actions were within what the Call, to use its own word, sought to "encourage;" and that the Call was, to repeat, in the words of the Court in *Bond,* "a call to unlawful refusal to be drafted."

This is not to deny that the Call contained many lawful criticisms of the war, lawful adjurations and expressions of sympathy and support for persons who acted illegally, and contemplated conduct of an entirely lawful character. It is also true, as Spock points out, that the Call stated that funds would be used "in whatever ways may seem appropriate." From this he argues that the persons signing the Call "reserve to themselves the determination of 'what ways may seem appropriate.' " While this may be so, nonetheless the Call on its face indicated that some signers considered the illegal to be the appropriate. *Cf.* Truax v. Corrigan, 1921, 257 U.S. 312, 327-328, 42 S.Ct. 124, 66 L.Ed. 254. We adopt the description given in the perceptive brief of the Unitarian Universalist Association, amicus on behalf of Ferber. The Call had "a double aspect: in part it was a denunciation of governmental policy and, in part, it involved a public call to resist the duties imposed by the Act."

The Evidence of Specific Intent

There remains the question whether it could have been found, within the strict test laid down by the cases *supra,* that the individual defendants personally agreed to employ the illegal means contemplated by the agreement including counselling unlawful refusal to be drafted or other violations of the Selective Service Act. We will begin with Goodman and his affirmative statement regarding counselling contained in "Civil Disobedience," written by him and signed by Coffin, quoted *supra.* In describing this paper, Coffin argues, as he did with the Call, that it "cannot be interpreted as a call to unlawful *refusal* to be drafted." "One may counsel *against* conscription by urging the claiming of exemption or deferment. . . . [O]nly counselling of *evasion* or *refusal* is unlawful, not counselling of *avoidance*. Avoidance may be entirely lawful—as by claiming lawful exemption or deferment." (Emphasis in orig.) This appraisal seems divorced from the realities. No defendant either here or at any time, used the word "avoidance." There is not even a reference in Civil Disobedience to "exemption or deferment," except for an expression of approval of those who voluntarily waive such. Nor does anyone explain the reference to long jail sentences, if "refusing . . . to serve when called" means lawful refusal.[27]

In addition, Goodman's remarks at the Washington demonstration were pari passu. There, after referring to the continuing activities of the Resistance in their successful solicitation of "draft resisters," Goodman stated that those of the older generation were present "because *we* want specifically to form an alliance with these young men which *we* will persist in, at least as long as the war lasts, in which *we* will encourage them and aid and abet and counsel them in every way we know how." (emphasis suppl.) The ambiguity in the original agreement was clarified, as to Goodman, by his own statements. Because a properly instructed jury could have found Goodman had the requisite specific intent he was not entitled to an acquittal.[28]

Coffin also signed Civil Disobedience, but if it could be thought that in some manner he is not to be personally charged therewith we quote his remarks at Washington, when it was sought to present turned-in cards to the Attorney General, again, like Goodman, speaking in terms of a joint undertaking.

> "The law of the land is clear. Section 12 of the National Selective Service Act declares that anyone 'who knowingly counsels, aids, or abets another to refuse or evade registration or service in the armed forces . . . shall be liable to imprisonment for not more than five years or a fine of ten thousand dollars or both.'
>
> "We hereby publicly counsel these young men to continue in their refusal to serve in the armed forces as long as the war in Vietnam continues, and we pledge ourselves to aid and abet them in all the ways we can. This means that if they are now arrested for failing to comply with a law that violates their consciences, we too must be arrested, for in the sight of that law we are now as guilty as they.
>
> "It is a longstanding tradition, sanctioned by American democracy, that the dictates of government must be tested on the anvil of individual conscience. This is what we now undertake to do—not as a first but as a last resort. And in accepting the legal punishment we are, in fact, supporting, not subverting, the legal order.
>
> "Still, to stand in this fashion against the law and before our fellow Americans is a difficult and even fearful thing. But in the face of what to us is insane and inhuman we can fall neither silent no servile. Nor can we educate young men to be conscientious only to desert them in their hour of conscience. So we are resolved, as they are resolved, to speak out clearly and to pay up personally."[29]

[15] Finally, at the Arlington Street Church ceremony on October 16 Coffin not only spoke but assisted in the collection of draft cards. This participation and assistance could well have been found to be aiding and abetting nonpossession.[30] Because it was this very type of resistance that the agreement might have been found to contemplate, a properly instructed jury could find that Coffin had the requisite specific intent. The jury was not obliged to view his conduct as he would have it on appeal. Before us he argues, "It is no crime . . . to *agree* to deliver turned-in draft

cards to the Attorney General. . . . [T]his action was completely law-abiding—Rev. Coffin accurately viewed it as the delivery to the law of evidence of a crime." (emphasis suppl.) We do not think of Coffin as one to run with the hare and hold with the hounds. In any event, he was not entitled to an acquittal.

[16] The principle of *strictissimi juris* requires the acquittal of Spock. It is true that he was one of the drafters of the Call, but this does not evidence the necessary intent to adhere to its illegal aspects. Nor does his admission to a government agent that he was willing to do "anything" asked to further opposition to the war. Specific intent is not established by such a generalization. Whatever the reason[31] the fact is that his speech was limited to condemnation of the war and the draft, and lacked any words or content of counselling. The jury could not find proscribed advocacy from the mere fact, which he freely admitted, that he hoped the frequent stating of his views might give young men "courage to take active steps in draft resistance." This is a natural consequence of vigorous speech.

Similarly, Spock's actions lacked the clear character necessary to imply specific intent under the First Amendment standard. He was not at the Arlington Street Church meeting; in fact he knew nothing of it until afterwards. Although he was at the Washington demonstration he had, unlike Goodman and Coffin, no part in its planning. He contributed nothing, even by his presence, to the turning in of cards. Nor, finally, did his statements in the course of the Washington demonstration extend at all beyond the general anti-war, anti-draft remarks he had made before. His attendance is as consistent with a desire to repeat this speech as it is to aid a violation of the act.

[17] The dissent would fault us for drawing such distinctions, but it forgets the teaching of Bond v. Floyd and other cases that expressing one's views in broad areas is not foreclosed by knowledge of the consequences, and the important lesson of *Noto, Scales* and *Yates* that one may belong to a group, knowing of its illegal aspects, and still not be found to adhere thereto. Viewing the record as a whole we feel we would be doing poor service to the rule of *strictissimi juris,* and to the principle that there must be substantial evidence, Yoffe v. United States, 1 Cir., 1946, 153 F.2d 570, and not a mere scintilla, Magnat Corp. v. B & B Electroplating Co., 1 Cir., 1966, 358 F.2d 794, to warrant submitting a case to the jury if we failed to hold Spock entitled to an acquittal.[32] *Cf.* Hellman v. United States, 9 Cir., 1961, 298 F.2d 810.[33]

The defendant Michael Ferber presents a different situation. Ferber was a draft-age student. His activities were limited to assisting in the burning and surrender of draft cards. Although he made an address at the Arlington Street Church, it was not counselling draft resistance, or even the surrendering of cards. Not only did he not sign the Call, or the cover letter, or attend the press conference, but the evidence did not warrant a finding that through other statements or conduct he joined the larger conspiracy for which the other defendants were prosecuted. The fact that he made incidental use of the services of some of the other defendants for his own purposes does not mean that he evidenced an attachment to all of theirs. It may be that Ferber engaged in a smaller conspiracy. This does not mean that he should be convicted for the larger one. Daily v. United States, 9 Cir., 1960, 282 F.2d 818. He must be acquitted.[34]

* * *

---

[1]A fifth defendant was acquitted, and will not be further referred to.

[2]In addition, considerable evidence was introduced of Spock's participation in a sit-in in front of the Whitehall induction center in New York City. We will assume with the defendants and now, apparently, the government as well, that this was token activity and protected political expression. *See* Brown v. Louisiana, 1966, 383 U.S. 131, 141-142, 86 S.Ct. 719, 15 L.Ed.2d 637; *but cf.* Adderley v. Florida, 1966, 385 U.S. 39, 87 S.Ct. 242, 17 L.Ed.2d 149; Cox v. Louisiana, 1965, 379 U.S. 559, 85 S.Ct. 476, 13 L.Ed.2d 487. Because of our resolution of the case on other grounds we need not pursue this matter, or explore the possibility of prejudice arising from the introduction of this evidence.

[3]Hereinafter, without distinction, draft cards.

[4]We do not understand the government to interpret 50 App. U.S.C. § 462(a) to cover hindering or interfering with the nonrecruitment activities of the armed services. Such action would be criminal under the Espionage Act, 18 U.S.C. §§ 2387, 2388(a), 2391.

[5]The brief of the Unitarian Universalist Association, amicus, is the only one which envisages that, although the defendants may have committed illegal acts, their conviction might impermissibly affect First Amendment rights of third parties. In considering this matter we are not troubled by questions of standing. *Compare* Dombrowski v. Pfister, 1965, 380 U.S. 479, 85 S.Ct. 1116, 14 L.Ed.2d 22, *with* United States v. Raines, 1960, 362 U.S. 17, 80 S.Ct. 519, 4 L.Ed.2d 524.

[6]Because of the identity of surname with one of the defendants, we will hereafter refer to Judge Coffin simply as the dissent.

[7]In Direct Sales Co. v. United States, 1943, 319 U.S. 703, 63 S.Ct. 1265, 87 L.Ed. 1674, for example, the agreement was embodied in catalogues widely distributed through the mails, and in order blanks the form of which was prescribed by the Secretary of the Treasury and which were, by law, retained for government inspection. Indeed, periodic reports, some monthly, some weekly, were made by Direct Sales to the government disclosing the names of purchasers and the amounts of purchases. The dissent supports its attachment to overtness with a dictum by Mr. Justice Harlan in Grunewald v. United States, 1957, 353 U.S. 391, 402, 77 S.Ct. 963, 972, 1 L.Ed.2d 931 ("every conspiracy is by its very nature secret"). With great respect to the Justice, this was a somewhat casual remark in a case dealing with a plainly illegal conspiracy, and is erroneous, as even the dissent's citations demonstrate. We may be pardoned for observing that more affection seems to be exhibited for this dictum than for some of the Justice's holdings in connection with agreements that are partly legal and partly not.

[8]Other cases in which the conspiracy itself was to a large degree public include Wells v. United States, 9 Cir., 1919, 257 F. 605 (meetings, apparently public, and circulars widely distributed demanding "Resist! Refuse!"); Haywood v. United States, 7 Cir., 1920, 268 F. 795, cert. denied 256 U.S. 689, 41 S.Ct. 449, 65 L.Ed. 1172; Anderson v. United States, 8 Cir., 1921, 273 F. 20, cert. denied 257 U.S. 647, 42 S.Ct. 56, 66 L.Ed. 415; United States v. Gordon, 7 Cir., 1943, 138 F.2d 174, cert. denied 320 U.S. 798, 64 S.Ct. 266, 88 L.Ed. 481. *See also* Pierce v. United States, 1920, 252 U.S. 239, 40 S.Ct. 205, 64 L.Ed. 542; Schenck v. United States, 1919, 249 U.S. 47, 39 S.Ct. 247, 63 L.Ed. 470.

[9]Neither can the claim that the conspiracy was "non-cohesive." If any cohesive motive be thought necessary where there already was a written document, *cf.* Interstate Circuit, Inc. v. United States, 1939, 306 U.S. 208, 222, 59 S.Ct. 467, 83 L.Ed. 610, there was ample common purpose here. The dissent's emphasis upon "discipline" again confuses means and result. Discipline may be needed for a secret conspiracy in order to keep it secret. The thrust of conspiracy, however, is in the agreement for joint action, not in the method of accomplishing it.

[10]The "general principle [is] that society, having the power to punish dangerous behavior, cannot be powerless against those who work to bring about that behavior." Scales v. United States, 1961, 367 U.S. 203, 225, 81 S.Ct. 1469, 1484, 6 L.Ed.2d 782.

[11]"Throughout our decisions there has recurred a distinction between the statement of an idea which may prompt its hearers to take unlawful actions, and advocacy that such action be taken." Justice Frankfurter concurring in Dennis v. United States, 1951, 341 U.S. 494, 545, 71 S.Ct. 857, 885, 95 L.Ed. 1137, quoted in Yates v. United States, 1957, 354 U.S. 298, 322, 77 S.Ct. 1064, 1 L.Ed.2d 1356, and again in Noto v. United States, 1961, 367 U.S. 290, 297, 81 S.Ct. 1517, 6 L.Ed.2d 836. *Cf.* Gitlow v. New York, 1925, 268 U.S. 652, 673, 45 S.Ct. 625, 69 L.Ed. 1138 (Holmes, J., dissenting) ("Every idea is an incitement.")

[12]The occasionally asserted judicial hostility to conspiracy prosecutions, Krulewitch v. United States, 1949, 336 U.S. 440, 445, 69 S.Ct. 716, 93 L.Ed. 790 (Jackson, J., concurring); United States v. Falcone, 2 Cir., 1940, 109 F.2d 579, 581, aff'd, 311 U.S. 205, 61 S.Ct. 204, 85 L.Ed. 128, springs largely from the government's overenthusiastic use of some of the procedures of conspiracy law rather than from a rejection of the public interest served by that law. Indeed, Justice Jackson, author of the *Krulewitch* concurrence, noted in Dennis v. United States, 341 U.S. at 577, 71 S.Ct. at 901: "There is no constitutional right to 'gang up' on the Government."

[13]The issue may perhaps be more objectively considered if we approach it in terms other than the present case where it may be easy to sympathize with many of the defendants' aims and be tempted to overlook, as incidental and peripheral, the illegal aspects of some of the means. It is not difficult to visualize conspirators whose basic ends are plainly illegal but who color them in order to obtain needed support of others, innocent and well intentioned, by adding lawful and popular objects.

[14]"I have never suggested or counseled or advocated that any one other person burn their draft card. In fact, I have mine in my pocket and will produce it if you wish. I do not advocate that people should break laws. What I simply try to say was that I admired the courage of someone who could act on his convictions knowing that he faces pretty stiff consequences." 385 U.S. at 134, 87 S.Ct. at 348.

[15]*See generally,* Richardson, Freedom of Expression and the Function of Courts, 65 Harv.L.Rev. 1 (1951).

[16]We note Spock's candid statement that direct urging of draft violations would in his opinion be "poor psychological practice."

[17]Justice Harlan noted in *Scales,* 367 U.S. at 229, 81 S.Ct. at 1486, "[A] technical conspiracy . . . is defined by its criminal purpose, so that *all* knowing association with the conspiracy is a proper subject for criminal proscription as far as First Amendment liberties are concerned." (emphasis in the original). *See* United States v. Borelli, 2 Cir., 1964, 336 F.2d 376, 384-385, cert. denied Cinquegrano v. United States, 379 U.S. 960, 85 S.Ct. 647, 13 L.Ed.2d 555; United States v. Falcone, 2 Cir., 1940, 109 F.2d 579, 581, aff'd 311 U.S. 205, 61 S.Ct. 204, 85 L.Ed. 128; United States v. Peoni, 2 Cir., 1938, 100 F.2d 401; Developments in the Law—Criminal Conspiracy, 72 Harv.L.Rev. 920, 925-27 (1959).

[18]The Court said in *Scales,* 367 U.S. at 229-230, 81 S.Ct. at 1486, "Thus the member for whom the organization is a vehicle for the advancement of legitimate aims and policies does not fall within the ban of the statute: he lacks the requisite specific intent 'to bring about the overthrow of the government as speedily as circumstances would permit.' Such a person may be foolish, deluded, or perhaps merely optimistic, but he is not by this statute made a criminal." *See also* Elfbrandt v. Russell, 384 U.S. at 15-17, 86 S.Ct. 1238.

[19]*Accord,* Hellman v. United States, 9 Cir., 1961, 298 F.2d 810. *See also* Nowak v. United States, 1958, 356 U.S. 660, 665-668, 78 S.Ct. 955, 2 L.Ed.2d 1048; Hartzel v. United States, 1944, 322 U.S. 680, 686-687, 64 S.Ct. 1233, 88 L.Ed. 1534; United States v. Tramaglino, 2 Cir., 1952, 197 F.2d 928, 930-931, cert. denied 344 U.S. 864, 73 S.Ct. 105, 97 L.Ed. 670; *cf.* United States v. Bruno, 2 Cir., 1939, 105 F.2d 921, rev'd on other grounds, 308 U.S. 287, 60 S.Ct. 198, 84 L.Ed. 257.

[20]We do not believe that section 462(a) is overbroad or vague. *See* Gara v. United States, 6 Cir., 1949, 178 F.2d 38, aff'd by an equally divided court, 340 U.S. 857, 71 S.Ct. 87, 95 L.Ed. 628; Warren v. United States, 10 Cir., 1949, 177 F.2d 596, cert. denied 338 U.S. 947, 70 S.Ct. 485, 94 L.Ed. 584; Kiyoshi Okamoto v. United States, 10 Cir., 1945, 152 F.2d 905, 906-907; *cf.* Singer v. United States, 1945, 323 U.S. 338, 65 S.Ct. 282, 89 L.Ed. 285. A special obligation exists as to federal statutes to construe them so to avoid unconstitutionality, Scales v. United States, *supra,* so long as such does not result in substantial re-writing. *See* Aptheker v. Secretary of State, 1964, 378 U.S. 500, 515-516, 84 S.Ct. 1659, 12 L.Ed.2d 992. The fact that a seemingly normal criminal statute, by virtue of its prohibition of conspiracy and crime counselling, may in some instances apply to affect freedom of association or freedom of speech does not invalidate the statute. *See* United States v. O'Brien, 1968, 391 U.S. 367, 88 S.Ct. 1673, 20 L.Ed.2d 672. The court's obligation is, rather, to make sure that such a statute does not improperly infringe upon speech in any particular instance. *See, e.g.,* Street v. New York, U.S., April 21, 1969, 394 U.S. 576, 89 S.Ct. 1354, 22 L.Ed.2d 572. Nor do we believe the indictment failed in its function of informing the defendants of the crime with which they were charged. *See* Wong Tai v. United States, 1927, 273 U.S. 77, 47 S.Ct. 300, 71 L.Ed. 545.

[21]Because we are discussing only the evidence of an agreement, the government's vacillation about which part of the evidence it relied on cannot, without some special showing, be taken to have prejudiced the defendants. On the contrary, the government is entitled to rely on whatever agreement is shown by the evidence. Glasser v. United States, 1942, 315 U.S. 60, 80, 62 S.Ct. 457, 86 L.Ed. 680. The defendants do not destroy the government's case by themselves showing a somewhat different but equally illegal agreement.

[22]The Call and the cover letter are reproduced in full in an appendix hereto.

[23]*See also* n. 9, *supra.* By the same token, nothing is taught by the frequently stressed fact that the signatories were in many instances persons of prominence, or that, apart from their common opposition to the war and to the draft, they were of disparate backgrounds and interests. *See* United States v. Lester, 3 Cir., 1960, 282 F.2d 750, 752-753, cert. denied 364 U.S. 937, 81 S.Ct. 385, 5 L.Ed.2d 368; Carbo v. United States, 9 Cir., 1963, 314 F.2d 718, 734, cert. denied Palmero v. United States, 377 U.S. 953, 84 S.Ct. 1625, 12 L.Ed.2d 498.

[24]In *Frania* the court said, 255 F. at 34, "This case is one of the simplest instances of proper proof in limine of combination ever brought to a court's attention. If, as per advertisement, an audience is gathered before a platform containing intending speakers, and is called to order by a chairman, who announces the object of the gathering, again, as per advertisement, it is impossible not to infer a combination in thought among the platform occupiers and their helpers." The rule of *strictissimi juris* may well require greater proof today of a defendant's specific intent, but in distinguishing *Fraina* on this ground the dissent confuses consensual principles with the ascertainment of what was consented to. The principles remain. *See* Yates v. United States, *supra,* 354 U.S. at 333, 77 S.Ct. 1064.

[25]Bozza v. United States, 1947, 330 U.S. 160, 165, 67 S.Ct. 645, 91 L.Ed. 818; Glasser v. United States, *supra* n. 21; White v. United States, 9 Cir., 1968, 394 F.2d 49, 53.

[26]The Call, which was printed as a paid advertisement in two national publications, and circulated separately, underwent a few changes. In all instances in describing "forms of resistance" it stated, "[a]mong those already in the armed forces some are refusing to obey specific illegal and immoral orders." In some editions it added, "some are absenting themselves without official leave." Neither of these methods connotes legal resistance.

[27]Additionally, we note that defendant Goodman's printed statement at the October 2 press conference contained the following: "The activity of the Resistance groups will be continuing beyond October 16, as more *draft refusers* come forward. It is our intention to parallel that development with continuing private and public activity in support of them." (Emphasis suppl.).

[28]Were it necessary to go any further, the Washington demonstration, planned by Goodman and Coffin, completed the surrender of draft cards; those who "surrendered" them at the Arlington Street Church having been told that they had a right of recall. This act, of course, was not mere speech, and could be found to satisfy the requirement of a "course of conduct clearly undertaken for the specific purpose of rendering effective" the illegal objects of the agreement. Scales v. United States, 367 U.S. at 234, 81 S.Ct. 1469.

[29]In spite of this final remark, made then and at other times, by both Coffin and Goodman, they argue now that they were not guilty if they believed that their actions were legal and that any conviction would be unconstitutional. For this they cite Keegan v. United States, 1945, 325 U.S. 478, 65 S.Ct. 1203, 89 L.Ed. 1745. The opinions there, however, are far from clear as to the extent of such a principle; nor have other courts reached a consensus. *Compare* Holdridge v. United States, 8 Cir., 1960, 282 F.2d 302, 310-311, and Kiyoshi Okamoto v. United States, 10 Cir., 1945, 152 F.2d 905, *with* Lantis v. United States, 9 Cir., 1950, 186 F.2d 91, 92-93, *and* Warren v. United States, 10 Cir., 1949, 177 F.2d 596, 600, cert. denied 338 U.S. 947, 70 S.Ct. 485, 94 L.Ed. 584. A defendant's motive in testing an act might properly go to sentence, but these defendants are contending that, having violated the statute, they should, in effect, be subject only to a riskless declaratory judgment. No such purpose was made known until the defendants reached the courtroom. Before that time, they publicly asserted that they were placing their own necks on the block. They should not now be heard to say that no axe was involved.

[30]Willful nonpossession of a draft card is criminal. O'Brien v. United States, 1 Cir., 1967, 376 F.2d 538, rev'd on other grounds, 391 U.S. 367, 88 S.Ct. 1673, 20 L.Ed.2d 672. One "who contributed consciously to furthering that illicit enterprise aided and abetted its commission." United States v. Johnson, 1943, 319 U.S. 503, 515, 63 S.Ct. 1233, 1239, 87 L.Ed. 1546. *Accord,* United States v. Williams, 1951, 341 U.S. 58, 64, 71 S.Ct. 595, 95 L.Ed. 747; Nye & Nissen v. United States, 1949, 336 U.S. 613, 619, 69 S.Ct. 766, 93 L.Ed. 919; *see also* United States v. Peoni, 2 Cir., 1938, 100 F.2d 401. Coffin was not merely present in the church, Hicks v. United States, 1893, 150 U.S. 442, 449-450, 14 S.Ct. 144, 37 L.Ed. 1137; Long v. United States, 1966, 124 U.S. App. D.C. 14, 360 F.2d 829, 835, he was an active, knowing participant. Wyatt v. United States, 10 Cir., 1968, 388 F.2d 395; Moore v. United States, 5 Cir., 1966, 356 F.2d 39; *cf.* United States v. Manna, 2 Cir., 1965, 353 F.2d 191, cert. denied, 384 U.S. 975, 86 S.Ct. 1868, 16 L.Ed.2d 685.

[31]*See* n. 16, *supra.*

[32]This, too, dissatisfies the dissent, which is unhappy whatever we do. Viz., because we recognize the necessity of special protection, thereby letting some defendants go free, we should not punish conspiracies in the field of speech at all; it is improper to apply the *Scales* and *Noto* safeguard because it is not strict enough; here we have applied it too strictly. Continuing with Ferber, *infra,* this conspiracy is too broad, it might have been proper to prosecute Ferber for a conspiracy limited to the Arlington Street Church matter; it is over-generous not to regard Arlington Street as a joining of the larger conspiracy. Basically, all this means is that the dissent refuses to draw distinctions.

[33]A similar situation involving a demonstrably active, as opposed to passive, participant in a bifarious organization, was faced in Hellman v. United States, *supra* note 19. While "Hellman was an

exceedingly active member of the Party," 298 F.2d at 813, the court found that there was insufficient proof, given a *strictissimi juris* standard, to show specific intent to further the Party's illegal, as opposed to legal, methods. "[T]he activity portrayed is explainable on the basis that he intended to bring about the Party's ultimate goals through peaceable means."

[34]The government has not raised the point, nor do we see independently any reason to suppose that a new trial would result in a stronger case for the government.

Spence v. Washington

418 U.S. 405 (1974)

Per Curiam.

Appellant displayed a United States flag, which he owned, out of the window of his apartment. Affixed to both surfaces of the flag was a large peace symbol fashioned of removable tape. Appellant was convicted under a Washington statute forbidding the exhibition of a United States flag to which is attached or superimposed figures, symbols, or other extraneous material. The Supreme Court of Washington affirmed appellant's conviction. *State v. Spence,* 81 Wash. 2d 788, 506 P. 2d 293 (1973). It rejected appellant's contentions that the statute under which he was charged, on its face and as applied, contravened the First Amendment, as incorporated by the Fourteenth Amendment, and was void for vagueness. We noted probable jurisdiction. 414 U.S. 815 (1973). We reverse on the ground that as applied to appellant's activity the Washington statute impermissibly infringed protected expression.

I

On May 10, 1970, appellant, a college student, hung his United States flag from the window of his apartment on private property in Seattle, Washington. The flag was upside down, and attached to the front and back was a peace symbol (*i.e.,* a circle enclosing a trident) made of removable black tape. The window was above the ground floor. The flag measured approximately three by five feet and was plainly visible to passersby. The peace symbol occupied roughly half of the surface of the flag.

Three Seattle police officers observed the flag and entered the apartment house. They were met at the main door by appellant, who said, "I suppose you are here about the flag. I didn't know there was anything wrong with it. I will take it down." Appellant permitted the officers to enter his apartment, where they seized the flag and arrested him. Appellant cooperated with the officers. There was no disruption or altercation.

Appellant was not charged under Washington's flag-desecration statute. See Wash. Rev. Code § 9.86.030, as amended.[1] Rather, the State relied on the so-called "improper use" statute, Wash. Rev. Code § 9.86.020. This statute provides, in pertinent part:

> "No person shall, in any manner, for exhibition or display:
>
> "(1) Place or cause to be placed any word, figure, mark, picture, design, drawing or advertisement of any nature upon any flag, standard, color, ensign or shield of the United States or of this state . . . or
>
> "(2) Expose to public view any such flag, standard, color, ensign or shield

> upon which shall have been printed, painted or otherwise produced, or to which shall have been attached, appended, affixed or annexed any such word, figure, mark, picture, design, drawing or advertisement. . . ."[2]

Appellant initially was tried to the bench in a local justice court, where he was found guilty and sentenced to 90 days' confinement, with 60 days suspended. Appellant exercised his right to be tried *de novo* in King County Superior Court, where he received a jury trial.

The State based its case on the flag itself and the testimony of the three arresting officers, who testified that they had observed the flag displayed from appellant's window and that on the flag was superimposed what they identified as a peace symbol. Appellant took the stand in his own defense. He testified that he put a peace symbol on the flag and displayed it to public view as a protest against the invasion of Cambodia and the killings at Kent State University, events which occurred a few days prior to his arrest. He said that his purpose was to associate the American flag with peace instead of war and violence:

> "I felt there had been so much killing and that this was not what America stood for. I felt that the flag stood for America and I wanted people to know that I thought America stood for peace."

Appellant further testified that he chose to fashion the peace symbol from tape so that it could be removed without damaging the flag. The State made no effort to controvert any of appellant's testimony.

The trial court instructed the jury in essence that the mere act of displaying the flag with the peace symbol attached, if proved beyond a reasonable doubt, was sufficient to convict. There was no requirement of specific intent to do anything more than display the flag in that manner. The jury returned a verdict of guilty. The court sentenced appellant to 10 days in jail, suspended, and to a $75 fine. The Washington Court of Appeals reversed the conviction. 5 Wash. App. 752, 490 P. 2d 1321 (1971). It held the improper-use statute overbroad and invalid on its face under the First and Fourteenth Amendments. With one justice dissenting and two concurring in the result, the Washington Supreme Court reversed and reinstated the conviction. 81 Wash. 2d 788, 506 P. 2d 293 (1973).

II

A number of factors are important in the instant case. First, this was a privately owned flag. In a technical property sense it was not the property of any government. We have no doubt that the state or national governments constitutionally may forbid anyone from mishandling in any manner a flag that is public property. But this is a different case. Second, appellant displayed his flag on private property. He engaged in no trespass or disorderly conduct. Nor is this a case that might be analyzed in terms of reasonable time, place, or manner restraints on access to a public area. Third, the record is devoid of proof of any risk of breach of the peace. It was not appellant's purpose to incite violence or even stimulate a public demonstration. There is no evidence that any crowd gathered or that appellant made any effort to attract attention beyond hanging the flag out of his own window. Indeed, on the facts stipulated by the parties there is no evidence that anyone other than the three police officers observed the flag.

Fourth, the State concedes, as did the Washington Supreme Court, that appellant engaged in a form of communication.[3] Although the stipulated facts fail to show that any member of the general public viewed the flag, the State's concession is inevitable on this record. The undisputed facts are that appellant "wanted people to know that I thought America stood for peace." To be sure, appellant did not choose to articulate his views through printed or spoken words. It is therefore necessary to determine whether his activity was sufficiently imbued with elements of communication to fall within the scope of the First and Fourteenth Amendments, for as the Court noted in *United States v. O'Brien,* 391 U.S. 367, 376 (1968). "[w]e cannot accept the view that an apparently limitless variety of conduct can be labeled 'speech' whenever the person engaging in the conduct intends thereby to express an idea." But the nature of appellant's activity, combined with the factual context and environment in which it was undertaken, lead to the conclusion that he engaged in a form of protected expression.

The Court for decades has recognized the communicative connotations of the use of flags. *E.g., Stromberg v. California,* 283 U.S. 359 (1931). In many of their uses flags are a form of symbolism comprising a "primitive but effective way of communicating ideas, . . ." and "a short cut from mid to mind." *Board of Education v. Barnette,* 319 U.S. 624, 632 (1943). On this record there can be little doubt that appellant communicated through the use of symbols. The symbolism included not only the flag but also the superimposed peace symbol.

Moreover, the context in which a symbol is used for purposes of expression is important, for the context may give meaning to the symbol. See *Tinker v. Des Moines School District,* 393 U.S. 503 (1969). In *Tinker,* the wearing of black armbands in a school environment conveyed an unmistakable message about a contemporaneous issue of intense public concern—the Vietnam hostilities. *Id.,* at 505-514. In this case, appellant's activity was roughly simultaneous with and concededly triggered by the Cambodian incursion and the Kent State tragedy, also issues of great public moment. Cf. *Scheuer v. Rhodes,* 416 U.S. 232 (1974). A flag bearing a peace symbol and displayed upside down by a student today might be interpreted as nothing more than bizarre behavior, but it would have been difficult for the great majority of citizens to miss the drift of appellant's point at the time that he made it.

It may be noted, further, that this was not an act of mindless nihilism. Rather, it was a pointed expression of anguish by appellant about the then-current domestic and foreign affairs of his government. An intent to convey a particularized message was present, and in the surrounding circumstances the likelihood was great that the message would be understood by those who viewed it.

We are confronted then with a case of prosecution for the expression of an idea through activity. Moreover, the activity occurred on private property, rather than in an environment over which the state by necessity must have certain supervisory powers unrelated to expression. Cf. *Procunier v. Martinez,* 416 U.S. 396 (1974); *Healy v. James,* 408 U.S. 169 (1972); *Tinker v. Des Moines School District, supra.* Accordingly, we must examine with particular care the interests advanced by appellee to support its prosecution.

We are met at the outset with something of an enigma in the manner in which the case was presented to us. The Washington Supreme Court rejected any reliance on a breach-of-the-peace rationale. 81 Wash. 2d. at 796 n. 1, 506 P. 2d, at 299 n. 1. It based its result primarily on the ground that "the nation and state both have a recognizable interest in preserving the flag as a symbol of the nation. . . ."[4] Yet counsel for the State declined to support the highest state court's principal rationale in argument before us.[5] He pursued instead the breach-of-the-peace theory discarded by the state court. Indeed, that was the only basis on which he chose to support the constitutionality of the state statute.

Despite counsel's approach, we think it appropriate to review briefly the range of various state interests that might be thought to support the challenged conviction, drawing upon the arguments before us, the opinions below, and the Court's opinion in *Street v. New York,* 394 U.S. 576, 590-594 (1969). The first interest at issue is prevention of breach of the peace. In our view, the Washington Supreme Court correctly rejected this notion. It is totally without support in the record.

We are also unable to affirm the judgment below on the ground that the State may have desired to protect the sensibilities of passersby. "It is firmly settled that under our Constitution the public expression of ideas may not be prohibited merely because the ideas are themselves offensive to some of their hearers." *Street v. New York, supra,* at 592. Moreover, appellant did not impose his ideas upon a captive audience. Anyone who might have been offended could easily have avoided the display. See *Cohen v. California,* 403 U.S. 15 (1971). Nor may appellant be punished for failing to show proper respect for our national emblem. *Street v. New York, supra,* at 593; *Board of Education v. Barnette, supra.*[6]

We are brought, then, to the state court's thesis that Washington has an interest in preserving the national flag as an unalloyed symbol of our country. The court did not define this interest; it simply asserted it. See 81 Wash. 2d, at 799, 506 P. 2d, at 300. The dissenting opinion today, see *post,* at 420-422, adopts essentially the same approach. Presumably, this interest might be seen as an effort to prevent the appropriation of a revered national symbol by an individual, interest group, or enterprise where there was a risk that association of the symbol with a particular product or viewpoint might be taken erroneously as evidence of governmental endorsement.[7] Alternatively, it might be argued that the interest asserted by the state court is based on the uniquely universal character of the national flag as a symbol. For the great majority of us, the flag is a symbol of patriotism, of pride in the history of our country, and of the service, sacrifice, and valor of the millions of Americans who in peace and war have joined together to build and to defend a Nation in which self-government and personal liberty endure. It evidences both the unity and diversity which are America. For others the flag carries in varying degrees a different message. "A person gets from a symbol the meaning he puts into it, and what is one man's comfort and inspiration is another's jest and scorn." *Board of Education v. Barnette,* 319 U.S., at 632-633. It might be said that we all draw something from our national symbol, for it is capable of conveying simultaneously a spectrum of meanings. If it may be destroyed or permanently disfigured, it could be argued that it will lose its capability of mirroring the sentiments of all who view it.

But we need not decide in this case whether the interest advanced by the court below is valid.[8] We assume, *arguendo,* that it is. The statute is nonetheless unconstitutional as applied to appellant's activity.[9] There was no risk that appellant's acts would mislead viewers into assuming that the Government endorsed his viewpoint. To the contrary, he was plainly and peacefully[10] protecting the fact that it did not. Appellant was not charged under the desecration statute, see n. 1, *supra,* nor did he permanently disfigure the flag or destroy it. He displayed it as a flag of his country in a way closely analogous to the manner in which flags have always been used to convey ideas. Moreover, his message was direct, likely to be understood, and within the contours of the First Amendment. Given the protected character of his expression and in light of the fact that no interest the State may have in preserving the physical integrity of a privately owned flag was significantly impaired on these facts, the conviction must be invalidated.[11]

The judgment is reversed.

It is so ordered.

Mr. Justice Blackmun concurs in the result.

Mr. Justice Douglas, concurring. . . .

Mr. Chief Justice Burger, dissenting. . . .

Mr. Justice Rehnquist, with whom The Chief Justice and Mr. Justice White join, dissenting. . . .

---

[1]This statute provides in part:

"No person shall knowingly cast contempt upon any flag, standard, color, ensign or shield . . . by publicly mutilating, defacing, defiling, burning, or trampling upon said flag, standard, color, ensign or shield."

[2]Wash. Rev. Code § 9.86.010 defines the flags and other symbols protected by the desecration and improper-use statutes as follows: "The words flag, standard, color, ensign or shield, as used in this chapter, shall include any flag, standard, color, ensign or shield, or copy, picture or representation thereof, made of any substance or represented or produced thereon, and of any size, evidently purporting to be such flag, standard, color, ensign or shield of the United States or of this state, or a copy, picture or representation thereof."

[3]Brief for Appellee 3; 81 Wash. 2d, at 799, 800, 506 P. 2d.

[4]81 Wash. 2d, at 799, 506 P. 2d, at 300. A subsidiary ground relied on by the Washington Supreme Court must be rejected summarily. It found the inhibition on appellant's freedom of expression "minuscule and trifling" because there are "thousands of other means available to [him] for the dissemination of his personal views. . . ." *Id.*, at 799, 800, 506 P. 2d, at 300, 301. As the Court noted in, *e.g., Schneider v. State,* 308 U.S. 147, 163 (1939), "one is not to have the exercise of his liberty of expression in appropriate places abridged on the plea that it may be exercised in some other place."

[5]Brief for Appellee 6; Tr. of Oral Arg. 31-32.

[6]Counsel for the State conceded that promoting respect for the flag is not a legitimate state interest. Tr. of Oral Arg. 30.

[7]Undoubtedly such a concern underlies that portion of the improper-use statute forbidding the utilization of representations of the flag in a commercial context. Indeed, the third subparagraph of the improper-use statute, Wash. Rev. Code § 9.86.020(3), which is not at issue here, is aimed directly at commercial exploitation of our national symbol. There is no occasion in this case to address the application of the challenged statute to commercial behavior. Cf. *Halter v. Nebraska,* 205 U.S. 34 (1907). The dissent places major reliance on *Halter,* see *post,* at 418-420, despite the fact that *Halter* was decided nearly 20 years before the Court concluded that the First Amendment applies to the States by virtue of the Fourteenth Amendment. See *Gitlow v. New York,* 268 U.S. 652 (1925).

[8]If this interest is valid, we note that it is directly related to expression in the context of activity like that undertaken by appellant. For that reason and because no other governmental interest unrelated to expression has been advanced or can be supported on this record, the four-step analysis of *United States v. O'Brien,* 391 U.S. 367, 377 (1968), is inapplicable.

[9]Because we agree with appellant's as-applied argument, we do not reach the more comprehensive overbreadth contention he also advances. But it is worth noting the nearly limitless sweep of the Washington improper-use flag statute. Read literally, it forbids a veteran's group from attaching, *e.g.,* battalion commendations to a United States flag. It proscribes photographs of war heroes standing in front of the flag. It outlaws newspaper mastheads composed of the national flag with superimposed print. Other examples could easily be listed.

Statutes of such sweep suggest problems of selective enforcement. We are, however, unable to agree with appellant's void-for-vagueness argument. The statute's application is quite mechanical, particularly when implemented with jury instructions like the ones given in this case. The law in Washington, simply put, is that *nothing* may be affixed to or superimposed on a United States flag or a representation thereof. Thus, if selective enforcement has occurred, it has been a result of prosecutorial discretion, not the language of the statute. Accordingly, this case is unlike *Smith v.*

Goguen, 415 U.S. 566 (1974), where the words of the statute at issue ("publicly . . . treats contemptuously") were themselves sufficiently indefinite to prompt subjective treatment by prosecutorial authorities.

[10]Appellant's activity occurred at a time of national turmoil over the introduction of United States forces into Cambodia and the deaths at Kent State University. It is difficult now, more than four years later, to recall vividly the depth of emotion that pervaded most colleges and universities at the time, and that was widely shared by young Americans everywhere. A spontaneous outpouring of feeling resulted in widespread action, not all of it rational when viewed in retrospect. This included the closing down of some schools, as well as other disruptions of many centers of education. It was against this highly inflamed background that appellant chose to express his own views in a manner that can fairly be described as gentle and restrained as compared to the actions undertaken by a number of his peers.

[11]The similarity of our holding to that of the Iowa Supreme Court in *State v. Kool*, 212 N. W. 2d 518 (1973), merits note. In that case, the defendant displayed a replica of the United States flag upside down in his window, superimposing a peace symbol to create an effect identical to that achieved by Spence. Recognizing the communicative character of the defendant's activity, the Iowa Supreme Court reversed his conviction for flag misuse and held the statute unconstitutional as applied. The court eschewed an overbreadth analysis, and it rejected a number of the state interests we have found unavailing in the instant case.

The Right to Become and to Remain a Citizen

COMMENTARY

The Supreme Court has consistently recognized that citizenship is a valuable status on which many other basic rights are founded. The denial or removal of citizenship is a grave decision, which requires proper substantive and procedural safeguards before the courts will uphold it. The right of native-born and naturalized citizens to maintain their citizenship has, of course, been afforded greater protection than the right of an alien to become a citizen. However, even in the latter case the Supreme Court has been unwilling to yield without examination to executive decisions founded on claims of national security.

In 1946 the Court held that an individual could not be denied citizenship merely because he refused on religious grounds to bear arms, though he was willing to serve in the armed forces in a non-combatant role.[1] The Court held that Congress had not explicitly required that a would-be citizen be willing to bear arms, and that it would not read such a requirement into the act or permit the executive branch to do so.

In 1958, two cases forced the Supreme Court to delineate the circumstances under which the interests of national defense and foreign policy would permit the government to strip an individual of his citizenship. The Court was badly divided and reached opposite results in the two cases. In *Perez v. Brownell*, a five-man majority held that Congress could authorize the executive to strip citizenship from one who voted in a foreign election. Justice Frankfurter, writing for the Court, noted that:

> "Broad as the power in the National Government to regulate foreign affairs must be, it is not without limitation. The restrictions confining Congress in the exercise of any of the powers expressly delegated to it in the Constitution apply with equal vigor when that body seeks to regulate our relations with other nations."[2]

He went on to find that there was a rational nexus between Congress' foreign policy power and the embarrassment that might result from having American citizens vote in a foreign election. The Court declined to reach the other issue raised in *Perez, viz.*, whether a person who remained outside the United States to avoid the draft could be deprived of his citizenship.

In the second case, *Trop. v. Dulles* 356 U.S. 86 (1958), the Court held that a person could not be stripped of his citizenship for deserting in wartime. Three Justices (Warren, Black and Douglas) took the broad position, as they had in *Perez,* that under the Fourteenth Amendment "the Government is without power to take citizenship away from a native-born or lawfully naturalized American." Four Justices took the position that the desertion law was a penal statute, and that stripping a person of his citizenship for deserting was a cruel and unusual punishment in violation of the Eighth Amendment. Justice Brennan, who had joined the majority in *Perez,* took the position that the government had not demonstrated the requisite nexus between the war power and the policy of stripping a deserter of his citizenship in addition to imposing the ordinary penalties.

The issue which the Court avoided in *Perez*—whether remaining outside the United States to avoid the draft was sufficient grounds to deprive a person of his citizenship—was decided by the Court four years later. In *Kennedy v. Mendoza-Martinez,* 372 U.S. 144 (1962), the Court held that stripping a person of his citizenship for avoiding the draft was a punishment which could be handed out only under due procedural safeguards. It found that those safeguards were not available under the law and that the statute was therefore unconstitutional.

Justice Arthur Goldberg, in his opinion for the five-Justice majority, noted in passing that the Constitution "is not a suicide pact." Since this phrase is often quoted in government briefs to justify executive branch action, it is worth noting the context in which the statement was made:

> The powers of Congress to require military service for the common defense are broad and far-reaching, for while the Constitution protects against invasions of individual rights, it is not a suicide pact. . . .
>
> The great powers of Congress to conduct war and to regulate the nation's foreign relations are subject to the constitutional requirements of due process.[3]

In the light of these three decisions, the law seemed to be that persons could be deprived of citizenship if the penalty was rationally related to a legitimate governmental policy and if proper procedures were followed. However, in 1967 the Supreme Court over-ruled *Perez* and held that the Fourteenth Amendment is an absolute bar to depriving a person of citizenship without his or her consent.[4] Thus no matter how compelling the national security interest is said to be, the government can no longer strip any person of his or her citizenship.

---

[1] *Girouard v. United States,* 328 U.S. 61 (1946).

[2] *Perez v. Brownell,* 356 U.S. 44 (1958), at 58.

[3] 372 U.S. 159-60, 164-65.

[4] *Afroyim v. Rusk,* 387 U.S. 253 (1967).

STATUTES

Immigration and Naturalization Act

8 U.S.C. §1481

Loss of Nationality by Native-Born or Naturalized Citizen; Voluntary Action; Burden of Proof; Presumptions

(a) From and after the effective date of this chapter a person who is a national of the United States whether by birth or naturalization, shall lose his nationality by—

(1) obtaining naturalization in a foreign state upon his own application, upon an application filed in his behalf by a parent, guardian, or duly authorized agent, or through the naturalization of a parent having legal custody of such person: *Provided,* That nationality shall not be lost by any person under this section as the result of the naturalization of a parent or parents while such person is under the age of twenty-one years, or as the result of a naturalization obtained on behalf of a person under twenty-one years of age by a parent, guardian, or duly authorized agent, unless such person shall fail to enter the United States to establish a permanent residence prior to his twenty-fifth birthday: *And provided further,* That a person who shall have lost nationality prior to January 1, 1948, through thc naturalization in a foreign state of a parent or parents, may, within one year from the effective date of this chapter, apply for a visa and for admission to the United States as a nonquota immigrant under the provisions of section 1101(a) (27) (E) of this title; or

(2) taking an oath or making an affirmation or other formal declaration of allegiance to a foreign state or a political subdivision thereof; or

(3) entering, or serving in, the armed forces of a foreign state unless, prior to such entry or service, such entry or service is specifically authorized in writing by the Secretary of State and the Secretary of Defense: *Provided,* That the entry into such service by a person prior to the attainment of his eighteenth birthday shall serve to expatriate such person only if there exists an option to secure a release from such service and such person fails to exercise such option at the attainment of his eighteenth birthday; or

(4) (A) accepting, serving in, or performing the duties of any office, post, or employment under the government of a foreign state or a political subdivision thereof, if he has or acquires the nationality of such foreign state; or (B) accepting, serving in, or performing the duties of any office, post, or employment under the government of a foreign state or a political subdivision thereof, for which office, post, or employment an oath, affirmation, or declaration of allegiance is required; or

(5) voting in a political election in a foreign state or participating in an election or plebiscite to determine the sovereignty over foreign territory; or

(6) making a formal renunciation of nationality before a diplomatic or consular officer of the United States in a foreign state, in such form as may be prescribed by the Secretary of State; or

(7) making in the United States a formal written renunciation of

nationality in such form as may be prescribed by, and before such officer as may be designated by, the Attorney General, whenever the United States shall be in a state of war and the Attorney General shall approve such renunciation as not contrary to the interests of national defense; or

(8) deserting the military, air, or naval forces of the United States in time of war, if and when he is convicted thereof by court martial and as the result of such conviction is dismissed or dishonorably discharged from the service of such military, air, or naval forces: *Provided,* That, notwithstanding loss of nationality or citizenship under the terms of this chapter or previous laws by reason of desertion committed in time of war, restoration to active duty with such military, air, or naval forces in time of war or the reenlistment or induction of such a person in time of war with permission of competent military, air, or naval authority shall be deemed to have the immediate effect of restoring such nationality or citizenship heretofore or hereafter so lost; or

(9) committing any act of treason against, or attempting by force to overthrow, or bearing arms against, the United States, violating or conspiring to violate any of the provisions of section 2383 of Title 18, or willfully performing any act in violation of section 2385 of Title 18, or violating section 2384 of Title 18 by engaging in a conspiracy to overthrow, put down, or to destroy by force the Government of the United States, or to levy war against them, if and when he is convicted thereof by a court martial or by a court of competent jurisdiction; or

(10) departing from or remaining outside of the jurisdiction of the United States in time of war or during a period declared by the President to be a period of national emergency for the purpose of evading or avoiding training and service in the military, air, or naval forces of the United States. For the purposes of this paragraph failure to comply with any provision of any compulsory service laws of the United States shall raise the presumption that the departure from or absence from the United States was for the purpose of evading or avoiding training and service in the military, air, or naval forces of the United States.

(b) Any person who commits or performs any act specified in subsection (a) of this section shall be conclusively presumed to have done so voluntarily and without having been subjected to duress of any kind, if such person at the time of the act was a national of the state in which the act was performed and had been physically present in such state for a period or periods totaling ten years or more immediately prior to such act.

(c) Whenever the loss of United States nationality is put in issue in any action or proceeding commenced on or after September 26, 1961 under, or by virtue of, the provisions of this chapter or any other Act, the burden shall be upon the person or party claiming that such loss occurred, to establish such claim by a preponderance of the evidence. Except as otherwise provided in subsection (b) of this section, any person who commits or performs, or who has committed or performed, any act of expatriation under the provisions of this chapter or any other Act shall be presumed to have done so voluntarily, but such presumption may be rebutted upon a showing, by a preponderance of the evidence, that the act or acts committed or performed were not done voluntarily.

June 27, 1952, c. 477, Title III, ch. 3, § 349, 66 Stat. 267; Sept. 3, 1954, c. 1256, § 2, 68 Stat. 1146; Sept. 26, 1961, Pub.L. 87-301, § 19, 75 Stat. 656.

8 U.S.C. §1482

Dual Nationals; Divestiture of Nationality

A person who acquired at birth the nationality of the United States and of a foreign state and who has voluntarily sought or claimed benefits of the nationality of any foreign state shall lose his United States nationality by hereafter having a continuous residence for three years in the foreign state of which he is a national by birth at any time after attaining the age of twenty-two years unless he shall—

(1) prior to the expiration of such three-year period, take an oath of allegiance to the United States before a United States diplomatic or consular officer in a manner prescribed by the Secretary of State; and

(2) have his residence outside of the United States solely for one of the reasons set forth in paragraph (1), (2), (4), (5), (6), (7), or (8) of section 1485 of this title, or paragraph (1) or (2) of section 1486 of this title: *Provided, however,* That nothing contained in this section shall deprive any person of his United States nationality if his foreign residence shall begin after he shall have attained the age of sixty years and shall have had his residence in the United States for twenty-five years after having attained the age of eighteen years.

June 27, 1952, c. 477, Title III, ch. 3, § 350, 66 Stat. 269.

8 U.S.C. §1483

Restrictions on Expatriation

(a) Except as provided in paragraph (7), (8), and (9) of section 1481 of this title, no national of the United States can expatriate himself, or be expatriated, under this chapter while within the United States or any of its outlying possessions, but expatriation shall result from the performance within the United States or any of its outlying possessions of any of the acts or the fulfillment of any of the conditions specified in this part if and when the national thereafter takes up a residence outside the United States and its outlying possessions.

(b) A national who within six months after attaining the age of eighteen years asserts his claim to United States nationality, in such manner as the Secretary of State shall by regulation prescribe, shall not be deemed to have expatriated himself by the commission, prior to his eighteenth birthday, of any of the acts specified in paragraphs (2), (4), (5), and (6) of section 1481(a) of this title.

June 27, 1952, c. 477, Title III, ch. 3, § 351, 66 Stat. 269.

8 U.S.C. §1484

Loss of Nationality by Naturalized National

(a) A person who has become a national by naturalization shall lose his nationality by—

(1) having a continuous residence for three years in the territory of a

foreign state of which he was formerly a national or in which the place of his birth is situated, except as provided in section 1485 of this title, whether such residence commenced before or after the effective date of this chapter;

(2) having a continuous residence for five years in any other foreign state or states, except as provided in sections 1485 and 1486 of this title, whether such residence commenced before or after the effective date of this chapter.

(b) (1) For the purpose of paragraph (1) of subsection (a) of this section, the time during which the person had his residence abroad solely or principally for a reason or purpose within the scope of any provision of section 1485 of this title shall not be counted in computing quantum of residence.

(2) For the purpose of paragraph (2) of subsection (a) of this section, the time during which the person had his residence abroad solely or principally for a reason or purpose within the scope of any provision of sections 1485 and 1486 of this title shall not be counted in computing quantum of residence.

June 27, 1952, c. 477, Title III, ch. 3, § 352, 66 Stat. 269.

8 U.S.C. §1485

Inapplicability of Section 1484 to Certain Persons

Section 1484(a) of this title shall have no application to a national who—

(1) has his residence abroad in the employment of the Government of the United States; or

(2) is receiving compensation from the Government of the United States and has his residence abroad on account of disability incurred in its service; or

(3) shall have had his residence in the United States for not less than twenty-five years subsequent to his naturalization and shall have attained the age of sixty years when the foreign residence is established; or

(4) had his residence abroad on October 14, 1940, and temporarily has his residence abroad, or who thereafter has gone or goes abroad and temporarily has his residence abroad, solely or principally to represent a bona fide American educational, scientific, philanthropic, commercial, financial, or business organization, having its principal office or place of business in the United States, or a bona fide religious organization having an office and representative in the United States, or an international agency of an official character in which the United States participates, for which he receives a substantial compensation; or

(5) has his residence abroad and is prevented from returning to the United States exclusively (A) by his own ill health; or (B) by the ill health of his parent, spouse, or child who cannot be brought to the United States, whose condition requires his personal care and attendance: *Provided,* That in such case the person having his residence abroad shall, at least every six months, register at the appropriate Foreign Service office and submit evidence satisfactory to the Secretary of State that his case continues to meet the requirements of this subparagraph; or (C) by reason of the death of his parent, spouse, or child: *Provided,* That in the case of the death of such parent, spouse, or child the person having his residence abroad shall return to the United States within six months after the death of such relative; or

(6) has his residence abroad for the purpose of pursuing a full course of study of a specialized character or attending full-time an institution of learning of a grade above that of a preparatory school: *Provided,* That such residence does not exceed five years; or

(7) is the spouse or child of, or has a son or daughter who is, an American citizen, and who has his residence abroad for the purpose of being with his American citizen spouse, parent, or son or daughter who has his residence abroad for one of the objects or considerations specified in paragraph (1), (2), (3), (4), (5), or (6) of this section, or paragraph (2) of section 1486 of this title; or

(8) is the spouse or child of an American national by birth who while under the age of twenty-one years had his residence in the United States for a period or periods totaling ten years, and has his residence abroad for the purpose of being with said spouse or parent; or

(9) was both in the United States or one of its outlying possessions, who originally had American nationality and who, after having lost such nationality through marriage to an alien, reacquired it; or

(10) has, by Act of Congress or by treaty, United States nationality solely by reason of former nationality and birth or residence in an area outside the continental United States: *Provided,* That subsections (b) and (c) of section 404 of the Nationality Act of 1940, as amended, shall not be held to be or to have been applicable to persons defined in this paragraph.

June 27, 1952, c. 477, Title III, ch. 3, § 353, 66 Stat. 270;
Aug. 4, 1959, Pub.L. 86-129, § 1, 73 Stat. 274.

8 U.S.C. §1486

Inapplicability of Section 1484(a) (2) to Certain Persons

Section 1484(a) (2) of this title shall have no application to a national—

(1) who is a veteran of the Spanish-American War, World War I, or World War II, or of the Korean hostilities (having served honorably in an active-duty status in the military, air, or naval forces of the United States during a period beginning June 25, 1950, and ending July 1, 1955), and the spouse, children, and dependant parents of such veteran whether such residence in the territory of a foreign state or states commenced before or after the effective date of this chapter: *Provided,* That any such veteran who upon June 27, 1952, has had his residence continuously in the territory of a foreign state of which he was formerly a national or in which the place of his birth is situated for three years or more, and who has retained his United States nationality solely by reason of the provisions of section 406(h) of the Nationality Act of 1940, shall not be subject to the provisions or requirements of section 1484(a) (1) of this title: *Provided further,* That the provisions of section 404(c) of the Nationality Act of 1940, as amended, shall not be held to be or to have been applicable to veterans of World War II;

(2) who has established to the satisfaction of the Secretary of State, as evidenced by possession of a valid unexpired United States passport or other valid document issued by the Secretary of State, that his residence is temporarily outside of the United States for the purpose of (A) carrying on a

commercial enterprise which in the opinion of the Secretary of State will directly and substantially benefit American trade or commerce; or (B) carrying on scientific research on behalf of an institution accredited by the Secretary of State and engaged in research which in the opinion of the Secretary of State is directly and substantially beneficial to the interests of the United States; or (C) engaging in such work or activities, under such unique or unusual circumstances, as may be determined by the Secretary of State to be directly and substantially beneficial to the interests of the United States;

(3) who is the widow or widower of a citizen of the United States and who has attained the age of sixty years, and who has had a residence outside of the United States and its outlying possessions for a period of not less than ten years during all of which period a marriage relationship has existed with a spouse who has had a residence outside of the United States and its outlying possessions in an occupation or capacity of the type designated in paragraphs (1), (2), (3), (4), or (5) (A) of section 1485 of this title, or paragraphs (1), (2) or (4) of this section;

(4) who has attained the age of sixty years, and has had a residence outside the United States and its outlying possessions for not less than ten years, during all of which period he has been engaged in an occupation of the type designated in paragraphs (1), (2), or (4) of section 1485 of this title, or paragraph (2) of this section, and who is in bona fide retirement from such occupation; or who is the spouse or child of the national described in this paragraph and who has his residence abroad for the purpose of being with such American citizen spouse or parent; or

(5) who shall have had his residence in the United States for not less than fifteen years subsequent to his naturalization and prior to the establishment of his foreign residence; or who prior to attaining the age of twenty-one years, shall have had his residence in the United States for not less than fifteen years subsequent to his lawful admission for permanent residence.

June 27, 1952, c. 477, Title III, ch. 3, § 354, 66 Stat. 271;
Aug. 4, 1959, Pub.L. 86-129, §§ 2, 3, 73 Stat. 274;
Sept. 26, 1961, Pub.L. 87-301, § 20, 75 Stat. 656.

8 U.S.C. §1487

Loss of American Nationality Through Parents' Expatriation; Not Effective Until Persons Attain Age of Twenty-Five Years

A person having United States nationality, who is under the age of twenty-one and whose residence is in a foreign state with or under the legal custody of a parent who hereafter loses United States nationality under section 1482 or 1484 of this title, shall also lose his United States nationality if such person has or acquires the nationality of such foreign state: *Provided,* That, in such case, United States nationality shall not be lost as the result of loss of United States nationality by the parent unless and until the person attains the age of twenty-five years without having established his residence in the United States.

June 27, 1952, c. 477, Title III, ch. 3, § 355, 66 Stat. 272.

8 U.S.C. §1488

Nationality Lost Solely from Performance of Acts or Fulfillment of Conditions

The loss of nationality under this part shall result solely from the performance by a national of the acts or fulfillment of the conditions specified in this part.

June 27, 1952, c. 477, Title III, ch. 3, § 356, 66 Stat. 272.

CASES

Kennedy v. Mendoza-Martinez

372 U.S. 144 (1962)

Mr. Justice Goldberg delivered the opinion of the Court.

We are called upon in these two cases to decide the grave and fundamental problem, common to both, of the constitutionality of Acts of Congress which divest an American of his citizenship for "[d]eparting from or remaining outside of the jurisdiction of the United States in time of war or . . . national emergency for the purpose of evading or avoiding training and service" in the Nation's armed forces.

* * *

IV. The Constitutional Issues.

A. Basic Principles.

Since the validity of an Act of Congress is involved, we begin our analysis mindful that the function we are now discharging is "the gravest and most delicate duty that this Court is called upon to perform." *Blodgett v. Holden,* 275 U.S. 142, 148 (separate opinion of Holmes, J.). This responsibility we here fulfill with all respect for the powers of Congress, but with recognition of the transcendent status of our Constitution.

We deal with the contending constitutional arguments in the context of certain basic and sometimes conflicting principles. Citizenship is a most precious right. It is expressly guaranteed by the Fourteenth Amendment to the Constitution, which speaks in the most positive terms. The Constitution is silent about the permissibility of involuntary forfeiture of citizenship rights. While it confirms citizenship rights, plainly there are imperative obligations of citizenship, performance of which Congress in the exercise of its powers may constitutionally exact. One of the most important of these is to serve the country in time of war and national emergency. The powers of Congress to require military service for the common defense are broad and far-reaching, for while the Constitution protects against invasions of individual rights, it is not a suicide pact. Similarly, Congress has broad power under the Necessary and Proper Clause to enact legislation for the regulation of foreign affairs. Latitude in this area is necessary to ensure effectuation of this indispensable function of government.

These principles, stemming on the one hand from the precious nature of the constitutionally guaranteed rights of citizenship, and on the other from the powers of Congress and the related obligations of individual citizens, are urged upon us by the parties here. The Government argues that §§ 401 (j) and 349 (a) (10) are valid as an exercise of Congress' power over foreign affairs, of its war power, and of the inherent sovereignty of the Government. Appellees urge the provisions' invalidity as not within any of the powers asserted, and as imposing a cruel and unusual punishment.

We recognize at the outset that we are confronted here with an issue of the utmost import. Deprivation of citizenship—particularly American citizenship, which is "one of the most valuable rights in the world today," Report of the President's Commission on Immigration and Naturalization (1953), 235—has grave practical consequences. An expatriate who, like Cort, had no other nationality becomes a stateless person—a person who not only has no rights as an American citizen, but no membership in any national entity whatsoever. "Such individuals as do not possess any nationality enjoy, in general, no protection whatever, and if they are aggrieved by a State they have no means of redress, since there is no State which is competent to take up their case. As far as the Law of Nations is concerned, there is, apart from restraints of morality or obligations expressly laid down by treaty . . . no restriction whatever to cause a State to abstain from maltreating to any extent such stateless individuals." 1 Oppenheim, International Law (8th ed., Lauterpacht, 1955), § 291, at 640. The calamity is "[n]ot the loss of specific rights, then, but the loss of a community willing and able to guarantee any rights whatsoever. . . ." Arendt, The Origins of Totalitarianism (1951), 294. The stateless person may end up shunted from nation to nation, there being no one obligated or willing to receive him, or, as in Cort's case, may receive the dubious sanctuary of a Communist regime lacking the essential liberties precious to American citizenship.

B. The Perez and Trop Cases.

The basic principles here involved, the gravity of the issue, and the arguments bearing upon Congress' power to forfeit citizenship were considered by the Court in relation to different provisions of the Nationality Act of 1940 in two cases decided on the same day less than five years ago: *Perez v. Brownell,* 356 U.S. 44, and *Trop v. Dulles,* 356 U.S. 86.

In *Perez,* § 401 (e), which imposes loss of nationality for "[v]oting in a political election in a foreign state or participating in an election or plebiscite to determine the sovereignty over foreign territory," was upheld by a closely divided Court as a constitutional exercise of Congress' power to regulate foreign affairs. The Court reasoned that since withdrawal of citizenship of Americans who vote in foreign elections is reasonably calculated to effect the avoidance of embarrassment in the conduct of foreign relations, such withdrawal is within the power of Congress, acting under the Necessary and Proper Clause. Since the Court sustained the application of § 401 (e) to denationalize Perez, it did not have to deal with § 401 (j), upon which the Government had also relied, and it expressly declined to rule on the constitutionality of that section, 356 U.S., at 62. There were three opinions written in dissent. The principal one, that of The Chief Justice, recognized "that citizenship may not only be voluntarily renounced through exercise of the right of expatriation but also by other actions in derogation of undivided allegiance to this country," *id.,* at 68, but concluded that "[t]he mere act of voting in a foreign election, however, without regard to the circumstances attending the participation, is not sufficient to show a voluntary abandonment of citizenship," *id.,* at 78.

In *Trop,* § 401 (g), forfeiting the citizenship of any American who is guilty of "[d]eserting the military or naval forces of the United States in time of war, provided he is convicted thereof by court martial and as the result of such conviction is dismissed or dishonorably discharged, . . ." was declared unconstitutional. There was no opinion of the Court. The Chief Justice wrote an opinion for four members of the Court, concluding that § 401 (g) was invalid for the same reason that he had urged as to § 401 (e) in his dissent in *Perez,* and that it was also invalid as a cruel and unusual punishment imposed in violation of the Eighth Amendment. Justice Brennan conceded that it is "paradoxical to justify as constitutional the expatriation of the citizen who has committed no crime by voting in a Mexican political election, yet find unconstitutional a statute which provides for the expatriation of a soldier guilty of the very serious crime of desertion in time of war," 356 U.S., at 105. Notwithstanding, he concurred because "the requisite rational relation between this statute and the war power does not appear, . . ." *id.,* at 114. Justice Frankfurter, joined by three other Justices, dissented on the ground that § 401 (g) did not impose punishment at all, let alone cruel and unusual punishment, and was within the war powers of Congress.

C. Sections 401 (j) and 349 (a) (10) as Punishment.

The present cases present for decision the constitutionality of a section not passed upon in either *Perez* or *Trop*—§ 401 (j), added in 1944, and its successor and present counterpart, § 349 (a) (10) of the Immigration and Nationality Act of 1952. We have come to the conclusion that there is a basic question in the present cases, the answer to which obviates a choice here between the powers of Congress and the constitutional guarantee of citizenship. That issue is whether the statutes here, which automatically—without prior court or administrative proceedings—impose forfeiture of citizenship, are essentially penal in character, and consequently have deprived the appellees of their citizenship without due process of law and without according them the rights guaranteed by the Fifth and Sixth Amendments, including notice, confrontation, compulsory process for obtaining witnesses, trial by jury, and assistance of counsel. This issue was not relevant in *Trop* because, in contrast to §§ 401 (j) and 349 (a) (10), § 401 (g) required conviction by court-martial for desertion before forfeiture of citizenship could be inflicted. In *Perez* the contention that § 401 (e) was penal in character was impliedly rejected by the Court's holding, based on legislative history totally different from that underlying §§ 401 (j) and 349 (a) (10), that voting in a political election in a foreign state "is regulable by Congress under its power to deal with foreign affairs." 356 U.S., at 59. Compare *Dent v. West Virginia,* 129 U.S. 114; *Hawker v. New York,* 170 U.S. 189; *Flemming v. Nestor,* 363 U.S. 603. Indeed, in *Trop* The Chief Justice observed that

"Section 401 (j) decrees loss of citizenship without providing any semblance of procedural due process whereby the guilt of the draft evader may be determined before the sanction is imposed, . . ." 356 U.S., at 94, and Justice Frankfurter in dissent alluded to the due process overtones of the requirement in § 401 (g) of prior conviction for desertion by court-martial, *id.*, at 116-117.

It is fundamental that the great powers of Congress to conduct war and to regulate the Nation's foreign relations are subject to the constitutional requirements of due process. The imperative necessity for safeguarding these rights to procedural due process under the gravest of emergencies has existed throughout our constitutional history, for it is then, under the pressing exigencies of crisis, that there is the greatest temptation to dispense with fundamental constitutional guarantees which, it is feared, will inhibit governmental action. "The Constitution of the United States is a law for rulers and people, equally in war and in peace, and covers with the shield of its protection all classes of men, at all times, and under all circumstances." *Ex parte Milligan,* 4 Wall. 2, 120-121. The rights guaranteed by the Fifth and Sixth Amendments are "preserved to every one accused of crime who is not attached to the army, or navy, or militia in actual service." *Id.,* at 123. "[I]f society is disturbed by civil commotion—if the passions of men are aroused and the restraints of law weakened, if not disregarded—these safeguards need, and should receive, the watchful care of those intrusted with the guardianship of the Constitution and laws. In no other way can we transmit to posterity unimpaired the blessings of liberty, consecrated by the sacrifices of the Revolution." *Id.,* at 124.

We hold §§ 401 (j) and 349 (a) (10) invalid because in them Congress has plainly employed the sanction of deprivation of nationality as a punishment—for the offense of leaving or remaining outside the country to evade military service—without affording the procedural safeguards guaranteed by the Fifth and Sixth Amendments. Our forefathers "intended to safeguard the people of this country from punishment without trial by duly constituted courts. . . . And even the courts to which this important function was entrusted were commanded to stay their hands until and unless certain tested safeguards were observed. An accused in court must be tried by an impartial jury, has a right to be represented by counsel, [and] must be clearly informed of the charge against him. . . ." *United States v. Lovett,* 328 U.S. 303, 317. See also *Chambers v. Florida,* 309 U.S. 227, 235-238.

As the Government concedes, §§ 401 (j) and 349 (a) (10) automatically strip an American of his citizenship, with concomitant deprivation "of all that makes life worth living," *Ng Fung Ho v. White,* 259 U.S. 276, 284-285, whenever a citizen departs from or remains outside the jurisdiction of this country for the purpose of evading his military obligations. Conviction for draft evasion, as Cort's case illustrates, is not prerequisite to the operation of this sanction. Independently of prosecution, forfeiture of citizenship attaches when the statutory set of facts develops. It is argued that the availability after the fact of administrative and judicial proceedings, including the machinery the Court approved last Term in *Rusk v. Cort,* 369 U.S. 367, to contest the validity of the sanction meets the measure of due process. But the legislative history and judicial expression with respect to every congressional enactment relating to the provisions in question dating back to 1865 establish that forfeiture of citizenship is a penalty for the act of leaving or staying outside the country to avoid the draft. This being so, the Fifth and Sixth Amendments mandate that this punishment cannot be imposed without a prior criminal trial and all its incidents, including indictment, notice, confrontation, jury trial, assistance of counsel, and compulsory process for obtaining witnesses. If the sanction these sections impose is punishment, and it plainly is, the procedural safeguards required as incidents of a criminal prosecution are lacking. We need go no further.

The punitive nature of the sanction here is evident under the tests traditionally applied to determine whether an Act of Congress is penal or regulatory in character, even though in other cases this problem has been extremely difficult and elusive of solution. Whether the sanction involves an affirmative disability or restraint, whether it has historically been regarded as a punishment, whether it comes into play only on a finding of *scienter,* whether its operation will promote the traditional aims of punishment—retribution and deterrence, whether the behavior to which it applies is already a crime, whether an alternative purpose to which it may rationally be connected is assignable for it, and whether it appears excessive in relation to the alternative purpose assigned are all relevant to the inquiry, and may often point in differing directions. Absent conclusive evidence of congressional intent as to the penal nature of a statute, these factors must be considered in relation to the statute on its face. Here, although we are convinced that application of these criteria to the face of the statutes supports the conclusion that they are punitive, a detailed examination along such lines is unnecessary, because the objective manifestations of congressional purpose indicate conclusively that the provisions in question can only be interpreted as punitive. A study of the history of the predecessor of § 401 (j), which "is worth a volume of logic," *New York Trust Co. v. Eisner,* 256 U.S. 345, 349, coupled with a reading of Congress' reasons for enacting § 401 (j), compels a conclusion that the statute's primary function is to serve as an additional penalty for a special category of draft evader. Compare *Trop v. Dulles, supra,* 356 U.S., at 107-110 (Brennan, J., concurring).

* * *

2. The Present Statutes.

The immediate legislative history of § 401 (j) confirms the conclusion, based upon study of the earlier legislative and judicial history, that it is punitive in nature. The language of the section was, to begin with, quite obviously patterned on that of its predecessor, an understandable fact since the draft of the bill was submitted to the Congress by Attorney General Biddle along with a letter to Chairman Russell of the Senate Immigration Committee, in which the Attorney General referred for precedent to the 1912 reenactment of the 1865 statute. This letter, which was the impetus for the enactment of the bill, was quoted in full text in support of it in both the House and Senate Committee Reports, H. R. Rep. No. 1229, 78th Cong., 2d Sess. 2-3 (1944); S. Rep. No. 1075, 78th Cong., 2d Sess. 2 (1944), and is set out in the margin. The Senate Report stated that it "fully explains the purpose of the bill." S. Rep. No. 1075, *supra,* at 1. The letter was couched entirely in terms of an argument that citizens who had left the country in order to escape military service should be dealt with, and that loss of citizenship was a proper way to deal with them. There was no reference to the societal good that would be wrought by the legislation, nor to any improvement in soldier morale or in the conduct of war generally that would be gained by the passage of the statute. The House Committee Report and the sponsors of the bill endorsed it on the same basis. The report referred for support to the fact that the FBI files showed "over 800 draft delinquents" in the El Paso area alone who had crossed to Mexico to evade the draft. H. R. Rep. No. 1229, *supra,* at 2. The obvious inference to be drawn from the report, the example it contained, and the lack of mention of any broader purpose is that Congress was concerned solely with inflicting effective retribution upon this class of draft evaders and, no doubt, on others similarly situated. Thus, on the floor of the House, Representative Dickstein of New York, the Chairman of the House Committee on Immigration and Naturalization, explained the bill solely as a means of dealing with "draft dodgers who left this country knowing that there was a possibility that they might be drafted in this war and that they might have to serve in the armed forces. . . ." He implied that the bill was necessary to frustrate their "idea of evading military service and of returning after the war is over, and taking their old places in our society." 90 Cong. Rec. 3261 (1944). Senator Russell, who was manager of the bill as well as Chairman of the Senate Immigration Committee, explained it in similar terms:

> "Certainly those who, having enjoyed the advantages of living in the United States, were unwilling to serve their country or subject themselves to the Selective Service Act, should be penalized in some measure. . . . Any American citizen who is convicted of violating the Selective Service Act loses his citizenship. This bill would merely impose a similar penalty on those who are not subject to the jurisdiction of our courts, the penalty being the same as would result in the case of those who are subject to the jurisdiction of our courts." 90 Cong. Rec. 7629 (1944).

The Senate and House debates, together with Attorney General Biddle's letter, brought to light no alternative purpose to differentiate the new statute from its predecessor. Indeed, as indicated, the Attorney General's letter specifically relied on the predecessor statute as precedent for this enactment, and both the letter and the debates, consistent with the character of the predecessor statute, referred to reasons for the enactment of the bill which were fundamentally retributive in nature. When all of these considerations are weighed, as they must be, in the context of the incontestibly punitive nature of the predecessor statute, the conclusion that § 401 (j) was itself dominantly punitive becomes inescapable. The legislative history of § 349 (a) (10) of the Immigration and Nationality Act of 1952, which re-enacted § 401 (j), adds nothing to disturb that result. Our conclusion from the legislative and judicial history is, therefore, that Congress in these sections decreed an additional punishment for the crime of draft avoidance in the special category of cases wherein the evader leaves the country. It cannot do this without providing the safeguards which must attend a criminal prosecution.

V. Conclusion.

It is argued that our holding today will have the unfortunate result of immunizing the draft evader who has left the United States from having to suffer any sanction against his conduct, since he must return to this country before he can be apprehended and tried for his crime. The compelling answer to this is that the Bill of Rights which we guard so jealously and the procedures it guarantees are not to be abrogated merely because a guilty man may escape prosecution or for any other expedient reason. Moreover, the truth is that even without being expatriated, the evader living abroad is not in a position to assert the vast majority of his component rights as an American citizen. If he wishes to assert those rights in any real sense he must return to this country, and by doing that he will subject himself to prosecution. In fact, while he is outside the country evading prosecution, the United States may, by proper refusal to exercise its largely discretionary power to afford him diplomatic protection, decline to invoke its sovereign power on his behalf. Since the substantial benefits of American citizenship only come into play upon return to face prosecution, the draft evader who wishes to exercise his citizenship rights will inevitably come home and pay his debt, which within constitutional limits Congress has the power to define. This is what Mendoza-Martinez did, what Cort says he is willing to do, and what others have done. Thus our holding today does not frustrate the effective handling of the problem of draft evaders who leave the United States.

We conclude, for the reasons stated, that §§ 401 (j) and 349 (a) (10) are punitive and as such cannot constitutionally stand, lacking as they do the procedural safeguards which the Constitution commands. We recognize that draft evasion, particularly in time of war, is a heinous offense, and should and can be properly punished. Dating back to Magna Carta, however, it has been an abiding principle governing the lives of civilized men that "no freeman shall be taken or imprisoned or disseised or outlawed or exiled . . . without the judgment of his peers or by the law of the land. . . ." What we hold is only that, in keeping with this cherished tradition, punishment cannot be imposed "without due process of law." Any lesser holding would ignore the constitutional mandate upon which our essential liberties depend. Therefore the judgments of the District Courts in these cases are

Affirmed.

Mr. Justice Douglas and Mr. Justice Black, while joining the opinion of the Court, adhere to the views expressed in the dissent of Mr. Justice Douglas, in which Mr. Justice Black joined, in *Perez v. Brownell,* 356 U.S. 44, 79, that Congress has no power to deprive a person of the citizenship granted the native-born by § 1, cl. 1, of the Fourteenth Amendment.

Mr. Justice Brennan, concurring. . . .

Mr. Justice Harlan, whom Mr. Justice Clark joins, dissenting. . . .

Mr. Justice Stewart, with whom Mr. Justice White joins, dissenting. . . .

The Right to Travel

COMMENTARY

International travel, the Supreme Court has held, is a constitutionally protected right—an aspect of Fifth Amendment liberty that may be restricted only to protect a substantial public interest which can be met in no other way. Applying this principle, the Court has permitted the government to refuse to validate passports for travel to certain designated areas. But it has upheld the citizen's right to undertake such travel without a passport, and prohibited the imposition of criminal penalties for travel to unauthorized areas. As a practical matter, Americans are free to travel anywhere they choose, subject only to the knowledge that if they travel to restricted areas the State Department may not be able and would not be obliged to provide the services it is otherwise required by law to provide for American citizens.

These principles evolved in a series of cases reviewing government efforts to prevent alleged Communists from travelling abroad. In 1952 the State Department issued regulations under a 1926 Act, denying passports to members of the Communist Party and others traveling to advance the interests of the Communist movement. In *Kent v. Dulles,* 357 U.S. 116 (1958), the Court held that Congress had not authorized the withholding of passports on the basis of beliefs.

Six years later the court faced the constitutional issue squarely. In the Internal Security Act of 1950, 50 U.S.C. §785, Congress had specifically directed the withholding of passports from members of designated political organizations. The Court found the statute unconstitutional on its face, since its broad sweep covered not only situations in which the national security interest might justify restrictions on travel, but many innocuous situations as well. The statute, the Court noted, failed to distinguish between knowing and unknowing members of listed organizations, and failed to take into account the purpose of the travel or the areas into which the individual intended to go.[1]

The reasoning in *Aptheker* foreshadowed the later upholding by the Court of regulations permitting the Secretary of State to refuse to validate passports for travel to Cuba.[2] While affirming its holding in *Kent v. Dulles* that the right to travel is a protected liberty, the Court held that it could be abridged when the limitations were not based on the beliefs of the traveller, but rather on national security considerations applying equally to all citizens. The Court examined the national security rationale for prohibiting travel to Cuba and noted that "the Secretary (of State) has justifiably concluded that travel to Cuba by American citizens might involve the Nation in dangerous international incidents."

The impact of this holding was substantially softened when the Court held shortly afterward that, although the State Department could refuse to validate the passport for travel to a certain area, no legitimate national security purpose was served by allowing criminal penalties on those who chose to travel without State Department protection.[3] A Court of Appeals narrowed the government's ability to prevent travel to closed areas even further, when it held that the State Department could not deny a passport to an individual because of the belief that he intended to go to a closed area while on his trip.[4]

---

[1]*Aptheker v. Secretary of State,* 378 U.S. 550 (1963).

[2]*Zemel v. Rusk,* 381 U.S. 1 (1964).

[3]*United States v. Laub,* 385 U.S. 475 (1967).

[4]*Lynd v. Rusk,* 389 F.2d 940 (D.C. Cir. 1967).

CASES

Kent et.al. v. Dulles, Secretary of State

357 U.S. 116 (1957)

Mr. Justice Douglas delivered the opinion of the Court.

This case concerns two applications for passports, denied by the Secretary of State. One was by Rockwell Kent who desired to visit England and attend a meeting of an organization known as the "World Council of Peace" in Helsinki, Finland. The Director of the Passport Office informed Kent that issuance of a passport was precluded by § 51.135 of the Regulations promulgated by the Secretary of State on two grounds:[1] (1) that he was a Communist and (2) that he had had "a consistent and prolonged adherence to the Communist Party line." The letter of denial specified in some detail the facts on which those conclusions were based. Kent was also advised of his right to an informal hearing under § 51.137 of the Regulations. But he was also told that whether or not a hearing was requested it would be necessary, before a passport would be issued, to submit an affidavit as to whether he was then or ever had been a Communist.[2] Kent did not ask for a hearing but filed a new passport application listing several European countries he desired to visit. When advised that a hearing was still available to him, his attorney replied that Kent took the position that the requirement of an affidavit concerning Communist Party membership "is unlawful and that for that reason and as a matter of conscience," he would not supply one. He did, however, have a hearing at which the principal evidence against him was from his book It's Me O Lord, which Kent agreed was accurate. He again refused to submit the affidavit, maintaining that any matters unrelated to the question of his citizenship were irrelevant to the Department's consideration of his application. The Department advised him that no further consideration of his application would be given until he satisfied the requirements of the Regulations.

Thereupon Kent sued in the District Court for declaratory relief. The District Court granted summary judgment for respondent. On appeal the case of Kent was heard with that of Dr. Walter Briehl, a psychiatrist. When Briehl applied for a passport, the Director of the Passport Office asked him to supply the affidavit covering membership in the Communist Party. Briehl, like Kent, refused. The Director then tentatively disapproved the application on the following grounds:

> "In your case it has been alleged that you were a Communist. Specifically it is alleged that you were a member of the Los Angeles County Communist Party; that you were a member of the Bookshop Association, St. Louis, Missouri; that you held Communist Party meetings; that in 1936 and 1941 you contributed articles to the Communist Publication 'Social Work Today'; that in 1939, 1940 and 1941 you were a sponsor to raise funds for veterans of the Abraham Lincoln Brigade in calling on the President of the United States by a petition to defend the rights of the Communist Party and its members; that you contributed to the Civil Rights Congress bail fund to be used in raising bail on behalf of convicted Communist leaders in New York City; that you were a member of the Hollywood Arts, Sciences and Professions Council and a

contact of the Los Angeles Committee for Protection of Foreign Born and a contact of the Freedom Stage, Incorporated."

The Director advised Briehl of his right to a hearing but stated that whether or not a hearing was held, an affidavit concerning membership in the Communist Party would be necessary. Briehl asked for a hearing and one was held. At that hearing he raised three objections: (1) that his "political affiliations" were irrelevant to his right to a passport; (2) that "every American citizen has the right to travel regardless of politics"; and (3) that the burden was on the Department to prove illegal activities by Briehl. Briehl persisted in his refusal to supply the affidavit. Because of that refusal Briehl was advised that the Board of Passport Appeals could not under the Regulations entertain an appeal.

Briehl filed his complaint in the District Court which held that his case was indistinguishable from Kent's and dismissed the complaint.

The Court of Appeals heard the two cases *en banc* and affirmed the District Court by a divided vote. 101 U.S. App. D. C. 278, 239, 248 F. 2d 600, 561. The cases are here on writ of certiorari. 355 U.S. 881.

The Court first noted the function that the passport performed in American law in the case of *Urtetiqui v. D'Arbel,* 9 Pet. 692, 699, decided in 1835:

> "There is no law of the United States, in any manner regulating the issuing of passports, or directing upon what evidence it may be done, or declaring their legal effect. It is understood, as matter of practice, that some evidence of citizenship is required, by the secretary of state, before issuing a passport. This, however, is entirely discretionary with him. No inquiry is instituted by him to ascertain the fact of citizenship, or any proceedings had, that will in any manner bear the character of a judicial inquiry. It is a document, which, from its nature and object, is addressed to foreign powers; purporting only to be a request, that the bearer of it may pass safely and freely; and is to be considered rather in the character of a political document, by which the bearer is recognized, in foreign countries, as an American citizen; and which, by usage and the law of nations, is received as evidence of the fact."

A passport not only is of great value—indeed necessary—abroad; it is also an aid in establishing citizenship for purposes of re-entry into the United States. See *Browder v. United States,* 312 U.S. 335, 339; 3 Moore, Digest of International Law (1906), § 512. But throughout most of our history—until indeed quite recently—a passport, though a great convenience in foreign travel, was not a legal requirement for leaving or entering the United States. See Jaffe, The Right to Travel: The Passport Problem, 35 Foreign Affairs 17. Apart from minor exceptions to be noted, it was first[3] made a requirement by § 215 of the Act of June 27, 1952, 66 Stat. 190, 8 U. S. C. § 1185, which states that, after a prescribed proclamation by the President, it is "unlawful for any citizen of the United States to depart from or enter, or attempt to depart from or enter, the United States unless he bears a valid passport."[4] And the Proclamation necessary to make the restrictions of this Act applicable and in force has been made.[5]

Prior to 1952 there were numerous laws enacted by Congress regulating passports and many decisions, rulings, and regulations by the Executive Department concerning them. Thus in 1803 Congress made it unlawful for an official knowingly to issue a passport to an alien certifying that he is a citizen. 2 Stat. 205. In 1815, just prior to the termination of the War of 1812, it made it illegal for a citizen to "cross the frontier" into enemy territory, to board vessels of the enemy on waters of the United States or to visit any of his camps within the limits of the United

States, "without a passport first obtained" from the Secretary of State or other designated official. 3 Stat. 199-200. The Secretary of State took similar steps during the Civil War. See Dept. of State, The American Passport (1898), 50. In 1850 Congress ratified a treaty with Switzerland requiring passports from citizens of the two nations. 11 Stat. 587, 589-590. Finally in 1856 Congress enacted what remains today as our basic passport statute. Prior to that time various federal officials, state and local officials, and notaries public had undertaken to issue either certificates of citizenship or other documents in the nature of letters of introduction to foreign officials requesting treatment according to the usages of international law. By the Act of August 18, 1856, 11 Stat. 52, 60-61, 22 U. S. C. § 211a, Congress put an end to those practices.[6] This provision, as codified by the Act of July 3, 1926, 44 Stat., Part 2, 887, reads,

> "The Secretary of State may grant and issue passports . . . under such rules as the President shall designate and prescribe for and on behalf of the United States, and no other person shall grant, issue, or verify such passports."

Thus for most of our history a passport was not a condition to entry or exit.

It is true that, at intervals, a passport has been required for travel. Mention has already been made of the restrictions imposed during the War of 1812 and during the Civil War. A like restriction, which was the forerunner of that contained in the 1952 Act, was imposed by Congress in 1918.

The Act of May 22, 1918, 40 Stat. 559, made it unlawful, while a Presidential Proclamation was in force, for a citizen to leave or enter the United States "unless he bears a valid passport." See H. R. Rep. No. 485, 65th Cong., 2d Sess. That statute was invoked by Presidential Proclamation No. 1473 on August 8, 1918, 40 Stat. 1829, which continued in effect until March 3, 1921. 41 Stat. 1359.

The 1918 Act was effective only in wartime. It was amended in 1941 so that it could be invoked in the then-existing emergency. 55 Stat. 252. See S. Rep. No. 444, 77th Cong., 1st Sess. It was invoked by Presidential Proclamation No. 2523, November 14, 1941, 55 Stat. 1696. That emergency continued until April 28, 1952. Proc. No. 2974, 66 Stat. C31. Congress extended the statutory provisions until April 1, 1953. 66 Stat. 54, 57, 96, 137, 330, 333. It was during this extension period that the Secretary of State issued the Regulations here complained of.[7]

Under the 1926 Act and its predecessor a large body of precedents grew up which repeat over and over again that the issuance of passports is "a discretionary act" on the part of the Secretary of State. The scholars,[8] the courts,[9] the Chief Executive,[10] and the Attorneys General,[11] all so said. This long-continued executive construction should be enough, it is said, to warrant the inference that Congress had adopted it. See *Allen v. Grand Central Aircraft Co.,* 347 U.S. 535, 544-545; *United States v. Allen-Bradley Co.,* 352 U.S. 306, 310. But the key to that problem, as we shall see, is in the manner in which the Secretary's discretion was exercised, not in the bare fact that he had discretion.

The right to travel is a part of the "liberty" of which the citizen cannot be deprived without due process of law under the Fifth Amendment. So much is conceded by the Solicitor General. In Anglo-Saxon law that right was emerging at least as early as the Magna Carta.[12] Chafee, Three Human Rights in the Constitution of 1787 (1956), 171-181, 187 *et seq.,* shows how deeply engrained in our history this freedom of movement is. Freedom of movement across frontiers in either direction, and inside frontiers as well, was a part of our heritage. Travel abroad, like travel within the country, may be necessary for a livelihood. It may be as close to the heart of the individual as the choice of what he eats, or wears, or reads. Freedom of movement is basic in our scheme of values. See *Crandall v. Nevada,* 6 Wall. 35, 44; *Williams v. Fears,* 179 U.S. 270, 274; *Edwards v. California,* 314 U.S. 160. "Our nation," wrote Chafee, "has thrived on the principle that, outside areas of plainly harmful conduct, every American is left to shape his own life as he thinks best, do what he pleases, go where he pleases." *Id.,* at 197.

Freedom of movement also has large social values. As Chafee put it:

> "Foreign correspondents and lecturers on public affairs need first-hand information. Scientists and scholars gain greatly from consultations with colleagues in other countries. Students equip themselves for more fruitful careers in the United States by instruction in foreign universities.[13] Then there are reasons close to the core of personal life—marriage, reuniting families, spending hours with old friends. Finally, travel abroad enables American citizens to understand that people like themselves live in Europe and helps them to be well-informed on public issues. An American who has crossed the ocean is not obliged to form his opinions about our foreign policy merely from what he is told by officials of our government or by a few correspondents of American newspapers. Moreover, his views on domestic questions are enriched by seeing how foreigners are trying to solve similar problems. In many different ways direct contact with other countries contributes to sounder decisions at home." *Id.,* at 195-196. And see Vestal, Freedom of Movement, 41 Iowa L. Rev. 6, 13-14.

Freedom to travel is, indeed, an important aspect of the citizen's "liberty." We need not decide the extent to which it can be curtailed. We are first concerned with the extent, if any, to which Congress has authorized its curtailment.

The difficulty is that while the power of the Secretary of State over the issuance of passports is expressed in broad terms, it was apparently long exercised quite narrowly. So far as material here, the cases of refusal of passports generally fell into two categories. First, questions pertinent to the citizenship of the applicant and his allegiance to the United States had to be resolved by the Secretary, for the command of Congress was that "No passport shall be granted or issued to or verified for any other persons than those owing allegiance, whether citizens or not, to the United States." 32 Stat. 386, 22 U. S. C. § 212. Second, was the question whether the applicant was participating in illegal conduct, trying to escape the toils of the law, promoting passport frauds, or otherwise engaging in conduct which would violate the laws of the United States. See 3 Moore, Digest of International Law (1906), § 512; 3 Hackworth, Digest of International Law (1942), § 268; 2 Hyde, International Law (2d rev. ed.), § 401.

The grounds for refusal asserted here do not relate to citizenship or allegiance on the one hand or to criminal or unlawful conduct on the other. Yet, so far as relevant here, those two are the only ones which it could fairly be argued were adopted by Congress in light of prior administrative practice. One can find in the records of the State Department rulings of subordinates covering a wider range of activities than the two indicated. But as respects Communists these are scattered rulings and not consistently of one pattern. We can say with assurance that whatever may have been the practice after 1926, at the time the Act of July 3, 1926, was adopted, the administrative practice, so far as relevant here, had jelled only around the two categories mentioned. We, therefore, hesitate to impute to Congress, when in 1952 it made a passport necessary for foreign travel and left its issuance to the discretion of the Secretary of State, a purpose to give him unbridled discretion to grant or withold a passport from a citizen for any substantive reason he may choose.

More restrictive regulations were applied in 1918 and in 1941 as war measures. We are not compelled to equate this present problem of statutory construction with problems that may arise under the war power. Cf. *Youngstown Sheet & Tube Co. v. Sawyer,* 343 U.S. 579.

In a case of comparable magnitude, *Korematsu v. United States,* 323 U.S. 214, 218, we allowed the Government in time of war to exclude citizens from their homes and restrict their freedom of movement only on a showing of "the gravest imminent danger to the public safety." There the Congress and the Chief Executive moved in coordinated action; and, as we said, the Nation was then at war. No such condition presently exists. No such showing of extremity, no such showing of joint action by the Chief Executive and the Congress to curtail a constitutional right of the citizen has been made here.

Since we start with an exercise by an American citizen of an activity included in constitutional protection, we will not readily infer that Congress gave the Secretary of State unbridled discretion to grant or withhold it. If we were dealing with political questions entrusted to the Chief Executive by the Constitution we would have a different case. But there is more involved here. In part, of course, the issuance of the passport carries some implication of intention to extend the bearer diplomatic protection, though it does not more than "request all whom it may concern to permit safely and freely to pass, and in case of need to give all lawful aid and protection" to this citizen of the United States. But that function of the passport is subordinate. Its crucial function today is control over exit. And, as we have seen, the right of exit is a personal right included within the word "liberty" as used in the Fifth Amendment. If that "liberty" is to be regulated, it must be pursuant to the law-making functions of the Congress. *Youngstown Sheet & Tube Co. v. Sawyer, supra.* And if that power is delegated, the standards must be adequate to pass scrutiny by the accepted tests. See *Panama Refining Co. v. Ryan,* 293 U.S. 388, 420-430. Cf. *Cantwell v. Connecticut,* 310 U.S. 296, 307; *Niemotko v. Maryland,* 340 U.S. 268, 271. Where activities or enjoyment, natural and often necessary to the well-being of an American citizen, such as travel, are involved, we will construe narrowly all delegated powers that curtail or dilute them. See *Ex parte Endo,* 323 U.S. 283, 301-302. Cf. *Hannegan v. Esquire, Inc.,* 327 U.S. 146, 156; *United States v. Rumely,* 345 U.S. 41, 46. We hesitate to find in this broad generalized power an authority to trench so heavily on the rights of the citizen.

Thus we do not reach the question of constitutionality. We only conclude that § 1185 and § 211a do not delegate to the Secretary the kind of authority exercised here. We deal with beliefs, with associations, with ideological matters. We must remember that we are dealing here with citizens who have neither been accused of crimes nor found guilty. They are being denied their freedom of movement solely because of their refusal to be subjected to inquiry into their beliefs and associations. They do not seek to escape the law nor to violate it. They may or may not be Communists. But assuming they are, the only law which Congress has passed expressly curtailing the movement of Communists across our borders has not yet become effective.[14] It would therefore be strange to infer that pending the effectiveness of that law, the Secretary has been silently granted by Congress the larger, the more pervasive power to curtail in his discretion the free movement of citizens in order to satisfy himself about their beliefs or associations.

To repeat, we deal here with a constitutional right of the citizen, a right which we must assume Congress will be faithful to respect. We would be faced with important constitutional questions were we to hold that Congress by § 1185 and § 211a had given the Secretary authority to withhold passports to citizens because of their beliefs or associations. Congress has made no such provision in explicit terms; and absent one, the Secretary may not employ that standard to restrict the citizens' right of free movement.

Reversed.

Mr. Justice Clark, with whom Mr. Justice Burton, Mr. Justice Harlan, and Mr. Justice Whittaker concur, dissenting. . . .

---

[1]22 CFR § 51.135 provides:

"In order to promote the national interest by assuring that persons who support the world Communist movement of which the Communist Party is an integral unit may not, through use of United States passports, further the purposes of that movement, no passport, except one limited for direct and immediate return to the United States, shall be issued to:

"(a) Persons who are members of the Communist Party or who have recently terminated such membership under such circumstances as to warrant the conclusion—not otherwise rebutted by the evidence—that they continue to act in furtherance of the interests and under the discipline of the Communist Party;

"(b) Persons, regardless of the formal state of their affiliation with the Communist Party, who engage in activities which support the Communist movement under such circumstances as to warrant the conclusion—not otherwise rebutted by the evidence—that they have engaged in such activities as a result of direction, domination, or control exercised over them by the Communist movement;

"(c) Persons, regardless of the formal state of their affiliation with the Communist Party, as to whom there is reason to believe, on the balance of all the evidence, that they are going abroad to engage in activities which will advance the Communist movement for the purpose, knowingly and wilfully of advancing that movement."

[2]Section 51.142 of the Regulations provides:

"At any stage of the proceedings in the Passport Division or before the Board, if it is deemed necessary, the applicant may be required, as a part of his application, to subscribe, under oath or affirmation, to a statement with respect to present or past membership in the Communist Party. If applicant states that he is a Communist, refusal of a passport in his case will be without further proceedings."

[3]Sections 2 and 6 of the Act of September 23, 1950, known as the Internal Security Act of 1950, 64 Stat. 987, 993, 50 U. S. C. §§ 781, 785, provided that it shall be unlawful, when a Communist organization is registered under the Act or when "there is in effect a final order of the Board requiring an organization to register," for any member having knowledge of such registry and order to apply for a passport or for any official to issue him one. But the conditions precedent have not yet materialized.

[4]That section provides in relevant part:

"(a) When the United States is at war or during the existence of any national emergency proclaimed by the President, . . . and the President shall find that the interests of the United States require that restrictions and prohibitions in addition to those provided otherwise than by this section be imposed upon the departure of persons from and their entry into the United States, and shall make public proclamation thereof, it shall, until otherwise ordered by the President or the Congress, be unlawful—

"(1) for any alien to depart from or enter or attempt to depart from or enter the United States except under such reasonable rules, regulations, and orders, and subject to such limitations and exceptions as the President may prescribe;

* * *

"(3) for any person knowingly to make any false statement in an application for permission to depart from or enter the United States with intent to induce or secure the granting of such permission either for himself or for another;

* * *

"(b) After such proclamation as is provided for in subsection (a) has been made and published and while such proclamation is in force, it shall, except as otherwise provided by the President, and subject to such limitations and exceptions as the President may authorize and prescribe, be unlawful for any citizen of the United States to depart from or enter, or attempt to depart from or enter, the United States unless he bears a valid passport."

[5]Proc. No. 3004, 67 Stat. C31.

[6]See 9 Op. Atty. Gen. 350, 352.

[7]Dept. Reg. No. 108.162, effective August 28, 1952, 17 Fed. Reg. 8013.

[8]See 2 Hyde, International Law (2d rev. ed. 1945), § 399; 3 Hackworth, Digest of International Law (1942), § 268.

[9]See *Perkins v. Elg,* 307 U.S. 325, 350.

[10]Exec. Order No. 654, June 13, 1907; *id.,* No. 2119-A, Jan. 12, 1915; *id.,* No. 2286-A, Dec. 17, 1915; *id.,* No. 2362-A, Apr. 17, 1916; *id.,* No. 2519-A, Jan. 24, 1917; *id.,* No. 4382-A, Feb. 12, 1926; *id.,* No. 4800, Jan. 31, 1928; *id.,* No. 5860, June 22, 1932; *id.,* No. 7856, Mar. 31, 1938, 3 Fed. Reg. 681, 22 CFR § 51.75. The present provision is that last listed and reads in part as follows:

"The Secretary of State is authorized in his discretion to refuse to issue a passport, to restrict a passport for use only in certain countries, to restrict it against use in certain countries, to withdraw or cancel a passport already issued, and to withdraw a passport for the purpose of restricting its validity or use in certain countries."

The Department, however, did not feel that the Secretary of State could exercise his discretion willfully without cause. Acting Secretary Wilson wrote on April 27, 1907, "The issuance of passports is a discretionary act on the part of the Secretary of State, and he may, for reasons deemed by him to be sufficient, direct the refusal of a passport to an American citizen; but a passport is not to be refused to an American citizen, even if his character is doubtful, unless there is reason to believe that he will put the passports to an improper or unlawful use." Foreign Relations of the United States, Pt. II (1910), 1083. See 3 Moore, Digest of International Law (1906), § 512. Freund, Administrative Powers over Persons and Property (1928), 97, states ". . . in practice it is clear that the Department of State acts upon the theory that it must grant the passport unless there is some circumstance making it a duty to refuse it. Any other attitude would indeed be intolerable; it would mean an executive power of a political character over individuals quite out of harmony with traditional American legislative practice."

[11]13 Op. Atty. Gen. 89, 92; 23 Op. Atty. Gen. 509, 511.

[12]Article 42 reads as follows:

"It shall be lawful to any person, for the future, to go out of our kingdom, and to return, safely and securely, by land or by water, saving his allegiance to us, unless it be in time of war, for some short space, for the common good of the kingdom: excepting prisoners and outlaws, according to the laws of the land, and of the people of the nation at war against us, and Merchants who shall be treated as it is said above." And see Jaffe, *op. cit. supra,* 19-20; Sibley, The Passport System, 7 J. Soc. Comp. Leg. (N. S.) 26, 32-33; 1 Blackstone Commentaries 134-135.

[13]The use of foreign travel to promote educational interests is reviewed by Francis J. Colligan in 30 Dept. State Bull. 663.

[14]See note 3, *supra.*

Aptheker et.al. v. Secretary of State

378 U.S. 500 (1963)

Mr. Justice Goldberg delivered the opinion of the Court.

This appeal involves a single question: the constitutionality of § 6 of the Subversive Activities Control Act of 1950, 64 Stat. 993, 50 U. S. C. § 785. Section 6 provides in pertinent part that:

"(a) When a Communist organization[1] . . . is registered, or there is in effect a final order of the Board requiring such organization to register, it

> shall be unlawful for any member of such organization, with knowledge or notice that such organization is so registered or that such order has become final—
>
> "(1) to make application for a passport, or the renewal of a passport, to be issued or renewed by or under the authority of the United States; or
>
> "(2) to use or attempt to use any such passport."[2]

Section 6 became effective, with respect to appellants, on October 20, 1961, when a final order of the Subversive Activities Control Board issued directing the Communist Party of the United States to register under § 7 of the Subversive Activities Control Act. The registration order had been upheld earlier in 1961 by this Court's decision in *Communist Party of the United States v. Subversive Activities Control Board,* 367 U.S. 1. Prior to issuance of the final registration order both appellants, who are native-born citizens and residents of the United States, had held valid passports. Subsequently, on January 22, 1962, the Acting Director of the Passport Office notified appellants that their passports were revoked because the Department of State believed that their use of the passports would violate § 6. Appellants were also notified of their right to seek administrative review of the revocations under Department of State regulations.

Appellants requested and received hearings to review the revocations of their passports. The respective hearing examiners concluded that "the Department of State had reason to believe that [appellants are] within the purview of Section 6 (a) (2) of the Subversive Activities Control Act . . . and as a result thereof . . . use of a passport would be in violation of the law." On the basis of this conclusion the examiners recommended that the passport revocations be sustained.[3] Both appellants appealed to the Board of Passport Appeals which recommended affirmance of the revocations. The Secretary of State subsequently approved the recommendations of the Board. The Secretary stated that he "relied solely on the evidence in the record" and that, as the basis of his decision, he:

> "specifically adopted as his own the [Board's] finding of fact that 'at all material times [appellants were members] of the Communist Party of the United States with knowledge or notice that such organization had been required to register as a Communist organization under the Subversive Activities Control Act.' "

Appellants thereupon filed separate complaints seeking declaratory and injunctive relief in the United States District Court for the District of Columbia. The complaints, which have been considered together, asked that judgments be entered declaring § 6 of the Subversive Activities Control Act unconstitutional and ordering the Secretary of State to issue passports to appellants. Each appellant-plaintiff alleged that § 6 was unconstitutional as, *inter alia,* "a deprivation without due process of law of plaintiff's constitutional liberty to travel abroad, in violation of the Fifth Amendment to the Constitution of the United States."[4] Appellants conceded that the Secretary of State had an adequate basis for finding that they were members of the Communist Party of the United States and that the action revoking their passports was proper if § 6 was constitutional. The parties agreed that all administrative remedies had been exhausted and that it would be futile, and indeed a criminal offense, for either appellant to apply for a passport while remaining a member of the Communist Party.

The three-judge District Court, which was convened to review the constitutional question, rejected appellants' contentions, sustained the constitutionality of § 6 of the Control Act, and granted the Secretary's motion for summary judgment. 219 F. Supp. 709. The court concluded that:

> "the enactment by Congress of section 6, which prohibits these plaintiffs from obtaining passports so long as they are members of an organization—in this case the Communist Party—under a final order to register with the Attorney General . . . is a valid exercise of the power of Congress to protect and preserve our Government against the threat posed by the world Communist movement and that the regulatory scheme bears a reasonable relation thereto." *Id.*, at 714.

This Court noted probable jurisdiction. 375 U.S. 928.

Appellants attack § 6, both on its face and as applied, as an unconstitutional deprivation of the liberty guaranteed in the Bill of Rights. The Government, while conceding that the right to travel is protected by the Fifth Amendment, contends that the Due Process Clause does not prevent the reasonable regulation of liberty and that § 6 is a reasonable regulation because of its relation to the danger the world Communist movement presents for our national security. Alternatively, the Government argues that "whether or not denial of passports to some members of the Communist Party might be deemed not reasonably related to national security, surely Section 6 was reasonable as applied to the top-ranking Party leaders involved here."

We hold, for the reasons stated below, that § 6 of the Control Act too broadly and indiscriminately restricts the right to travel and thereby abridges the liberty guaranteed by the Fifth Amendment.

I.

In 1958 in *Kent v. Dulles,* 357 U.S. 116, 127, this Court declared that the right to travel abroad is "an important aspect of the citizen's 'liberty' " guaranteed in the Due Process Clause of the Fifth Amendment. The Court stated that:

> "The right to travel is a part of the 'liberty' of which the citizen cannot be deprived without due process of law under the Fifth Amendment. . . . Freedom of movement across frontiers in either direction, and inside frontiers as well, was a part of our heritage. Travel abroad, like travel within the country, . . . may be as close to the heart of the individual as the choice of what he eats, or wears, or reads. Freedom of movement is basic in our scheme of values."[5] *Id.*, at 125-126.

In *Kent,* however, the Court concluded that Congress had not conferred authority upon the Secretary of State to deny passports because of alleged Communist beliefs and associations. Therefore, although the decision protected the constitutional right to travel, the Court did not examine "the extent to which it can be curtailed." *Id.*, at 127. The Court, referring to § 6 of the Subversive Activities Control Act, noted that "the only law which Congress has passed expressly curtailing the movement of Communists across our borders has not yet become effective." *Id.*, at 130. Two years later in *Communist Party of the United States v. Subversive Activities Control Board, supra,* this Court reviewed and upheld the registration requirement of § 7of the Control Act. The Court, however, did not pass upon the "various consequences of the Party's registration for its individual members," *id.*, at 70, because:

> "It is wholly speculative now to foreshadow whether, or under what conditions, a member of the Party may in the future *apply for a passport,* or seek government or defense-facility or labor-union employment, or, being an

> alien, become a party to a naturalization or a denaturalization proceeding. None of these things may happen. If they do, appropriate administrative and judicial procedures will be available to test the constitutionality of applications of particular sections of the Act to particular persons in particular situations. Nothing justifies previsioning those issues now." *Id.,* at 79. (Emphasis added.)

The present case, therefore, is the first in which this Court has been called upon to consider the constitutionality of the restrictions which § 6 imposes on the right to travel.

The substantiality of the restrictions cannot be doubted. The denial of a passport, given existing domestic and foreign laws, is a severe restriction upon, and in effect a prohibition against, world-wide foreign travel. Present laws and regulations make it a crime for a United States citizen to travel outside the Western Hemisphere or to Cuba without a passport. By its plain import § 6 of the Control Act effectively prohibits travel anywhere in the world outside the Western Hemisphere by members of any "Communist organization"—including "Communist-action" and "Communist-front" organizations.[6] The restrictive effect of the legislation cannot be gain-said by emphasizing, as the Government seems to do, that a member of a registering organization could recapture his freedom to travel by simply in good faith abandoning his membership in the organization. Since freedom of association is itself guaranteed in the First Amendment,[7] restrictions imposed upon the right to travel cannot be dismissed by asserting that the right to travel could be fully exercised if the individual would first yield up his membership in a given association.

Although previous cases have not involved the constitutionality of statutory restrictions upon the right to travel abroad, there are well-established principles by which to test whether the restrictions here imposed are consistent with the liberty guaranteed in the Fifth Amendment. It is a familiar and basic principle, recently reaffirmed in *NAACP v. Alabama,* 377 U.S. 288, 307, that "a governmental purpose to control or prevent activities constitutionally subject to state regulation may not be achieved by means which sweep unnecessarily broadly and thereby invade the area of protected freedoms." See, *e.g., NAACP v. Button,* 371 U.S. 415, 438; *Louisiana ex rel. Gremillion v. NAACP,* 366 U.S. 293; *Shelton v. Tucker,* 364 U.S. 479, 488; *Schware v. Board of Bar Examiners,* 353 U.S. 232, 239; *Martin v. Struthers,* 319 U.S. 141, 146-149; *Cantwell v. Connecticut,* 310 U.S. 296, 304-307; *Schneider v. State,* 308 U.S. 147, 161, 165. In applying this principle the Court in *NAACP v. Alabama, supra,* referred to the criteria enunciated in *Shelton v. Tucker, supra,* at 488:

> "[E]ven though the governmental purpose be legitimate and substantial, that purpose cannot be pursued by means that broadly stifle fundamental personal liberties when the end can be more narrowly achieved. The breadth of legislative abridgment must be viewed in the light of less drastic means for achieving the same basic purpose."

This principle requires that we consider the congressional purpose underlying § 6 of the Control Act.[8] The Government emphasizes that the legislation in question flows, as the statute itself declares, from the congressional desire to protect our national security. That Congress under the Constitution has power to safeguard our Nation's security is obvious and unarguable. Cf. *Kennedy v. Mendoza-Martinez,* 372 U.S. 144, 159-160. As we said in *Mendoza-Martinez,* "while the Constitution protects against invasions of individual rights, it is not a suicide pact." *Id.,* at 160. At the same time the Constitution requires that the powers of government "must be so exercised as not, in attaining a permissible end, unduly to infringe" a constitutionally protected freedom. *Cantwell v. Connecticut, supra,* at 304.

Section 6 provides that any member of a Communist organization which has registered or has been ordered to register commits a crime if he attempts to use or obtain a United States passport. The section applies to members who act "with knowledge or notice" that the organization is under a final registration order. "Notice" is specifically defined in § 13 (k). That section provides that publication in the Federal Register of the fact of registration or of issuance of a final registration order "shall constitute notice to all members of such organization that such order has become final." Thus the terms of § 6 apply whether or not the member actually knows or believes that he is associated with what is deemed to be a "Communist-action" or a "Communist-front" organization. The section also applies whether or not one knows or believes that he is associated with an organization operating to further aims of the world Communist movement and "to establish a Communist totalitarian dictatorship in the countries throughout the world. . . ." 64 Stat. 987, 50 U. S. C. § 781 (1). The provision therefore sweeps within its prohibition both knowing and unknowing members. In related contexts this Court has had occasion to consider the substantiality of the relationship between an individual and a group where, as here, the fact of membership in that group has been made the sole criterion for limiting the individual's freedom. In *Wieman v. Updegraff,* 344 U.S. 183, the Court held that the due process guarantee of the Constitution was violated when a State, in an attempt to bar disloyal individuals from its employ, excluded persons solely on the basis of organizational memberships without regard to their knowledge concerning the organizations to which they had belonged. The Court concluded that: "Indiscriminate classification of innocent with knowing activity must fall as an assertion of arbitrary power." *Id.,* at 191.

Section 6 also renders irrelevant the member's degree of activity in the organization and his commitment to its purpose. These factors, like knowledge, would bear on the likelihood that travel by such a person would be attended by the type of activity which Congress sought to control. As the Court has elsewhere noted, "men in adhering to a political party or other organization notoriously do not subscribe unqualifiedly to all of its platforms or asserted principles." Cf. *Schneiderman v. United States,* 320 U.S. 118, 136. It was in this vein that the Court in *Schware v. Board of Bar Examiners,* 353 U.S., at 246, stated that even "[a]ssuming that some members of the Communist Party . . . had illegal aims and engaged in illegal activities, it cannot automatically be inferred that all members shared their evil purposes or participated in their illegal conduct." Section 6, however, establishes an irrebuttable presumption that individuals who are members of the specified organizations will, if given passports, engage in activities inimical to the security of the United States.[9]

In addition to the absence of criteria linking the bare fact of membership to the individual's knowledge, activity or commitment, § 6 also excludes other considerations which might more closely relate the denial of passports to the stated purpose of the legislation. The prohibition of § 6 applies regardless of the purposes for which an individual wishes to travel. Under the statute it is a crime for a notified member of a registered organization to apply for a passport to travel abroad to visit a sick relative, to receive medical treatment, or for any other wholly innocent purpose.[10] In determining whether there has been an abridgment of the Fifth Amendment's guarantee of liberty, this Court must recognize the danger of punishing a member of a Communist organization "for his adherence to lawful and constitutionally protected purposes, because of other and unprotected purposes which he does not necessarily share." *Noto v. United States,* 367 U.S. 290, 299-300; *Scales v. United States,* 367 U.S. 203, 229-230. In addition it must be noted that § 6 applies to a member regardless of the security-sensitivity of the areas in which he wishes to travel. As a result, if a notified member of a registered organization were to apply for a passport to visit a relative in Ireland, or to read rare manuscripts in the Bodleian Library of Oxford University, the applicant would be guilty of a crime; whereas, if he were to travel to Canada or Latin America to carry on criminal activities directed against the United States, he could do so free from the prohibitive reach of § 6.

In determining the constitutionality of § 6, it is also important to consider that Congress has within its power "less drastic"[11] means of achieving the congressional objective of safeguarding our national security. *Shelton v. Tucker,* 364 U.S., at 488. The Federal Employee Loyalty Program, which was before this Court in *Joint Anti-Fascist Refugee Comm. v. McGrath,* 341 U.S. 123, provides an example. Under Executive Order No. 9835, membership in a Communist organization is not considered conclusive but only as one factor to be weighed in determining the loyalty of an applicant or employee.[12] It is relevant to note that less than a month after the decision in *Kent v. Dulles, supra,* President Eisenhower sent a message to Congress stating that: "Any limitations on the right to travel can only be tolerated in terms of overriding requirements of our national security, and must be subject to substantive and procedural guaranties." Message from the President—Issuance of passports, H. Doc. No. 417, 85th Cong., 2d Sess.; 104 Cong. Rec. 13046. The legislation which the President proposed did not make membership in a Communist organization, without more, a disqualification for obtaining a passport. S. 4110, H. R. 13318, 85th Cong., 2d Sess. Irrespective of views as to the validity of this or other such proposals, they demonstrate the conviction of the Executive Branch that our national security can be adequately protected by means which, when compared with § 6, are more discriminately tailored to the constitutional liberties of individuals.

In our view the foregoing considerations compel the conclusion that § 6 of the Control Act is unconstitutional on its face. The section, judged by its plain import and by the substantive evil which Congress sought to control, sweeps too widely and too indiscriminately across the liberty guaranteed in the Fifth Amendment. The prohibition against travel is supported only by a tenuous relationship between the bare fact of organizational membership and the activity Congress sought to proscribe. The broad and enveloping prohibition indiscriminately excludes plainly relevant considerations such as the individual's knowledge, activity, commitment, and purposes in and places for travel. The section therefore is patently not a regulation "narrowly drawn to prevent the supposed evil," cf. *Cantwell v. Connecticut,* 310 U.S., at 307, yet here, as elsewhere, precision must be the touchstone of legislation so affecting basic freedoms, *NAACP v. Button,* 371 U.S., at 438.

II.

The Government alternatively urges that, if § 6 cannot be sustained on its face, the prohibition should nevertheless be held constitutional as applied to these particular appellants. The Government argues that "surely Section 6 was reasonable as applied to the top-ranking Party leaders involved here."[13] It is not disputed that appellants are top-ranking leaders: Appellant Aptheker is editor of *Political Affairs,* the "theoretical organ" of the Party in this country and appellant Flynn is chairman of the Party.[14]

It must be remembered that "[a]lthough this Court will often strain to construe legislation so as to save it against constitutional attack, it must not and will not carry this to the point of perverting the purpose of a statute . . ." or judicially rewriting it. *Scales v. United States, supra,* at 211. To put the matter another way, this Court will not consider the abstract question of whether Congress might have enacted a valid statute but instead must ask whether the statute that Congress did enact will permissibly bear a construction rendering it free from constitutional defects.

The clarity and preciseness of the provision in question make it impossible to narrow its indiscriminately cast and overly broad scope without substantial rewriting. The situation here is different from that in cases such as *United States v. National Dairy Products Corp.,* 372 U.S. 29, where the Court is called upon to consider the content of allegedly vague statutory language. Here, in contrast, an attempt to "construe" the statute and to probe its recesses for some core of constitutionality would inject an element of vagueness into the statute's scope and application; the plain words would thus become uncertain in meaning only if courts proceeded on a case-by-case basis to separate out constitutional from unconstitutional areas of coverage. This course would not be proper, or desirable, in dealing with a section which so severely curtails personal liberty.

Since this case involves a personal liberty protected by the Bill of Rights, we believe that the proper approach to legislation curtailing that liberty must be that adopted by this Court in *NAACP v. Button,* 371 U.S. 415, and *Thornhill v. Alabama,* 310 U.S. 88. In *NAACP v. Button* the Court stated that:

> "[I]n appraising a statute's inhibitory effect upon such rights, this Court has not hesitated to take into account possible applications of the statute in other factual contexts besides that at bar. *Thornhill v. Alabama,* 310 U.S. 88, 97-98; *Winters v. New York,* [333 U.S. 507], 518-520. Cf. *Staub v. City of Baxley,* 355 U.S. 313. . . . The objectionable quality of vagueness and overbreadth does not depend upon absence of fair notice to a criminally accused or upon unchanneled delegation of legislative powers, but upon the danger of tolerating, in the area of First Amendment freedoms, the existence of a penal statute susceptible of sweeping and improper application. Cf. *Marcus v. Search Warrant,* 367 U.S. 717, 733. These freedoms are delicate and vulnerable, as well as supremely precious in our society. The threat of sanctions may deter their exercise almost as potently as the actual application of sanctions." 371 U.S., at 432-433.

For essentially the same reasons this Court had concluded that the constitutionality of the statute in *Thornhill v. Alabama* should be judged on its face:

> "An accused, after arrest and conviction under such a statute [on its face unconstitutionally abridging freedom of speech], does not have to sustain the burden of demonstrating that the State could not constitutionally have written a different and specific statute covering his activities as disclosed by the charge and the evidence introduced against him." 310 U.S., at 98.[15]

Similarly, since freedom of travel is a constitutional liberty closely related to rights of free speech and association, we believe that appellants in this case should not be required to assume the burden of demonstrating that Congress could not have written a statute constitutionally prohibiting their travel.[16]

Accordingly the judgment of the three-judge District Court is reversed and the cause remanded for proceedings in conformity with this opinion.

Reversed and remanded.

Mr. Justice Black, concurring. . .

Mr. Justice Douglas, concurring. . . .

Mr. Justice Clark, whome Mr. Justice Harlan joins and whom Mr. Justice White joins in part, dissenting. . . .

---

[1]Paragraph 5 of § 3 of the Act provides that: "For the purposes of this suchapter . . . [t]he term 'Communist organization' means any Communist-action organization, Communist-front organization, or Communist-infiltrated organization." 64 Stat. 990, as amended, 68 Stat. 777, 50 U. S. C. § 782.

[2]Section 6 (b) provides that:

"When an organization is registered, or there is in effect a final order of the Board requiring an organization to register, as a Communist-action organization, it shall be unlawful for any officer or employee of the United States to issue a passport to, or renew the passport of, any individual knowing or having reason to believe that such individual is a member of such organization."

The criminal penalties for violations of § 6 are specified in § 15 (c) of the Act which provides in pertinent part that:

"Any individual who violates any provision of section 5, 6, or 10 of this title shall, upon conviction thereof, be punished for each such violation by a fine of not more than $10,000 or by imprisonment for not more than five years, or by both such fine and imprisonment." 64 Stat. 1003, 50 U. S. C. § 794 (c).

[3]Appellants do not question that the hearings afforded them procedural due process of Law. Cf. *Greene v. McElroy,* 360 U.S. 474.

[4]Each complaint further alleged that § 6 was unconstitutional as:

"(b) an abridgement of plaintiff's freedoms of speech, press and assembly, in violation of the First Amendment, (c) a penalty imposed on plaintiff without a judicial trial, and therefore a bill of attainder, in violation of Article I, section 9 of the Constitution, (d) a deprivation of plaintiff's right to trial by jury as required by the Fifth and Sixth Amendments and Article III, section 2, clause 3 of the Constitution, and (e) the imposition of a cruel and unusual punishment in violation of the Eighth Amendment."

Our disposition of this case makes it unnecessary to review these contentions.

[5]In *Bolling v. Sharpe,* 347 U.S. 497, 499-500, this Court stated that: "Although the Court has not assumed to define 'liberty' with any great precision, that term is not confined to mere freedom from bodily restraint. Liberty under law extends to the full range of conduct which the individual is free to pursue, and it cannot be restricted except for a proper governmental objective."

[6]See note 1, *supra.*

[7]*E.g., Brotherhood of Railroad Trainmen v. Virginia State Bar,* 377 U.S. 1; *Gibson v. Florida Legislative Investigation Comm.,* 372 U.S. 539; *NAACP v. Button,* 371 U.S. 415; *Louisiana ex rel. Gremillion v. NAACP,* 366 U.S. 293; *Shelton v. Tucker,* 364 U.S. 479; *Bates v. City of Little Rock,* 361 U.S. 516; *NAACP v. Alabama ex rel. Patterson,* 357 U.S. 449; *Schneider v. State,* 308 U.S.

[8]The purpose of the Act is stated in § 2. 64 Stat. 987, 50 U. S. C. § 781. Congress found, as is generally stated in § 2 (1), that there "exists a world Communist movement . . . whose purpose it is, by treachery, deceit, infiltration, . . . espionage, sabotage, terrorism, and any other means deemed necessary, to establish a Communist totalitarian dictatorship in the countries throughout the world through the medium of a world-wide Communist organization." Congress concluded, as stated in § 2 (15), that the "Communist organization in the United States" and the world Communist movement present a danger to the security of the United States, a danger requiring legislative action. The congressional purpose in adopting § 6 is more specifically stated in § 2 (8):

"Due to the nature and scope of the world Communist movement, with the existence of affiliated constituent elements working toward common objectives in various countries of the world, travel of Communist members, representatives, and agents from country to country facilitates communication and is a prerequisite for the carrying on of activities to further the purposes of the Communist movement."

[9]The provision in question cannot, as the Government admits, be limited by adopting an interpretation analogous to this Court's interpretation of the so-called "membership clause" in the Smith Act. In *Scales v. United States,* 367 U.S. 203, the Smith Act, which imposes criminal penalties for

membership, was interpreted to include only " 'active' members having also a guilty knowledge and intent." *Id.*, at 228. The membership clause in that case, however, explicitly required "that a defendant must have knowledge of the organization's illegal advocacy." *Id.*, at 221. That requirement was intimately connected with the construction limiting membership to "active" members. With regard to the Control Act, however, as the Government concedes, "neither the words nor history of Section 6 suggests limiting its application to 'active' members."

[10]In denying appellants passports the Secretary of State made no finding as to their purposes in traveling abroad. The statute, as noted, supports the Secretary's implicit conclusion that such a finding was irrelevant. Appellants, however, in their respective complaints stated their purposes. Appellant Aptheker alleged that:

"He desires to travel to countries of Europe and elsewhere for study and recreation, to observe social, political and economic conditions abroad, and thereafter to write, publish, teach and lecture in this country about his observations. He also desires to travel abroad in order to attend meetings of learned societies and to fulfill invitations to lecture abroad."

Appellant Flynn alleged that:

"[She] desires to travel to countries of Europe and elsewhere for recreation and study, to observe social, political and economic conditions abroad, and thereafter to write, publish and lecture about her observations."

[11]The abridgment of liberty involved in this case is more "drastic" than, and distinguishable from, that involved in *American Communications Assn. v. Douds,* 339 U.S. 382. In *Douds* the Court upheld § 9 (h) of the National Labor Relations Act as amended by the Taft-Hartley Act, 61 Stat. 136, 146, 29 U. S. C. § 159 (h), which conditions trade-union access to the facilities of the National Labor Relations Board upon the submission of non-Communist affidavits by officers of the union. Although the requirement undoubtedly discouraged unions from choosing officers with Communist affiliations, it did not prohibit their election and did not affect basic individual rights to work and to union membership.

[12]In 1950 the Assistant to the Attorney General of the United States, Peyton Ford, expressed to Congress the views of the Department of Justice with regard to a proposed government loyalty bill which predicated a conclusive presumption of disloyalty on the fact of organizational membership. Mr. Ford said:

"A world of difference exists, from the standpoint of sound policy and constitutional validity, between making, as the bill would, membership in an organization designated by the Attorney General a felony, and recognizing such membership, as does the employee loyalty program under Executive Order 9835, as merely one piece of evidence pointing to possible disloyalty. The bill would brand the member of a listed organization a felon, no matter how innocent his membership; the loyalty program enables the member to respond to charges against him and to show, in a manner consistent with American concepts of justice and fairness, that his membership is innocent and does not reflect upon his loyalty.

"... It does not appear, therefore, necessary, even if constitutionally possible, to add to existing law and regulations at the present time a penal statute such as proposed in the bill.

"The foregoing comments represent the considered views of this Department, having in mind that it is the duty of the Attorney General to protect the rights of individuals guaranteed by the Constitution, as well as to protect the Government from subversion." Hearings on H. R. 3903 and H. R. 7595 before the House Committee on Un-American Activities, 81st Cong., 2d Sess., 2125.

[13]The Government recognizes, however, that: "Membership, or even leadership, in the Communist Party is not automatically a crime." Brief for Petitioner on Petition for a Writ of Certiorari, p. 11, *United States v. Communist Party of the United States,* No. 1027, O. T. 1963, *cert. denied,* 377 U.S. 968

[14]For appellants' alleged purposes in traveling, see note 10, *supra.*

[15]See Freund, The Supreme Court of the United States (1961), pp. 67-69; Note, 61 Harv. L. Rev. 1208 (1948); Note, 109 U. Pa. L. Rev. 67, 75-85 (1960).

[16]Nor in our opinion should the Secretary of State or other government officers be exposed to the risk of criminal penalties for violating § 6 (b) by issuing a passport to a member of a registered Communist-action organization who is subsequently found by a court to be a person whose travel, contrary to the belief of the government officer, could constitutionally be prohibited.

The Right to Work

COMMENTARY

Time and again during the McCarthy era the Court was asked to review the use of loyalty oaths by State and Federal governments and their procedures for firing employees suspected of being security risks—procedures which in other areas would have failed to meet acceptable standards of due process. Each time the Court found a way to avoid deciding the fundamental constitutional issues, while often, but not always, affording protection to those whom the government sought to fire.

One of the earliest cases to come before the Court in this area, *Peters v. Hobby,* 349 U.S. 331 (1955) set the pattern. Peters, a doctor, had been denied a government position because of a finding by the Loyalty Review Board, established under Executive Order 9835, that there was a reasonable doubt to his loyalty. The Board acted on its own initiative after an agency review board within the Department of Health, Education and Welfare had declined to make such a finding.

In bringing the case before the Supreme Court, Peters asked the Court to decide several major constitutional questions. First was the right to confront and cross-examine accusers. Peters had been charged by annonymous informants of being a member of the Communist Party and a supporter of its activities. This was the entire case against him. Second, Peters argued that to deny him government employment simply because of his alleged political beliefs violated his First Amendment rights. This argument appeared to be particularly strong since Peters was not seeking a position that required a clearance or access to national security information, and there was no suggestion that his political views, whatever they may have been, would have affected the giving of medical advice required of him.

The Court specifically refused to reach the constitutional issues. It found that the Loyalty Board's power was limited by the terms of the Executive Order to situations in which an agency board had recommended dismissal. Thus the Board's action in this case went beyond the authority granted to it by the President.

One year later the Court again declined to decide the constitutional questions presented by a summary dismissal.[1] Congress in 1950 had given to the heads of certain agencies summary suspension and unreviewable dismissal powers when deemed necessary "in the interest of the national security of the United States."

The Act had given this power only to the heads of a few specified agencies involved directly with national security matters, but had authorized the President to grant this power to other agencies. Pursuant to this authority the President granted the suspension and dismissal powers of the act to *all* Federal agencies. Subsequently petitioner Cole was suspended and then discharged from his job in the Food and Drug Administration, on the grounds that his continued employment was not "clearly consistent with the interests of national security." After a careful review of the law Justice Harlan writing for the Court found:

> (1) that the term "national security" is used in the Act in a definite and limited sense and relates only to those activities which are directly concerned with the Nation's safety, as distinguished from the general welfare; and (2) that

> no determination has been made that petitioner's practice was affected with the "national security" as that term is used in the Act.[2]

Thus the summary dismissal was not authorized by Congress, because the President's blanket extension of these procedures needed to be justified in each case; and the petitioner in this case, it was found, was entitled to all the procedural safeguards normally afforded government employees.

Three members of the Court in dissent urged the Court to consider whether the President had the inherent power, even without Congressional sanction, to authorize summary dismissals; but it declined to do so.

Nor did the Court reach this question in 1959, when confronted with a case involving the denial of a clearance to a professional employee of a government contractor. In *Greene v. McElroy,* 360 U.S. 474 (1959), the Court simply asked whether the Defense Department had in fact been authorized, by either the President or the Congress, to establish a program in which decisions to deny clearances, and hence employment in private industry, were made without "the traditional, procedural safeguards of confrontation and cross-examination." The Court, in an opinion by Chief Justice Warren, concluded that neither Congress nor the President had authorized such action and hence it did not have to reach the question of whether they could constitutionally do so. The Court held that where it was confronted with a procedure that deprived a person of an important right without normal due process, it would require at minimum an explicit legal mandate for the program. Passive acquiescence in the program by continued grant of appropriations to the agency and failure to express disapproval might be sufficient to ratify executive action in other areas, but was not acceptable where constitutional rights of individuals were at stake.

In what appeared to be a very similar case a few years later, the Court sustained the government's refusal to permit an employee of a contractor to enter a military base. While this case, *Cafeteria Workers v. McElroy,* 367 U.S. 886 (1961), is one of those cited by the government as upholding the exercise of inherent Presidential powers in the national security field, the opinion of the Court was narrowly drawn and emphasized the special facts of the case.

One Rachel Brawner was denied the pass she needed to enter the military base where she worked in the cafeteria. The revocation of her pass was made by the base commander on the grounds that she failed to meet the security requirements for access to the base.

Justice Stewart in his opinion for the Court noted that the President had authority to determine who would enter military bases and that he had specifically authorized the issuance of the regulations under which Brawner's access was denied. Hence unlike the situation in *Greene v. McElroy,* the Court had to consider the constitutionality of the program, which did not provide for a hearing at which the person denied a permit could speak in her own defense.

The Court stressed the absolute control of access to military bases given to base commanders throughout American history. It noted also that the petitioner's deprivation was not severe, since she could practice her trade as a short order cook elsewhere, and since she had not explicitly been branded with the label of loyalty risk. Four Justices dissented, arguing that some procedural safeguards were required.

As the tide of McCarthyism receded the Court became less reluctant to reach constitutional issues, and began to render decisions that cut back on the implications of *Cafeteria Workers.* In 1950 Congress had provided that when an organization is under a formal order to register before the Subversive Activities Control Board, it shall be unlawful for any member of the organization "to engage in any employment in any defense facility." Robel, an admitted member of the Communist Party, which had been so ordered to register, was indicted for continuing to work in a plant designated as a defense facility. In *United States v. Robel,* 389 U.S. 258 (1967), the Court held the statute unconstitutionally overbroad, for failing to distinguish among persons with varying degrees of commitment to the goals of the organization, and among jobs of varying degress of sensitivity. The Court noted that

> the phrase 'war power' cannot be invoked as a talismanic incantation to support any exercise of Congressional power which can be brought within its control. '[E]ven the war power does not remove constitutional limitation safeguarding essential liberties.'[3]

Chief Justice Warren went on to note that when one of Congress' enumerated process clashes with the liberties protected by the Bill of Rights, the Court must "determine whether the resulting restriction on freedom can be tolerated." The Court held in effect that Congress could bar those who were personally committed to violent revolution from sensitive government positions, but it could not on the basis of mere membership bar an individual from all government positions. In a footnote, the Court denied that it was balancing conflicting interests. Rather it stated it was simply requiring the Congress to draw its legislation more narrowly to avoid the conflict.[4]

In an earlier opinion that same year, the Court had applied the same reasoning in holding unconstitutional a state law barring members of the Communist Party, regardless of their specific beliefs, from teaching in the State University system.[5] Following this decision, the Court struck down most loyalty oaths asking prospective employees to certify that they were not members of particular groups or holders of certain political views; but it did uphold others requiring support for the constitution.[6]

---

[1]*Cole v. Young,* 351 U.S. 536 (1956).

[2]351 U.S. 543.

[3]*Home Building and Loan Association v. Blaisdell,* 290 U.S. 398, 426 (1934).

[4]389 U.S. at 268, n. 20.

[5]*Keyishian v. Board of Regents,* 385 U.S. 589 (1967).

[6]See *Cole v. Richardson,* 405 U.S. 676 (1972).

STATUTES

Executive Order 10450

Whereas the interests of the national security require that all persons privileged to be employed in the departments and agencies of the Government, shall be reliable, trustworthy, of good conduct and character, and of complete and unswerving loyalty to the United States; and

Whereas the American tradition that all persons should receive fair, impartial, and equitable treatment at the hands of the Government requires that all persons seeking the privilege of employment or privileged to be employed in the departments and agencies of the Government be adjudged by mutually consistent and no less than minimum standards and procedures among the departments and agencies governing the employment and retention in employment of persons in the Federal service:

Now, therefore, by virtue of the authority vested in me be the Constitution and statutes of the United States, including section 1753 of the Revised Statutes of the United States (5 USC 631); the Civil Service Act of 1883 (22 Stat. 403; 5 USC 632, et seq.); section 9A of the act of August 2, 1939, 53 Stat. 1148 (5 USC 118j); and the act of August 26, 1950, 64 Stat. 476 (5 USC 22-1, et seq.), and as President of the United States, and deeming such action necessary in the best interests of the national security, it is hereby ordered as follows:

Sec. 1. In addition to the departments and agencies specified in the said act of August 26, 1950, and Executive Order No. 10237 of April 26, 1951, the provisions of that act shall apply to all other departments and agencies of the Government.

Sec. 2. The head of each department and agency of the Government shall be responsible for establishing and maintaining within his department or agency an effective program to insure that the employment and retention in employment of any civilian officer or employee within the department or agency is clearly consistent with the interests of the national security.

Sec. 3. (a) The appointment of each civilian officer or employee in any department or agency of the Government shall be made subject to investigation. The *scope* of the investigation shall be determined in the first instance according to the degree of adverse effect the occupant of the position sought to be filled could bring about, by virtue of the nature of the position, on the national security, but in no event shall the investigation include less than a national agency check (including a check of the fingerprint files of the Federal Bureau of Investigation), and written inquiries to appropriate local law-enforcement agencies, former employers and supervisors, references, and schools attended by the person under investigation: *Provided,* that upon request of the head of the department or agency concerned, the Civil Service Commission may, in its discretion, authorize such less investigation as may meet the requirements of the national security with respect to per-diem, intermittent, temporary, or seasonal employees, or aliens employed outside the United States. Should there develop at any stage of investigation information indicating that the employment of any such person may not be clearly consistent with the interests of the national security, there shall be conducted with respect to such person a full field investigation, or such less investigation as shall be sufficient to enable the head of the department or agency concerned to determine whether retention of such person is clearly consistent with the interests of the national security.

(b) The head of any department or agency shall designate, or cause to be designated, any position within his department or agency the occupant of which could bring about, by virtue of the nature of the position, a material adverse effect on the national security as a sensitive position. Any position so designated shall be filled or occupied only by a person with respect to whom a full field investigation has been conducted: *Provided,* that a person occupying a sensitive position at the time it is designated as such may continue to occupy such position pending the completion of a full field investigation, subject to the other provisions of this order: *And provided further,* that in case of emergency a sensitive position may be filled for a limited period by a person with respect to whom a full field preappointment investigation has not been completed if the head of the department or agency concerned finds that such action is necessary in the national interest, which finding shall be made a part of the records of such department or agency.

Sec. 4. The head of each department and agency shall review, or cause to be reviewed, the cases of all civilian officers and employees with respect to whom there has been conducted a full field investigation under Executive Order No. 9835 of March 21, 1947, and, after such further investigation as may be appropriate, shall re-adjudicate, or cause to be re-adjudicated, in accordance with the said act of August 26, 1950, such of those cases as have not been adjudicated under a security standard commensurate with that established under this order.

Sec. 5. Whenever there is developed or received by any department or agency information indicating that the retention in employment of any officer or employee of the Government may not be clearly consistent with the interests of the national security, such information shall be forwarded to the head of the employing department or agency or his representative who, after such investigation as may be appropriate, shall review, or cause to be reviewed, and, where necessary, re-adjudicate, or cause to be re-adjudicated, in accordance with the said act of August 26, 1950, the case of such officer or employee.

Sec. 6. Should there develop at any stage of investigation information indicating that the employment of any officer or employee of the Government may not be clearly consistent with the interests of the national security, the head of the department or agency concerned or his representative shall immediately suspend the employment of the person involved if he deems such suspension necessary in the interests of the national security and, following such investigation and review as he deems necessary, the head of the department or agency concerned shall terminate the employment of such suspended officer or employee whenever he shall determine such termination necessary or advisable in the interests of the national security, in accordance with the said act of August 26, 1950.

Sec. 7. Any person whose employment is suspended or terminated under the authority granted to heads of departments and agencies by or in accordance with the said act of August 26, 1950, or pursuant to the said Executive Order No. 9835 or any other security or loyalty program relating to officers or employees of the Government, shall not be reinstated or restored to duty or reemployed in the same department or agency and shall not be reemployed in any other department or agency, unless the head of the department or agency concerned finds that such reinstatement, restoration, or reemployment is clearly consistent with the interests of the national security, which finding shall be made a part of the records of such department or agency: *Provided,* that no person whose employment has been terminated under such authority thereafter may be employed by any other department or agency except after a determination by the Civil Service Commission that such person is eligible for such employment.

Sec. 8. (a) The investigations conducted pursuant to this order shall be designed to develop information as to whether employment or retention in employment in the Federal service of the person being investigated is clearly consistent with the interests of the national security. Such information shall relate, but shall not be limited, to the following:

(1) Depending on the relation of the Government employment to the national security:

(i) Any behavior, activities, or associations which tend to show that the individual is not reliable or trustworthy.

(ii) Any deliberate misrepresentations, falsifications, or omissions of material facts.

(iii) Any criminal, infamous, dishonest, immoral, or notoriously disgraceful conduct, habitual use of intoxicants to excess, drug addiction, or sexual perversion.

(iv) Any illness, including any mental condition, of a nature which in the opinion of competent medical authority may cause significant defect in the judgment or reliability of the employee, with due regard to the transient or continuing effect of the illness and the medical findings in such case.

(v) Any facts which furnish reason to believe that the individual may be subjected to coercion, influence, or pressure which may cause him to act contrary to the best interests of the national security.

(2) Commission of any act of sabotage, espionage, treason, or sedition, or attempts thereat or preparation therefor, or conspiring with, or aiding or abetting, another to commit or attempt to commit any act of sabotage, espionage, treason or sedition.

(3) Establishing or continuing a sympathetic association with a saboteur, spy, traitor, seditionist, anarchist, or revolutionist, or with an espionage or other secret agent or representative of a foreign nation, or any representative of a foreign nation whose interests may be inimical to the interests of the United States, or with any person who advocates the use of force or violence to overthrow the government of the United States or the alteration of the form of government of the United States by unconstitutional means.

(4) Advocacy of use of force or violence to overthrow the government of the United States, or of the alteration of the form of government of the United States by unconstitutional means.

(5) Knowing membership with the specific intent of furthering the aims of, or adherence to and active participation in, any foreign or domestic organization, association, movement, group, or combination of persons (hereinafter referred to as organizations) which unlawfully advocates or practices the commission of acts of force or violence to prevent others from exercising their rights under the Constitution or laws of the United States or of any State, or which seeks to overthrow the Government of the United States or any State or subdivision thereof by unlawful means. (As amended by E.O. 11785, dated June 4, 1974, 39 Fed. Reg. 110.)

(6) Intentional, unauthorized disclosure to any person of security information, or of other information disclosure of which is prohibited by law, or willful violation or disregard of security regulations.

(7) Performing or attempting to perform his duties, or otherwise acting, so as to serve the interests of another government in preference to the interests of the United States.

(8) Refusal by the individual, upon the ground of constitutional privilege against self-incrimination, to testify before a congressional committee regarding charges of his alleged disloyalty of other misconduct.

(b) The investigation of persons entering or employed in the competitive service shall primarily be the responsibility of the Civil Service Commission, except in cases in which the head of a department or agency assumes that responsibility pursuant to law or by agreement with the Commission. The Commission shall furnish a full investigative report to the department or agency concerned.

(c) The investigation of persons (including consultants, however employed), entering employment of, or employed by, the Government other than in the competitive service shall primarily be the responsibility of the employing department or agency. Departments and agencies without investigative facilities may use the investigative facilities of the Civil Service Commission, and other departments and agencies may use such facilities under agreement with the Commission.

(d) There shall be referred promptly to the Federal Bureau of Investigation all investigations being conducted by any other agencies which develop information indicating that an individual may have been subjected to coercion, influence, or pressure to act contrary to the interests of the national security, or information relating to any of the matters described in subdivisions (2) through (8) of subsection (a) of this section. In cases so referred to it, the Federal Bureau of Investigation shall make a full field investigation.

Sec. 9. (a) There shall be established and maintained in the Civil Service Commission a security-investigations index covering all persons as to whom security investigations have been conducted by any department or agency of the Government under this order. The central index established and maintained by the Commission under Executive Order No. 9835 of March 21, 1947, shall be made a part of the security-investigations index. The security-investigations index shall contain the name of each person investigated, adequate identifying information concerning each such person, and a reference to each department and agency which has conducted an investigation concerning the person involved or has suspended or terminated the employment of such person under the authority granted to heads of departments and agencies by or in accordance with the said act of August 26, 1950.

(b) The heads of all departments and agencies shall furnish promptly to the Civil Service Commission information appropriate for the establishment and maintenance of the security-investigations index.

(c) The reports and other investigative material and information developed by investigations conducted pursuant to any statute, order, or program described in section 7 of this order shall remain the property of the investigative agencies conducting the investigations, but may, subject to considerations of the national security, be retained by the department or agency concerned. Such reports and other investigative material and information shall be maintained in confidence, and no access shall be given thereto except, with the consent of the investigative agency concerned, to other departments and agencies conducting security programs under the authority granted by or in accordance with the said act of August 26, 1950, as may be required for the efficient conduct of Government business.

Sec. 10. Nothing in this order shall be construed as eliminating or modifying in any way the requirement for any investigation or any determination as to security which may be required by law.

Sec. 11. On and after the effective date of this order the Loyalty Review Board established by Executive Order No. 9835 of March 21, 1947, shall not accept agency findings for review, upon appeal or otherwise. Appeals pending before the Loyalty Review Board on such date shall be heard to final determination in accordance with the provisions of the said Executive Order No. 9835, as amended. Agency determinations favorable to the officer or employee concerned pending before the Loyalty Review Board on such date shall be acted upon by such Board, and whenever the Board is not in agreement with such favorable determination the case shall be remanded to the department or agency concerned for determination in accordance with the standards and procedures established pursuant to this order. Cases pending before the regional loyalty boards of the Civil Service Commission on which hearings have not been initiated on such date shall be referred to the department or agency concerned. Cases being heard by regional loyalty boards on such date shall be heard to conclusion, and the determination of the board shall be forwarded to the head of the department or agency concerned: *Provided,* that if no specific department or agency is involved, the case shall be dismissed without prejudice to the applicant. Investigations pending in the Federal Bureau of Investigation or the Civil Service Commission on such date shall be completed, and the reports thereon shall be made to the appropriate department or agency.

(a) Executive Order No. 9835 of March 21, 1947, as amended is hereby revoked.

(b) The head of each department and agency shall be furnished by the Attorney General with the name of each organization which shall be or has been heretofore designated under this order. Except as specifically provided hereafter, nothing contained herein shall be construed in any way to affect previous designations made pursuant to Executive Order No. 10450, as amended.

(c) The Subversive Activities Control Board shall, upon petition of the Attorney General, conduct appropriate hearings to determine whether any organization is totalitarian, fascist, communist, subversive, or whether it has adopted a policy of unlawfully advocating the commission of acts of force or violence to deny others their rights under the Constitution or laws of the United States or of any State, or which seeks to overthrow the government of the United States or any State or subdivision thereof by unlawful means.

(d) The Board may determine that an organization has adopted a policy of unlawfully advocating the commission of acts of force or violence to deny others their constitutional or statutory rights or that an organization seeks to overthrow the government of the United States or any State or subdivision thereof by unlawful means if it is found that such group engages in, unlawfully advocates, or has among its purposes or objectives, or adopts as a means of obtaining any of its purposes or objectives.

(1) The commission of acts of force or violence or other unlawful acts to deny others their rights or benefits guaranteed by the Constitution or laws of the United States or of the several States or political subdivisions thereof; or

(2) The unlawful damage or destruction of property; or injury to persons; or

(3) The overthrow or destruction of the government of the United States or the government of any State, Territory, district, or possession thereof, or the government of any political subdivision therein, by unlawful means; or

(4) The commission of acts which violate laws pertaining to treason, rebellion or insurrection, riots or civil disorders, seditious conspiracy, sabotage, trading with the enemy, obstruction of the recruiting and enlistment service of the United States, impeding officers of the United States, or related crimes or offenses.

(e) The Board may determine an organization to be 'totalitarian' if it is found that such organization engages in activities which seek by unlawful means the establishment of a system of government in the United States which is autocratic and in which control is centered in a single individual, group, or political party, allowing no effective representation to opposing individuals, groups, or parties and providing no practical opportunity for dissent.

(f) The Board may determine an organization to be 'facist' if it is found that such organization engages in activities which seek by unlawful means the establishment of a system of government in the United States which characterized by rigid one-party dictatorship, forcible suppression of the opposition, ownership of the means of production under centralized governmental control and which fosters racism.

(g) The Board may determine an organization to be 'communist' if it is found that such organization engages in activities which seek by unlawful means the establishment of a government in the United States which is based upon the revolutionary principles of Marxism-Leninism, which interprets history as a relentless class war aimed at the destruction of the existing society and the establishment of the dictatorship of the proletariat, the government ownership of the means of production and distribution of property, and the establishment of a single authoritarian party.

(h) The Board may determine an organization to be 'subversive' if it is found that such organization engages in activities which seek the abolition or destruction by unlawful means of the government of the United States or any State, or subdivision thereof.

(i) The Board may further determine, after consideration of the evidence, that an organization has ceased to exist. Upon petition of the Attorney General or upon petition of any organization which has been designated pursuant to this section the Board after appropriate hearings may determine that such organization does not currently meet the standards for designation. The Attorney General shall appropriately revise or modify the information furnished to departments and agencies consistent with the determinations of the Board.

(j) The Board shall issue appropriate regulations for the implementation of this section. (As amended by E.O. 11605, dated July 2, 1971, 36 Fed. Reg. 131.)

Sec. 12. Executive Order No. 9835 of March 21, 1947, as amended, is hereby revoked. (As amended by E.O. 11785, dated June 4, 1974, 39 Fed. Feg. 110.)

Sec. 13. The Attorney General is requested to render to the heads of departments and agencies such advice as may be requisite to enable them to establish and maintain an appropriate employee security program.

CASES

Cole v. Young

351 U.S. 536 (1956)

Opinion of the Court by Mr. Justice Harlan, announced by Mr. Justice Burton.

This case presents the question of the meaning of the term "national security" as used in the Act of August 26, 1950, giving to the heads of certain departments and agencies of the Government summary suspension and unreviewable dismissal powers over their civilian employees, when deemed necessary "in the interest of the national security of the United States."

Petitioner, a preference-eligible veteran under § 2 of the Veterans' Preference

Act of 1944, 58 Stat. 387, as amended, 5 U. S. C. § 851, held a position in the classified civii service as a food and drug inspector for the New York District of the Food and Drug Administration, Department of Health, Education, and Welfare. In November 1953, he was suspended without pay from his position, pending investigation to determine whether his employment should be terminated. He was given a written statement of charges alleging that he had "a close association with individuals reliably reported to be Communists" and that he had maintained a "sympathetic association" with, had contributed funds and services to, and had attended social gatherings of an allegedly subversive organization.

Although afforded an opportunity to do so, petitioner declined to answer the charges or to request a hearing, as he had the right to do. Thereafter, the Secretary of the Department of Health, Education, and Welfare, after "a study of all the documents in [petitioner's] case," determined that petitioner's continued employment was not "clearly consistent with the interests of national security" and ordered the termination of his employment. Petitioner appealed his discharge to the Civil Service Commission, which declined to accept the appeal on the ground that the Veterans' Preference Act, under which petitioner claimed the right of appeal, was inapplicable to such discharges.

Petitioner thereafter brought an action in the District Court for the District of Columbia seeking a declaratory judgment that his discharge was invalid and that the Civil Service Commission had improperly refused to entertain his appeal, and an order requiring his reinstatement in his former position. The District Court granted the respondents' motion for judgment on the pleadings and dismissed the complaint. 125 F. Supp. 284. The Court of Appeals, with one judge dissenting, affirmed. 96 U.S. App. D. C. 379, 226 F. 2d 337. Because of the importance of the questions involved in the field of Government employment, we granted certiorari. 350 U.S. 900.

Section 14 of the Veterans' Preference Act, 58 Stat. 390, as amended, 5 U. S. C. § 863, provides that preference eligibles may be discharged only "for such cause as will promote the efficiency of the service" and, among other procedural rights, "shall have the right to appeal to the Civil Service Commission," whose decision is made binding on the employing agency. Respondents concede that petitioner's discharge was invalid if that Act is controlling. They contend, however, as was held by the courts below, that petitioner's discharge was authorized by the Act of August 26, 1950, *supra,* which eliminates the right of appeal to the Civil Service Commission. Thus the sole question for decision is whether petitioner's discharge was authorized by the 1950 Act.

> "may, in his absolute discretion and when deemed necessary in the interest of national security, suspend, without pay, any civilian officer or employee of [his agency]. . . . The agency head concerned may, following such investigation and review as he deems necessary, terminate the employment of such suspended civilian officer or employee whenever he shall determine such termination necessary or advisable in the interest of the national security of the United States, and such determination by the agency head concerned shall be conclusive and final: . . ."

The Act was expressly made applicable only to the Departments of State, Commerce, Justice, Defense, Army, Navy, and Air Force, the Coast Guard, the Atomic Energy Commission, the National Security Resources Board, and the National Advisory Committee for Aeronatics. Section 3 of the Act provides, however, that the Act may be extended "to such other departments and agencies of the

Government as the President may, from time to time, deem necessary in the best interests of national security," and the President has extended the Act under this authority "to all other departments and agencies of the Government."[2] While the validity of this extension of the Act depends upon questions which are in many respects common to those determining the validity of the Secretary's exercise of the authority thereby extended to her,[3] we will restrict our consideration to the latter issue and assume, for purposes of this decision, that the Act has validly been extended to apply to the Department of Health, Education, and Welfare.

The Act authorizes dismissals only upon a determination by the Secretary that the dismissal is "necessary or advisable in the interest of the national security." That determination requires an evaluation of the risk of injury to the "national security" that the employee's retention would create, which in turn would seem necessarily to be a function, not only of the character of the employee and the likelihood of his misconducting himself, but also of the nature of the position he occupies and its relationship to the "national security." That is, it must be determined whether the position is one in which the employee's misconduct would affect the "national security." That, of course, would not be necessary if "national security" were used in the Act in a sense so broad as to be involved in *all* activities of the Government, for then the relationship to the "national security" would follow from the very fact of employment. For the reasons set forth below, however, we conclude (1) that the term "national security" is used in the Act in a definite and limited sense and relates only to those activities which are directly concerned with the Nation's safety, as distinguished from the general welfare; and (2) that no determination has been made that petitioner's position was affected with the "national security," as that term is used in the Act. It follows that his dismissal was not authorized by the 1950 Act and hence violated the Veterans' Preference Act.

I.

In interpreting the 1950 Act, it is important to note that that Act is not the only, nor even the primary, source of authority to dismiss Government employees. The general personnel laws—the Lloyd-LaFollette[4] and Veterans' Preference Acts[5]—authorize dismissals for "such cause as will promote the efficiency of the service," and the ground which we conclude was the basis for petitioner's discharge here—a reasonable doubt as to his loyalty—was recognized as a "cause" for dismissal under those procedures as early as 1942.[6] Indeed, the President's so-called Loyalty Program, Exec. Order No. 9835, 12 Fed. Reg. 1935, which prescribed an absolute standard of loyalty to be met by all employees regardless of position, had been established pursuant to that general authority three years prior to the 1950 Act and remained in effect for nearly three years after its passage.[7] Thus there was no want of substantive authority to dismiss employees on loyalty grounds, and the question for decision here is not whether an employee *can* be dismissed on such grounds but only the extent to which the summary *procedures* authorized by the 1950 Act are available in such a case.

As noted above, the issue turns on the meaning of "national security," as used in the Act. While that term is not defined in the Act, we think it clear from the statute as a whole that that term was intended to comprehend only those activities of the Government that are directly concerned with the protection of the Nation from internal subversion or foreign aggression, and not those which contribute to the strength of the Nation only through their impact on the general welfare.

Virtually conclusive of this narrow meaning of "national security" is the fact that, had Congress intended the term in a sense broad enough to include all activities of the Government, it would have granted the power to terminate employment "in the interest of the national security" to all agencies of the Government. Instead, Congress specified 11 named agencies to which the Act should apply, the character of which reveals, without doubt, a purpose to single out those agencies which are directly concerned with the national defense and which have custody over information the compromise of which might endanger the country's security, the so-called "sensitive" agencies. Thus, of the 11 named agencies, 8 are concerned with military operations or weapons development, and the other 3, with international relations, internal security, and the stock-piling of strategic materials. Nor is this conclusion vitiated by the grant of authority to the President, in § 3 of the Act, to extend the Act to such other agencies as he "may, from time to time, deem necessary in the best interests of national security." Rather, the character of the named agencies indicates the character of the determination required to be made to effect such an extension. Aware of the difficulties of attempting an exclusive enumeration and of the undesirability of a rigid classification in the face of changing circumstances, Congress simply enumerated those agencies which it determined to be affected with the "national security" and authorized the President, by making a similar determination, to add any other agencies which were, or became, "sensitive." That it was contemplated that this power would be exercised "from time to time" confirms the purpose to allow for changing circumstances and to require a selective judgment, necessarily implying that the standard to be applied is a less than all-inclusive one.

The limitation of the Act to the enumerated agencies is particularly significant in the light of the fact that Exec. Order No. 9835, establishing the Loyalty Program, was in full effect at the time of the consideration and passage of the Act. In that Order, the President had expressed his view that it was of "vital importance" that *all* employees of the Government be of "complete and unswerving loyalty" and had prescribed a minimum loyalty standard to be applied to all employees under the normal civil service procedures. Had Congress considered the objective of insuring the "unswerving loyalty" of all employees, regardless of position, as a matter of "national security" to be effectuated by the summary procedures authorized by the Act, rather than simply a desirable personnel policy to be implemented under the normal civil service procedures, it surely would not have limited the Act to selected agencies. Presumably, therefore, Congress meant something more by the "interest of the national security" than the general interest the Nation has in the loyalty of even "non-sensitive" employees.

We can find no justification for rejecting this implication of the limited purpose of the Act or for inferring the unlimited power contended for by the Government. Where applicable, the Act authorizes the agency head summarily to suspend an employee pending investigation and, after charges and a hearing, finally to terminate his employment, such termination not being subject to appeal. There is an obvious justification for the summary suspension power where the employee occupies a "sensitive" position in which he could cause serious damage to the national security during the delay incident to an investigation and the preparation of charges. Likewise, there is a reasonable basis for the view that an agency head who must bear the responsibility for the protection of classified information committed to his custody should have the final say in deciding whether to repose his trust in an employee who has access to such information. On the other hand, it is difficult to justify summary suspensions and unreviewable dismissals on loyalty grounds of employees who are not in "sensitive" positions and who are thus not situated where they could bring about any discernible adverse effects on the Nation's security. In the absence of an immediate threat of harm to the "national security," the normal dismissal procedures seem fully adequate and the justification for summary powers disappears. Indeed, in view of the stigma attached to persons dismissed on loyalty grounds, the need for procedural safeguards seems even greater than in other cases, and we will not lightly assume that Congress intended to take away those safeguards in the absence of some overriding necessity, such as exists in the case of employees handling defense secrets.

The 1950 Act itself reflects Congress' concern for the procedural rights of employees and its desire to limit the unreviewable dismissal power to the minimum scope necessary to the purpose of protecting activities affected with the "national security." A proviso to § 1 of the Act provides that a dismissal by one agency under the power granted by the Act "shall not affect the right of such officer or employee to seek or accept employment in any other department or agency of the Government," if the Civil Service Commission determines that the employee is eligible for such other employment. That is, the unreviewable dismissal power was to be used only for the limited purpose of removing the employee from the position in which his presence had been determined to endanger the "national security"; it could affect his right to employment in other agencies only if the Civil Service Commission, after review, refused to clear him for such employment. This effort to preserve the employee's procedural rights to the maximum extent possible hardly seems consistent with an intent to define the scope of the dismissal power in terms of the indefinite and virtually unlimited meaning for which the respondents contend.

Moreover, if Congress intended the term to have such a broad meaning that all positions in the Government could be said to be affected with the "national security," the result would be that the 1950 Act, though in form but an exception to the general personnel laws, could be utilized effectively to supersede those laws. For why could it not be said that national security in that sense requires not merely loyal and trustworthy employees but also those that are industrious and efficient? The relationship of the job to the national security being the same, its demonstrated inadequate performance because of inefficiency or incompetence would seem to present a surer threat to national security, in the sense of the general welfare, than a mere doubt as to the employee's loyalty.

Finally, the conclusion we draw from the face of the Act that "national security" was used in a limited and definite sense is amply supported by the legislative history of the Act.

In the first place, it was constantly emphasized that the bill, first introduced as S. 1561 in the 80th Congress and passed as H. R. 7439 in the 81st Congress, was intended to apply, or to be extended, only to "sensitive" agencies, a term used to imply a close and immediate concern with the defense of the Nation.[8] Thus the Senate Committee on Armed Services, in reporting out S. 1561, stated:

> "This bill provides authority to terminate employment of indiscreet or disloyal employees who are employed in areas of the Government which are sensitive from the standpoint of national security.
>
> * * *
>
> "[Section 3 will permit] the President to determine additional sensitive areas and include such areas in the scope of the authorities contained in this bill.
>
> * * *

"Insofar as the [addition of § 3] is concerned, it was recognized by all witnesses that there were other sensitive areas within the various departments of the Government which are now, or might in the future become, deeply involved in national security. . . . In view . . . of the fact that there are now and will be in the future other sensitive areas of equal importance to the national security, it is believed that the President should have authority to make a finding concerning such areas and by Executive action place those areas under the authorities contained in this act."[9]

The House Committee on Post Office and Civil Service reported that "The provisions of the bill extend only to departments and agencies which are concerned with vital matters affecting the national security of our Nation."[10] The committee reports on H. R. 7439 in the next Congress similarly referred to the bill as granting the dismissal power only to the heads of the "sensitive" agencies.[11] While these references relate primarily to the agencies to be covered by the Act, rather than to the exercise of the power within an agency, the standard for both is the same—in the "interests of the national security"—and the statements thus clearly indicate the restricted sense in which "national security" was used. In short, "national security" is affected only by "sensitive" activities.

Secondly, the history makes clear that the Act was intended to authorize the suspension and dismissal only of persons in sensitive positions. Throughout the hearings, committee reports, and debates, the bill was described as being designed to provide for the dismissal of "security risks."[12] In turn, the examples given of what might be a "security risk" always entailed employees having access to classified materials; they were security risks because of the risk they posed of intentional or inadvertent disclosure of confidential information.[13]

It is clear, therefore, both from the face of the Act and the legislative history, that "national security" was not used in the Act in an all-inclusive sense, but was intended to refer only to the protection of "sensitive" activities. It follows that an employee can be dismissed "in the interest of the national security" under the Act only if he occupies a "sensitive" position, and thus that a condition precedent to the exercise of the dismissal authority is a determination by the agency head that the position occupied is one affected with the "national security." We now turn to an examination of the Secretary's action to show that no such determination was made as to the position occupied by petitioner.

* * *

II.

The Secretary's action in dismissing the petitioner was expressly taken pursuant to Exec. Order No. 10450, 18 Fed. Reg. 2489,[16] promulgated in April 1953 to provide uniform standards and procedures for the exercise by agency heads of the suspension and dismissal powers under the 1950 Act. That Order prescribes as the standard for dismissal, and the dismissal notice given to petitioner contained, a determination by the Secretary that the employee's retention in employment "is not clearly consistent with the interests of national security."[17] Despite this verbal formula, however, it is our view that the Executive Order does not in fact require the agency head to make any determination whatever on the relationship of the employee's retention to the "national security" if the charges against him are within the categories of the charges against petitioner—that is, charges which reflect on the employee's loyalty. Rather, as we read the Order, it enjoins upon the agency heads the duty of discharging any employee of doubtful loyalty, *irrespective* of the character of his job and its relationship to the "national security." That is, the Executive Order deems an adverse determination as to loyalty to satisfy the requirements of the statute without more.

We therefore interpret the Executive Order as meaning that, when "loyalty" charges are involved, an employee may be dismissed regardless of the character of his position in the Government service, and that the agency head need make no evaluation as to the effect which continuance of his employment might have upon the "national security." We recognize that this interpretation of the Order rests upon a chain of inferences drawn from less than explicit provisions. But the Order was promulgated to guide the agency heads in the exercise of the dismissal power, and its failure to state explicitly what determinations are required leaves no choice to the agency heads but to follow the most reasonable inferences to be drawn. Moreover, whatever the practical reasons that may have dictated the awkward form of the Order, its failure to state explicitly what was meant is the fault of the Government. Any ambiguities should therefore be resolved against the Government, and we will not burden the employee with the assumption that an agency head, in stating no more than the formal conclusion that retention of the employee is not "clearly consistent with the interest of national security," has made any subsidiary determinations not clearly required by the Executive Order.

* * *

From the Secretary's determination that petitioner's employment was not "clearly consistent with the interests of national security," therefore, it may be assumed only that the Secretary found the charges to be true and that they created a reasonable doubt as to petitioner's loyalty. No other subsidiary finding may be inferred, however, for, under the Executive Order as we have interpreted it, no other finding was required to support the Secretary's action.[19]

From our holdings (1) that not all positions in the Government are affected with the "national security" as that term is used in the 1950 Act, and (2) that no determination has been made that petitioner's position was one in which he could adversely affect the "national security," it necessarily follows that petitioner's discharge was not authorized by the 1950 Act. In reaching this conclusion, we are not confronted with the problem of reviewing the Secretary's exercise of discretion, since the basis for our decision is simply that the standard prescribed by the Executive Order and applied by the Secretary is not in conformity with the Act.[20] Since petitioner's discharge was not authorized by the 1950 Act and hence violated the Veterans' Preference Act, the judgment of the Court of Appeals is reversed and the case is remanded to the District Court for further proceedings not inconsistent with this opinion.

Reversed and remanded.

---

[2]§ 1, Exec. Order No. 10450, 18 Fed. Reg. 2489, set forth in the Appendix, *post,* p. 558.

[3]Secretary Folsom, the present Secretary of the Department of Health, Education, and Welfare, has been substituted as respondent for the former Secretary Hobby.

[4]§ 6, 37 Stat. 555, as amended, 5 U. S. C. § 652.

[5]§ 14, 58 Stat. 390, as amended, 5 U. S. C. § 863.

[6]Civil Service War Regulations, § 18.2 (c) (7), September 26, 1942, 5 CFR, Cum. Supp., § 18.2 (c) (7).

[7]Employees dismissed under the Loyalty Program were entitled to review by the Civil Service Commission's Loyalty Review Board, thus satisfying the requirements of § 14 of the Veteran's Preference Act. See *Kutcher v. Gray,* 91 U.S. App. D. C. 266, 199 F. 2d 783 (C.A.D.C. Cir.).

[8]Congress' reluctance to extend such powers to all agencies of the Government is also indicated by the prior legislation. At various times since 1942, similar summary dismissal statutes, of limited duration, had been enacted, but these had been limited to the obviously "sensitive" military departments, 56 Stat. 1053, 63 Stat. 1023, and the State Department, 60 Stat. 458. The 1950 Act, introduced at the request of the Department of Defense, was designed to make the authority permanent, include several other "sensitive" agencies, and afford greater flexibility by permitting the President to extend the Act to other agencies which became "sensitive." H. R. Rep. No. 2330, 81st Cong., 2d Sess., p. 3; S. Rep. No. 1155, 80th Cong., 2d Sess., p. 4.

[9]S. Rep. No. 1155, 80th Cong., 2d Sess., pp. 2-4.

[10]H. R. Rep. No. 2264, 80th Cong., 2d Sess., p. 2.

[11]H. R. Rep. No. 2330, 81st Cong., 2d Sess., pp. 2-5; S. Rep. No. 2158, 81st Cong., 2d Sess., p. 2.

[12]*E.g.*, S. Rep. No. 2158, 81st Cong., 2d Sess., p. 2: "The purpose of the bill is to increase the authority of the heads of Government departments engaged in sensitive activities to summarily suspend employees considered to be bad security risks. . . ."

[13]For example, Mr. Murray, the Chairman of the Committee on Post Office and Civil Service, which had reported the bill, gave the following illustration of the purpose of the bill in opening the debate in the House: "For instance, an employee who is working in some highly sensitive agency doing very confidential, secret defense work and who goes out and gets too much liquor may unintentionally or unwittingly, because of his condition, confide to someone who may be a subversive, secret military information about the character of work he is doing in that department. He is, by his conduct, a bad security risk and should be discharged." 96 Cong. Rec. 10017.

[16]The relevant portions of the Executive Order, as it stood at the time of petitioner's suspension and discharge, are printed in the Appendix, *post*, p. 558.

[17]Section 6 of the Order, which formally prescribes the standards for "termination," in terms adopts the very language of the statute, "necessary or advisable in the interests of the national security." Section 7, however, provides that a suspended employee "shall not be reinstated" unless the agency head determines that reinstatement is "clearly consistent with the interests of the national security." Since nonreinstatement of a suspended employee is equivalent to the termination of his employment, it is apparent that the "clearly consistent" standard of § 7 is the controlling one. See also §§ 2, 8, and 3 (a). In the view we take of the case, we need not determine whether the "clearly consistent" standard is, as petitioner contends, a more onerous one than the "necessary or advisable" standard.

[19]That the Secretary similarly interpreted the Executive Order and did not in fact determine that petitioner's job was a "sensitive" one is confirmed by the respondents' concession that petitioner "did not have access to Government secrets or classified material and was not in a position to influence policy against the interests of the Government." Respondents' Brief, pp. 3-4; Record, p. 40.

[20]No contention is made that the Executive Order might be sustained under the President's executive power even though in violation of the Veterans' Preference Act. There is no basis for such an argument in any event, for it is clear from the face of the Executive Order that the President did not intend to override statutory limitations on the dismissal of employees, and promulgated the Order solely as an implementation of the 1950 Act. Thus § 6 of the Order purports to authorize dismissals only "in accordance with the said Act of August 26, 1950," and similar references are made in § 4, 5, and 7. This explicit limitation in the substantive provisions of the Order is of course not weakened by the inclusion of the "Constitution," as well as the 1950 and other Acts, in the omnibus list of authorities recited in the Preamble of the Order; it is from the Constitution that the President derives any authority to implement the 1950 Act at all. When the President expressly confines his action to the limits of statutory authority, the validity of the action must be determined solely by the congressional limitations which the President sought to respect, whatever might be the result were the President ever to assert his independent power against that of Congress.

Greene v. McElroy

360 U.S. 474 (1959)

Mr. Chief Justice Warren delivered the opinion of the Court.

This case involves the validity of the Government's revocation of security clearance granted to petitioner, an aeronautical engineer employed by a private manufacturer which produced goods for the armed services. Petitioner was discharged from his employment solely as a consequence of the revocation because his access to classified information was required by the nature of his job. After his discharge, petitioner was unable to secure employment as an aeronautical engineer and for all practical purposes that field of endeavor is now closed to him.

Petitioner was vice president and general manager of Engineering and Research Corporation (ERCO), a business devoted primarily to developing and manufacturing various mechanical and electronic products. He began this employment in 1937 soon after his graduation from the Guggenheim School of Aeronautics and, except for a brief leave of absence, he stayed with the firm until his discharge in 1953. He was first employed as a junior engineer and draftsman. Because of the excellence of his work he eventually became a chief executive officer of the firm. During his career with ERCO, he was credited with the expedited development of a complicated electronic flight simulator and with the design of a rocket launcher, both of which were produced by ERCO and long used by the Navy.

During the post-World War II period, petitioner was given security clearances on three occasions. These were required by the nature of the projects undertaken by ERCO for the various armed services. On November 21, 1951, however, the Army-Navy-Air Force Personnel Security Board (PSB) advised ERCO that the company's clearances for access to classified information were in jeopardy because of a tentative decision to deny petitioner access to classified Department of Defense information and to revoke his clearance for security reasons. ERCO was invited to respond to this notification. The corporation, through its president, informed PSB that petitioner had taken an extended furlough due to the Board's action. The ERCO executive also stated that in his opinion petitioner was a loyal and discreet United States citizen and that his absence denied to the firm the services of an outstanding engineer and administrative executive. On December 11, 1951, petitioner was informed by the Board that it had "decided that access by you to contract work and information [at ERCO] . . . would be inimical to the best interests of the United States." Accordingly, the PSB revoked petitioner's clearances. He was informed that he could seek a hearing before the Industrial Employment Review Board (IERB), and he took this course. Prior to the hearing, petitioner received a letter informing him that the PSB action was based on information indicating that between 1943 and 1947 he had associated with Communists, visited officials of the Russian Embassy, and attended a dinner given by an allegedly Communist Front organization.

On January 23, 1952, petitioner, with counsel, appeared before the IERB. He was questioned in detail concerning his background and the information disclosed in the IERB letter. In response to numerous and searching questions he explained in substance that specific "suspect" persons with whom he was said to have associated were actually friends of his ex-wife. He explained in some detail that during his first marriage, which lasted from 1942 through 1947, his then wife held views with which he did not concur and was friendly with associates and other persons with whom he had little in common. He stated that these basic disagreements were the prime reasons that the marriage ended in failure. He attributed to his then wife his attendance at the dinner, his membership in a bookshop association which purportedly was a "front" organization, and the presence in his home of "Communist" publications. He denied categorically that he had ever been a "Communist" and he spoke at length about his dislike for "a theory of Government which has for its object the common ownership of property." Lastly, petitioner explained that his visits to persons in various foreign embassies (including the Russian Embassy) were made in connection with his attempts to sell ERCO's products to their Governments. Petitioner's witnesses, who included top-level executives of ERCO and a number of military officers who had worked with petitioner in the past, corroborated many of petitioner's statements and testified in substance that he was a loyal and discreet citizen. These top-level executives of ERCO, whose right to clearance was never challenged, corroborated petitioner's testimony concerning his reasons for visiting the Russian Embassy.

The Government presented no witnesses. It was obvious, however, from the questions posed to petitioner and to his witnesses, that the Board relied on confidential reports which were never made available to petitioner. These reports apparently were compilations of statements taken from various persons contacted by an investigatory agency. Petitioner had no opportunity to confront and question persons whose statements reflected adversely on him or to confront the government investigators who took their statements. Moreover, it seemed evident that the Board itself had never questioned the investigators and had never seen those persons whose statements were the subject of their reports.

On January 29, 1952, the IERB, on the basis of the testimony given at the hearing and the confidential reports, reversed the action of the PSB and informed petitioner and ERCO that petitioner was authorized to work on Secret contract work.

On March 27, 1953, the Secretary of Defense abolished the PSB and IERB and directed the Secretaries of the three amred services to establish regional Industrial Personnel Security Boards to coordinate the industrial security program. The Secretaries were also instructed to establish uniform standards, criteria, and procedures. Cases pending before the PSB and IERB were referred to these new Boards. During the interim period between the abolishment of the old program and the implementation of the new one, the Secretaries considered themselves charged with administering clearance activities under previously stated criteria.

On April 17, 1953, respondent Anderson, the Secretary of the Navy, wrote ERCO that he had reviewed petitioner's case and had concluded that petitioner's "continued access to Navy classified security information [was] inconsistent with the best interests of National Security." No hearing preceded this notification. He requested ERCO to exclude petitioner "from any part of your plants, factories or sites at which classified Navy projects are being carried out and to bar him access to all Navy classified information." He also advised the corporation that petitioner's case was being referred to the Secretary of Defense with the recommendation that the IERB's decision of January 29, 1952, be overruled. ERCO had no choice but to comply with the request. This led to petitioner's discharge. ERCO informed the Navy of what had occurred and requested an opportunity to discuss the matter in view of petitioner's importance to the firm. The Navy replied that "[a]s far as the Navy Department is concerned, any further discussion on this problem at this time will serve no useful purpose."

Petitioner asked for reconsideration of the decision. On October 13, 1953, the Navy wrote to him stating that it had requested the Eastern Industrial Personnel Security Board (EIPSB) to accept jurisdiction and to arrive at a final determination concerning petitioner's status. Various letters were subsequently exchanged between petitioner's counsel and the EIPSB. These resulted finally in generalized charges, quoted in the margin, incorporating the information previously discussed with petitioner at his 1952 hearing before the IERB.

On April 28, 1954, more than one year after the Secretary took action, and for the two days thereafter, petitioner presented his case to the EIPSB and was cross-examined in detail. The hearing began with a statement by the Chairman, which included the following passage:

> "The transcript to be made of this hearing will not include all material in the file of the case, in that, it will not include reports of investigation conducted by the Federal Bureau of Investigation or other investigative agencies which are confidential. Neither will it contain information concerning the identity of confidential informants or information which will reveal the source of confidential evidence. The transcript will contain only the Statement of Reasons, your answer thereto and the testimony actually taken at this hearing."

Petitioner was again advised that the revocation of his security clearance was based on incidents occurring between 1942 and 1947, including his associations with alleged Communists, his visits with officials of the Russian Embassy, and the presence in his house of Communist literature.

Petitioner, in response to a question, stated at the outset of the hearing that he was then employed at a salary of $4,700 per year as an architectural draftsman and that he had been receiving $18,000 per year as Vice President and General Manager or ERCO. He later explained that after his discharge from ERCO he had unsuccessfully tried to obtain employment in the aeronautics field but had been barricaded from it because of lack of clearance.

Petitioner was subjected to an intense examination similar to that which he experienced before the IERB in 1952. During the course of the examination, the Board injected new subjects of inquiry and made it evident that it was relying on various investigatory reports and statements of confidential informants which were not made available to petitioner. Petitioner reiterated in great detail the explanations previously given before the IERB. He was subjected to intense cross-examination, however, concerning reports that he had agreed with the views held by his ex-wife.

Petitioner again presented a number of witnesses who testified that he was loyal, that he had spoken approvingly of the United States and its economic system, that he was a valuable engineer, and that he had made valuable and significant contributions to this country's war efforts during World War II and the Korean War.

Soon after the conclusion of the hearing, the EIPSB notified petitioner that it had affirmed the Secretary's action and that it had decided that the granting of clearance to petitioner for access to classified information was "not clearly consistent with the interests of national security." Petitioner requested that he be furnished with a detailed statement of findings supporting the Board's decision. He was informed, however, that security considerations prohibited such disclosure. On September 16, 1955, petitioner requested review by the Industrial Personnel Security Review Board. On March 12, 1956, almost three years after the Secretary's action and nearly one year after the second hearing, he received a letter from the Director of the Office of Industrial Personnel Security Review informing him that the EIPSB had found that from 1942-1947 petitioner associated closely with his then wife and her friends, knowing that they were active in behalf of and sympathized with the Communist Party, that during part of this period petitioner maintained a sympathetic association with a number of officials of the Russian Embassy, that during this period petitioner's political views were similar to those of his then wife, that petitioner had been a member of a suspect bookshop association, had invested money in a suspect radio station, had attended a suspect dinner, and had, on occasion, Communist publications in his home, and that petitioner's credibility as a witness in the proceedings was doubtful. The letter also stated that the doubts concerning petitioner's credibility affected the Board's evaluation of his trustworthiness and that only trustworthy persons could be afforded access to classified information. The EIPSB determination was affirmed.

After the EIPSB decision in 1954, petitioner filed a complaint in the United States District Court for the District of Columbia asking for a declaration that the revocation was unlawful and void and for an order restraining respondents from acting pursuant to it. He also asked for an order requiring respondents to advise ERCO that the clearance revocation was void. Following the affirmance of the EIPSB order by the Industrial Personnel Review Board, petitioner moved for summary judgment in the District Court. The Government cross-filed for dismissal of the complaint or summary judgment. The District Court granted the Government's motion for summary judgment, 150 F. Supp. 958, and the Court of Appeals affirmed that disposition, 103 U.S. App. D. C. 87, 254 F. 2d 944.

The Court of Appeals recognized that petitioner had suffered substantial harm from the clearance revocation. But in that court's view, petitioner's suit presented no "justiciable controversy"—no controversy which the courts could finally and effectively decide. This conclusion followed from the Court of Appeals' reasoning that the Executive Department alone is competent to evaluate the competing considerations which exist in determining the persons who are to be afforded security clearances. The court also rejected petitioner's claim that he was deprived of his livelihood without the traditional safeguards required by "due process of law" such as confrontation of his accusers and access to confidential reports used to determine his fitness. Central to this determination was the court's unwillingness to order the Government to choose between disclosing the identities of informants or giving petitioner clearance.

Petitioner contends that the action of the Department of Defense in barring him from access to classified information on the basis of statements of confidential informants made to investigators was not authorized by either Congress or the President and has denied him "liberty" and "property" without "due process of law" in contravention of the Fifth Amendment. The alleged property is petitioner's employment; the alleged liberty is petitioner's freedom to practice his chosen profession. Respondents admit, as they must, that the revocation of security clearance caused petitioner to lose his job with ERCO and has seriously affected, if not destroyed, his ability to obtain employment in the aeronautics field. Although the right to hold specific private employment and to follow a chosen profession free from unreasonable governmental interference comes within the "liberty" and "property" concepts of the Fifth Amendment, *Dent v. West Virginia,* 129 U.S. 114; *Schware v. Board of Bar Examiners,* 353 U.S. 232; *Peters v. Hobby,* 349 U.S. 331, 352 (concurring opinion); cf. *Slochower v. Board of Education,* 350 U.S. 551; *Truax v. Raich,* 239 U.S. 33, 41; *Allgeyer v. Louisiana,* 165 U.S. 578, 589-590; *Powell v. Pennsylvania,* 127 U.S. 678, 684, respondents contend that the admitted interferences which have occurred are indirect by-products of necessary governmental action to protect the integrity of secret information and hence are not unreasonable and do not constitute deprivations within the meaning of the Amendment. Alternatively, respondents urge that even if petitioner has been restrained in the enjoyment of constitutionally protected rights, he was accorded due process of law in that he was permitted to utilize those procedural safeguards consonant with an effective clearance program, in the administration of which the identity of informants and their statements are kept secret to insure an unimpaired flow to the Government of information concerning subversive conduct. But in view of our conclusion that this case should be decided on the narrower ground of "authorization," we find that we need not determine the answers to these questions.

The issue, as we see it, is whether the Department of Defense has been authorized to create an industrial security clearance program under which affected persons may lose their jobs and may be restrained in following their chosen professions on the basis of fact determinations concerning their fitness for clearance made in proceedings in which they are denied the traditional procedural safeguards of confrontation and cross-examination.

Prior to World War II, only sporadic efforts were made to control the clearance of persons who worked in private establishments which manufactured materials for national defense. Report of the Commission on Government Security, 1957, S. Doc. No. 64, 85th Cong., 1st Sess. 236. During World War II the War Department instituted a formalized program to obtain the discharge from war plants of persons engaged in sabotage, espionage, and willful activity designed to disrupt the national defense program. *Id.,* at 237. In 1946, the War Department began to require contractors, before being given access to classified information, to sign secrecy agreements which required consent before their employees were permitted access to Top Secret or Secret Information. *Id.,* at 238. At the outset, each armed service administered its own industrial clearance program. *Id.,* at 239. Later, the PSB and IERB were established by the Department of Defense and the Secretaries of the armed services to administer a more centralized program. *Ibid.* Confusion existed concerning the criteria and procedures to be employed by these boards. *Ibid.* Eventually, generalized procedures were established with the approval of the Secretaries which provided in part that before the IERB "[t]he hearing will be conducted in such manner as to protect from disclosure information affecting the national security or tending to compromise investigative sources or methods. . . ." See "Procedures Governing Appeals to the Industrial Employment Review Board, dated 7 November 1949," note 4, *supra,* § 4(c). After abolition of these boards in 1953, and the establishment of the IPSB, various new sets of procedures were promulgated which likewise provided for the non-disclosure of information "tending to compromise investigative sources or methods or the identity of confidential informants."

All of these programs and procedures were established by directives issued by the Secretary of Defense or the Secretaries of the Army, Navy, and Air Force. None was the creature of statute or of an Executive Order issued by the President.

Respondents maintain that congressional authorization to the President to fashion a program which denies security clearance to persons on the basis of confidential information which the individuals have no opportunity to confront and test is unnecessary because the President has inherent authority to maintain military secrets inviolate. And respondents argue that if a statutory grant of power is necessary, such a grant can readily be *inferred* "as a necessarily implicit authority from the generalized provisions" of legislation dealing with the armed services. But the question which must be decided in this case is not whether the President has inherent power to act or whether Congress has granted him such a power; rather, it is whether either the President or Congress exercised such a power and delegated to the Department of Defense the authority to fashion such a program.

Certain principles have remained relatively immutable in our jurisprudence.

One of these is that where governmental action seriously injures an individual, and the reasonableness of the action depends on fact findings, the evidence used to prove the Government's case must be disclosed to the individual so that he has an opportunity to show that it is untrue. While this is important in the case of documentary evidence, it is even more important where the evidence consists of the testimony of individuals whose memory might be faulty or who, in fact, might be perjurers or persons motivated by malice, vindictiveness, intolerance, prejudice, or jealousy. We have formalized these protections in the requirements of confrontation and cross-examination. They have ancient roots. They find expression in the Sixth Amendment which provides that in all criminal cases the accused shall enjoy the right "to be confronted with the witnesses against him." This Court has been zealous to protect these rights from erosion. It has spoken out not only in criminal cases, *e.g., Mattox v. United States,* 156 U.S. 237, 242-244; *Kirby v. United States,* 174 U.S. 47; *Motes v. United States,* 178 U.S. 458, 474; *In re Oliver,* 333 U.S. 257, 273, but also in all types of cases where administrative and regulatory actions were under scrutiny. *E.g., Southern R. Co. v. Virginia,* 290 U.S. 190; *Ohio Bell Telephone Co. v. Public Utilities Commission,* 301 U.S. 292; *Morgan v. United States,* 304 U.S. 1, 19; *Carter v. Kubler,* 320 U.S. 243; *Reilly v. Pinkus,* 338 U.S. 269. Nor, as it has been pointed out, has Congress ignored these fundamental requirements in enacting regulatory legislation. *Joint Anti-Fascist Committee v. McGrath,* 341 U.S. 168-169 (concurring opinion).

Professor Wigmore, commenting on the importance of cross-examination, states in his treatise, 5 Wigmore on Evidence (3d ed. 1940) § 1367:

> "For two centuries past, the policy of the Anglo-American system of Evidence has been to regard the necessity of testing by cross-examination as a vital feature of the law. The belief that no safeguard for testing the value of human statements is comparable to that furnished by cross-examination, and the conviction that no statement (unless by special exception) should be used as testimony until it has been probed and sublimated by that test, has found increasing strength in lengthening experience."

Little need be added to this incisive summary statement except to point out that under the present clearance procedures not only is the testimony of absent witnesses allowed to stand without the probing questions of the person under attack which often uncover inconsistencies, lapses of recollection, and bias, but, in addition, even the members of the clearance boards do not see the informants or know their identities, but normally rely on an investigator's summary report of what the informant said without even examining the investigator personally.

We must determine against this background, whether the President or Congress has delegated to the Department of Defense the authority to by-pass these traditional and well-recognized safeguards in an industrial security clearance program which can operate to injure individuals substantially by denying to them the opportunity to follow chosen private professions. Respondents cite two Executive Orders which they believe show presidential delegation. The first, Exec. Order No. 10290, 16 Fed. Reg. 9795, was entitled "Prescribing Regulations Establishing Minimum Standards For The Classification, Transmission, And Handling, By Departments And Agencies Of The Executive Branch, Of Official Information Which Requires Safeguarding In The Interest Of The Security Of The United States." It provided, in relevant part:

* * *

The second, Exec. Order No. 10501, 18 Fed. Reg. 7049, which revoked Exec. Order No. 10290, is entitled "Safeguarding Official Information In The Interests Of The Defense Of The United States" and provides in relevant part:

* * *

Clearly, neither of these orders empowers any executive agency to fashion security programs whereby persons are deprived of their present civilian employment and of the opportunity of continued activity in their chosen professions without being accorded the chance to challenge effectively the evidence and testimony upon which an adverse security determination might rest.

Turning to the legislative enactments which might be deemed as delegating authority to the Department of Defense to fashion programs under which persons may be seriously restrained in their employment opportunities through a denial of clearance without the safeguards of cross-examination and confrontation, we note that Government's own assertion, made in its brief, that "[w]ith petitioner's contention that the Industrial Security Program is not explicitly authorized by statute we may readily agree. . . ."

The first proffered statute is the National Security Act of 1947, as amended, 5 U. S. C. § 171 *et seq.* That Act created the Department of Defense and gave to the Secretary of Defense and the Secretaries of the armed services the authority to administer their departments. Nowhere in the Act, or its amendments, is there found specific authority to create a clearance program similar to the one now in effect.

Another Act cited by respondents is the Armed Service Procurement Act of 1947, as amended. It provides in 10 U. S. C. § 2304 that:

* * *

Respondents argue that these statutes, together with 18 U. S. C. § 798, which makes it a crime willfully and knowingly to communicate to unauthorized persons information concerning cryptographic or intelligence activities, and 50 U. S. C. § 783 (b), which makes it a crime for an officer or employee of the United States to communicate classified information to agents of foreign governments or officers and members of "Communist organizations," reflect a recognition by Congress of the existence of military secrets and the necessity of keeping those secrets inviolate.

Although these statutes make it apparent that Congress recognizes the existence of military secrets, they hardly constitute an authorization to create an elaborate clearance program which embodies procedures traditionally believed to be inadequate to protect affected persons.

Lastly, the Government urges that if we refuse to adopt its "inferred" authorization reasoning, nevertheless, congressional ratification is apparent by the continued appropriation of funds to finance aspects of the program fashioned by the Department of Defense. Respondents refer us to Hearings before the House Committee on Appropriations on Department of Defense Appropriations for 1956, 84th Cong., 1st Sess. 774-781. At those hearings, the Committee was asked to approve the appropriation of funds to finance a program under which reimbursement for lost wages would be made to employees of government contractors who were temporarily denied, but later granted, security clearance. Apparently, such reimbursements had been made prior to that time out of general appropriations. Although a specific appropriation was eventually made for this purpose, it could not conceivably constitute a ratification of the hearing procedures, for the procedures were in no way involved in the special reimbursement program.

Respondents' argument on delegation resolves itself into the following: The President, in general terms, has authorized the Department of Defense to create procedures to restrict the dissemination of classified information and has apparently acquiesced in the elaborate program established by the Secretary of Defense even where application of the program results in restraints on traditional freedoms without the use of long-required procedural protections. Similarly, Congress, although it has not enacted specific legislation relating to clearance procedures to be utilized for industrial workers, has acquiesced in the existing Department of Defense program and has ratified it by specifically appropriating funds to finance one aspect of it.

If acquiescence or implied ratification were enough to show delegation of authority to take actions within the area of questionable constitutionality, we might agree with respondents that delegation has been shown here. In many circumstances, where the Government's freedom to act is clear, and the Congress or the President has provided general standards of action and has acquiesced in administrative interpretation, delegation may be inferred. Thus, even in the absence of specific delegation, we have no difficulty in finding, as we do, that the Department of Defense has been authorized to fashion and apply an industrial clearance program which affords affected persons the safeguards of confrontation and cross-examination. But this case does not present that situation. We deal here with substantial restraints on employment opportunities of numerous persons imposed in a manner which is in conflict with our long-accepted notions of fair procedures. Before we are asked to judge whether, in the context of security clearance cases, a person may be deprived of the right to follow his chosen profession without full hearings where accusers may be confronted, it must be made clear that the President or Congress, within their respective constitutional powers, specifically has decided that the imposed procedures are necessary and warranted and has authorized their use. Cf. *Watkins v. United States,* 354 U.S. 178; *Scull v. Virginia,* 359 U.S. 344. Such decisions cannot be assumed by acquiescence or non-action. *Kent v. Dulles,* 357 U.S. 116; *Peters v. Hobby,* 349 U.S. 331; *Ex parte Endo,* 323 U.S. 283, 301-302. They must be made explicitly not only to assure that individuals are not deprived of cherished rights under procedures not actually authorized, see *Peters v. Hobby, supra,* but also because explicit action, especially in areas of doubtful constitutionality, requires careful and purposeful consideration by those responsible for enacting and implementing our laws. Without explicit action by lawmakers, decisions of great constitutional import and effect would be relegated by default to administrators who, under our system of government, are not endowed with authority to decide them.

Where administrative action has raised serious constitutional problems, the Court has assumed that Congress or the President intended to afford those affected by the action the traditional safeguards of due process. See *e.g., The Japanese Immigrant Case,* 189 U.S. 86, 101; *Dismuke v. United States,* 297 U.S. 167, 172; *Ex parte Endo,* 323 U.S. 283, 299-300; *American Power Co. v. Securities and Exchange Comm'n,* 329 U.S. 90, 107-108; *Hannegan v. Esquire,* 327 U.S. 146, 156; *Wong Yang Sung v. McGrath,* 339 U.S. 33, 49. Cf. *Anniston Mfg. Co. v. Davis,* 301 U.S. 337; *United States v. Rumely,* 345 U.S. 41. These cases reflect the Court's concern that traditional forms of fair procedure not be restricted by implication or without the most explicit action by the Nation's lawmakers, even in areas where it is possible that the Constitution presents no inhibition.

In the instant case, petitioner's work opportunities have been severely limited on the basis of a fact determination rendered after a hearing which failed to comport with our traditional ideas of fair procedure. The type of hearing was the product of administrative decision not explicitly authorized by either Congress or the President. Whether those procedures under the circumstances comport with the Constitution we do not decide. Nor do we decide whether the President has inherent authority to create such a program, whether congressional action is necessary, or what the limits on executive or legislative authority may be. We decide only that in the absence of explicit authorization from either the President or Congress the respondents were not empowered to deprive petitioner of his job in a proceeding in which he was not afforded the safeguards of confrontation and cross-examination.

Accordingly, the judgment is reversed and the case is remanded to the District Court for proceedings not inconsistent herewith.

It is so ordered.

Mr. Justice Frankfurter, Mr. Justice Harlan and Mr. Justice Whittaker concur in the judgment on the ground that it has not been shown that either Congress or the President authorized the procedures whereby petitioner's security clearance was revoked, intimating no views as to the validity of those procedures.

Mr. Justice Harlan, concurring specially. . . .

Mr. Justice Clark, dissenting. . . .

Cafeteria and Restaurant Workers Union v. McElroy

367 U.S. 886 (1961)

Mr. Justice Stewart delivered the opinion of the Court.

In 1956 the petitioner Rachel Brawner was a short-order cook at a cafeteria operated by her employer, M & M Restaurants, Inc., on the premises of the Naval Gun Factory[1] in the city of Washington. She had worked there for more than six years, and from her employer's point of view her record was entirely satisfactory.

The Gun Factory was engaged in designing, producing, and inspecting naval ordnance, including the development of weapons systems of a highly classified nature. Located on property owned by the United States, the installation was under the command of Rear Admiral D. M. Tyree, Superintendent. Access to it was restricted, and guards were posted at all points of entry. Identification badges were issued to persons authorized to enter the premises by the Security Officer, a naval officer subordinate to the Superintendent. In 1956 the Security Officer was Lieutenant Commander H. C. Williams. Rachel Brawner had been issued such a badge.

The cafeteria where she worked was operated by M & M under a contract with the Board of Governors of the Gun Factory. Section 5 (b) of the contract provided:

> ". . . In no event shall the Concessionaire engage, or continue to engage, for operations under this Agreement, personnel who
>
> * * *
>
> "(iii) fail to meet the security requirements or other requirements under applicable regulations of the Activity, as determined by the Security Officer of the Activity."

On November 15, 1956, Mrs. Brawner was required to turn in her identification badge because of Lieutenant Commander Williams' determination that she had failed to meet the security requirements of the installation. The Security Officer's determination was subsequently approved by Admiral Tyree, who cited § 5 (b) (iii) of the contract as the basis for his action. At the request of the petitioner Union, which represented the employees at the cafeteria, M & M sought to arrange a meeting with officials of the Gun Factory "for the purpose of a hearing regarding the denial of admittance to the Naval Gun Factory of Rachel Brawner." This request was denied by Admiral Tyree on the ground that such a meeting would "serve no useful purpose."

Since the day her identification badge was withdrawn Mrs. Brawner has not been permitted to enter the Gun Factory. M & M offered to employ her in another restaurant which the company operated in the suburban Washington area, but she refused on the ground that the location was inconvenient.

The petitioners brought this action in the District Court against the Secretary of Defense, Admiral Tyree, and Lieutenant Commander Williams, in their individual and official capacities, seeking, among other things, to compel the return to Mrs. Brawner of her identification badge, so that she might be permitted to enter the Gun Factory and resume her former employment. The defendants filed a motion for summary judgment, supported by various affidavits and exhibits. The motion was granted and the complaint dismissed by the District Court. This judgment was affirmed by the Court of Appeals for the District of Columbia, sitting *en banc.* Four judges dissented.[2] We granted certiorari because of an alleged conflict between the Court of Appeals' decision and *Greene v. McElroy,* 360 U.S. 474. 364 U.S. 813.

As the case comes here, two basic questions are presented. Was the commanding officer of the Gun Factory authorized to deny Rachel Brawner access to the installation in the way he did? If he was so authorized, did his action in excluding her operate to deprive her of any right secured to her by the Constitution?

I.

In *Greene v. McElroy, supra,* the Court was unwilling to find, in the absence of explicit authorization, that an aeronautical engineer, employed by a private contractor on private property, could be barred from following his profession by governmental revocation of his security clearance without according him the right to confront and cross-examine hostile witnesses. The Court in that case found that neither the Congress nor the President had explicitly authorized the procedure which had been followed in denying Greene access to classified information. Accordingly we did not reach the constitutional issues which that case otherwise would have presented. We proceed on the premise that the explicit authorization found wanting in *Greene* must be shown in the present case, putting to one side the Government's argument that the differing circumstances here justify less rigorous standards for measuring delegation of authority.

It cannot be doubted that both the legislative and executive branches are wholly legitimate potential sources of such explicit authority. The control of access to a military base is clearly within the constitutional powers granted to both Congress and the President. Article I, § 8, of the Constitution gives Congress the power to "provide and maintain a navy;" to "make rules for the government and regulation of the land and naval forces;" to "exercise exclusive legislation . . . over all places purchased by the consent of the legislature of the state in which the same shall be, for the erection of forts, magazines, arsenals, dock-yards, and other needful buildings;" and to "make all laws which shall be necessary and proper for carrying into execution the foregoing powers. . . ." Broad power in this same area is also vested in the President by Article II, § 2, which makes him the Commander in Chief of the Armed Forces.

Congress has provided that the Secretary of the Navy "shall administer the Department of the Navy" and shall have "custody and charge of all . . . property of the Department." 10 U. S. C. § 5031 (a) and (c). In administering his Department, the Secretary has been given statutory power to "prescribe regulations, not inconsistent with law, for the government of his department, . . . and the custody, use, and preservation of the . . . property appertaining to it." 5 U. S. C. § 22. The law explicitly requires that United States Navy Regulations shall be approved by the President, 10 U. S. C. § 6011, and the pertinent regulations in effect when Rachel Brawner's identification badge was revoked had, in fact, been expressly approved by President Truman on August 9, 1948.

The requirement of presidential approval of Navy regulations is of ancient vintage.[3] The significance of such presidential approval has often been recognized by this Court. *Smith v. Whitney,* 116 U.S. 167, 181; *Johnson v. Sayre,* 158 U.S. 109, 117; *United States Grain Corp. v. Phillips,* 261 U.S. 106, 109; *Denby v. Berry,* 263 U.S. 29, 37.[4] We may take it as settled that Navy Regulations approved by the President are, in the words of Chief Justice Marshall, endowed with "the sanction of the law." *United States v. Maurice,* 2 Brock. 96, 105.[5] And we find no room for substantial doubt that the Navy Regulations in effect on November 15, 1956, explicitly conferred upon Admiral Tyree the power summarily to deny Rachel Brawner access to the Gun Factory.

Article 0701 of the Regulations delineates the traditional responsibilities and duties of a commanding officer. It provides in part as follows:

> "The responsibility of the commanding officer for his command is absolute, except when, and to the extent, relieved therefrom by competent authority, or as provided otherwise in these regulations. The authority of the commanding officer is commensurate with his responsibility, subject to the limitations prescribed by law and these regulations. . . ."

Article 0734 of the Regulations provides:

> "In general, dealers or tradesmen or their agents shall not be admitted within a command, except as authorized by the commanding officer:
>
> "1. To conduct public business.
>
> "2. To transact specific private business with individuals at the request of the latter.
>
> "3. To furnish services and supplies which are necessary and are not otherwise, or are insufficiently, available to the personnel of the command."

It would be difficult to conceive of a more specific conferral of power upon a commanding officer, in the exercise of his traditional command responsibility, to exclude from the area of his command a person in Rachel Brawner's status. Even without the benefit of the illuminating gloss of history, it could hardly be doubted that the phrase "tradesmen or their agents" covered her status as an employee of M & M with explicit precision.[6] But the meaning of the regulation need not be determined *in vacuo.* It is the verbalization of the unquestioned authority which commanding officers of military installations have exercised throughout our history.[7]

An opinion by Attorney General Butler in 1837 discloses that the power of a military commanding officer to exclude at will persons who earned their living by working on military bases was even then of long standing. Speaking of the Superintendent of the Military Academy, the Attorney General's opinion stated:

> "[H]e has always regarded the citizens resident within the public limits—such as the sutler, keeper of the commons, tailor, shoemaker, artificers, etc., even though they own houses on the public grounds, or occupy buildings belonging to the United States . . .—as *tenants at will,* and liable to be removed whenever, in the opinion of the superintendent, the interests of the academy require it. 'This,' he observes, 'has been the practice since I have been in command; and such, I am told, was the usage under the administration of my predecessors.' " 3 Op. Atty. Gen. 268, 269.

This power has been expressly recognized many times. "The power of a military commandant over a reservation is necessarily extensive and practically exclusive, forbidding entrance and controlling residence as the public interest may demand." 26 Op. Atty. Gen. 91, 92. "[I]t is well settled that a post commander can, in his discretion, exclude all persons other than those belonging to his post from post and reservation grounds." JAGA 1904/16272, 6 May 1904. "It is well settled that a Post Commander can, under the authority conferred on him by statutes and regulations, in his discretion, exclude private persons and property therefrom, or admit them under such restrictions as he may prescribe in the interest of good order and military discipline (1918 Dig. Op. J. A. G. 267 and cases cited)." JAGA 1925/680.44, 6 October 1925.

Under the explicit authority of Article 0734 of the Navy Regulations, and in the light of the historically unquestioned power of a commanding officer summarily to exclude civilians from the area of his command, there can remain no serious doubt of Admiral Tyree's authority to exclude Rachel Brawner from the Gun Factory upon the Security Officer's determination that she failed to meet the "security requirements . . . of the Activity." Her admittance to the installation in the first place was permissible, in the commanding officer's discretion, only because she came within the exception to the general rule of exclusion contained in the third paragraph of Article 0734 of the Regulations. And the plain words of Article 0734 made absolute the commanding officer's power to withdraw her permission to enter the Gun Factory at any time.

II.

The question remains whether Admiral Tyree's action in summarily denying Rachel Brawner access to the site of her former employment violated the requirements of the Due Process Clause of the Fifth Amendment. This question cannot be answered by easy assertion that, because she had no constitutional right to be there in the first place, she was not deprived of liberty or property by the Superintendent's action. "One may not have a constitutional right to go to Baghdad, but the Government may not prohibit one from going there unless by means consonant with due process of law." *Homer v. Richmond,* 110 U.S. App. D. C. 226, 229, 292 F.

2d 719, 722. It is the petitioners' claim that due process in this case required that Rachel Brawner be advised of the specific grounds for her exclusion and be accorded a hearing at which she might refute them. We are satisfied, however, that under the circumstances of this case such a procedure was not constitutionally required.

The Fifth Amendment does not require a trial-type hearing in every conceivable case of government impairment of private interest. "For, though 'due process of law' generally implies and includes *actor, reus, judex,* regular allegations, opportunity to answer, and a trial according to some settled course of judicial proceedings, . . . yet, this is not universally true." *Murray's Lessee v. Hoboken Land and Improvement Co.,* 18 How. 272, 280. The very nature of due process negates any concept of inflexible procedures universally applicable to every imaginable situation. *Communications Comm'n v. WJR,* 337 U.S. 265, 275-276; *Hannah v. Larche,* 363 U.S. 420, 440, 442; *Hagar v. Reclamation District No. 108,* 111 U.S. 701, 708-709. " '[D]ue process,' unlike some legal rules, is not a technical conception with a fixed content unrelated to time, place and circumstances." It is "compounded of history, reason, the past course of decisions. . . ." *Joint Anti-Fascist Comm. v. McGrath,* 341 U.S. 123, 162-163 (concurring opinion).

As these and other cases make clear, consideration of what procedures due process may require under any given set of circumstances must begin with a determination of the precise nature of the government function involved as well as of the private interest that has been affected by governmental action. Where it has been possible to characterize that private interest (perhaps in oversimplification)[8] as a mere privilege subject to the Executive's plenary power, it has traditionally been held that notice and hearing are not constitutionally required. *Oceanic Navigation Co. v. Stranahan,* 214 U.S. 320, 340-343; *Knauff v. Shaughnessy,* 338 U.S. 537; *Jay v. Boyd,* 351 U.S. 345, 354-358; cf. *Buttfield v. Stranahan,* 192 U.S. 470, 497.

What, then, was the private interest affected by Admiral Tyree's action in the present case? It most assuredly was not the right to follow a chosen trade or profession. Cf. *Dent v. West Virginia,* 129 U.S. 114; *Schware v. Board of Bar Examiners,* 353 U.S. 232; *Truax v. Raich,* 239 U.S. 33. Rachel Brawner remained entirely free to obtain employment as a short-order cook or to get any other job, either with M & M or with any other employer. All that was denied her was the opportunity to work at one isolated and specific military installation.

Moreover, the governmental function operating here was not the power to regulate or license, as lawmaker, an entire trade or profession, or to control an entire branch of private business, but, rather, as proprietor, to manage the internal operation of an important federal military establishment. See *People v. Crane,* 214 N.Y. 154, 167-169, 108 N.E. 427, 431-432 (per Cardozo, J.); cf. *Perkins v. Lukens Steel Co.,* 310 U.S. 113, 129. In that proprietary military capacity, the Federal Government, as has been pointed out, has traditionally exercised unfettered control.

Thus, the nature both of the private interest which has been impaired and the governmental power which has been exercised makes this case quite different from that of the lawyer in *Schware, supra,* the physician in *Dent, supra,* and the cook in *Raich, supra.* This case, like *Perkins v. Lukens Steel Co.,* 310 U.S. 113, involves the Federal Government's dispatch of its own internal affairs. The Court has consistently recognized that an interest closely analogous to Rachel Brawner's, the interest of a government employee in retaining his job, can be summarily denied. It has become a settled principle that government employment, in the absence of legislation, can be revoked at the will of the appointing officer. *In the Matter of*

Hennen, 13 Pet. 230, 246, 259; *Crenshaw v. United States,* 134 U.S. 99, 108; *Parsons v. United States,* 167 U.S. 324, 331-334; *Keim v. United States,* 177 U.S. 290, 293-294; *Taylor and Marshall v. Beckham (No. 1),* 178 U.S. 548, 575-578. This principle was reaffirmed quite recently in *Vitarelli v. Seaton,* 359 U.S. 535. There we pointed out that Vitarelli, an Interior Department employee who had not qualified for statutory protection under the Civil Service Act, "could have been summarily discharged by the Secretary at any time without the giving of a reason. . . ." 359 U.S., at 539.

It is argued that this view of Rachel Brawner's interest is inconsistent with our decisions in *United Public Workers v. Mitchell,* 330 U.S. 75, and *Wieman v. Updegraff,* 344 U.S. 183. In those two cases an individual's interest in government employment was recognized as entitled to constitutional protection, and it is contended that what the Court said in deciding them would require us to hold that Rachel Brawner was entitled to notice and hearing in this case. In *United Public Workers* the Court observed that "[n]one would deny" that "Congress may not 'enact a regulation providing that no Republican, Jew or Negro shall be appointed to federal office, or that no federal employee shall attend Mass or take any active part in missionary work.' " 330 U.S., at 100. In *Wieman* the Court held unconstitutional a statute which excluded persons from state employment solely on the basis of membership in alleged "Communist-front" or "subversive" organizations, regardless of their knowledge concerning the activities and purposes of the organizations to which they had belonged. In the course of its decision the Court said, "We need not pause to consider whether an abstract right to public employment exists. It is sufficient to say that constitutional protection does extend to the public servant whose exclusion pursuant to a statute is patently arbitrary or discriminatory." 344 U.S., at 192.

Nothing that was said or decided in *United Public Workers* or *Wieman* would lead to the conclusion that Rachel Brawner could not be denied access to the Gun Factory without notice and an opportunity to be heard. Those cases demonstrate only that the state and federal governments, even in the exercise of their internal operations, do not constitutionally have the complete freedom of action enjoyed by a private employer. But to acknowledge that there exist constitutional restraints upon state and federal governments in dealing with their employees is not to say that all such employees have a constitutional right to notice and a hearing before they can be removed. We may assume that Rachel Brawner could not constitutionally have been excluded from the Gun Factory if the announced grounds for her exclusion had been patently arbitrary or discriminatory—that she could not have been kept out because she was a Democrat or a Methodist. It does not follow, however, that she was entitled to notice and a hearing when the reason advanced for her exclusion was, as here, entirely rational and in accord with the contract with M & M.

Finally, it is to be noted that this is not a case where government action has operated to bestow a badge of disloyalty or infamy, with an attendant forecloseure from other employment opportunity. See *Weiman v. Updegraff,* 344 U.S. 183, 190-191; *Joint Anti-Fascist Comm. v. McGrath,* 341 U.S. 123, 140-141; cf. *Bailey v. Richardson,* 86 U.S. App. D. C. 248, 182 F. 2d 46, aff'd by an equally divided Court, 341 U.S. 918.[9] All this record shows is that, in the opinion of the Security Officer of the Gun Factory, concurred in by the Superintendent, Rachel Brawner failed to meet the particular security requirements of that specific military installation. There is nothing to indicate that this determination would in any way impair Rachel

Brawner's employment opportunities anywhere else. As pointed out by Judge Prettyman, speaking for the Court of Appeals, "Nobody has said that Brawner is disloyal or is suspected of the slightest shadow of intentional wrongdoing. 'Security requirments' at such an installation, like such requirements under many other circumstances, cover many matters other than loyalty." 109 U.S. App. D. C., at 49, 284 F. 2d, at 183. For all that appears, the Security Officer and the Superintendent may have simply thought that Rachel Brawner was garrulous, or careless with her identification badge.

For these reasons, we conclude that the Due Process Clause of the Fifth Amendment was not violated in this case.

Affirmed.

Mr. Justice Brennan, with whom The Chief Justice, Mr. Justice Black and Mr. Justice Douglas join, dissenting. . . .

---

[1]The name of the Naval Gun Factory has now been officially changed to Naval Weapons Plant. It will be referred to as the "Gun Factory" in this opinion.

[2]The appeal was originally heard by a panel of three judges, and the District Court's judgment was reversed, one judge dissenting. After rehearing *en banc,* the original opinion was withdrawn, and the District Court's judgment was affirmed. 109 U.S. App. D. C. 39, 284 F. 2d 173.

[3]See R. S. § 1547 (1875) which was derived from the Act of July 14, 1862, c. 164, § 5, 12 Stat. 565. See also the Act of April 24, 1816, c. 69, § 9, 3 Stat. 298; the Act of March 3, 1813, c. 52, § 5, 2 Stat. 819.

[4]See also 25 Op. Atty. Gen. 270.

[5]The absence of presidential approval was relied upon in one case as a basis for finding certain administrative action unauthorized. See *Phillips v. United States Grain Corp.,* 279 F. 244, 248-249, rev'd on other grounds, 261 U.S. 106. See also 25 Op. Atty. Gen. 270, 275.

[6]A tradesman has been defined by Webster as "a shopkeeper; also, one of his employees." Webster, New International Dictionary (Second Edition, Unabridged, 1958), 2684.

[7]The contrast with the history of the security program involved in *Greene v. McElroy* is striking. There it was pointed out that "[p]rior to World War II, only sporadic efforts were made to control the clearance of persons who worked in private establishments which manufactured materials for national defense." 360 U.S., at 493.

[8]See Davis, The Requirement of a Trial-Type Hearing, 70 Harv. L. Rev. 193, 222-224.

[9]Compare Davis, The Requirement of a Trial-Type Hearing, 70 Harv. L. Rev. 193, 229-230, and Note, The Supreme Court, 1950 Term, 65 Harv. L. Rev. 107, 156-158, with Richardson, Problems in the Removal of Federal Civil Servants, 54 Mich. L. Rev. 219, 240-241.

United States v. Robel

389 U.S. 258 (1967)

Mr. Chief Justice Warren delivered the opinion of the Court.

This appeal draws into question the constitutionality of § 5 (a)(1)(D) of the Subversive Activities Control Act of 1950, 64 Stat. 992, 50 U. S. C. § 784 (a)(1)(D),[1] which provides that, when a Communist-action organization[2] is under a final order to register, it shall be unlawful for any member of the organization "to engage in any employment in any defense facility." In *Communist Party v. Subversive Activities*

Control Board, 367 U.S. 1 (1961), this Court sustained an order of the SACB requiring the Communist Party of the United States to register as a Communist-action organization under the Act. The Board's order became final on October 20, 1961. At that time appellee, a member of the Communist Party, was employed as a machinist at the Seattle, Washington, shipyard of Todd Shipyards Corporation. On August 20, 1962, the Secretary of Defense, acting under authority delegated by § 5 (b) of the Act, designated that shipyard a "defense facility." Appellee's continued employment at the shipyard after that date subjected him to prosecution under § 5 (a)(1)(D), and on May 21, 1963, an indictment was filed charging him with a violation of that section. The indictment alleged in substance that appellee had "unlawfully and willfully engage[d] in employment" at the shipyard with knowledge of the outstanding order against the Party and with knowledge and notice of the shipyard's designation as a defense facility by the Secretary of Defense. The United States District Court for the Western District of Washington granted appellee's motion to dismiss the indictment on October 4, 1965. To overcome what it viewed as a "likely constitutional infirmity" in § 5 (a)(1)(D), the District Court read into that section "the requirements of active membership and specific intent." Because the indictment failed to allege that appellee's Communist Party membership was of that quality, the indictment was dismissed. The Government, unwilling to accept that narrow construction of § 5 (a)(1)(D) and insisting on the broadest possible application of the statute,[3] initially took its appeal to the Court of Appeals for the Ninth Circuit. On the Government's motion, the case was certified here as properly a direct appeal to this Court under 18 U. S. C. § 3731. We noted probable jurisdiction. 384 U.S. 937.[4] We affirm the judgment of the District Court, but on the ground that § 5 (a)(1)(D) is an unconstitutional abridgment of the right of association protected by the First Amendment.[5]

We cannot agree with the District Court that § 5 (a)(1)(D) can be saved from constitutional infirmity by limiting its application to active members of Communist-action organizations who have the specific intent of furthering the unlawful goals of such organizations. The District Court relied on *Scales v. United States,* 367 U.S. 203 (1961), in placing its limiting construction on § 5 (a)(1)(D). It is true that in *Scales* we read the elements of active membership and specific intent into the membership clause of the Smith Act.[6] However, in *Aptheker v. Secretary of State,* 378 U.S. 500 (1964), we noted that the Smith Act's membership clause required a defendant to have knowledge of the organization's illegal advocacy, a requirement that "was intimately connected with the construction limiting membership to 'active' members." Id., at 511, n. 9. *Aptheker* involved a challenge to § 6 of the Subversive Activities Control Act, 50 U. S. C. § 785, which provides that, when a Communist organization is registered or under a final order to register, it shall be unlawful for any member thereof with knowledge or notice thereof to apply for a passport. We held that "[t]he clarity and preciseness of the provisions in question make it impossible to narrow its indiscriminately cast and overly broad scope without substantial rewriting." *Id.,* at 515. We take the same view of § 5 (a)(1)(D). It is precisely because that statute sweeps indiscriminately across all types of association with Communist-action groups, without regard to the quality and degree of membership, that it runs afoul of the First Amendment.

In *Aptheker,* we held § 6 unconstitutional because it too broadly and indiscriminately infringed upon constitutionally protected rights. The Government has argued that, despite the overbreadth which is obvious on the face of § 5 (a)(1)(D), *Aptheker* is not controlling in this case because the right to travel is a more basic freedom than the right to be employed in a defense facility. We agree that *Aptheker* is not controlling since it was decided under the Fifth Amendment. But we cannot agree with the Government's characterization of the essential issue in this case. It is true that the specific disability imposed by § 5 (a)(1)(D) is to limit the employment opportunities of those who fall within its coverage, and such a limitation is not without serious constitutional implications. See *Greene v. McElroy,* 360 U.S. 474, 492 (1959). But the operative fact upon which the job disability depends is the exercise of an individual's right of assocation, which is protected by the provisions of the First Amendment.[7] Wherever one would place the right to travel on a scale of constitutional values, it is clear that those rights protected by the First Amendment are no less basic in our democratic scheme.

The Government seeks to defend the statute on the ground that it was passed pursuant to Congress' war power. The Government argues that this Court has given broad deference to the exercise of that constitutional power by the national legislature. That argument finds support in a number of decisions of this Court.[8] However, the phrase "war power" cannot be invoked as a talismanic incantation to support any exercise of congressional power which can be brought within its ambit. "[E]ven the war power does not remove constitutional limitations safeguarding essential liberties." *Home Bldg. & Loan Assn. v. Blaisdell,* 290 U.S. 398, 426 (1934). More specifically in this case, the Government asserts that § 5 (a)(1)(D) is an expression "of the growing concern shown by the executive and legislative branches of government over the risks of internal subversion in plants on which the national defense depend[s]."[9] Yet, this concept of "national defense" cannot be deemed an end in itself, justifying any exercise of legislative power designed to promote such a goal. Implicit in the term "national defense" is the notion of defending those values and ideals which set this Nation apart. For almost two centuries, our country has taken singular pride in the democratic ideals enshrined in its Constitution, and the most cherished of those ideals have found expression in the First Amendment. It would indeed be ironic if, in the name of national defense, we would sanction the subversion of one of those liberties—the freedom of association—which makes the defense of the Nation worthwhile.

When Congress' exercise of one of its enumerated powers clashes with those individual liberties protected by the Bill of Rights, it is our "delicate and difficult task" to determine whether the resulting restriction on freedom can be tolerated. See *Schneider v. State,* 308 U.S. 147, 161 (1939). The Government emphasizes that the purpose of § 5 (a)(1)(D) is to reduce the threat of sabotage and espionage in the Nation's defense plants. The Government's interest in such a prophylactic measure is not insubstantial. But it cannot be doubted that the means chosen to implement that governmental purpose in this instance cut deeply into the right of association. Section 5 (a)(1)(D) put appellee to the choice of surrendering his organizational affiliation, regardless of whether his membership threatened the security of a defense facility,[10] or giving up his job.[11] When appellee refused to make that choice, he became subject to a possible criminal penalty of five years' imprisonment and a $10,000 fine.[12] The statute quite literally establishes guilt by association alone, without any need to establish that an individual's association poses the threat feared by the Government in proscribing it.[13] The inhibiting effect on the exercise of First Amendment rights is clear.

It has become axiomatic that "[p]recision of regulation must be the touchstone in an area so closely touching our most precious freedoms." *NAACP v. Button,* 371 U.S. 415, 438 (1963); see *Aptheker v. Secretary of State,* 378 U.S. 500, 512-513;

Shelton v. Tucker, 364 U.S. 479, 488 (1960). Such precision is notably lacking in § 5 (a)(1)(D). That statute casts its net across a broad range of associational activities, indiscriminately trapping membership which can be constitutionally punished[14] and membership which cannot be so proscribed.[15] It is made irrelevant to the statute's operation that an individual may be a passive or inactive member of a designated organization, that he may be unaware of the organization's unlawful aims, or that he may disagree with those unlawful aims.[16] It is also made irrelevant that an individual who is subject to the penalties of § 5 (a)(1)(D) may occupy a non-sensitive position in a defense facility.[17] Thus, § 5 (a)(1)(D) contains the fatal defect of overbreadth because it seeks to bar employment both for association which may be proscribed and for association which may not be proscribed consistently with First Amendment rights. See *Elfbrandt v. Russell,* 384 U.S. 11; *Aptheker v. Secretary of State, supra; NAACP v. Alabama ex rel. Flowers,* 337 U.S. 288 (1964); *NAACP v. Button, supra.* This the Constitution will not tolerate.

We are not unmindful of the congressional concern over the danger of sabotage and espionage in national defense industries, and nothing we hold today should be read to deny Congress the power under narrowly drawn legislation to keep from sensitive positions in defense facilities those who would use their positions to disrupt the Nation's production facilities. We have recognized that, while the Constitution protects against invasions of individual rights, it does not withdraw from the Government the power to safeguard its vital interests. *Kennedy v. Mendoza-Martinez,* 372 U.S. 144, 160 (1963). Spies and saboteurs do exist, and Congress can, of course, prescribe criminal penalties for those who engage in espionage and sabotage.[18] The Government can deny access to its secrets to those who would use such information to harm the Nation.[19] And Congress can declare sensitive positions in national defense industries off limits to those who would use such positions to disrupt the production of defense materials. The Government has told us that Congress, in passing § 5 (a)(1)(D), made a considered judgment that one possible alternative to that statute—an industrial security screening program—would be inadequate and ineffective to protect against sabotage in defense facilities. It is not our function to examine the validity of that congressional judgment. Neither is it our function to determine whether an industrial security screening program exhausts the possible alternatives to the statute under review. We are concerned solely with determining whether the statute before us has exceeded the bounds imposed by the Constitution when First Amendment rights are at stake. The task of writing legislation which will stay within those bounds has been committed to Congress. Our decision today simply recognizes that, when legitimate legislative concerns are expressed in a statute which imposes a substantial burden on protected First Amendment activities, Congress must achieve its goal by means which have a "less drastic" impact on the continued vitality of First Amendment freedoms.[20] *Shelton v. Tucker, supra;* cf. *United States v. Brown,* 381 U.S. 437, 461 (1965). The Constitution and the basic position of First Amendment rights in our democratic fabric demand nothing less.

Affirmed.

Mr. Justice Marshall took no part in the consideration or decision of this case.

Mr. Justice Brennan, concurring in the result. . . .

Mr. Justice White, with whom Mr. Justice Harlan joins, dissenting. . . .

[1]The Act was passed over the veto of President Truman. In his veto message, President Truman told Congress, "The Department of Justice, the Department of Defense, the Central Intelligence Agency, and the Department of State have all advised me that the bill would seriously damage the security and the intelligence operations for which they are responsible. They have strongly expressed the hope that the bill would not become law." H. R. Doc. No. 708, 81st Cong., 2d Sess., 1 (1950).

President Truman also observed that "the language of the bill is so broad and vague that it might well result in penalizing the legitimate activities of people who are not Communists at all, but loyal citizens." *Id.,* at 3.

[2]Section 3 (3)(a) of the Act, 50 U. S. C. § 782 (3)(a), defines a "Communist-action organization" as: "any organization in the United States (other than a diplomatic representative or mission of a foreign government accredited as such by the Department of State) which (i) is substantially directed, dominated, or controlled by the foreign government or foreign organization controlling the world Communist movement . . . and (ii) operates primarily to advance the objectives of such world Communist movement. . . ."

[3]The Government has persisted in this view in its arguments to this Court. Brief for the Government 48-56.

[4]We initially heard oral argument in this case on November 14, 1966. On June 5, 1967, we entered the following order:

"Case is restored to the calendar for reargument and counsel are directed to brief and argue, in addition to the questions presented, the question whether the delegation of authority to the Secretary of Defense to designate 'defense facilities' satisfies pertinent constitutional standards." 387 U.S. 939. We heard additional arguments on October 9, 1967.

[5]In addition to arguing that § 5 (a)(1)(D) is invalid under the First Amendment, appellee asserted the statute was also unconstitutional because (1) it offended substantive and procedural due process under the Fifth Amendment; (2) it contained an unconstitutional delegation of legislative power to the Secretary of Defense; and (3) it is a bill of attainder. Because we agree that the statute is contrary to the First Amendment, we find it unnecessary to consider the other constitutional arguments.

[6]18 U. S. C. § 2385.

[7]Our decisions leave little doubt that the right of association is specifically protected by the First Amendment. *E.g., Aptheker v. Secretary of State, supra,* at 507; *Gibson v. Florida Legislative Investigation Committee,* 372 U.S. 539, 543 (1963); *Bates v. City of Little Rock,* 361 U.S. 516, 522-523 (1960); *NAACP v. Alabama ex rel. Patterson,* 357 U.S. 449, 460 (1958). See generally Emerson, Freedom of Association and Freedom of Expression, 74 Yale L. J. 1 (1964).

[8]See, *e.g., Lichter v. United States,* 334 U.S. 742, 754-772 (1948); *Hirabayashi v. United States,* 320 U.S. 81, 93 (1943).

[9]Brief for the Government 15.

[10]The appellee has worked at the shipyard, apparently without incident and apparently without concealing his Communist Party membership, for more than 10 years. And we are told that, following appellee's indictment and arrest, "he was released on his own recognizance, and immediately returned to his job as a machinist at the Todd Shipyards, where he has worked ever since." Brief for Appellee 6, n. 8. As far as we can determine, appellee is the only individual the Government has attempted to prosecute under § 5 (a)(1)(D).

[11]We recognized in *Greene v. McElroy,* 360 U.S., at 492, that "the right to hold specific private employment and to follow a chosen profession free from unreasonable governmental interference comes within the 'liberty' and 'property' concepts of the Fifth Amendment."

[12]50 U. S. C. § 794 (c).

[13]The Government has insisted that Congress, in enacting § 5 (a)(1)(D), has not sought "to punish membership in 'Communist-action' . . . organizations." Brief for the Government 53. Rather, the Government asserts, Congress has simply sought to regulate access to employment in defense facilities. But it is clear the employment disability is imposed only because of such membership.

[14]See *Scales v. United States,* 367 U.S. 203 (1961).

[15]See *Elfbrandt v. Russell,* 384 U.S. 11 (1966).

[16]A number of complex motivations may impel an individual to align himself with a particular organization. See *Gibson v. Florida Legislative Investigation Committee,* 372 U.S. 539, 562-565 (1963) (concurring opinion). It is for that reason that the mere presence of an individual's name on an organization's membership rolls is insufficient to impute to him the organization's illegal goals.

[17]See *Cole v. Young,* 351 U.S. 536, 546 (1956): "[I]t is difficult to justify summary suspensions and unreviewable dismissals on loyalty grounds of employees who are not in 'sensitive' positions and who are

thus not situated where they could bring about any discernible adverse effects on the Nation's security."

[18]Congress has already provided stiff penalties for those who conduct espionage and sabotage against the United States. 18 U. S. C. §§ 792-798 (espionage); §§ 2151-2156 (sabotage).

[19]The Department of Defense, pursuant to Executive Order 10865, as amended by Executive Order 10909, has established detailed procedures for screening those working in private industry who, because of their jobs, must have access to classified defense information. 32 CFR Part 155. The provisions of those regulations are not before the Court in this case.

[20]It has been suggested that this case should be decided by "balancing" the governmental interests expressed in § 5 (a)(1)(D) against the First Amendment rights asserted by the appellee. This we decline to do. We recognize that both interests are substantial, but we deem it inappropriate for this Court to label one as being more important or more substantial than the other. Our inquiry is more circumscribed. Faced with a clear conflict between a federal statute enacted in the interests of national security and an individual's exercise of his First Amendment rights, we have confined our analysis to whether Congress has adopted a constitutional means in achieving its concededly legitimate legislative goal. In making this determination we have found it necessary to measure the validity of the means adopted by Congress against both the goal it has sought to achieve and the specific prohibitions of the First Amendment. But we have in no way "balanced" those respective interests. We have ruled only that the Constitution requires that the conflict between congressional power and individual rights be accommodated by legislation drawn more narrowly to avoid the conflict. There is, of course, nothing novel in that analysis. Such a course of adjudication was enunciated by Chief Justice Marshall when he declared: "Let the end be legitimate, let it be within the scope of the constitution, and all means which are appropriate, which are plainly adapted to that end, *which are not prohibited, but consist with the letter and spirit of the constitution,* are constitutional." *M'Culloch v. Maryland,* 4 Wheat. 316, 421 (1819) (Emphasis added.) In this case, the means chosen by Congress are contrary to the "letter and spirit" of the First Amendment.

RIGHTS OF SPECIAL GROUPS

RIGHTS OF SPECIAL GROUPS

Rights of Aliens

COMMENTARY

Most of the protections provided by the Constitution and the Bill of Rights apply equally to all "persons" who are within the borders of the United States or otherwise subject to its jurisdiction. However, the Courts have looked upon certain categories of persons as having diminished rights because of special requirements of national defense and foreign policy.

The Supreme court in the last years of the nineteenth century laid down a constitutional doctrine of plenary governmental power regarding aliens which has remained unchanged in its essentials. In the *Chinese Exclusion Case,* 130 U.S. 581 (1889), the Court upheld legislation that nullified a treaty with China and barred Chinese laborers who had returned home with assurances that they would be able to re-enter the United States. In 1893, the Court upheld a law expelling resident Chinese aliens from the country; the power of Congress so to legislate was said to be absolute and unqualified.[1] However, in the *Japanese Immigrant Case,* 189 U.S. 86 (1903), the Court held that an alien within the United States could not be deported without some requirements of procedural due process being met. In general, an alien is entitled to a deportation hearing with notice of the charges, an opportunity to cross-examine witnesses, and to have a decision based solely on the evidence presented.[2]

Beginning in 1917, Congress has enacted statutes providing for the deportation of aliens who hold particular political beliefs. These deportations have been almost uniformly upheld, provided the proscribed beliefs were still held at the time of the deportation and provided that the requisite due process was observed.[3]

In exclusion cases, the requirements of due process continue to be minimal indeed. After World War II, the Supreme Court was confronted with a number of immigration cases growing out of wartime marriages and the effort to exclude communists from entering the United States. *Knauff v. Shaughnessy,* 338 U.S. 537

(1950), involved a decision to exclude a war bride. The Court took the occasion to reiterate its previous position that the right of entry is a privilege and the alien seeking admission stands without rights. "The exclusion of aliens is a fundamental act of sovereignty. The right to do so stems not alone from legislative power but is inherent in the executive power to control the foreign affairs of the nation."[4] Thus, "Whatever the procedure authorized by Congress is, it is due process as far as an alien denied entry is concerned."[5] An alien could, as in this case, be excluded for unspecified "security" reasons based on "confidential" information.

The issue of due process in deportation, as opposed to exclusion cases recurred two years later, when the government sought to expel aliens for membership in the Communist Party, including those whose membership terminated prior to the 1940 statute which authorized such expulsion. The Court reiterated the government's broad right to terminate the residence of an alien on grounds ostensibly related to national security concerns.

> War, of course, is the most usual occasion of extensive resort to the power [to expel aliens]. Though the resident alien may be personally loyal to the United States, if his nation becomes our enemy his allegiance prevails over his personal preference and makes him also our enemy, liable to expulsion or internment, and his property becomes subject to seizure and perhaps confiscation. But it does not require war to bring the power of deportation into existence or to authorize its exercise. Congressional apprehension of foreign or internal dangers short of war may lead to its use. So long as the alien elects to continue the ambiguity of his allegiance his domicile here is held by a precarious tenure.[6]

The Court went on to hold that the political activities in question were not protected by the First Amendment, even as to citizens; and that the due process clause did not permit the Court to substitute its judgment for that of Congress as to what political activity should be grounds for deportation. The Court's discussion implied that perhaps aliens could not be deported for conduct protected by the First Amendment.

The First Amendment issue arose in a different context when a group of Americans sought to compel the government to admit a distinguished Belgian Marxist scholar on the grounds that they wanted to hear his views and debate public issues with him. In *Kleindienst v. Mandel,* 408 U.S. 753 (1972) the Court adhered to the line of cases giving the political branches complete discretion to determine the conditions under which aliens would be denied admission. That discretion having been exercised "on the basis of a facially legitimate and bona fide reason, the courts will neither look behind the exercise of that discretion, nor test it by balancing its justification against the First Amendment interests of those who seek personal communication with the applicant."[7]

A separate line of cases relates to the right of aliens to equal treatment when the government is not seeking to deport them. In general, discrimination against aliens will be upheld only if it has a rational basis in some appropriate governmental objective. The national security interest may supply such a basis; but it does not automatically do so. Thus, the Civil Service Commission cannot, without explicit authorization from the President or Congress, condition all government employment on citizenship, since the Commission has no national security functions which might justify such a decision.[8]

[1]*Fong Yue Ting v. United States,* 149 U.S. 698 (1893).
[2]*Japanese Immigrant Case,* 8 U.S.C. §1252(b).
[3]40 Stat. 1012, 66 Stat. 163, 68 Stat. 1146.
[4]*Knauff v. Shaugnessy,* 338 U.S. 537 (1950) at 542.
[5]*Id.* at 544.
[6]*Harisiades v. Shaughnessy,* 342 U.S. 580, 587 (1952).
[7]*Kleindienst v. Mandel,* 408 U.S. 753 (1972), at 770.
[8]*Hampton v. Mow Sun Wong,* 426 U.S. 88 (1976).

STATUTES

1918 Alien Act

40 Stat. 1012

Chap. 186.—An Act To exclude and expel from the United States aliens who are members of the anarchistic and similar classes.

Be it enacted by the Senate and House of Representatives of the United States of America in Congress assembled, That aliens who are anarchists; aliens who believe in or advocate the overthrow by force or violence of the Government of the United States or of all forms of law; aliens who disbelieve in or are opposed to all organized government; aliens who advocate or teach the assassination of public officials; aliens who advocate or teach the unlawful destruction of property; aliens who are members of or affiliated with any organization that entertains a belief in, teaches, or advocates the overthrow by force or violence of the Government of the United States or of all forms of law, or that entertains or teaches disbelief in or opposition to all organized government, or that advocates the duty, necessity, or propriety of the unlawful assaulting or killing of any officer or officers, either of specific individuals or of officers generally, of the Government of the United States or of any other organized government, because of his or their official character, or that advocates or teaches the unlawful destruction of property shall be excluded from admission into the United States.

Sec. 2. That any alien who, at any time after entering the United States, is found to have been at the time of entry, or to have become thereafter, a member of any one of the classes of aliens enumerated in section one of this Act, shall, upon the warrant of the Secretary of Labor, be taken into custody and deported in the manner provided in the immigration Act of February fifth, nineteen hundred and seventeen. The provisions of this section shall be applicable to the classes of aliens mentioned in this Act irrespective of the time of their entry into the United States.

Sec. 3. That any alien who shall, after he has been excluded and deported or arrested and deported in pursuance of the provisions of this Act, thereafter return to or enter the United States or attempt to return to or to enter the United States shall be deemed guilty of a felony, and upon conviction thereof shall be punished by imprisonment for a term of not more than five years; and shall, upon the termination of such imprisonment, be taken into custody, upon the warrant of the Secretary of

Labor, and deported in the manner provided in the immigration Act of February fifth, nineteen hundred and seventeen.

Approved, October 16, 1918.

Immigration and Nationalization Act of 1952

66 Stat. 163

Title II, Chapter 2—Qualifications for Admission of Aliens; Travel Control of Citizens and Aliens

* * *

General Classes of Aliens Ineligible to Receive Visas and Excluded from Admission

Sec. 212. (a) Except as otherwise provided in this Act, the following classes of aliens shall be ineligible to receive visas and shall be excluded from admission into the United States:

* * *

(28) Aliens who are, or at any time have been, members of any of the following clases:

(A) Aliens who are anarchists;

(B) Aliens who advocate or teach, or who are members of or affiliated with any organization that advocates or teaches, opposition to all organized government;

(C) Aliens who are members of or affiliated with (i) the Communist Party of the United States, (ii) any other totalitarian party of the United States, (iii) the Communist Political Association, (iv) the Communist or any other totalitarian party of any State of the United States, of any foreign state, or of any political or geographical subdivision of any foreign state, (v) any section, subsidiary, branch, affiliate, or subdivision of any such association or party, or (vi) the direct predecessors or successors of any such association or party, regardless of what name such group or organization may have used, may now bear, or may hereafter adopt: *Provided,* That nothing in this paragraph, or in any other provision of this Act, shall be construed as declaring that the Communist Party does not advocate the overthrow of the Government of the United States by force, violence, or other unconstitutional means;

(D) Aliens not within any of the other provisions of this paragraph who advocate the economic, international, and governmental doctrines of world communism or the establishment in the United States of a totalitarian dictatorship, or who are members of or affiliated with any organization that advocates the economic, international, and governmental doctrines of world communism or the establishment in the United States of a totalitarian dictatorship, either through its own utterances or through any written or printed publications issued or published by or with the permission or consent of or under the authority of such organization or paid for by the funds of, or funds furnished by, such organization;

(E) Aliens not within any of the other provisions of this paragraph, who are members of or affiliated with any organization during the time it is registered or required to be registered under section 7 of the Subversive Activities Control Act of 1950, unless such aliens establish that they did not have knowledge or reason to believe at the time they became members of or affiliated with such an organization (and did not thereafter and prior to the date upon which such organization was so registered or so required to be registered have such knowledge or reason to believe) that such organization was a Communist organization;

(F) Aliens who advocate or teach or who are members of or affiliated with any organization that advocates or teaches (i) the overthrow by force, violence, or other unconstitutional means of the Government of the United States or of all forms of law; or (ii) the duty, necessity, or propriety of the unlawful assaulting or killing of any officer or officers (either of specific individuals or of officers generally) of the Government of the United States or of any other organized government, because of his or their official character; or (iii) the unlawful damage, injury, or destruction of property; or (iv) sabotage;

(G) Aliens who write or publish, or cause to be written or published, or who knowingly circulate, distribute, print, or display, or knowingly cause to be circulated, distributed, printed, published, or displayed, or who knowingly have in their possession for the purpose of circulation, publication, distribution, or display, any written or printed matter, advocating or teaching opposition to all organized government, or advocating or teaching (i) the overthrow by force, violence, or other unconstitutional means of the Government of the United States or of all forms of law; or (ii) the duty, necessity, or propriety of the unlawful assaulting or killing of any officer or officers (either of specific individuals or of officers generally) of the Government of the United States or of any other organized government, because of his or their official character; or (iii) the unlawful damage, injury, or destruction of property; or (iv) sabotage; or (v) the economic, international, and governmental doctrines of world communism or the establishment in the United States of a totalitarian dictatorship;

(H) Aliens who are members of or affiliated with any organization that writes, circulates, distributes, prints, publishes, or displays, or causes to be written, circulated, distributed, printed, published, or displayed, or that has in its possession for the purpose of circulation, distribution, publication, issue, or display, any written or printed matter of the character described in paragraph (G);

(I) Any alien who is within any of the classes described in subparagraphs (B), (C), (D), (E), (F), (G), and (H) of this paragraph because of membership in or affiliation with a party or organization or a section, subsidiary, branch, affiliate, or subdivision thereof, may, if not otherwise ineligible, be issued a visa if such alien establishes to the satisfaction of the consular officer when applying for a visa and the consular officer finds that (i) such membership or affiliation is or was involuntary, or is or was solely when under sixteen years of age, by operation of law, or for purposes of obtaining employment, food rations, or other essentials of living and where necessary for such purposes, or (ii) (a) since the termination of such membership or affiliation, such alien is and has been, for at least five years prior to the date of the application for a visa, actively opposed to the doctrine, program, principles, and ideology of such party or organization or the section, subsidiary, branch, or affiliate or subdivision thereof, and (b) the admission of such alien into the United States would be in the public interest. Any such alien to whom a visa has been issued under the provisions of this subparagraph may, if not otherwise inadmissible, be admitted into the United States if he shall establish to the satisfaction of he Attorney General when applying for admission to the United States and the Attorney General finds that (i) such membership or affiliation is or was involuntary, or is or was solely when under sixteen years of age, by operation of law, or for purposes of obtaining employment, food rations, or other essentials of living and when necessary for such purposes, or (ii) (a) since the termination of such membership or affiliation, such alien is and has been, for at least five years prior to the date of the application for admission actively opposed to the doctrine, program, principles, and ideology of such party or organization or the section, subsidiary, branch, or affiliate or subdivision thereof, and (b) the admission of such alien into the United States would be in the public interest. The Attorney General shall promptly make a detailed report to the Congress in the case of each alien who is or shall be admitted into the United States under (ii) of this subparagraph;

(29) Aliens with respect to whom the consular officer or the Attorney General knows or has reasonable ground to believe probably would, after entry, (A) engage in activities which would be prohibited by the laws of the United States relating to espionage, sabotage, public disorder, or in other activity subversive to the national security, (B) engage in any activity a purpose of which is the opposition to, or the control or overthrow of, the Government of the United States, by force, violence, or other unconstitutional means, or (C) join, affiliate with, or participate in the activities of any organization which is registered or required to be registered under section 7 of the Subversive Activities Control Act of 1950:

* * *

Travel Control of Aliens and Citizens in Time of War or National Emergency

Sec. 215. (a) When the United States is at war or during the existence of any national emergency proclaimed by the President, or, as to aliens, whenever there exists a state of war between or among two or more states, and the President shall find that the interests of the United States require that restrictions and prohibitions in addition to those provided otherwise than by this section be imposed upon the departure of persons from and their entry into the United States, and shall make public proclamation thereof, it shall, until otherwise ordered by the President or the Congress, be unlawful—

(1) for any alien to depart from or enter or attempt to depart from or enter the United States except under such reasonable rules, regulations, and orders, and subject to such limitations and exceptions as the President may prescribe;

(2) for any person to transport or attempt to transport from or into the United States another person with knowledge or reasonable cause to believe

that the departure or entry of such other person is forbidden by this section;

(3) for any person knowingly to make any false statement in an application for permission to depart from or enter the United States with intent to induce or secure the granting of such permission either for himself or for another;

(4) for any person knowingly to furnish or attempt to furnish or assist in furnishing to another a permit or evidence of permission to depart or enter not issued and designed for such other person's use;

(5) for any person knowingly to use or attempt to use any permit or evidence of permission to depart or enter not issued and designed for his use;

(6) for any person to forge, counterfeit, mutilate, or alter, or cause or procure to be forged, counterfeited, mutilated, or altered, any permit or evidence of permission to depart from or enter the United States;

(7) for any person knowingly to use or attempt to use or furnish to another for use any false, forged, counterfeited, mutilated, or altered permit, or evidence of permission, or any permit or evidence of permission which, though originally valid, has become or been made void or invalid.

(b) After such proclamation as is provided for in subsection (a) has been made and published and while such proclamation is in force, it shall, except as otherwise provided by the President, and subject to such limitations and exceptions as the President may authorize and prescribe, be unlawful for any citizen of the United States to depart from or enter, or attempt to depart from or enter, the United States unless he bears a valid passport.

* * *

1954 Expatriation Act

68 Stat. 1164

An Act to Amend the Immigration and Nationality Act to Provide for the Loss of Nationality of Persons Convicted of Certain Crimes.

Be it enacted by the Senate and House of Representatives of the United States of America in Congress assembled, That this Act may be cited as the "Expatriation Act of 1954".

Sec. 2. Paragraph (9) of subsection (a) of section 349 of the Immigration and Nationality Act (66 Stat. 163, 268; 8 U. S. C. 1481 (a) (9)) is amended to read as follows:

> "(9) committing any act of treason against, or attempting by force to overthrow, or bearing arms against, the United States, violating or conspiring to violate any of the provisions of section 2383 of title 18, United States Code, or willfully performing any act in violation of section 2385 of title 18, United States Code, or violating section 2384 of said title by engaging in a conspiracy to overthrow, put down, or to destroy by force the Government of the United States, or to levy war against them, if and when he is convicted thereof by a court martial or by a court of competent jurisdiction; or".

Approved September 3, 1954

Rights of Conscientious Objectors

COMMENTARY

The Constitution guarantees the right to bear arms, but the Quaker community of colonial times failed in their attempt to include a guarantee of the right *not* to bear arms. Except for the period of the civil war, however, compulsory military service did not become a reality until modern times.

In 1918, the Supreme Court held that a requirement of compulsory military service did not exceed the war powers of Congress.[1] Because Congress had provided that members of certain sects might be exempted because of their religious beliefs, the question of a clash between the war power and the First Amendment did not arise. Subsequently, the lower courts upheld provisions requiring conscientious objectors to perform alternative civilian service under indirect governmental control, and the Supreme Court refused to intervene.[2]

In 1965, the Court was obliged to consider the case of individuals who did not belong to a pacifist sect, and who did not even believe in God in a traditional sense, but who nevertheless claimed to be opposed to participation in war in any form, by reason of their religious beliefs. Avoiding the constitutional questions that might be raised if Congress explicitly sought to exclude such individuals from conscientious objector status, the Court held that Congress had intended no such discrimination.[3] This approach was extended five years later to make persons whose beliefs were essentially ethical in character eligible for exemption as well.[4]

As the tide of opposition to the war in Vietnam led applications for conscientious objector status to unprecedented heights, the Court was confronted with a new class of applicants: those whose unwillingness to bear arms extended only to wars they deemed unjust. At this point the Court discerned a direct threat to the government's ability to conduct an effective foreign policy and provide for the common defense; and it held that Congress had not intended to permit individuals to avoid military service on the basis of their opposition to a particular war. It would be impossible in practice, the Court said, to distinguish moral and religious objectors from purely political ones in such a case.[5]

If opposition to the draft or to the nation's foreign policy did not automatically entitle one to an exemption from military service, however, neither did it make it proper to single out such persons for accelerated induction. In *Oestereich v. Local Board No. 11,* 393 U.S. 233 (1968), the Court struck down a policy of the Selective Service System, not expressly authorized by Congress, under which "delinquents" (including persons who turned in their draft cards to express opposition to the war or to the draft) were stripped of any deferments to which they might have been entitled, and placed in the highest priority class of persons eligible to be drafted. This policy, the Court held, was tantamount to using military service as a punishment for one's political views, and bore no rational relationship to the System's function of meeting the military's manpower needs.[6] The Court did not, however, decide in this case whether Congress could, consistently with the First Amendment, make it a crime to destroy one's draft card as a gesture of political protect. On this issue see *United States v. O'Brien,* discussed in the section on Political Crimes.

In addition to confronting these areas of direct conflict between military service and First Amendment rights, the courts were also asked in a number of cases to review the procedures of the Selective Service System and determine their compatibility with notions of due process. Initially the courts took the view that the need of the nation to respond quickly to an emergency should not be obstructed by allowing individuals to delay their induction with procedural wrangles. Moreover, the local draft boards were not ordinary government agencies but "little groups of neighbors" serving as volunteers, who could not be expected to observe the ordinary standards of administrative regularity.

However, in 1946 the Supreme Court held that the courts did have power to determine whether the decision of a draft board to deny a deferment had any basis in fact, and whether the Selective Service System had followed its own regulations.[7]

Over the years the right of registrants to such basic procedural protections as a statement of the reasons for denial of a deferment became established through judicial review. Congress, however, had expressly barred the courts from intervening prior to the date set for induction, and the Court upheld this bar as generally valid.[8] Thus a registrant who believed his induction order was invalid was faced with the unpleasant choice between obeying the order and seeking relief by way of habeas corpus, or disobeying the order and testing his claim in the context of a criminal prosecution.

The further development of the law respecting the procedural rights of draft registrants was cut short by the advent of the all-volunteer army in 1973.

---

[1]*Selective Draft Law Cases,* 245 U.S. 366 (1918).

[2]See *e.g., Hart v. United States,* 391 U.S. 956 (1968) (Douglas, J., dissenting).

[3]*United States v. Seeger,* 380 U.S. 163 (1965).

[4]*Welsh v. United States,* 398 U.S. 333 (1970).

[5]*United States v. Gillette,* 401 U.S. 437 (1971).

[6]See also *Gutknecht v. United States,* 396 U.S. 295 (1970), and *Breen v. Local Board No. 16,* 396 U.S. 460 (1970).

[7]*Estep v. United States,* 327 U.S. 114 (1946).

[8]*Clark v. Gabriel,* 393 U.S. 256 (1968).

The Rights of Armed Forces Members

COMMENTARY

Members of the Armed Forces are subject to the Uniform Code of Military Justice enacted by Congress under its constitutional power to provide regulations for the Army and Navy. Infractions are tried by courts-martial in the military justice system. However, court-martial convictions, if constitutionally defective, may be appealed by various routes to the civilian courts.

The leading Supreme Court decision setting the boundaries of constitutional rights for members of the armed services is *Parker v. Levy,* 417 U.S. 733 (1974). Levy was a medical doctor and an Army captain who refused to obey an order to train special forces units en route to Vietnam, and who made public statements to enlisted men on base urging them not to go to Vietnam. Levy was tried by court-martial and convicted under what are known as the "general articles," 133 and 134, which prohibit "conduct unbecoming an officer" and conduct involving a neglect of good order and discipline. He sought to overturn his conviction by arguing that these articles were unconstitutional, in that the offenses defined there were both vague and overbroad, and his conviction thereunder infringed his right to freedom of speech. The Supreme Court, with Justice Rehnquist writing for a five-man majority, disagreed. The Court did, for the first time, hold explicitly that the protection of the First Amendment applies to officers on active duty; but it sharply qualified the extent of that protection in the military context.

> While members of the armed forces are not excluded from the protection granted by the First Amendment, the different character of the military community and of the military mission require a different application of those protections. The fundamental necessity for obedience, and the consequent necessity for imposition of discipline, may render permissible within the military that which would be constitutionally impermissible outside it.[1]

Applying this reasoning, the Court found that the "general articles" were not unconstitutionally vague or overbroad; and it upheld Levy's punishment for speech that in civilian life might well be protected by the First Amendment.

The jurisdiction of the courts-martial does not extend to civilian dependents of servicemen overseas;[2] nor does it extend to servicemen whose criminal activity is not "service-connected."[3] Yet when a serviceman sought to enjoin his pending court-martial for selling marijuana off-base on grounds that the offense was not service-connected, the Supreme Court held that the federal courts should not intervene until all remedies within the military justice system have been exhausted.[4]

Continuing its policy of deferring to the special claims of the military, the Court held that a military base commander could prohibit the distribution by civilians of political leaflets on what was otherwise an open military base, so long as there was no suggestion that the prohibition was being applied arbitrarily because of the content of the publications.[5]

---

[1]*Parker v. Levy,* 417 U.S. 733 (1974), at 23-24.

[2]*Reid v. Covert,* 354 U.S. 1 (1957).

[3]*O'Callahan v. Parker,* 395 U.S. 258 (1959).

[4]*Schlesinger v. Councilman,* 420 U.S. 738 (1974).

[5]*Greer v. Spock,* 424 U.S. 828 (1976).

CIVIL REMEDIES

CIVIL REMEDIES

COMMENTARY

Courts become involved in balancing constitutional rights against claims of national security in a variety of ways, notably when a citizen sues the government, or officials of the government, alleging violations of constitutional rights. There are formidable barriers to success in such litigation.

The Need for a Statutory Basis

Congress can by statute authorize the courts to award damages for injuries caused by governmental officials. It has provided such remedies when state officials conspire to deprive a citizen of his or her constitutional rights, (18 U.S.C. 1974) and it has provided a remedy also for certain specified actions of federal officials, most notably in the area of electronic surveillance (18 U.S.C. 2520). It has not, however, legislated a general right to damages for violations of constitutional rights by federal officials.

Until 1971, it was not entirely clear whether, in the absence of statute, a right to relief in court for violations of constitutional rights could be said to arise from the Constitution itself. The Supreme Court confronted the question of whether it had the inherent power to award damages in a case involving the violation of Fourth Amendment rights by agents of the Federal narcotics bureau. The Court, in a 6-3 opinion, held that no statute was required to create a cause of action for such a wrong, and that petitioner was "entitled to recover money damages for any injuries he has suffered as a result of the agents' violation of the (Fourth) Amendment."[1] The Court quoted from *Marbury v. Madison*: "The very essence of civil liberty certainly consists in the right of every individual to claim the protection of the laws whenever he receives an injury."[2] Thus, injunctive relief as well as damages should be available in suitable cases. However, there are other doctrinal obstacles to obtaining civil remedies for constitutional wrongs. For example, the Court in *Bivens* specifically left open the question of whether the government might be immune from suit in certain circumstances or be able to put forward an affirmative defense.

Standing

Three times the Burger Court has invoked the doctrine of standing to sue to avoid a direct balancing of constitutional claims against alleged interests of national security. Standing to sue is a refinement of the notion that courts will not decide abstract questions, but only the claims of a party whose personal interests are directly injured. In *Laird v. Tatum*, 408 U.S. 1 (1971) the Court denied standing to a group of plaintiffs who complained of an unlawful domestic surveillance program conducted by the United States army. The Court refused to decide whether the program was lawful. The question, said the Court, was:

> whether the jurisdiction of a federal court may be invoked by a complainant who alleges that the exercise of his First Amendment rights is being chilled by the mere existence, without more, of a governmental investigative and data gathering activity that is alleged to be broader in scope than is reasonably necessary for the accomplishment of a valid governmental purpose.[3]

Because plaintiffs had been subjected to no governmental action of a "regulatory, proscriptive, or compulsory" nature,they had suffered no concrete harm and lacked standing to sue. This case initially appeared to be a major stumbling block to establishing judicial remedies against abuses by the intelligence agencies. However, the Watergate and intelligence agency investigations have now produced substantial evidence of conduct directly injurious to individual citizens, and a number of recent cases have survived in lower court motions to dismiss that relied on the standing criteria laid out in *Tatum*.[4]

Two other recent Supreme Court decisions have applied the standing doctrine to refuse judicial enforcement of security-related constitutional provisions that do not confer a right directly on specific persons. In these cases, plaintiffs can claim injury only in their capacity as citizens and taxpayers, and the Court has seen fit to direct them to the other branches of government for a remedy. *United States v. Richardson*, 418 U.S. 166 (1974) involved an attempt by a taxpayer to compel the government to publish the CIA's budget, pursuant to the requirement of Art. I sec. 9 that there be a public accounting of all expenditures. The Court stated that "the subject matter is committed to the surveillance of Congress, and ultimately to the political process."[5] In a case decided the same day, the Court refused on similar grounds to decide whether membership in the reserves by members of Congress violates Art. I, sec. 6, cl. 2 of the Constitution, which prohibits a member of Congress from holding any other "office."[6]

These two cases establish a powerful bar to taxpayer or citizen suits on national security issues, except where there have been violations of the personal constitutional rights of those suing or where, as in the case of the Freedom of Information Act, Congress has by statute authorized the suits.

Sovereign Immunity and Affirmative Defenses

Even where standing to sue can be established, the law may raise other stumbling blocks to the action. Although immunity and defenses against damages are often treated together, they are significantly different. If officials are immune from suit, actions against them must be dismissed based on the pleadings alone, and the government can avoid a trial on the evidence. Affirmative defenses on the other hand, must be established at trial; even if the government ultimately prevails, important information may thereby be made public.

Historically, many courts had adopted the position, put in its classic form by Judge Learned Hand in *Gregoire v. Biddle*, 177 F.2d 579 (2d Cir. 1949), that the society benefitted from allowing public officials to perform their functions without fear of personal liability for damages, and that this good was far more important than the right of a particular citizen to collect damages. In endorsing this position in a defamation suit against a government official, however, the Supreme Court limited its holding to cases in which constitutional rights had not been violated.[7] Later, the Court of Appeals for the Fourth Circuit applied the reasoning of *Barr* to a case involving a deliberate defamation done by a secret CIA agent at the direction of the CIA. Juri Raus and Eerik Heine were politically active Estonian emigrants. Raus accused Heine of being an agent of the KGB. Heine sued for slander, and Raus replied that he had made the charge at the direction of the CIA. Raus's position was supported by affidavits from CIA officials. The court sustained a formal claim of state secrets privilege in permitting the CIA not to answer questions put to it by the plaintiff. It went on to hold that if Raus made his statement at the direction of a high CIA official, he had an absolute immunity. But the right claimed by plaintiff to have been violated was not a constitutional right.

The doctrine of absolute immunity has been applied to a few situations involving violations of constitutional rights, but only in very narrow circumstances. Such immunity has been granted to members of Congress, whose immunity is explicitly provided for in the Constitution, see *Gravel v. United States*, 408 U.S. 606 (1972); to judges, *Pierson v. Ray*, 386 U.S. 547 (1967); and to prosecutors, (at least when they are acting as agents of the court), *Imbler v. Pachtman*, 424 U.S. 409 (1976). However, other state and federal officials, even at the highest level, do not have absolute immunity from suits arising from violations of constitutional rights. Rather they have available an affirmative defense—a right to prove that they acted on a good faith and reasonable belief that their actions were not unconstitutional.[8]

Scheuer was a suit against the Governor of Ohio arising from the Kent State shootings, and the Supreme Court laid down a two-pronged test for the existence of the affirmative defense. The first test, the so-called subjective test, is whether the defendant actually believed that what he was doing was constitutional. The second, objective test, is whether it was reasonable for him to have that belief. If the action violated a clearly established constitutional doctrine, then the defendant does not have a good faith defense, whatever his personal belief. In a later decision, Justice White said "an act violating a student's constitutional rights can be no more justified by ignorance or disregard of settled, indisputable law on the part of one entrusted with supervision of students' daily lives than by the presence of actual malice."[9]

The test enunciated in these cases has recently been applied in a lawsuit arising from a warrantless wiretap which defendants sought to justify on national security grounds, as part of a program authorized by the President. Both former-President Richard Nixon, and then-Attorney General John Mitchell have been held liable for damages on the ground that their conduct was not so observant of well-known constitutional standards as to justify application of the good faith defense.[10]

---

[1] *Bivens v. Six Unknown Named Agents*, 403 U.S. 388, 397 (1971).

[2] 1 Cranch 137, 163 (1803).

[3] *Laird v. Tatum*, 408 U.S. 1 (1971) at 10.

[4] *Berlin Democratic Club v. Rumsfeld*, 416 F. Supp. 144 (D.D.C., 1976).

[5] *United States v. Richardson*, 418 U.S. 166 (1974) at 179.

[6] *Schlesinger v. Reservists Comm. to Stop the War*, 418 U.S. 208 (1974).

[7] *Barr v. Matteo*, 360 U.S. 564 (1959).

[8] *Scheuer v. Rhodes*, 416 U.S. 232 (1973).

[9] *Wood v. Strickland*, 420 U.S. 308 (1975).

[10] *Halperin v. Kissenger*, 424 F. Supp. 838 (D.D.C., 1976).

CASES

Heine v. Raus

399 F.2d 785 (1968)

Haynsworth, Chief Judge:

In this slander action, the plaintiff appeals from an order of summary judgment entered against him, on the ground of governmental privilege, after a partial disclosure limited by invocation by the Central Intelligence Agency of the governmental privilege against disclosure of state secrets. The controversy, thus partially surfaced, arose out of the Central Intelligence Agency's intelligence and counterintelligence activities and its attempt to expose the plaintiff as a Soviet KGB agent, a defamation which the plaintiff alleges to be false.

The plaintiff, Eerik Heine, is an Estonian emigre residing in Canada. With an apparant history as a "freedom fighter" in Estonia, he was an occasional lecturer in the United States and an exhibitor of an anti-communist film. As such, he was known to the leaders of Estonian emigres in the United States and apparently entitled to their confidence.

The defendant, Juri Raus, is also an Estonian emigre. He resides in the United States and is the National Commander of the Legion of Estonian Liberation. He readily admits that he told the Board of Directors of the Legion that he was reliably informed by an official agency of the United States that Heine was a Soviet agent or collaborator and that the Legion should not cooperate with him. This, the plaintiff charges, made his film and his lecture no longer salable and brought him into disgrace in the Estonian communities in the United States and Canada.

In his initial answer, Raus claimed only a qualified privilege. He claimed that he had spoken, without malice, only as an officer of the Legion and only on privileged occasions to privileged persons. There was no indication of any involvement of the CIA. Later, however, an amended answer was tendered, supported by a series of affidavits executed by the Director or Deputy Director of the CIA, in which the absolute executive privilege was claimed. In those documents it was alleged that Raus was an undercover or secret agent of the CIA,[1] had executed special assignments for it in the past and acted under the instructions of the CIA when he "warned" his fellow Legionnaires that Heine was a Soviet agent. Earlier disclosure of these circumstances was said to have been prevented by a CIA secrecy agreement, to which Raus had subscribed and which purported to carry with it punishment for violations under 18 U.S.C.A. §§ 793 and 794, including life imprisonment or death. When the first answer was filed, counsel for the CIA had refused permission to Raus to disclose his CIA connection.

Thereafter, the plaintiff sought to take Raus' deposition in order to obtain additional information about his employment by the CIA. The Director of the CIA, through his General Counsel, appeared for the taking of the deposition,[2] and, on a question by question basis, in the presence of the Judge, invoked the government's privilege against disclosure of state secrets. Raus was allowed to state that he had been paid, directly or indirectly, for services he had rendered the CIA, but the privilege was sustained to prevent probing of the details of his employment.

Otherwise, it appears from affidavits of the Director of the CIA that Raus and other Estonian emigres in the United States had been sources of foreign intelligence and that the purpose of the instruction to Raus to discredit Heine was to protect the integrity of the CIA's sources of foreign intelligence within Estonian emigre groups or developed through them.

In that state of the litigation, the District Court granted a motion for summary judgment.[3] It was of the opinion that the absolute governmental privilege was available to a government employee such as Raus, who faithfully executed his instructions, as to one of higher authority exercising discretionary functions within the outer perimeter of his authority.[4] We agree, provided the instructions were issued by one having authority to issue them.

I

[1] At the outset it is well to put to one side of the question of the CIA's right to invoke the government's privilege of silence with respect to "state secrets."

"The privilege belongs to the Government and must be asserted by it; it can neither be claimed nor waived by a private party. It is not to be lightly invoked. There must be a formal claim of privilege, lodged by the head of the department which has control over the matter, after actual personal consideration by that officer. The court itself must determine whether the circumstances are appropriate for the claim of privilege, and yet do so without forcing a disclosure of the very thing the privilege is designed to protect. The latter requirement is the only one which presents real difficulty." *United States v. Reynolds,* 345 U.S. 1, 7-8, 73 S.Ct. 528, 532, 97 L.Ed. 727 (1953).

The District Court was quite correct in its allowance of the governmental claim of the privilege of secrecy. It was properly invoked generally by the Director of the CIA. The Court made sufficient inquiry—some of it *in camera*—to assure that it had not been done lightly, without pressing so far as to reveal the very state secrets the privilege is intended to protect. When the deposition of Raus was taken, he ruled upon each question calling for information arguably within the privilege, requiring Raus to answer those which the Court thought would not impair the privilege while foreclosing answers to those questions which apparently would. In his conduct of the proceedings, we think he balanced, as fairly as possible, the conflicting interests and was faithful to the "formula of compromise" taught by *Reynolds.*

We affirm the right of the CIA in this case to invoke the governmental privilege against disclosure of state secrets and its allowance, to the extent it was allowed, by the District Court.[5]

II

On the question of executive privilege in defamation suits, we also agree generally with the District Court, its analysis of *Barr v. Matteo* and its reasoning, though we come to the conclusion that one more detail should have been supplied before entry of summary judgment.

In *Barr v. Matteo,* it was held that the Acting Director of the Office of Rent Stabilization was entitled to the protection of the absolute executive privilege. Responding to congressional criticism of the agency, Barr issued a press release announcing his intention to suspend two subordinate officials and placing upon their shoulders responsibility for the payouts under criticism. Three justices joined Mr. Justice Harlan in the leading opinion in which the governmental interest in having officials, exercising discretionary authority, assured freedom to act in the interest of the agency without fear of having to defend actions for defamation was balanced against the interest of the individual plaintiffs in seeking judicial rehabilitation of their reputations. With reliance upon the analysis and justification of Judge Learned Hand in *Gregorie v. Biddle,* 2 Cir., 177 F.2d 579, 581, quoted also by the District Court in its opinion in this case, preference was given to the governmental interest. Mr. Justice Black, emphasizing the interest of the public in being informed of such matters, concurred. Mr. Justice Stewart agreed with the analysis of the leading opinion, but dissented because he thought Barr had acted to save his own hide by diverting criticism from himself to the plaintiffs, and not in the interest of the agency. The Chief Justice and Justices Douglas and Brennan dissented generally on the ground that the absolute executive privilege should be limited to the President and cabinet officers[6] and, possibly, other appointed officials directly responsible to the President.

If "*Barr v. Matteo* extended the earlier decisions of this Court to what I and others considered to be the breaking point," as Mr. Chief Justice Warren observed when dissenting from the denial of a writ of certiorari in *Becker v. Philco Corp.,* 389 U.S. 979, 980, 88 S.Ct. 408, 409, 19 L.Ed.2d 473, this case is much closer to the earlier precedents if we assume that the actor was the Director, himself.

Unlike Mr. Barr, the Director of the CIA is appointed by the President of the United States with the advice and consent of the Senate. He is responsible to the President through the National Security Council. His office is not of cabinet rank, but it is a highly sensitive position. Necessarily, the Director must work in close collaboration with the President, himself, and with such cabinet officers as the Secretary of State and the Secretary of Defense. He is closer by far to the White House than an acting Director of Rent Stabilization, a subordinate official under the Director of Economic Stabilization.

In *Barr v. Matteo,* too, there was room for Mr. Justice Stewart's view that Barr acted not so much to protect the agency from criticism as to divert the criticism from his shoulders to those of his two subordinates. Here, in contrast, we have no such possibility. While we cannot penetrate the cloak of secrecy which surrounds the CIA, there is no reason to suppose the defamation had any relation to the Director's personal career or his reputation or to those of his subordinates. For all that appears, it was done entirely out of consideration of the national interest.

The CIA and its Director are specifically charged with the duty and responsibility of protecting sources of foreign intelligence and methods of collecting such intelligence from unauthorized disclosure.[7] That aliens within this country are sources of foreign intelligence, as claimed by the Director, has been recognized by the Congress. If the Director determines that an alien's entry for permanent residence in the United States is in the interest of national security or essential to the Agency's intelligence mission, the entry of the alien and his family is allowed though they would be otherwise inadmissible.[8] Unlike Barr, who acted under no direction or specific authorization to issue press releases, action here to protect the integrity of sources of foreign intelligence was explicitly directed by Congress.

If it be said that the defamation here was deliberate, and it was, it was no more deliberate than the defamation in *Barr v. Matteo,* and its purpose was loftier. While the veil of secrecy hampers our appraisal of the situation confronting the CIA, enough appears to relate the defamation to governmental interests.

The Director has sworn in his affidavits that Raus and other Estonian emigres in this country had been sources of foreign intelligence and that other sources of such intelligence had been developed through them. Plainly implicit in the Director's affidavits and the testimony is the receipt by the CIA of information, believed reliable, that Heine was a secret Soviet agent. Such agents do not wear the guise of their masters and if one could successfully infiltrate the Estonian emigre sources in this country he could expect to discover the foreign sources of intelligence developed through them. In such circumstances, is the CIA to seek an indictment on charges it cannot prove if the sources of its information are its own secret agents in the Soviet Republic? Is it to sit idly by, suffering a pollution of its sources of foreign intelligence and the intimidation, arrest and persecution of its foreign agents? Or can it protect its sources of information, as required by the statute, by "warning" its own sources that the infiltrator is, or may be, a Soviet agent? In a sensitive area, closely touching national defense, the latter choice seems the one demanded by the national interest, notwithstanding the devastating impact of the warning upon the one thus accused of espionage. While the effect of the defamation upon the plaintiff here may have been greater than the harm suffered by the plaintiffs in *Barr v. Matteo,* the relation of the defamation to the national interest is much closer.

While the claim of secrecy prevents our obtaining a clear view of the entire scene, the Director's sworn, but undocumented, claims are enough to support the claim of governmental privilege. That ought to be enough when the statements are those of an official in so responsible an office and a requirement of further documentation and elaboration would violate the privilege of state secrets or greatly burden its exercise.

Thus far, our analysis of the problem is deficient, for we have assumed that the Director, himself, was the author of the defamation. The present record does not show that he was, though it is certainly inferable that the instructions to Raus were given by one having authority from the Director to issue them. In appraising this case in comparison with *Barr v. Matteo,* however, it has been useful to start with the assumption that the Director, himself, uttered the defamation, for it should follow, as of course, that the subordinate who acts with the authorization of the superior is entitled to claim the same privilege as the superior.

[2] If, in defamation cases, recognition of an absolute privilege for judges, legislators and highly placed executive officers of the government, when acting in line of duty, is to serve its intended purpose, it must extend to subordinate officials and employees who execute the official's orders. There would be little purpose to a cloak of immunity for Mr. Barr if Mr. Matteo were allowed to maintain an action for defamation against all of those subordinates in his office who "published" the defamation in the course of handling and distributing the press release. There would be no advantage in protection to a judge against actions for defamation founded upon statements made by him in an official opinion written for his court, if such actions could readily be maintained against his secretary who, at his direction, typed and transmitted the opinion, or against the clerk of the court who published it. If the circumstances impose a compelling moral obligation upon the superior to defend and indemnify the subordinates, immunization of the superior alone from direct defamation actions would be a useless formalism.

[3] Recognition of an absolute privilege of the subordinate by attribution of the superior thus appears to be a necessary corollary of the superior's privilege. It is generally recognized that an agent, acting within the scope of his authority, does have whatever privilege the principal would have enjoyed if he had acted for himself.[9] The principle is applicable in defamation actions[10] and, if an authorized agent would have been privileged, subsequent ratification confers the privilege upon an unauthorized agent.[11] Applicability of the principle to this case has been suggested in an article generally critical of the District Court's decision.[12]

[4] We conclude that the absolute privilege is available to Raus if his instructions were issued with the approval of the Director or of a subordinate authorized by the Director, in the subordinate's discretion, to issue such instructions, or if the giving of the instructions was subsequently ratified and approved by such an official.

[5] Though the Director's affidavits state that Raus acted under instructions of the CIA, which certainly strongly implies that the instructions were given by, or with the approval of, a responsible, authorized official of the Agency and though the Director's appearance in the case carries with it a strong implication of his personal ratification and approval, it is said that on the present record there is still a permissible inference that the instructions were given by an unauthorized underling and that his action has never had the approval of a responsible official of the Agency having authority to issue or approve such instructions. The inference seems unlikely, but we cannot say it is foreclosed by the present record.

[6] Since summary judgment was issued, we will vacate the judgment so that, if the plaintiff represents to the District Court serious reliance upon the inference, further inquiry may be had and additional findings made. The inquiry should be directed to the identity of the official within the Agency who authorized or approved the instructions to Raus. Disclosure of the identity of the individual who dealt with Raus is not required; the answer to be sought is whether or not the Director or a Deputy Director or a subordinate official, having authority to do so, authorized, approved or ratified the instructions. If such disclosures are reasonably thought by the District Judge to violate the claimed privilege for state secrets, they may be made *in camera,* to that extent. Disclosures *in camera* are inconsistent with the normal rights of a plaintiff of inquiry and cross-examination, of course, but if the two interests cannot be reconciled, the interest of the individual litigant must give way to the government's privilege against disclosure of its secrets of state.

Finally, we may observe that while we generally approve entry of summary judgment for the defendant, subject only to the limited additional inquiry we direct, the plaintiff would fare no better if the defendant's privilege were held to be not absolute, but only qualified. Heine cannot controvert the claim of Raus, supported by the CIA, that he acted under instructions of that Agency.[13] Heine claims no publication exceeding the instructions. He has no basis for a showing of malice. If summary judgment is appropriate after the additional, limited inquiry we direct, it will avoid the necessity of a trial and possible compromise of state secrets which the government is entitled to preserve.

Vacated and remanded.

---

[1]His overt employment was in the Bureau of Public Roads in Washington.

[2]Earlier, in an affidavit, the Director, himself, had sought to invoke the secrecy privilege generally as to any information in addition to that disclosed in the affidavits.

[3]*Heine v. Raus,* D.C.Md., 261 F.Supp. 570.

[4]*Barr v. Matteo,* 360 U.S. 564, 79 S.Ct. 1335, 3 L.Ed.2d 1434; *Howard v. Lyons,* 360 U.S. 593, 79 S.Ct. 1331, 3 L.Ed.2d 1454.

[5]In addition to requiring Raus to Answer some questions, the District Court rejected the first affidavits of the Director of the CIA as insufficient to support the claim of absolute governmental privilege. As a result, additional affidavits containing additional information were filed.

[6]See *Spalding v. Vilas,* 161 U.S. 483, 16 S.Ct. 631, 40 L.Ed. 780.

[7]50 U.S.C.A. §§ 403(d) (3), 403g.

[8]50 U.S.C.A. § 403h.

[9]Restatement (Second), Agency § 345 (1958).

[10]*Ibid.* Illustration 2.

[11]*Ibid.* Comment (e).

[12]Spying and Slandering: An Absolute Privilege for the CIA Agent? 67 Col.L.Rev. 752.

[13]Here, it would matter not if the instructions were unauthorized within the Agency as long as Raus believed them to be.

Craven, Circuit Judge (concurring and dissenting):

I agree with the court that summary judgment was improvidently entered. In addition to the deficiency pointed out by Chief Judge Haynsworth in the majority opinion, I suggest there are others, especially the failure to develop the scope of Raus' duty. Indeed, it seems to me the affidavits and meager information elicited from Raus by deposition are merely conclusory and not at all sufficient to support summary judgment. I believe it error to accept general assertions[1] as a basis for summary judgment where the opposing party is without access to information normally available to test the affidavits because of the invocation of the state secrets privilege. Cf. Fed.R.Civ.P. 56(f).

The court says that if executive immunity "is to serve its intended purpose, it must extend to subordinate officials and employees who execute the officials' orders." This means that millions of federal employees are accorded absolute immunity from any liability whatsoever for *intentional* defamation either because such employees fall within the definition of "official" or "officer" as defined in *Barr v. Matteo,* 360 U.S. 564, 79 S.Ct. 1335, 3 L.Ed. 1434 (1959), or, like Raus, take orders from those who do. On remand, there is to be no further inquiry as to Raus' "scope of duty." It seems to me the court is assuming[2] that the publication of defamation is within his official duties, or it is holding that so long as he did what he was told to do the privilege extends even to conduct outside the scope of employment. I cannot believe that the latter is intended[3] and, therefore, conclude the court must be making the assumption. But the burden of proof is upon Raus to show that he is entitled to executive immunity, and there is no presumption to aid him. Prosser, Torts § 111 at 823 (3rd ed. 1964). Clearly, it seems to me, he has failed to sustain his burden. That he may have failed to do so because of (a) his secrecy agreement with CIA or (b) CIA's invocation of the executive privilege to protect state secrets are appealing factors that furnish no leverage for decision. Raus does not attack the secrecy agreement if, indeed, he could do so. We are agreed that we may not invalidate the state secrecy privilege. If the result be that Raus cannot show that he acted within the scope of his employment and is thus entitled to a derivative privilege, it does not seem to me that the court ought to assume what he cannot establish. To do so is to put upon Heine a burden of proof that is not his and which he cannot possibly sustain: to show that Raus is *not* entitled to executive immunity.

The National Security Act specifically delegates to the *Director,* and not to the Agency, the statutory power relied on by the CIA and the district judge to justify the defamatory statements, and the affidavits do not suggest that the Director personally instructed Raus to defame Heine, nor is there any showing that the Director approved the defamation of Heine or properly delegated his responsibility to protect intelligence sources.[4] On remand, surely a probing inquiry into this matter can be accomplished without compelling disclosure of "state secrets." I do not view the omission as one sure to be remedied by the filing of another conclusory affidavit.

The court today, it seems to me, extends *Barr* beyond its breaking point. I would not go so far for several reasons, one of which is the court's concession that it is not necessary to do so, and that a qualified privilege would adequately protect the government employee in this case. I agree that such a result seems likely, and I would be content if Raus were accorded only that privilege and Heine given the opportunity to prove, if he can, actual malice.

What distinguishes this case for me from *Barr* and its progeny is the deliberate choice by the Central Intelligence Agency of defamation of character as an instrument of national policy. Such a factor alone seems to me to adequately distinguish *Barr* and all other cases with which I am familiar. I do not believe the Supreme Court in *Barr* intended that the immunity there recognized should extend to intentional defamation as an instrument of governmental policy. But if I am wrong about that, I suggest that a rule must be fashioned to limit the exercise of intentional defamation to responsible officers and officials. To immunize millions of government subordinate employees from liability for intentionally slandering private persons upon their mere explanation that they were told to do it, and the assertion that it was within the scope of employment, destroys, in my opinion, the balance that was struck in *Barr*. If the CIA must defame someone in order to protect national security, it seems to me it could be done more effectively by the Director himself rather than a secret underling—and with far less danger to a free society.

Justifying factors found in recent cases where absolute executive immunity has been sustained are not present in this case. See Spying and Slandering: An Absolute Privilege for the CIA Agent? 67 Colum.L.Rev. 752, 766-768 (1967). There is here no comment which served the interest of discussion and criticism of government activity or foreign relations. Not involved here are intra-departmental confidential communications necessary to the intelligent functioning of government. Nor is there any possibility here of scrutiny by an alternative remedial procedure in which Heine might vindicate himself or rehabilitate his reputation.[5] The privilege is sought by one who is not subject—as are most federal employees—to normal public scrutiny and sanctions for improper conduct. Since Raus was instructed to defame Heine, it is scarcely to be supposed he will be reprimanded by CIA for doing so.

Unlike *Barr v. Matteo* and other typical defamation cases, there was here deliberate use of defamatory material, said even now, after the event, to have been authorized by an agency of government (not simply done by an "unworthy" individual employee) for the very purpose of destroying the influence and effectiveness of an individual. *Barr* was not intended to protect the oppressive use of governmental power. Nor was the rule in *Barr* formulated for the protection of the "unworthy" officer of government. The protection afforded such an officer was given to him, not because he deserved to have it but because of fear that if he was denied it, there might result a deterrent effect upon honest and well intentioned officers of government that would hamper government operation. The premise of *Barr* is that because of human foible officers of government may sometimes unfortunately defame innocent individuals and that protection of such an officer is a necessary evil in order to protect worthy officers from the fear of private civil libel actions. *Barr* envisioned defamation and possible slander as the occasional failures of fallible human beings acting as government officers and not as instruments of governmental policy. I think the immunity conferred in *Barr* has no application to a fact situation where defamation is chosen by a government agency as deliberate policy.[6] That CIA may adopt a policy of defamation for the reason that it thinks such a policy is in the best interest of the United States is implicit in the silence of the Federal Tort Claim Act[7] and the undoubted power of the executive to invoke the "state secrets" privilege in a proper case. All that I would hold is that the individual person who publishes such defamation will not thereafter be entitled to *absolute* executive immunity under the doctrine enunciated in *Barr* as I understand it.

I would reverse and remand to the district court to consider whether or not Raus by reason of his position in the Estonian Legion is entitled to assert the qualified privilege commonly granted to those who have a special interest to preserve. See Prosser, Torts § 110 (3rd ed. 1964). I would also ask the district court to consider whether Heine was such a public figure as to afford defendant the privilege allowed under *New York Times Co. v. Sullivan,* 376 U.S. 254, 84 S.Ct. 710, 11 L.Ed.2d 686 (1964), and its progeny. Surely, as the court suggests, one or the other of these ought to be enough.

---

[1]Rule 56(e) contemplates that a sufficient affidavit shall "set forth such facts as would be admissible in evidence."

[2]It is true that Helms' affidavit contains the assertion that Raus was "acting within the scope and course of his employment" and was instructed to publish the defamatory words. Without factual averments, i.e., job description, the statement is simply a legal conclusion, unless one is willing to say employment is always co-extensive with instructions of the employer.

[3]If Raus had shot Heine, presumably no court would exonerate him of tort liability on the ground he was told to do it—not even for the purpose of shielding the government official who told him. "When 007 plinks an enemy with a well directed projectile from his trusty Walther PPK .32, aficionados give no thought to his possible legal liability; we are all aware that Bond is licensed to kill. In the real world, however, intelligence agents often strike not with guns but with words—allegations that destroy reputations, families, careers. And the question of their responsibility before the law is not nearly so settled as it is in the Fleming phantasmagoria." Comment, Spying and Slandering: An Absolute Privilege for the CIA Agent? 67 Colum.L.Rev. 752 (1967), citing I. Fleming, Goldfinger 29 (1959).

[4]Helms' affidavit of April 1, 1966, shows a broad delegation of powers to the Deputy Director effective April 28, 1965—long after the defamation of Heine occurred in 1963 and 1964.

[5]Indeed, Heine presented himself in Washington for arrest on the theory that if he were in fact a Communist, he would be guilty of failing to register under the Federal Foreign Agents Registration Act. 22 U.S.C.A. §§ 611-621 (1964) as amended (Supp. 1966). Neither the FBI nor the CIA made any response. N.Y. Times, April 28, 1966, at 29, col. 1; id., April 29, 1966, at 19, col. 1; id., May 14, 1966, at 2, col. 3.

[6]*See* Comment, 77 Yale L.J. 367, 387 (1967), where in discussing legislative immunity under U.S. Const. art. I, § 6, it is suggested that a defamed person ought to have "redress against conduct that no rationale for the constitutional privilege purports to justify: the exercise of public power with intent to inflict injury on private citizens or with reckless disregard for their interests."

[7]28 U.S.C.A. § 2680(h) excludes slander and libel actions.

Bivens v. Six Unknown Agents of Federal Bureau of Narcotics

403 U.S. 388 (1971)

Mr. Justice Brennan delivered the opinion of the Court.

The Fourth Amendment provides that:

> "The right of the people to be secure in their persons, houses, papers, and effects, against unreasonable searches and seizures, shall not be violated. . . ."

In *Bell v. Hood,* 327 U.S. 678 (1946), we reserved the question whether violation of that command by a federal agent acting under color of his authority gives rise to a cause of action for damages consequent upon his unconstitutional conduct. Today we hold that it does.

This case has its origin in an arrest and search carried out on the morning of November 26, 1965. Petitioner's complaint alleged that on that day respondents, agents of the Federal Bureau of Narcotics acting under claim of federal authority, entered his apartment and arrested him for alleged narcotics violations. The agents manacled petitioner in front of his wife and children, and threatened to arrest the entire family. They searched the apartment from stem to stern. Thereafter, petitioner was taken to the federal courthouse in Brooklyn, where he was interrogated, booked, and subjected to a visual strip search.

On July 7, 1967, petitioner brought suit in Federal District Court. In addition to the allegations above, his complaint asserted that the arrest and search were effected without a warrant, and that unreasonable force was employed in making the arrest; fairly read, it alleges as well that the arrest was made without probable cause.[1] Petitioner claimed to have suffered great humiliation, embarrassment, and mental suffering as a result of the agents' unlawful conduct, and sought $15,000 damages from each of them. The District Court, on respondents' motion, dismissed the complaint on the ground, *inter alia,* that it failed to state a cause of action.[2] 276 F. Supp. 12 (EDNY 1967). The Court of Appeals, one judge concurring specially,[3] affirmed on that basis. 409 F. 2d 718 (CA2 1969). We granted certiorari. 399 U.S. 905 (1970). We reverse.

I

Respondents do not argue that petitioner should be entirely without remedy for an unconstitutional invasion of his rights by federal agents. In respondents' view, however, the rights that petitioner asserts—primarily rights of privacy—are creations of state and not of federal law. Accordingly, they argue, petitioner may obtain money damages to redress invasion of these rights only by an action in tort, under state law, in the state courts. In this scheme the Fourth Amendment would serve merely to limit the extent to which the agents could defend the state law tort suit by asserting that their actions were a valid exercise of federal power: if the agents were shown to have violated the Fourth Amendment, such a defense would be lost to them and they would stand before the state law merely as private individuals. Candidly admitting that it is the policy of the Department of Justice to remove all such suits from the state to the federal courts for decision,[4] respondents nevertheless urge that we uphold dismissal of petitioner's complaint in federal court, and remit him to filing an action in the state courts in order that the case may properly be removed to the federal court for decision on the basis of state law.

We think that respondents' thesis rests upon a unduly restrictive view of the Fourth Amendment's protection against unreasonable searches and seizures by federal agents, a view that has consistently been rejected by this Court. Respondents seek to treat the relationship between a citizen and a federal agent unconstitutionally exercising his authority as no different from the relationship between two private citizens. In so doing, they ignore the fact that power, once granted, does not disappear like a magic gift when it is wrongfully used. An agent acting—albeit unconstitutionally—in the name of the United States possesses a far greater capacity for harm than an individual trespasser exercising no authority other than his own. Cf. *Amos v. United States,* 255 U.S. 313, 317 (1921); *United States v. Classic,* 313 U.S. 299, 326 (1941). Accordingly, as our cases make clear, the Fourth Amendment operates as a limitation upon the exercise of federal power regardless of whether the State in whose jurisdiction that power is exercised would prohibit or penalize the identical act if engaged in by a private citizen. It guarantees to citizens of the United States the absolute right to be free from unreasonable searches and seizures carried out by virtue of federal authority. And "where federally protected rights have been invaded, it has been the rule from the beginning that courts will be alert to adjust their remedies so as to grant the necessary relief." *Bell v. Hood,* 327 U.S., at 684 (footnote omitted); see *Bemis Bros. Bag Co. v. United States,* 289 U.S. 28, 36 (1933) (Cardozo, J.); *The Western Maid,* 257 U.S. 419, 433 (1922) (Holmes, J.).

First. Our cases have long since rejected the notion that the Fourth Amendment proscribes only such conduct as would, if engaged in by private persons, be condemned by state law. Thus in *Gambino v. United States,* 275 U.S. 310 (1927), petitioners were convicted of conspiracy to violate the National Prohibition Act on the basis of evidence seized by state police officers incident to petitioners' arrest by those officers solely for the purpose of enforcing federal law. *Id.,* at 314. Notwithstanding the lack of probable cause for the arrest, *id.,* at 313, it would have been permissible under state law if effected by private individuals.[5] It appears, moreover, that the officers were under direction from the Governor to aid in the enforcement of federal law. *Id.,* at 315-317. Accordingly, if the Fourth Amendment reached only to conduct impermissible under the law of the State, the Amendment would have had no application to the case. Yet this Court held the Fourth Amendment applicable and reversed petitioners' convictions as having been based upon evidence obtained through an unconstitutional search and seizure. Similarly, in *Byars v. United States,* 273 U.S. 28 (1927), the petitioner was convicted on the basis of evidence seized under a warrant issued, without probable cause under the Fourth Amendment, by a state court judge for a state law offense. At the invitation of state law enforcement officers, a federal prohibition agent participated in the search. This Court explicitly refused to inquire whether the warrant was "good under the state law . . . since in no event could it constitute the basis for a *federal* search and seizure." *Id.,* at 29 (emphasis added).[6] And our recent decisions regarding electronic surveillance have made it clear beyond peradventure that the Fourth Amendment is not tied to the niceties of local trespass laws. *Katz v. United States,* 389 U.S. 347 (1967); *Berger v. New York,* 388 U.S. 41 (1967); *Silverman v. United States,* 365 U.S. 505, 511 (1961). In light of these cases, respondents' argument that the Fourth Amendment serves only as a limitation on federal defenses to a state law claim, and not as an independent limitation upon the exercise of federal power, must be rejected.

Second. The interests protected by state laws regulating trespass and the invasion of privacy, and those protected by the Fourth Amendment's guarantee against unreasonable searches and seizures, may be inconsistent or even hostile. Thus, we may bar the door against an unwelcome private intruder, or call the police if he persists in seeking entrance. The availability of such alternative means for the protection of privacy may lead the State to restrict imposition of liability for any consequent trespass. A private citizen, asserting no authority other than his own, will not normally be liable in trespass if he demands, and is granted, admission to another's house. See W. Prosser, The Law of Torts § 18, pp. 109-110 (3d ed. 1964); 1 F. Harper & F. James, The Law of Torts § 1.11 (1956). But one who demands admission under a claim of federal authority stands in a far different position. Cf. *Amos v. United States,* 255 U.S. 313, 317 (1921). The mere invocation of federal power by a federal law enforcement official will normally render futile any attempt to resist an unlawful entry or arrest by resort to the local police; and a claim of authority to enter is likely to unlock the door as well. See *Weeks v. United States,* 232 U.S. 383, 386 (1914); *Amos v. United States, supra.*[7] "In such cases there is no safety for the citizen, except in the protection of the judicial tribunals, for rights which have been invaded by the officers of the government, professing to act in its name. There remains to him but the alternative of resistance, which may amount to crime." *United States v. Lee,* 106 U.S. 196, 219 (1882).[8] Nor is it adequate to answer that state law may take into account the different status of one clothed with the authority of the Federal Government. For just as state law may not authorize federal agents to violate the Fourth Amendment, *Byars v. United States, supra; Weeks v. United States, supra; In re Ayers,* 123 U.S. 443, 507 (1887), neither may state law undertake to limit the extent to which federal authority can be exercised. *In re Neagle,* 135 U.S. 1 (1890). The inevitable consequence of this dual limitation on state power is that the federal question becomes not merely a possible defense to the state law action, but an independent claim both necessary and sufficient to make out the plaintiff's cause of action. Cf. *Boilermakers v. Hardeman,* 401 U.S. 233, 241 (1971).

Third. That damages may be obtained for injuries consequent upon a violation of the Fourth Amendment by federal officials should hardly seem a surprising proposition. Historically, damages have been regarded as the ordinary remedy for an invasion of personal interests in liberty. See *Nixon v. Condon,* 286 U.S. 73 (1932); *Nixon v. Herndon,* 273 U.S. 536, 540 (1927); *Swafford v. Templeton,* 185 U.S. 487 (1902); *Wiley v. Sinkler,* 179 U.S. 58 (1900); J. Landynski, Search and Seizure and the Supreme Court 28 *et seq.* (1966); N. Lasson, History and Development of the Fourth Amendment to the United States Constitution 43 *et seq.* (1937); Katz, The Jurisprudence of Remedies: Constitutional Legality and the Law of Torts in *Bell v. Hood,* 117 U. Pa. L. Rev. 1, 8-33 (1968); cf. *West v. Cabell,* 153 U.S. 78 (1894); *Lammon v. Feusier,* 111 U.S. 17 (1884). Of course, the Fourth Amendment does not in so many words provide for its enforcement by an award of money damages for the consequences of its violation. But "it is . . . well settled that where legal rights have been invaded, and a federal statute provides for a general right to sue for such invasion, federal courts may use any available remedy to make good the wrong done." *Bell v. Hood,* 327 U.S., at 684 (footnote omitted). The present case involves no special factors counselling hesitation in the absence of affirmative action by Congress. We are not dealing with a question of "federal fiscal policy," as in *United States v. Standard Oil Co.,* 332 U.S. 301, 311 (1947). In that case we refused to infer from the Government-soldier relationship that the United States could recover damages from one who negligently injured a soldier and thereby caused the Government to pay his medical expenses and lose his services during the course of his hospitalization. Noting that Congress was normally quite solicitous where the federal purse was involved, we pointed out that "the United States [was] the party plaintiff to the suit. And the United States has power at any time to create the liability." *Id.,* at 316; see *United States v. Gilman,* 347 U.S. 507 (1954). Nor are we asked in this case to impose liability upon a congressional employee for actions contrary to no constitutional prohibition, but merely said to be in excess of the authority delegated to him by the Congress. *Wheeldin v. Wheeler,* 373 U.S. 647 (1963). Finally, we cannot accept respondents' formulation of the question as whether the availability of money damages is necessary to enforce the Fourth Amendment. For we have here no explicit congressional declaration that persons injured by a federal officer's violation of the Fourth Amendment may not recover money damages from the agents, but must instead be remitted to another remedy, equally effective in the view of Congress. The question is merely whether petitioner, if he can demonstrate an injury consequent upon the violation by federal agents of his Fourth Amendment rights, is entitled to redress his injury through a particular remedial mechanism normally available in the federal courts. Cf. *J. I. Case Co. v. Borak,* 377 U.S. 426, 433 (1964); *Jacobs v. United States,* 290 U.S. 13, 16 (1933). "The very essence of civil liberty certainly consists in the right of every individual to claim the protection of the laws, whenever he receives an inqury." *Marbury v. Madison,* 1 Cranch 137, 163 (1803). Having concluded that petitioner's complaint states a cause of action under the Fourth Amendment, *supra,* at 390-395, we hold that petitioner is entitled to recover money damages for any injuries he has suffered as a result of the agents' violation of the Amendment.

II

In addition to holding that petitioner's complaint had failed to state facts making out a cause of action, the District Court ruled that in any event respondents were immune from liability by virtue of their official position. 276 F. Supp., at 15. This question was not passed upon by the Court of Appeals, and accordingly we do not consider it here. The judgment of the Court of Appeals is reversed and the case is remanded for further proceedings consistent with this opinion.

So ordered.

Mr. Justice Harlan, concurring in the judgment.

Mr. Chief Justice Burger, dissenting. . . .

Mr. Justice Black, dissenting. . . .

Mr. Justice Blackmun, dissenting. . . .

---

[1]Petitioner's complaint does not explicitly state that the agents had no probable cause for his arrest, but it does allege that the arrest was "done unlawfully, unreasonably and contrary to law." App. 2. Petitioner's affidavit in support of his motion for summary judgment swears that the search was "without cause, consent or warrant," and that the arrest was "without cause, reason or warrant." App. 28.

[2]The agents were not named in petitioner's complaint, and the District Court ordered that the complaint be served upon "those federal agents who it is indicated by the records of the United States Attorney participated in the November 25, 1965, arrest of the [petitioner]." App. 3. Five agents were ultimately served.

[3]Judge Waterman, concurring, expressed the thought that "the federal courts can . . . entertain this cause of action irrespective of whether a statute exists specifically authorizing a federal suit against federal officers for damages" for acts such as those alleged. In his view, however, the critical point was recognition that some cause of action existed, albeit a state-created one, and in consequence he was willing "*as of now*" to concur in the holding of the Court of Appeals. 409 F. 2d, at 726 (emphasis in original).

[4]"[S]ince it is the present policy of the Department of Justice to remove to the federal courts all suits in state courts against federal officers for trespass or false imprisonment, a claim for relief, whether based on state common law or directly on the Fourth Amendment, will ultimately be heard in a federal court." Brief for Respondents 13 (citations omitted); see 28 U. S. C. § 1442 (a); *Willingham v. Morgan,* 395 U.S. 402 (1969). In light of this, it is difficult to understand our Brother Blackmun's complaint that our holding today "opens the door for another avalanche of new federal cases." *Post,* at 430. In estimating the magnitude of any such "avalanche," it is worth noting that a survey of comparable actions against state officers under 42 U. S C. § 1983 found only 53 reported cases in 17 years (1951-1967) that survived a motion to dismiss. Ginger & Bell, Police Misconduct Litigation—Plaintiff's Remedies, 15 Am. Jur. Trials 555, 580-590 (1968). Increasing this figure by 900% to allow

for increases in rate and unreported cases, every federal district judge could expect to try one such case every 13 years.

[5]New York at that time followed the common-law rule that a private person may arrest another if the latter has in fact committed a felony, and that if such is the case the presence or absence of probable cause is irrelevant to the legality of the arrest. See *McLoughlin v. New York Edison Co.*, 252 N. Y. 202, 169 N. E. 227 (1929); cf. N. Y. Code Crim. Proc. § 183 (1958) for codification of the rule. Conspiracy to commit a federal crime was at the time a felony. Act of March 4, 1909, § 37, 35 Stat. 1096.

[6]Conversely, we have in some instances rejected Fourth Amendment claims despite facts demonstrating that federal agents were acting in violation of local law. *McGuire v. United States*, 273 U.S. 95 (1927) (trespass *ab initio*); *Hester v. United States*, 265 U.S. 57 (1924) ("open fields" doctrine); cf. *Burdeau v. McDowell*, 256 U.S. 465 (1921) (possession of stolen property).

[7]Similarly, although the Fourth Amendment confines an officer executing a search warrant strictly within the bounds set by the warrant, *Marron v. United States*, 275 U.S. 192, 196 (1927); see *Stanley v. Georgia*, 394 U.S. 557, 570-572 (1969) (Stewart, J., concurring in result), a private individual lawfully in the home of another will not normally be liable for trespass beyond the bounds of his invitation absent clear notice to that effect. See 1 F. Harper & F. James, The Law of Torts § 1.11 (1956).

[8]Although no State has undertaken to limit the common-law doctrine that one may use reasonable force to resist an unlawful arrest by a private person, at least two States have outlawed resistance to an unlawful arrest sought to be made by a person known to be an officer of the law. R. I. Gen. Laws § 12-7-10 (1969); *State v. Koonce*, 89 N. J. Super. 169, 180-184, 214 A. 2d 428, 433-436 (1965).

Laird v. Tatum et al

408 U.S. (1972)

Mr. Chief Justice Burger delivered the opinion of the Court.

Respondents brought this class action in the District Court seeking declaratory and injunctive relief on their claim that their rights were being invaded by the Department of the Army's alleged "surveillance of lawful and peaceful civilian political activity." The petitioners in response described the activity as "gathering by lawful means . . . [and] maintaining and using in their intelligence activities . . . information relating to potential or actual civil disturbances [or] street demonstrations." In connection with respondents' motion for a preliminary injunction and petitioners' motion to dismiss the complaint, both parties filed a number of affidavits with the District Court and presented their oral arguments at a hearing on the two motions. On the basis of the pleadings,[1] the affidavits before the court, and the oral arguments advanced at the hearing, the District Court granted petitioners' motion to dismiss, holding that there was no justiciable claim for relief.

On appeal, a divided Court of Appeals reversed and ordered the case remanded for further proceedings. We granted certiorari to consider whether, as the Court of Appeals held, respondents presented a justiciable controversy in complaining of a "chilling" effect on the exercise of their First Amendment rights where such effect is allegedly caused, not by any "specific action of the Army against them, [but] only [by] the existence and operation of the intelligence gathering and distributing system, which is confined to the Army and related civilian investigative agencies." 144 U.S. App. D. C. 72, 78, 444 F. 2d 947, 953. We reverse.

(1)

There is in the record a considerable amount of background information regarding the activities of which respondents complained; this information is set out primarily in the affidavits that were filed by the parties in connection with the District Court's consideration of respondents' motion for a preliminary injunction and petitioners' motion to dismiss. See Fed. Rule Civ. Proc. 12(b). A brief review of that information is helpful to an understanding of the issues.

The President is authorized by 10 U. S. C. §331[2] to make use of the armed forces to quell insurrection and other domestic violence if and when the conditions described in that section obtain within one of the States. Pursuant to those provisions, President Johnson ordered federal troops to assist local authorities at the time of the civil disorders in Detroit, Michigan, in the summer of 1967 and during the disturbances that followed the assassination of Dr. Martin Luther King. Prior to the Detroit disorders, the Army had a general contingency plan for providing such assistance to local authorities, but the 1967 experience led Army authorities to believe that more attention should be given to such preparatory planning. The data-gathering system here involved is said to have been established in connection with the development of more detailed and specific contingency planning designed to permit the Army, when called upon to assist local authorities, to be able to respond effectively with a minimum of force. As the Court of Appeals observed,

> "In performing this type function the Army is essentially a police force or the back-up of a local police force. To quell disturbances or to prevent further disturbances the Army needs the same tools and, most importantly, the same information to which local police forces have access. Since the Army is sent into territory almost invariably unfamiliar to most soldiers and their commanders, their need for information is likely to be greater than that of the hometown policeman.
>
> "No logical argument can be made for compelling the military to use *blind* force. When force is employed it should be intelligently directed, and this depends upon having reliable information—in time. As Chief Justice John Marshall said of Washington, 'A general must be governed by his intelligence and must regulate his measures by his information. It is his duty to obtain correct information. . . .' So we take it as undeniable that the military, *i.e.*, the Army, need a certain amount of information in order to perform their constitutional and statutory missions." 144 U.S. App. D. C., at 77-78, 444 F. 2d, at 952-953 (footnotes omitted).

The system put into operation as a result of the Army's 1967 experience consisted essentially of the collection of information about public activities that were thought to have at least some potential for civil disorder, the reporting of that information to Army Intelligence headquarters at Fort Holabird, Maryland, the dissemination of these reports from headquarters to major Army posts around the country, and the storage of the reported information in a computer data bank located at Fort Holabird. The information itself was collected by a variety of means, but it is significant that the principal sources of information were the news media and publications in general circulation. Some of the information came from Army Intelligence agents who attended meetings that were open to the public and who wrote field reports describing the meetings, giving such data as the name of the sponsoring organization, the identity of speakers, the approximate number of persons in attendance, and an indication of whether any disorder occurred. And still other information was provided to the Army by civilian law enforcement agencies.

The material filed by the Government in the District Court reveals that Army Intelligence has field offices in various parts of the country; these offices are staffed in the aggregate with approximately 1,000 agents, 94% of whose time[3] is devoted to the organization's principal mission,[4] which is unrelated to the domestic surveillance system here involved.

By early 1970 Congress became concerned with the scope of the Army's domestic surveillance system; hearings on the matter were held before the Subcommittee on Constitutional Rights of the Senate Committee on the Judiciary. Meanwhile, the Army, in the course of a review of the system, ordered a significant reduction in its scope. For example, information referred to in the complaint as the "blacklist" and the records in the computer data bank at Fort Holabird were found unnecessary and were destroyed, along with other related records. One copy of all the material relevant to the instant suit was retained, however, because of the pendency of this litigation. The review leading to the destruction of these records was said at the time the District Court ruled on petitioners' motion to dismiss to be a "continuing" one (App. 82), and the Army's policies at that time were represented as follows in a letter from the Under Secretary of the Army to Senator Sam J. Ervin, Chairman of the Senate Subcommittee on Constitutional Rights:

> "[R]eports concerning civil disturbances will be limited to matters of immediate concern to the Army—that is, reports concerning outbreaks of violence or incidents with a high potential for violence beyond the capability of state and local police and the National Guard to control. These reports will be collected by liaison with other Government agencies and reported by teletype to the Intelligence Command. They will not be placed in a computer. . . . These reports are destroyed 60 days after publication or 60 days after the end of the disturbance. This limited reporting system will ensure that the Army is prepared to respond to whatever directions the President may issue in civil disturbance situations and without 'watching' the lawful activities of civilians." (App. 80.)

In briefs for petitioners filed with this Court, the Solicitor General has called our attention to certain directives issued by the Army and the Department of Defense subsequent to the District Court's dismissal of the action; these directives indicate that the Army's review of the needs of its domestic intelligence activities has indeed been a continuing one and that those activities have since been significantly reduced.

(2)

The District Court held a combined hearing on respondents' motion for a preliminary injunction and petitioners' motion for dismissal and thereafter announced its holding that respondents had failed to state a claim upon which relief could be granted. It was the view of the District Court that respondents failed to allege any action on the part of the Army that was unlawful in itself and further failed to allege any injury or any realistic threats to their rights growing out of the Army's actions.[5]

In reversing, the Court of Appeals noted that respondents "have some difficulty in establishing visible injury":

> "[They] freely admit that they complain of no specific action of the Army against them. . . . There is no evidence of illegal or unlawful surveillance activities. We are not cited to any clandestine intrusion by a military agent. So far as is yet shown, the information gathered is nothing more than a good newspaper reporter would be able to gather by attendance at public meetings and the clipping of articles from publications available on any newstand." 144 U.S. App. D. C., at 78, 444 F. 2d, at 953.

The court took note of petitioners' argument "that nothing [detrimental to respondents] has been done, that nothing is contemplated to be done, and even if some action by the Army against [respondents] were possibly foreseeable, such would not present a presently justiciable controversy." With respect to this argument, the Court of Appeals had this to say:

> "This position of the [petitioners] does not accord full measure to the rather unique argument advanced by appellants [respondents]. While [respondents] do indeed argue that in the future it is possible that information relating to matters far beyond the responsibilities of the military may be misused by the military to the detriment of these civilian [respondents], yet [respondents] do not attempt to establish this as a definitely foreseeable event, or to base their complaint on this ground. Rather, [respondents] contend that the *present existence of this system* of gather and distributing information, allegedly far beyond the mission requirements of the Army, constitutes an impermissible burden on [respondents] and other persons similarly situated which exercises a *present inhibiting effect* on their full expression and utilization of their First Amendment rights. . . ." *Id.,* at 79, 444 F. 2d, at 954. (Emphasis in original.)

Our examination of the record satisfies us that the Court of Appeals properly identified the issue presented, namely, whether the jurisdiction of a federal court may be invoked by a complainant who alleges that the exercise of his First Amendment rights is being chilled by the mere existence, without more, of a governmental investigative and data-gathering activity that is alleged to be broader in scope than is reasonably necessary for the accomplishment of a valid governmental purpose. We conclude, however, that, having properly identified the issue, the Court of Appeals decided that issue incorrectly.[6]

In recent years this Court has found in a number of cases that constitutional violations may arise from the deterrent, or "chilling," effect of governmental regulations that fall short of a direct prohibition against the exercise of First Amendment rights. *E.g., Baird v. State Bar of Arizona,* 401 U.S. 1 (1971); *Keyishian v. Board of Regents,* 385 U.S. 589 (1967); *Lamont v. Postmaster General,* 381 U.S. 301 (1965); *Baggett v. Bullitt,* 377 U.S. 360 (1964). In none of these cases, however, did the chilling effect arise merely from the individual's knowledge that a governmental agency was engaged in certain activities or from the individual's concomitant fear that, armed with the fruits of those activities, the agency might in the future take some *other* and additional action detrimental to that individual. Rather, in each of these cases, the challenged exercise of governmental power was regulatory, proscriptive, or compulsory in nature, and the complainant was either presently or prospectively subject to the regulations, proscriptions, or compulsions that he was challenging.

For example, the petitioner in *Baird v. State Bar of Arizona* had been denied admission to the bar solely because of her refusal to answer a question regarding the organizations with which she had been associated in the past. In announcing the judgment of the Court, Mr. Justice Black said that "a State may not inquire about a man's views or associations solely for the purpose of withholding a right or benefit because of what he believes." 401 U.S., at 7. Some of the teachers who were the complainants in *Keyishian v. Board of Regents* had been discharged from employment by the State, and the others were threatened with such discharge, because of their political acts or associations. The Court concluded that the State's "complicated and intricate scheme" of laws and regulations relating to teacher loyalty could not withstand constitutional scrutiny; it was not permissible to inhibit

First Amendment expression by forcing a teacher to "guess what conduct or utterance" might be in violation of that complex regulatory scheme and might thereby "lose him his position." 385 U.S., at 604. *Lamont v. Postmaster General* dealt with a governmental regulation requiring private individuals to make a special written request to the Post Office for delivery of each individual mailing of certain kinds of political literature addressed to them. In declaring the regulation invalid, the Court said: "The addressee carries an affirmative obligation which we do not think the Government may impose on him." 381 U.S., at 307. *Baggett v. Bullitt* dealt with a requirement that an oath of vague and uncertain meaning be taken as a condition of employment by a governmental agency. The Court said: "Those with a conscientious regard for what they solemnly swear or affirm, sensitive to the perils posed by the oath's indefinite language, avoid the risk of loss of employment, and perhaps profession, only by restricting their conduct to that which is unquestionably safe. Free speech may not be so inhibited." 377 U.S., at 372.

The decisions in these cases fully recognize that governmental action may be subject to constitutional challenge even though it has only an indirect effect on the exercise of First Amendment rights. At the same time, however, these decisions have in no way eroded the

> "established principle that to entitle a private individual to invoke the judicial power to determine the validity of executive or legislative action he must show that he has sustained or is immediately in danger of sustaining a direct injury as the result of that action. . . ." *Ex parte Lévitt,* 302 U.S. 633, 634 (1937).

The respondents do not meet this test; their claim, simply stated, is that they disagree with the judgments made by the Executive Branch with respect to the type and amount of information the Army needs and that the very existence of the Army's data-gathering system produces a constitutionally impermissible chilling effect upon the exercise of their First Amendment rights. That alleged "chilling" effect may perhaps be seen as arising from respondents' very perception of the system as inappropriate to the Army's role under our form of government, or as arising from respondents' beliefs that it is inherently dangerous for the military to be concerned with activities in the civilian sector, or as arising from respondents' less generalized yet speculative apprehensiveness that the Army may at some future date misuse the information in some way that would cause direct harm to respondents.[7] Allegations of a subjective "chill" are not an adequate substitute for a claim of specific present objective harm or a threat of specific future harm; "the federal courts established pursuant to Article III of the Constitution do not render advisory opinions." *United Public Workers v. Mitchell,* 330 U.S. 75, 89 (1947).

Stripped to its essentials, what respondents appear to be seeking is a broad-scale investigation, conducted by themselves as private parties armed with the subpoena power of a federal district court and the power of cross-examination, to probe into the Army's intelligence-gathering activities, with the district court determining at the conclusion of that investigation the extent to which those activities may or may not be appropriate to the Army's mission. The following excerpt from the opinion of the Court of Appeals suggests the broad sweep implicit in its holding:

> "Apparently in the judgment of the civilian head of the Army not everything being done in the operation of this intelligence system was necessary to the performance of the military mission. *If the Secretary of the Army can formulate and implement such judgment based on facts within his Departmental knowledge, the United States District Court can hear evidence,*

ascertain the facts, and decide what, if any, further restrictions on the complained-of activities are called for to confine the military to their legitimate sphere of activity and to protect [respondents'] allegedly infringed constitutional rights." 144 U.S. App. D. C., at 83, 444 F. 2d, at 958. (Emphasis added.)

Carried to its logical end, this approach would have the federal courts as virtually continuing monitors of the wisdom and soundness of Executive action; such a role is appropriate for the Congress acting through its committees and the "power of the purse"; it is not the role of the judiciary, absent actual present or immediately threatened injury resulting from unlawful governmental action.

We, of course, intimate no view with respect to the propriety or desirability, from a policy standpoint, of the challenged activities of the Department of the Army; our conclusion is a narrow one, namely, that on this record the respondents have not presented a case for resolution by the courts.

The concerns of the Executive and Legislative Branches in response to disclosure of the Army surveillance activities—and indeed the claims alleged in the complaint—reflect a traditional and strong resistance of Americans to any military intrusion into civilian affairs. That tradition has deep roots in our history and found early expression, for example, in the Third Amendment's explicit prohibition against quartering soldiers in private homes without consent and in the constitutional provisions for civilian control of the military. Those prohibitions are not directly presented by this case, but their philosophical underpinnings explain our tradition insistence on limitations on military operations in peacetime. Indeed, when presented with claims of judicially cognizable injury resulting from military intrusion into the civilian sector, federal courts are fully empowered to consider claims of those asserting such injury; there is nothing in our Nation's history or in this Court's decided cases, including our holding today, that can properly be seen as giving any indication that actual or threatened injury by reason of unlawful activities of the military would go unnoticed or unremedied.

Reversed.

Mr. Justice Douglas, with whom Mr. Justice Marshall concurs, dissenting. . . .

Mr. Justice Brennan, with whom Mr. Justice Stewart and Mr. Justice Marshall join, dissenting. . . .

---

[1]The complaint filed in the District Court candidly asserted that its factual allegations were based on a magazine article: "The information contained in the foregoing paragraphs numbered five through thirteen [of the complaint] was published in the January 1970 issue of the magazine *The Washington Monthly*. . . ."

[2]"Whenever there is an insurrection in any State against its government, the President may, upon the request of its legislature or of its governor if the legislature cannot be convened, call into Federal service such of the militia of the other States, in the number requested by that State, and use such of the armed forces, as he considers necessary to suppress the insurrection."

The constitutionality of this statute is not at issue here; the specific authorization of such use of federal armed forces, in addition to state militia, appears to have been enacted pursuant to Art. IV, § 4, of the Constitution, which provides that "[t]he United States . . . shall protect each of [the individual States] . . . on Application of the Legislature, or of the Executive (when the Legislature cannot be convened) against domestic Violence."

In describing the requirement of 10 U. S. C. § 331 for the use of federal troops to quell domestic disorders, Attorney General Ramsey Clark made the following statements in a letter sent to all state governors on August 7, 1967:

"There are three basic prerequisites to the use of Federal troops in a state in the event of domestic violence:

"(1) That a situation of serious 'domestic violence' exists within the state. While this conclusion should be supported with a statement of factual details to the extent feasible under the circumstances, there is no prescribed wording.

"(2) That such violence cannot be brought under control by the law enforcement resources available to the governor, including local and State police forces and the National Guard. The judgment required here is that there is a definite need for the assistance of Federal troops, taking into account the remaining time needed to move them into action at the scene of violence.

"(3) That the legislature or the governor requests the President to employ the armed forces to bring the violence under control. The element of request by the governor of a State is essential if the legislature cannot be convened. It may be difficult in the context of urban rioting, such as we have seen this summer, to convene the legislature.

"These three elements should be expressed in a written communication to the President, which of course may be a telegram, to support his issuance of a proclamation under 10 U. S. C. § 334 and commitment of troops to action. In case of extreme emergency, receipt of a written request will not be a prerequisite to Presidential action. However, since it take several hours to alert and move Federal troops, the few minutes needed to write and dispatch a telegram are not likely to cause any delay.

"Upon receiving the request from a governor, the President, under the terms of the statute and the historic practice, must exercise his own judgment as to whether Federal troops will be sent, and as to such questions as timing, size of the force, and federalization of the National Guard.

"Preliminary steps, such as alerting the troops, can be taken by the Federal government upon oral communications and prior to the governor's determination that the violence cannot be brought under control without the aid of Federal forces. Even such preliminary steps, however, represent a most serious departure from our traditions of local responsibility for law enforcement. They should not be requested until there is a substantial likelihood that the Federal forces will be needed."

This analysis of Attorney General Clark suggests the importance of the need for information to guide the intelligent use of military forces and to avoid "overkill."

[3]Translated in terms of personnel, this percentage figure suggests that the total intelligence operation concerned with potential civil disorders hardly merits description as "massive," as one of the dissents characterizes it.

[4]That principal mission was described in one of the documents filed with the District Court as the conducting of "investigations to determine whether uniformed members of the Army, civilian employees [of the Army] and contractors' employees should be granted access to classified information." App. 76-77.

[5]In the course of the oral argument, the District Judge sought clarification from respondents' counsel as to the nature of the threats perceived by respondents; he asked what exactly it was in the Army's activities that tended to chill respondents and others in the exercise of their constitutional rights. Counsel responded that it was

"precisely the threat in this case that *in some future civil disorder* of some kind, the Army is going to come in with its list of troublemakers . . . and go rounding up people and putting them in military prisons somewhere." (Emphasis added.)

To this the court responded that "we still sit here with the writ of habeas corpus." At another point, counsel for respondents took a somewhat different approach in arguing that "*we're not quite sure exactly what they have in mind* and that is precisely what causes the chill, the chilling effect." (Emphasis added.)

[6]Indeed, the Court of Appeals noted that it had reached a different conclusion when presented with a virtually identical issue in another of its recently decided cases, *Davis v. Ichord,* 143 U.S. App. D. C. 183, 442 F. 2d 1207 (1970). The plaintiffs in *Davis* were attacking the constitutionality of the House of Representatives Rule under which the House Committee on Internal Security conducts investigations and maintains files described by the plaintiffs as a "political blacklist." The court noted that any chilling effect to which the plaintiffs were subject arose from the mere existence of the Committee and its files and the mere possibility of the misuse of those files. In affirming the dismissal of the complaint, the court concluded that allegations of such a chilling effect could not be elevated to a justiciable claim merely by alleging as well that the challenged House Rule was overly broad and vague.

In deciding the case presently under review, the Court of Appeals distinguished *Davis* on the ground that the difference in the source of the chill in the two cases—a House Committee in *Davis* and the Army in the instant case—was controlling. We cannot agree that the jurisdictional question with which we are here concerned is to be resolved on the basis of the identity of the parties named as defendants in the complaint.

[7]Not only have respondents left somewhat unclear the precise connection between the mere existence of the challenged system and their own alleged chill, but they have also cast considerable doubt on whether they themselves are in fact suffering from any such chill. Judge MacKinnon took cogent note of this difficulty in dissenting from the Court of Appeals' judgment, rendered as it was "on the facts of the case which emerge from the pleadings, affidavits and the admissions made to the trial court." 144 U.S. App. D. C., at 84, 444 F. 2d, at 959. At the oral argument before the District Court, counsel for respondents admitted that his clients were "not people, obviously, who are cowed and chilled"; indeed, they were quite willing "to open themselves up to public investigation and public scrutiny." But, counsel argued, these respondents must "represent millions of Americans not nearly as forward [and] courageous" as themselves. It was Judge MacKinnon's view that this concession "constitutes a basic denial of practically their whole case." *Ibid.* Even assuming a justiciable controversy, if respondents themselves are not chilled, but seek only to represent those "millions" whom they believe are so chilled, respondents clearly lack that "personal stake in the outcome of the controversy" essential to standing. *Baker v. Carr,* 369 U.S. 186, 204 (1962). As the Court recently observed in *Moose Lodge No. 107 v Irvis,* 407 U.S. 163, 166, a litigant "has standing to seek redress for injuries done to him, but may not seek redress for injuries done to others."

United States v. Richardson

418 U.S. 166 (1974)

Mr. Chief Justice Burger delivered the opinion of the Court.

We granted certiorari in this case to determine whether the respondent has standing to bring an action as a federal taxpayer[1] alleging that certain provisions concerning public reporting of expenditures under the Central Intelligence Agency Act of 1949, 63 Stat. 208, 50 U. S. C. § 403a *et seq.,* violate Art. I, § 9, cl. 7, of the Constitution which provides:

> "No Money shall be drawn from the Treasury, but in Consequence of Appropriations made by Law; and a regular Statement and Account of the Receipts and Expenditures of all public Money shall be published from time to time."

Respondent brought this suit in the United States District Court on a complaint in which he recites attempts to obtain from the Government information concerning detailed expenditures of the Central Intelligence Agency. According to the complaint, respondent wrote to the Government Printing Office in 1967 and requested that he be provided with the documents "published by the Government in compliance with Article I, section 9, clause (7) of the United States Constitution." The Fiscal Service of the Bureau of Accounts of the Department of the Treasury replied, explaining that it published the document known as the Combined Statement of Receipts, Expenditures, and Balances of the United States Government. Several copies of the monthly and daily reports of the office were sent with the letter. Respondent then wrote to the same office and, quoting part of the CIA Act, asked whether this statute did not "cast reflection upon the authenticity of the Treasury's Statement." He also inquired as to how he could receive further information on the expenditures of the CIA. The Bureau of Accounts replied stating that it had no other available information.

In another letter, respondent asserted that the CIA Act was repugnant to the Constitution and requested that the Treasury Department seek an opinion of the Attorney General. The Department answered declining to seek such an opinion and this suit followed. Respondent's complaint asked the court to "issue a permanent injunction enjoining the defendants from publishing their 'Combined Statement of Receipts, Expenditures and Balances of the United States Government' and representing it as the fulfillment of the mandates of Article I Section 9 Clause 7 until same fully complies with those mandates."[2] In essence, the respondent asked the federal court to declare unconstitutional that provision of the Central Intelligence Agency Act which permits the Agency to account for its expenditures "solely on the certificate of the Director. . . ." 50 U. S. C. § 403j (b). The only injury alleged by respondent was that he "cannot obtain a document that sets out the expenditures and receipts" of the CIA but on the contrary was "asked to accept a fraudulent document." The District Court granted a motion for dismissal on the ground respondent lacked standing under *Flast v. Cohen,* 392 U.S. 83 (1968), and that the subject matter raised political questions not suited for judicial disposition.

The Court of Appeals sitting en banc, with three judges dissenting, reversed, 465 F. 2d 844 (CA3 1972), holding that the respondent had standing to bring this action.[3] The majority relied chiefly on *Flast v. Cohen, supra,* and its two-tier test that taxpayer standing rests on a showing of (a) a "logical link" between the status as a taxpayer and the challenged legislative enactment, *i.e.,* an attack on an enactment under the taxing and spending clause of Art. I, § 8, of the Constitution; and (b) a 'nexus" between the plaintiff's status and a specific constitutional limitation imposed on the taxing and spending power. 392 U.S., at 102-103. While noting that the respondent did not directly attack an appropriations act, as did the plaintiff in *Flast,* the Court of Appeals concluded that the CIA statute challenged by the respondent was "integrally related," 465 F. 2d, at 853, to his ability to challenge the appropriations since he could not question an appropriation about which he had no knowledge. The Court of Appeals seemed to rest its holding on an assumption that this case was a prelude to a later case challenging, on the basis of information obtained in this suit, some particular appropriation for or expenditure of the CIA; respondent stated no such an intention in his complaint. The dissenters took a different approach urging denial of standing principally because, in their view, respondent alleged no specific injury but only a general interest common to all members of the public.

We conclude that respondent lacks standing to maintain a suit for the relief sought and we reverse.

I

As far back as *Marbury v. Madison,* 1 Cranch 137 (1803), this Court held that judicial power may be exercised only in a case properly before it—a "case or controversy" not suffering any of the limitations of the political-question doctrine, not then moot or calling for an advisory opinion. In *Baker v. Carr,* 369 U.S. 186, 204 (1962), this limitation was described in terms that a federal court cannot

> " 'pronounce any statute, either of a State or of the United States, void, because irreconcilable with the Constitution, except as it is called upon to adjudge the legal rights of litigants in actual controversies.' *Liverpool Steamship Co. v. Commissioners of Emigration,* 113 U.S. 33, 39."

Recently in *Association of Data Processing Service Organizations, Inc. v. Camp,* 397 U.S. 150 (1970), the Court, while noting that "[g]eneralizations about standing to sue are largely worthless as such," *id.*, at 151, emphasized that "[o]ne generalization is, however, necessary and that is that the question of standing in the federal courts is to be considered in the framework of Article III which restricts judicial power to 'cases' and 'controversies.'"[4]

Although the recent holding of the Court in *Flast v. Cohen, supra*, is a starting point in an examination of respondent's claim to prosecute this suit as a taxpayer, that case must be read with reference to its principal predecessor, *Frothingham v. Mellon*, 262 U.S. 447 (1923). In *Frothingham*, the injury alleged was that the congressional enactment challenged as unconstitutional would, if implemented, increase the complainant's future federal income taxes.[5] Denying standing, the *Frothingham* Court rested on the "comparatively minute],] . . . remote, fluctuating and uncertain," *id.*, at 487, impact on the taxpayer, and the failure to allege the kind of direct injury required for standing.

> "The party who invokes the [judicial] power must be able to show not only that the statute is invalid but that he has sustained or is immediately in danger of sustaining some direct injury as the result of its enforcement, and not merely that he suffers in some indefinite way in common with people generally.' *Id.*, at 488.

When the Court addressed the question of standing in *Flast*, Mr. Chief Justice Warren traced what he described as the "confusion" following *Frothingham* as to whether the Court had announced a constitutional doctrine barring suits by taxpayers challenging federal expenditures as unconstitutional or simply a policy rule of judicial self-restraint. In an effort to clarify the confusion and to take into account intervening developments, of which class actions and joinder under the Federal Rules of Civil Procedure were given as examples, the Court embarked on "a fresh examination of the limitations upon standing to sue in a federal court and the application of those limitations to taxpayer suits." 392 U.S., at 94. That re-examination led, however, to the holding that a "taxpayer will have standing *consistent with Article III* to invoke federal judicial power when he alleges that congressional action under the taxing and spending clause is in derogation of those constitutional provisions *which operate to restrict the exercise of the taxing and spending power.*" *Id.*, at 105-106. (Emphasis supplied.) In so holding, the Court emphasized that Art. III requirements are the threshold inquiry:

> "The 'gist of the question of standing' is whether the party seeking relief has 'alleged such a personal stake in the outcome of the controversy as to assure that concrete adverseness . . . upon which the court so largely depends for illumination of difficult constitutional questions.'" *Id.*, at 99, citing *Baker v. Carr*, 369 U.S., at 204.

The Court then announced a two-pronged standing test which requires allegations: (a) challenging an enactment under the taxing and spending clause of Art. I § 8, of the Constitution; and (b) claiming that the challenged enactment exceeds specific constitutional limitations imposed on the taxing and spending power. 392 U.S., at 102-103. While the "impenetrable barrier to suits against Acts of Congress brought by individuals who can assert only the interest of federal taxpayers," *id.*, at 85, had been slightly lowered, the Court made clear it was reaffirming the principle of *Frothingham* precluding a taxpayer's use of "a federal court as a forum in which to air his generalized grievances about the conduct of government or the allocation of power in the Federal System." *Id.*, at 106. The narrowness of that holding is emphasized by the concurring opinion of Mr. Justice Stewart, in *Flast*:

> "In concluding that the appellants therefore have standing to sue, we do not undermine the salutary principle, established by *Frothingham* and reaffirmed today, that a taxpayer may not 'employ a federal court as a forum in which to air his generalized grievances about the conduct of government or the allocation of power in the Federal System.' " (Citation omitted.) *Id.*, at 114.

II

Although the Court made it very explicit in *Flast* that a "fundamental aspect of standing" is that it focuses primarily on the *party* seeking to get his complaint before the federal court rather than "on the issues he wishes to have adjudicated," *id.*, at 99, it made equally clear that

> "in ruling on [taxpayer] standing, it is both appropriate and necessary to look to the substantive issues for another purpose, namely, to determine whether there is a logical nexus between the status asserted and the claim sought to be adjudicated." *Id.*, at 102.[6]

We therefore turn to an examination of the issues sought to be raised by respondent's complaint to determine whether he is "a proper and appropriate party to invoke federal judicial power," *ibid.*, with respect to those issues.

We need not and do not reach the merits of the constitutional attack on the statute; our inquiry into the "substantive issues" is for the limited purpose indicated above. The mere recital of the respondent's claims and an examination of the statute under attack demonstrate how far he falls short of the standing criteria of *Flast* and how neatly he falls within the *Frothingham* holding left undisturbed. Although the status he rests on is that he is a taxpayer, his challenge is not addressed to the taxing or spending power, but to the statutes regulating the CIA, specifically 50 U. S. C. § 403j (b). That section provides different accounting and reporting requirements and procedures for the CIA, as is also done with respect to other governmental agencies dealing in confidential areas.[7]

Respondent makes no claim that appropriated funds are being spent in violation of a "specific constitutional limitation upon the . . . taxing and spending power. . . ." 392 U.S., at 104. Rather, he asked the courts to compel the Government to give him information on precisely how the CIA spends its funds. Thus there is no "logical nexus" between the asserted status of taxpayer and the claimed failure of the Congress to require the Executive to supply a more detailed report of the expenditures of that agency.[8]

The question presented thus is simply and narrowly whether these claims meet the standards for taxpayer standing set forth in *Flast*; we hold they do not. Respondent is seeking "to employ a federal court as a forum in which to air his generalized grievances about the conduct of government." 392 U.S., at 106. Both *Frothingham* and *Flast, supra,* reject that basis for standing.

III

The Court of Appeals held that the basis of taxpayer standing

> "need not always be the appropriation and the spending of [taxpayer's] money for an invalid purpose. The personal stake may come from an injury in fact even if it is not directly economic in nature. Association of Data Processing Organizations, Inc. v. Camp, [397 U.S. 150,] 154 (1970)." 465 F. 2d, at 853.[9]

The respondent's claim is that without detailed information on CIA expenditures—and hence its activities—he cannot intelligently follow the actions of Congress or the Executive, nor can he properly fulfill his obligations as a member of the electorate in voting for candidates seeking national office.

This is surely the kind of a generalized grievance described in both *Frothingham* and *Flast* since the impact on him is plainly undifferentiated and "common to all members of the public." *Ex parte Levitt,* 302 U.S. 633, 634 (1937); *Laird v. Tatum,* 408 U.S. 1, 13 (1972). While we can hardly dispute that this respondent has a genuine interest in the use of funds and that his interest may be prompted by his status as a taxpayer, he has not alleged that, as a taxpayer, he is in danger of suffering any particular concrete injury as a result of the operation of this statute. As the Court noted in *Sierra Club v. Morton,* 405 U.S. 727 (1972),

> "a mere 'interest in a problem,' no matter how longstanding the interest and no matter how qualified the organization is in evaluating the problem, is not sufficient by itself to render the organization 'adversely affected' or 'aggrieved' within the meaning of the APA." *Id.,* at 739.

Ex parte Lévitt, supra, is especially instructive. There Levitt sought to challenge the validity of the commission of a Supreme Court Justice who had been nominated and confirmed as such while he was a member of the Senate. Levitt alleged that the appointee had voted for an increase in the emoluments provided by Congress for Justices of the Supreme Court during the term for which he was last elected to the United States Senate. The claim was that the appointment violated the explicit prohibition of Art. I, § 6, cl. 2, of the Constitution.[10] The Court disposed of Levitt's claim, stating:

> "It is an established principle that to entitle a private individual to invoke the judicial power to determine the validity of executive or legislative action he must show that he *has sustained or is immediately in danger of sustaining a direct injury* as the result of that action and it is not sufficient that he has merely a general interest common to all members of the public." 302 U.S., at 634. (Emphasis supplied.)

Of course, if Lévitt's allegations were true, they made out an arguable violation of an explicit prohibition of the Constitution. Yet even this was held insufficient to support standing because, whatever Levitt's injury, it was one he shared with "all members of the public." Respondent here, like the petitioner in *Lévitt,* also fails to clear the threshold hurdle of *Baker v. Carr,* 369 U.S., at 204. See *supra,* at 171, and *Flast, supra.*[11]

It can be argued that if respondent is not permitted to litigate this issue, no one can do so. In a very real sense, the absence of any particular individual or class to litigate these claims gives support to the argument that the subject matter is committed to the surveillance of Congress, and ultimately to the political process. Any other conclusion would mean that the Founding Fathers intended to set up something in the nature of an Athenian democracy or a New England town meeting to oversee the conduct of the National Government by means of lawsuits in federal courts. The Constitution created a *representative* Government with the representatives directly responsible to their constituents at stated periods of two, four, and six years; that the Constitution does not afford a judicial remedy does not, of course, completely disable the citizen who is not satisfied with the "ground rules" established by the Congress for reporting expenditures of the Executive Branch. Lack of standing within the narrow confines of Art. III jurisdiction does not impair the right to assert his views in the political forum or at the polls. Slow, cumbersome, and unresponsive though the traditional electoral process may be thought at times, our system provides for changing members of the political branches when dissatisfied citizens convince a sufficient number of their fellow electors that elected representatives are delinquent in performing duties committed to them.

As our society has become more complex, our numbers more vast, our lives more varied, and our resources more strained, citizens increasingly request the intervention of the courts on a greater variety of issues than at any period of our national development. The acceptance of new categories of judicially cognizable injury has not eliminated the basic principle that to invoke judicial power the claimant must have a "personal stake in the outcome," *Baker v. Carr, supra,* at 204, or a "particular, concrete injury," *Sierra Club, supra,* at 740-741, n. 16, or "a direct injury," *Ex parte Levitt, supra,* at 634; in short, something more than "generalized grievances," *Flast, supra,* at 106. Respondent has failed to meet these fundamental tests; accordingly, the judgment of the Court of Appeals is

Reversed.

Mr. Justice Brennan, dissenting. . . .

Mr. Justice Powell, concurring. . . .

Mr. Justice Stewart, with whom Mr. Justice Marshall concurs, dissenting. . . .

---

[1]Respondent's complaint alleged that he was "a member of the electorate, and a loyal citizen of the United States." At the same time, he states that he "does not challenge the formulation of the issue contained in the petition for certiorari." Brief for Respondent in Opposition to Pet. for Cert. 1. The question presented there was: "Whether a federal taxpayer has standing to challenge the provisions of the Central Intelligence Act which provide the appropriations to and expenditures by that Agency shall not be made public, on the ground that such secrecy contravenes Article I, section 9, clause 7 of the Constitution." Pet. for Cert. 2.

[2]App. 15-16. Respondent's complaint also asked for a three-judge district court and this application was denied by a single District Judge with directions to place the case on the calander in the usual manner. The Court of Appeals, in the judgment under review, ordered that, on remand, the case be considered by a three-judge court. The District Court has granted a stay of the respondent's motion to convene a three-judge court, pending disposition of this petition for writ of certiorari. On September 26, 1972, the Third Circuit denied a petition for mandamus, filed by respondent, to compel the immediate convening of a three-judge court.

[3]The majority found that the respondent had standing to bring this suit as a taxpayer. One judge held that he had standing as a citizen. This case was originally argued before a panel consisting of two Circuit Judges and one District Judge sitting by designation. After a second round of briefs, the Court of Appeals determined *sua sponte* to hear the case en banc without further argument. The District Judge sat with the Court of Appeals en banc. This point was not raised in the question presented in the petition for certiorari but the Solicitor General, in a footnote, called attention to the District Judge's participation. He expressed the view that, although 28 U. S. C. § 46 (c) limits en banc hearings to Circuit Judges in active service (and any retired Circuit Judge who participated in the initial hearing), the error was harmless. Brief for United States 5-6, n. 4. In these circumstances we need not reach the question.

[4]397 U.S., at 151. See also K. Davis, Administrative Law Treatise § 22.09-6, p. 753 (Supp. 1970).

[5]In *Frothingham,* the plaintiff sought to enjoin enforcement of the Federal Maternity Act of 1921, 42 Stat. 224, which provided for financial grants to States with programs for reducing maternal and infant mortality. She alleged violation of the Fifth Amendment's Due Process Clause on the ground that the legislation encroached on an area reserved to the States.

[6]In some cases, the operative effect of this "look at the substantive issues" could lead to the conclusion that the "substantive issues" were nonjusticiable and in consequence no one would have standing. See *Gilligan v. Morgan,* 413 U.S. 1, 9 (1973); *Flast v. Cohen,* 392 U.S. 83, 95 (1968); *Poe v. Ullman,* 367 U.S. 497, 508-509 (1961).

[7]See 28 U. S. C. § 537 (Federal Bureau of Investigation); 31 U. S. C. § 107 (foreign affairs); 42 U. S. C. § 2017 (b) (Atomic Energy Commission).

[8]Congress has taken notice of the need of the public for more information concerning governmental operations, but at the same time it has continued traditional restraints on disclosure of confidential

information. See Freedom of Information Act, 5 U. S. C. § 552; *Environmental Protection Agency v. Mink,* 410 U.S. 73 (1973).

[9]The Court of Appeals thus appeared to rely on *Association of Data Processing Service Organizations, Inc. v. Camp,* 397 U.S. 150 (1970). Abstracting some general language of that opinion from the setting and controlling facts of that case, the Court of Appeals overlooked the crucial factor that standing in that case arose under a specific statute, Bank Service Corporation Act of 1962, 76 Stat. 1132, 12 U. S. C. § 1861. The petitioners in *Data Processing* alleged competitive economic injury to private business enterprise due to a ruling by the Comptroller of the Currency permitting national banks to sell their data processing services to other banks and to bank customers whose patronage the data processing companies sought. We recognized standing for those private business proprietors who were engaged in selling the same kind of services the Comptroller allowed banks to sell; we held only that the claims of impermissible competition were "arguably . . . within the zone of interests protected" by § 4 of the Bank Service Corporation Act. 397 U.S., at 156. In short, Congress had provided competitor standing. The Court saw no indication that Congress had sought to preclude judicial review of *adminstrative rulings* of the Comptroller of the Currency as to the limitations Congress placed on national banks.

[10]"No Senator or Representative shall, during the Time for which he was elected, be appointed to any civil Office under the Authority of the United States, which shall have been created, or the Emoluments whereof shall have been encreased during such time. . . ."

[11]Although we need not reach or decide precisely what is meant by "a regular Statement and Account," it is clear that Congress has plenary power to exact any reporting and accounting it considers appropriate in the public interest. It is therefore open to serious question whether the Framers of the Constitution ever imagined that general directives to the Congress or the Executive would be subject to enforcement by an individual citizen. While the available evidence is neither qualitatively nor quantitatively conclusive, historical analysis of the genesis of cl. 7 suggests that it was intended to permit some degree of secrecy of governmental operations. The ultimate weapon of enforcement available to the Congress would, of course, be the "power of the purse." Independent of the statute here challenged by respondent, Congress could grant standing to taxpayers or citizens, or both, limited, of course, by the "cases" and "controversies" provisions of Art. III.

Not controlling, but surely not unimportant, are nearly two centuries of acceptance of a reading of cl. 7 as vesting in Congress plenary power to spell out the details of precisely when and with what specificity Executive agencies must report the expenditure of appropriated funds and to exempt certain secret activities from comprehensive public reporting. See 2 M. Farrand, The Records of the Federal Convention of 1787, pp. 618-619 (1911); 3 *id.,* at 326-327; 3 J. Elliot, Debates on the Federal Constitution 462 (1836); D. Miller, Secret Statutes of the United States 10 (1918).

Index to Cases

Index to Statutes

Index to Executive Orders